D1564366

Eric Voegelin

and the Foundations of
Modern Political Science

Eric Voegelin

and the Foundations of
Modern Political Science

Barry Cooper

University of Missouri Press

COLUMBIA AND LONDON

Library of Congress Cataloging-in-Publication Data

Cooper, Barry, 1943–
Eric Voegelin and the foundations of modern political science /
  Barry Cooper.
     p. cm.
  Includes bibliographical references.
  ISBN 0-8262-1229-8 (alk. paper)
    1. Voegelin, Eric, 1901– — Contributions in political science.
  I. Voegelin, Eric, 1901– .
  JC263.V632C65   1999
  320'.092—dc21   99–24837
                                                               CIP

Text design: Elizabeth K. Young
Jacket design: Mindy Shouse
Typesetter: BookComp, Inc.
Printer and binder: Edwards Brothers, Inc.
Typefaces: Palatino, Caslon

For Denise, Meghan, and Brendan
Encore!

And to John C. Kerr, O.B.C.
Long-standing fishing companion,
brother twice over,
and the world's most generous friend

φιλοσοφοῦμεν ἄνευ μαλακίας

The more I read the more I doubted whether Izaak Walton gave a coot's hoot whether one fished with a flyrod, plunking poles, trot-lines, harpoons or gill-nets. The more I read the more obvious it became that there was only one thing he cared for deeply—a thing completely alien to my experience, a thing that made me most uncomfortable, a thing too vague to grasp but too frequently alluded to to ignore. The more I read, the more it seemed that *The Compleat Angler* was almost casually and incidentally a fishing book. Its deepest *raison d'être* was not love for Angling, but love for that nebulous Personage men call *God*.

David James Duncan, *The River Why*

Contents

Preface

This book is the first of two studies on the political science of Eric Voegelin. Several studies of Voegelin's work have appeared, some even prior to his death in 1985. Since then, the professional attention of scholars has resulted not only in an enormous growth in the secondary literature but also in the creation of several specialized centers for the study of Voegelin's thought, the establishment of two ordered archival collections, one at Stanford and the other in Munich, and a major publishing project, supported by two university presses, to bring out an English-language edition of Voegelin's *Collected Works*. A more modest publishing program is in place in German. It is not simply a result of this activity that one may argue that Voegelin was the most important political scientist of the century—though somebody must be. Rather, what Northrop Frye once called the "circumference" and what others have called the "depth" of the thought of a poet or philosopher constitutes a measure of greatness. With Voegelin both spatial metaphors are apt. The most general purpose of this study is to indicate as clearly as possible the depths or the circumference of Voegelin's political science. I have attempted an exposition, not a critique, on the grounds that, before one is in a position to criticize, it is necessary to be reasonably secure in one's understanding.

The foundations indicated in the title are found chiefly in Voegelin's *History of Political Ideas*. In a talk to the Eric Voegelin Society, which meets annually as part of the American Political Science Association, Paul Caringella, who served as Voegelin's assistant during the final years of his life, suggested that the *History* was Voegelin's first anamnesis, a recollection of the evocations and disorders of Western political history. At a similar gathering of Voegelin scholars in Manchester, Mendo Henriques, a Portuguese student of Voegelin's political science, observed that the *History* bears comparison with Saint Augustine's *City of God* or Bodin's *Six Books of the Republic* in that all three were motivated by a major political and spiritual upheaval. Indeed, Voegelin has said as much in the opening pages of his best-known book, *The New Science of Politics*.

My reading of the *History,* and of related work from Voegelin's hand during and after World War II, is congruent with the observations of Caringella and Henriques. This large text does, indeed, recollect the history of Western political ideas. In the present study, I have tried to convey the notion that Voegelin learned *from* Vico or Bodin, Schelling or

Toynbee, as well as *about* these thinkers. In general, it is my view that because Voegelin had learned from such people—and many others—he was able to respond to the critical events of the day with the insights that he had. The result, the *History of Political Ideas*, was more than a *livre de circonstance*, as were the books of his predecessors. It was, in my view, the solid empirical foundation for Voegelin's restoration of political science to a genuine science of order in politics, consciousness, and history. The last named element accounts for the adjective *modern* in the title: the importance of the "historical singularity" of political institutions, evocations, and interpretative symbols, which Voegelin learned from Vico, is surely the hallmark of the modern world. Voegelin's understanding of history, I argue, is one of the ways that his political science may be distinguished from that of Leo Strauss, who also undertook an enormous task of recovery. Having said that the *History* is the foundation, one must add that the finished structure, Voegelin's mature and meditative science, rose above it. In his later work, for example, he explained why the term *history of ideas* was to be avoided. However, it seems to me that a study of the foundations will help scholars understand the significance of Voegelin's later work. It nearly goes without saying that no introduction, no matter how complete, can be a substitute for the original. This book may serve as a guide to Voegelin's writing before, during, and just after World War II.

Voegelin's scholarly career began nearly twenty years before the writings we consider here, and a good case could be made to begin with his dissertation, his early publications on jurisprudence or sociology, and so on. In fact, I have provided a brief sketch of some of Voegelin's publications from the 1930s, but the purpose of this study is much more modest than anything approaching an intellectual biography or an analysis of the entirety of Voegelin's work.

The procedure I used was itself "Voegelinian," in the sense that I worked through the materials and tried to allow patterns of meaning to emerge. "The materials," a locution characteristically used by Voegelin, were his publications, but also a sizable collection of documents and correspondence in the Voegelin Papers, Hoover Institution, Stanford. Most of these writings are, naturally enough, from the 1940s, though I also make occasional reference to *Order and History* and *The New Science of Politics*. The later writings are cited to show where there is a critical continuity or where later formulations throw light on earlier ones. Some chapters—Chapter 7, for example—take into account a good deal of contemporary and specialized scholarship in order to make clear the significance of Voegelin's work in this area. Consulting specialists is a procedure Voegelin often recommended. In other chapters, such as

Chapter 9, it was sufficient to refer to contemporary scholarship in foot-notes since (in my opinion) Voegelin's work of a generation ago is to be preferred, simply on the grounds of being superior scholarship. Finally, there are occasional diversions from the main line of interpretation, as with the discussion of Emil Fackenheim in Chapter 10, because (again, in my opinion) the formulations are clearer than those that Voegelin achieved with respect to the problem under analysis.

In writing a big book over several years with documentation from far-flung archival deposits, a number of personal and financial obliga-tions are always contracted. It is a particular pleasure for an author to acknowledge such debts. On the financial side, I would like to thank the Alexander von Humboldt Foundation for granting me the Konrad Adenauer Award, the Deutscher Akademischer Austauschdienst and the Social Science and Humanities Research Council of Canada for major grants to examine materials in Germany, and the Earhart Foundation and the Donner Canadian Foundation for grants used to consult the Voegelin Collection or papers at the Hoover Institution, Stanford. I was also recip-ient of a Killam Research Fellowship, which provided release time from teaching, and a University of Calgary Sabbatical Fellowship. These same granting agencies and the University of Calgary International Travel Grant Committee have enabled me to take part in several international conferences on Voegelin's work. I am also grateful to Liberty Fund, Inc., for supporting two conferences on Voegelin to which I was invited.

Personal debts are equally numerous, and are usually incurred in-dependently of financial ones. Ellis Sandoz, whose energy and orga-nizational skills have sustained the publication of Voegelin's *Collected Works*, is rightly mentioned with honor by all who have studied Voegelin. In addition I have benefited from his encouragement and criticism in a wide variety of venues, from Antoine's to the Rose Valley Hotel. Paul Caringella has been equally encouraging and helpful, though our conversations have taken place in more conventional circumstances. In Germany, Jürgen Gebhardt, Tilo Schabert, and Peter Opitz have all provided generously of their time and have opened their institutions to me. At Stanford, Linda Bernard at the Hoover Institution has been a most helpful guide, as was Helmut Klumpjan at the Voegelin Library in Erlangen. In one way or another I would also like to thank Allison Bowes, Leah Bradshaw, Jodi Cockerill, Tom Darby, Peter Emberley, Tom Flanagan, Michael Franz, Thomas Heilke, Manfred Henningsen, John Kirby, David Levy, Ken Minogue, Tony Peacock, Zdravko Planinc, Jene Porter, Geoffrey Price, Brendan Purcell, Bart Testa, Helen Trimpi, Wesley Trimpi, Jim Wiser, and David Walsh. Carolyn Andres, of the Political

Science Department at the University of Calgary, has processed countless words, for which I am especially thankful.

It is a common failure of university teachers, as of other mortals, that they seldom count their blessings. I have been lucky in that my wife, Denise Guichon, and the children, Meghan and Brendan, who have again put up with an often absent, sometimes absentminded, and occasionally irritable member of the family, have not failed to remind me that it is a great privilege to be able to write scholarly books.

Abbreviations

CW *The Collected Works of Eric Voegelin.* Edited by Paul Caringella, Jürgen Gebhardt, Thomas A. Hollweck, Ellis Sandoz. 34 volumes.

HI Hoover Institution Archives, Voegelin Papers; citation to box and folder.

HPI *History of Political Ideas.*

Vol. I. *Hellenism, Rome, and Early Christianity.* Edited by Athanasios Moulakis. *CW,* vol. 19.

Vol. II. *The Middle Ages to Aquinas.* Edited by Peter von Sivers. *CW,* vol. 20.

Vol. III. *The Later Middle Ages.* Edited by David Walsh. *CW,* vol. 21.

Vol. IV. *Renaissance and Reformation.* Edited by David L. Morse and William M. Thompson. *CW,* vol. 22.

Vol. V. *Religion and the Rise of Modernity.* Edited by James L. Wiser. *CW,* vol. 23.

Vol. VI. *Revolution and the New Science.* Edited by Barry Cooper. *CW,* vol. 24.

Vol. VII. *The New Order and Last Orientation.* Edited by Jürgen Gebhardt and Thomas A. Hollweck. *CW,* vol. 25.

Vol. VIII. *Crisis and the Apocalypse of Man.* Edited by David Walsh. *CW,* vol. 26.

NSP *The New Science of Politics.* Chicago: University of Chicago Press, 1952.

OH *Order and History.* Available Columbia: University of Missouri Press, 1999.

Vol. 1. *Israel and Revelation.* 1956.

Vol. 2. *The World of the Polis.* 1957.

Vol. 3. *Plato and Aristotle.* 1957.

Vol. 4. *The Ecumenic Age.* 1974.

Vol. 5. *In Search of Order.* 1987.

RF Rockefeller Foundation, correspondence; citation to collection, box, and folder.

Eric Voegelin

and the Foundations of

Modern Political Science

1

Escape and Arrival

Eric Voegelin left Austria within four months of the *Anschluss*, the forcible incorporation of the country into the German Reich. The circumstances of his leaving exemplified the age-old conflict between the philosopher and the tyrant, and the story of his arrival in the United States and eventual settlement at Louisiana State University was filled with contingencies and not a little drama. The biographical details of Voegelin's departure from Europe and arrival in the United States are important for an understanding of his political science because, as he remarked in his *Autobiographical Reflections*, "the motivations of my work are simple, they arise from the political situation."[1] At no time was the political situation more perilous to Voegelin than in March 1938, after the German army had crossed the Austrian frontier and occupied Vienna. Voegelin had been aware of the connection between revolutionary political actions and political ideologies for the previous fifteen years. Behind the Bolshevik revolution was Marxism, and behind Marxism, the writings of Marx. In the late twenties and early thirties the phenomena of Fascism and National Socialism provided additional reasons to examine the problem of ideologies and their genesis.

National Socialism—or, rather, its ideological doctrine—was the topic of analysis in two books published in 1933, *Rasse und Staat* and *Die Rassenidee in der Geistesgeschichte von Ray bis Carus*.[2] The publication of these two books, and other prewar texts, ensured his name would be enrolled among the proscribed once Nazi rule of Austria had been consolidated. A brief summary of this material is, therefore, in order.

---

1. Voegelin, *Autobiographical Reflections*, ed. Ellis Sandoz, 93.
2. These volumes have been translated by Ruth Hein as *Race and State* and *The History of the Race Idea: From Ray to Carus*, both edited with an introduction by Klaus Vondung, and published as *CW*, vols. 2 and 3 (1997; available Columbia: University of Missouri Press, 1999). A systematic and detailed exegesis of the two books is Thomas W. Heilke, *Voegelin on the Idea of Race: An Analysis of Modern European Racism*. See also Heilke, "Science, Philosophy, and Resistance: On Eric Voegelin's Practice of Opposition."

By analyzing the biological, ethnological, and anthropological contents of the "race-idea," Voegelin showed in *Race and State* that it was not a scientific theory but an instrument of propaganda and thus a practical mechanism for organizing a political community for action. The *concept* of race, in contrast, was formally defined in the specialized biological and ethnological sciences. It referred to a specific, limited object that was studied according to formalized methods and according to the conventions of the particular sciences in question, chiefly ethnology and biology. Even within that context the scientific worth of the concept was highly questionable; the notion that the race idea was itself scientific was characterized by Voegelin as a superstition. The introductory chapter of *Race and State* justified this characterization by a methodological argument centered on what Voegelin conceptualized as the "primal way of seeing." Commitment to a "primal way of seeing" that enabled one to consider the race idea as a product of science was not merely an epistemological mistake or a cognitive error but rather the manifestation of a real spiritual disorder. The distinction between concepts, the meaning of which was conditioned by an analytic or scientific discursive context, and symbols that expressed experiences of reality, including perverse and imaginary experiences, was upheld by Voegelin throughout his scholarly life.

The second book, *Die Rassenidee,* began with the words, "The knowledge of man is out of joint." Evidence for this state of affairs was found in current "race-theory," which was an example, he said, of "inauthentic thinking." In this case the initial inauthenticity was found in the scientific assumption that human existence was something other than the substantive unity of body and soul. Action taken on the basis of an assumption that a human being was reducible to genetic or other material constituents could end only in disaster. Voegelin sought to understand this disaster by analyzing the history of race ideas as they had developed during the previous two centuries. Such "ideas," Voegelin argued, were not ideas of anything, in the sense of *opinions about* something or other, because there existed no single biological or ethnological substance or reality to which the "idea" might refer or give linguistic expression. The phenomena studied by biologists and ethnographers had nothing to do with the dogmatic superstition of the race idea. Indeed the race idea amounted to an imaginary transformation of biological phenomena into a source of meaning for individual and collective life. Because the transformation was imaginary, it could not achieve what it sought to achieve. The inevitability of a scientific or philosophical failure, however, was independent of the ability of such ideas to motivate human beings to act, which action can cause great havoc.

In the particular instance of the Nazi race idea Voegelin recognized the distorted millenarianism that transformed Germans into the salvific bearers of the "Nordic Idea" and the Jews into the diabolic bearers of the "anti-idea." This millenarianism promised purity and perfection as a historical and pragmatic possibility. The combination of millenarian activism and scientistic reductionism required the physical liquidation of the bearers of the Jewish "anti-idea" so that the "Nordic Idea" might triumph. In commonsense terms, Voegelin had exposed the National Socialist recipe for state-organized mass murder.

Behind the murderous ideological program Voegelin elaborated the historical and anthropological context. Conventionally one would speak of a postmedieval, post-Christian, or, indeed, a modern understanding of human existence. As a first approximation, with regard to Voegelin's work during the 1930s, this is not a misleading characterization. We will see in detail in the following chapters that Voegelin's political science, as a historical as well as an anthropological science, must inevitably be modern, though not in the sense that modernity is a deformation of the anthropology and philosophy of history of the Christian middle ages. For the present, it is enough to note that, for Voegelin, a decisive change took place with the break from "the rational glorification of fundamental Christian experiences." In place of that rational glorification, Voegelin discovered the manifold substitution of a nonrational and even irrational exploration of intramundane "nature," both human and nonhuman. Because, however, human existence is not simply an intramundane reality, distortions in the "primal way of seeing" were introduced into Western intellectual and spiritual life that then were expressed in "inauthentic thinking" and imaginary transformations of reality. It was not until much later in his life that Voegelin found the conceptual vocabulary adequate to analyze these problems. Even so, he was made aware of them before the force of circumstances compelled him to escape from the murderous practical implications.

In 1936, Voegelin published an analysis of the Austrian regime, *Der autoritäre Staat: Ein Versuch über das österreichische Staatsproblem.*[3] Again, political events lay at the origin of this work, in particular the social and political unrest of 1934 and the establishment of the corporate constitution as a response to those disorders. The chief sociological problem was that, while Austria was endowed with the legal apparatus of a state and contained an ethnically homogeneous population, it was not a

---

3. This volume has been translated by Ruth Hein as *The Authoritarian State: An Essay on the Problem of the Austrian State,* edited with an introduction by Gilbert Weiss, and published as *CW,* vol. 4 (Columbia: University of Missouri Press, 1999).

nation-state in the Western European sense, because that population had never existed as a political society capable of historical action. Austria had existed as part of the medieval empire and as part of the Hapsburg monarchy; after World War I the other successor states could plausibly claim to be the products of a historical development toward national existence. Often, as with Czechoslovakia, these claims were contentious, but in the case of Austria the claim was nonexistent. The Austrian state was, as it were, left over when the succession states were carved off from the realm of the Hapsburgs.

More specifically, Austria lacked the will to maintain an independent political existence in the face of the external ideological appeals of international socialism and Germanic ethnic solidarity. The interests of the contending parties were placed before those of national independence. The legal constitution, which assumed the existence of a people represented in a parliament, was incompatible with the constitutional reality, or regime. This tension between the legal constitution and the actual regime rendered Austria incapable of responding in a unified manner to the escalating European political disorder. Parliament was less a representative institution than an assembly of parties that used the letter of the constitution against its spirit in the hope of achieving narrow ideological and partisan domination. By 1933 there existed an *imperium in imperio* or, rather, several *imperia in imperio,* in the form of party armies; the German Revolution that brought the National Socialists to power exacerbated matters further. In February 1934, a short civil war was ended by the "authoritarian state," which may be seen as its result.

From 1934 to 1936 or 1937 the state acted in a manner that was at some variance with the "democratic" constitution of 1918. The aim of these policies, which included the banning of the Communist Party, the National Socialist Party, and the Social Democratic Party as well as the disbanding of the party militias, was to preserve the political unit against destruction by parties that claimed to be defending the letter of the constitution. That their words were not to be trusted was clear enough to Voegelin because they also said that once they had sufficient power they would abolish the constitution. In contrast to the regime that preceded it, the authoritarian state clearly had the political will to exist in defiance of the international and national socialists. The spiritual substance of the will-to-exist as a political unit was provided by Catholic "ideas" of the person, society, and humanity; this spiritual substance was opposed by the "ideas" held by international and national collectivists of the person, society, and humanity, which, to complicate matters further, were opposed to one another.

The authoritarian state promised to provide the shelter within which the development of an Austrian people in the Western European sense might take place. If such a people was in fact to become a reality, the legal constitution of 1918 might then be an appropriate legal expression or "articulation" of it. In the meantime, the internal organization of the regime according to the corporatist model was intended to undermine any appeals to class or ethnic conflict by organizing a plurality of quasi-autonomous social units along functional lines. Conflicting interests would be settled by a decision taken by the state authority. Whatever its deficiencies, it seemed clear that the authoritarian creation of a will-to-exist had temporarily removed the danger of political instability at the heart of Central Europe, which would have followed in the wake of the disappearance of Austria.

In the course of writing his study of the race idea, Voegelin analyzed the contemporary symbols of "authoritarian" and "total" (though not the term *totalitarian*, which first had been used by Mussolini in 1926). These linguistic phenomena were "ideas" in the sense developed in the earlier books, and so part of the political reality to be analyzed. Voegelin insisted that the currently popular Catholic ideas of the person, society, and humanity were badly deformed in the direction of Averroism.[4] This deformation was evident in the assumption that the intramundane collectivity of human beings called "Austrians" constituted a "totality" that the state "authority" could treat as beings subordinate to itself, to be directed according to the "ideas" of whoever held "authority." Again, the mechanical reduction of human beings to the constituents of the state alone indicated a disfiguration with potentially calamitous consequences.

Voegelin's analytic principle was the same as the one he had used in the discussion of the race idea. Linguistic phenomena such as "authoritarian" and "totality" were to be distinguished from the concepts of political science. These concepts in turn served as the linguistic instruments by which the analysis was carried out. This insight, along with the institutional analysis of Maurice Hauriou upon which Voegelin had relied for his conceptualization of the problems, was elaborated after the war in his most famous book, *The New Science of Politics*. The Austrian political events of the midthirties, however, provided the experiential context for the postwar analysis.

Voegelin's reliance on the arguments of Hauriou in *The Authoritarian State* brought him into conflict with his former teacher Hans Kelsen.

---

4. Voegelin had been aware of the importance of Averroism for the development of Western political ideas for at least a decade. A short report on some of this work is his "Siger de Brabant." See also *HPI,* II:178–204.

Kelsen's pure theory of law, which Voegelin never ceased to admire within its own sphere, was evidently no substitute for a theoretical account of the legitimate power of government. The first purpose of government power, he said, is to maintain the body politic as a being capable of action. That action, in turn, is directed by an "idea" capable of realization. Law is derived from the authority enjoyed by a government that has the support of the members of the political unit undertaking the realization of the "idea." Legitimate government, therefore, is not a matter of simply following the legal form but, more fundamentally, of expressing and realizing the "idea" of the body politic. It follows that, when the legal form does not correspond to the political reality, no amount of legal analysis will aid in understanding the political problem. Nor could it provide the experiential substance on the basis of which the existing deformations could be opposed.

More specifically, when new regimes such as the Austrian "authoritarian state" are created, their viability will depend not upon the legality of the foundation, because the regime establishes the foundation, but upon the degree to which the regime is capable of protecting the population from external disturbances and encouraging the growth of a genuine body politic. In his *Autobiographical Reflections,* Voegelin compared his approach to Austrian constitutional problems to the sentiments expressed by Justice Jackson in his dissent in the Terminiello case: the Bill of Rights is not a suicide pact.[5] During the midthirties the Austrian state was able to defend the Austrian population against the ideological fanaticism of national and international collectivists, and for that reason received Voegelin's qualified support. Moreover, Voegelin's journalism, including contributions to the *Neue Freie Presse,* the leading newspaper in Vienna, may be seen as a practical attempt to help form public opinion to resist the propaganda of those who, he said later, were concerned only with the abolition of democracy.[6]

Voegelin's last prewar book, *Die politischen Religionen,* was published in Vienna in March 1938 and was immediately confiscated by the Gestapo. This action by the Nazis made his exile or his death a virtual certainty. In 1939 an edition was brought out by the same publisher, Bermann-Fischer, by then relocated in Stockholm. The publication of the second

5. *Autobiographical Reflections,* 54. See also *NSP,* 144.
6. Voegelin's later reflections on this point are contained in a letter to Taylor Cole, at the time editor of the *Journal of Politics* (HI 9/23). Voegelin's newspaper articles discussed the new constitution, its courts, the formation and expression of public opinion, propaganda, utopian political speculation, and so on. See the references in Geoffrey Price, "Eric Voegelin: A Classified Biography," 17–18.

edition provided Voegelin with the opportunity to add a new preface, detailing the publication history and responding to "fundamental questions" raised by his critics. Of those positions worthy of response, chief among them was the opinion that, in his analysis of National Socialism, Voegelin was too "objective" and that, in consequence, his position was insufficiently clear. Voegelin replied that, there were, of course, "political intellectuals" who announced their deep hatred of National Socialism and led, or would like to lead, a struggle against it. Voegelin, too, could have written a moralizing tract. His opposition to every sort of political collectivism, he said, was obvious to anyone who could read. But he did not follow such a course and, as he had good reasons not to have done so, he would make those reasons, or rather, the main reason, clear. It was straightforward: political collectivism was not just a moral or a political phenomenon but contained a more fundamental "religious element." When one concentrated on the merely disreputable surface phenomena, the more basic reality would be obscured by the resulting literary analysis, which then becomes an additional obstacle to understanding. What is worse as a practical matter, moral and political denunciation is bound to be overwhelmed by the emotional appeal of the more basic religious elements. Accordingly, moral and political denunciation would be both unscientific and ineffective.

Voegelin's radical analysis, in contrast, took account of fundamental religious experiences. There is, he said, evil in the world—not in the sense of an absence of good or a defective mode of being, but in the sense of a real, effective, satanic force and substance in the world that cannot be adequately opposed by moralism alone. Rather, it can be resisted only by an equally strong but religiously good substance. A genuine renewal could proceed only from the efforts of great religious personalities; all a scholar or a philosopher can do is prepare the soil from which resistance against evil may arise. This aspect of the problem is precisely what moralizing intellectuals failed to understand, chiefly because they were unaware that the process of decay that has enabled religious movements of the Nationalist Socialist type to flourish is one of secularization, the same process of secularization that resulted in the humanistic moralism that is so ineffective in its opposition to religiously inspired collectivists. For such intellectuals, "the religious question is taboo." For this reason, Voegelin said, it was important to break the taboo and discuss basic religious questions as well as surface appearances of political evils. The book "would have been worthless if one were left with the impression that it dealt only with morally dubious, stupid, barbaric, or contemptible matters. That I do not regard the power of evil as a power of good is obvious in this book to anyone who is not insensitive to religious questions."[7] In contemporary language, Voegelin argued that the ideological fanaticism of the Nazis was not just a moral or political mistake but a spiritual perversion. Understanding ideology in this way also indicated to Voegelin the likely course that resistance to it might take—not least of all in his own person.

In making his analysis Voegelin drew upon Max Scheler's philosophical anthropology, discussed in more detail in Chapter 5. Evidence was taken from the religious reforms of Akhen-Aton, from medieval accounts of spiritual and temporal power, from Hobbes, and from National Socialist symbolism. All such evidence was "religious" in the sense that it was an expression of, or was related to the experience of, *realia*, to instances of being that carry a heightened meaning because they are recognized as having been infused with the substance of a "Beyond" or of the "Divine." These experiences, in turn, are ordered by reference to the *realissimum*, the highest reality or the most real thing there is. Within the category of the "religious," Voegelin made a further distinction between "the spiritual religions" that found the *realissimum* in the ground of being, which he termed world-transcendent religions, and all other religions. These latter found the *realissimum* in the things of the world and therefore were called "world-immanent religions."

A similar distinction applied to the human being undergoing religious experience. The will, the intellect, sentiments, spirituality—all are accentuated in the human being who apprehends a Beyond. Human beings can transcend their existence in any number of ways, from the movement of the soul toward the *unio mystica* with God to several forms of ecstasy: mundane communal festivals, devotion to the tribe, or drugs, the instinctive convulsions of sexual activity, blood-lust, and so on. Moreover, the symbolism used to express these experiences reveals both structural parallels and historical continuity. Hierarchy and order, in which the sacred substance is transmitted from the *realissimum* to the believers; the universal and particular *ekklesia* as the carriers of the sacred substance; the kingdom of God and the kingdom of Satan; the principle of the Leader and of the new apocalypse: all these can be found throughout the range of religious phenomena. To neglect one or another of these attributes would signify a failure to recognize the full meaning of the spiritual disorder constituted by political religions.

So far as the political religions of the twentieth century were concerned, the meaning or substance of religious phenomena, Voegelin

---

7. Voegelin, *Die politischen Religionen*, 9. This volume will appear as *Political Religions* in vol. 5 of *CW*, ed. Manfred Henningsen (Columbia: University of Missouri Press, 1999).

said, has moved away from fulfillment in a supernatural community of the spirit and toward the imaginary fantasies of world-immanent apocalyptic visions. These fantasies are not always recognized for what they are because the image of an earthly condition of perfected humanity is usually invoked in "scientific" language. Moreover, the conflict in detail between the visions of the two major collectivist parties, the Nazis and the Bolsheviks, has tended to obscure the essential sameness of their religious attitudes. The pressure of ideological conflict, however, leads not to an abandonment of apocalyptic visions but to a transformation of them from naive visions (in the Kantian sense) to conscious ones. In commonsense language, there occurs a quantum leap in the degree of mendacity involved. One need no longer believe in the truth of the apocalyptic vision but only in its effectiveness in promoting a political regime free of the ambiguities and pragmatic difficulties of the historical situation. The next step is to declare that whatever promotes the existence of the regime is the new apocalyptic truth. In this way propaganda, parades, the preparation for war, and death in battle are all intramundane or disfigured forms of the *unio mystica*. Voegelin provided a detailed analysis of Gerhard Schumann's *Lieder vom Reich* to illustrate the actual movements in the soul from which a political religion can be constructed and the political unit capable of action in history can be created. The religious ecstasies involved are not spiritual but instinctive and are expressed not in the search for the ground of being but in the collectivist intoxication of action. In this way enthusiasm is diverted from its sacred source in order to mobilize support for the revolutionary transformation of human existence. Voegelin's postwar analysis of the phenomena of totalitarianism continued the argument developed with regard to political religions.

The race books, then, and especially *Political Religions,* were analyses that exposed the mendacity and apocalyptic fantasies of National Socialism. Voegelin was under no illusion that making clear the spiritual perverseness of Nazism would in any way inhibit its effectiveness. Anyone spiritually integrated enough to understand Voegelin's argument would not be moved by Nazi appeals anyhow. Those who were intoxicated by collectivist action and the ecstasies of ideological belief would see in Voegelin only an enemy to be overcome.

We saw above that Voegelin's account of ideological political movements and of their animating political religions focused on the experience of the renunciation of God and the attempt imaginatively to divinize an intramundane political project. We should note an additional feature of this act: the creation of intramundane symbolisms bearing the same structural attributes as the world-transcendent religions has the effect of concealing the most essential features of reality. The new political religion cuts off the way toward the reality of God and perverts the relationship of the beings that exist under God. In other words, human beings undertake imaginatively to recast God's relationship to creation. In reality, as distinct from their own imaginative self-understanding, such persons become organized centers of disturbance and of resistance to reality as it has been vouchsafed to human beings. In one form or another, Voegelin made this argument in the next forty years of his work.

As noted, Voegelin's analysis of Nazi collectivism in *Political Religions* proceeded on the assumption that evil exists in the world, that God's creation contains evil, that the majesty of being is dimmed by the misery of creatures, that communities can be built on hatred and murder, and that humans can turn away from God. Moreover, the identification of the Nazis as a satanic force for evil was sufficiently unambiguous even for the most dull-witted employee of the Gestapo to realize that the author was not on side. Voegelin was, therefore, not at all surprised that he had been marked as an enemy, though he was very much surprised (and angered) that the Western powers would make such an obvious blunder as to permit the occupation of Austria in March 1938. The Germans were thereby given the opportunity of conquering Czechoslovakia, which would create a strategic situation clearly unfavorable to the West in the event of an increasingly probable general war. Voegelin realized immediately that he had to make preparations to leave.

His first task was to get money out of Austria. Currency restrictions made it impossible to send money abroad directly, so Voegelin arranged to pay the salary of his friend Alex von Muralt, a Swiss journalist resident in Vienna, while von Muralt's salary would be left in the hands of a Zurich lawyer. The four months following the German invasion were unpleasant for Voegelin and his wife. He had been expecting to be appointed as a full professor at the University of Graz in the fall of 1938 but had been summarily dismissed from his post at the university and had been informed by the minister of education that his future prospects for employment were nonexistent. He was encouraged to emigrate to the United States and quickly formed several plans to do so.

However difficult his own circumstances, they were nothing as compared to what befell the Voegelins' Jewish friends. A year later he wrote from his new home recalling the events of the summer of 1938.

> Daily there was news of our acquaintances, of one that he had killed himself, of another that a death notice from a concentration camp had been received. An old friend, a woman of sixty-five years, was in prison for three months and wrote us the most touching letters. Particularly dreadful was the fate of our Jewish friends: nearly all of them were in jail for shorter or longer

periods, and many are still there. We have received some news that one or another has come out. One, who was in Dachau for seven months, arrived in Ghent; another was released with frozen and festering legs; another, more fortunate, after a seven-hour flight through the snowy Ardennes arrived in Brussels. Many were beaten and spat upon by the SA troopers and at night hauled away from their homes to prison. An old couple, with half an hour warning, were driven from their home and forced to abandon everything. A very rich couple (the husband was 80), were completely plundered and left the country with two suitcases; the 70-year-old wife died shortly thereafter of a heart attack. The old gentleman found refuge at a small family estate in Czechoslovakia and is now again homeless because, with the destruction of Czechoslovakia, the land came under German rule. These are just cases that we ourselves have experienced in our circle of acquaintances.[8]

Within a month of the occupation, Voegelin had begun arrangements to leave Austria and secure a position abroad. On April 5, 1938, he wrote to Tracy Kittredge, assistant director of the European office of the Rockefeller Foundation, whom Voegelin had known since the 1920s, when he was the recipient of a Laura Spellman Rockefeller Fellowship, which enabled him to spend two years in the United States and a third year in Paris.[9] He explained that he had six months to find a position in North America or Britain and that he was qualified to teach "any routine course" in sociology and political science. "Furthermore, I am a specialist for political ideas of the French 16th century; for the relations between European and Oriental political ideas from the 13th to 18th century; and for European political ideas of the present time."[10] He asked for Kittredge's help in alerting his American contacts to his qualifications and availability.

Because the American government had established a quota to limit the number of emigrants from Austria, Voegelin's prospects for admittance to the United States as an ordinary immigrant were dim. If he was offered employment, however, he would be eligible for a nonquota visa. Accordingly, during the spring of 1938, he dispatched letters, similar to the one sent to Kittredge, to the Carnegie Endowment, to about twenty North American universities, as well as to the London School of Economics, the Geneva Research Center, the Institute for International

8. This letter was written by Eric in the spring of 1939 to Lissy Voegelin's relatives and was signed by her. See also "The Totalitarian Climate," HI 55/39, probably also written in 1939.

9. See the editors' introduction to *CW*, vol. 1, *On the Form of the American Mind*, ed. Jürgen Gebhardt and Barry Cooper (1995; available Columbia: University of Missouri Press, 1999), for additional details.

10. HI 30/14.

Education in New York, and the Foreign Policy Association, also in New York.[11] Letters went out as well to Viennese friends already living abroad and to Americans he had met during his tenure as a Rockefeller fellow. Early in May, Voegelin learned that the Rockefeller Foundation would pay half of his salary for three years to any American university that offered him employment. Prospects for the future gave ground for hopes, but the present situation remained bleak.

These were not happy times for Voegelin. Typical of the letters he wrote was one to Frederick A. Ogg, the head of the political science department at Wisconsin, where he had studied a little more than a decade before:

> My dear sir:
>   In case there is an opening in your department I beg you to consider this letter as an application for the position.
>   I was born on January 3, 1901, at Cologne, my father being German, and my mother Viennese. In 1910 my father came to Vienna, and I had my secondary education in that city. After having graduated from a Viennese *Realgymnasium* with honors, I matriculated in the Law Faculty of Vienna, and received the degree of *Dr.rer.pol.* with honours in 1922. My thesis dealt with a problem of theoretical sociology. In 1922 I attended the summer session at Oxford, and, among other things, took a course in English Grammar under Dr. Gilbert Murray. During the year 1922–23 I was the holder of a Weininger Fellowship,

11. Because Voegelin had known Kittredge for several years and was aware of the high regard in which he was held by the Rockefeller Foundation, he presented Kittredge with an abbreviated list of his qualifications. (In fact, Kittredge considered Voegelin "probably one of the ablest of our former Austrian fellows"; see RF 1:1/705/5/49.) To Professor John B. Whitton, director of the Geneva Research Center, he provided a more detailed statement: "As to my qualifications, I am holding at present, as you know, the rank of an associate professor in the University of Vienna. I am able to give any general and special courses in the fields of general political science, history of political ideas, comparative government, legal theory, sociology, social philosophy, social ethics, and all questions of methodology of the social sciences. My special fields are: recent European political ideologies; influence of Oriental political ideas on Europe since the 13th century; French 16th century political ideas, particularly Jean Bodin. I could give a particularly interesting course, or series of lectures, on the Mongolian Empire of the 13th century, its political ideas and constitutional law, with social reference to the letters of the Mongol Khans to European powers which I am just now about to publish. During the last two years I have engaged in a new line of research on the religious element in political thought; my work is covering all periods from antiquity up to the present; and I think I am, as far as I know, the only scholar who masters the subject under all its aspects—the historical and political as well as the theological and psychological. A little book on 'Political Religions' is already printed and ready for issue, but will come out only in fall due to difficulties of a technical order. This new research work is the most important contribution I am able to make at the moment, and I think it would be an excellent subject for a series of lectures or a course" (HI 41/18).

and studied in the Universities of Berlin and Heidelberg under Professors Heinrich Triepel, Alfred Vierkandt, Rudolf Smend, Gerhard Anschütz, Alfred Waber, Edgar Salin, Karl Jaspers, and Friedrich Gundolf. In 1923–24 I was an Assistant in public law in the University of Vienna, working under Professor Hans Kelsen. In 1924 I accepted a Rockefeller Fellowship, which was later extended to two more years. I spent the first of the three years (1924–26) in the United States, and the year 1926–27 in France. In America I studied at Columbia, Harvard, Yale and at your University. In Columbia I took Dr. Powell's course in American constitutional law, Dr. Macmahon's course in political science, Dr. John Dewey's course in philosophy, Dr. Irwin Edman's course in metaphysics, and Dr. W. C. Mitchell's course in history of economic theory. In Harvard I took Dean Roscoe Pound's course in legal philosophy, Dr. Holcombe's course in government, one of Dr. A. N. Whitehead's courses in philosophy, and Dr. Ally A. Young's seminar in economic theory. In your University I worked chiefly under Dr. John R. Commons in the fields of American social history, American trade unionism, and the social and economic implications of American constitutional law. At Yale I took courses in legal theory under Drs. Arthur L. Corbin and Walter Wheeler Cook. While in America I was in addition to my Rockefeller Fellowship, given a research fellowship in economics at Harvard, and an honorary fellowship in your University. After finishing my work at these universities I took trips to the Pacific coast and to the South, and made a special study of the educational problem of Kentucky mountaineers in Berea College.

The academic year 1926–27 was spent in Paris, where I took courses in economics, political science, and philosophy at the Sorbonne. Most of my time I devoted, however, to collecting materials in French constitutional history in the *Bibliothèque Nationale*. Immediately after returning to Vienna I published my book on *Die Form des Amerikanischen Geistes*, (number 1 of the enclosed list of my publications). While in America and France, I partly wrote and partly prepared articles number 9, 10, and 12–22 of the enclosed list.

Upon my return to Austria, I again became Assistant in public law in the University of Vienna, working at first under Professor Hans Kelsen, and then under Professors Adolf Merkla and Ludwig von Adamovich. In 1928 I was appointed *Privatdozent* in general political science and sociology, and, in 1935, I received the title of *a.o. Universitätsprofessor*. I am holding this position at present, or, I should rather say, I held it until three weeks ago. In addition, I made frequent trips for research purposes to Berlin, Heidelberg, Paris, London, and Rome. In 1931 I also gave a series of lectures on the differences of national types of mind and the subsequent difficulties of international understanding at the Geneva University Institute for International Studies. These lectures were given in English. Since 1928 I have given courses in government, sociology, and social ethics at the Vienna Workers' High School (*Volkshochschule*), and since 1936 I have been head of the political science department of this School. The School has 10,000 students. Since 1936 I have furthermore been secretary of the Austrian Coordinating Committee for International Studies, and for the Tenth International Studies Conference. In Paris in 1937, I organized a special study group on the Austrian problem.

During the last few years I have done work in several different fields. In the field of recent European political ideas I have published a book entitled *Rasse und Staat* (number 2 of the list of publications), and another one on *Die Rassenidee in der Geistesgeschichte* (number 3 of the list of publications). In comparative government I published my book on *Der autoritäre Staat* (number 4 of list of publications). On the influence of Eastern political ideas and institutions on the West since the thirteenth century I published an article on Tamerlane's influence on the Renaissance (number 32 of the list of publications), and a book on the constitutions and the political concept of the Mongol Empire in the thirteenth century is in preparation. In addition, I am working on a survey of Mongolian influences upon European political thought which I hope to have published in about two years. I have also collected the materials for a volume on Jean Bodin, and hope to have it published soon. A book entitled "Political Religions" and dealing with a history of the religious element in political ideas from antiquity up to the present has already been printed and is ready for issue. Because of technical difficulties this book will, however, not appear until this fall.

In the University of Vienna I have, during the last ten years, given courses in general political science, sociology, history of political ideas, comparative government, legal theory, constitutional law, methodological questions, and recent political ideologies. In addition I have given many single lectures to various scientific societies.

I have an excellent reading and speaking knowledge of English and French, an excellent reading knowledge of Italian, and a fairly good reading knowledge of Spanish and Russian.

I feel qualified to give general and special courses on the subjects mentioned above, and in addition courses in social psychology, social ethics, and social philosophy. I have particularly done a vast amount of reading in the history of political ideas from antiquity to the present, and am especially in a position to build up courses in comparative government which will include American as well as European problems.

Mr. Kittredge, Assistant Director of the Rockefeller Foundation, has informed me that the Foundation is ready to pay one-half of the salary, for three years, of any appointment offered to me by an American University. I should be glad to accept any position above the rank of instructor, and with any salary with which it would be possible for a small family to live on.

As for personal references I may give Professor Charles E. Merriam and Harold D. Lasswell, University of Chicago; Professor Edin M. Borchard, Yale University; and Professor Gottfried von Haberler, Harvard.

Hoping to have the pleasure of meeting you at some future date,

I remain,

Sincerely yours,

Dr. Erich Voegelin

I. Stadiongasse 4

Vienna, Germany.[12]

---

12. HI 27/30.

By the end of May, Voegelin's income had dropped to zero. "The situation," he wrote his friend Fritz Machlup, who was at that time teaching at Buffalo, "is, therefore, getting somewhat close from a financial point of view."[13] By early June, responses to his letters of application were arriving in Vienna. They were not encouraging. Professor Ogg, for example, expressed great interest in Voegelin's career and admiration for his scholarship. However, budgetary arrangements for the year had been made "and there is simply no possibility at all of securing money with which to make additional appointments."[14] Nothing was said of the Rockefeller Foundation's support. Gottfried Haberler, listed as a reference in the letter to Ogg, and another of Voegelin's Viennese friends, was teaching in the economics department at Harvard. Voegelin had written him in April and early in May received an encouraging inquiry: would he be interested in working with William Elliott on certain problems in international relations? He replied immediately that it would be splendid to collaborate with Elliott, whom he had also met during his earlier time at Harvard, though it was not clear exactly what problems they would be working on. Voegelin included a résumé of his own career and added a "table of problems" he would like to work on. It outlined the genesis and growth of immanent, secular political religions and the transformation of them into totalitarian mass movements.

On June 3, 1938, Haberler wrote back, apologizing for the delay in response but including the good news that Voegelin had been awarded "a grant of $2,000.00 for one year to undertake a study in the International Aspects of Political Religions."[15] Voegelin would hold the grant under the auspices of the Bureau of International Research at Harvard, which explained, in Haberler's words, the "rather childish" description. "Practically, you can do what you want," he said. An official letter would be in Voegelin's hands shortly and perhaps the offer of an instructorship as well. Failing that, Joseph Schumpeter had agreed to sponsor him, and an affidavit to that effect would also be forthcoming. Haberler urged Voegelin not to reject the modest offer of the bureau since it would enable him to live while he searched for a better position. "I should like to ask you not to tell other people of this matter," he said. "They would think that I can easily find jobs for everybody. Unfortunately

---

13. HI 24/7. Other letters referred to in this paragraph are also in HI.

14. HI 27/30.

15. Kittredge attempted to get the Rockefeller Foundation to provide Voegelin with "a small supplement to the [Harvard] stipend" but was unsuccessful in persuading his colleagues at the foundation that this would be a good investment. See RF 1:1/705/5/49.

that is not the case. That something could be found for you is entirely due to Elliott's enthusiasm for you and that has its solid foundation in the singular qualifications and reputation of yours, which is not easy to duplicate."[16] Voegelin accepted the offer and began making arrangements to leave for the United States. Emigration, however, was both difficult and dangerous.

Shortly after the occupation in March, Voegelin came to the attention of the Gestapo, which dispatched an agent to search his apartment for incriminating material. The agent made off with his address book and his copies of Marx and Lenin. He declined to take Voegelin's copy of *Mein Kampf,* notwithstanding Voegelin's assurance that it was the same kind of document as *Das Kapital.* The inspection of Voegelin's library and the occasional surveillance were part of a "well organized and cleverly released wave of terror, calculated to encircle the individual existence closer and closer to the point of extinction—meaning thereby emigration or suicide." One of the effects, Voegelin reported later, was stress-induced insomnia.[17] Despite this harassment, Voegelin's plans for escape proceeded at a leisurely pace. Things changed on Wednesday, July 13. Voegelin earlier had placed a newspaper notice advertising furniture for sale. On Tuesday a man posing as a prospective buyer called, looked at the furniture, and asked the Voegelins a number of questions relating to their reasons for departure. The Voegelins suspected something was amiss since the alleged buyer seemed more interested in them than in their furniture. The next day, around noon, another agent of the Gestapo arrived and demanded Voegelin's passport, explaining that all professors and other "competent personalities" would have their passports confiscated so as to prevent them from leaving. By a stroke of good fortune, neither Voegelin nor his passport was at home. Lissy Voegelin's brother was a director of a large shipping company with close ties to the government. One of the services the company provided was to take care of visa formalities for its clients without passing them through the hands of the Gestapo; her brother had agreed to include the Voegelins' passports along with a large number of others when he next visited the regular police to secure the required visas, and the documents were in his hands. Mrs. Voegelin was able honestly to inform the Gestapo agent that the police already had their passports. She telephoned her brother who had, in fact, just received the passports back from the police. Mrs. Voegelin immediately retrieved the passports, informed her husband what had taken place, and urged him to leave on the next train.

16. HI 15/33.
17. See Voegelin, "The Totalitarian Climate," HI 55/39.

Having now checked with the Austrian police, the Gestapo learned that Voegelin was in possession of his passport. On Thursday afternoon the Gestapo agent was back looking for Voegelin and his passport. Voegelin was again blessed by good fortune and was out of the house, saying good-bye to an elderly friend who lived in the suburbs of Vienna. Mrs. Voegelin told her visitor that she did not know where he was. She then took the tram to the suburban terminus in the hope of meeting him before he returned to their apartment. Lissy arrived as Eric was climbing aboard an inbound tram; she persuaded him that matters were now very serious, and he agreed to leave that night.

The Gestapo agent had said he would be back at 7:00 A.M. Friday morning and that if Voegelin was not there he would ensure that the borders were sealed against his departure. Voegelin spent the rest of the day in cafés and took the evening train to Switzerland, crossing the frontier around 10:30 P.M.[18] In the meantime, the Gestapo had posted one of its men outside the Voegelins' apartment building. A few minutes before Lissy Voegelin received a telegram from her husband in Zurich, the watcher disappeared. A few days later she flew to Zurich to join Eric.[19]

Escaping Austria put them out of immediate danger, but they had still to get into the United States. A research appointment was insufficient to obtain a nonquota visa. It was not until the middle of August that a letter arrived from Arthur N. Holcombe, chairman of the department of government at Harvard, attesting that Voegelin would be appointed instructor with the duties of tutor.[20] At last eligible for a visa, his only task now was to obtain one.

Voegelin had discussed the question with American consular officials in Vienna prior to his escape. Because the Vienna office was swamped with applications, it was suggested that he apply in Paris. Early in July he had written Leo Gross in Paris to make inquiries at the American consulate about obtaining a visa there.[21] Gross was secretary of the International Institute for Intellectual Cooperation, an organization connected to the League of Nations and financed in part by the Rockefeller

18. This account is taken from a letter Voegelin wrote to Leo Gross, HI 15/21. It was repeated to several other correspondents. Additional details were supplied in conversation by Lissy Voegelin.

19. This initiative by the local Gestapo apparently left no records in the Reich Security Service Archive that survived either at the Bundesarchiv Koblenz or Potsdam. *Findbuch Reichssicherheitshauptamt,* Pst. 3 (Potsdam: Bundesarchiv), 92–93.

20. HI 16/17. See also Harvard University, *Directory of Officers and Students* (Cambridge: Harvard University Press, 1938).

21. HI 15/21.

Foundation. In the spring of 1937 the institute had sponsored a conference in Paris at which Voegelin had presented a paper on Austrian politics. Moreover, Voegelin had served as secretary of the Austrian Coordinating Committee for International Studies from October 1937 until its dissolution the following spring, and that organization had been supported by the International Institute. Gross replied to Voegelin's query that, while the American consulate was not as busy in Paris as in Vienna, the French authorities would grant transit visas only to persons who were already in possession of an American visa. Kittredge's letter to the American consulate in Paris, which included an offer on behalf of the Rockefeller Foundation to pay Voegelin's living expenses, was of no use if he was unable to enter France.

In the event, Gross offered to pay Voegelin in Zurich by way of the International Institute. Since Voegelin had already sufficient funds in Zurich he declined, fully expecting to be able to use the money in Paris. Meanwhile he had also received an offer of support from Friedrich Hayek at the London School of Economics. Voegelin again declined the offer, but suggested that Hayek might wish to consider helping Friedrich Engel-Janosi, who soon would be in great need. Engel-Janosi had been forced to sell the Austrian factory owned by his family and would not be permitted to leave until he had trained the new owners. He had no money outside the Reich and would be impoverished when he left. Moreover, he was under close surveillance, and Voegelin suggested that Hayek write him through a relative in Switzerland.[22]

The American consul in Zurich was, Voegelin said later, "a very nice Harvard boy," but deeply suspicious of Voegelin's past. Being neither a Communist, a Catholic, nor a Jew, Voegelin had no apparent reason to be fleeing Austria unless he was a criminal. Nothing could therefore be done about an American visa, and so no transit visa through France could be obtained, until the matter of Voegelin's possible criminal record was cleared up. When the letter from Holcombe arrived, confirming Voegelin's appointment, it was sufficient to overcome the "Harvard boy's" doubts. Voegelin and his wife received their nonquota visas and booked passage on the SS *Washington*, leaving Le Havre on September 8. By the end of August, the French had again changed their regulations and Voegelin was permitted to stay in Paris, but only overnight.

22. HI 17/3. Eventually Engel-Janosi reached the United States and taught for several years at Johns Hopkins University. He read the chapters of Voegelin's *History of Political Ideas* as they were written and provided him with extensive criticism. See HI 11/7.

Voegelin's time in Zurich had not been wasted. On August 20, he wrote to Elliott that he had made some interesting discoveries in the Zurich city library. Among their holdings were seventeenth-century materials on Mongol questions. "Apparently the theologians and historians of German 17th century considered the Mongol empire and expansion as a religious phenomenon. They speak of the religion of 'Genghiskhanism', treating it on the same level as Mohammedanism, Paganism, Judaism etc. The wars of Tamerlane are considered to be a chapter of ecclesiastical history of the Mediterranean. That fits nicely in with my problem of political religions, and I am quite delighted now about the delay in Zurich."[23]

The crossing coincided with the Munich crisis, the flight of Prime Minister Chamberlain to the Reich, and his return bearing a piece of paper that promised "peace in our time." Voegelin mentioned to a fellow passenger, Harold Laski, whom Voegelin had first met during the 1920s,[24] that Britain was going the way of Austria. Laski was furious and refused to speak with him for the remainder of the voyage. Among the other news items carried by the shipboard wire report was a story that the president of Louisiana State University had been forced to flee into the bayous in order to escape from supporters of Gov. Huey Long who were intent on beating him up. Mrs. Voegelin was apprehensive about the country to which they were immigrating if university presidents were treated in such a way. Voegelin assured her that they would be living far from Louisiana. The Voegelins spent the week of September 15–21 in New York. A few days later they reached Boston by boat because a hurricane had struck Long Island and New England, interrupting road and rail transportation. In later life Voegelin went out of his way to emphasize that he had no regrets in leaving Vienna.[25] Even so, the Voegelins' future in the United States must have looked far from secure.

Voegelin had become an enemy of the National Socialists purely on his own merits. His scholarly and popular writings ensured that he would be arrested sooner rather than later. His escape from Austria, in contrast, depended greatly on the efforts of others and not inconsiderably upon chance. Voegelin's brother-in-law's position in the shipping company and his willingness (despite his own support for the Reich) to assist the Voegelins were essential to their obtaining exit visas; Voegelin was

23. HI 11/2.
24. In 1930, Voegelin translated Laski's article on law and the state; "Das Recht und der Staat," *Zeitschrift für öffentliches Recht* 10 (1930): 1–27.
25. See for example, Voegelin's interview with Andrew Baird of *Fortune Magazine*, HI 7/7.

fortunate in having a means of obtaining money outside the Reich; the timing of the visits by the Gestapo was a matter of sheer good luck. Moreover, the calmness of Lissy Voegelin under highly distressing circumstances was also essential for their escape. His ability to secure entry to the United States rested not so much upon fortune as upon the same personal factors that brought him to the notice of the National Socialists, namely his personal integrity and achievements as a scholar. He would not have known the Americans who now were able to help him had he not obtained the traveling fellowship from the Rockefeller Foundation fifteen years earlier. He would not have retained the active support of Elliott and Haberler at Harvard had he not undertaken to publish the work that he did. Nor would he have been able to call upon the good offices of Kittredge and Gross had he failed to produce a solid body of scholarship. One may say, therefore, that while his exit may have been simply a matter of fortune, his arrival in the United States had been prepared by years of sustained scholarly achievement. As Haberler had said, Voegelin's qualifications and reputation were not easy to duplicate.

Voegelin's position at Harvard was temporary. His chairman, Arthur Holcombe, indicated that while he was pleased to have him in Cambridge, he hoped he would use his year profitably for research and quickly secure a position someplace else. One of the first letters Voegelin dispatched was to Robert Hall, director of the Institute of Far Eastern Studies at the University of Michigan.[26] Voegelin sought a position teaching summer school and indicated to Hall that he had been concentrating his research work in recent years on Mongol questions, in particular on Chinggis Qan and Temür. Indeed, the first major research project Voegelin undertook in the United States was an edition and analysis of the thirteenth-century Mongol orders of submission to the European powers.[27] It was part of a long-term interest in the relationship between political events in Asia and those of Europe. In his letter to Hall, Voegelin emphasized that he was competent to discuss Mongol constitutional law, ideas of leadership, state-theology, and the influences from China on the Mongols and of the Mongols on European cultural history. In the event, nothing was available at Michigan.

26. HI 19/6.
27. The study was eventually published in *Byzantion* 15 (1941): 378–413. During 1938 and 1939 Voegelin reported in his correspondence that Professor Samuel Hazard Cross, the editor of *Speculum*, had accepted it for publication in that journal. The significance of this work for Voegelin's political science is discussed in Chapter 7.

Over the next few months he sent out over forty additional letters. There were already three Germans on the teaching staff of the department of government at Harvard, including his contemporary Carl Friedrich. Even if Holcombe had not been so explicit, Voegelin knew a Harvard job was not in the cards. Elsewhere in the East, matters were not much better. "The difficulty," Voegelin wrote to Tracy Kittredge at the Rockefeller Foundation early in December 1938, "is apparently that every college is already provided with a German refugee; the Berlin Hochschule für Politik seems to have an enormous staff, sufficient to furnish a considerable number of colleges with at least one man."[28] Bennington College had apparently not yet received its allotment from the Berlin Hochschule, and early in February, Robert Leigh, the college president, offered Voegelin employment for the next term, starting two weeks later.[29] Voegelin accepted the offer to teach American and comparative government, constitutional law, and public administration. He kept his position at Harvard and commuted each Wednesday from Vermont to conduct his tutorials.

Voegelin's search for a summer school job was eventually successful. About the same time as the Bennington offer, he received one from Northwestern to teach an eight-week course on modern political theory, from Rousseau to the present.[30] He accepted and mentioned that the subject matter "coincides very agreeably with work I have just under hand: I am publishing a History of Political Ideas." One term at Bennington convinced him that he did not wish to teach there permanently. In his *Autobiographical Reflections* he cited several reasons.[31] The first was that he found the liberal, Marxist, and even communist ideological climate no more congenial than the National Socialist atmosphere he had recently left. Second, having put Austria behind him, he was determined to become an American, not an émigré living in America. Since most European scholars seemed to prefer New England and the Atlantic states, if Voegelin were to settle outside the established émigré communities, he would have to search for a position outside the Northeast. In fact, for Voegelin, this was by no means a hardship. Several times he wrote acquaintances and friends in Chicago, Cincinnati, or Minnesota of his desire to see the "real" America again. A final reason was that Voegelin knew he wanted to become an American political scientist, which meant learning by teaching American government. He felt, probably quite

28. HI 30/14.
29. HI 8/3.
30. HI 27/19.
31. *Autobiographical Reflections,* 57–58.

rightly, that no large eastern university would permit a foreigner to undertake such on-the-job training.

Among the letters sent out in the fall of 1938 was one to the University of Alabama in Tuscaloosa. Shortly after he accepted the one-term appointment at Bennington, Alabama made him an offer. As with the other applications he had sent out, the Rockefeller Foundation would pay for one-half his salary for three years, which meant that Alabama obtained Voegelin's services for the sum of $1,250.00 per annum. Voegelin was appointed as an assistant professor. He expected to be reappointed as an associate professor for two additional years with an indefinite tenure after that. As he wrote to Kittredge on February 24, "you can imagine how happy Mrs. Voegelin and I myself are about the development," a remark he repeated in a letter to his older friend from Vienna, Oskar Morgenstern, then at Princeton.[32] Not least among the reasons was that he would be able to teach American government. In addition, he was to teach courses in comparative government, diplomatic history, and international relations; he also organized a "private seminar" along Viennese lines and gave a large number of speeches to fraternities, veterans' organizations, womens' clubs, and the like.

In mid-April 1939, Bennington realized what a prize it had secured in Voegelin and offered to continue his appointment at more than twice the salary he would receive at Alabama. He wrote to Morgenstern later that month that "things are developing very nicely here. The President has made me an offer for three years with a top salary, but I think I had better go now at least for one year to Alabama." A. R. Hatton, chairman of the department of political science at Northwestern, offered the advice that Alabama was to be preferred, "if salaries are in any way comparable," because it would be easier to move from Alabama to a college more desirable even than Bennington, because a coeducational institution would be a "better experience," and because of the presence at Alabama of scholars such as Roscoe Martin who were raising the standards of political science teaching there.[33]

In a letter to William Elliott in June, Voegelin remarked that some of his Bennington colleagues were surprised and apparently insulted that he would turn down such a magnificent offer from their college.[34] Voegelin expressed his regrets at their response and said he was sorry to leave behind any ill will. After he left, matters grew tangibly worse. Bennington had paid Voegelin for only five months, even though he

32. HI 30/14, 25/36. See also RF, 1:1/200/411/4862.
33. HI 25/36, 8/3, 27/19.
34. HI 11/2.

worked for half a year at an annual salary of $3,000. "I did a half-year's work," he wrote in mid-August to Mrs. Rose Ryan, assistant to the comptroller, "and I expected actually a half-year's pay. The number of installments has nothing to do with the matter as far as I can see, and is not mentioned in the contract." He pointed out that if Mrs. Ryan's interpretation was correct, "the yearly salary for any instructor at Bennington College is a nominal figure only, while actually he would receive only as many twelfths of that amount as there are months in which teaching is going on." And that, Voegelin said, is unheard of.[35]

Voegelin's summer seminar at Northwestern was concerned with totalitarian movements and democratic resistance to them. Social and economic factors were considered, but the emphasis was on interpreting totalitarianism as a "political religion." Contemporary political movements, he said, "are primarily important as phases in the process of disintegration of the Christian unity of the Western world." Particular attention was paid to the political philosophers whose doctrines guided the formation of the modern secular state and to the more fundamental religious "ideas" that had been discussed in *Political Religions*.[36]

In late May, Voegelin received a request from the director of the summer session at Northwestern, Ernest Hahne, to prepare a fifteen-minute radio talk on "Democracy and the Individual," to be broadcast on the Red Network of NBC. Five days later Voegelin had sent a text back to Hahne, an achievement that reflects equally well on his industry and on the efficiency of the postal service in 1939.[37] His written submission, more detailed than the transcript of the broadcast, was a splendid piece of commonsense analysis. He began by observing that the right to vote was fundamental in a democracy but that it was not enough. Equally important was the Aristotelian requirement of the right to rule and be ruled by turns. This means that, under modern conditions, one must be able to vote *against* as well as to vote *for* a party or candidate. To do so responsibly citizens must have access to accurate information and be protected from state interference in their ability to speak and assemble freely, to petition for the redress of grievances, and to join or found a

35. HI 8/3. A search of the records of the Bennington College Comptroller's Office would be necessary to determine whether Voegelin received his final $250, for no record of subsequent correspondence seems to exist in HI.

36. HI 27/19. Voegelin also took part in a standard summer school symposium on "The Groups of Refugees Forced to Leave Germany" and gave an interview to the *Northwestern News Magazine* (published in the issue of July 21, 1939) outlining the circumstances of his dismissal from Vienna. A copy is in the Voegelin Library, Erlangen. See also HI 56/2.

37. HI 56/4.

political party. Equally important, rulers in a democracy must be both reasonably secure in office but not so secure as to form a caste.

The corresponding dangers threatening democracy likewise concern the relationship of rulers and ruled. When large numbers of people shirk their democratic duties of being well informed and disputative, or if they are prevented from acting democratically, it will be increasingly difficult to recruit leaders willing or able to assume their democratic responsibilities. The German example was a useful illustration of what takes place when individuals no longer wish to be democratic citizens. Voegelin's point was that the National Socialists did not destroy otherwise healthy democratic institutions. On the contrary, they and the Communists, acting together on the basis of a common hatred of democracy, prevented, by their so-called blocking majority, any democratic government action. In fact, the antidemocratic majority in the Reichtag was elected by a majority of voters under strictly democratic rules.

What made the Central European experience so important for modern democracy was that the factors that combined to create an antidemocratic majority were present elsewhere. The most important condition for the existence of modern democracy, so far as individuals are concerned, is that they be reasonable, in the sense of being capable of dealing with personal problems, but capable as well of seeing what their interests are and having sufficient courage and self-respect to press for them by speaking up and offering an opinion on a desirable policy. It may be granted that these conditions were sufficiently present during the founding of the American republic, Voegelin said, but it must also be granted that those conditions obtain less widely in the twentieth century.

Technological changes associated with the industrial revolution had changed the structure of society by decreasing the independence of citizens. Often these changes have been praised as promoting interdependence, but they may be more accurately and more simply described as promoting dependence. Under modern industrial and organizational conditions, less is required by way of personal responsibility and initiative, and more by way of discipline and precision in the execution of orders. The immediate experiences of dependence enhance the appeal of discipline, organization, and planning—planning done by somebody else—as recipes for individual and collective greatness. Moreover, given the complexity of economic and technological problems, most citizens have grown incapable of forming a proper understanding of the issues involved; the reasonableness of their opinion and even of their involvement was thereby diminished.

Voegelin illustrated his argument by reference to the Central European social groups to whom totalitarian politics appealed: lower and middle ranges of large-scale organizations, professionals in the applied sciences, those whose vocation is alien to democratic experience, such as army officers, and those who are economically vulnerable. It was equally important to be aware of the centers of resistance to totalitarianism. Two were emphasized, the peasants and the churches. The teaching of the churches concerning the Christian personality was obviously incompatible with collectivism. Peasants and others whose life is associated with agriculture traditionally have been hostile to regimentation. But just because both the churches and the peasantry were to some degree hostile to the triumphant forces of technological industrialism, it did not follow that they would be effective sources of resistance to totalitarianism. Voegelin was not, in any event, concerned with the practical restoration of peasant yeomen or with an evangelical revival.

His concern, rather, was with the experiential bases for the centers of resistance, namely a sense of individuality and responsibility for matters of genuine significance. If experiences of dependency induce anxieties that undermine individual capacities for action, then social institutions would have to be changed in such a way that individuals could experience greater security. Certain aspects of what has become the welfare state, such as health and unemployment insurance, would, Voegelin argued, relieve individuals from the necessity of taking stands on economic measures the complex implications of which they do not understand. Politics might then be concerned with discussion of policies and laws relative to the ethical structure of society, not questions of economic administration. Voegelin added that he did not expect the experts charged with carrying out the administration of welfare to avoid costly mistakes but that such mistakes might be seen as "the price which has to be paid for creating a society with security of status for the individual." Moreover, Voegelin emphasized that it was equally important to ensure that the government did not expand the welfare "safety net" into ongoing interference in the economy. Such interference, initiated in the name of "planning," led, to use a term later made famous by Hayek, down the road to serfdom.

Summer school at Northwestern ended in mid-August 1939. Voegelin bought a 1936 Ford, learned to drive it with the assistance of the salesman, and promptly smashed a fender. Mrs. Voegelin drove most of the way to Tuscaloosa. At Alabama, Voegelin taught American government and American diplomatic history as well as political philosophy. Life in Tuscaloosa, Voegelin wrote to Talcott Parsons early in the new year, "is very pleasant. But the social environment, being rather different from the East or the Middle West, is still somewhat bewildering."[38] By April

38. HI 28/12.

he knew he would be reappointed for an additional two years as an associate professor.

The scholarly ambience of Tuscaloosa in 1940 was not always as supportive of Voegelin's work as he might have wished. In the fall of the year, for example, Voegelin wrote his dean with a request for a grant of a hundred dollars to acquire books for the library that would be useful for his research. The volumes requested were standard monographs unlikely to be available through interlibrary loan because they were the kinds of books that were usually placed permanently on reserve. A little more than a month later the dean replied that Voegelin's request "raised a rather delicate question," namely whether books were, properly speaking, "supplies." Decanal authority was insufficient to resolve a question of such complexity, and it was referred to the president of the university, who, "while also sympathetic," feared the establishment of an undesirable precedent. The request for a hundred dollars was denied, and Voegelin was told to redirect his request to the library or to his department—which, of course, he had already done.[39]

The Voegelins spent most of the summer of 1941 in Tuscaloosa. In August they drove north through the Appalachians, crossed the Smokies into North Carolina, and continued south again along the coast, touring the ports of the Old South. In September 1941 Voegelin returned to his teaching duties. Despite the difficulties of learning by teaching and of learning to speak idiomatic English to southerners, Voegelin was a very successful teacher. In June 1941 his students had won a regional prize for their essays on American foreign policy.[40] Yet his encounter with the dean and president was symptomatic of the difficulty a thinker of Voegelin's ability would inevitably encounter at an undistinguished and poorly funded state university. "Alabama is charming," he wrote Parsons, "but it is not particularly stimulating."[41]

During wartime it was inevitable that Voegelin's support would be sought for various political or military purposes. As early as May 1941, Gregor Sebba invited him to join the editorial board of *Austrian Action*.[42] He refused because, he said, "I simply have decided for my own person

39. HI 38/18.
40. HI 90/1.
41. HI 28/12.
42. Voegelin and Sebba had been students at the University of Vienna Law School during the 1920s. Sebba served in the British Army and in the OSS as well as on the board of *Austrian Action*. See his "Autobiographical Note" in *The Dream of Descartes*, ed. Richard A. Watson (Carbondale: Southern Illinois University Press, 1987), and Richard Macksey, foreword to *The Collected Essays of Gregor Sebba: Truth, History and the Imagination*, ed. H. Sebba, A. A. Bueno, and H. Boers.

to go in for American action." Six months later he was asked to join the Free Austrian National Council. Again he refused but, upon hearing from Willibald Ploechl, one of the organizers, that it was supported by the Department of State, Voegelin wrote Adolf Berle, at the time an assistant secretary of state, for his advice. He had no interest in Austrian politics, he told Berle, and had no desire to do anything that might delay or jeopardize his receiving American citizenship, but "if my membership on [the Council] seems desirable to the Department, I shall, of course, consider it my duty to join it." Berle replied, quite correctly, that Voegelin was free to join the Free Austrian National Council or any other group to plead whatever cause he liked so long as it was consistent with the laws of the United States. "On the other hand," Berle said, "foreigners who have entered this country and who propose to become a permanent part of it may very well feel that their efforts might be more usefully directed toward entering the main stream of American life." Voegelin then responded to Ploechl that it was clear to him, at least, that the support of the Department of State was "not strong enough to find expression in writing." Accordingly, he would not give up his "hitherto clear intention of complete Americanization" in order "to adopt voluntarily the doubtful status of a foreign agent."[43]

Later in the year he was twice approached by Austrians living in exile. The first attempt to recruit him was again undertaken by Ploechl, who asked if Voegelin would care to join an Austrian cabinet-in-exile that had been formed in Toronto under a former minister from the Schuschnigg cabinet named Rott. Voegelin declined the honor. The second approach was from Austrian Action, now no longer just a magazine, of which Sebba was secretary. On November 6, 1941, the chairman, Count Ferdinand Czernin, asked for Voegelin's opinion regarding the legality of Rott's ability to act as a representative of the former Austrian government by virtue of his status as a former minister.

Voegelin played his cameo role in this Viennese comic opera with aplomb. "It is a great pleasure for me to be at your service" he said, but, considering the nature of Count Czernin's question, "I shall have to make a few reservations." First, he did not have sufficient materials "to make a formal responsible statement." Second, he noted that the question of the legality of Rott's status was "a very delicate one" and referred Czernin to pages 150–60 of *Der autoritäre Staat* for a thorough discussion of the topic. The delicacy in question lay in the distinction between legitimacy and legality. Voegelin cited as authorities on this question "The National Socialist, Carl Schmitt, . . . The French Republican, Maurice Hauriou," and

43. HI 7/2.

just about every other leading constitutional theorist. He was, therefore, "greatly astonished" that the matter was even raised. Before giving his exegesis of the letter of Austrian constitutional law, which concluded that Rott could claim no legal warrant for his pretensions to office, Voegelin requested that they not damage his reputation by quoting him as an authority on legal matters that had absolutely no political relevance or importance.[44]

Ten days later Count Czernin wrote back, oblivious to the absurdity of the gavotte. Voegelin's presentation of the legal problems, he said, "would greatly help to calm down the excitement created by Mr. Rott's coup d'état." He asked permission to quote Voegelin's "legal opinion" to the Department of State and to the Canadian, British, and Czech governments. Voegelin agreed, "provided that your covering letter states clearly that I do not consider the question of legality as relevant for the authority of government," and that his name not be attached to any remarks destined for a wider audience. Czernin agreed; three weeks later he asked Voegelin to write a legal memorandum on the basis of which an Austrian "War Council" could enter upon negotiations with the British and American governments as "trustee of the Austrian people's right to freedom and independence until such time as it can again exercise its democratic right of self-determination." Voegelin ended the comedy by pointing out to the count that legal questions "have only a comparatively subordinate role" in matters of high policy, such as the future of states after a war of such ferocity and duration as the present one.

As a postscript to the efforts of Austrian exiles to involve Voegelin in their politics, a curious incident took place in 1942. Count Degenfeld, secretary to Otto of Hapsburg, wrote Voegelin asking for his signature on a proclamation by which an Austrian military unit might be formed under the aegis of the U.S. Army. It was with great regret, Voegelin said, that he declined to support such a proclamation. The reason was not that he objected to the dissociation of Austria from the Reich. His reason was purely personal, namely that he expected to be drafted early in 1943 and intended to fight as an American, not an Austrian, soldier. He would, furthermore, be quite willing to support the restoration of Austria when that seemed likely. "I have," wrote Voegelin, "voluntarily taken my stand for Austria in the years before 1938 to the extent of destroying my position and of being compelled to emigrate in order to escape the concentration camp. In the critical moment those who were supposed to lead the fight surrendered or ran away. Two of the members of the cabinet that did not fight have signed the Proclamation.

44. HI 7/2.

I am delighted to give them a chance to fight this time and by the fight they show to acquire the authority for asking others to join them." He ended by offering his respects to His Majesty. A few days later he wrote Talcott Parsons that, since the proclamation seemed to imply that all inhabitants of the Hapsburg empire prior to 1918 were "Austrians," the whole business was bound to end badly.[45]

Because Voegelin was not then a U.S. citizen and could not aid the war effort directly, the option of service in Washington was closed to him. He did, however, make a few modest contributions. In early 1942 he wrote a "Memorandum Concerning a Program of Study for the Public Service." The memorandum addressed the problem of training American civil and military administrators for postwar overseas duties in Europe, Japan, and Africa. He outlined a liberal arts curriculum that combined elements of European civil service training "with items necessitated by the special problem of American administration in foreign countries," such as the need to familiarize students with foreign languages and literatures. In April, Louisiana State University was approached by the army to provide instruction to staff officers on German, Italian, and Japanese political beliefs, and Voegelin was asked to do most of the work.[46]

In June 1942, Voegelin received a letter from Taylor Cole, who was on leave from Duke University serving in the Military Intelligence Service of the War Department.[47] Cole asked Voegelin's advice on two questions: first, how the Allies might impede German military operations by enhancing intergroup conflicts within the Reich; and second, how to indicate to enemy soldiers, particularly those recruited from Austria, that an Allied victory would be preferable to continued struggle under the control of the National Socialists. Voegelin provided a seven-page reply. The principal intergroup conflict was between the National Socialists and all other ideological, institutional, and social groupings. There was, moreover, considerable overlap among group categories where dissension might be profitably exploited.

Three "ideological groupings" existed from the pre-Hitler period, Voegelin said: the Marxists, the democrats, and the Christians. It was doubtful whether a successful appeal could be made to individuals included in either of the first two categories. On the one hand, the language of American democracy would be unintelligible to the handful of democrats in the Reich; on the other, the Soviet Union had a monopoly on the appeal to Communists, who were the only brand of Marxists

45. HI 25/22, 28/12.
46. HI 23/27.
47. HI 38/16. See also Cole, *The Recollections of R. Taylor Cole*, 70 ff.

that might respond. Regarding an appeal to Christians, Voegelin was more hopeful. There were obvious difficulties in making an appeal to German Christians on the grounds of a common religious faith: the alliance with the Soviet Union was one such difficulty, and the weakness of Christianity, compared to "national will to power and resentment against the Japanese attack," as motive forces for the American war effort, was another. Nevertheless, "the idea of a defense of Christianity is one that would seriously cut into the unity of the German nation and engage considerable parts of the nation against the communist effort." Regarding institutional groupings, only the army and the churches were significant, and the fate of the former was clearly tied to the fate of the regime. The institutional interests of the churches, however, were enormous, "and the danger to the Church as an institution is the one Christian problem that has penetrated even to the Holy See and stirred it to do occasional mild action." As for social and economic groupings, nothing much could be expected until the war had clearly turned against the Reich, and then the most likely groups to which appeals might be made were peasants and workers. In Austria, only Christian socialist peasants would be likely to respond to Allied propaganda that promised "protection against totalitarian regulation from the right or the left." Cole gave a cordial response to Voegelin's analysis.

In the meantime, Voegelin's position at the University of Alabama had become precarious. By the end of the fall semester of 1941, the significance of the refusal by Voegelin's administrative superiors to grant his request for one hundred dollars worth of books was plain: they were seriously considering firing him. Fortunately, at the 1939 meeting of the Southern Political Science Association, Voegelin had met Robert J. Harris, chairman of the LSU Political Science Department. He was invited to Baton Rouge to deliver a lecture in the spring of 1941 and was invited to teach there as a visiting professor for the first semester of 1942. A number of irregularities ensued. First, Roscoe Martin, the chairman at Alabama, asked Voegelin to see if the Rockefeller Foundation could delay the second half of the third year's payment, scheduled for the spring of 1942, until the fall. Kittredge replied that he did not see how this would benefit the University of Alabama, which would have to replace Voegelin at full salary anyhow, and such a change was, in any event, not possible. Kittredge then suggested that the Rockefeller Foundation continue to contribute to Voegelin's salary, as before, but that he pay for his replacement at Alabama with his LSU salary. This proved impossible for Alabama. In the end, it was agreed that the Rockefeller Foundation contribution to Voegelin's salary would be used to pay his replacement; but, when the day came, enrollment had dropped at the university and the course Voegelin had taught at Alabama was dropped as well. Then, shortly after Voegelin accepted the offer to teach at LSU, he was informed by Martin that he was not likely to be rehired the following fall. En-rollment had been dropping throughout the university, the Rockefeller subsidy was about to end, and the university president had a distinct preference for Alabamans, however modest their pretensions to scholar-ship, over foreigners, however brilliant. "All this," Voegelin wrote Elliott, "is rather disquieting and makes it advisable to look for an opening elsewhere before I stand all of a sudden penniless in the world."[48]

The publication of his article on the Mongols in *Byzantion* gave Voe-gelin the opportunity in April 1942 to send reprints to his friends and acquaintances and to ask for their aid in securing employment. During February and March he had had a frank exchange of views with the administration in Tuscaloosa.[49] As he wrote John Ramsay in the history department at Alabama, "I had to go pretty far in explaining what I thought about accepting a Rockefeller grant in payment for my salary and then to dismiss me on the day when it expired, while the grant was given with the purpose of securing permanency of tenure; and I elaborated the problem generally into indicating that it looked like sabotage to me if in a time like this the good men were dismissed while the permanent sitters, whom nobody wanted, should be retained under the pretext of tenure."[50] Voegelin's plain speech had the effect that Alabama offered to hire him for one more year. In the meantime he was looking actively for a position elsewhere.

During the late spring and early summer of 1942 Voegelin discussed with Harris the possibility of moving permanently to LSU. Harris as-sured him of a position as soon as one of their colleagues, Alex Daspit, confirmed his departure for Washington. Daspit departed in mid-July, but he would not ask for a leave of absence for the duration of the war until he decided whether he enjoyed his work in Washington. Voegelin replied a week later from Cambridge, where he was again at work on his *History*, that he would accept a definite offer from LSU. "As to the salary," he wrote, "you know that I am greedy: if you give me the choice between $3200.00 or more, I take more." A week later Harris replied that he had recommended another four hundred dollars; in the first week in August the dean refused and countered with a hundred dollar increase for 1942–1943.[51]

48. RF, 1:1/200/411/4862–3, HI 24/22, 11/2.
49. HI 38/19.
50. HI 29/34.
51. HI 16/15.

On August 8, Voegelin wrote to Martin, asking to be released from his commitments to Alabama, and to Harris, agreeing to the terms of his appointment at LSU. Martin wrote back expressing his pleasure that Voegelin's abilities were being more adequately recognized but also his regret that he would be leaving. "I do not hesitate to say that your going will damage the professional standing of this Department very seriously, though I would entertain the hope that at some future date we might resume our progress toward scholarship." He then asked whether Voegelin sought a leave of absence or wished to resign, and Voegelin sought assurance from Harris that their correspondence constituted a contract. Harris sent Voegelin a telegram: "Offer final contract being prepared in presidents office will be mailed on receipt of data requested in letter this morning. Safe to resign." On August 18, 1942, Voegelin resigned from Alabama, and on August 19 he was appointed visiting associate professor of government at Louisiana State University. He remained at Baton Rouge until 1958, when he moved to the University of Munich in order to establish the Institute for Political Science.

2

War and
Political Ideas

By the start of the academic year 1942–1943, Voegelin was settled in a permanent position at Louisiana State University. Since 1939, he had been actively taking part in the activities of the political science community. Voegelin had been trained at the University of Vienna in political science rather than in law. Even so, he completed his dissertation under the joint supervision of the classical scholar Othmar Spann and of Hans Kelsen, author of the Austrian Constitution of 1920 and of the "pure theory of law" to which he owed his lasting fame.[1] It is not surprising, therefore, that Voegelin maintained a serious and continuous intellectual interest in problems of jurisprudence and the systematic study of the law, or "legal science," which was Voegelin's English for the German concept of *Rechtslehre*. As late as 1976, for example, Voegelin was corresponding with editors at Notre Dame University Press concerning the possibility of publishing a manuscript written twenty years earlier as the text for a course in jurisprudence at LSU.[2] During the 1940s, Voegelin was often called upon to review books on legal matters for political science journals. In these pieces, Voegelin addressed many of the same questions concerning method and the criteria for the sound interpretation of texts that he considered in his discussion of the course of the war. We will consider Voegelin's scientific analyses of legal theory in the following chapter. Over the next few years Voegelin produced four articles on

1. Voegelin's first article in English was "Kelsen's Pure Theory of Law" (1927). Many of his early articles in German concerned various aspects of law and jurisprudence, and substantial parts of his books on the United States and on Austria dealt with legal matters. Moreover, during his last years in Vienna he began work on a book dealing with the basic concepts of *Staatslehre*.
2. HI 38/26. *The Nature of the Law,* ninety-eight pages in typescript in 1957, was subsequently published in *The Nature of the Law and Related Legal Writings,* ed. Robert Anthony Pascal, James Lee Babin, and John William Corrington, *CW,* vol. 27 (1991; available Columbia: University of Missouri Press, 1999).

interrelated aspects of the war and began work on his *History of Political Ideas*. The articles clearly reflected the immediate political and strategic concerns of the day; the *History*, as we will see in subsequent chapters, was Voegelin's more comprehensive account of the genesis and nature of the spiritual disorder of which the destructive violence of the war and the incoherence of ideology were but phenomenal manifestations.

The first of the four articles, "Extended Strategy: A New Technique in Dynamic Relations," was initially presented at the November 1939 meeting of the Southern Political Science Association.[3] The term *extended strategy* was taken from Hermann Rauschning's *The Revolution of Nihilism* and referred to techniques of political expansion, such as subversion, economic pressure, and propaganda. These techniques were not part of the process of peaceful diplomacy but were properly understood as strategic instruments preparatory to the application of armed force in the conquest of territory and population. Voegelin proposed to give an analysis of the background of the strategy and of the historical conditions that enabled it to operate with such success. The chief characteristic of the technique was that it was hidden; the first stage in the analysis, therefore, was to discuss the "screen techniques" that had been employed by the National Socialists to hide their real purposes. Voegelin's argument thus combined shrewd analysis with a presentation of historical evidence.

The initial phase consisted in the restoration of internal German sovereignty through rearmament, conscription, and reoccupation of the Rhineland, all of which were violations of explicit provisions in the Treaty of Versailles. The success of these moves depended on two things: first, the widespread opinion in Germany that the Versailles Treaty violated the conventions governing the appropriate treatment of sovereign states and, second, the fact that Germany understood itself as a sovereign state. For anyone who had observed the National Socialist revolution with care it was apparent that invocations of German sovereignty, national honor, and so forth were simply used to obscure an aggressive revolutionary dynamic. In contrast, politically effective public opinion at first in Germany, but later in the West as well, considered the Nazis as reformers in a hurry who, while beset with certain unfortunate attitudes and an understandable impatience, were really just like prepubescent adolescents, going through a phase: once the anomalies of Versailles were removed, things would simmer down, and Germany would again start behaving like a "normal" state.

The strategy entered a second phase when the language of national self-determination replaced the language of internal sovereignty. If one

3. Quotations are from the identical version published in *Journal of Politics*.

accepted at face value the language of national self-determination, it would not be difficult to convince oneself that the annexation of Austria and of the Sudeten-German area of Czechoslovakia was simply an internal affair of the German nation in the process of attaining the proper form of a state, and again simply correcting some of the regrettable oversights of 1918–1919. With the annexation of the remainder of Czechoslovakia in the spring of 1939 a new symbolic screen was widely accepted by Western public opinion: *Lebensraum.* Translating the term as literally "living-space" is unintelligible in commonsense English. After all, Germans had the space of Germany in which to live, and the space of Czechoslovakia that had been appropriated by them was already being lived in by Czechs and Slovaks. The biological, collectivist, geopolitical, and metaphysical connotations of the term in German were inadequately understood, to say the least, by Western interpreters. To think through the implications of the symbolism of *Lebensraum* would have entailed a reconsideration of the language of national self-determination and even of internal state sovereignty, which no one seemed prepared to do.

Instead, most Western observers directed their attention to the surface aspect of the doctrine, namely the extension of jurisdiction over areas and populations, and concluded that *Lebensraum* really meant imperialism. Unlike national self-determination and internal sovereignty, most Western observers had decided that imperialism was no longer a legitimate political pursuit. Accordingly, the change from the allegedly peaceful second-phase screen, namely national self-determination, to the unacceptable third-phase screen, *Lebensraum,* was sufficient to induce the Western powers to abandon the attempt to deal with the revolutionaries through appeasement, and they declared war. Apart from an intense but vague feeling that they were in peril, the actual reasons the Western powers declared war were but dimly apprehended.

On the National Socialists' side, other ancillary techniques were employed to sustain the strategy of dynamic expansion. Chief among them was the use of the plebiscite. The advantage of this technique was that it met an abstract democratic standard and thereby appealed to those Western opinion-leaders for whom democracy had also become abstract. These were people who had forgotten that the essential problem of democratic government, as Voegelin had observed in his NBC speech quoted in Chapter 1, was the substantive relation of the governors to the governed. At the same time, those who were aware of the problem of democracy, as with those who were aware of the nature of the National Socialist revolution, were also politically marginalized.

In the Austrian example, the same technique of destroying the democratic substance while adhering to democratic forms resulted in the curious spectacle of Western intellectuals denouncing the Austrian government for its formally nondemocratic efforts to shelter the fragile democratic substance of Austrian politics from the attacks of the Austrian National Socialists and Communists. At the time, Voegelin reflected later, he was amazed and angered at the criminal thoughtlessness of the Western leaders and intellectuals.[4] Apart from the obvious strategic implications, it was simple common sense that, when genuine democrats noticed that the government was incapable of defending them against the antidemocratic collectivists, they would likely withdraw their support from the regime. Thus, the abstract criticisms of Western intellectuals could serve only to strengthen the antidemocratic forces and do nothing for Austrian democracy, whether formal or substantive.

Other ancillary screening techniques included an anti-Bolshevik appeal to the fearful but credulous wealthy and a continuing story that Germany was "frustrated" because it had been wronged. That the latter interpretation of events was widely believed to be self-evident speaks volumes about the stupidity and cowardice of Western leaders, which in turn must be counted among the major factors contributing to the success of the National Socialists' strategy. Apart from the dubiousness of employing a category of individual psychology to account for the behavior of nations, the connection between frustration and aggression is by no means obvious even for individuals. On the one hand, human beings are frustrated all the time without responding by outbursts of violence and aggression. Moreover, when individuals cannot handle their frustrations and respond by aggressive behavior, it is customary to put them in criminal detention facilities. On the other hand, aggression is not simply a consequence of frustration. Individuals and nations may be tempted to act aggressively, for instance, as a response to weakness. But it was by no means obvious that aggression can be controlled by appeasement. The old Roman maxim, *qui desiderat pacem, praeparet bellum*, had lost none of its truth during the 1930s.

A final screen device was erected not by the National Socialists but by Western political leaders. After the annexation of Czechoslovakia following the Munich agreement, the opinion that Hitler was a habitual, pathological liar gained currency in the West. If a lie is a statement uttered by someone who knows it is untrue, Hitler cannot be called a liar. According to National Socialist epistemology, Voegelin said, truth is what is in the interests of the German people as interpreted by the National Socialists. Promises cannot be broken because they are not, properly speaking, points of stabilization but tactical elements in the

4. *Autobiographical Reflections*, 40.

revolutionary process. Lenin expressed the same epistemology in his aphorism, "words are weapons." What was least excusable about the Western response derived from the fact that both the National Socialists and the Bolsheviks were sufficiently plainspoken on this point that involuntary misunderstanding was unlikely.

As a postscript to this analysis of Western complicity in National Socialist expansion, Voegelin delivered a short speech at LSU in February 1942 on "British War Aims."[5] Everyone was clear that the Western powers had to win the war militarily or they would not survive.

> Beyond this clear purpose of preservation, however, the meaning of the war becomes doubtful. The confusion is due to the particular development which political aims in general have taken in the Western democracies in the recent decades. The aims of all workers are to improve the conditions of wages and hours; the aims of our businessmen are business as usual and normalcy; the aims of our middle class are the freedom from want and fear, the abundant life and the enjoyment of comfort. Important as well [sic] these aims are, none of them is political in the technical sense of assertion and expansion of power.

For this reason the Soviet, German, and Japanese governments had a considerable advantage: they were controlled by rulers who had definite power aims.

Voegelin sent reprints of his article to several people. Karl Loewenstein responded with the observation: "I feel that one should emphasize less the lack of understanding of such screen verbiage by others [in the West] than the utter disingenuity and faithlessness of the Nazis in using them."[6] Carl Friedrich was equally anxious to condemn the National Socialists and excuse the Western leaders:

> Thanks very much for sending me your reprint on "Extended Strategy." While I in general agree with you I would maintain that the inclination to use screen language is very common in any kind of politics that addresses itself to large groups and necessarily so. The analysis which symbolic logic and what is popularly known as semantics had made of the use of words is clearly indicative of this universal trend. The peculiarity of the Nazis is not that they use screen language but what kind of screen they use, and what is the screen. On the whole I think the peculiar characteristic is rather the extraordinary recklessness in which any connection between the screen and what is being screened is being disregarded. And this, to be sure, is characteristic of any group which goes as far as the Nazis do in their contempt for their followers.[7]

5. This speech exists only in manuscript, HI 61/14.
6. HI 23/23.
7. HI 13/16.

The response by these two German-born political scientists could not have been reassuring to Voegelin.

It was also in 1940 that Voegelin published "The Growth of the Race Idea." The contents summarized and recast the arguments of the two prewar books on race; the work was, however, more precise and explicit regarding the methodological issues involved in the analysis of political ideas. The greater analytic precision resulted from Voegelin's systematic reflection on the purpose and function of a political idea. The occasion for these reflections was Voegelin's writing of an "Introduction" to the first version of his *History of Political Ideas.* The origin of the *History* may be dated in the fall or early winter of 1938–1939, when Voegelin was still at Harvard. There he met Fritz Morstein Marx, who at the time edited a textbook series in political science for the McGraw-Hill Book Company. Morstein Marx asked Voegelin if he would contribute a college textbook, around two hundred pages in length. In February 1939, Voegelin signed a "Memorandum of Agreement" to produce, by September 1940, *A History of Political Ideas.*[8] And so began the long, sometimes frustrating, sometimes rewarding, sometimes even amusing story of the growth, revision, regrowth, and recasting of a manuscript that appeared in part during the 1950s as *Order and History,* in part half a century later as a major element in Voegelin's *Collected Works,* and in part during the later 1940s as independently published scholarly articles.[9] In short, from 1939 to the publication of *The New Science of Politics* in 1952, the manuscript was Voegelin's chief preoccupation and the major work from his hand. As we shall see, several chapters of *History of Political Ideas* constitute the most important building blocks in Voegelin's construction of a modern foundation to political science.

Sometime during the spring of 1940, Voegelin wrote his "Introduction," which considered the fundamental question of just what sort of thing a political idea was, such that he might presume to write its history.[10] The establishment of a government, Voegelin began, "is an essay in world creation." From a shapeless chaos of conflicting desires

8. HI 24/24, 24/32.
9. The philological details are ably presented by Thomas A. Hollweck and Ellis Sandoz in their "General Introduction to the Series," *HPI,* I:3–16.
10. The holograph was written in English in Voegelin's almost unreadable and cramped hand, HI 56/9. Thomas Hollweck deciphered Voegelin's writing and published it as "Appendix A" in *HPI,* I:225–37. The date, the spring of 1940, is assigned on the basis of Voegelin's correspondence with another of his Viennese friends, Max Mintz; a letter of March 23, 1940, quotes Voegelin's "Introduction" exactly (HI 25/23). Quotations in the text are from the "Introduction." I have followed Hollweck's transcription except for a couple of minor changes.

rises "a little world of order, a cosmic analogy, a cosmion." Its existence is precarious; ultimately it can be maintained only by the threat and the application of violence—internally by means of the police and the justice system, externally by military power. The use of violence, however, is instrumental only for the preservation of order, *cosmos:* "the function proper of order is the creation of a shelter in which man may give to his life a semblance of meaning." One of the tasks of political science, therefore, is to give an account of political institutions, along with an appropriate philosophy of history that traces the steps by which political society evolved from tribe and clan to "the power-units whose rise and decline constitute the drama of history." Among Voegelin's contemporaries, as we shall see in Chapter 8, Toynbee was often cited as the great exemplar, notwithstanding the reservations that Voegelin on occasion expressed concerning aspects of Toynbee's work. Voegelin proceeded on the assumption that, along with the history of these power-units, whether tribal or imperial, "we can trace also, in continuity, the attempts to rationalize the shelter-function of the cosmion, the little world of order, by what are commonly called political ideas."[11] The details may vary, but the purpose remains constant—to rationalize the shelter that gives meaning to human life against the forces of disintegration and chaos, a shelter that, in the end, is maintained by force.

Furthermore, Voegelin said, these ideas are configured into three "sets." The first concerns the constitution of the cosmos as a whole; the second, its internal order; and the third, the "status of the cosmion in the simultaneous world and in history." Again the details vary enormously in their concrete specificity, but all have a determinate place in the general structure of meaning.[12] If political ideas were exhausted by an analysis of the "shelter-function" in any particular context, it would be a relatively straightforward task to write their history. One need only specify the purpose, use, or function of an idea beforehand and then apply this "conceptual framework," to use the contemporary jargon, to the appropriate "data" in order to find what one has decided to look for. Apart from its a priori circularity, however, this "utilitarian argument," which starts and ends with a consideration of the use and

11. Voegelin's use of the term *cosmion* was borrowed from Adolf Stöhr's *Wege des Glaubens* (1921). See Hollweck and Sandoz, "General Introduction," 18 and references, especially Voegelin's letter to Schütz, October 6, 1945, HI 34/10, and Schütz, "On Multiple Realities," in *Collected Papers,* ed. M. Natanson, 1:207.

12. Voegelin made much the same point in rather different language in his 1928 book on America when he drew attention to the concrete and specific differences between the composition and treatment of theater tickets (for example) in Paris and in New York (*CW,* 1:5).

configuration of political ideas, "does not reach the emotional center of the cosmion."

Looking to that emotional center one first encounters a manifold of desire: to create a meaningful world out of chaos and disorder, to unite a fragmentary life by making it part of a more comprehensive social unit, to overcome the limitations of individual achievement by making it part of a group purpose. Indeed, the anxieties that arise "when the possibility of the utter senselessness of a life ending in annihilation is envisaged" can find any number of means to express themselves. The problem, however, is that the cosmion is, in reality, finite, whereas the cosmos of which it is the ordered analog is not. One may indicate this negative characteristic paradoxically with the observation that, as infinite, the cosmos is not just cosmos in the simple sense of ordered whole. It is also disorder, chaos. From its chaotic element springs the aforementioned anxiety. This peculiarity of reality, which Voegelin considered and analyzed in several different formulations, was illustrated on this occasion by comparing the achievement of a "finite cosmos of meaning" with its rejection by some individuals as being in one way or another an inadequate representation of reality. "There have always been men," Voegelin said, "who have held the belief that out of the perishable qualities of human existence no earthly structure of intrinsic meaning can be built, that every attempt at creating a cosmion is futile, and that man has to undergo the trial of life only as a preparation for a life of meaning beyond his earthly existence." When translated into the organization of personal life, this belief can assume forms ranging from revolutionary communism to the so-called Protestant work ethic to anchoritic mysticism. All of them, however, Voegelin called apolitical.

The coexistence or tension between apolitical and political attitudes reveals to everyone that the "little world of order" is not the complete, absolute, and divine cosmos but a finite, relative, and humanly created imaginative analog. Because of its imaginative character, the cosmion is "always exposed to the recognition of that character by man," which leads to an ongoing political problem, amply illustrated by Voegelin's own experience, namely that those who adopt the "political" attitude are apt to forget or suppress their awareness of the fact that the cosmion is not absolute. "The important point in any system of political ideas is, therefore, the speculative" because speculation is concerned with resolving the problem of the basic and fundamental conflict between the finiteness of the cosmion and the infinite cosmos that is concretely manifest in the particular analog. A simple but nevertheless elegant solution was achieved by the Mongols who so interested Voegelin at the time: God is represented on earth by Chinggis Qan, who mediates the divine order by his command of an efficient cavalry whose divinely appointed task is to conquer the world, and thereby convert chaos and disorder into an ordered cosmion under their dominion. Polytheistic, monotheistic, and atheistic solutions are all possible. In each instance the aim is to connect or mediate the finite with the infinite. The end point came, Voegelin said, with the totalitarian "systems of ideas" that attempt to eliminate entirely the apolitical experiences and "to substitute the cosmion for the cosmos; in this respect, as an attempt to create an absolute cosmos out of the finite forces of human desire and will, it may be called magic."

The conclusion Voegelin drew from this argument concerned less the precariousness of organized power in maintaining the existence of a political society than the limited degree to which a political idea is descriptive of any sort of reality. "Its primary function," he said, "is not a cognitive, but a formative one. The political idea is not an instrument of description of a political unit, but an instrument of its creation. Or, as Schelling has put it in his *Philosophy of Mythology*, it is not the nation that produces a myth, but the myth that produces a nation." The creation of a political cosmion and the symbolization of the ordered relationship between ruler and ruled was called by Voegelin an act of evocation. Such evocations transform an amorphous field of human energies and anxieties into an ordered unit capable of action. The "magic" of an evocation is not, therefore, confined to the Mongols or the totalitarians but enters into the constitution of any political regime. The most familiar example is that of the king, a human being who nevertheless symbolizes political order through the unity of the human personality.

The evocative power of language, with the presumption that when a term is used it actually refers to something, leads to further complications because the evocative use of language is not usually distinguished from the descriptive. Yet language can result in "elaborate systems of thought" on the basis of terms that "empirically denote nothing." Moreover, since those individuals who are engaged in the evocative process are usually of the view that they are describing rather than evoking reality, the history of political ideas contains a vast array of misunderstandings and conflicting uses of language "ranging from purely evocative symbols through numerous intermediate shades to primarily descriptive language and ending in purely empirical descriptions of political reality."[13] Because there is generally a lack of awareness between the evocative and

13. Voegelin was using the term *empirical* in its Aristotelian sense of *empeiria*, which we usually translate as *experience*. See, for example, *The History of Animals*, 532b20 ff., *EN*, 1143b10 ff., *Prior Analytics*, 46a15 ff., *Posterior Analytics*, 100a3 ff. See also my

the descriptive use of language, political science is obliged to follow a fairly complex procedure of distinguishing the several usages from one another.

First is the "primary purpose of the political idea," which is to evoke the political unit, the "cosmion of order," and bring it into existence. Once it has come into being, the political unit, which now may act as a real social and political force, can be described "as something not magically but empirically real." This second use of language, which attempts to describe a magical evocation empirically, must inevitably lead to failure of one sort or another because the cosmion is *essentially* a magic rather than an empirical unit. Third, however, the trail of failures—from mechanical forces to biological units, from spiritual units and collective souls to contracting parties—constitutes much of the subject matter of textbooks on the history of political thought. Fourth is the special instance of a magic adventure undertaken during times "when the magic forces give out and men do not quite believe what they say." Under these conditions they simply pronounce "that nothing has to be evoked and everything is already there." Voegelin examined many such so-called theories and argued that, in fact, they were simply ancillary props to the ongoing evocative process. Moreover, since the duplicity of uttering disenchanted statements of belief is relatively easy to detect, one commonly finds a fifth and skeptical response alongside the pragmatic but mendacious "explanations" that explain nothing. On the other hand, when confronted with the corrosive and disenchanting language of skepticism, the ancillary so-called theories may simply reinforce themselves and create a sixth kind of language that ranges from an ideological weapon to a utopian dream.

All of these usages "have a claim to be called political ideas," but that is not the end of the story. A so-called political thinker or political theorist "who interprets man may detest the phenomenon of political order and wish to eradicate it, but he cannot ignore it. He has to take into account the experience of life and death, of the anxiety of existence, and of the desire and force to create out of perishable existence a cosmic analogy. The problem of politics has to be considered in the larger setting of an interpretation of human nature." We will consider systematically the question of Voegelin's philosophical anthropology in Chapter 5. In this "Introduction" to *History of Political Ideas*, Voegelin simply described "the function of political theory in the development of political ideas."

"Eric Voegelin, Empirical Political Scientist," in *The Restoration of Political Science and the Crisis of Modernity*, 271–82.

The term *theory,* Voegelin said, has often been loosely used to denote a political idea in one of the several senses just distinguished. But such usage can be confusing, and in the interest of clarity it is advisable to use it to mean "contemplation, *theoria* in the Aristotelian sense. A political theory, then, would be the product of detached contemplation of political reality." Such contemplation is a rare, individual, and nonadditive achievement. "Certainly there is no continuous process by which a theory of politics evolves and grows into a system, as theoretical physics does." Just as important, a political theorist is also a particular human being who was born into, and raised within, a particular political cosmion; as with other such particular human beings, he or she participates meaningfully in the evocative forces of the environment. Indeed, one may expect that the theorist takes a greater interest in politics than the average individual precisely because of a greater sensitivity regarding the political evocation. "In most cases," Voegelin observed,

> the theoretical attempt ends with a compromise, and this accounts for the vast body of political thought that has to be classified under the head of ancillary evocative ideas. The theorist reaches, in those cases, a certain degree of detachment and is able to take a larger view of the political process than his fellow citizens who are engrossed in the daily struggle, but the basic evocative ideas of his own cosmion prove to be the limit that he cannot transgress.

Voegelin mentioned Aristotle, Thomas Aquinas, and Bodin as examples of genuine theorists—but even they were conditioned by the evocative forces of the disintegrating polis, the expansive Christian empire, and the nascent national state.

The experiential relationship between political theory and the political idea, namely contemplation and evocation, is, then, necessarily one of conflict. "When contemplative analysis is carried to its limits, it has to explain the cosmion as what it is, as a magical entity, existing through the evocative forces of man; it has to explain its relativity, and its essential inability to accomplish what it intends to do—that is, to render an absolute shelter of meaning." Considered from the perspective of the evocative political idea, the contemplative attitude of the theorist will be understood as an attack on the meaning of political life. Political theory, therefore, is, *eo ipse,* an act of disenchantment, an undoing of the web of evocative ideas that for nearly everyone constitute the little island of order in a sea of chaos.

> Every serious attempt at contemplation will meet, therefore, with the resistance of the political forces in the cosmion as soon as it receives publicity and influence. It is too well known a fact to need specific illustration that,

for instance, certain mythical elements in national history are taboo and that scholars tampering with them by detached investigation arouse public resentment.

These remarks are certainly congruent with the approximately contemporary observations of Leo Strauss on the art of writing practiced by political philosophers.

The conclusion Voegelin drew was that such developments as occur in political science can be the result only of the efforts of outstanding individuals. Accordingly, political science cannot itself evoke the substance of a community of political philosophers or political scientists. It is an individual enterprise because cooperation would require institutions that "could not exist without social consent, and it is unimaginable that any political society would support, or even tolerate, an intellectual enterprise that questions the value of its cosmic analogy—at least no political society in history has ever done so." So far as Voegelin himself was concerned, the purpose of political science was neither to overcome this conflict nor even fully to comprehend it; still less was it to question the evocative ideas of any particular cosmion. Rather, it was to raise the issue of whether these ideas constituted a meaningful pattern and, if so, to describe it. That was the task he set for himself in the analysis of Nazi techniques of using "screen language" in the article "Extended Strategy," and it was continued in the article on the race idea.[14]

As we have just seen, the implications of the race idea have nothing to do with organized knowledge of biological or ethnographic phenomena. The idea is, rather, an element in a modern creed movement used to integrate a community spiritually and politically. There was simply no point in measuring a creed by the standards of science. "Such criticism is correct," Voegelin said, but "without meaning because it is not the function of an idea to describe social reality but to assist in its constitution." Images and symbols are related to reality but only as expressions of a diffuse field in terms of a comparatively simple representative unit. The disjunction between the diffuse field and the simplified symbol or idea (Voegelin here used the terms interchangeably) meant that polemics reflected a typical structure and division. Those who accepted the symbol as meaningful would assert the presence of the reality expressed in it; those who did not would point out the discrepancies between the symbolic representation of the reality and the reality itself and, on the basis of that insight, criticize those who accepted it as valid for believing in errors, myths, utopias, and so on.

14. Quotations that follow in the text are from "The Growth of the Race Idea."

Voegelin provided an exegesis of three examples of "body ideas," the polis, the mystical body of Christ, and the race idea. The methodological question that emerged from his account of these ideas concerns the question of evil and how evil is to be treated in political science. Voegelin's analysis contrasted the account of human existence, the anthropology, expressed in Christianity with the modern "scientific" anthropologies, of which the evocation of the race idea shared pride of place with that of "scientific socialism." With respect to evil, according to Christian anthropology, humans are imperfect beings burdened with original sin, which may be understood in this context as the Christian equivalent of the experience of chaos (within the cosmos) discussed earlier as the source of anxiety regarding existence. Human beings, according to the Christian anthropology, live their lives "under the categories of grace and repentance, damnation and salvation." Evil is both general and particular, and no one is exempt from responsibility for human sinfulness. Under the impact of secularization, the structure of this anthropology shifted: "progress" referred no longer to the way of the pilgrim toward the heavenly kingdom but to the way that consumers are able to enjoy longer and ever more comfortable self-preservation.

Transformations of this kind, Voegelin said, are symptoms of a process he identified as the externalization of evil. "The idea of evil becomes dissociated from its Christian context of human imperfection and sin, and is transferred from an internal problem of the soul to the external problem of an unsatisfactory state of things, which may be overcome by intelligent and concerted action of man." Matters can be simplified even further by particularizing evil in terms of identifiable others. In this way the Christian spiritual realm of darkness, equivalent in meaning to the cosmological chaos-within-cosmos, is transmogrified into an existing worldly political enemy. Modern political movements characteristically balance their own positive evocative "idea" with a "counter-idea" that is appropriately diabolical.[15]

15. In November 1952, Voegelin received a request from Edgar J. Thompson, a sociologist at Duke University, to translate "The Jew as Counter-Idea," pt. II, chap. 7, from *Race and State,* under the title "The Jew as Contrast-Conception." Voegelin indicated he was too busy to revisit obsolete arguments, recommended *The New Science of Politics* as a development of the problems "in their present theoretical setting," and stated he was "rather horrified by your information that a gentleman by the name of Copeland apparently has used the concept and mistranslated it as 'contrast concept' instead of 'counter idea.'" The older book was based on the "distinction between science in race questions and political ideas. The chapter on the Jews as a 'Counter-Idea' is distinctly part of the analysis of ideas, not of concepts. A counter-idea belongs in the realm of *doxa* in the Platonic sense, not in the realm of

With respect to the race idea in particular, the Christian distinction between body and soul had to be replaced with a "scientific" account that conceived bodily characteristics as somehow determining the personality of both the members of the new religious community and the members of the new diabolical countercommunity. As Voegelin had observed in the prewar race books, these "scientific" accounts are not, in fact, scientific at all but evocative community ideas or symbols that for other reasons are called scientific by those who accept them. Voegelin's point was not simply that Nazi "race ideas" were evil but that they were an example of a specific spiritual deformation, which he here identified as the externalization of evil, and that the status of such ideas as deformations did not in the least impair their ability to assist in the constitution of a political community. Such a community, moreover, could be very successful in undertaking to act in the world, as the National Socialists, along with Bolshevik "scientific socialists," have proved well enough. Furthermore, Voegelin pointed out, as he did in *Political Religions*, that moralizing lamentation over the existence of evil was no substitute for analysis of its genesis and characteristics. Such analysis, he said, not only could be undertaken by political science but was a central concern.

The third of Voegelin's analyses on the war was the most realistic, in the sense that it addressed directly the course of European political events.[16] By 1941 it was clear that the German government had successfully transformed the greater part of Europe into a powerful political structure. Because this structure had not been consolidated, it was impossible to give an unambiguous account of the institutions of government or of the principles upon which they were based. The reasons were clear enough: on the one hand, the internal development of the National Socialist revolution had not ended; on the other, the outcome of the war precipitated by German expansion was unpredictable. "All a scholar can do responsibly at such a juncture," Voegelin said, "is to outline and depict some of the essential features of the situation which will probably have a bearing on any future settlement, whatever the outcome of the armed struggle."

The first of three "essential features" was the general power structure of the Western world, that is, of America and Europe west of Russia.

---

science and concepts. Further elaboration of this fundamental problem of the social sciences you will also find in the previously mentioned recent book. The substitution of contrast concept for counter idea makes unmitigated nonsense of the work I have done. The idea that, through the generosity of Mr. Copeland, I receive 'credit' for such theoretical amateurishness does not exhilarate me at all" (HI 37/21).

16. Voegelin, "Some Problems of German Hegemony." The following quotations in the text are from this source.

The familiar and static prewar structure of legally coordinated units, differing in power but qualitatively equal as sovereign states, must be supplemented by taking into consideration the "very dynamic historic structure of the Western world." The center of Western expansion was the old German empire around which were grouped the old national states, some of which established their own empires. In the case of the United States, what was once a fragment of a geographically peripheral European empire had developed an empire of its own.

The wars that accompanied national imperial expansion took place on the geographic periphery of Europe and in the colonies. When they were concluded and imperial rivalries settled down into spheres of interest, the old imperial core, which had been preoccupied with the disintegration of the old imperial structure, undertook to become a national state under the creative expansion of Prussia. Nineteenth-century Germany, however, unlike the geographically peripheral national states during the previous two centuries, and unlike the contemporaneous United States, had nowhere to expand. The first phase of imperial expansion was modeled on the French and British precedents; the end of the maritime dream in 1919 initiated a second phase of overland expansion, modeled perhaps on the continental conquests of the United States.

Given Germany's geographic position in central Europe, either it would be constricted by the imperial expansion of the maritime states on the periphery or, if it undertook to expand its power overland, a considerable diminution of the Atlantic empires was implied as a result of German control of the internal strategic lines of the Western world. These geopolitical facts were well known and fully appreciated by both German and non-German political thinkers. Since 1938, the additional implication had been indicated by events: the expansion of German control through the zone of national states had altered the structure of the colonial zone as well. A consolidated Europe would place North America between "the European-African coast on the one side and the Japanese-dominated Asiatic coast on the other side in an isolation which might not be to the liking of even the most ardent American isolationist."

The second essential feature concerned the problems of organizing Eastern Europe on the basis of German power. The German empire had been a great power since 1870. Moreover, Germany was the original home, dating from the days of the medieval *sacrum imperium*, of the European imperial idea. Germany, therefore, was bound to act like any other great imperial Western power and not like Norway or Portugal. Only force could prevent some kind of German hegemony in Europe east of France in the same way that only force could have prevented the continental expansion of the United States or the expansion of French and British maritime power into Africa and Asia. Prior to 1919, German hegemony over central and southeast Europe was exercised by means of agreements with the Austrian empire, and the "nationalities question," which led to the postwar succession states, was handled by way of domestic Austrian policy. Regional interstate conflicts were thus confined to the small states of the Balkans. One may say, therefore, that whatever else the Austrian nationalities policy may have signified, it was an important instrument of German hegemony.

Following the 1919 settlements at Versailles and St. Germain, that particular policy instrument was no longer available. Moreover, the succession states would remain free of German hegemony only so long as Germany was too weak to resume the "drive to the east" or was forcibly prevented from so doing. Politically speaking, therefore, the succession states constituted a power vacuum kept in existence by the influence of the Western European maritime and Eastern European Soviet powers that surrounded Germany. In order for peaceful change to occur in the area, a federation in eastern and southeastern Europe would have had to have been created to replace the Austrian empire. If Germany had not become a totalitarian regime such evolution might have been possible once those whom Voegelin called the "national self-determination fanatics" had disappeared from the scene. The options, therefore, were three. First, if Germany was to exist as a great power it would exercise hegemony over Europe. Second, if it did not so exist, Central and Eastern Europe would have to be organized by the Atlantic powers on the basis of military occupation. The third possibility was that Western Europe might be organized under Russian hegemony.[17] The "day-dream of Western statesmen," Voegelin said, namely the coexistence of a nonhegemonic Germany along with a power vacuum to the southeast, was simply impossible.

The third essential factor was the totalitarian outcome of the National Socialist revolution. Unlike the seventeenth- and eighteenth-century revolutions in Britain and France, the nineteenth-century revolutions of Germany took place in a newly founded state without the representative dynastic legitimacy of the Western nation-states. As a result, Germany lacked both a ruling class comparable to the Western one and a people that had gradually acquired political liberties. Moreover, the political attitudes and ideas of the German lower middle class and workers were touched neither by liberalism nor by religious reform, as in Britain and

17. It is worth noting that Voegelin spoke of Russian rather than Soviet hegemony, no doubt because the former term referred to a civilizational reality whereas the latter depended for its existence on a highly volatile commitment to an ideological fantasy.

the United States, nor by the secular French ideas of 1789. Generally speaking, the sentiments sustaining German political ideas were collectivist. The workers were formed chiefly by Marxist collectivist sentiments and the lower middle class by nationalist collectivist sentiments. Neither type showed much respect for the individual person.

Four additional political contingencies resulting from the settlement of 1919 were important. Just as the destruction of the Austrian empire and the erection of the nationalities into sovereign states did not make the establishment of a supranational organization in southeast Europe any easier, neither was the destruction of the monarchy in Germany a prudent step toward democracy. It seemed highly improbable, Voegelin said, "that a man with the personal behavior and characteristics of Hitler could ever have achieved any importance in a society whose standards of personal conduct were determined in the last instance by the Prussian court." Likewise the destruction of the German army removed both a military and an educational organization. It was Voegelin's opinion that "the particularly repulsive atrocities of the National Socialists" were in part a result of the fact that they were committed "by civilians who had not gone through the school of the Prussian army." A third contingency was the aforementioned democratic constitution imposed on a people who were without any substantive democratic sentiments. In consequence, formal democracy served as a vehicle by which the antidemocratic masses gained power. Finally, the conservative bourgeoisie, which might have developed into a democratic political force, was ruined by the postwar inflation.[18]

In 1941 it was still impossible to say what the immediate military and political consequences of the National Socialists' rise to power would be. A few things, however, were obvious enough. First, the revolution brought to the top of German society persons who were nearly untouched by German civilizing influences. Second, the population increase between 1870 and 1910 of nearly 50 percent added to the numbers of those who were least integrated into the existing national community. The combined result of these two facts had been to achieve "a severe break in the civilizational tradition" of the German nation. With respect to the ongoing question of German hegemony, the ideological impact of the National Socialists on Central and Eastern Europe was akin to the Stalinist formula of a national form and socialist content, with the

18. This last point, plus a technical comment on the Bismarck constitution ("Some Problems of German Hegemony," 163 n. 1), was suggested to Voegelin by the former chancellor of the Weimar Republic, Heinrich Bruening, whom Voegelin had met at Harvard. HI 8/50.

important difference that there was not even the pretense of international egalitarianism. The result of both the Stalinist and the National Socialist nationalities policies was, however, comparable insofar as they shared the objective of obliterating entire historic civilizations.

The long-term consequences of the attempted destruction of the non-German nations would be, Voegelin said, incalculable. If Germany remained in a position to suppress the resistance of conquered populations to its rule, Germany would be the agent of large-scale massacres. If resistance was successful, the massacres would be directed against the Germans and their allies, not by them. More important perhaps than his indication of such gory possibilities, Voegelin was clear in his expectations that, following a German defeat, "in order to prevent a Russian expansion it would be necessary for the sea powers to occupy the continent and to organize the indescribable wreck themselves." It is, perhaps, an indication of Voegelin's tough-minded political realism and powers of analysis that, prior to the U.S. entry into the war, he could anticipate the necessity both of an alliance of the maritime powers, which came into being as the North Atlantic Treaty Organization, and of massive economic reconstruction, which materialized as the Marshall Plan. By Voegelin's analysis, therefore, the options remained the same in 1930 as they were in 1910 or as they became in 1950: German hegemony *or* occupation by the Atlantic powers *or* Russian hegemony.

Voegelin's last article devoted extensively to an analysis of the war was a discussion of Nietzsche, "the only philosopher who ever has been considered the major cause of a world war."[19] Voegelin proposed to consider the reasons and motives for attributing such influence to him and to outline Nietzsche's own interpretation of the crisis of the age and its wars.

The influence of political philosophers on political affairs is, at most, indirect and subtle. Their efforts may have an educational impact on politically involved individuals, but it is usually very difficult to anticipate what that impact might be. In any event, it is certainly inadmissible in political science to argue that predicting an event causes it. In fact, anyone who is sensitive to the process of spiritual decay can see the likely course ahead. Nietzsche used the term *nihilism* to describe the pathological attitude between the death of the old spiritual order and the birth of

19. Voegelin, "Nietzsche, the Crisis, and the War." Subsequent quotations are from this source. Voegelin's other discussions of Nietzsche were also highly focused. The most comprehensive is the essay "Nietzsche and Pascal," HI 61/14. It has been edited by Peter Opitz and published in *Nietzsche-Studien* and appears as well in *HPI*, VII:251–303. See also *CW*, vol. 12, *Published Essay, 1966–1985*, ed. Ellis Sandoz (1990; available Columbia: University of Missouri Press, 1999), chap. 13.

the new. By naming the crisis Nietzsche did not evoke it but simply brought into focus his experience of contemporary European spirituality. By so doing, Nietzsche challenged his readers to overcome nihilism by undertaking a kind of conversion. We know from both Plato and Paul that only a few individuals are capable of accepting the challenge to turn their souls around. If conversion on a large scale were possible, there would be no spiritual crisis in the first place because such crises consist precisely in the absence of resistance to spiritual dissolution. Under the circumstances, therefore, most people respond by denying the existence of a spiritual crisis or, since in fact the crisis does exist and its existence is well known, attempting to avoid its consequences.

The type of person who expressed his attitude toward the crisis by ridiculing the one who named it was called by Nietzsche the "last man." The consequence of the attitude of the last man, however, was not the condition where he imagined his small desires would be satisfied. Nietzsche's great insight was that when the spiritual order of the soul disintegrated the result was not a despiritualized happiness but disorder and chaos. It is for this reason, in *Will to Power*, for example, that Nietzsche predicted immense wars and revolutions accompanied only by the sentiment of excitement without purpose. According to Voegelin, Nietzsche's words were by no means hyperbole; they were a sober description of events. Moreover, these events were accompanied by the kinds of denials that Nietzsche also anticipated.

Consider the evidence: following World War I, responsibility for the outburst of violence and revolution was attributed to Germany by using the symbol "war-guilt." By declaring the cause to be specific and particular, nothing further, particularly in the West, needed to be brought to consciousness regarding any more general a crisis. When the publication of prewar diplomatic correspondence indicated there was no evidence for a specifically German responsibility, the lesson was obvious: "the state of the Western World proved so chaotic that a general war could erupt without a clear political purpose on the part of the participating Great Powers." After the war there followed very little conscious reflection on its significance. Rather, the realization that the "war-guilt" attribution was a kind of mistake helped sustain an attitude of hesitancy among Western statesmen and an unwillingness to acknowledge the reality of the threat posed by the National Socialists. One may say, therefore, that the crisis about which Nietzsche wrote appeared prior to 1914 as a combination of paralysis with respect to preventive action and fatalistic acceptance of purposeless violence.[20] After 1919, these two factors were

20. This aspect of the war was most poignantly expressed in the literature and poetry of soldiers on both sides of no-man's land. Much of the havoc portrayed in

dissociated, but they remained mutually determinative insofar as the violence of the National Socialists could not have been undertaken in the absence of paralysis on the other side.

Voegelin's analysis of the Western crisis as a confirmation of Nietzsche's predictions also confirmed the importance of Nietzsche's diagnosis. The next step was to provide a critical account of alternative interpretations of Nietzsche that attempted to associate him with the crisis in a causal way. Voegelin began by considering two highly effective but philosophically primitive approaches. The first, which enacted Nietzsche's parable of the last man, lived more or less comfortably within the crisis and derided Nietzsche, the analyst of it. A second primitive approach was again to externalize evil by trying to localize it in the political alignment of one side or another in the conflict. Not "guilt" for starting the Great War, this time, but a flaw in the German national character accounted for the crisis. This interpretation, incidentally, carried with it dire consequences for the continued existence of Germany as a national culture. If the flaw was in the German national character, either Germans would have to go or their character would have to change, which is to say: one way or another they would have to stop being (flawed) Germans. Less primitive, but no more satisfactory, was the attempt to make a criticism of Nietzsche from within the crisis that he had sought to transcend. There is something faintly comic, for example, in liberal outrage that Nietzsche refused to be a peace-loving progressive democrat.

Two additional interpretations, by spiritual personalities of some stature, were also analyzed by Voegelin. The first, by George Santayana, saw in Germany an extreme exemplification of the general crisis. The criterion of the crisis in both its Western and its German form was, for Santayana, "the loss of experience and wisdom that was embodied in Christianity." It was, Santayana said, a social rather than an individual crisis: "the fountains of wisdom and self-knowledge remain, and we may still drink at them in solitude." Perhaps one day mankind will drink at them again in society—so ended his *Egotism in German Philosophy*, in a prayer. Santayana's position, Voegelin said, was "ultimate in the sense that it reflects an immediate mystical experience beyond the crisis. It is not ultimate, however, in the sense that no other fundamental position is possible." In particular, while Santayana's

---

the literature of the first two decades of the twentieth century has been recapitulated in the literature, at least in English, of the closing two decades, which suggests that, to those still sensitive to the spiritual catastrophe expressed in World War I, Nietzsche's analysis has not lost its importance.

intellectual mysticism anticipated the truth of the last solitude of existence, it necessarily ignored the experiences of the spiritualization of life in society.

In connection with Nietzsche, Voegelin said, Santayana's attitude was hostile to his "Platonism," by which Voegelin meant Nietzsche's attempt to regenerate society spiritually by imaginatively evoking the true order of man and society and then indicating how the substance of society in its existing configuration could realistically be altered to conform more closely to the true order. Prior to 1876 Nietzsche was of the opinion that civilizational disintegration could be retarded or even reversed through a re-creation of the German people thanks to the efforts of Wagner and Bismarck. After 1876 his "Platonism" was broken by despair at the disintegration of the German spirit, but it was also destroyed by the peculiar demonism of Nietzsche's own unique spiritual life, the hardening of his heart, to use a Christian symbol.

Once Voegelin had formulated the problem this way, the outline of a response more adequate than Santayana's or Nietzsche's became visible. If the human substance could be awakened "in society," as Santayana had prayed, and if the soul of the individual making the attempt was not demonically closed, then Nietzsche's Platonism might be resumed. According to Voegelin, "this man appeared in the person of Stefan George."[21]

In his poem of 1917, "Der Krieg," George expressed his experience that the war was a symptom of the crisis, a bloody externality, not the crisis itself. "He is unable to participate," Voegelin said, "in the emotions of the people who find out that something is wrong only when they have at least a world war to convince them." For George the crisis was a Western not a German event and "the execution of a judgment passed on a guilty mankind because mankind is expiating through it a common guilt." George was, according to Voegelin, the only great figure of the preceding generation to have entered into Nietzsche's spirit in the sense that he sought to continue Nietzsche's task. He was, therefore, a sufficient

---

21. Leo Strauss, incidentally, agreed with Voegelin on this point. Voegelin wrote to Strauss on April 22, 1951, that the members of the George Circle saw clearly the importance of the erotic formation of a spiritual community. "To see the image of the beautiful-good man (the *kalos k'agathos* [gentleman]) in the other, to awaken it and draw it out (complicated by the mystery that the image in the other is one's own image), is possible only through the eroticism of conversation." Strauss replied on June 4, 1951: "You are quite right: [Stefan] George understood more of Plato than did Wilamowitz, Jaeger, and the whole gang." See *Faith and Political Philosophy: The Correspondence between Leo Strauss and Eric Voegelin, 1934–1964*, ed. and trans. Peter Emberley and Barry Cooper, 86, 90.

safeguard against misunderstanding Nietzsche as a National Socialist before his time.

Yet one can hardly deny that Nietzsche was rather easily appropriated by the National Socialists. His immoderate rhetoric has been noticed by virtually all his readers. Most of this inappropriate language was employed in his analysis of nihilism and of despiritualized society and, in fact, detracted from the splendid empirical analysis. His use of the term *slavery* to describe democrats, for instance, betrays an inability to recall or to experience the Christian "idea" of the singularity and spiritual dignity of the individual soul. And that "idea," which referred to experiences of world-transcendent realities, did not touch Nietzsche's sentiments. One could say, however, that the Christian idea of individual dignity remained a positive, albeit diluted, force at the heart of the democratic movement. Nietzsche was wrong, therefore, to claim democrats were exclusively motivated by resentment. Second, Nietzsche's "vitiated Platonism," his insistence on creating an image of right order from his own will without any experience of "the light of the transcendent idea," as Plato experienced, or "the faith in the social substance," as Stefan George experienced, made the possibility of real reform very slight. It is for this reason that one finds such strange images in Nietzsche, of the ruler as beast, for instance, who is characterized only by his willful opposition to the herd. As a result, it is perhaps not surprising that National Socialists may have misunderstood and appropriated some of Nietzsche's more extravagant remarks.

It is often forgotten that Nietzsche knew nothing of the wars of the twentieth century, so uncanny was his foresight. It is true nonetheless that he was concerned only with the wars of his own time and the perspective opened to him on the future from his present. The year 1876 was earlier mentioned as being a pivotal date. Prior to that year, and especially after the Franco-Prussian War, Nietzsche's "Platonism" was expressed in his high hope for German and, indeed, European regeneration, as was mentioned, under the political and spiritual guidance of Bismarck and Wagner. After 1876 his disappointment was also focused on Bismarck and Wagner.

The strategic position of Germany, as Voegelin had explained in "Extended Strategy," was that German territory had been excluded from great-power politics by the imperial consolidations of Russia and by those of the Atlantic nations. With the destruction of the legitimacy of the old order by the French Revolution, Nietzsche was led to envisage the possibility of a European consciousness that had overcome the allegiance to a specific and particular *patria*. When Germany turned toward middle-class nationalism following the defeat of France, Nietzsche's hopes for a spiritual force sufficient to oppose Russia (and the United States) evaporated. Because he made no attempt to stem the tide of German deculturation, Bismarck was attacked by Nietzsche with splendid vituperative enthusiasm, as was Wagner, whom Nietzsche saw as the most obnoxious expression of German/European baseness. Nietzsche came to see himself, especially after 1888, as the source of true order in German/European society, and therefore directly in competition with Bismarck and Wagner, or perhaps Bismarck-Wagner, a composite being that symbolized the political-spiritual disorder.

Nietzsche's "Platonism" found extravagant expression in his later writings, and in consequence it is easy to ridicule. By so doing (and perhaps this was Nietzsche's objective), one declares oneself among the herd of last men. Nietzsche's extravagant rhetoric, that is, expressed perfectly his position as the dominant philosophical and religious personality of the age. From Voegelin's analysis one may draw the conclusion that much of the misunderstanding of Nietzsche is an expression of the spiritual disorders that Nietzsche so brilliantly analyzed.

The defeat of the German armies in World War II did not alter the fundamental geopolitical structure of Europe. There was considerable chaos in European societies as a consequence of material destruction, but there was also considerable intellectual confusion, much as Nietzsche had anticipated. Voegelin conscientiously reviewed some of this literature of second-rate opinion. His reviews extended from the perfunctory ("the book may have a function in the present struggle in France, but its importance does not extend further") to the generous: "Count Sforza's optimistic appraisal of fascism as an adventure from which the nation will return to its traditions seems of doubtful validity; and the doubts are aroused precisely by the contrast between the qualities of the author and the qualities which determine the politics of our time."[22] Occasionally a particularly ill-informed or ideologically perverse book would provide a more diverting engagement. In 1947, for example, Voegelin reviewed F. S. C. Northrop's influential *The Meeting of East and West*. The subtitle of the book, *An Inquiry Concerning World Understanding,* indicated that it was not a work of scholarship but a political tract proposing a solution to a pragmatic political problem. Accordingly, the historical material was introduced for the purpose of supporting and illustrating Northrop's solution. The "world" within which "understanding" was sought was

22. Reviews of J. Boissonet, *La misère par la Surabondance: Karl Marx, père de la crise mondiale* (1938), and Count Carlo Sforza, *Contemporary Italy: Its Intellectual and Moral Origins* (1945).

the power-configuration of 1946. The chief cause of a lack of understanding, Northrop said, was ideological conflict. To achieve a peaceful world, one must, first, establish the content of the competing ideologies; second, determine the extent to which they are mutually compatible; and third, "develop a composite ideology that will combine the better parts of all of them and hence will be acceptable to everybody." Developing such a composite ideology was the task Northrop set for himself.

The importance of the book lay in the author's attempt to transcend Western and American provincialism. Its defects were all of a technical or theoretical nature: his neo-Comtian philosophy of history, his view of science as the driving force behind "ideological" development, and, most important, his uncritical use of the term *ideology* itself. By Northrop's lights, ideology embraced religion, philosophy, art, political and economic theory, and philosophy of nature. "Such simplification," Voegelin said, "is hardly excusable." One of the consequences was that by reducing all cultural experiences to "theory" or "aesthetics," the basis for differentiating physics from religious studies or political science, namely the differentiation of reality itself as matter, politics, worship, and so on, was overlooked. Likewise, the whole range of spiritual distinctions was completely ignored. This led Northrop to the startling conclusion that the "ideology" of Einstein and Planck had made Christian "ideology" obsolete and outmoded. The result of these theoretical lapses, not to say dubious taste, was to obscure the most important problem of Western history, the differentiation of the spiritual personality. Such experiences were apparently beyond Northrop's horizon of understanding.

Northrop was at least sincere in attempting to deal with a real problem, Western provincialism. Two other books, appearing around the same time and bearing titles that indicated they ostensibly served the same goal as Northrop, seemed to Voegelin to be even more questionable. The general context may be indicated by Voegelin's observation that the defeat of the Axis powers did not conclude Nietzsche's wars of the spirit. Europe remained divided between territory and people living under the influence of the Russian empire or under the influence of the Western maritime empires. The spiritual struggle, which we conventionally call the cold war, continued. Indeed, that struggle may be said to have continued even after the collapse of the Soviet Union.

The first book under review, entitled *The Lesson of Germany*, had been written by individuals who had been active in the German labor movement and sought to provide the Marxist faithful with an edifying account.[23] Voegelin observed at the outset that, under the pressure of

23. Review of Gerhart Eisler, Albert Norden, and Albert Schreiner, *The Lesson of Germany: A Guide to Her History* (1946).

competing totalitarian creeds, one must expect "a good deal of rewriting of history to suit the various party-lines." For the authors, human history is the struggle of good and evil, of progressives and reactionaries. The history of Germany was a sad chapter in this struggle because the reactionaries did so well, at least temporarily. "The lesson is that terrible things will happen again in the future if Germany from now on is not run by Communists." The sources used in compiling the materials from which the lesson was drawn were, naturally enough, selected with great care. "On the whole," Voegelin concluded, "we may say that to the faithful this type of history will be greatly edifying, while to the scholar it is a farce and to the reviewer a pest." As a symptom of ideological disorientation it was easy enough to spot.

In 1946 Voegelin reviewed a second volume that belongs to this same category but was more cleverly disguised as a work of scholarship. Frederick L. Schuman's *Soviet Politics: At Home and Abroad* was a "comprehensive volume" destined to remain "the representative treatise for quite some time to come." It was filled with information and stylishly written. However, "it is a book of opinion, not scientific analysis." The author attempted to make a sympathetic but also objective political judgment about the Soviet regime. The result, however, was a "skillful apology" the importance of which consisted in the fact that it was part of "a trend in contemporary political science." Schuman proceeded on the assumption that a rational, scientific approach to political reality did not exist and that one was either for or against the Soviet Union for emotional reasons. Hence "objectivity means a middle course between Marxism and crypto-fascism." In practice, this meant that all criticism of Marxism had to be ignored.

The result was a very peculiar book. Schuman, for example, wrote: "the greatest glory of the Soviet state is its achievement of effective equality in rights and opportunities for peoples of all races, languages and culture." To which observation Voegelin remarked: "If we do not hear more of the unspeakable misery inflicted by this 'greatest glory,' which resulted, for instance, in the wholesale massacre of nomads who did not care to become factory workers, the reason is that the nationalities in question are mostly on a primitive level which prevents them from being sufficiently vociferous to be heard beyond the Soviet border." A bizarre comparison by Schuman of Soviet indirect elections with the U.S. Electoral College was evidence of a "hair-raising" disregard of reality.

The cornerstone of Schuman's apology was Stalin's dogma of capitalist encirclement. "The misery inflicted by the Soviet regime on the Russian people and the terroristic suppression of all opposition that arouse the resentment of the West, have to be understood as a reaction to the threatening attitude assumed by the outside world toward

Communism since the October Revolution." The attitude of the Western powers was all the more inexcusable because of the heroic Soviet victory against Germany. The problem with Schuman's argument was not that the Soviet effort should be overlooked, but that events must be placed in a larger historical context if they were to be properly understood. The political scientist would have to raise the very question that Schuman had explicitly prohibited, namely the importance of Marxism as a disturbing factor in Western politics.

With the perspective afforded by the evidence of the twentieth century, one may say that the socially disruptive and irresponsible gibberish uttered by half-baked intellectuals about class wars, dictatorships of the proletariat, and so forth has created a symbolism and provided the patterns for the solution of political problems that, once they were launched on their public course, were at the disposition of anyone. They could be used, Voegelin remarked, not only by the intellectuals who created them, and not only in the interest of the working class for whom they were originally meant; they could also be used by the lower middle class for waging war against the proletariat and for the establishment of Fascist dictatorships. Once the patterns of violence and atrocity were set, one could never know what effects they would produce. The ways of causation in these matters were tortuous and often incredible. Those who screamed in horror at the Nazi gas chambers, for instance, might have read *Mein Kampf* with profit and learned when and where Hitler's idea of judicious extermination of political enemies by means of poison gas germinated.[24] Voegelin was suggesting, in fact, that Hitler was in some respects a sound interpreter of Marx. In particular, once the vulgarities of the Bolsheviks became the common currency of political discourse, there was no reason to think they could be kept out of the mouths of the National Socialists. Indeed, the textual links from Marx through Sorel to Mussolini can be traced by any competent scholar.[25]

Schuman, however, was apparently unaware of those connections. There was no commonsense awareness that "the deeds of hatred have a habit of growing into further deeds of hatred with an increasing ferocity," nor that the end of the escalation may not have been reached. On the contrary, Voegelin said, "Professor Schuman adopts an ethics of *raison d'état* which connives unconditionally in atrocities and approves the

24. The reference was to chap. 15 of *Mein Kampf*, where Hitler reflected on Marxism and the possibility of exterminating one's enemies. The use of poison gas for the job was taken from Hitler's experience in World War I.

25. See for example the recent account by Paul Johnson, *Modern Times: The World from the Twenties to the Eighties* (New York: Harper and Row, 1983), 54–58.

pattern of hatred" at least insofar as it served communist ends. If the majority of the Russian people were peasants who were unpersuaded by what they considered to be the strange ideas of communist intellectuals, there was no thought that the peasants should be left alone rather than be butchered until the survivors saw the light and allowed themselves to be organized in collective enterprises. An apologetic tone in discussing this historical catastrophe was evidence enough of the author's lack of respect for the victims of the communist terror. Even so, Schuman's book remained the best treatment of Soviet politics available, which was, Voegelin said, "the worst condemnation conceivable of the present state of political science."[26]

In June 1946, Roscoe Martin, Voegelin's former colleague at Alabama, wrote him that his review of Schuman's book "was really a 'lulu,'" and that he was courting the enmity of reviewers of his own *History of Political Ideas.* Voegelin replied that "the leftist intelligentsia will be up in arms anyway and condemn it as one of the worst atrocities of the century. Hence: why not pummel them right away?"[27]

Not all the material that came under Voegelin's public notice was of the dubious quality of Schuman and Eisler. In 1944, for example, he reviewed John H. Hallowell's *The Decline of Liberalism as an Ideology, with Particular Reference to German Politico-Legal Thought.* Hallowell traced the liberal idea from its beginnings in seventeenth-century Germany through its decline in the nineteenth century and to its utter disintegration in the twentieth. As a measure by which to judge decline and disintegration, Hallowell developed a concept of "integral liberalism." The concept combined "the idea of the autonomous individual with the belief in an objective order of values." So long as the individual conscience was responsive to that order, limits were placed on the autonomy of the individual. A decline of liberalism occurred when contact with it was lost and the awareness of limits disappeared. The end point was reached when an unlimited individual force was left to operate within a morally neutral legal framework. During the process of decline, the chief topic of jurisprudence shifted from a concern with substantive justice to a concern with legal form to which any substantive content could be applied.

---

26. The book review editor at *Journal of Politics,* V. O. Key, toned down some of Voegelin's remarks in the printed version. Waldemar Gurian, who earlier had edited Voegelin's reviews in *Review of Politics,* wrote Voegelin: "I have just read your excellent review of Schuman. I fully agree and I hope that readers will understand the irony of the last paragraph. I am afraid that the second part of the first sentence in the last paragraph [indicating that Schuman's book was the best available] will be widely used for propaganda purposes" (HI 15/27).

27. HI 24/22.

In Voegelin's view "the problem is aptly stated and presented; the study is to be recommended particularly for its insight that the totalitarian ideas are not an event superseding liberalism, but the logical outcome of the initial inconsistencies of the liberal position." Voegelin indicated where Hallowell did "not quite go far enough" in his analysis but recommended the book for two reasons. First, Hallowell recognized that an adequate discussion of political principles must "be based on a solid and well-reasoned religious position." Second, "the greatest merit of the book is the recognition of the fact that the inconsistencies of liberalism which led to its decline had their roots in a faultiness of its religious and metaphysical basis. A recovery of liberalism, accordingly, is possible only by the creation of a more solid basis in the religious experiences and the metaphysics which lend validity to its principal tenets." Unlike the other works that dealt with one or another aspect of European politics, Hallowell had undertaken an analysis based on a genuine philosophical anthropology.

In Chapter 1 we suggested that Voegelin's chief motivation for writing *History of Political Ideas* may have been to make sense of the Western catastrophe. Necessarily he was aware that the completion of the book would establish him as a major American political scientist. In 1946 he was promoted to full professor at LSU, and his position, at last, was secure. His research expenses, however, were high so that one may also say he was underpaid. Moreover, as an eminent scholar, he was a likely candidate for recruitment by other universities. In the late summer of 1946 and again in 1947 Alabama tried unsuccessfully to hire him back. The salary was attractive, but Voegelin wished to finish *History of Political Ideas* and could not afford the disruption of moving. His former mentor at Harvard, W. Y. Elliott, thought he might be able to replace Carl Friedrich for a semester, and he received an indication that Illinois was interested in hiring him, but the most attractive (and best documented) offer came from Yale, early in 1948. The invitation from P. E. Corbett asked if he was prepared to speak on "the common philosophy, if there is one, of the Catholic Democratic Parties in various countries of Europe" or, failing that, on "Corporativism." Voegelin replied that he shared Corbett's skepticism regarding the existence of a common philosophy and suggested instead "a survey of the Western revolutionary movements and of the reaction of the established institutions towards them. Since the Church is one of the most important of these institutions, the subject of the Catholic democratic reaction would have to be treated."[28]

28. HI 24/22, 38/18, 11/2, 62/25.

On the same day Corbett's letter arrived, Voegelin received another, from his friend Cleanth Brooks, who had left LSU for Yale a few years earlier. "The invitation," wrote Brooks "means, of course, that Yale is very much interested in making you an offer." Brooks added that he knew "from direct sources" that Yale was prepared to do so. The "direct source" was Willmore Kendall, who also informed Voegelin that the political science department was enthusiastic and that one of its members, Cecil Driver, had read the manuscript of Voegelin's *History* and had pronounced it "a great book." Finally, Brooks declared that he was delighted "with the library, the general 'tone' of the university here, and that of the intellectual community." There was, he said, "a minimum of snobbery and the old Yale inertia. You would be regarded as a great acquisition, and rightly so." Voegelin replied that he was pleased with the information Brooks's letter contained, but he had some reservations regarding the salary and the lower rank that Brooks had indicated, in confidence, that Kendall, in confidence, had told him about. Moreover, he had a sabbatical coming up and an offer to give some guest lectures in Vienna, which would pay for a research trip to Paris. There were, therefore, "a good number of points to be considered"; because the terms Brooks had indicated were "just close enough to the lowest edge to cause hesitations," he was unable simply to jump at the opportunity.[29] In the event, Voegelin delivered his lecture on March 12, 1948.

On March 15, Voegelin wrote to Corbett expressing his thanks and his favorable impression of the students who attended his lecture. The same day he wrote Brooks indicating the same opinion, but adding that "nothing was said about such sordid things as the possibility of a job or, *horrible dictu,* salaries, etc. Corbett only indicated most pleasantly that correspondence might ensue." He expressed again his doubts regarding the salary Brooks had said was likely and added "it was a funny feeling. I must say, of being handed around and sniffed over by everybody concerned. I only regretted that the situation did not permit me to do a little sniffing for myself."[30]

In addition to Cleanth Brooks, Voegelin had become a friend of Robert Heilman when Heilman, too, had taught in the English department at LSU.[31] Indeed, the correspondence between the two extended over the next thirty years. As is often the case with such friendships, the epistolary

29. HI 8/46, 20/39.
30. HI 62/25, 8/46.
31. For Heilman's memoir of the 1940s at LSU, see "The State of Letters: Baton Rouge and L.S.U. Forty Years After," esp. 133–34. See also Heilman's "Eric Voegelin: Reminiscences."

exchanges were witty and frank. On March 19, 1948, Voegelin wrote Heilman bringing him up to date about some lively and curious goings-on at LSU and the "slightly more exciting" news about Yale. "The lecture looked to me like a great success; with discussion it lasted for two hours and could have gone on for another hour." Despite the "lousy" salary, he said he would accept an offer if one were made.[32]

Voegelin had thanked Kendall for his hospitality and efforts, and on April 2 Kendall replied that Voegelin had "made a deep impression upon [his] listeners," particularly the graduate students and younger faculty. However, the decision was wholly in the hands of "the colonels in the department," and on that score Kendall was "not optimistic: every attempt in recent years to move the department away from its bets upon mediocrity, unproductiveness, and drift has smashed itself against the colonels' determination to parlay those numbers into a fortune or bust, and I shall be as astonished as pleased if it proves any different this time." A couple of weeks later Kendall again wrote, this time confessing his dismay at the inaction of the Yale department. He confessed as well that "what was in question, *ab initio,* was an attempt on the part of the younger group to change the department into a different kind of enterprise; if you like, to carry through a revolution; and this meant either consent or abdication on the part of the full professors." Two of the "colonels," whom Kendall named, were opposed to Voegelin.[33]

Voegelin explained what had happened in a letter to Heilman: "I am afraid of even answering Kendall's letter because I have no intention of getting involved even faintly into any idiotic conspiracy which Kendall or Brooks, or both, have cooked up. On the other hand, since there is no word from Corbett, I am completely in the dark. I miss you very much in this contingency." Heilman responded immediately to his friend's request for advice with a shrewd appraisal of Yale's academic politics and of what Kendall and Brooks had done. The danger of being associated with a conspiracy against the colonels was obvious, and Heilman suggested a tone of "discreet neutrality. . . . You know, cordiality, and agreeableness, and a noncommittal indication that you are always interested in knowing about interesting things going on at Yale."[34]

On May 19, more than two months after he had delivered his lecture, Voegelin received a note from Corbett. Corbett expressed his "sorrow and surprise" when, upon reviewing his files, he discovered he had not thanked Voegelin for his "very interesting talk." He excused himself

32. HI 17/9.
33. HI 20/39.
34. HI 17/9.

for the usual reasons: teaching and administration. Voegelin's visit, he said, awakened a lively interest in his interpretation of revolutionary movements. "Needless-to-say, not all of us were convinced that your pattern of interpretation is fully established," but everybody admired his scholarship. He ended by indicating that Yale was highly interested in his work, "and we shall look forward very keenly to a publication of your 'Theory of Politics,' if I may coin a name."[35] Voegelin replied to Corbett with "discreet neutrality," and nothing further was heard from Yale.

A few days earlier Voegelin had written Heilman to thank him for his advice on the Yale matter and to tell him "something about the rackets and intrigue in the academic world in Europe." The intrigue concerned his summer visit to Vienna and whether he was welcome among the economists who composed the rest of the group. Heilman commented: "the Hayek story is lovely; we are delighted. Patterns of academic conduct are apparently the same."[36] In the event Voegelin visited the University of Vienna later that year. He made contact with scholars specializing in topics covered in his *History* and prepared to return to Europe for sabbatical research early in 1949.

By the end of World War II, Voegelin had settled in to American life and American political science. He was a regular participant at meetings of the Southern and the American Political Science Associations and had published in the respective journals of those associations. He had developed a theoretically astute argument to judge the significance of political ideas both as evocative symbols and in the several subordinate senses. He also had been exposed to the Byzantine complexities of recruitment to the great, or at least prestigious, universities of America.

More important for his subsequent work, he had established professional and then personal contact with Waldemar Gurian at the *Review of Politics*. This journal in particular, established at Notre Dame University, was a vehicle for much of the best political science to be published during and after the war. Gurian and his colleagues were congenial to Voegelin's understanding of the most important prerequisite for political science: it must be founded on an idea of man, a philosophical anthropology. In addition, as is indicated in the following chapters, it must be based on a comprehensive understanding of "the materials." For Voegelin, the

35. HI 62/25.
36. HI 17/9, 17/3. Voegelin's correspondence with Heilman during 1949 and 1950 indicates that he also considered moving to the University of Washington and actually gave an interview lecture at Johns Hopkins. Nothing came of either exploratory move, and Voegelin remained in Baton Rouge.

materials meant both the great speculative and analytical texts of political philosophy and the narrative texts of political history. Moreover, as he explained in the "Introduction" to *History of Political Ideas,* the two sets of texts were related.[37]

Because the chief function of a political idea is, as we saw, to create a cosmion, such ideas must be deeply intertwined with particular political units. "They are," Voegelin wrote, "so closely worked into the pattern of political history that a separation of ideas from the reality which they help to create may not be possible at all." This was why a philosopher such as Hegel could use the development of political ideas as the guiding principle for the understanding of political history. However one judges the result of Hegel's speculation or of any of the other philosophers of history, the question of the pattern of political history and its connection to political ideas is a real one. This reality is acknowledged by two well-known conventions. On the one hand, we often divide the history of Western political ideas into the well-known blocks associated with the Greek polis, the medieval Christian empire, and the modern national state. On the other, there is the convention of organizing the history of political ideas around the great personalities: Plato, Augustine, Thomas, Hobbes, Hegel, and so on. These divisions make sense, according to Voegelin,

> because the political units of these periods conform to certain general types of cosmic analogy and the rationalizing and theoretical attempts of these periods show tendencies of convergence toward an ideal theoretical system representative of the period. A common stock of evocative ideas forming the basis, the theorists of each period are occupied with the task of contemplative analysis of the common stock.

On the basis of these more or less uncontroversial observations, which can be confirmed by a glance at the tables of contents of readily available textbooks on the history of political ideas, Voegelin developed several "rules" for organizing the materials for his *History.* In place of a catalog of evocative ideas or an equally evocative continuity or "tradition" of theoretical contemplation associated with great names, a comprehensive history "will, then, have to show the gradual growth of theory out of an evocative situation; it will have to lead up to the limits reached within a situation of that kind and, then, show the dissolution and [abandonment] of theoretical thought under the pressure of new evocations."

In the actual text of Voegelin's *History* this meant beginning not, as is usually done, with the Greeks but with the chronologically earlier

---

37. Subsequent quotes are from this text, *HPI,* I:232–37 ("Appendix A").

developments of Egypt and Mesopotamia. Indeed, he said, "there could be made even a good point for starting with an analysis of more primitive stages of human society, because their traces can be found in the later history." Certainly the current of ideas that was initiated with Alexander continued the evocation or the theory not of the polis but of the Asiatic empires.

Voegelin's divergence from the conventional patterns of a history of political ideas was guided by his desire not simply to trace patterns of political history or to pen a series of essays on important theoretical achievements, but to trace the connections between one evocation and another, and to pay particular attention to "the point where a new evocative element enters the scene and either splits up or sums up the accumulated materials." So, for example, the ancient Near Eastern and Greek developments, which were to a degree separate one from another, came together in the period of Alexander and the Diadochic empires. Likewise, as we shall see in detail in Chapter 7, even Western political history must take into account contemporary non-Western developments: political history, in the end, is world, not European, political history. In his study of Machiavelli, for example, Voegelin argued that the imagery of the savior-prince introduced by Machiavelli in chapter 26 of *The Prince* owed its origin to the political history and associated imagery of Temür and his victory over Bayezid at Chubuq over a century before. The beginning of what we conventionally call the modern period is thus rendered more complicated than we usually think because the restoration of contacts between Europe and Asia, which led to the renaissance of the Eastern intellectual heritage in the West, coincided with the dissolution of the Western empire and the growth of the national state.

Scholars may dispute the details, but there is a consensus that the national state is a type of political organization distinct from its predecessors. No interpretative consensus, however, exists with respect to more recent developments:

> the majority, it seems, hold the opinion that we are still [in 1940] in the period of radical nationalism; but the suspicion is growing that the idea of the national state may be decaying and that, for at least two centuries, new types of evocation are developing slowly but distinctly. The horrible noise with which the national states are filling the political stage may well be their agony. I rather incline toward this interpretation, and I have tried, therefore, to [unite] in the final chapter all the signs that I believe to be indicative of new evocative orders, although their final shape cannot be more than surmised.

What Voegelin had in mind for the final chapter, if one had been written in 1940, also cannot be surmised. It was clear, however, to Voegelin that the evocation of the national state was under considerable stress. National myths and evocative national ideas, no less than the alleged rationality of the state, were being challenged by new evocations for which no conventional nomenclature had yet developed. That was the intellectual and political reality that Voegelin experienced. The actual contents of the *History of Political Ideas*, as we shall indicate, aimed at providing an analysis of the patterns of evocation and disintegration. Based on the work he had done in German, Voegelin's notion of a political idea was a provisionally satisfactory analytical instrument. It enabled him to make sense of the political realities he experienced along with everyone else, and it provided him with a basis for criticism of alternative methods of analysis. In the context of postwar political science, the chief alternative was conventionally called positivism.

3

Positivism and the Destruction of Science

O ne of the reasons for the enduring position of *The New Science of Politics* in the canon of contemporary political science is the powerful analysis and criticism in its introductory chapter of "the destruction of science which characterized the positivistic era in the second half of the nineteenth century."[1] This destruction was made clear to Voegelin on a number of occasions both prior to the publication of the *New Science* and afterward. We will consider some of Voegelin's encounters with positivism in American political science in this chapter. We begin, however, with the position Voegelin reached in 1952.

The destruction of science by positivism, he said, resulted from the widespread acceptance of two erroneous assumptions regarding the impressive results obtained by the sciences of natural phenomena. The first, a "harmless idiosyncrasy," was the assumption that the successes of the natural sciences could be attributed, at least in part, to the mathematical or quasi-mathematical methods they employed and, therefore, the acceptance of such methods as paradigmatic and the application of them by practitioners of other sciences would result in comparable achievements.

The second assumption was not harmless but a "real source of danger." It maintained that a "study of reality could qualify as scientific only if it used the methods of the natural sciences." If a study did not use such methods, it was *eo ipse* unscientific. Moreover, the subject matter examined by such "nonscientific" procedures was often dismissed as illusionary, which meant either it was simply nonexistent or it was capable of being transformed by scientific suspicion and reduction into a form suitable for scientific analysis. One of the implications of Voegelin's understanding of positivism or the positivist era is that the term *positivism* is to be understood in a large and capacious sense.

1. Unless otherwise indicated, quotations are from *NSP*, "Introduction," 1–26.

In contrast to the positivist understanding, for Voegelin and for a Voegelinian understanding of political science, the term *science* meant the "study of reality" or "a search for truth concerning the nature of the various realms of being," the interrelationship between or among these "realms," and so on. Facts are relevant to this activity insofar as knowledge of them illuminates meanings; methodological relevance is determined not a priori but in terms of the contribution that any particular procedure makes to the study or search. In short, "different objects require different methods." This commonsense observation may be generalized as the principle of theoretical relevance.

If, however, one subordinates this principle to the a priori requirements of method, the result is a perversion of the meaning of science. If one operates on the basis of the two positivist assumptions and erects a particular method, whatever it may be, into the criterion of science, "then the meaning of science as a truthful account of the structure of reality, as the theoretical orientation of man in his world, and as the great instrument for man's understanding of his own position in the universe" is destroyed. These three elements constitute the meaning of science; all are required because there also exist untruthful accounts of the structure of reality, nontheoretical and antitheoretical orientations of man in his world, and alternative, noncognitive instruments for the understanding of the place of humanity in the universe.[2] This understanding of what science is was not Voegelin's private definition. Rather, it was a restoration or a recovery of the full amplitude of science following the destructive activity of positivism. Voegelin often indicated that his understanding of political science was, with respect to the personal and social dimensions of reality, very close to the *episteme politike* of Plato and Aristotle.

The conclusion to which one is drawn is that, for Voegelin, positivism was first of all a matter of principle, namely the perversion of science. Like any perversion, it was the result of an act, in this case an intellectual act of subordinating theoretical relevance to method. This principle of perverse subordination, then, constitutes the methodological core of the problem, which implies that the manifestations of positivism through particular doctrines are secondary. Accordingly, if one focused on the matter of doctrine, rather than on principle, phenomena that were in principle related might not be recognized as such "because on the level of doctrine the adherents of different model methods are apt to oppose each other."

2. In *Truth and Method*, first published in German in 1960, Hans-Georg Gadamer developed a similar argument at great length. See also Jürgen Gebhardt, "The Vocation of a Scholar."

Voegelin then sketched the logical development of positivist doctrine. First of all, the principle that method constitutes the criterion of science would lead directly and logically to the result that, so long as they are generated by the appropriate method, all propositions concerning facts will be considered scientific, which opens up the possibility of generating massive amounts of "scientific" trivia. In the event, this has occurred more rarely than might be expected since even the most committed positivist need not entirely abandon his or her common sense when it comes to selecting topics for treatment. What occurs with some regularity, however, is that "the operation on relevant materials" is undertaken on the basis of "defective principles," which is to say, principles for which no theoretical foundations exist. What Voegelin had in mind as examples of defective principles were those "derived from the *Zeitgeist*, political preferences or personal idiosyncrasies." When applied to the factual materials, analyses undertaken on the basis of such principles are usually accurate enough, in the sense that they are not sheer fiction, but are inadequate because of what is omitted. Worse, uncritical interpretative principles do not permit the interpreter to recognize the significance of what is left out.

The most common manifestation of positivism, which still influences the conduct of contemporary political scientists, appears in the development of methodology. Practically by definition, methodologists share the opinion that method determines the status of a science. However, when they generalize the procedure and take the inevitable step of reflection, the concern with methodology "regained the understanding of the specific adequacy of different methods for different sciences." Here Voegelin mentioned Husserl and Cassirer in passing but focused chiefly on the life and work of Max Weber.[3] Weber marked the end point in the internal development of problems raised by "the attempt at making political science (and the social sciences in general) 'objective' through a methodologically rigorous exclusion of all 'value judgments.' "

The chief difficulty concerning "values" and "value judgments" is well known and develops from the internal logic of the argument that

3. Voegelin's relationship to Max Weber is considerably more complex than admiration for his scholarship coupled with reservations regarding his methodological reflections. In fact, Voegelin wrote three articles on Weber: "Über Max Weber," *Deutsche Vierteljahresschrift für Literaturewissenschaft und Geistesgeschichte* 3:2 (1925): 177–93; "Max Weber," *Kölner Vierteljahrshefte für Soziologie* 9:1/2 (1930): 1–16; "Die Grosse Max Webers," in *Ordnung, Bewusstsein, Geschichte*, ed. Peter J. Opitz (Stuttgart: Klett-Cotta, 1988), 78–98. Peter J. Opitz, "Max Weber und Eric Voegelin," provides a thorough analysis of the changes in Voegelin's relationship to Weber and reproduces several interesting letters from the 1930s between Voegelin, Leopold von Wiese, and Marianne Weber.

supports the distinction. The dichotomy of value judgment and fact judgment developed during the nineteenth century in the wake of the positivist assumption that only propositions concerning facts of the phenomenal world could count as being "objective" and therefore scientific. Value judgments expressed only preferences and decisions and so were "subjective." The difficulty with this argument and with the whole "fact/value question" is that, in reality, the classical and Christian "science of man" did not contain value judgments at all but elaborated, "empirically and critically, the problems of order, which derive from philosophical anthropology as part of a general ontology." The solution was to turn classical philosophy, Christianity, and much else besides into "values" of one sort or another. But this could be done only by doing violence not to the structure of reality but to the intellectual operation that sought to understand it, which meant ignoring, forgetting, or otherwise eclipsing ontology as a science. In the process, ethics and politics ceased to be what they were, for example, for Aristotle, namely rational accounts, sciences, of the order within which human beings actualize themselves. Instead, ethics and politics became indistinguishable from preferences, idiosyncrasies, and subjective, uncritical opinion, *doxa* in the sense of the term used by Plato and Aristotle.

The methodological disputes of the nineteenth century were, in Voegelin's view, attempts to move beyond uncritical opinion about "values."[4] The effort had the undoubted virtue of awakening "the consciousness of critical standards," even though the use of the concept of value judgment had the malign consequence of eclipsing "the whole body of classic and Christian metaphysics, and especially of philosophical anthropology." Looking back, the great methodological battles appeared to be doxic disputes over assumptions, axioms, and hypotheses. Where there was widespread agreement regarding a "value"—the state, for example— then the danger of sinking into "a morass of relativism" might appear remote. One could undertake what looked like an objective study by exploring the facts—the motivations, actions, and conditions—that had a bearing on the "value" of the state. But when there existed different opinions regarding what is valuable, there were bound to be as many political sciences as there were individuals with differing views. Accordingly, a conservative would select facts in accord with conservative values, and a Marxist would do the same regarding Marxist values.

---

4. For an account of Voegelin's position in the history of this methodological struggle between neo-Kantian *Kulturwissenschaft* and Dilthey's *Geisteswissenschaft,* see "Editors' Introduction," *CW,* 1:ix–xxxv. For the general context, see Fritz Ringer, *The Decline of the German Mandarins: The German Academic Community, 1890–1933.*

If the result was not simply chaotic, the reason lay in the pressure exerted by "a civilizational tradition which held the diversification of uncritical opinion within its general frame." But once such conventions and traditions were unable to exert the necessary pressure, the alternatives became clear: the "morass of relativism" or a science of order. Max Weber stood between the two options and, as Nietzsche said of Kant, performed the role of the great delayer.

For Weber, value-free science meant an exploration of the causality of action by means of ideal types. His science could not say whether it was better to be a Marxist revolutionary or a liberal constitutionalist, but it could indicate what the consequences would be if someone tried to translate ideological preferences into political action. Weber searched for an appropriate language to express his apprehension of the problem of theoretical relevance. He did so through the categories of "responsibility" and "demonism." The task of science with respect to "demonic" values was to make politicians "aware of the consequences of their actions and [to awaken] in them the sense of responsibility." As a practical activity this was, no doubt, worthwhile. But if the values were truly demonic, there is no reason anyone should wake up to responsibility, particularly when they could fall back upon what Weber himself identified as an "ethics of intention" that dismissed the problem of consequences altogether.

Analysis based on categories derived from the *vita activa* led, therefore, to an impasse. The problem could be dealt with only on the basis of a philosophical anthropology, a *theory* of human existence, and not on the basis of types of human action. Yet, Voegelin said, by "entering into rational conflict with [demonic] values through the mere fact of his enterprise" of analysis, Weber was able to escape the relativism and nihilism toward which his argument seemed to lead. Voegelin's question was: how?

The methodological issue is still alive in contemporary political science, so it may be useful to restate it. According to the pre-Weberian methodologists, a historical or political science could be value-free because its object of study was constituted by "reference to a value." The plurality of values, as we noted, contained the possibility of constituting a plurality of objects of study. The sheer fact of the matter was, however, that for Weber some values and some studies undertaken with reference to them were better than others. They simply were more scientific or better science.

The greatest and best-known example was capitalism: Weber showed beyond question that religious convictions, not class struggles, were decisive, whatever an intellectual who had demonically chosen Marxism as his value might believe and whatever facts he might select with reference to that value to support his views on the significance of class struggle. Weberian science was possible, therefore, not on the basis of arguments advanced by its author but almost in spite of them. If Weber was a scientist in Voegelin's sense of the term, as he undoubtedly was, the reasons lay first in Weber's intellectual integrity but second in the fact that the structure of reality was accessible to such an intellect. In Voegelin's words, Weberian science was advanced on the basis of "the authentic principles of order as they had been discovered and elaborated in the history of mankind." As a practical matter, in the actual writing of his great books, Weber discovered that specific truths about order had a real, concrete presence in the order of reality, even though he was unable to account theoretically for his discoveries by the procedures he used.

In the example of capitalism Weber showed that the Marxists' "historical materialistic" interpretation was simply wrong.[5] There must, therefore, exist a standard of truth in science that is independent of the constitution of the subject matter of a science by referring facts to the value of historical materialism. Voegelin drew out an obvious implication: "if critical objectivity made it impossible for a scholar to be a Marxist," how could anyone be a Marxist without also "surrendering the standards of critical objectivity that he would be obliged to observe as a responsible human being?" For Voegelin the question was rhetorical. It answered itself; for Weber there was no answer.

The significance of Weber's work, however, was plain: "he had reduced the principle of value-free science *ad absurdum*," because in terms of a value-free science the value of science was worth no more than the value of ideological nonsense. Because of his "positivistic hangover," there could be for Weber no genuine *episteme,* so that "the principles of order had to be introduced as historical facts." But even with regard to historical development, Weber achieved a kind of self-canceling result: the last phase in Weber's account of the evaluation of rational action was also an account of the disenchantment and dedivinization of the world. Sooner or later scholars would realize that the disenchantment derived not from reality but from the aforementioned positivistic hangover. In Voegelin's words, one could simply "turn around and rediscover the rationality of metaphysics in general and of philosophical anthropology in particular, that is, the areas of science from which Max Weber had kept studiously aloof." Voegelin's own political science was intended to do just that.

_____

5. See Karl Löwith, "Max Weber und Karl Marx," *Archiv für Sozialwissenschaft und Sozialpolitik* 67 (1932): 53–99, 175–214.

Many of the methodological problems that Voegelin discussed so eloquently in *The New Science of Politics* had been discussed previously in the course of conducting the usual obligations of a scholar to appraise the work of others. During the early 1940s, Voegelin was called upon with some regularity to review books on law and jurisprudence as well as on politics. It has been suggested by the editors of his *The Nature of the Law* that, at the time, Voegelin was unsure "whether he would settle in a political science faculty or a law faculty."[6] Indeed, *The Nature of the Law* is in many respects a complement to *The New Science of Politics*, not least of all as a critique of positivism.

As early as 1941, in a review of N. S. Timasheff's *An Introduction to the Sociology of Law* and E. Bodenheimer's *Jurisprudence*, Voegelin provided a comprehensive description of what an "adequate science of law" entailed. Over the previous century and a half, a broad understanding of jurisprudence had been elaborated by several generations of fine legal minds.

> It is not exhausted by a history of institutions or a blueprint of a just order, nor by an analysis of the logical structure of legal rules nor by a classification of social behavior, nor by an inquiry into power structures nor by an analysis of the judicial process. It ranges from the biological characteristics of man to the ethical and religious background of a civilization, from the economic system of a community to the logic of normative judgments, from the expansiveness of the human being (symbolized in the concept of liberty) and its shrinking in anxiety (symbolized in the concept of fear) to delicate technical discussions on the best way of achieving a certain social end by means of regulation. None of these topics is unimportant in a full presentation of the object, none of them can be neglected as only incidental; every one of them requires the full mastery of the materials as well as of the methods employed in their interpretation.[7]

Voegelin's procedure as a reviewer of scholarly books, as distinct from the kinds of ideological pamphlets and opinion pieces that we noticed in previous chapters, was a model of analysis. He began by characterizing a problem and indicating the requirements for a thorough analysis of it. "Mastery of the materials as well as of the methods employed in their interpretation" remained the standard for all political science, including Voegelin's.

The two works under review in this case were of sufficient scholarly merit that they could profitably be measured by such an exacting standard. Both authors had a comprehensive understanding of jurisprudence

6. "Editors' Introduction," *CW*, 27:xxii.
7. Voegelin, "Two Recent Contributions to the Science of Law." Quotations without further reference are from the reprint of this article in *CW*, 27:87–94.

and "agree that law is not an aprioric structure of the human mind nor, therefore, a phenomenon to be found invariably at all stages of civilization, but that it has a historical status." Accordingly, the most satisfactory way to arrive at a conceptually precise definition of law is "to form an ideal type of the fully developed stage and to characterize other types of community order through their difference from the mature type of law." This essentially Weberian procedure depended for its successful execution on the systematic development of criteria of relevance.

In spite of the undoubted merits of both books, neither author provided an adequate methodological justification of the criteria by which he had selected his materials and ordered them into categories for analysis. Their respective shortcomings were, in a sense, complementary: Timasheff was systematic but abstract, whereas Bodenheimer was "practical" in the sense that his selection of evidence was guided by the actual configuration of legal materials as they may be found in the historical environment. Timasheff, Voegelin said, "opens his book with definitions of concepts without revealing how he arrived at them and why he puts them forward, then passes on and finds to his agreeable surprise that they fit reality and have not been introduced in vain after all, leaving his reader to ponder on the miracle of the pre-established harmony." In other words, Timasheff's "positivistic notion of science" simply avoided the question of criteria of relevance by making relevance a matter of initial conceptual definition. According to Voegelin, following Weber, conceptually precise definitions should conclude a survey of materials collected on the basis of an articulate theory of relevance, and eventually on the basis of a philosophical anthropology.

In contrast, Bodenheimer's approach was entirely satisfactory, but only as a "first delimitation" because it began with "the object as it occurs in history and tries to penetrate from the obvious occurrence to the elements that may have entered into the composition of the complex result." It is a commendable approach, Voegelin said, because it starts from "the self-interpretation of historical reality through the persons who express their metaphysical, political and ethical preferences in a given situation." The "first approach" to the question of relevance, then, must be "what the members of legally ordered communities think to be relevant." Unfortunately, Bodenheimer went no further than this "first approach" or "first delimitation." His account remained "the first and not the last effort of a science of law," because, in the end, the purpose of his system of jurisprudence was to justify the view that law had the function of "limiting the actions of the individuals to behavior patterns that are mutually compatible with one another, and it limits the actions of rulers so that the plain members of the community may be reasonably secure against the unexpected, arbitrary governmental interference in their private spheres." In consequence, the ideal type advanced by Bodenheimer was "the model of the Western constitutional governments," though not, perhaps, in the closest accord with the self-interpretation of social reality even in the West. This was no problem for Bodenheimer because he "wishes to monopolize the term *law* for constitutional governments and to deny it to the legal order of dictatorships." So long as the differences between legal or constitutional regimes and dictatorships were carefully worked out in detail, this apparent restriction remained scientifically unimportant.

The bulk of the book consisted of "a report of doctrines on the several aspects of law," suitably arranged so as to constitute a useful survey of the topic. "The treatment assumes the form of a short and, on the whole, correct report of the theories, followed by concise and pertinent critical remarks that lead beyond the theories in question into the systematic problems—though not very far." The most systematically penetrating sections accordingly dealt with the most systematically penetrating thinkers, namely those who had a "comprehensive philosophical education." After the end of the eighteenth century and the "division of labor in social sciences," the survey became more barren. That is, the subject matter, not the author's own philosophical acumen, determined the theoretical or scientific value of the work.

Timasheff's positivism and Bodenheimer's historicism detracted from the scientific value of their works insofar as the methods implied by those terms were inappropriate or inadequate for the materials under analysis. The value of their books was simply a consequence of their workmanlike intellectual competence.

In his review of J. B. Scott's *Law, the State, and the International Community*, Voegelin considered a more serious methodological problem.[8] Scott's book, he said, was "an outstanding achievement in the dogmatic literature on the subjects of law and international order." The procedure employed by Scott was to isolate the legal order from the context of social and political reality and to treat it "as if it were a realm to itself to be established sooner or later on this earth after certain obstacles have been overcome in the course of evolution." Scott combined the methodological defects of Timasheff and Bodenheimer in the sense that he began with a "creed." By this term Voegelin indicated the vulgarian equivalent to Timasheff's a priori and abstract definition of relevance. Scott then proceeded to the historical materials, but unlike Bodenheimer, he did so in order to invoke "the authority of congenial thinkers."

8. Voegelin, "Right and Might" (1941); reprinted in *CW*, 27:84–86.

Ransacking the past in search of support for one's "creed" inevitably meant that unsupportive evidence would be distorted or ignored altogether. Accordingly, "there is no point in measuring it by the standards of science."[9] The scientist could do no more than identify and analyze the chief assumptions that governed the credal system, which Voegelin proceeded to do.

The first assumption was that an evolution toward the goal of a peaceful order of law existed. For this dogma to be accepted one must also assume the existence of a "historic era" that included some civilizations, such as that of the contemporary West, and excluded others. "Minor items like China, India, Egypt, and Byzantine Empire are apparently relegated with the Primitives to the limbo of prehistory." But even within the historic era, Scott was compelled to introduce supplementary dogmas to cover gaps or temporary retrogressions. The period of the Great Migrations was therefore passed over in silence; nothing was said of the centuries between Saint Augustine and John of Salisbury. Moreover, the evidence presented as "contributions towards an order of law" was discussed in such a way that the unpeaceful and disordered historical context was also overlooked. The Stoics, who made a splendid "contribution," were contemporaries of Alexander; Cicero lived amid the great imperial expansion of Rome; the development of the much applauded international law beginning in the sixteenth century occurred during the conquest of America.

This last observation, which was excised by the journal editor, pointed to some highly unpleasant implications of Scott's progressivist creed. In his argument regarding the legitimacy of the Spanish conquests, Francisco de Vitoria rejected

> the more crudely materialistic argument for the suppression and exploitation of the Indians, but produced gentle arguments instead that the resources of this earth were destined by God for all men, that the Spaniards had a right to exploit the raw materials of America, that they had a right to settle there undisturbed, that they might start the conversion of natives to Christianity, that they had a right of forceful intervention when the native rulers would discriminate against their converted Christian subjects and that they could, if necessary for the protection of the Christians, replace the native government by Spanish rule. May I humbly ask the unenlightened question, what exactly is the difference between these acknowledged great contributions to

9. These words were removed, along with similar observations noted below, by Waldemar Gurian, the editor of *Review of Politics*. The version printed in *The Nature of the Law* was taken from the printed text, not the typescript. Voegelin's remarks are reproduced here from the typescript.

international law, and the claims advanced by the National Socialist party to send their propaganda agents to foreign countries, to disintegrate the political community from within by converting sections of the population to their ideas, to assume the protection of the converts, and, if necessary, to intervene with force and to abolish an unenlightened native government when it discriminates against its National Socialist citizens?

For Scott, the difference between the Nazis and the Conquistadores was simple: we are a Christian civilization and our expansion is desirable, whereas the expansion of other creeds is to be resisted. In response, Voegelin asked whether the expansion of Christian civilizational order, "as of any order, is not linked to the use of force against unwilling or helpless minorities, as favored by Vitoria, and approved by Professor Scott?" Notwithstanding Voegelin's moral language, his main criticism was methodological. In a serious work of political science it was unacceptable to separate ideas of order from the realities of power. "The problem of right order," Voegelin said, "is not a problem of peace, but of the principles on which it is built, if necessary by force." This is not to say that might makes right; it remains true, nevertheless, that might does make an order, "and that without it an order can neither be created nor maintained."[10] Voegelin concluded his review with the observation that further discussion of the problem of order, power, and justice would have to call into question the assumptions that sustained Scott's doctrine.

The following year, 1942, Voegelin had an opportunity to consider at greater length the question of science in connection with a short book by Huntington Cairns, *The Theory of Legal Science.*[11] Voegelin was "baffled" by the book, he said, because the title led him to expect an account of the epistemological and methodological foundations of an existing science, whereas the author "is of the opinion that legal science does not exist at all" and that its creation is a desideratum. Cairns proceeded to outline what such a legal science might be, if it could be created, and Voegelin pointed out that the work of Max Weber actually constituted such an achievement. Despite the baffling aspects of a book that both called for the creation of an as yet nonexistent science of social order and rejected the body of legal science that did exist, Cairns's book was nevertheless valuable because it dealt with "the crucial problem of any science of social order." Accordingly, a critical analysis of the author's arguments would bring into focus the "theoretical situation of our time."

---

10. Here again the printed text varies from the original, which happens to be rather clearer.
11. Voegelin, "The Theory of Legal Science: A Review"; reprinted in *CW*, 27:95–112.

Underlying Cairns's theoretical analysis was a "model" of science, based on natural science, that formulated general laws on the basis of which events may be predicted, the more accurately the better, where accuracy was understood in terms of mathematical exactness. Voegelin repeated his simple and obvious observation that the use "of the formal apparatus of mathematics in the couching of propositions in any science, is not a matter of choice but of ontological possibility." One does not use mathematics in the discussion of the routinization of charisma because the structure or the reality of the subject matter does not lend itself to mathematically exact formulations. Legal science, as political science, has its own standards of precision, and they are not mathematical.

Cairns did not consider the question of the applicability of mathematical exactness as a criterion of scientific adequacy but simply made the assumption that "the subject matter of social order has the same structure as the subject matter of organic nature." The assumption was unclear because Cairns spoke not of distinct realms of being, namely social order and organic nature, but of a kind of composite category, the external world. But the ontological status of the "external world" is precisely what was at issue. That is, it was questionable for Voegelin whether there existed an external world that exhibited a uniform and homogeneous structure of subject matter in such a way that a single method of analysis was appropriate and thus fit for the designation "science." To begin with, "organic nature" *looked* rather different from "social order." Cairns had some hesitation in deciding this question, and Voegelin drew the obvious conclusion: if the structure of the "external world" was not uniform and homogeneous, then the relevance of mathematicized physical science to the scientific understanding of social order was highly questionable, which introduced the "crucial problem of any science of social order," namely the problem of relevance.

In order to discuss what is relevant in the external world and in society for any science of social order, one must develop a "philosophy of man and of his place in society and the world at large." Without an "idea of man," Voegelin said, "we have no frame of reference for the designation of human phenomena as relevant or irrelevant. Man is engaged in the creation of social order physically, biologically, psychologically, intellectually, and spiritually," and only some of these engagements admit of "general laws." Accordingly, the criteria of relevance for the constitution of political, social, or legal science is properly developed on the basis of philosophical anthropology, not legal generality and not mathematical or quasi-mathematical predictability.

If the first concern of a political scientist must be with the relevance of the subject matter with respect to criteria determined by principles of philosophical anthropology, one must face up to a genuine difficulty: "we do not all have the same idea of man and our principles of selection of relevant subject matter may differ widely." This being the case, "do we have to accept the consequence that there never will be a social science in steady progress to ever higher perfection of the system like the natural sciences?" Voegelin's answer was "an emphatic yes."

Conflicting principles of philosophical anthropology did not, how-ever, mean the triumph of subjectivism and relativism. First, because of the "weight of social institutions," the "civilizational tradition" of *The New Science of Politics* served as a corrective to wildly arbitrary observations "insofar as the idea of man embodied in them will influence the amplitude of the socially possible disagreement." Second, within this context, there existed the "corrective discussion of social science" based on a "stock of knowledge" that a social scientist cannot disregard without exposing himself to the charge of incompetence. "Through all disagreements among philosophers," Voegelin observed, "there is a con-vergence towards standards that makes it impossible to claim the suc-cessful construction of a system unless the anthropology underlying it gives due weight to the various elements of human nature." In principle, therefore, if in a piece of critical scholarship one points out and analyzes the incompetence of a social or political or legal scientist by drawing attention to facts that have been overlooked, to logical lapses, and so on, one is actually engaged in the practice of corrective discussion.

Voegelin engaged in corrective discussion of the text under review by indicating to Cairns and anyone else who cared to notice that such discussion was to be distinguished from any notion of scientific progress. He provided two reasons. First, "the idea of man is not a datum in the external world but a creation of the human spirit, undergoing historical changes, and it has to be recreated every generation and by every single person." For example, Christianity has added to the idea of man as elab-orated in classical philosophy the dimension of "spiritual singularity." Consequently, one cannot develop a science of political or legal order based simply on the anthropology of Plato or Aristotle. Similarly, within Christianity since the Renaissance there has been added the dimension of "historic singularity." Voegelin did not specify further the meaning of these "dimensions" beyond indicating that they were derivative of "the fundamental religious attitudes of the thinkers who created and transformed them." In short, Voegelin was using the additive imagery of dimensions to describe the process of consciousness that he later formu-lated in terms of the compactness and differentiation of the experience and symbolization of reality. The trail of symbols left by human beings as the residue of their efforts to clarify the structure of reality is the chief source of evidence that the creative activities of the human spirit are historically distinct. Comparing these distinctive symbolizations of experience is, of course, possible, but it involves additional methodological reflection, as we shall see in subsequent chapters.

Voegelin's immediate concern, however, was to emphasize once again that the physical and social sciences differ profoundly in their respective epistemologies. Material reality, Voegelin said, "is, in a sense, static, and the progress we can make in its exploration is the progress in the dissection of a corpse that holds still; the realm of man and society is relatively much more alive and the degree of understanding will be determined by the amplitude of the idea of man that is at the disposition of a scholar through environmental tradition and through the breadth of his personality." Accordingly, the fundamental attitude of an author with respect to the idea of man also had a significant bearing on the quality of the result of his reflections. In Voegelin's later work, this methodological requirement of social science became thematic in the concept, borrowed from Plato and Aristotle, of participation. In the present context, corrective discussion is not necessarily persuasive because the breadth of personality or of consciousness of the individual being corrected may be insufficient to understand or accept correction. Accordingly, there is no expectation that corrective discussion will be a success, in the sense of engendering a more differentiated consciousness of participation in reality, which is not what advocates of progress mean by the term anyway.

So far as Cairns's study was concerned, there was no explicit account of his "idea of man," which absence gravely impaired his understanding of relevance. "Cairns," Voegelin said, "does not see that relevancies change with the idea of man and that this idea has its roots in the sphere of the self-reflective personality, in which the attitudes of man toward the world are constituted." Instead, Cairns assumed there was but one legitimate system of relevancy, namely that of the natural sciences, and therefore that human beings must be "a part of the external world, along with other natural phenomena, seen from the outside." Accordingly, spiritually significant aspects of the human person, which are empirically important for political, legal, and social order, were excluded on the grounds that they were unobservable in the "external world."

One may characterize Cairns's system of relevance with the observation that he had replaced human spiritual singularity with human biological fungibility. By doing so a "science of general rules becomes possible" and thereby as well the possibility of rational organization of society under the categories of his as yet nonexistent theory of legal science. According to Voegelin, however, matters were rather more complex: the problem of social, political, or legal order lay precisely in the fact that "ideas of man" differed and could not simply be substituted for one another. The experience of human reality expressed in the notion of the spiritual singularity of the self-reflective personality could not be reduced to a single interchangeable human characteristic. All that could happen in the attempt to do so was that the experience of spiritual singularity would be ignored or perhaps extinguished, if necessary by extinguishing the human beings who had ordered their lives through such experience. Voegelin, therefore, described Cairns's attitude as characteristic of a socially benevolent technician or engineer whose sentiments were sustained by the invalid assumption "that we all know what we want, that we all want the same, and that the problem of social order does *not* lie precisely in the fact that our ideas of order differ in correspondence to our ideas of man." Cairns was not unaware that there were certain problems connected to social engineering, namely that even the most elaborate system of rules of behavior does not tell us the right thing to do. Accordingly, to the project of developing a science of law he added a "science of ethical rules," the achievement of which was to take place entirely in the future. At the present time this science, like the science of the law, was nonexistent. For this reason Voegelin described Cairns's attitude as one of "spiritual nihilism."

Voegelin concluded that spiritual nihilism was symptomatic as well as idiosyncratic: the anxiety that replaced the annihilation of the sentiments of historical and spiritual singularity typically drives an individual to seek the shelter of the order of natural science, often because such science seems to be all that makes sense. The creative forces of the soul as the source of spiritual order have been eclipsed by "invention" and the purposiveness of calculative action. The intensity of the new sentiments carries with it the conviction that humans are interchangeable parts and opens the possibility of rational social control understood as a process of invention. But, asked Voegelin, "what is that whole order good for, once we have it? Nobody knows. It is an order without meaning, an order at any cost born out of the anxieties of a lost man." Accordingly, Cairns's book was both a "touching personal document" and a "terrifying symptom of the disorder in which we live." In 1942 there were other more apparent symptoms of disorder than the academic confusions and spiritual nihilism of a Huntington Cairns. For Voegelin, however, the two complexes of disorder, the personal and the political, were related.[12]

12. Cairns provided a short reply (pp. 571–72) in the *Louisiana Law Review*. He did not engage Voegelin's criticism nor even his analysis but declared simply that his

The 1946 annual meeting of the American Political Science Association (APSA) was held in Cleveland just after Christmas. It provided an additional opportunity to develop and discuss the question of method and the implications of positivism for political science. During the fall, Arnold Brecht organized a roundtable discussion, entitled "Beyond Relativism in Political Theory," and invited Voegelin to take part.[13] Early in November, Voegelin received a copy of Brecht's "Introductory Remarks." These were designed, he said, as a "technical help" to avoid unnecessary repetitions and "to help us technically in our effort to keep the debate on a high level." More to the point, Brecht asked the participants "to use the draft as an agenda in preparing your own contributions to the discussion." A draft of the announcement of the session, which was included in the program without any changes, was also included. "It is not the purpose of this roundtable," wrote Brecht,

> to minimize the merits of relativism or of what is usually called the scientific method. Its purpose is rather (1) to take stock of the *opinions* held by participants and audience regarding the possibility of advancing beyond relativism in political theory, (2) to clarify the precise meaning of the different views, and (3) to discuss the legitimate functions of political theory under the competing *opinions* in the *struggle of ideas*.

Brecht had been a senior official in the German and Prussian governments prior to the advent of the Third Reich and knew almost by instinct the importance of agenda-setting.[14] His introductory remarks, no less than the description of the purpose of the roundtable, had the objective of constraining the discussion within the parameters of his particular understanding of "political theory."

Brecht's position, evident from the program announcement, equated "relativism" and "the scientific method." This position was one regarding which several opinions could be identified and disagreements specified. By clarifying the several opinions involved and by making positions explicit so that the grounds for dispute are plain, he said, science gets

---

book spoke for itself and that he would not discuss "Voegelin's ontology," which was, of course, the heart of Voegelin's criticism.

13. The other participants were J. Roland Pennock, who acted as secretary; Francis G. Wilson, chairman of the APSA Political Theory Research Panel; Gabriel Almond; Francis W. Coker; John H. Hallowell; Hans Kelsen; Benjamin Lippincott; and Benjamin Wright. Unless otherwise indicated, quotations are taken from HI 6/15. The discussion was to take place over two sessions, Friday and Saturday mornings, December 27–28. Voegelin was able to attend only the second session.

14. See Brecht, *The Political Education of Arnold Brecht: An Autobiography, 1884–1970.*

done.[15] Several implications were drawn out in Brecht's "Introductory Remarks." First, political theory is "relative" in the sense that it is related to the law, political institutions, historical and sociological conditions, purposes actually being pursued, and so on. "Relative questions of cause and effect, and of the adequacy of means for the achievement of definite purposes, are legitimate subjects of political theory." However, Brecht continued, "no scientific method has yet been devised to determine the superiority of any ends or purposes over any other ends or purposes in absolute terms." Accordingly, one can discuss only the efficiency of one or another goal as a means to some other goal about which "scientific methods" must remain silent. This did not mean, Brecht said, "that actually there *are* no differences in the value of any ends or purposes" but "only" that the "realm of values" is "inaccessible to scientific methods" and so cannot be communicated "to other men in forms of proof or conclusive demonstration." That is, one may espouse certain convictions, but they do not constitute "intersubjective proof." This statement was a paraphrase of the first and greatest Weberian commandment.

A second was like unto it: science alone is capable of what today would be called "values clarification." Two procedures are involved: analysis and clarification of the meaning of a conviction or "value," and examination of the consequences of holding such convictions. This position Brecht identified with "higher-level relativists," and he invoked the name of Max Weber as first among them. On the basis of these two points, Brecht then proposed a consideration of a "research program" to investigate the "meaning and implications" of various political ideologies, which is to say, an investigation of the values to which the adherents of ideologies are committed and the implications of those commitments. After having elaborated this "research program" it would be allowable to consider "research programs based on any *other* method or methods" to deal with ideologies. It was understood by Brecht that, whatever these other methods might be, they could not possibly be called scientific. His final two points were practical: ought individual scholars strive to be neutral or ought they "take sides" (and, of course, tell their audience that they have taken sides on the basis of no "intersubjective proof of the validity of our assumptions"); likewise, ought "we scholars," that is, the community of scholars, actually do something "in the political fight that is going on in the world among ideologies?"

15. Brecht argued for this position, opinion, or view at considerable length in his *Political Theory: The Foundations of Twentieth-Century Political Thought,* in which he also offered critical remarks against what he took to be Voegelin's position, opinion, or view developed in *The New Science of Politics.*

Brecht ended his introduction by informing the audience "of a decision we have made regarding the technique of this discussion," namely that it would consist only in taking stock "of the various opinions that prevail among us at the present historical juncture" and, if the meaning of those opinions is doubtful, clarifying them. Certainly "it is not our purpose to decide on the divergencies of opinion among us or to convince one another or the audience that we are right."

About a month after Voegelin received a copy of Brecht's "Introductory Remarks" he received another letter with additional "technical points" for his consideration. In this circular of November 30, 1946, Brecht informed the participants that they would have about five minutes each hour to state their views. To expedite matters, he requested that the panelists develop a "short thesis" of their opinions. From Voegelin in particular Brecht asked for a brief written statement, and, after the event, he asked for "a short write-up" of the points made. Early in January 1947, Voegelin complied.

The "write-up" of his remarks began with a consideration of Brecht's third point, the question of a "research program," because that point led directly to the current difficulties and bewilderment expressed in the title of the panel. "Research," Voegelin said, is a dubious term, "a vague designation for the various operations of a scholar who is engaged in elaborating a problem in science." If one ignores the context of scientific problems, research turns into "indulgence in irrelevancies." This is particularly apt to occur when one discusses "research programs" or "research projects" because such items cannot sensibly be found "by casting around for topics of interest, for a 'topic' is not a 'problem,'" and science is concerned with the elaboration or analysis of problems. A problem, Voegelin went on, arises for a scholar during the course of his study of existing materials in light of the existing theoretical accounts of them. "If the emerging problem is of sufficient systematic importance to warrant the theorization or retheorization of a body of materials, the scholar may proceed to do so" and may, indeed, call his enterprise a project. But that designation comes at the end of the analysis and after the problem has emerged, not before.[16]

---

16. The distinction between a topic and a problem is fundamental to Voegelinian political science but is also often overlooked. More than once Voegelin responded to a request to deliver a lecture on a particular topic with the abrupt response that he was a scientist concerned with the analysis of problems. To one such request, for example, he replied: "Your first letter had led me to believe that your group was seriously interested to see what problems in political science look like when treated by a man who moves in the Christian and classic tradition of philosophizing. In

Voegelin then provided a brief phenomenology of the emergence of problems. Problems arise for specific scholars during the course of a concrete intellectual effort that, in turn, takes place "in an intellectual environment, which we may call 'the present state of science.'" Phenomenologically considered, science is "a process in writing" that is related to "the state of science" as manifest in the writing of those who have dealt with the problem previously. That is, no one can discuss a problem in political theory without relating one's discussion to the state of science concerning this problem. Specifically, this means that any new account of a problem gains its scientific legitimacy by being critically differentiated from existing accounts that actually constitute "the state of science."

Voegelin added an example from the roundtable discussion. One of the panelists had remarked that "we do not possess a 'philosophy of democracy.'" This may be true, Voegelin allowed, but it is no more than an abstract complaint so far as the state of political science is concerned. Properly stated, the proposition would indicate that existing theoretical accounts of the institutions and ideas of democracy are defective and that not much has been done about it in recent years. Assuming the truth of such a claim, the next thing for a scholar to consider would be whether he or she should take up the "problem of democracy" where it had been left by scholars such as Tocqueville or Mill, Renan or Le Bon, Jaspers, Toynbee, Mannheim, or Laski. Wherever one decides to start, one nevertheless starts somewhere and proceeds by way of a "concrete critique of concrete works of science which are sufficiently important to warrant such discussion."

On the basis of such reflections, Voegelin then considered Brecht's first two questions:

1. Is intersubjective proof possible regarding the validity or invalidity of value judgments in political matters?
2. Can political theory contribute to the dispute about political value judgments other than by clarifying the meaning of proposed evaluations and examining the consequences of political actions based on these evaluations?

In order to discuss these or any other such questions in a sensible way one must, as Voegelin had already indicated, relate them to the state of

your second letter you suggest 'topics' instead of problems—and the substitution of topics for problems happens to be the cardinal sin from which the lecture industry in our academic life suffers. I certainly would not touch a topic like 'Biblical Faith and Democratic Political Order,' or a more specific topic of the same nature, with a barge pole. That is precisely the sort of thing from which I try to get away" (HI 19/10).

science. Yet if one actually does so, it turns out that the present state of science (in 1946) no longer considers such questions significant. Brecht's questions, as his earlier references to Max Weber made plain, belonged to the state of "a certain sector of the social sciences in the opening years of this century." Max Weber's great essays on method and objectivity in the social sciences had been superseded

> by the developments of the last fifty years in the fields of philosophical anthropology, through the exploration of the relation between ethics and ontology, through the exploration of the myth, through the establishment of spiritual processes as the determinants in the formation of "horizons" of values, through the historicization of the problems of politics and the abolition of the problem of the "best" form of government, through the rise of the philosophy of existence, and so forth.

In consequence, science is simply not concerned with the nonproblem of value judgments nor with the nonproblem of relativism, without, however, "having landed in any absolutism." The answer to Brecht's two questions was, therefore, clear: political science has, indeed, contributed a good deal to the "dispute about political value-judgments." So much, in fact, that the first question has become obsolete. Sensible programmatic suggestions, therefore, would have to begin from an awareness of the present state of science.

Voegelin sent a polite note to Brecht along with his "write-up" in which he expressed regret at having "to disagree with you on some points." To Francis Wilson, the panel chairman, he was more frank:

> Among ourselves, however, I should like to say that I am rather shocked by the turn which these discussions on research and programs are taking. On the one hand, the Program of the Association contains a grandiose Foreword on the importance of the time and the responsibilities incumbent on political scientists; on the other hand, we show a levity and irresponsibility in handling theoretical issues which is tantamount to the abandonment of any serious work altogether. It is a disgrace that a Round Table of the American Political Science Association can be conducted as if the whole development of the last fifty years in theory were nonexistent.[17]

He concluded by proposing a remedy: "to abandon for a while the gassing about programs and to arrange, on the occasion of such meetings, for the delivery of serious work by two or three persons."

Brecht's "position" was impervious to Voegelin's criticism. The dogmatic and self-referential nature of "scientific value-relativism," which

17. HI 42/5.

was so evident in Brecht's "technical remarks," could be "refuted" only in practice, by ceasing to have any appeal to younger scholars. That, after all, is the normal result of obsolescence.[18] Obsolescent or not, Brecht was still a gentleman and a scholar; in his "Theses" delivered prior to the panel, Voegelin paid him the compliment of a more serious analysis and characterization of the issue.

To approach the question of relativism in political theory in terms of the verification of value judgments, Voegelin began, "does not touch the real problem involved." Indeed, such an approach is nothing more than an expression, in gentlemanly and scholarly terms to be sure, of the question it attempts to analyze. The real problem concerns "the origin of political theory in philosophical existence," which is, in the first instance, a historical problem: political theory, or political science, has its origin in the contemplative life of the Greek philosophers, chiefly Plato and Aristotle. "The *bios theoretikos* is for Aristotle the condition for a view of man in society that can be called the theoretical view in the technical sense." From this theoretical perspective, *stricto sensu*, "the differentiation of human existence into its biological, utilitarian and noetic strata becomes visible." To Aristotle's theory three major additional insights, each of which also occurred on a specific or "concrete" historical occasion, have been added: the differentiation of the spiritual personality in Christianity, the development during and after the fourteenth century of toleration based upon *theologia mystica,* and the articulation of a meaning to profane history distinct from sacred history after Vico's *New Science* in the eighteenth century. The complex of Aristotelian "theory" and the insights gained during the Christian centuries, Voegelin said, constitute "the principle 'immediate experiences' that form the classical basis of political theory."

In addition to, and distinct from, that understanding of "classical" political science, there exist several other interpretations of politics that are less comprehensive but nevertheless structured by specific and politically significant experiences that "may bring into clearer view special

18. When Brecht's *Political Theory* was published, Voegelin was asked by John D. Lewis to review it for the *APSR.* To Lewis's observation that he had had some difficulty in finding a reviewer, Voegelin somewhat impishly replied: "After all, there are Strauss and Friedrich, and there are the incumbents of the chairs for Political Theory in Yale and Princeton who would be both competent and happy to review a major monograph in their field. The book should be quite interesting to these people because its position is that of value relativism. That, incidentally, is the reason why the book should not be reviewed by me, as I am somewhat out of sympathy with that attitude. It would be fairer to Brecht to have his book reviewed by somebody who fundamentally agrees with his position" (HI 23/10).

problems in the vast field of human existence in society." Voegelin again used the term *political idea* to describe such interpretations and gave as examples the Lockean "bourgeois" and Marxian "proletarian" interpretations of politics.[19] Insofar as the political scientist is unable to acknowledge as true or valid or exhaustive the interpretations advanced by the advocate of one or another political idea, conflict between the two is likely to occur. This conflict is inevitable when two partial political views that claim to be absolute are advanced with the enthusiasm that is inspired by the certainty of commitment to dogma.

Two kinds of conflict have a bearing on the question of relativism because of the following considerations. First, the conflict between the political idea and political science is, concretely, a conflict between a human being who lives a theoretical and philosophical existence and one who lives a dogmatic and political one. The only "solution" is for the theorist to "surrender the *bios theoretikos* and become a political dogmatist" or for the dogmatist to abandon his restrictive horizon and become a theorist or scientist. The conflict between different political ideas originates in different modes of political existence. It can be resolved only "if one of the two opponents surrenders his position and joins the former enemy." Rational discussion of the problem of conflicting interpretations can take place only between human beings "who live existentially in the *bios theoretikos*" and so not among political dogmatists, or between them and a political scientist. So far as the last pair is concerned, the political dogmatist (or the intellectual dogmatist for that matter) will always be for the political scientist a problem to be analyzed, not a partner in discussion. In this context, Voegelin concluded, a relativist is someone who is aware of the conflicting political dogmas and their claims to absolute validity, is "sufficiently sensitive to the *bios theoretikos* not to join blindly and dogmatically one of the partial interpretations," but who nevertheless is unable to live in the mode of the *bios theoretikos*.

With Brecht it was possible to indicate that science had, as it were, moved on and left him behind, still beavering away on questions that had been dealt with a half century earlier. Brecht at least seemed to be aware of what Voegelin called "the obligations of the *bios theoretikos*," and he was certainly aware of the history of Western political theory,[20]

---

19. Readers of *The New Science of Politics* will recognize an alternative formulation of the distinction between "symbols by which political societies interpret themselves" and concepts used "in the economy of science" (*NSP*, 1, 29).

20. In his circular letter of November 30, 1946, Brecht instructed the panelists on the "technical point" that they were not to undertake "excursions into aspects that can be supposed to be such of general knowledge, at least among professors

even if he was unable to live the theoretical life, in Aristotle's sense of the term.

Others among Voegelin's contemporaries shared Brecht's restricted and obsolescent opinions regarding the meaning of science but lacked both Brecht's sensitivity and his scholarly command of the texts. The vulgarian version of Brecht's "scientific value-relativism," which is conventionally called behavioralism, did not, in Voegelin's view, even qualify as obsolete science. These individuals effectively had no notion of what the *bios theoretikos* meant either as an attitude or as a way of life. Unlike Brecht, no appeal could be made to the lost treasure of political philosophy because such persons did not know it to be treasure or that it was lost. Indeed, they looked upon Brecht's work as the finest sort of "political theory," and may themselves be characterized as the finest living proof of "the destruction of science" to which Voegelin referred in the opening pages of *The New Science of Politics.* At the same time such individuals were apt to think of themselves as the finest fruit of scientific progress, which poses a curious analytical problem for a Voegelinian political scientist. As we shall see, Voegelin dealt with it by distancing himself from the highly uncongenial enterprise or by satire. The method is still to be recommended.

In November 1949, the managing editor of the *APSR,* Taylor Cole, wrote Voegelin asking him to review a paper submitted by David Easton on the work of Harold Lasswell. In his reply Voegelin wondered whether he was the best person to offer advice on the publication: "The subject-matter bores me to death. The idea of exploring the epigonic flounderings of Lasswell from Weber, through Freud and Pareto, to something like a Schmittian decisionism, rigged up to serve the ends of democracy—is slightly nauseating." His "personal advice" to Easton was to forget about Lasswell and do something worthwhile. "Besides, the author's positivistic jargon about 'conceptual frameworks,' 'structured materials,' and his conviction that political science should deal with problems of 'social significance' (whatever that means) and 'must not tolerate' anything else (whatever that means) is not inviting." Even so, Easton's paper could serve as "documentary evidence" of the greatness of the political science department at the University of Chicago, which, he remarked, *Time* magazine had recently identified as "mankind's most central center of learning." Moreover, "within the 'conceptual framework' of Chicago positivism" the article was first-rate and the author was both "obviously

---

of political theory, and we must assume familiarity with the whole literature both political and philosophic."

intelligent" and competent in handling the topic. "Besides, he seems to have discovered, like Lasswell, that one cannot do without 'values,' though he does not yet quite know what the strange animal is."[21]

Voegelin's sarcastic letter to Cole indicated his opinion of the "behavioral persuasion." It was one he maintained even after he came to the attention of several prominent behavioralists with the publication of *The New Science of Politics*. In 1973, for example, Voegelin wrote to Ellis Sandoz, chiding him for involving his work in a criticism of behavioralism. "Please," wrote Voegelin,

> try to get it out of your head that the behaviorists are any concern of mine. I do not live in solitude but in international communication with scholars so numerous that I must severely husband my time to maintain all the contacts. The behaviorists you have in mind are simply outside science and, as I also on occasion have remarked, I find them never quoted in any of the works I have to use in the course of my work; they are entirely unknown to scholars internationally. Moreover, I do not feel the slightest obligation to engage in extended polemics or criticisms because most of the literature to which you refer is far below the level that would deserve critical attention. I am afraid you are a bit too much impressed by what you consider the great position or repute of behaviorists among themselves and their followers.[22]

A few years later, in response to a request that he participate in a symposium on the question of methodology in the social sciences, Voegelin generalized his view of the unscientific status of the "social sciences." Methodologies, he said, were no longer even the partially scientific enterprises they were during the 1920s but had become "preconceived models of reality which do not fit the reality in which human beings live." Instead of being debatable, as they once had been, methodologies had become devices "to kill off philosophical and historical knowledge in order to leave the field open to the pluralism of emotional ideologies." The result is an institutional, not a scientific, problem because so many members of "social science" faculties are faced with enormous amounts of empirical material that the methodologies to which they are devoted

---

21. HI 6/16. Cole apparently took Voegelin's advice and rejected the submission. Eventually, Easton published "Harold Lasswell: Policy Scientist for a Democratic Society" in *Journal of Politics* 12 (1950): 450–77. At the time Voegelin was a "Section Editor" for *Journal of Politics*, but in the area of comparative politics, not political philosophy. Readers can judge how far Easton had moved beyond what Voegelin called his "budding insights" by the time of his presidential address to the APSA: Easton, "The New Revolution in Political Science," *APSR* 63 (1969): 1051–61.

22. HI 32/1. See Sandoz, "Voegelin Read Anew: Political Philosophy in the Age of Ideology."

cannot handle. The institutional problem, he said, "is formidable, but it is not a problem for scholars and it cannot be solved by 'debate.'"[23]

As a postscript to Voegelin's encounter with the most prominent school or doctrine in American political science, let us consider an incident that took place in February 1976. Voegelin had been invited to the University of Southern California to speak on the "political implications" of behavior control.[24] He described the meetings as a "revelation" because, for the first time, he saw "behaviorists in the flesh." He noted that they disagreed with one another and appeared to be ignorant of "the latest advances in the historical and philosophical sciences." The conference seemed "to be obsessed with drugs" and yet unaware of the analysis of the addiction to happiness that Swift had undertaken in *A Tale of a Tub*. According to Swift, he went on, in such a society "everyone is either a knave or a fool: the knave must be mad in order to find pleasure in controlling other people's behavior, and the fool must be mad in order to permit his behavior to be controlled by knaves." Equally significant, he said, was Thomas Mann's version of the question. In every society, Mann said, one finds a few people who are willing to explore the uncertainties of truth and many who prefer certainty, even if it is untrue, "because it obscures that which is uncertain and cannot be faced." This constant problem is serious "in the sense that if a piece of nonsense falls into an empty head as a certainty, it can have terrible consequences," particularly if the empty head is nevertheless convinced it has the solution to every affliction and is greatly aggrieved. A good example, Voegelin said, was Lenin.

As a matter of principle, however, "behavior control only works on empty-headed people." The political problem that follows from this principle is the fact that "the general level of the population consists of empty-headed people who feel uncertain and want a certainty, and you can give them a certainty by telling them, for instance, something about psychoanalysis. Then they are happy—on their level, which doesn't mean that they will become intelligent." He went on to point to the importance of the history of sadism as expressed in Camus's *The Rebel*,

---

23. HI 37/14. In 1982 Voegelin received a questionnaire regarding "political theorists" in the United States from a German academic, Jürgen Falter. It was accompanied by an encouraging letter from Karl W. Deutsch, Stanfield Professor of International Peace, Department of Government, Harvard, and a former president of the APSA. Voegelin refused to answer and pointed out to Professor Falter that Falter was engaged in an ideological enterprise that was a waste of time; he should, said Voegelin, read *The New Science of Politics* or *Order and History* if he was interested in political philosophy (HI 12/8).

24. Henry Clark, ed., *The Ethics of Experience and Behavior Control*. The conference proceedings and Voegelin's correspondence with Clark are in HI 9/17.

of Schiller's discussion of problems of identity and immorality in his *Lectures on Universal History,* and of the concept of division of labor with its implications for personal and social stability and independence.

Voegelin's remarks were followed by those of L. Keith Millar, who described himself as having been "a social activist for twenty years in everything from banning the bomb to stopping the [Vietnam] war and everything in between." He concluded his talk with the following words:

> Let me share my fantasy of how behavior analysis may help in shaping our world. I visualize people living in a network of small self-governed villages. These villages would have a decentralized form of leadership and equitable distribution of work and rewards. It would teach people how to live happily and productively, not how to consume and race to their death. It would seem to live in harmony with its environment. It would constantly experiment with better methods and it would gather data to evaluate its program. It would permit us to control our social environment as we have increasingly controlled our physical environment.

What Voegelin's audience made of his remarks and those of Millar may be indicated by the questions he was asked.

> Q: It seems to me that you, Dr. Voegelin, are characterizing some behavior controllers as people who want dominance out of insecurity. And, you say, this kind of thing would only be effective on those with empty heads. At the same time we heard Dr. Miller describe a rather utopian, idealistic kind of existence for the betterment of mankind, for peaceful and cooperative living. Would you accept that?
>
> A: (Voegelin) These are all nice words but they are completely empty. They don't mean anything in concrete terms.
>
> Q: Well, Dr. Miller works with concrete individuals in concrete situations.
>
> A: (Voegelin) Well, I work also with concrete individuals, with my students. The students with whom I have to deal are the victims of that kind of utopianism. Because they are not quite empty, they resist, but are prevented from intellectual effectiveness in their resistance by an academic environment in which the process of science is deliberately impeded. That is a very important factor. The university has in Western society become the iron curtain that prevents the young people from finding out what is going on in scientific scholarship.

Voegelin returned to Stanford and sent Professor Clark a letter thanking him for the opportunity to witness "behaviorists in action" against their foes, the "humanists," represented on this occasion by the psychologist Rollo May. Rational discussion and "dialogue" proved impossible, but precisely for that reason "I believe I owe you a report on the case you permitted me to observe." The report, which contained what he called

"Swiftian traces," illustrated the same problem Voegelin encountered thirty years before at the APSA roundtable.[25] By 1976, however, he took a more detached view of the enterprise, rather akin to that of Gulliver on his third voyage.

The general structure of the encounter was well known to Voegelin from previous meetings with ideologists, "National Socialists, Hegelians, Western Marxists, or Russian Communists." Typically, the ideologists never budge, which means the nonideological representatives of common sense or of the Western intellectual and spiritual culture must either submit or engage in "energetic disagreement." Nonideologists ought to know this, since the evidence is so overwhelming, which raises the question: why do they bother? "The atmospheric condition that causes such meetings and surrounds their futility has always a touch of the enigmatic." In the encounter between the behaviorists and the humanists Voegelin detected "a sincere concern about the morality of controlling the behavior of your fellowman by chemical or psychological manipulation on a massive scale." He was unsure, however, of its origin, and suggested four possibilities: the behaviorists may be nervous because the totalitarian implications of their enterprise had been discussed even in mass-circulation magazines; the humanists may be nervous because they have remained silent about the spread of this totalitarian movement; both sides may be nervous about each other and have decided that the situation may be defused by talk; or, last, both sides may have retained sufficient common sense to recognize the potential for violence in the enterprise of behavior control as in other ideological movements.

Whatever the motives, the problem remains: the humanists are supposed to get together with representatives "of a vicious attack on the standards of reason and spirit," individuals who "want to suffocate the dignity of man with social processes under the direction of their pathologically deformed existence." The "enigmatic" point of such meetings is found in the fact that there is no common intellectual or rational ground on which the partners to the discussion can expect to meet. Yet the fact that they do meet and do discuss something means that some sort of common ground exists, even if it is not reason. Voegelin borrowed Whitehead's term "climate of opinion" to indicate what the two sides shared.[26]

25. Voegelin used the phrase in a letter to Gerald Chapman; he added that "it is impossible today to write technical satire, because the reality is more grotesque than the imaginative exaggeration of a satirist can be" (HI 10/5).

26. See Alfred North Whitehead, *Science and the Modern World* (New York: Macmillan, 1925).

Whatever the decency and goodwill of the humanists, they are still able to overlook the fact that their opponents, in this case the behaviorists, have no interest in a genuine discussion. That is, they connive in their own defeat, and do so with a good conscience. This "enigmatic" point can be understood not by examining the good or bad faith of the participants. The entire encounter "must also be critically examined with regard to the observation or nonobservation of intellectual and spiritual standards."

So far as intellectual standards were concerned, Voegelin was able to observe in the Los Angeles meeting the "all too obvious" symptoms of deculturation. For example, in order even to discuss the project of producing "happiness" by means of chemical and psychological engineering, one must overlook the reductionist fallacy, that is, "the assumption that the higher strata in the hierarchy of being are fully determined by processes on the lower level." No one did; indeed, accepting the fallacy was the condition for the discussion. The only things at issue were whether these technologies worked, which ones were more effective, and by what right they were employed.

The questionable spirituality of the participants was expressed not in their cultural illiteracy but in the aggressive pride they took in it. "This structure in the discourse can no longer be classified as a variety of regrettable ignorance that can plead poor education and the intellectual dryrot of the university system as extenuating circumstances." On the contrary, aggressive ignorance is the face of the *libido dominandi*. "The ideologist," Voegelin said,

> whether Racist, Marxist, or Behaviorist, in order to have his engineering way with human beings, must first suppress our experiences of the nature and dignity of man, as well as the symbols by which we express these experiences. . . . The libidinous savagery reached its climax, and at the same time betrayed its motivations, in the attack on Rollo May, who happens to be aware of such problems, accompanied by the threat that he will be "left behind" if he does not join the Behaviorists in their merry ride on the wave of the future.

Voegelin concluded by recalling additional manifestations of ignorance and aggressiveness and insisted on paying his own airfare "because I feel uneasy about being counted as a participant in an event of this kind. I want to preserve as much of my status as an independent observer as I can."

The response of the conference organizers to Voegelin's analysis was not anger or even mild discomfort: it would, they hoped, provide an opportunity for a further round of talk. Voegelin had sent a copy of his letter to Clark to Harvey Wheeler of the Institute for Higher Studies in Santa Barbara. Wheeler wrote Clark urging him to take Voegelin's letter "seriously" because "it may provide you with an excellent opportunity to derive further benefit from the conference." That dividend would take the form of "a follow-up debate—perhaps a round robin literary debate—between the various participants." Clark then passed on Wheeler's suggestion to Voegelin, asking him for his opinion of it and for permission to circulate the original letter. Voegelin dryly replied that he had no objections and that, in addition to having sent a copy of the letter to Wheeler, he had shown it only to the Stanford chaplain. On the other hand, if Clark was interested in Voegelin's analysis of ideological movements, he might consult *From Enlightenment to Revolution,* or, if he cared to learn about dogma, there was *The Ecumenic Age* to consider. To these two academic entrepreneurs, interested in staging a round-robin debate, like a peewee hockey jamboree or a little league baseball tournament, any concern for the actual content of the commodities in which they trafficked, namely uncritical opinion, was absent. So too was Voegelin's irony lost on them.

As with Gulliver's voyage to Laputa, Voegelin's "Swiftian traces" carried a serious meaning. First of all, the argument advanced in *The New Science of Politics* regarding the destruction of science by positivism had been prepared by Voegelin's analyses of legal texts as well as by his encounter with the gentlemanly obsolescence of Arnold Brecht.[27] The encounter with the behavioralists, intoxicated with grandiose dreams, confirmed in practice what Voegelin long had known: this otherwise "harmless idiosyncrasy" could become a real irritant to the conduct of science because it had captured emotions and sentiments that inspired individuals to undertake their perverse activities with a good conscience.

The genealogy of libidinous and perverse behavioralists from "scientific value-relativism" and the destructive effects of nineteenth-century positivism may be taken as established. But the individuals Voegelin encountered "in action" were but late additions to what Hegel beautifully described as the spiritual bestiary, *das geistige Tierreich.* The spiritual genealogy of the problem, to be considered in the balance of this chapter, began much earlier.

In *The New Science of Politics* Voegelin alluded to this question with an offhand reference to "the impression which the Newtonian system made

27. Indeed, these issues had been discussed as well in Voegelin's German publications beginning with the introduction to *On the Form of the American Mind.* See also the discussion by Peter Opitz, "Max Weber und Eric Voegelin."

on Western intellectuals like Voltaire." The assumption that mathematical physics alone can claim to be science, that the sciences concerned with human and social order are not sciences, and that the subject matter with which such sciences are concerned, namely the order of consciousness, does not exist antedates Voltaire's enthusiasm for Newton. Voegelin discussed this larger problem in several places in *History of Political Ideas* and in a 1948 article published in *Social Research*.[28] In these texts Voegelin illustrated what the practice of political science entailed as well as provided an analysis of the historical context of positivist opinion, which is conventionally described as the growth of scientism. It nearly goes without saying that there is no presumption that the contemporary denizens of this particular compound within the spiritual bestiary have any awareness of their own antecedents. On the contrary, as Voegelin indicated, ignorance, even if deliberate, goes some distance to explain an irrational devotion to certainty, even if the votary is more or less aware of the untruth of the object of his or her devotions.

Accepting the conventional term used to describe this complex of sentiments, commitments, and intellectual positions, Voegelin argued that the "origins of scientism" lay in the intellectual atmosphere of the late sixteenth century. The erosion of the medieval view of human being and of the world was well underway, but the systematic alternative, which conventionally is indicated by the term *modern*, had not yet crystallized. That Voegelin was aware of the complexity of the problem of modernity is indicated in the hesitations he experienced in organizing the materials for *History of Political Ideas*. The same chapters were gathered together at different times as "Part Six: Transition" and "Part Seven: The New Order" but also as "Part Four: The Modern World." The first problem to consider, Voegelin argued, was the growth of sectarian spirituality to the point that it was sufficiently effective in European society to split the medieval unit of the church into a plurality of churches, each of which claimed to represent the true faith. In turn, ecclesiastical pluralism became an independent factor in the development of mystical theology, in contrast to dogmatic theology, but also in the development of tolerance, skepticism, agnosticism, and atheism.[29] A second complex of factors surrounded the humanistic revival of classical learning: the first effect was to shatter the self-evident and self-contained standards of civilization. A plurality of civilizations was fully as disconcerting as a plurality of churches. One must, therefore, take into consideration

28. Voegelin, "The Origins of Scientism." Much of this article was taken directly from the manuscript of *History*.

29. These reflections are found in "Man in History and Nature," *HPI*, V:134–79. Quotations in the text without attribution are from this source.

not only the acceptance and revival of antiquity in opposition to the middle ages but also the rejection of antiquity in the name of modern achievements. Third, the renewal of classical learning was not simply a restoration of scholarly awareness of hitherto unknown texts. It included a revival of Hellenistic cosmology, including astrology. "From the ancient celestial myth, with its cult of the central sun-god, seems to have arrived a component, however attenuated, of the sentiments that motivated the heliocentric conception of the cosmos." At the same time, the mathematical expression of heliocentrism, which was "anti-astrological" in its intent, was also instrumental in overcoming biblical cosmology.

This intricate pattern nevertheless converged on the understanding that human being was the source of meaning in the universe, which is to say that the old world of stable, given, objective meaning created by God had come to an end. The hierarchy of heaven and earth gave way to an infinitely extended universe "evoked as a projection of the human mind and of its infinity into space." In addition, the Christian idea of providential or sacred history, bounded by God's creation of the world according to the narrative in Genesis and the eschatological end as foretold in Revelation, was gradually replaced by an intramundane idea of history determined by "the same natural forces as man himself."[30] The gradual nature of the change meant that there was no grandiose evocation of the modern world or of the modern age by a single mind. Indeed, the process unfolded in a series of steps, each marked by an accompanying sentiment—from despondency stemming from an awareness that an age was drawing to an end along with anxiety in the face of an unknown future, to confidence in one's own self-conscious action and exhilaration at the prospect of discovery and creation.

In later chapters, we shall consider Voegelin's analysis of the changes in the Western understanding of the meaning of history insofar as they became constituents of his own philosophy of history. So far as the question of nature is concerned, we may begin with a consideration of astrology and the observation that, at the end of the fifteenth century, both Pico della Mirandola and Savonarola issued protests against it, the one in the name of the secular dignity of human being, the other in the name of Christian spiritual freedom.

Savonarola claimed to have relied upon Pico but, more important, he addressed a wider audience and provided a more thorough clarification of the theoretical issues.[31] Reliance on astrological guidance or

30. This was essentially the same story that Voegelin told in *The History of the Race Idea,* though the focus was much more comprehensive.
31. Pico's *Disputationes adversus astrologiam* was published in 1496; Savanarola's *Trattato contra gli astrologi* in 1497. See the account in Eugenio Garin, *Astrology in the*

advice regarding a course of action or its timing, Savonarola said, both undermined ethical responsibility and destroyed the free personality. Predictive or "judicial" astrology contradicted both empirical science and Christian theology. On the one hand, human beings can predict effects only where causal necessities are at work; on the other, knowledge of the future regarding contingencies such as human or divine acts and initiatives is available only to God because God embraces all time in eternity so that, for him, the future is as present as the past.

The contrast between the two understandings of nature was distinctly drawn. For Christians, nature did not include the soul; for "pagan" astrology, the rhythms of nature influenced (or determined) not only the body but the soul as well. Savonarola's purpose was to distinguish the realm of the soul or of human spirituality from that of nature, but "it serves inevitably also the methodological purification of the object of science. And the purification of the object of science may result, once the sentiments are bent in an intramundane direction, not in a renewed life of the soul but in a submission of the soul to the categories of science thus purified." In the event, of course, that is just what did result.

The beginning of the process was marked by the quest for a simplified mathematical description of celestial movements and by the fulfillment of that quest in the heliocentric model developed by Copernicus in *De Revolutionibus Orbium Coelestium* (1543). It is certainly true that Copernicus praised the sun "holding court as it were on a royal throne," but the emphasis was on the clarity and certainty of mathematical order.[32] Such order, however, was of no interest to a contemporary nonmathematician such as Bodin, who nevertheless was as interested as Copernicus in finding in nature, in the cosmos, a "certain" order to replace the manifestly uncertain order of disintegrating political and religious institutions. We shall consider Bodin's importance for Voegelin's political science in more detail in Chapter 6.

Notwithstanding his efforts, in the aftermath of the seventeenth century, "certainty" was more often sought by analogy with mathematical physics than with Bodin's *cosmos empsychos*, though there are notable exceptions, Fludd, Bruno, Schelling, and Nietzsche in particular. The

---

Renaissance: The Zodiac of Life, trans. C. Jackson and J. Allen; Lynn Thorndike, "The True Place of Astrology in the History of Science"; Anthony J. Parel, *The Machiavellian Cosmos*, chap. 1.

32. See Alexandre Koyré, *From the Closed World to the Infinite Universe*, chap. 2. Voegelin cited Koyré's 1943 article on Copernicus and sent early drafts of his argument to George Jaffé, a physicist at Berkeley, for his comments (HI 20/7). See also Keith Hutchinson, "Towards a Political Iconology of the Copernican Revolution."

difference, however, with these later figures is that for them, unlike Bodin and Copernicus, the cosmos was no longer the closed Hellenic world but a speculatively infinite universe. In the transformation of attitude, celestial observation played a part, but a minor one. In 1572, a new star appeared in the constellation of Cassiopeia, that is, in the ethereal region of the fixed stars, which was supposed to be immutable, unlike the mutable sublunar regions. Five years later a new comet appeared, which Tycho Brahe showed did not move in the sublunar regions but, like the nova, altered the ethereal region; moreover, it plowed right through the crystal spheres that, ever since Aristotle, were held to support the celestial bodies. The effect of these new observations was to assist in the creation of an atmosphere of readiness to consider and to accept a new understanding and interpretation of the cosmos.

Starting with Kepler, that interpretation was supplied by mathematics so that nature was understood exhaustively in terms of mathematical relations. Accordingly, one finds, for example, in Kepler's famous debate with Fludd, the astronomer saying he was content to describe the motion of the planets rather than evoke the meaning of intelligible harmonies sought by the alchemist. Indeed, Kepler confessed himself unable to comprehend such an enterprise.[33] The problem was, however, more complex than the triumph of science over superstition. Alchemy and hermeticism may not be acceptable as science, but they are not without meaning for the life of the spirit.[34] In particular, the destruction of Christian spirituality and of its redemptive impulse toward human being ignored the problem of the life of the spirit in nature, which was precisely the focus of alchemy and hermeticism, but also of the speculations of Giordano Bruno.

The conflict between the incipient mathematization of science and the soon-to-be eclipsed philosophy of nature provided the context and, indeed, the impetus for Bruno's remarkable metaphysical speculations.[35] So far as he was concerned, mathematized science was inferior to natural philosophy because it attended only to the accidental and phenomenal aspects of nature. Copernicus's achievement lay in the astronomer's emphasis on the human intellect as the ordering center of systematic knowledge of the external world. This break with traditional authority

33. For details see Barry Cooper, *Action into Nature: An Essay on the Meaning of Technology,* chap. 3.

34. See Stephen A. McKnight, *Sacralizing the Secular: The Renaissance Origins of Modernity* and "Eric Voegelin, The Renaissance *Prisca Theologica* Tradition, and Changing Perspectives on the Gnostic Features of Modernity."

35. For details, see Cooper, *Action into Nature,* 93–97, and references.

was, for Bruno, both an intellectual liberation and a manifestation of the activity of nature in human being.

Bruno's speculations may be characterized as the resumption of an inquiry into the fundamental substance of the cosmos "at the one point at which the substance of nature is given to man in its immediacy, that is, in the spirit of man himself." In this way, Bruno avoided the twin errors of hermeticism, which claimed to grasp the substance of nature by human means, and scientism, which treated human substance as if it were a natural phenomenon. According to Bruno, the cosmos is one in substance but many in form; one of those forms, the spirit, is the self-consciousness of that substance. In Voegelin's summary:

> In man the cosmos becomes self-reflection and reveals its substance as spiritual: the cosmos is the life of a spiritual soul, as a whole and in all its parts, from matter as the lowest rank in the hierarchy, through vegetable and animal forms, to man himself. . . . The identity of the spiritual substance throughout the cosmos, in the manifold of the differentiated forms, is the decisive point in the speculation of Bruno. By virtue of this identity, nature is spirit and the spirit in man is a manifestation of nature.

Bruno went on to speculate on the relationship between the spirit that animates the manifold forms, namely God, and the finite spirit of human beings. Humans can know not God but only the traces or "accidences" of God as the manifold forms; humans can know scientifically only the phenomenal accidences of the forms, the "accidences of the accidences." In contrast, human beings can, by an imaginative act, project finite experience into the infinite—but it is a substantive or speculative infinite, not a phenomenal or physical one. In this context the Copernican concern as to whether the sun moves around the earth or vice versa is irrelevant for the relation between celestial bodies, whether earth or sun, and their animating substance.

Not until Schelling did a major philosopher resume the type of metaphysical speculation initiated by Bruno. Instead, mathematized science swept the field, and philosophers focused on the epistemological puzzles that such a science raised when directed not only at phenomena but, more important, at questions of substance. Because of this restriction in focus, the intellectual efforts of philosophers prepared for the triumph of positivism.

In his 1948 article, Voegelin began with a preliminary characterization of scientism as an intellectual movement that began with a fascination with mathematical physics, leading to the three-part positivist dogma we have already encountered.[36] The most important consequence of the widespread acceptance of the doctrines of scientism was that the quest for substance in nature, man, and society as well as in divine, cosmic-transcendent reality was no longer considered to be science. Using the traditional philosophical language of Bruno, Voegelin distinguished sciences of phenomena and sciences of substance. Accordingly, the issue formulated in the context of Copernican astronomy remained "the core of the scientistic problem today." Voegelin then provided a summary definition of scientism as "the attempt to treat substance (including man in society and history) as if it were phenomenon."[37] The significance of scientism, so clearly displayed in the 1946 APSA roundtable and in the 1976 encounter with the behaviorists, lay in its social effectiveness as a widespread intellectual attitude. The chief source of that effectiveness, as Voegelin hinted in a passage from *The New Science of Politics* quoted earlier, was the prestige surrounding the name of Newton and his system.

That Newtonian natural science could serve as a model for all science (including political science) was possible because of the generally defective condition of political science at the start of the seventeenth century.[38] The medieval institutions of church and empire were in a state of advanced decay, and the new mystical bodies politic, the nations, were not yet sufficiently established to be able to sustain a coherent body of political thought. "Between the empire and the national state," wrote Voegelin, "man was left alone. The tabula rasa of Descartes was more than the methodological principle of a philosopher; it was the actual state of man without the shelter of a cosmion." With the disintegration of medieval institutions came the disintegration of the medieval evocation of a world created by God "giving status to every human being in the Mystical Body of Christ according to his charisma and uniting the unequal through the bond of love." Cast onto the surface of the world in

36. In "Origins of Scientism," 462, Voegelin summarized what he there called a scientistic creed: (1) that mathematical science of natural phenomena is a model science to which all other sciences ought to conform; (2) that all realms of being are accessible to the methods of the sciences of phenomena; and (3) that all reality which is not accessible to sciences of phenomena is either irrelevant or, in the more radical form of the dogma, illusionary. This was essentially the creed of nineteenth-century positivism discussed above.

37. Voegelin's distinction between substance and phenomenon, as with his distinction between a topic and a problem, was fundamental, was taken from the traditional vocabulary of Western philosophy, and was apt to be overlooked or ignored by most political scientists.

38. See Voegelin's account, "Tabula Rasa," in *HPI*, VII:47–52.

particular fragments of humanity, namely the nations, the human being had been reduced, like Lear, to "a poor, bare, forked animal" endowed with powers of memory, foresight, and pragmatic reasoning but filled with the fear of violent death. With this endowment, human beings "had to create a preliminary order and then to reconquer, in a slow process, the realms of spirit, of conscience and moral obligation, of history, of his relation to God and to the universe." Science, by which is meant the science of natural phenomena, was understood as an aid in the process of reconstruction.

Initially the methods of geometry rather than physics were understood to supply the most robust model and technique; later, during the nineteenth century, the new sciences of biology and psychology came to the fore. Whatever the model, the problem remained one of restoring to human existence all that had been stripped away in the reduction of humanity to its "natural elements." That meant the long and difficult recovery of human passions and sentiments, of conscience and historicity, and of the relationship between human and divine being. In order to provide a coherent and comprehensive account simply of human being, these elements of reality had to be rationally and hierarchically ordered. The entire process of evoking a new cosmion, Voegelin said, "culminated, in the late nineteenth and early twentieth centuries, in philosophical anthropology becoming the center of political thought." We will discuss Voegelin's understanding of philosophical anthropology and its importance for political science in Chapter 5.

The methodological problem of using inapt naturalistic linguistic formulas to express political problems cannot be separated from the problem of accounting for the development and internal order of the new parochial political bodies. Looked at in terms of the disintegration of Western, Christian political ideas, the national communities take on the attributes of schismatic politico-religious units. At the same time, however, these national communities understood their specific and local political problems as universal; likewise, the analyses made and the ideas evoked in response were held to be of general, not limited, significance and application. The pragmatic consequences of schismatic parochialism are as obvious today as they were during the immediate postwar period. Only the pragmatic configuration of forces has changed. To use Voegelin's language:

> The idea of a Western, if not human, validity for the national schismatic developments then hardened into intransigent national missions with the catastrophic consequence that the attempts to realize the claim of universality through imperial expansion were opposed by the prospective victims in

prolonged wars. The French Revolution with its climax in Napoleon's imperialism and the German Revolution with its climax in Hitler's imperialism
had to be defeated—with the result that the Anglo-Saxon powers with their
claim of universality for the English and American variant of democracy
have now to face a non-Western civilization, with a universal claim of its
own, across the battlefields of Europe.[39]

Voegelin first explored the connection between scientism as a socially
effective intellectual movement and the growth of parochial and anti-
spiritual political bodies in his consideration of English political ideas
as they developed during the eighteenth century. The aftermath of the
Puritan Revolution, the Restoration, and the Glorious Revolution was a
profoundly exhausted and disoriented English society, the intellectual
articulation of which had evidently lost contact not only with the realities
of divine transcendence and reason but with the reality of everyday
existence as well. Voegelin described the condition, using a term of
Bishop Berkeley, as a loss of the "concrete."[40]

The dissolution of England during the "gin age" was extensive enough
to be reflected demographically; Voegelin's focus, however, was on the
one English political institution that had actually ceased to function, an
institution "the functioning of which was of the greatest importance for
the preservation of the intellectual and spiritual substance of the nation,
that is, the Church of England." The evisceration of the Anglican Church
was achieved first by the regulation and suppression of Nonconformist
clergy during the Restoration and then by the removal of "nonjurors" after the Glorious Revolution. The purge of what Stalin would have called
left and right deviationists had "destructive effects on the substance of
the nation similar to the destructions worked by later revolutions of
this type."

Notwithstanding the material prosperity of England, two symptoms
indicated the degree to which a "loss of the concrete" had come to
characterize English life. First, "the concrete is lost with regard to the
fundamental orientation of existence through faith, and [second] it is
lost with regard to the system of symbols and concepts in which the
orientation of existence is expressed." The two symptoms were mutually
reinforcing: the actual loss of orientation through faith blocks the creation
of appropriate symbols, and the existing deformation of symbols blocks
any recollection of the orienting experiences. The result is an impressive
confusion, the cause of which was diagnosed by Voegelin under the

39. Voegelin, "The English Quest for the Concrete," in *HPI*, VI:149–215. Quotations
in the text without attribution are from this source.
40. George Berkeley, *Works*, ed. T. E. Jessop, vol. 2, *Principles of Human Knowledge*.

headings of the psychologization of the self and the materialization of the external world.[41] The first term, for Voegelin, meant "the misapprehension that through reflection on the stream of the consciousness, and on the experiences given in it, the nature of man or the substance of the self can become known." In a sense, this misapprehension was entirely appropriate because, in the absence of the experience of substantial participation in the order of the cosmos, all that remained was the perceiving self and the perceived structure of the world. This is why, as we noted earlier, much of Western philosophy after the seventeenth century consisted in proposing solutions to epistemological puzzles, the origin of which lay in the initial misapprehension.

A disturbance of the elementary experience of participation in the cosmos can be apprehended most clearly with respect to the question of world-transcendent divine reality. Regarding material reality, one can be assured of its existence through the pragmatic tests of observation and experiment—kicking the stone assures you it exists. Regarding transcendent reality matters are rather different: "only the genuine participation through the trembling experience of faith as substance and proof of things unseen (Hebrews 11:1)."[42] When faith is extinguished as a mode of participation, then one is left with nothing but a series of propositions of doubtful logical coherence. And it is the incoherence of the dogma, not the absence of an illuminating inner light of faith, that is most obvious to the external light of reason. Once reason is understood as an autonomous faculty capable of generating propositions about transcendent reality (and not the result of faith) then the expressions of faith become reduced to the interpretation of documents. Instead of openness toward God as the condition for reason to operate, reason, secular reason, is held to be the sole means of orienting existence within the world.

The evocation of secular reason as the judge of the truth of revelation was Locke's achievement in his *Essay Concerning Human Understanding*.[43] For Locke, reason was simply a natural faculty. Such an understanding had as its chief consequence the eclipse of the experiences that historically have generated mythic and religious symbols of a beyond. Revelation is transformed from an experience of the presence of transcendent reality that must be regained concretely by faith by every individual into a series of propositions examined analytically by reason. This particular "loss of the concrete" meant that for those who followed Locke's dogma

41. These two categories were Voegelin's version of Berkeley's "Materialism" and "Free Thought." See Berkeley, *Works*, vol. 3, *Alciphron or the Minute Philosopher*, esp. Dialogue I, "On Free-Thinking and the General Good," 31–64.

42. See also Voegelin, *NSP*, 122 ff.

43. Book IV, 18:5–11; ed. Peter H. Nidditch (Oxford: Clarendon, 1975), 691–96.

regarding the topic of reason and revelation, discussion of the reality of experience became impossible. Henceforth, all one could do is look at the consistencies and inconsistencies of doctrine, a pastime that grows boring quickly enough. Once the concreteness of the *cognitio fidei* has been obliterated, a whole realm of experience can be trashed as unreasonable. More timid souls, fearing the starkness of "free thinking," express but also hide their anxieties with veils of piety and reverence.

Voegelin's characterization of the loss of the concrete was that it is a spiritual disease, a *nosos* in the classical sense. Faith turns into sentimental reverence toward religious symbols, and the meaning of the symbols is exhausted in doctrinal propositions. "As a residuum of reality there remains only the structure and content of consciousness, that is, of a self no longer open toward transcendental reality." In place of transcendental reality is the reality described by mathematical physics, which in turn becomes the vehicle by which all realms of being are reduced to the reality of matter.

Notwithstanding the importance of the fallacies surrounding the psychologization of the self, in the present context, the materialization of the external world is perhaps even more significant. By that phrase Voegelin meant "the misapprehension that the structure of the external world as it is constituted in the system of mathematized physics is the ontologically real structure of the world." We have already indicated Bruno's response to the problem posed by Copernicus's heliocentrism. Historically matters were made more complex by the conflict of Galileo with Cardinal Bellarmine and the Inquisition. Bellarmine was willing to accept any scientific theory so long as it raised no challenge to a symbolism that considered the earth to be the symbolic center of the cosmos. The spatial or phenomenal center of the cosmos, if such a thing can even be conceived, must be considered irrelevant for a symbolism the origin of which lies in the experiences of the soul and in speculation regarding the soul's spiritual destiny. "The shift of the spatial center," Voegelin wrote, "becomes an attack on the experiences of the spiritual drama if the shift is construed as the displacement of the 'real' center in the symbolic sense." Bellarmine was unable to show Galileo that the function of phenomenal science was, in principle, limited; and Galileo could not conceive that the splendid Copernican theory was no more than a hypothesis to account for phenomena, and that its truth or certainty was an artifact of the method used to produce it.

Voegelin's account of the issue of absolutism versus relativity has been recapitulated by historians of science.[44] Specifically, the Newtonian

44. See the references in Cooper, *Action into Nature*, 270 ff.

doctrine of absolute space, a necessary assumption for his universal mechanics, seemed to justify the "fallacy of misplaced concreteness," as Whitehead called it. As a result of the acceptance of this doctrine, "The belief that science is the key to the understanding of nature in an ontological sense has entered as a decisive ingredient into every one of our political mass movements—liberalism, progressivism, Darwinism, Communism, National Socialism. The historical root of this belief is the Newtonian theory of space."[45] The historical consequence of the theory of absolute space, Voegelin said, was to seal "the system ontologically against God; and by virtue of this character, the Newtonian system became socially effective."[46] In turn, the eclipse of God by Newton's system profoundly influenced the political and economic structure of the world, beginning in England but moving soon enough to embrace the globe.

The principal features of the changes to which Voegelin adverted are so well known that little more than a partial enumeration is necessary to indicate their importance: the transformation of science into technology, the industrialization of the economy, population increase, urbanization, economic and social interdependence, increased productivity and political power in technical and industrial states, and so on. The usefulness of science and the technology for the increase in the power of a state hardly needs elaboration. Even so, "the idea that structure and problems of human existence can be superseded in historical society by the utilitarian segment of existence is certainly plain nonsense; it is equivalent to the idea that the nature of man can be abolished without abolishing man, or that the spiritual order can be taken out of existence without disordering existence."[47] The most apparent contemporary manifestation of this destructive obsession is the opinion that the cure for the damage caused by science and technology is more science and technology.

The advocates of this opinion, however, appear to be unaware of two fundamental truths: first, that the effects of science and technology are a consequence of the structure of phenomenal reality, "which permits the introduction of human action into the chain of cause and effect once the law of the chain has been discovered," and, second, that this same structure does not obtain beyond phenomenal reality—and, in particular, is quite alien to the reality of human spirituality. If, nevertheless, one

45. See the exposition in "Origins of Scientism," esp. 465–73. In HI 50/13 there exists a supplementary but fragmentary exposition of Leibniz's account of time that complements Leibniz's criticism of Newton's understanding of space.
46. Voegelin, "Origins of Scientism," 473.
47. Ibid., 487.

attempts to operate in the area of human substance as if it belonged wholly to the realm of phenomena, "that is the definition of magic." The experiential source of this "gigantic outburst of magic imagination," Voegelin said, lay in the atrophy and primitivization of the intellectual and spiritual culture associated with the middle ages. The attribution of certainty and absoluteness to the mechanics of a Galileo or a Newton also expressed the unwillingness of the attributing personality to orient its own existence through the experience of openness to transcendent reality.

More than a personal failing or a personal tragedy is involved when such refusals are generalized into the doctrine that mathematical exactness and experimental verification are self-sufficient standards of truth for all areas of experience. The most obvious result is the opinion that no knowledge beyond that brought to light by mathematics and experimentation needs to be cultivated by human beings. In consequence, the growth of science and technology has been accompanied by "an unspeakable advance of mass ignorance with regard to the problems that are existentially the important ones."[48] Second, this ignorance has become socially reproductive through technologically inspired educational institutions that reward (and tempt) those who embody the "scientistic pathos." As a more adequate characterization of the personality attracted to the pathos of scientism, as well as of the society where such personalities are socially predominant, Voegelin suggested the term *spiritual eunuchism*. Historically speaking, the nineteenth century in Europe was the scene of a remarkable civilizational transformation by the "eunuch type," which prepared the way for the "spiritual anarchy" of the twentieth century.

A third result of the institutionalization of spiritual and philosophical ignorance is that scientistic dilettantes assume their own condition to be normal and project it onto others. The degree to which they are able to act successfully on this assumption has varied in space and time. Moreover, by the time that Einstein was able to revise the foundations of physics so that they conformed more or less to the philosophical position of Leibniz, the damage had been done, in the sense that the scientistic pathos had migrated far beyond the concerns of physics and cosmology. In consequence, and notwithstanding differences that exist throughout the globe regarding the possibility of an individual escaping from the

48. In vulgar terms, the more the technological society has been able to actualize itself, the less it has known what technology is "for." This question has also concerned Hans Jonas; see his *Philosophical Essays: From Ancient Creed to Technological Man* and *The Imperative of Responsibility: In Search of an Ethics for the Technological Age*.

confines of scientism, the hope for individual spiritual freedom "should not obscure the realistic insight that we who are living today shall never experience freedom of the spirit in society."[49] The most one can expect, under such circumstances, is to discover or analyze a complex of ideas that furnishes a stable point from which to develop a critical analysis of the problem. For Voegelin, the person and work of Schelling provided "a point of orientation for the understanding of the crisis because they are not engulfed in the crisis themselves."[50] What Voegelin said of Schelling, that he resumed the *philosophia perennis*, could be said as well of Voegelin. Neither Schelling nor Voegelin, however, could halt or even reduce the momentum of scientism. Civilizational restoration is evidently a different matter from the theoretical penetration of a spiritual crisis and of its accompanying political disorder.[51]

Voegelin's analysis of Schelling's philosophy was preceded by a chapter bearing the title "Phenomenalism." It was Voegelin's view that "the complex of phenomenalism has never been isolated as a component factor in the intellectual and spiritual life of modern man, as far as we know, and there exists no monograph on the subject to which we could refer the reader." Aspects of the reality to which Voegelin's terminological innovation referred had, of course, been noted by other historians and philosophers.[52]

49. Voegelin, "Origins of Scientism," 494.

50. Voegelin, "Introductory Remarks" to "Last Orientation," in *HPI*, VII:175–77. Subsequent quotations are from chap. 1, "Phenomenalism," 178–92. The importance of Schelling for Voegelin's political science is treated at greater length in Chapter 10.

51. The difficulty is illustrated in an exchange between Voegelin and his old Viennese friend Fritz Machlup. Machlup wrote: "I would not be able to tell them [Scientists] exactly what it is that they cannot see, what it is that they reject as metaphysics and that anybody must see before he can tackle the main problems in the social sciences," a sentiment that was no doubt widespread, even among Voegelin's sympathetic readers. Voegelin replied, first, that the physicists would not change because of the "schism" between "science," meaning the natural science of phenomena, and metaphysics, which is part of the "civilizational crisis"; second, that the request for a "metaphysical" statement cannot be met because metaphysics has been the result of contemplation, at least from the time of Plato and Aristotle, but physicists have not read them—or if they had, it would be as part of a "field," that is, as a topic and not as a "dimension of thought"; third, that the "institutionalized stupidity" of scientism could be compared to the previous two waves of political stupidity, communism and Nazism (HI 24/7).

52. See, for example, Paul Hazard, *The European Mind, 1680–1715*, trans. J. L. May, 314 ff., and the discussion in Cooper, *Action into Nature*, chap. 3. See also the remarks by Hannah Arendt on "The Discovery of the Archimedean Point" in *The Human Condition*, 257–68, 284–86.

The importance of phenomenalism in the present context, however, concerns the analytic arguments that distinguish this problem from other aspects of modern intellectual and spiritual life. To use a decidedly modern formulation, one may say that scientism is to phenomenalism as epistemology is to ontology. Leaving aside for a moment the incompleteness of the first two terms, the argument runs as follows: reality, according to phenomenalism, is what appears, but what does not appear is not real; on the other hand, what does appear does not appear to everybody and, if it does so appear, nevertheless does not necessarily appear in the same way; hence, phenomenalism is supported by a method of looking at appearances, an epistemology, that ensures that what does appear looks the same to everyone who cares to look; the appropriate method, narrowly conceived or in principle, is mathematics; more generally conceived, it is scientism.

Such a formulation is not misleading. It is more accurate, however, to follow Voegelin's strict usage: "phenomenalism" refers to the complex of "sentiments, imaginations, beliefs, ideas, and speculations, as well as patterns of conduct determined by them" that have arisen in the wake of the advancement of scientism rather than to a discursive account of reality. Voegelin first recalled Bruno's formula, that the natural sciences in fact dealt with "the accidences of the accidences," not the substance of nature or of history, and second, that phenomenalism was one expression of a large complex of intramundane sentiments and attitudes that emerged to replace Christian spirituality as the latter atrophied, especially during the course of the nineteenth century. Voegelin's third point was more complex. Phenomenalist sentiments and ideas were labeled "materialist" in the nineteenth century. This was usually undertaken in a polemical context by individuals seeking to defend one or another aspect of Christian doctrine. The confusion of phenomenalism and materialism was intelligible inasmuch as the religious polemicists had as their opponents chiefly persons devoted to the science of material phenomena, namely physics. The distinction between material phenomena and the substance, namely matter, for which the material phenomena were substituted within the economy of physics was, however, apt to be overlooked

A genuine materialism, which assumes that matter is the substance of reality, entails a metaphysical argument of much greater subtlety and complexity than is found in the defense of phenomenalist notions. In this respect, the choice of substance, whether matter or spirit, is of less significance than the distinction, and the awareness of the distinction, between substance and accidence or substance and phenomenon. In any particular thinker, the choice to postulate spirit or matter as the substance of reality may well be itself an accident—and just for that reason the results may be experientially equivalent. "True materialism," Voegelin said,

> is rare, and the philosophers who turn toward it are among the most distinguished minds of their age. In our time the great materialists are George Santayana and Paul Valéry, both strongly under the influence of Lucretius. Materialism does not imply a negation or even a contempt of the spirit. On the contrary, a great spiritual sensitiveness alone can induce the fatigue of spiritual existence, disillusionment with its symbols as substances, and their acceptance as aesthetic expressions of the substantial mystery of life.

Having clarified the problem by indicating what phenomenalism is not, Voegelin offered a preliminary set of definitions. First, phenomenalism itself is "the complex of sentiments and ideas that cluster around the tendency to interpret the phenomenal relations that are the object of science as a substantial order of things." Once the intellectual act of making a commitment to phenomenalism has been undertaken, a number of additional possibilities follow. Second, therefore, is the designation of the result of imaginatively taking phenomena for substance, which Voegelin termed "phenomenal reality." Third, phenomenal reality can be treated as an object of speculation in the same way as substantive reality: such speculation Voegelin called "phenomenal speculation." Likewise "phenomenal projections" are the result of transferring hopes and fears and similar experiential relations that properly belong to substantive reality, and "phenomenal obsessions" are the effect that such projections have on human beings. Last, when individuals act on the basis of phenomenal speculations and under the compulsion of phenomenal obsessions, the resulting conduct and attitudes Voegelin termed "phenomenal action" and "phenomenal activism."

This rather abstract set of distinctions between parallel terms was followed by a summary of the supporting historical evidence. By the middle of the seventeenth century, Bruno's speculation had been phenomenalized. For Bruno, the infinite was a projection of the human spirit, but a projection the meaning of which was to assure the projector of his connection to the divine. The advancement of astronomy and physics had appealed to sections of the educated public in such a way that they could contemplate in their imagination "unlimited horizons of knowledge of the external world." Such knowledge, moreover, was accompanied by the belief that it would decisively affect the place of human being in the cosmos and thereby invalidate the Christian understanding of human nature and destiny.

The implications of phenomenalism were bound to provoke resistance from thinkers still formed by Christian anthropology. For example, in his *Pensées*,[53] Pascal provided his own interpretation of the growth of phenomenal science. The purpose was not to celebrate human pride of achievement but to contemplate the relative insignificance of human being as a prelude to the Christian recollection of human creatureliness. The meditative exercise was relatively straightforward: consider, for example, the sun in relation to the relatively insignificant earth, and then the fixed stars in relation to the relatively insignificant sun. But then what? We are faced with something like the childhood game of imagining a wall at the outermost edge of the cosmos with a ladder leaning against it. What do you see when you climb the ladder and look over the wall? The imagination eventually must fail. A similar impasse is experienced if one tries to imagine ever smaller particles that begin to approach nothingness. Reflection on the results of these two speculations would, then, reveal human being suspended between the infinite and nothingness. Instead of considering the significance of human finitude, however, phenomenally obsessed or scientistically inspired human beings have assumed they are in possession of the principles necessary for the exploration of reality. But they are not: on the one hand, principles must arise from somewhere, but Pascal's meditative analysis has shown the basis of phenomena to be an incomprehensible nothingness. Moreover, principles must apply everywhere, including the infinite, which likewise passeth human understanding. Rejection of the implications of Pascal's meditative train typifies the attitude that transforms phenomenal science into a science of the real order of nature, of history, of reality as a whole.

Voegelin illustrated the consequences of phenomenalism with the examples of biology, economics, and psychology. Eighteenth-century biology considered a theory of evolution of forms of life;[54] it was relatively simple and contained a number of gaps and "missing links." But it was accompanied by the awareness "that the idea of an evolution of living forms did not bring us one step nearer to an understanding of the mystery of the substance that was evolving through the chain of forms." That is, eighteenth-century biologists by and large were aware that when they changed the ontological unit from the single Aristotelian species to the modern evolutionary chain, and even pushed the origin of organic forms back to inorganic matter, the essential mystery of life remained untouched. Darwin's theory, however, along with its ancillary doctrines of struggle for life, survival of the fittest, and natural selection,

---

53. *Les Pensées de Pascal,* ed. Francis Kaplan, no. 132, pp. 152–59.
54. See Stephen Jay Gould, *Ontogeny and Phylogeny,* esp. chap. 3. Much of this material was discussed in *The History of the Race Idea* as well.

to which may be added the more recent contributions of population and molecular biology, "had a popular success and became a mass creed for the semieducated." It was, in fact, accepted not as an account of the mechanics of evolution but as a revelation about the meaning of life, including politics.

The transformation of a theory about the phenomenal unfolding of substance, namely life, into a philosophy of substance and its widespread acceptance are symptomatic "of the critical split in the history of the Western mind between the narrowing main line along which the problems of substance move and the phenomenal mass movements that increasingly dominate the public scene and produce the moral and intellectual confusion of our time." In the example of Darwin, the reasons for the transformation of phenomenal relations into a phenomenal reality are well known: Darwin was a great empirical biologist who managed to order a large amount of data to create a new form of ordered knowledge, but at the same time his awareness of the relationship of his particular science to the problems of ontology and metaphysics was so slight as to be nonexistent. The will to create a phenomenal reality from the propositions of a science of biological phenomena was sustained by an anti-Christian and secular assumption, nowhere justified, that the interpretation of man as the final link on the evolutionary chain has a bearing on the question of human spirituality. As Nietzsche had occasion to point out,[55] the assumption that human being was the final product of evolution was entirely gratuitous. Indeed, the status of a human being "created in the image and likeness of God"[56] and apprehended by the cognition of faith was simply ignored by scientists and by those who promoted their achievements. Both sorts of individuals were strongly committed to understanding the human position in a world-immanent order as revealed by a science of phenomena. Because it does not quite go without saying, it bears repeating: such an anthropology rested upon phenomenalist assumptions that never have been justified. This was why Voegelin characterized such opinions as "a mass creed for the semieducated" or a symptom of the "intellectual confusion" of the present times.

The new phenomenal reality became the object of speculation, projection, obsession, and action directly when the biological mechanisms of struggle, survival, and selection were applied to politics and social life. In a competitive society, for example, the doctrine of natural selection could be invoked to indicate that those who succeed were also better examples of humanity, that their success was a manifestation of the natural order,

55. *Zarathustra*, esp. prologue and pt. I.
56. Genesis, 1, 26.

and that the results were for that reason just. In consequence, moral and spiritual issues, which in fact have their own bases of justification, may be eclipsed. And so, to take an example from Voegelin's works on race, when a diffuse but widespread biological phenomenalism was combined with a highly focused notion of racial differentiation, it was a simple matter to reinterpret history in terms of inferior and superior races, an interpretation that in turn became obsessive when it was turned into a rule for action.

Voegelin's second example, economics, in fact antedated the application of biology to social and political relations in a competitive society. As with a biological science that justified success independently of ethical or spiritual realities, so with a phenomenalist economic science, the ancillary doctrines of rational economic action, individual self-interest, and increased productivity of goods and services were necessarily silent regarding the desirability of an economic order that succeeded in maximizing wealth at the cost in other areas of human and natural life. Economics becomes obsessive, as does biology, when "the laws developed by a theory of economic action are erected into standards of action, when the theoretical system of economic relations is considered a right order of society that should not be disturbed by interventions." The most obvious symptom of this obsessiveness is the brutality of what is conventionally termed liberal economic order. That the majesty of the law protects alike the property of the rich and the poverty of the poor has long been a topic of shrewd comment by moralists, not all of whom, by any means, were socialists.[57]

Indeed, one of the components of the communist as well as the National Socialist revolution was "the desire to break the liberal economic obsession and to evolve a new substantial order." But these substantial revolutions, no less than the gentler changes associated with the growth of the welfare state, were overshadowed by the phenomenalism of planning.[58] For collectivists and socialists, whether national, international, or merely democratic, the plan for "welfare" is turned into an unquestioned absolute and is enforced with at least as much brutality as occurs when liberals treat the individual as a function of economic activity.[59] Not surprisingly, therefore, the response to the excesses of

57. See Voegelin's letter to Strauss, April 15, 1953, in *Faith and Political Philosophy*, 96.
58. This aspect of the antiliberal revolutions was emphasized by Voegelin's contemporary Friedrich A. Hayek in *The Road to Serfdom*.
59. Voegelin detected this sentiment even in Huntington Cairns and the benevolent technician who might (some day) apply a "science of ethical rules" along with a "science of the law" to achieve what Cairns doubtless considered to be justice.

welfare "planning" has occasionally been a return to apparently less oppressive, but just as obsessive, liberal economics.

Psychological phenomenalism, Voegelin's third example, is familiar from everyday experience as well as from special occasions such as Voegelin's meeting with the behaviorists noted earlier. The results are seen in the dissolution of the life of the spirit into various technologies of manipulation and management, including self-manipulation and self-management. From advertising, to entertainment, to news, "we have created a modern demonology by the side of which a medieval catalog of angels and demons looks a trifle shabby."

The consequences of the contemporary and somewhat syncretistic phenomenalism that Voegelin noted have grown even more obvious over the years. In literature, for example, the growth of science fiction as a genre parallels the growth of scientistic obsession. From Mary Shelley's *Frankenstein* to the commercialized success of generations of Star Trekers and Trekkies, it is not always clear what is supposed to be satirization of scientism and phenomenalist obsession and what is intended by the producers of such materials to be a presentation of what they consider to be the "serious" potentialities of science.[60] On the other hand, it is certainly true that scientistic obsessions can be translated into action in the form of technological achievements. "This technical realm," Voegelin said, "is becoming increasingly phenomenal and acquiring obsessional characteristics insofar as it tempts man to translate into reality what can be done by technical means without regard for the consequences in the realm of a substantial order." Indeed, technology can, and in the years since Voegelin wrote increasingly has, become a self-legitimizing order: what can be done should be done and will be done. In 1945, the results were perhaps clearer than they have become since, as human beings grew more adjusted to the technological society.[61]

> We must observe the transplantation and destruction of whole populations, the machine-gunning of fleeing civilians, terror-bombing and pulverization

---

60. There are, for example, serious (if not scholarly) studies of the physics of *Star Trek*, complete with footnotes and mathematical formulas. Contemporary examples go far beyond Voegelin's, which was the study by Hadley Cantril of the response by the American public to the famous broadcast by Orson Welles of H. G. Wells's tale of an invasion from Mars. "Among those who believed it," Voegelin wrote, "were two geologists from Princeton who set out heroically to investigate the invasion at the risk of their lives, as befits true scientists." Cantril's *The Invasion from Mars: A Study in the Psychology of Panic* revealed to Voegelin "the depth of the madness in which we live."

61. See Cooper, *Action into Nature*, pt. II.

of towns, and the horrors of extermination camps. The tools cease to be simple instruments of execution in the service of substantial purposes and gain a momentum of their own that bends the purposes to the technical possibilities. If the realm of purposes itself is drying up in substance, as it does in our time, and biological, economic, and psychological obsessions move into the place of purposes, the combination of the various phenomenalisms threatens to extinguish the last vestiges of substance. The National Socialist exterminations are the starkest manifestation of the victory of phenomenal obsession over spiritual order. There is a most intimate connection between the comic strip and the concentration camp. The man who runs away from an invasion from Mars because the comic strip and the broadcast have decomposed his personality and the SS man who garrotes a prisoner without compunction because he is dead to the meaning of his action in the order of spiritual reality are brothers under the skin. Phenomenalism has gone further toward transforming our society into the combination of a slaughterhouse with a booby hatch than many contemporaries are still sane enough to realize.

Shortly after Voegelin concluded this chapter the atomic bombing of Japan took place, and he appended a short note:

P.S. This chapter was finished six weeks before the atom bomb was dropped on Hiroshima—the date that has brought us one step nearer to the point where reality and comic strip become indistinguishable.

This has been a long and complex chapter, the length and complexity of which have in part been dictated by the Voegelinian dictum that one must follow where the materials lead. Let us conclude by drawing together the major points in Voegelin's argument. First, the evidence for the destruction of science during the positivist era was found in the contemporary work being undertaken in academic institutions nominally dedicated to scientific pursuits. The positivism of Timasheff, the historicism of Bodenheimer, the simple dogmatism of Scott, and the elaborate scientism of Cairns all contained distinct, but related, defects. Arnold Brecht's dogmatic "neo-Weberian" approach was long out of date, and the behaviorists were little more than ill-educated ideologues. Second, however, the source of the problem lay not with the methodological disputes of the nineteenth century. The foundations for the eclipse of substance in natural and in human being were laid during the sixteenth century. Voegelin's concern was not with the history of astronomy but with the spiritual disorientation that accompanied the "scientific revolutions," namely the loss of concrete experiences of reality and the replacement of such experiences with phenomenalist equivalents. Phenomenalism was Voegelin's summary definition of the ontological error characteristic of the positivist era, much as *spiritual eunuch* was the term he used to describe the type of human being characteristic of the positivist era.

The practical consequences of phenomenalist activism or of acting out phenomenalist obsessions, of which World War II was Voegelin's most immediate example, are massively present in everyone's daily life. The real difficulties, however, lie not with our experiences of such practical realities as atomic bombing or atomic pollution but in making sense of such things. Voegelin was after all a political philosopher, not an engineer. He was concerned first of all with—again, for instance—what the cold war or the "event" at Three Mile Island or Chernobyl *meant* and not with developing fail-safe systems for B-52s or nuclear reactors. Recollecting such basic facts is not otiose. In the example of biological phenomenalism, for instance, the popularity of Darwinism as a mass creed continued irrespective of the fact that one could be a "Darwinist" only by overlooking some rather elementary distinctions, such as that between the mechanism of the evolution of life and the meaning of life, the analysis of what living, as distinct from nonliving, being *is*. Such distinctions were made increasingly seldom, with the consequence, as Voegelin noted, that he and his contemporaries "shall never experience freedom of the spirit in society," whatever the greatness of an individual spiritual personality.

Voegelin provided several examples to illustrate the effects of the erosion and then the disappearance of spiritual communities. So long as they existed, such institutions preserved a tradition of spiritual order to which the words of a great thinker might occasionally give representative expression. The Dominican Order and its extensive network of Houses of Study, for example, was able to preserve into this century the standards of scholarship and traditions of metaphysical speculation created by Thomas Aquinas, notwithstanding the fact that, for instance, the *Summa Contra Gentiles* did not have the effect on the wider European stage for which it was written. Another example, to be discussed in Chapter 6, was Bodin. Unlike Thomas, he was unsupported by a scholastic institution to which he could hand over a Bodinian tradition, and yet his evocation of a national and royal state became part of French political life. By the eighteenth century, however, the flourishing of intense partisanship made it increasingly difficult for spiritually sensitive thinkers to find any receptive community at all. Philosophical schools and individual philosophies were entrepreneurial endeavors left to flourish or decay beyond the safeguards, the shelter, the continuity, and the authority of religious orders. In consequence, spiritual realists, as Voegelin called such thinkers as Bodin or Spinoza (and to whose number may perhaps be added Vico, Toynbee, and Voegelin himself), were increasingly isolated. Those philosophies that did appear were "the expression of parochial community substances, of particular aspects of the world as they came into view with the advancement of physics, chemistry, economics, biology, and psychology, and of idiosyncratic views of 'original' thinkers."

One symptom of this isolation was the breakdown of a common philosophical language. Once the shared universe of discourse dissolved, differences in attitudes, sentiments, and experiences became impenetrable barriers to understanding. "In the eighteenth and nineteenth centuries," Voegelin said, "the spiritual cleavage and decay begin to corrode the rational conceptual apparatus that is supposed to serve the adequate expression of ideas." Moreover, when people have difficulty understanding one another they grow less willing to make the attempt. In this way more or less rational discussion is supplanted by the massed choirs of chanting creed communities. One of the contributing factors in the erosion of a common philosophical language and the consequent isolation of the spiritual realist has been precisely the substitution of phenomenal relations for substantial reality—that is, phenomenalism.

Phenomenalism, in other words, is not manifest simply in such obvious and grotesque episodes as the gulag. It also is a metaphysically defective theory that confuses human beings by undermining their understanding of spiritual existence. The two elements are connected insofar as the practical effects would not have been produced in the first place had not the producers been phenomenally obsessed; so long as the spiritual dimension of human existence is neglected, the products of phenomenal obsession will not be properly understood. "A not inconsiderable part of the intellectual confusion of our time," Voegelin observed, "with its bitterness and irreconcilable hatreds between democrats and Fascists, Communists and liberals, is due to the fact that the philosophical dilettantes run amuck." The two symptoms, despiritualization of philosophical discourse and metaphysical irrationalism, or dilettantism, are two sides of the same coin. Without an adequate ontology that distinguishes intelligibly the substance and structure of different modes or realms of being, rational discourse is impossible.

Specifically regarding human spirituality, if one considers the operations of the spirit to be manifestations of material conditions, such as blood sugar levels, or psychological relations, or as the effects of economic conditions, the social situation, racial or ethnic determinants, the misfortune of a dysfunctional family, or an alcoholic great-grandmother, discourse becomes irrational because the various ontic realms become distorted in their own intelligible structure, because their relations to one another become distorted, and because things are not called by their proper names but by the names of something else. That is, spiritual disorders and pathologies are not understood as disorders of the soul but as manifestations, for example, of great-grandmother's taste for ardent spirits. In contrast, rationalism

> implies the acceptance of an ontology that recognizes the structure of reality in all its strata from matter to spirit, without attempts at reducing causally the phenomena of one realm of being to those of another; and it furthermore implies the representation of reality by language symbols that follow the stratification of being, without any attempts at applying the symbols for the phenomena in one realm of being to the phenomena of another realm.

In effect, phenomenalism attempts to destroy the structure of reality—or, more accurately, the phenomenalist ignores or denies the reality of the spirit that is, evidently, not a living force in his or her soul. But without a principle of spiritual order, there is no limit to spiritual disorder when institutions and the habits of thought and of conduct atrophy over time. Under such circumstance rationality comes to mean the technical capacity of connecting means to ends, whatever they may be, which is to say, however irrational, unjust, immoral, or silly they may be. Indeed, when the ends become sufficiently irrational, no amount of "technical rationality" can ever actualize them for the simple reason that they are plainly impossible. Plato has given the model account of the process in books 8 and 9 of his *Republic,* and Michael Oakeshott has restated the problem many times.[62]

The consequences of phenomenalism, especially its decapitation of ontology and its use of irrational terminology, are a major problem for political science in general and for the history of political ideas in particular. This is why, as Voegelin said, it is relatively easy to present the political ideas of Plato or Aristotle or Saint Thomas because, within the limits of one's interpretative abilities, the arguments of such great thinkers can be presented more or less using their own terms. Thomas and Plato developed excellent, if complex, ontologies and did so using masterly philosophical technique. The political scientist, therefore, will effectively be in the position of student, and one's interpretative problems will center on the question of fidelity to the philosopher's intention.

---

62. See in particular "Rationalism in Politics," in *Rationalism in Politics and Other Essays,* ed. Timothy Fuller. To the extent that the results of phenomenalism in the positivist era are described adequately by the metaphor of *nosos,* disease, Oakeshott's observation on the question is sobering indeed: "It is always depressing for a patient to be told that his disease is almost as old as himself and that consequently there is no quick cure for it, but (except for the infections of childhood) this is usually the case" (34).

On the other hand, a completely different sort of problem arises with "a technically miserable thinker" because, in order for such a person's ideas and arguments to make sense, they must constantly be referred to a rational standard that transcends that individual's thought. This means that one must develop a rational terminological apparatus to deal with the metaphysically defective and spiritually impoverished language of the analysand. Voegelin's prime example in this regard was Voltaire, whom we shall consider in more detail in Chapter 6.

Voegelin's analysis of the destructive effects of positivism had an obvious relevance to the fashionable application of mathematical and quasi-mathematical models to the study of political phenomena. As he explained in his letter to Sandoz quoted earlier, however, he really had little concern for "the behavioral persuasion." Indeed, many of the methodological problems raised by positivism had a more immediate connection to the "subfield" of political science conventionally identified as political theory. This was evident from the APSA roundtable presided over by Arnold Brecht; the problem appeared in another guise in Voegelin's reviews of Hannah Arendt's account of the horrors of the mid-twentieth century, *The Origins of Totalitarianism*, and Leo Strauss's more astringent analysis, *On Tyranny*, to a consideration of which we turn in the next chapter.

4

Method
Voegelin, Strauss,
and Arendt

Eric Voegelin, Leo Strauss, and Hannah Arendt were all forced to flee Germany when that country fell under the sway of the National Socialists. They have been grouped together by hostile critics and by those who admired their work; their interpersonal relations have been the subject of gossip, speculation, and occasional analysis. Whatever the motives one may have for an interest in the persons, the outstanding quality of their work was bound to attract the attention of scholars. It is regrettable that the public exchanges of these three thinkers were so few. In the event, Voegelin did have occasion to comment publicly on the work of both Arendt and Strauss, and they to reply. Moreover, the two books he reviewed were both concerned with understanding the significance of the war and of the evils that had appeared with two of the major participants, Nazi Germany and the Soviet Union.[1] Characteristically, Arendt's account of totalitarianism was direct and explicit, while Strauss's was indirect and implicit. Both of Voegelin's reviews (and the two authors' replies) raised important and serious questions regarding the proper method to be employed in political science, especially as concerns vile and evil regimes.

---

1. Voegelin usually sent both Arendt and Strauss copies of his major publications, and they usually responded with polite thanks. Strauss's *Natural Right and History* (Chicago: University of Chicago Press, 1953) is in Voegelin's library at Erlangen, but it is unmarked even by his usual light pencil lines in the margin. Strauss's copy of Voegelin's *New Science of Politics* in the Strauss Archive at the University of Chicago is accompanied by fourteen pages of notes evidently prepared with a view to writing a review. Voegelin agreed to review Strauss's book for *Review of Politics*, but if ever he completed the work it remained unpublished. Voegelin to Gurian, September 28, 1953, University of Notre Dame, Archives, URP06/Box 6.

The first edition of Strauss's *On Tyranny* appeared in 1948; Voegelin reviewed it the following year. Most of the commentary on this book has revolved around the issues raised by the "debate" between Strauss and Alexandre Kojève, who had known one another for many years and apparently agreed on the agenda of questions considered philosophically important, though not on the answers to them.[2] Whether the term *debate* is indeed *le mot juste,* whether the two participants did establish the fundamental alternatives, or whether theirs was properly speaking an intramural contest are all topics of considerable appeal as intellectual puzzles. Our present concern, however, is to make clear the terms of Voegelin's analysis of Strauss's political science, and to consider the general question of method.

In 1942 Voegelin had sent Strauss a copy of his review of Huntington Cairns's *Theory of Legal Science,* which was discussed in the previous chapter. Strauss thanked him and praised the excellence of Voegelin's refutation of Cairns but expressed a number of significant reservations concerning Voegelin's argument.[3] "The position you attack," wrote Strauss, "is only the last remnant of the science established by Plato and Aristotle," which he then characterized by enumerating five attributes, the first four of which concerned Strauss's understanding of the "position" of Plato and Aristotle. The fifth attribute of Platonic/Aristotelian science was "the impossibility of grounding science on religious faith." Cairns, according to Strauss, had derived his position from a rejection of Voegelin's position and thus indirectly, and perhaps unconsciously, from that of Plato and Aristotle. "Now, you will say," Strauss continued, "that the Platonic-Aristotelian concept of science was put to rest through Christianity and the discovery of history. I am not quite persuaded of that." Strauss's first objection, then, was that Voegelin had contaminated

2. Leo Strauss, *On Tyranny: An Interpretation of Xenophon's Hiero,* with a foreword by Alvin Johnson (New York: Macmillan, 1948); a second edition appeared in French six years later, *De La Tyrannie, par Léo Strauss, Précédé de Hiéron, de Xénophon et suivi de Tyrannie et sagesse par Alexandre Kojève,* trans. H. Kern (Paris: Gallimard, 1954), containing an edited version of the review by Kojève, which had originally appeared as "L'Action politique des philosophes," *Critique* 6 (1950): 41–42, 46–55, 138–55, along with Strauss's "Mise au point," which replied briefly to Voegelin and at greater length to Kojève. In 1963 an English translation, *On Tyranny: Revised and Enlarged,* ed. Allan Bloom (Glencoe: Free Press, 1963), was published, and a paperback was issued by Cornell University Press in 1968. Finally, there is a critical edition, *On Tyranny: Revised and Expanded Edition, Including the Strauss-Kojève Correspondence,* ed. Victor Gourevitch and Michael S. Roth. Reference is to the last text. Voegelin's review was published as "On Tyranny" in 1949.

3. Strauss to Voegelin, November 24, 1942, in *Faith and Political Philosophy,* 5–7. Other quotations are taken from this edition. Most of the letters are in HI 37/1.

the classical understanding of political science with considerations of "religious faith" and "history," which were in turn connected to a specific, historical religious faith, Christianity.

Strauss went on to say that he was persuaded by a "countercriticism of the Cartesian position," namely that it would be wrong to "adopt the thesis of Descartes and all his successors that Plato and Aristotle are fundamentally inadequate." Such a position would be intelligible and adequate only if it could be shown successfully that a "direct critique of Plato and Aristotle," based upon an "adequate understanding," had been completed. In the evident absence of such a critique, the central question of Plato and Aristotle versus Descartes must remain "entirely open." In other words, once philosophical questions were purged of religious faith and a concern with history, then a straight-ahead contrast between ancient and modern science was possible.

There remained, however, the possibility that an equivalent to religious faith might be found in Plato. If so, the prospect of a simple confrontation of ancients and moderns across the playing fields of "science" would have to be recast or augmented by "religious" questions. Strauss rejected that possibility: "I can especially not agree with you when you speak of Plato's attempt 'to create a new myth': his effort was directed toward grounding science anew and especially the science of the soul and of the state."

Voegelin replied in a letter dated December 9, 1942. He thanked Strauss for his "dear letter," agreed with his observation that Cairns's critique of positivism solved nothing, and indicated his desire to provide, "if not solutions, at least possibilities of clarification." As did Strauss, Voegelin found "the inevitable starting-point" in the Platonic-Aristotelian problem. Voegelin distinguished the two components in the following way: first, at the center of Platonic political thinking stand the fundamental experiences bound up with the person and death of Socrates. Specifically, the right ordering of the soul, the Platonic *dike*, was formed by the experiences of "catharsis through consciousness of death and the enthusiasm of eros." These fundamental experiences, moreover, were expressed through the great mythic representations in the *Phaedo, Symposium, Republic*, and *Laws*. Of secondary importance to the fundamental experiences and the expression of them through the form of the myth, therefore, was the "theoretical political-ethical achievement," because only after the fundamental order of the soul had been established could "the field of social relations determined by it be systematically ordered." For this reason Voegelin considered Platonic political science to be founded in myth. Moreover, the persuasiveness of the actual content of the Platonic myths as well as the suitability of the form for the expression of fundamental experiences was what made possible the " 'scientific' treatment of political and ethical problems," in Voegelin's view because the persuasive truths of the myths established "the stable point for the choice of the relevant materials." That is, myth, and its ability to persuade philosophers of its truth, was the analytical center of what would later be called philosophical anthropology. And for Voegelin a sound philosophical anthropology was a crucial element of political science.

In the second place, and in contrast to Platonic political science, Aristotle's *episteme politike* was founded not on the Socratic myth but on "the *bios theoretikos* of the intellectual mystic." The "system of relevance" achieved by the Socratic myth could be assumed by Aristotle to be valid; on the basis of that assumption, Aristotle was able to consider extensive empirical materials "under the now conceptualized mythical image."

Third, therefore, Voegelin did not agree with Strauss's paraphrase that Platonic-Aristotelian political science "was put to an end through Christianity and the discovery of history." Rather, he said, "the very possibilities of the Platonic-Aristotelian science already have their roots in myths and . . . Christianity and historical consciousness only changed them." The change wrought by Christianity was to replace "Hellenocentric man" by the individual, "the person in direct communication with God" rather than by way of the Delphic *omphalos*.[4] Precisely from the Hellenocentric position of Plato and Aristotle, therefore, "a universal political science is radically impossible." The universalization of the image of man in Christianity "is the decisive reason for the superiority of the Christian anthropology over the Hellenic."

Strauss replied on December 20, 1942, indicating his general disagreement with Voegelin's interpretation but adding, "it is so toweringly superior to nearly all that one gets to read about Plato and Aristotle, that I would greatly welcome its being presented to the American public." He then raised the specific objection that, even if Greek political science was not universalizable, which he denied, the universalization did not take place in the Renaissance but with its reception "by the Muslims and the Christians (from the ninth century on)."[5] So far as the sources

4. In his review of Cairns's book, Voegelin did not say that (in Strauss's words) "the Platonic-Aristotelian concept of science was put to rest through Christianity and the discovery of history." Voegelin wrote there substantially what he wrote in his letter to Strauss: "the appearance of Christ has *added* to the idea of man [in Plato and Aristotle] the dimension of the spiritual singularity of every human being, so that we cannot build a science of social order, for instance, on the anthropologies of Plato or Aristotle" (*CW*, 27:104; emphasis added).

5. Voegelin's point about the Renaissance concerned not the question of universality but rather that of its impossibility, owing to what, in his review of Cairns, he called the discovery of the "dimension of historic singularity," which was added to the

indicate, Voegelin did not reply to this observation of Strauss. He did, however, ask for Strauss's publication on Arabic and Jewish medieval political philosophy, and their epistolary conversation moved on to other things.[6]

In a letter dated October 16, 1946, Strauss asked for Voegelin's advice on finding a suitable venue for his "first attempt to interpret Xenophon's dialogue on tyrants (the *Hiero*)." A little more than two years later Voegelin had *On Tyranny* in hand, and Waldemar Gurian had asked him to review it.[7]

The "nucleus" of Strauss's book, Voegelin began in his review, was the analysis of Xenophon's much neglected dialogue *Hiero,* and in that respect it constitutes a valuable contribution to the history of political thought. Strauss's interpretation will compel revision of judgment with regard to Xenophon's "psychological subtlety and his skill of composition" but not with regard to his stature as a thinker. In addition to textual exegesis, Strauss reflected systematically on the broader problem of tyranny in ancient and modern times, on differences between ancient and modern political science, and on the connection between *Hiero* and *The Prince* of Machiavelli. "Every political scientist who tries to disentangle himself from the contemporary confusion over the problem of tyranny will be much indebted to this study and inevitably use it as a starting point." More specifically, according to Voegelin, Strauss was particularly interested in the problem "of freedom of intellectual criticism under a tyrannical government." In Hellenic antiquity, critics were adept at describing the defects of tyranny without being executed for their trouble. Strauss's mode of interpretation brought this and related problems into focus particularly well, Voegelin said. One of the related problems and "one of the finest parts of Professor Strauss's analysis concerns the subtle gradation of human ranks"—the wise man, the just man, the brave man, the gentleman, and so on, leading to "the socially relevant type which the tyrant must face in the mass" who "can be handled by various enticements and fears, by prizes for good conduct

---

spiritual singularity of Christianity (*CW,* 27:104). This problem is discussed in detail in connection with Vico in Chapter 9. In addition, and notwithstanding Voegelin's admiration for Strauss's access to the Arabic texts, Voegelin's understanding of the medieval Arabic *failasauf* did not accord with that of Strauss. Compare Voegelin, "Siger de Brabant," esp. 514 ff., with Strauss, "How Farabi Read Plato's *Laws*," in *What Is Political Philosophy? And Other Studies,* esp. 137–39.

6. Voegelin had been asked by *Social Research,* of which Strauss was an associate editor, to review a book on phenomenology, and the next topic the two men discussed was Husserl. The issues involved are discussed in Chapter 5.

7. Subsequent quotations are from *Review of Politics* 11 (1949): 241–44.

and by persuasion."[8] In general, therefore, Voegelin had great admiration for Strauss's achievement.

Even so, "we miss a proper evaluation" of the following point: for Xenophon, as for Plato, the problem of tyranny was "one of historical necessity" as well as a topic suitable for theoretical discussion. Notwithstanding the defective character of tyranny, it had become in Xenophon's day "the inevitable alternative to a democracy which had ceased to function effectively." Historically, of course, the "age of tyrants" preceded the development of Athenian democracy.[9] For Voegelin, though not for Strauss, this historical sequence was theoretically, methodologically, and scientifically significant. More specifically, Voegelin raised the question of whether, in the sequence tyranny-democracy-tyranny, the term *tyranny* meant the same thing in the sense of referring to substantially the same regime in both the pre- and postdemocratic context, which is to say in the pre- and postconstitutional context. Strauss's own textual analysis had pointed to the curious change in vocabulary: in the first part of the dialogue, " 'Tyrant' (and derivatives) occurs relatively much more frequently in the first part (83 times) than in the second part (7 times); on the other hand, 'ruling' (and derivatives) occurs much more frequently in the much shorter second part (12 times) than in the much more extensive first part (4 times)." This was significant because "the wise" Simonides "wants to induce Hiero to think of his position in terms of 'ruling' rather than in terms of 'tyranny.' "[10] Voegelin agreed with Strauss that the change in usage reflected the dramatic development of the dialogue but was of the view that something more was involved. The changing, or inconsistent, usage "may derive from the fact that a new political situation," one where a postdemocratic and postconstitutional regime appears to be necessary for public order, "is discussed in terms of 'tyranny' because a vocabulary more suitable to the new problems is not yet developed." The change from "tyrant" to "ruler," therefore, may indicate "the genuine necessity of dropping an inadequate term." This observation introduced the question of what an adequate term might be so that preconstitutional (and genuine) tyranny might be distinguished from the postconstitutional regime that had been identified by Xenophon and indicated indirectly through a change in the frequency of usage of

8. This aspect of Xenophon's dialogue was an important topic in the "debate" between Kojève and Strauss owing to its connection to the Hegelian notion of "recognition," which was central to Kojève's interpretation of Hegel. See Barry Cooper, *The End of History: An Essay on Modern Hegelianism*, 266–72.

9. See, for example, A. Andrewes, *The Greek Tyrants* and *Greek Society*, chap. 4, and N. G. L. Hammond, *A History of Greece to 322 B.C.*, 2d ed.

10. Strauss, *On Tyranny*, 65.

the two terms, *tyrant* and *ruler.* Only a "careful reader," to use a favored Straussian locution, would notice so subtle a hint.

Pushing this line of interpretation further, Voegelin then argued that the opposition Strauss maintained as existing between Xenophon's mirror of the prince, *Cyropaedia,* and the mirror of the tyrant, *Hiero,* was not the whole story. In one respect, the two dialogues were on the same side, namely, both texts explored the question of establishing a new rulership "that will make an end to the dreary overturning of democracies and tyrannies in the Hellenic polis." By this interpretation, the apparent opposition of the perfect king and the improved tyrant may be nothing more than an artifact of Xenophon's inadequate conceptual vocabulary. The comparison with Machiavelli, which was stressed by Strauss, sharpened the issue.

By Strauss's interpretation, the tendency of both *Hiero* and *The Prince* to neglect the distinction between king and tyrant was the closest and most important point of contact between ancient and modern political thought. For Strauss, Machiavelli's indifference to the distinction between king and tyrant was one of the deepest roots of modern political thought.[11] Voegelin did not disagree with Strauss's observation and provided the following explanation for it: the parallel between Xenophon and Machiavelli existed, he said, because both

> are in the position of "moderns" in their respective civilizations; the parallel between the two thinkers is due to the parallel between their historical situations. The distinction between king and tyrant is obliterated in *The Prince,* because Machiavelli, like Xenophon, was faced with the problem of a stabilizing and regenerating rulership after the breakdown of constitutional forms in the city-state; it is obliterated because Machiavelli, too, was in search of a type of ruler beyond the distinction of king and tyrant that is politically significant only *before* the final breakdown of the republican constitutional order.

The difference between Xenophon and Machiavelli lay in the fact that Machiavelli was able to discover a new term to designate the postconstitutional ruler, whereas Xenophon was able only to indicate that a new situation had arisen by means of the shift in usage that Strauss had noticed.

Machiavelli's new term was *armed prophet,* for which he claimed Xenophon's Cyrus (not Hiero) as a predecessor.[12] Within the new type of postconstitutional ruler, the old categories of good (royal) and bad

11. Ibid., 23–24.
12. Machiavelli, *The Prince,* chap. 6.

(tyrannical) reappeared.[13] Moreover, Voegelin added, there was an indirect influence of Xenophon on Machiavelli that Strauss overlooked. Machiavelli's image of an armed prophet and a savior prince drew upon several conventions, including a standardized *Life of Temür*, which we shall discuss in detail in Chapter 7. The pattern for the *Life of Temür*, which appeared most clearly in Machiavelli's *Life of Castruccio Castracani* (but also in the closing chapter of *The Prince*), was drawn from Xenophon's portrait of a young and ruthless Cyrus who compelled obedience through fear and terror.[14] In addition, however, Machiavelli incorporated non-Hellenic apocalyptic spiritual elements into his evocation of a postconstitutional prince. Accordingly, while Machiavelli and Xenophon were both "modern" with respect to their own civilizations, in the context of Western rather than Hellenic civilization, Machiavelli's "modernity" is "burdened with the tradition that leads from medieval and Renaissance Paracletes to the secularized Superman of the nineteenth century and after." We may note in passing that for Voegelin *ancient* and *modern* were terms that took their meaning from a historical or, as he said, following Toynbee, a "civilizational" context. We shall discuss this problem further in Chapter 8. For the present we would note only that, for Voegelin, the methodological distinction proper to the political and historical sciences involved was between Western and Hellenic civilizations, not ancient and modern (Western) civilization, which was the position of Strauss.

In January 1949, Voegelin sent Strauss a copy of his review. Strauss thanked him and expressed the hope that he might "argue out" their differences in print. In May 1949 Kojève wrote Strauss and suggested that they publish together a volume combining a French translation of Xenophon's dialogue and of Strauss's book, along with a review article that Kojève was in the midst of writing. In August 1950, Strauss informed Voegelin of Kojève's project and said he would begin his "Restatement" with a response to Voegelin's review. "I am not sticking strictly to what you expressly said," Strauss wrote, "I must come to terms with your unstated premises, which in part I know from your other publications, and in part presume."[15] By September 1950 Strauss had completed his

13. Ibid., chap. 8.
14. Xenophon, *Cyropaedia* I.4–5.
15. The correspondence is reproduced in *Faith and Political Philosophy,* 44–72. Voegelin wrote to Strauss that he was looking forward to learning "what the unstated presuppositions of my work are." Strauss replied to Voegelin: "My terrible handwriting must have brought about a terrible misunderstanding. How could you ever believe that I wrote that you will learn finally with clarity from my 'Restatement'

"Restatement" and sent it off to Kojève. As promised, the first few pages dealt with Voegelin's review.[16]

Strauss's "Restatement" was a mixture of reasoned disagreement regarding, for example, Voegelin's interpretation of Xenophon's intention in writing *Cyropaedia* or of Machiavelli's intention in writing *Life of Castruccio Castracani*, with transparently sophistic remarks on whether the distinction between good and bad rulers was not more fundamental than that between constitutional and postconstitutional situations, or whether such postconstitutional regimes as Voegelin said were justified by historical necessity were not thereby necessarily inferior to those that were inherently choiceworthy. Such statements may be called sophistic because, first, neither Voegelin nor anyone with a modicum of common sense would disagree with them and, second, Voegelin's remarks, in context, concerned the proper interpretation of a historical pattern or configuration, not a moral claim. In short, part of Strauss's "Restatement" was simply the rhetorical ploy of *suppresio veri suggestio falsi.*

The presupposition of Voegelin that Strauss considered to be the most questionable was the opinion that "what is decisive is not Xenophon's conscious intention, stated or implied, but the historical meaning of his work, the historical meaning of a work being determined by the historical situation as distinguished from the conscious intention of the author." Strauss believed that Voegelin subscribed to this doctrine and that, therefore, Voegelin was a historicist and subject to the standard, and in Strauss's view decisive, criticism, which Strauss leveled at all historicists, that they presumed to understand an author better than the author understood himself. This was, for Strauss, particularly to be regretted when it came to an ancient, classical, and Greek thinker. "After the experience of our generation," he wrote,

> the burden of proof would seem to rest on those who assert rather than on those who deny that we have progressed beyond the classics. And even if it were true that we could understand the classics better than they understood themselves, we would become certain of our superiority only after understanding them exactly as they understood themselves. Otherwise we might

what the unstated premises of your work are?" (71). Strauss probably possessed no copy of his handwritten letter and, in any event, did not provide a correction. Strauss's handwriting was notoriously hard to decipher, and it is entirely possible that he wrote something else. To Voegelin (and to the editors of the correspondence) his words *looked* to be what Voegelin took them to be.

16. See the correspondence reproduced in Strauss, *On Tyranny*, 241–63; Strauss's "Restatement" is available in *On Tyranny*, 178–85, reprinted from Strauss, *What Is Political Philosophy?*

mistake our superiority to our notion of the classics for superiority to the classics.

Strauss was genuinely concerned that Voegelin had fallen into error because he sent Voegelin a copy of his longer discussion, analysis, and refutation of historicism.[17]

From Voegelin's perspective, Strauss had accepted the system of relevance (to use the language of the last chapter) or the philosophical anthropology (to use the language of the next chapter) of classical political philosophy. It served Strauss well, and Voegelin maintained the highest regard for his scholarship.[18] Voegelin was particularly critical of attempts to turn Strauss's scholarly achievements into support for a conservative political agenda. In 1977, for example, he wrote to John P. East, in response to East's characterization of Strauss as a conservative:

> It was a pleasure to read your article; and I have no quarrel with its positive content. Still, I am not quite happy about it. For Strauss, after all, did not [do] the work he did, in order to extend comfort to Conservatives. He was a great scholar; and by the influence on his students he was instrumental in restoring a certain amount of serious scholarship to a field as sadly lacking in it as is political science. If one puts the weight as strongly as you do on the incompatibility of his classic and Judaeo-Christian tradition with the current isms, you underplay perhaps the fact that such a thing as "science" in the classic sense really exists, and that the various isms represented in our universities are not only immoral but objectively wrong. They are not euphemistically "utopian," they are phony, dilettantic, illiterate, and fraudulent. Whenever a utopian ismist cashes his salary-check, he takes money for merchandise which he cannot deliver. In every other profession but the academic that is called commercial fraud. A political theorist who cannot read the classics in his field because he is too lazy to learn Greek and Latin, should be immediately fired on elementary grounds of business ethics. I am expressing myself unequivocally, in order to make it clear that there is more at stake in a society than a liberal-conservative conflict when the universities become training centers for permissiveness, sloppy work, and intellectual confidence games. I am

17. Strauss, "Political Philosophy and History." See Voegelin's letter of March 12, 1949, in *Faith and Political Philosophy* as well as his blunt account of the whole business in a letter to Alfred Schütz, March 22, 1949, HI 34/11.

18. In addition to defending Strauss against ill-informed, presumptuous, and often ignorant critics, Voegelin on several occasions sent his best undergraduates from LSU to do graduate work at Chicago. He served on the examination committee of one of Strauss's Ph.D. students and wrote a strong letter to the William Volker Fund in support of Strauss's proposal to establish a political philosophy seminar at Chicago. For details see the correspondence between Voegelin and Edward Shils, HI 36/11; Willmore Kendall, April 8, 1948, HI 20/39; Richard Cornuelle of the Volker Fund, July 14, 1954, HI 42/1; James W. Fesler, March 20, 1957, HI 42/18.

far from agreeing with Strauss on everything, but he certainly has been a noticeable force in raising the awareness of standards in science.[19]

A year later, East was preparing a similar article on Voegelin's "contributions" to conservative thought. Voegelin's response to the article, as was his response to the behaviorists of southern California, was that East had assembled the materials for a satire. But, Voegelin said,

> The Satire itself has remained incomplete. In order to make it complete, you would have to confront the actual content and purpose of my work, which has nothing to do with conservative predilections, with these predilections as illustrated by your selection of quotations. Why you have left the satire incomplete, I am sure, you will know best yourself. But as a basis for satirical purposes your study merits high praise, and I shall use it perhaps sometime.[20]

Voegelin wrote similar letters on other occasions in an attempt to defend himself, Strauss, and other scholars against the smothering embrace of conservatives.[21] In short, neither Strauss nor Voegelin was a "conservative," notwithstanding the many, many publications and interpretations of their work that declare the opposite. As Voegelin observed, it is material for satire, which is a sophisticated as well as an acquired literary taste. The question of the use made by self-described "conservatives" of Strauss's and Voegelin's work is akin to the use made, for example, of Nietzsche or Hegel. A serious consideration of this problem would begin by an analysis of the status of terms such as *liberal* and *conservative*.[22] Because this is seldom if ever done, and because the work of the two political scientists is not distinguished from vulgarian appropriation by political activists, Voegelin's satirical reference to materials for satire adopted just the right tone.

In 1951, Hannah Arendt published *The Origins of Totalitarianism,* and Voegelin was again asked by Waldemar Gurian to write a review for

---

19. HI 10/23. East's article appeared in *Modern Age* 20 (1977).

20. HI 10/23.

21. See, for example, Voegelin to Russell Kirk, April 23, 1956, HI 21/6; Robert Heilman, October 8, 1960, HI 17/9; David Collier, *Modern Age,* May 12, 1961, HI 25/26; Peter Berger, *Social Research,* December 19, 1967, HI 36/29; Jeffrey M. Nelson, April 2, 1969, HI 27/1; Stephen J. Tonsor, April 3 and July 30, 1969, HI 37/27; Robert Schuettiger, October 13, 1969, HI 43/5; Ronald F. Docksai, *Young Americans for Freedom,* May 13, 1971, HI 42/19; Wolfram Ender, November 1, 1971, HI 44/11; Henry Regnery, June 14, 1972, HI 18/2; George H. Nash, December 9, 1974, HI 26/13; William F. Buckley, *National Review,* June 20, 1979, HI 26/19; Michael Berheide, March 9, 1981, HI 8/7.

22. See, however, Voegelin, "Liberalism and Its History," trans. Mary and Keith Algozin, and Strauss, *Liberalism: Ancient and Modern* (New York: Basic Books, 1968).

Review of Politics. The eight-and-a-half page review was then sent by Gurian to Arendt for her eight-page response, and Voegelin was given a final page to reply. It was, to say the least, an unusual procedure.[23]

Voegelin began by characterizing the significance of the phenomenon of "the totalitarian mass movements of our time." First, to all intents and purposes, the entire population of the world had been affected one way or another, even if only as potential victims. "The putrefaction of Western civilization, as it were, has released a cadaveric poison spreading its infection through the body of humanity" and has, in consequence, created something unprecedented, an ecumenic "community of suffering under the earthwide expansion of Western foulness." The chief problem, therefore, was confined to an analysis and theoretical understanding not of a complex and grandiose historical episode but of events that were fundamentally evil as well, a problem that had explicitly concerned Voegelin since the publication of *Political Religions* in 1939.

The methodological problem was, in principle, straightforward: the totalitarian phenomenon, as any other historical phenomenon, could be discussed by political science along the three different but coordinated interpretative lines of space, time, and subject matter. In space, one must have a knowledge of the pertinent facts regarding a plurality of civilizations; in time, one must be able to trace the genesis of the totalitarian movements within one civilizational area, the West, over the preceding millennium; in terms of subject matter, "the inquiry will have to range from religious experiences and their symbolization, through governmental institutions and the organization of terrorism, to the transformations of personality under the pressure of fear and habituation to atrocities." Unfortunately, Voegelin continued, political science was currently ill equipped to undertake such an analysis owing to "the insufficiency of theoretical instruments" that in turn was the great legacy of "the positivistic destruction of political science" to which reference has already been made in Chapter 3.

Voegelin identified three areas where inadequate theoretical instruments would lead to defective analysis. First, in the absence of a sound philosophical anthropology, it is difficult to construct adequate categories by which to classify and describe political phenomena, to say nothing of the significance of acts aiming at the transformation of the

23. See, however, Arendt, "The Personality of Waldemar Gurian," *Review of Politics* 17 (1955): 33–42. References to *The Origins of Totalitarianism* are to the "new edition." The Gurian-Voegelin correspondence is in HI 15/27. Voegelin's review, "The Origins of Totalitarianism," appeared in *Review of Politics* 15 (1953): 68–76; Arendt's "A Reply," 76–84; Voegelin's "Concluding Remark," 84–85.

personality under the pressure of fear and habituation to atrocity. Likewise, in the absence of a sound theory of the spirit, it is difficult to classify and describe phenomena of spiritual integration in the light of which spiritual disintegration appears on its own. What Voegelin was indirectly indicating by these observations he later identified as pneumopathology, as distinct from psychopathology. For example, certain personalities appeared to be perfectly habituated to atrocity but were not, for that reason alone, properly described as sadistic psychopaths. They were, however, spiritually disordered, and their disorder would not be properly diagnosed or properly described unless one had an adequate account of human spirituality available in light of which one might undertake the diagnosis. Finally, without a sound philosophy of history the revolutionary eruption of totalitarianism would appear unrelated to the long historical process of secularization.

The most obvious consequence of relying on inadequate theoretical instruments, therefore, is that one may be overwhelmed by the sheer magnitude of the horrendous events associated with totalitarian mass movements and totalitarian domination. Accordingly, one's preanalytic or conventional response to these events may make analytic, theoretical, or scientific understanding of totalitarian politics all but impossible. As we saw in Chapter 2, during the war there was considerable misunderstanding of the strategic objectives of the Nazis that, in Voegelin's view, resulted directly from the deficient theoretical instruments employed by political scientists. Postwar explanations of well-adjusted SS officers in terms of authoritarian personalities or more serious psychological disorders belong to this category of defective instrumentation as well. Whatever the condition of their science at midcentury, political scientists would be bound to give an account of the events of the preceding thirty years. The most obvious way of doing so would be to permit the phenomena to speak for themselves, as it were, even while the author of the narrative maintained an awareness of the danger that the sheer awfulness of events may prove overwhelming. If practiced by a scholar of intelligence, talent, and integrity, such an interpretative strategy would result in something like a phenomenology of totalitarian evil.

The Origins of Totalitarianism, Voegelin said, attempted to make contemporary phenomena intelligible by considering the development of totalitarianism from the eighteenth century, "thus establishing a time unit in which the essence of totalitarianism unfolded to its fullness." Arendt penetrated to the heart of the subject matter, but her analysis "bears the scars of the unsatisfactory state of theory to which we have alluded." Notwithstanding its "brilliant formulations and profound insights," the book was also characterized by embarrassing but instructive "derailments" that "reveal the intellectual confusion of the age, and show more convincingly than any argument why totalitarian ideas find mass acceptance and will find it for a long time to come." Arendt's book, therefore, achieved a certain clarity with respect to the phenomena but, from the more comprehensive perspective afforded by Voegelin's political science, was also significant as a symptom. Considered simply in terms of method, to the extent that Arendt provided a phenomenology of totalitarianism, it remained a prelude to scientific analysis—an indispensable prelude perhaps, but a prelude nonetheless.

The organization of the topics—anti-Semitism, imperialism, and totalitarianism—Voegelin observed, was roughly chronological; more important, it was also ordered by "increasing intensity and ferocity in the growth of totalitarian features toward the climax in the atrocities of the concentration camps." This organization, furthermore, was intelligible in light of its emotional motivation. The fate of human beings—of the Jews, of the victims of mass killings, of displaced persons—is a "center of emotional shock" from which derived Arendt's desire to understand the causes of similar events and how to stop them from recurring. The motivations of Arendt's procedure determined her treatment of the sequence of topics, namely the disintegration of political and social institutions along with modes of conduct appropriate to them, and the replacement of these institutions and modes of conduct, which we conventionally call Western civilization, with new ones—the "cadaveric poison" Voegelin mentioned earlier. Specifically, the governing theme of the book was the obsolescence or disintegration of the national state as the sheltering organization, the "cosmion" of Western political societies. Historical changes that made new sections of society "superfluous" reached the end point with "the disintegration of national societies and their transformation into aggregates of superfluous human beings."

By describing Arendt's book as having been motivated by emotional shock at the fate of human beings, Voegelin did not mean to imply that it was simply an "emotional"—that is, an irrational, sentimental, or polemical—book. On the contrary, Arendt's motivation was the source of its strength. In this context Voegelin drew attention to Thucydides' opening words in his *History of the War in the Peloponnese,* which illustrated, he said, the fact that sensitivity to the fate of others may be a motivating source of great historiography. "The emotion in its purity," Voegelin said, "makes the intellect a sensitive instrument for recognizing and selecting the relevant facts; and if the purity of the human interest remains untainted by partisanship, the result will be a historical study of respectable rank—as in the case of the present work, which in its substantive parts is remarkably free of ideological nonsense." In other words, Arendt's phenomenological efforts had produced a sound and detached account of the circumstances that occasioned the growth of totalitarian movements and totalitarian domination.[24]

Voegelin then provided a brief and favorable account of the subject matter covered "in order to convey an idea of the richness of the work." The value of this digest of enormous amounts of evidence was clear, but even so, "at this point a note of criticism will have to be allowed." The overarching source of the difficulties, in Voegelin's view, stemmed, as we have seen, from the destruction of science during the era of positivist ascendancy. This did not mean that Arendt was in any sense a positivist; indeed, if her work is to be categorized at all, it is part of the partial recovery of a sense of the problems that is conventionally associated with existentialism in general, and with Jaspers and Heidegger in particular.

Voegelin's "note of criticism," however, was directed not against any taint of positivism or against any theoretical difficulties of existentialism. Rather, he criticized Arendt on scholarly or methodological grounds for not using the "theoretical instruments" that were available to her. Had she used them, the organization of the subject matter might have been improved. Specifically, according to Voegelin, "her principle of relevance that orders the variegated materials into a story of totalitarianism is the disintegration of a civilization into masses of human beings without secure economic and social status; and her materials are relevant insofar as they demonstrate the process of disintegration." There is, of course, nothing wrong with using such a principle of relevance to tell the story of social disintegration. Voegelin's point was that such a story is, in fact, no more than a chapter in a book; it is not a self-sufficient little gem of meaning. "Obviously," he went on, "this process is the same as has been categorized by Toynbee as the growth of the internal and external proletariat. It is surprising that the author has not used Toynbee's highly differentiated concepts." If she had, Toynbee's work "would have substantially added to the weight of Dr. Arendt's analysis" by providing a more comprehensive principle of relevance than Arendt's univocal story line of disintegration—which, to be sure, was adequate so far as it went. Voegelin's point, to repeat, is that "the theoretical instruments which the present state of science puts at her disposition"—specifically, the arguments developed by Toynbee in *A Study of History*—would have

24. There were "nonemotional" studies of various aspects of totalitarianism, but they were, in Voegelin's view, defective in other respects. See his review of Maxine Sweezy, *The Structure of the Nazi Economy*, and Earnest Fraenkel, *The Dual State* (1942). Voegelin used Herman Rauschning's *The Revolution of Nihilism* in the summer school course he gave on totalitarianism at Northwestern in 1939 (HI 27/19).

enabled Arendt to carry her analysis further, had she availed herself of them. Voegelin's criticism of Arendt is similar to his criticism of Strauss inasmuch as he had no quarrel with what either had done, only with the fact that there was more to do, that the evidence that their analyses brought to light was not given adequate theoretical form.

Regarding Arendt, two "theoretical defects" followed from her limited principle of relevance. First, dealing with political and social institutions and types of conduct as determined by them "is apt to endow historical causality with an aura of fatality." Situations require but do not determine human responses: human character—the virtues, the range and intensity of passions, the element of personal spiritual freedom—also plays a part. "If conduct is not understood as the response of a man to a situation," Voegelin said, "and the varieties of response as rooted in the potentialities of human nature rather than in the situation itself, the process of history will become a closed stream, of which every crosscut at a given point of time is the exhaustive determinant of the future course." Now, Arendt knew this: social situations do not make people superfluous and superfluous people do not necessarily respond to their situation with resentment, hatred, and cruelty. She knew as well that the spiritual core of the human personality was crucial to the kind of response people make. As she remarked:

> Nothing perhaps distinguishes modern masses as radically from those of previous centuries as the loss of faith in a Last Judgment: the worst have lost their fear and the best have lost their hope. Unable as yet to live without fear and hope, these masses are attracted by every effort which seems to promise a man-made fabrication of the Paradise they had longed for and of the Hell they had feared.[25]

Voegelin made the following comment on this passage: "The spiritual disease of agnosticism is the peculiar problem of the modern masses, and the man-made paradises and man-made hells are its symptoms; and the masses have the disease whether they are in their paradise or their hell." Arendt's first "theoretical defect," therefore, was that she treated the story of Western disintegration as a fatal sequence, even though she was aware of the importance of human spirituality, and therefore of human freedom, in the process of disintegration. In terms of philosophical anthropology, spiritual diseases cannot be reduced to the conditions of their occurrence: they are not caused by superfluousness or resentment. On the contrary, superfluity and resentment are symptoms of the spiritual disease, identified here by Voegelin as agnosticism. Arendt was aware

25. Arendt, *Origins*, 446.

of the problem, or she would not have mentioned it. But she was not aware of its significance.

A second theoretical defect, therefore, followed from the first: because she did not acknowledge the significance of the spiritual disorder of agnosticism, her treatment of the vast array of materials she brought to light was out of focus. In short, Arendt's knowledge of the problem of spiritual disorder did not affect her treatment of the materials. If, as she rightly observed, the spiritual disease that hankered after fabricated paradises and stood in terror of fabricated hells was the problem, and not simply the institutional breakdown of society and modes of conduct, then one would reasonably expect the study of the origins of totalitarianism to be devoted to spiritual as well as to institutional questions. And then one would look not just to the fate of the nation-state but, more important, to "the rise of immanentist sectarianism since the high Middle Ages; and the totalitarian movements would not be simply revolutionary movements of functionally dislocated people, but immanentist creed movements in which medieval heresies have come to their fruition." And so, Voegelin concluded, Arendt "does not draw the theoretical conclusions from her own insights."

Before offering an account of why Arendt did not draw the proper theoretical conclusions from her own insights, Voegelin explored the problem further. To begin with, there was no doubt that Arendt was as aware of the spiritual and intellectual breakdown as she was of the institutional. "What totalitarian ideologies, therefore, aim at," she wrote, "is not the transformation of the outside world or the revolutionary transmutation of society, but the transformation of human nature itself."[26] Voegelin agreed: "This is, indeed, the essence of totalitarianism as an immanentist creed movement." Totalitarians, whether Nazis, Bolsheviks, or something else, are not, in fact, interested in social reformation "but want to create a millennium in the eschatological sense through the transformation of human nature." Not the grace of God but an act of human beings would, by the totalitarian vision, usher in a new heaven and a new earth—or rather, a heaven-on-earth. It is for this reason that Voegelin said that totalitarians are participants in immanentist creed movements in which medieval heresies, which also promised heaven-on-earth by substituting human action for divine grace, come to fruition.

At the end of the paragraph from which the above quotation was drawn, Arendt wrote: "Human nature as such is at stake, and even though it seems that these experiments succeed not in changing man

26. Ibid., 458.

but only in destroying him . . . one should bear in mind the necessary limitations to an experiment which requires global control in order to show conclusive results." The "experiment" to which Arendt referred involved the reduction of human beings to bundles of responses made to various stimuli under conditions of terror in concentration camps.[27] The pragmatic implication seemed to be: we cannot tell whether these experiments work because we have not yet achieved the necessary conditions for a proper experimental trial, namely the creation of a single ecumenic, totalitarian regime. The grave defect of the totalitarian "experiment," therefore, was the existence of nontotalitarian political regimes that, in one way or another, contaminated the results. The final contamination of the experimental results was achieved, in the example of the National Socialists, by a world war that ended with the destruction of the Nazi regime and the military occupation of Germany.

Voegelin was, of course, concerned with these grotesque pragmatic events.[28] His focus, however, was on the theoretical issue. "Nature," he said, "is a philosophical concept; it denotes that which identifies a thing as a thing of this kind and not another one." To use a familiar example: what makes the animal on the mat a cat is its catty nature, which it does not share with a dog; a dog is distinguished by its doggy nature, even though it, too, might share a place on the mat. Consequently, wrote Voegelin, "a 'nature' cannot be changed or transformed; a 'change of nature' is a contradiction in terms; tampering with the 'nature' of a thing means destroying the thing." For example, in order to transform a cat into a dog the catty nature of the specific and actual animal must be destroyed and replaced (somehow) with a doggy one.[29] The *fact* of the matter is, all humans can do is destroy a cat. Only God can "make" a dog, and the

---

27. Ibid., 459. "The concentration camps are the laboratories where changes in human nature are tested, and their shamefulness, therefore, is not just the business of their inmates and those who run them according to strict 'scientific' standards; it is the concern of all men" (ibid., 458).

28. The review copy, which is part of Voegelin's personal library, has numerous pencil lines in the margin of the concluding chapter, from which most of the quotations given in the text are drawn. Voegelin marked passages only very occasionally.

29. The qualification *somehow* is necessary in this imaginary example because "natures" are usually conceived as being uncreated by humans—though perhaps created by God. Obviously modern technological actions, which have fabricated new life-forms, have compelled a certain amount of qualification and elaboration of the problem. It is within the realm of possibility that one might genetically transform a cat into something that looked like a dog, barked like a dog, and so on. But would it *be* a dog? Or must dogs be begotten by dogs not made by humans from (former) cats? For a discussion of this question, see Oliver O'Donovan, *Begotten or Made?* (Oxford: Clarendon, 1984), and the discussion in Cooper, *Action into Nature*, 216 ff.

reason for this is philosophical, not theological, and not technological either. Voegelin was, therefore, surprised that Arendt would seriously entertain the possibility of undertaking a philosophically impossible act, namely the experimental transformation of human nature, by terror, in an ecumenic concentration camp. He, therefore, characterized her remark as "a symptom of the intellectual breakdown of Western civilization." Arendt, too, had apparently adopted "the immanentist ideology" that characterized the historical events she so thoroughly examined, which led to the following consequence: "she keeps an 'open mind' with regard to the totalitarian atrocities; she considers the question of a 'change of nature' a matter that will have to be settled by 'trial and error'; and since the 'trial' could not yet avail itself of the opportunities afforded by a global laboratory, the question must remain in suspense for the time being."

So as to prevent any misunderstanding, we should again stress that Voegelin's criticism concerned Arendt's "theoretical derailment," which had the effect of limiting the theoretical formulations of the insights her book contained. It was nevertheless a *serious* theoretical error to entertain as an intelligible anthropological possibility the "immanentist ideology" that, in Voegelin's view, characterized the "intellectual breakdown of Western civilization." Voegelin did not explain *why* Arendt adopted "the immanentist ideology" in the sense of providing a psychological explanation of her action, but he did indicate what her "theoretical derailment" meant.

As a conceptual, analytic, or scientific term, the adjective *immanent* takes its meaning in opposition to transcendent. In the particular example considered here, the noun so modified would be *world*. Accordingly, the phrase *immanentist ideology* refers to an act of ignoring, reducing, transfiguring, or perhaps explaining away the existence of experiences of world-transcendent reality, a reality conventionally described as "divine." In the context of the present problem, Voegelin said, "the true dividing line in the contemporary crisis does not run between liberals and totalitarians, but between the religious and philosophical transcendentalists on the one side, and the liberal and totalitarian immanentist sectarians on the other side." The implication, therefore, was that Arendt's theoretical derailment into "the immanentist ideology" was shared with the totalitarians whom she opposed vigorously as a matter of practice. That Arendt opposed totalitarianism has several times been averred, but we must emphasize: that was not the issue Voegelin raised. Indeed, her opposition to totalitarianism may serve as a textbook example of the problem discussed in the previous chapter that several positions might oppose one another in terms of doctrine, ethics, policy, or method but nevertheless be allied in principle.

Voegelin's conclusion was therefore clear: if the fundamental dividing line was between religious and philosophical transcendentalists and a rich variety of immanentist sectarians, Arendt clearly belonged among the latter. Her remarks regarding the concentration camp laboratories and their experiments with human nature, her "theoretical derailment," Voegelin said, might properly be characterized as reflecting "a typically liberal, progressive pragmatist attitude towards philosophical problems," and so reveal "how much ground liberals and totalitarians have in common; the essential immanentism which unites them overrides the differences of ethos which separate them." That is, liberals and totalitarians can find any number of intelligible grounds upon which to oppose one another, but a full understanding of their opposition would have to include an awareness of their shared spiritual immanentism. The contrast between Voegelinian and Arendtian political science with respect to this problem was expressed with considerable clarity by Arendt. "The criminal attempt to change the nature of man," she said, has provided her with the "trembling insight that no nature, not even the nature of man, can any longer be considered to be the measure of all things."[30] To this trembling insight a Voegelinian political scientist, conscious of the significance of philosophical or religious experiences of world-transcendent reality, might properly reply: the nature of man has not ceased to be the measure simply because a collection of spiritually disordered criminals has conceived of the project to change it and has succeeded in committing large-scale murder in the pursuit of its impossible project.

Voegelin concluded his review with an account of Arendt's evocation of a "nihilistic-nightmare" in place of "a well considered theory." It would be unfair, he said, "to hold the author responsible on the level of critical thought for what obviously is a traumatic shuddering under the impact of experiences that were stronger than the forces of spiritual and intellectual resistance." Indeed most of the book "is animated, if not penetrated, by the age-old knowledge about human nature and the life of the spirit," notwithstanding the unsatisfactory theoretical formulations that occurred chiefly in her conclusions. He ended with the proposal that we "take comfort in the unconscious irony of the closing sentence of the work where the author appeals, for the 'new' spirit of human solidarity, to Acts 16:28: 'Do thyself no harm; for we are all here.' Perhaps, when the author progresses from quoting to hearing these words, her nightmarish fright will end like that of the jailer to whom they were addressed."[31]

---

30. Arendt, *Origins,* 434 in the first edition. The remark, of more than philological interest, was omitted from subsequent editions.

31. In the story recounted in Acts 16, Paul and Silas are in jail; their prayers to be freed are apparently answered by an earthquake that opens the doors of the jail.

Voegelin's review considered several fundamental theoretical questions and was by no means simply an external summary of Arendt's text followed by a seal of approval or disapproval. And Hannah Arendt was not just a distinguished professor who happened to write a controversial book on a topic of considerable current interest. She was, along with Strauss and Voegelin, one of the great political thinkers of the century. When, therefore, Gurian received Voegelin's review, prudence alone might well have counseled him to ask for her response. Arendt agreed to respond because of the "general questions of method" and "general philosophical implications" that Voegelin discussed and because "I failed to explain the particular method which I came to use, and [failed] to account for a rather unusual approach . . . to the whole field of political and historical sciences as such."[32] What, then, was Arendt's approach?

She began, after some conventional introductory remarks, by indicating her view of the methodological question: "The problem originally confronting me was simple and baffling at the same time: all historiography is necessarily salvation and frequently justification; it is due to man's fear that he may forget and to his striving for something which is even more than remembrance." Working from this assumption, writing on the topic of totalitarianism posed a particular problem: she did not wish to preserve its memory but, on the contrary "felt engaged to destroy" it. One may say, therefore, that her book was not, properly speaking, a work of theory at all but had an immediately practical purpose.[33] Still, the question remained: how to write about this vile phenomenon?

Her solution "was to discover the chief elements of totalitarianism and to analyze them in historical terms, tracing these elements back in history as far as I deemed proper and necessary." By this account,

---

The jailer, in a panic, is about to commit suicide when Paul tells him not to worry because no one has escaped. The jailer then seeks salvation by conversion; Paul adds the jailer's family, and they are all baptized. It is perhaps worth noting that Arendt also changed this ending after the first edition.

32. These and subsequent quotations are taken from Arendt's "Reply" referred to above.

33. In the preface to *Origins*, Arendt wrote: "Comprehension does not mean denying the outrageous, deducing the unprecedented from precedents, or explaining phenomena by such analogies and generalities that the impact of reality and the shock of experience are no longer felt. It means, rather, examining and bearing consciously the burden which our century has placed on us—neither denying its existence nor submitting meekly to its weight. Comprehension, in short, means the unpremeditated, attentive facing up to, and resisting of, reality—whatever it may be." Heilke has argued in "Science, Philosophy, and Resistance" that Voegelin's books on Nazi "race ideas" served a similar, though less explicit, purpose.

Arendt's "principles of relevance" were simply what she deemed proper and necessary. *The Origins of Totalitarianism* was not, therefore, "a history of totalitarianism but an analysis in terms of history," not an account of the origins of totalitarianism but "a historical account of the elements which crystallized into totalitarianism" followed by "an analysis of the elemental structure of totalitarian movements and [of the structure of totalitarian] domination itself." The book, therefore, had a structure; Voegelin's criticism, however, was that its principle of relevance was overly narrow, and on that question Arendt was silent.[34]

A second methodological problem was, in Arendt's words, "a problem of 'style.'" According to Arendt, the morally abhorrent character of totalitarianism was descriptively part of the phenomenon. To describe concentration camps *sine ira* "is not to be 'objective', but to condone them." More generally, she said, "the problem of style is a problem of adequacy and of response." If one tries to be objective with morally repugnant phenomena, rather than to use one's imagination to grasp their significance, one renounces "the human faculty to respond to either. Thus the question of style is bound up with the problem of understanding." On the other hand, imaginative sensitivity to "differences of factuality," particularly as concerns totalitarianism, was, for Arendt, "all-important." Accordingly, "the 'phenomenal differences', far from 'obscuring' some essential sameness, are those phenomena which make totalitarianism 'totalitarian', which distinguishes this one form of government and movement from all others and, therefore, can alone help us in finding its essence. What is unprecedented in totalitarianism is not primarily its ideological content, but the *event* of totalitarian domination itself." Arendt's observation, considered as a historical aperçu, is true enough. Voegelin, it may be recalled, acknowledged the importance of the morally repugnant appearance of totalitarianism and indicated his views by using striking metaphors of putrefaction and cadaveric poison. His criticism of Arendt was obviously directed not at the area of their agreement regarding morally repugnant political phenomena but at the adequacy of her analysis of the intellectual and spiritual perversions that accounted for the phenomena. This question was not engaged by Arendt either.

Arendt then characterized her differences with Voegelin. "I proceed from facts and events," she said, "instead of intellectual affinities and

34. In *NSP,* chap. 1., Voegelin discussed the question of "elemental" analysis in connection with the problem of representation and indicated that such analysis dealt with only the external aspects of the problem; the internal aspects, which considered the question of meaning, required a critical or scientific approach based on a comprehensive philosophical anthropology.

influences," which was apparently the way she thought Voegelin proceeded. In particular, because totalitarianism did not exist factually or as an event prior to the twentieth century, Arendt did not see the point of Voegelin's remarks regarding immanentist sectarian creed movements in which medieval heresies had come to fruition. She simply "doubted" Voegelin's theory of medieval intellectual affinities and influences: "under no circumstances would I call any of them [the heretical medieval immanentist sectarian creed movements] totalitarian." Indeed, according to Arendt, trying to proceed by means of such affinities and influences places too much weight on "ideas" at the cost of ignoring "events."

Voegelin did not maintain that medieval heretics or modern liberals were totalitarians, though Arendt seemed to think he did ("Mr. Voegelin seems to think that totalitarianism is only the other side of liberalism, positivism and pragmatism"). Considered as political phenomena there is no reason anyone would confuse liberals and totalitarians or Anabaptists and Nazis. Voegelin's point was that phenomenal differences provided insufficient material for a comprehensive political science and that substantive and spiritual criteria and evidence were also required. This certainly entailed something more than "intellectual affinities and influences."

Indeed, phenomenal evidence, or a focus on "facts and events," was insufficient for Arendt as well. Nazis and Bolsheviks were also phenomenally distinguishable, yet both were identified by Arendt as totalitarian. Second, by the early 1950s considerable historical evidence had come to light regarding the continuity of medieval heretical sects with various enlightened, secular, and then revolutionary sects.[35] Voegelin relied on these interpretations in writing his *History of Political Ideas,* at least with respect to general strategies of textual and historical interpretation.

In the course of a review Voegelin obviously could not introduce these problems. In *History of Political Ideas,* however, he was able to argue *in extenso* for the position he had adopted regarding Arendt's interpretation. We will take as an example Voegelin's discussion of the sentiments surrounding the fourteenth-century clash between the papacy and France. This problem has the advantage of being concerned less with medieval heresies and the triumph of sectarians than with

---

35. For example: Henri de Lubac, *Drame de l'humanisme athée,* 2d ed. (1947); Hans Urs von Balthasar, *Apokalypse der deutschen Seele* (1937); Jakob Taubes, *Abenländische Eschatologie* (1947). Several times in his postwar correspondence Voegelin mentioned the work of these scholars as constituting genuine science. Often he would add, for the medieval period, the work of Étienne Gilson and Alois Dempf. See, for example, his letters to Kurt Wolff, HI 42/15.

relatively low-key intellectual and institutional shifts. Even with this conventional focus, however, several spiritual issues that had a direct bearing on the problem of totalitarianism were brought to light.

In 1302, the Bull *Unam Sanctam* asserted the supremacy of the papal spiritual power over all temporal powers.[36] It was issued at a time when the political affairs of the West, particularly those of the Atlantic powers, France and Britain, were separating from the politics of Christendom directed against the Muslim East. *Unam Sanctam* was not simply a diplomatic assertion of an obsolete papal power under circumstances that were growing increasingly inappropriate; it was also a document based on argumentation. It began from the statement of Saint Paul (Rom. 13:1) that all power is "ordered" and argued that order implied hierarchy, and mediation of powers from the divine, through the papal to the temporal. This doctrine, which had been introduced into the ongoing debate over spiritual and temporal authority by Bertrand of Bayonne half a century earlier, was based on two pseudo-Dionysian treatises dating from antiquity on the parallels between ecclesiastical and celestial hierarchies. The neo-Platonic doctrine was influential chiefly because it was attributed (in fact, wrongly) to Saint Paul's Athenian convert, Dionysius the Areopagite. In any event, Bertrand argued that the ecclesiastical hierarchy was an analog to the hierarchy of angels. The pope was the chief human hierarch from whom subordinate powers descended.

The importance of this doctrinal innovation was that it tended to eclipse the constitutional theory of the *sacrum imperium* according to which the charismata have been distributed by God directly, the spiritual and temporal functions were to be exercised within the *corpus mysticum* freely, and the members of the community have become bound together by mutual love in the sense indicated by Saint Paul (1 Cor. 13). Under the hierarchical theory of power, in contrast, the term *ecclesia*, for example, came to mean members of the church hierarchy rather than members of the Christian community. More broadly considered, Voegelin pointed out, the theory of the charismata and of the balance of spiritual and temporal power expressed in Pope Gelasius's doctrine of the two swords was historically and politically applicable only so long as a single imperial head could represent the temporal power more or less uncontested.

---

36. The discussion is in the chapter "The Absolute Papacy—Giles of Rome," in *HPI*, III:43–53. The papal document is widely reprinted. See, for example, Brian Tierney, ed., *The Crisis of Church and State, 1050–1300* (Englewood Cliffs: Prentice-Hall, 1964), 188 ff., or Ernest F. Henderson, ed., *Select Historical Documents of the Middle Ages* (London: Bell, 1903), 435 ff. See also Alois Dempf, *Sacrum Imperium: Geschichtes- und Staatsphilosophie des Mittelalters und der politischen Renaissance*, 449–55.

With the disintegration of the temporal power—evident, for example, in the ongoing conflicts between France and England—the danger that the new temporal political units would acquire the status of separate spiritual units became apparent as well. One method of maintaining the spiritual unit of the West appeared to be the establishment of an absolutistic hierarchy of power, centered on the papacy.

Important as the historical and diplomatic contexts were, the spiritual factors were at least as significant. "The evocation of Bertrand," wrote Voegelin, "constitutes a closed community, organized as a pyramid of ranks, with the power substance pervading the ranks from the top to the bottom."[37] Bertrand's theory was of a closed spiritual community, but it could be easily transferred to the closed administrative community, with the substance of power descending from the prince, through the bureaucratic hierarchy, to the people. Initially, the hierarchy was introduced as an analog to, and so justification for, spiritual and political liberty or individualism. But analogies move in both directions and, as Voegelin observed "the pendulum now seems to [have swung] in the direction of a new spiritual-temporal hierarchy in totalitarian communities."

In this respect, *Unam Sanctam* expanded Bertrand's construction, originally designed to justify the privileges of the Mendicant Orders, from the ecclesiastical order to a general theory of power, including temporal power. Giles of Rome's treatise *On Ecclesiastical Power* (1302) influenced the structure and the language of *Unam Sanctam*. Voegelin also detected (as did Dempf) the ambitions of an intellectual anxious for political rule. In his youth, Giles of Rome had written a defense of monarchic absolutism, *On Princely Rule* (1285), which argued the opposite position to that set out in the treatise of 1302. The Carlyles observed that this radical change in position was "arresting and even startling."[38] Voegelin commented that his change of heart "loses its enigmatic character if we recognize that Giles was less interested in spiritual or temporal power than in power as such. He was willing to advocate any power as absolute so long as he was associated with it. If Giles were placed in a modern environment we would have to say that he was a Fascist by temperament." Voegelin went on to explain analytically his use of an obvious anachronism. As soon as "the idea of the spiritual unity of mankind is translated from the free coexistence of Christians as members of the body of Christ into terms of a spiritual unity controlled by the holder of supreme power, the outlines of a form of government appear that today we are accustomed to calling totalitarian." Giles of Rome's contribution

---

37. "Siger de Brabant," in *HPI*, II:178–204.
38. R. W. and A. J. Carlyle, *A History of Medieval Political Theory in the West*, 5:403.

to Western political thought was to substitute for a doctrine of powers, in the plural, that was relative to purposes and institutions a doctrine of power, in the singular, that was applicable, in principle, to them all.

In the event, Egidius applied his doctrine to the papacy. A plenitude of material as well as spiritual power was in the hands of the pope, who exercised the spiritual power on his own account but directed the secular princes in the exercise of the material. All laws must conform to ecclesiastical laws; all organs of government were to be administered in conformity with the will of the church. The result was to create "a closed governmental system with respect to legislation, administration, and the use of instruments of coercion," at the head of which, and representing the whole, was the pope. At the same time, Egidius insisted on control over the hierarchy of sciences: philosophers were not to question theological doctrines but rather were to adapt their arguments to the service of the church. Finally, the intrusion of the church into the area of civil society was justified on the grounds that, through the Fall, human beings lost whatever rights they may have had by nature. "Such rights as they have," Voegelin observed, "they receive through their status in the sacramental order of the church, which has total dominion over all things. The whole sphere of natural law is abolished, and the legal status of men is made dependent on their obedient integration into the absolute governmental machine headed by the pope. The outlines of a totalitarian organization become recognizable."

The conclusion Voegelin drew from this analysis of medieval political theory did more than establish an intellectual pedigree for totalitarian activists. It illustrated as well a general methodological principle, that no account of power, including totalitarian power, would be complete if it ignored dimensions of spirituality and of the orientation of the spirit in a world-transcendent or intramundane direction. In the example of these medieval texts and events, Voegelin's insight was clear: once the case was made for the defense of an absolute church, it was a relatively simple matter to effect a transfer "to the secular political sphere when the particular national units had reached a degree of concentration that would permit the raising of spiritual claims in addition to the legal claims." The first occasion when the new theoretical arguments were elaborated in a context of national bodies politic was in the *Leviathan* of Hobbes, which even Arendt allowed had a connection with the origins of totalitarianism.[39]

With respect to the differences in method between Arendt and Voegelin, one may say that although Arendt could "analyze the element

39. Arendt, *Origins*, 139–41.

of expansion insofar as these elements were still clearly visible and played a decisive role in the totalitarian phenomenon itself" rather than write a history of anti-Semitism and a history of imperialism, she ignored the evolution of Western spirituality as an independent contributory element. If one asks *why* this omission was made, the most obvious, and perhaps the only, answer is: because it was not visible to her in the totalitarian phenomenon. And this consideration may serve to reemphasize Voegelin's point regarding the importance of philosophical anthropology, philosophy of the spirit, and philosophy of history as providing the necessary principles of relevance.[40]

An alternative way of formulating the differences between Arendt and Voegelin would be to say that Arendt's theorization was nominalistic whereas Voegelin's was realistic. As Voegelin pointed out in a letter to Francis Wilson, "nominalistic theories will be the best one can do in areas where penetration to essence is yet prevented by the state of science."[41] Nominalistic taxonomy or elemental analysis of the kind followed by Arendt would, therefore, distinguish totalitarian domination from liberal democracy, constitutional monarchy, classical tyranny, and so on. And, of course, Arendt did just that; indeed, she often insisted on the importance of making distinctions.[42] Distinctions are obviously important, and one must always begin with the phenomena that attract one's attention. Voegelin's point was that nominalistic theorization can indeed achieve a taxonomy of type concepts, but that such a result is no more than a first step. In contrast, "realistic theorization" moved "beyond the appearances of phenomena" by way of analysis to a definition of essence. Even so, Voegelin continued, "realistic theorization" is possible only in cases where the subject has genuine "ontological status." Accordingly, one could develop a realistic theory of "the nature of man or of society, or of the order of the human soul" but not of the "accidence of order" such as appear through a typology of regimes, including that of totalitarian domination.

---

40. Voegelin would not, therefore, accept without qualification Arendt's previously quoted statement that "all historiography is necessarily salvation and frequently justification." It is true that the sentiment can be extracted from Thucydides, and Arendt has done so in "The Concept of History: Ancient and Modern," in *Between Past and Future: Eight Exercises in Political Thought,* chap. 2, but for Voegelin the more immediate source is the "pathos" of the Renaissance historiographers. See Chapter 7 below.

41. HI 42/5.

42. In her response to Voegelin, for example, she wrote: "my chief quarrel with the present state of the historical and political sciences is their growing incapacity for making distinctions" ("A Reply," 82).

Voegelin made the same point in another paper published about the same time.[43] As is clear from his remarks on Egidius's temperament and his use of the term *totalitarian* in connection with his doctrine of power, Voegelin was not opposed to the critically justified use of anachronistic terminology provided it helped clarify a particular problem. In this as well, Voegelin and Arendt were likely to differ.[44] He was, however, opposed to the uncritical anachronistic use of the term *totalitarian*, particularly when it was applied by modern, secular intellectuals to aspects of medieval political thought that did not meet with their approval. Regarding an example of such usage Voegelin made the following remark:

> The term has arisen, in the 1920s, within the modern Gnostic mass movements. It does not denote the measures of extraordinary atrocity which these movements use in their expansion and domination, but the faith in human intramundane (not transcendent) perfection through political action by groups who are in possession of eschatological knowledge about the end of history. This substitution of human self-salvation, of something like a transfiguration of human nature through historical action, for the Christian idea of perfection through Grace in death is, indeed, a matter of principle insofar as it can be maintained only if the whole range of experiences of transcendence is disregarded. Totalitarian politics is based on an immanentist philosophical anthropology, as distinguished from Platonic-Aristotelian and Christian anthropologies which find the ordering center of human personality in the experiences of man's relation to transcendent reality. It seems to me impermissible to apply the term "totalitarianism" to both types alike, for such indiscriminate usage would obliterate the essential difference of principles and stress the non-essential similarity of prudential measures which, in various historical circumstances, may be used for the protection of a society against spiritual disintegration.[45]

Voegelin made his critical point on the basis of a realistic theory of the nature of man and of society that enabled him to distinguish violent measures taken on prudential grounds from violent measures taken on the basis of faith in the possibility of an intramundane transfiguration of

43. Voegelin, "The Oxford Political Philosophers" (1953).

44. See Arendt's remarks on the "unusual" distinction she made between labor and work based on striking "phenomenal evidence," namely "the simple fact that every European language, ancient and modern, contains two etymologically unrelated words for what we have come to think of as the same activity, and retains them in the face of their persistent synonymous usage" (*The Human Condition*, 79–80). For Arendt, the question of historical usage was particularly revealing; Voegelin would not disagree, but the demands of realistic theorization might necessitate the use of terms, such as *political society*, that for Arendt would in principle be avoided. Compare *NSP*, 1, with *The Human Condition*, 38 ff.

45. "Oxford Political Philosophers," 103.

human existence. Among other things, the first type of violence would in principle be limited whereas the second, because it is used in pursuit of an impossible goal, would be limitless.

In Arendt's opinion, the basis of the disagreement between the two lay elsewhere. According to her, Voegelin's "sharpest criticism" concerned Arendt's remarks on human nature. In response she wrote: "The problem of the relationship between essence and existence in Occidental thought seems to me to be a bit more complicated and controversial than Mr. Voegelin's statement on 'nature' (identifying 'a thing as a thing' and, therefore, incapable of change by definition) implies, but this I can hardly discuss here."[46] She did, however, amplify her remarks somewhat:

> I hardly proposed more change of nature than Mr. Voegelin himself in his book on *The New Science of Politics;* discussing the Platonic-Aristotelian theory of soul, he states: "one might almost say that before the discovery of psyche man had no soul." (p. 67) In Mr. Voegelin's terms, I could have said that after the discoveries of totalitarian domination and its experiments, we have reason to fear that man may lose his soul.

To this rhetorically powerful statement one must nevertheless raise a few objections. Voegelin's point was methodological and concerned precisely the distinction that Plato and Aristotle achieved in their analytical use of the term *psyche,* which was, moreover, grounded in a specific class of experiences that can be identified by the methods of classical philology.[47] Arendt was, of course, too well grounded in classical scholarship to be unaware of this problem; her usage, however, seemed to imply that the application of terror or the conduct of totalitarian "experiments" led to certain discoveries concerning souls. If, prior to Plato and Aristotle, "man had no soul," it was also true, according to Arendt, that after the "experiments" humans would also become without souls. But what did this mean? Obviously, souls were not things to be lost like marbles or teddy bears. Plato and Aristotle were fully aware that the imagery of

46. Arendt has, of course, had her defenders against Voegelin's criticism. One way of dealing with the issue of "human nature" and its changes that does not get lost in semantic divergencies was indicated by Voegelin himself. In a letter to Dal R. Evans (January 18, 1974, HI 12/6), he wrote: "The 'change' in the nature of man . . . is of course real, but a change is precisely what is called 'history' and the history of the differentiation is the content of *Order and History.* No differentiation of the psyche would be recognizable as such, unless it were the differentiation of something that was there before." Such an understanding of the meaning of the term *nature of man* is defensible in itself, but that was not what either Voegelin or Arendt meant in the exchange of 1953. The other possibility, derived from Schelling, has been given a systematic formulation by Emil Fackenheim and is discussed in Chapter 10.

47. See, for example, Bruno Snell, *The Discovery of the Mind: The Greek Origins of European Thought,* trans. T. G. Rosenmeyer.

losing one's soul referred to a kind of existential choice of injustice and ignorance over the desire for justice and wisdom. What Arendt had in mind may be indicated in one of her earlier accounts of the operation of the death factories:

> and they all died together, the young and the old, the weak and the strong, and the sick and the healthy; not as people, not as men and women, children and adults, boys and girls, not as good and bad, beautiful and ugly—but brought down to the lowest common denominator of organic life itself, plunged into the darkest and deepest abyss of primal equality, like cattle, like matter, like things that had neither body nor soul, nor even a physiognomy upon which death could stamp its seal.[48]

One is reminded in this account of the reduction of animal vitality to the stimulus-response organisms that emerged from the laboratories of Professor Pavlov. Human beings, like dogs, when placed in "experimental" conditions, can be destroyed, in the sense that the higher structures of consciousness can be reduced and suppressed. In this rather specific sense totalitarian experiments can, indeed, destroy souls along with bodies.[49]

Arendt meant something more than this, however, for it is also true that some survivors of the camps did not "lose their souls" and that the soul-destroying intentions of the camp operators could be frustrated.[50] Arendt's argument did not consider these possibilities, and in the following paragraph she amplified her remarks:

> In other words, the success of totalitarianism is identical with a much more radical liquidation of freedom as a political and as a human reality than anything we have ever witnessed before. Under these conditions, it will be hardly consoling to cling to an unchangeable nature of man and conclude that either man himself is being destroyed or that freedom does not belong to man's essential capabilities. Historically, we know of man's nature only insofar as it has existence, and no realm of eternal essences will ever console us if man loses his essential capabilities.

Her first sentence indicated again that totalitarian terror was highly effective in degrading human beings and that degraded human beings

48. Arendt, "The Image of Hell."
49. In the contemporary words of Everett Chance, "when you hold all the cards, erasing faith is easier than you might think. All you have to do is erase the mind it inhabits." Everett was speaking specifically about drug "therapy." David James Duncan, *The Brothers K* (New York: Bantam, 1992), 605.
50. Solzhenitsyn's testimony in *The Gulag Archipelago* provides evidence of this, as do the psychological studies of Bruno Bettelheim. In this connection see Cooper, *End of History*, chap. 8.

may be said to have "lost" their souls. But then one wonders whether they would be lost for good or could be "found" again. Arendt's language was clearly preanalytic, not to say mythic. Of course, it conveyed a meaning; but it did not follow that the mythic meaning would be altered even under conditions of ecumenic totalitarian experiments.

Her second sentence, however, took a different tack. She seemed, first, to imply that Voegelin was mistaken (or naive or perhaps cowardly) to "cling" to his insupportable views at a time when totalitarian experimenters were at large and at work. They must be stopped! The consolation of Voegelin's philosophy, she warned, would be short. Second, the conclusion she drew, "that either man himself is being destroyed or that freedom does not belong to man's essential capabilities," was an obvious non sequitur. To recall Voegelin's commonsensical point: totalitarian murderers succeeded only in killing people, not in "changing human nature." Accordingly, her last sentence, that we know of man's nature only insofar as it has existence, must be met by the rather strict observation Voegelin made in his review: it is "a sentence which, if it has any sense at all, can only mean that the nature of man ceases to be the measure when some imbecile conceives the notion of changing it. The author seems to be impressed by the imbecile and is ready to forget about the nature of man, as well as about all human civilization that has been built on its understanding." To put the matter in Arendtian terms, we in fact know man's nature to the degree we do because it is *not* exhausted in human existence. It is also "nonexistent" or "eternal" so that, to use a Platonic image, human existence does indeed participate in a "realm of eternal essences." Arendt then ended her response by restating her fears and linked them to the fears of Montesquieu rather than to the jailer of the apostles.

Voegelin's reply summarized the problem in astringent methodological terms. "It is the question of essence in history, the question of how to delimit and define phenomena of the class of political movements." Arendt's procedure was to deal with facts and events and to describe "well distinguished complexes of phenomena of the type of 'totalitarianism'; and [she] is willing to accept such complexes as ultimate, essential units." Voegelin, however, rejected this procedure because the presentation of factual configurations was insufficient. The state of science was not quite so inadequate as to preclude moving from nominalistic taxonomy to realistic analysis. "The investigation inevitably will start from the phenomena, but the question of theoretically justifiable units in political science cannot be solved by accepting the units thrown up by the stream of history at their face value." What is required for a proper theoretical justification of the units of analysis depends on the rational elaboration of principles of relevance developed for the purpose—hence Voegelin's remark that Arendt might have benefited from Toynbee. "What a unit is," he said in closing, "will emerge when the principles furnished by philosophical anthropology are applied to historical materials. It then may happen that political movements, which on the scene of history are bitterly opposed to one another, will prove to be closely related on the level of essence."

There was a postscript to this controversy. In the fall of 1952 Carl Friedrich was in the process of organizing a conference on totalitarianism. He wrote Gurian asking for his suggestions regarding participants. Gurian replied that Voegelin should be added to the list because he "could contribute to the verification of the historical and ideological background of totalitarianism." Friedrich thanked him for his advice, but Voegelin was not invited.[51] In the spring of 1953, however, Friedrich wrote to Voegelin:

> I have read your critical discussion of Hannah Arendt's book with a great deal of interest. I am afraid, though, I cannot agree with you either about her or about totalitarianism. I very much deprecate efforts to explain totalitarianism by reference to some antecedent theory or intellectual movement, be it Hegel, Hobbes, Protestantism, or now, with you, "immanentism." The arguments for these positions are always very intriguing, because there usually is *some* connection, and to that extent our understanding is illumined. I am convinced, however, that a genuine understanding of totalitarianism must start with the essential novelty and uniqueness of the phenomenon, and I strongly agree with Arendt's emphasis upon this. When, however, she in turn picks upon certain antecedents and then claims that they "crystallize" into totalitarianism, she is constructing the type of "explanation" which I question. I have not yet read your new book, but I hope to do so soon.[52]

For Voegelin, Friedrich labored under misconceptions heavier in some respects than those of Arendt. He replied,

> Thanks for your kind letter, and for the attention that you give to a rather occasional effort.
>   Much as I appreciate disagreement as a spice of life, I am afraid, on the particular count that you raise we must forgo the pleasure of the condiment. I do not try to explain totalitarianism, or anything of the sort, by reference to

51. Harvard University Archives, HUG(FP) 17, 12, Box 34; Gurian to Friedrich, November 12, 1952; Friedrich to Gurian, December 9, 1952. The conference proceedings were subsequently published under the editorship of Friedrich as *Totalitarianism: Proceedings of a Conference Held at the American Academy of Arts and Sciences, March 1953.*

52. HI 13/16.

antecedent theories. The term "immanentism" is an ontological type concept which derives its validity from the principles of philosophical anthropology. It denotes, not a theory, but a state of the psyche. There can only arise the question whether the concept is well constructed, and whether totalitarian movements can be subsumed under it.

Obviously, there arises the further question whether immanentist movements have a history in the sense that the adumbrated state of the psyche is slowly unfolding its potentialities, and spreading socially, over longer periods of time. But that is a plain empirical question which must be decided by reference to the materials. Balthasar, in his *Prometheus*, tried to show such an unfolding in Germany since 1775; more recently, Albert Camus has made a similar attempt in his *L'Homme Révolté* for France, for the same period. In my "New Science of Politics" I have tried to show that for certain components of the essence "immanentism" one must extend the continuity (of experience, *not* theory) even to certain movements of the twelfth century (following Burdach).

In no case, of course, does the existence of long-range psychic and social processes abolish the uniqueness of each sub-movement in its historical place. Here again I quite agree with you. Either Hannah Arendt should have stuck to the contemporary totalitarian movements as unique and been satisfied with a description; or, if she wanted to be ambitious, and tackle the difficult problem of long-range processes, she should have boned up on the highly developed methodology for handling such problems. As the book stands, it is a rather messy performance, valuable only for its historical materials.[53]

In his letter to Friedrich, but also from the tone of his review, it was clear that Voegelin's admiration for Arendt was far from unconditional. In fact, Voegelin's unadorned view was that *Origins* was "a messy performance, valuable only for its historical materials." In a letter to Gurian that accompanied his final response to Arendt's reply he expressed disappointment, even irritation, with Arendt's refusal or inability to engage in a serious discussion.

I cannot say that I am particularly happy about this development. But I must say that the fault is mine. The good lady, in spite of all her merits, has, I am afraid, not quite understood the explosive implications of what she is doing in theory. I have committed the mistake of honoring her with a careful review, taking her seriously, and entering into the issues. One shouldn't do that; it has cost me a lot of time to disentangle the decisive points from a rambling context, and the time seems to have been wasted.[54]

53. HI 13/16. I have found no record of Friedrich's reply to Voegelin's remarks either in Voegelin's papers at HI or in Friedrich's papers at Harvard.

54. HI 15/27. According to Arendt, however, she and Voegelin were united in their hatred of ideology but divided on the grounds that she was not a Christian (HI 6/23). See also Voegelin to Gurian, May 5, 1951, University of Notre Dame, Archives, URP06/Box 6.

A few months later Arendt published a longer discussion of ideology. Both from the title, "Ideology and Terror: A Novel Form of Government,"[55] and from the content it is evident that Arendt had not passed from nominalistic taxonomy to realistic analysis, notwithstanding the many interesting observations her article contained. After it had appeared, and several months following Voegelin's expression of his initial response to Arendt's position in the letter to Gurian, he had an occasion to reflect on the whole episode with more detachment and irony.

Marshall McLuhan had read Voegelin's *The New Science of Politics,* on the advice of Cleanth Brooks, and provided Voegelin with a lengthy exposition of the presence of Gnosticism in the arts. He complained at one point, "A person feels like an awful slacker to have spent twenty years of study on an 'art' which turns out to be somebody else's *ritual.*" Voegelin replied that the most interesting thing "is the fact that you have hit on the problem at all." Rather than complain about losing twenty years of work, McLuhan should take heart from the realization that it takes time to "disengage ourselves from the creeds of a dying world (I have lost more years than I care to remember with neo-Kantianism and Phenomenology, before I dropped the nonsense)." Besides, Voegelin said, the time is not really lost: one finds the right way more surely by oneself than if someone else just pointed it out. More to the point, who wants a "hearing" from the dead anyhow? You begin to live "with the Exodus from the civilizational realm of the dead, and the beginning begins with the discovery of the world as the Desert—if I may use well-known symbols."

Voegelin ended his remarks with some strategic advice on how to deal with such individuals: simply "know so much more, in a plain technical sense, than the others that they will be afraid to molest you. In detail, you will probably soon discover what I have discovered, that it is a lot of fun to bait the ungodly when they get impertinent" and make them "hopping mad." As an example, Voegelin included "the reprint of a little controversy I had recently, that will illustrate what I meant by having 'fun' with the ideologues. The good lady who was the subject of my critique was so disturbed by it, that she wrote a whole article clarifying her point after a fashion in a more recent issue of the same periodical."[56]

The controversy with Arendt illustrated a number of points. First, Voegelin's attitude changed from one of irritation that his efforts at a rational exposition of the problems had been turned aside by Arendt

55. The article was included as a chapter in subsequent editions of *The Origins of Totalitarianism.*
56. HI 25/3.

to one of detached resignation: at the end of the day, about all that anyone can really do with individuals who will not or cannot discuss the important questions is gain whatever enjoyment one can from the experience of sheer disagreement. In the history of political philosophy, ironic resignation to the incomprehension of one's potential interlocutor is not without precedent.[57]

Second, while at the end of the controversy with Arendt, Voegelin's attitude concerning her position was similar to that he held toward the behaviorists, he reached his conclusion by a different route and over a longer time. To recall an earlier observation: with the behaviorists, there was simply nothing to learn. Their actual commitments to scientism made their pretensions to science a bad joke.

Third, Voegelin's attitude regarding the approach of Leo Strauss reflected the possibility of honest disagreement between scholars who understood and respected one another. It was, therefore, a relatively straightforward problem to analyze and present the issues that arose in Voegelin's review of *On Tyranny*. Likewise in considering the disagreement regarding Plato and Aristotle or the difference made by Christianity to the conceptualization of political philosophy, misunderstandings were kept to a minimum. For example, both parties agreed that historical sequence mattered much more to Voegelin than to Strauss. Accordingly, the continuity of spiritual politics from medieval paracletes to the several varieties of supermen of the nineteenth century was for Voegelin a positive center of intellectual activism, whereas for Strauss it was sufficient to know that the doctrines espoused by such persons could be adequately comprehended and criticized from the standpoint of classical political philosophy.[58] Using Voegelin's language in his review of Arendt, if the real division was between immanentist sectarians and religious and philosophical transcendentalists, then Voegelin was in closer agreement with Strauss than with Arendt: no reasonable person would argue that Strauss was an immanentist sectarian. He was, as Voegelin said of himself, a scholar who knew his business.[59]

With *The Origins of Totalitarianism* Voegelin directly encountered a problem that was discussed somewhat abstractly in Chapter 3. Thinkers such as Plato or Aquinas, or even Strauss, present their arguments

57. See *Apology* 35e–38c. On other occasions as well Voegelin indicated that the appropriate response when pressed to discuss ideologically deformed topics is a firm refusal, a wry smile, and some consolation from Heraclitus B107: "The eyes and ears are bad witnesses for a man whose soul is barbarous" (HI 17/2).

58. For a discussion of these and related questions see *Faith and Political Philosophy*, pt. III.

59. HI 26/31.

in technically competent philosophical or theoretical language. In the absence of such competence, if one is to make sense of an author's ideas and arguments, they must be referred to a rational standard or to a philosophical, theoretical, or scientific context that transcends the one employed by the author. With Arendt, as with Voltaire, discussed in Chapter 6, this means that one must develop an adequate terminological apparatus to deal with a defective or spiritually impoverished language. The example of Arendt indicates that there is no guarantee that the author in question will accept the correction offered.

To illustrate Voegelin's understanding of what a properly scientific treatment of these questions might entail, let us conclude this chapter with a brief recollection of Voegelin's discussion of one aspect of to-talitarian domination, Nazi race ideas, introduced above in Chapter 2.[60] Voegelin began by distinguishing the concept of race, which may or may not prove useful in anthropology, natural science, population biology, and so on, from the idea of race, the purpose of which is to create an image of a group as a unit—because, as observable phenomena, groups dissolve into the actions, purposes, and motivations of individuals. Second, he further distinguished the race idea as one of a series of body ideas that have developed historically and proposed a nominalistic taxonomy of his own around the three types: the body politic created by the Greek polis, the mystical body of Christ, and the race idea. Third, however, Voegelin moved beyond the classification of types toward a realistic analysis of the human spiritual essence expressed in or through the body ideas. As with the discussion of Egidius, Voegelin was particularly concerned with the historical development of modern political ideas from medieval ones—or rather, from the one-sided interpretation of medieval ones.

In the symbolism of the mystical body of Christ, two antecedent elements came together. First, the idea of like-mindedness, *homonoia,* re-ferred generally to the bond of sentiment among members of any type of community. Second, however, the symbolism of Christ as a second Adam established the genealogical principle of a common ancestor: Christ was, however, a common spiritual rather than corporeal ancestor of humanity. The *idea* of the mystical body, in the technical sense that Voegelin used the term, "is based on an interpretation of the persons of Christ and of man. Both [Christ and ordinary human beings] consist of the body, the *soma,* and the mind [or spirit], the *pneuma."* The ontological basis for the union of Christ and the human community of Christians is the assumption (or

---

60. Voegelin, "The Growth of the Race Idea."

confession of faith) that the nature of Christ is both fully human and fully divine. Accordingly, in their like-mindedness all members of the community, the *ekklesia*, participate in the spirit, the *pneuma*, of Christ, which, being also fully divine, is centered beyond the range of ordinary earthly experience. That is, the unifying force, the ontologically real bond of the *ekklesia*, is the divine and world-transcendent personality of Christ. Voegelin drew a contrast with pre-Christian possessions by spirits (or demons), which were usually confined to a single other person; the fullness, the *pleroma*, of the spirit of Christ, however, meant that it may live in an indefinite number of others, beginning "when two or three are gathered together" in Christ's name, to use the formula of the Book of Common Prayer. With the emphasis on the *mystical* body, we may call this the more pneumatic account of the construction of the Christian community.

A second, and balancing, account, which lays the emphasis on the mystical *body* and which we may call the more somatic one, symbolizes Christ as "the head of the body, the *ekklesia*" (Col. 1:18). The point of this second version is to avert the obvious danger that the Christian community might consider that it was simply a collection of like-minded individuals. By analogy with the human body, the head does not exist apart from the body; by the same token, the relationship between head and body must be specified. Paul clarified this problem by means of the diversification of the one spirit of Christ into the *charismata*, the divine gifts, that determine the status and calling of the several members of the one body. In 1 Cor. 12, for example, Saint Paul begins by considering the diversities of the *charismata* but then remarks:

> But all these [gifts] worketh that one and selfsame Spirit, dividing to every man severally as he will. For as the body is one, and hath many members, and all the members of that one body, being many, are one body: so also is Christ. For by one Spirit are we all baptized into one body, whether we be Jews or Gentiles, whether we be bond or free; and have been all made to drink into one Spirit. For the body is not one member, but many. (1 Cor. 12:11–14)

As was mentioned above in the discussion of Egidius, the Pauline balance consists in the infusion of the more somatic account with the specifically Christian meaning expressed through the Christological interpretation of like-mindedness, which is to say, through what we have called the more pneumatic account. With the fragmentation of medieval Christian universalism into particular national or other communities, the more somatic interpretation, "which is most intimately dependent on the Christology, is referred to the background while the idea of the diversification of a spiritual unit into spiritual functions is transferred to spiritual substances other than the *pneuma* of Christ," such as, for example, the nation.

In other words, when the emphasis shifts from a balance of somatic and pneumatic to a heavily skewed pneumatic interpretation of community, the way is opened "for a reconstruction of the spiritual meaning of community along lines diverging from the Christian." The development was not toward a recovery of the polis symbolism or of the like-mindedness of the empire of Alexander the Great, but in a direction unconnected to symbols of family, kinship, or bloodline. Specifically, the fragmentation or particularization of the Christian community substituted for Christological like-mindedness the like-mindedness of particular national communities, each endowed with "a more or less systematized body of symbolic doctrine asserting the superior qualities of the several national spirits and their consequent particular mission in history." The new parochial symbolism, therefore, presupposes the Christian form of the mystical body and simply replaces the Christological content, substance, and reality with something else. Moreover, because these new communities are fragments of a Christian community, "they are capable of evolving almost any new set of symbols out of elements which are offered by the civilizational situation of the moment." Such "elements" might include economic factors, as in the case of the Bolsheviks, or biological ones, as in the case of the Nazis. In either instance, these real but fragmentary factors are endowed with an imaginary spiritual meaning that, as a political idea, can serve as an image to unite a group and motivate it to act.

We need not provide a detailed account of the changes from the medieval Christian symbols and experiences that, following Bergson, Voegelin called "open" to the modern intramundane or "closed" equivalents in order to understand what a properly scientific account of the dynamics of the changes entailed: "The formerly open group with spiritual threads running from every single member beyond the earthly reality into another ontological realm closes by the transfer of the center from the beyond into the very community itself."[61] The actual content of the symbolism of closure has, in turn, varied across the range of political societies. As a mere matter of fact, racial symbolism (in 1940) was more acceptable in Germany than in France or Britain. In order to account for this fact, Voegelin introduced historical considerations similar to those that marked a point of major divergence with Strauss.

Voegelin made the point in different contexts throughout his scholarly life, and we will encounter it again in the course of this study. In the

---

61. Ibid., 303. The details were in fact summarized in the article and set out at greater length in *The History of the Race Idea* and *Race and State*. Regarding the latter book, Arendt said it was "the best historical account of race-thinking in the pattern of a 'history of ideas'" (*Origins*, 158).

formulation of 1940, he used the phrase "the structure of institutions and ideas" to describe what might be called a three-dimensional type-construct. A two-dimensional categorization is familiar from Aristotle's *Politics*. Good and bad versions of rule by the one, the few, and the many (*Politics* 1279a25) can be plotted on a bivariate table. Similar categorizations can be drawn up for the national state or the Western democracy or the authoritarian state. These two-dimensional type-categories neglect, however, the importance of "the relative time position of the characteristics" and so neglect as well the "relative historical weight" of the various constituent elements of, for example, the category of regime classified as a national democracy.

An example may clarify Voegelin's point. In order to understand the French national democracy, one must not only look to the juridical construction of the French state but also bear in mind that the political unit of France was founded during late medieval times and to all intents and purposes was well established by the mid-seventeenth century. The bourgeois and democratic revolutions, which began in the eighteenth century, took place within a solid administrative structure established over the preceding centuries. Moreover, the political ideas that animated French society during the eighteenth-century revolutions were eighteenth-century ideas of the rights of man, not ideas of race or class.

In contrast, a country such as Germany or Italy may belong to the same two-dimensional juridical type as France; indeed, it may even have a constitution that is modeled on the constitution of France. At the same time, however, it may "have a perfectly different time structure when the fixation of the territory and political independence follow the awakening of national consciousness of the bourgeois stratum of society, instead of preceding it, as in the case in Germany and Italy, and in the Central and Eastern European states." National groups attaining statehood without the weight of centuries to provide stability to the regime are apt to have different political ideas than did the eighteenth-century French who established the legal state that was subsequently copied elsewhere.

Specifically, the increased virulence of totalitarian domination in Italy, Germany, and Russia was, in Voegelin's view, "strictly determined by the time structure of their democratic periods." In Italy the period of liberal republicanism preceded national unification by decades; in Germany national unification coincided with the Prussian wars, which were conducted independently of the liberal republicanism of the 1840s. "And the totalitarian revolution in Russia is probably the most complete one because the effective liberal revolution preceded the communistic one only by a few months." A relatively long duration of a liberal democratic regime may act as a kind of inoculation against the totalitarian "virus."

Using less metaphorical language, Voegelin observed that

> racial symbolism has comparatively little chance in a society which has gone
> through an eighteenth century revolution, because the collective element of
> racialism is hardly compatible with the belief in the value of the sovereign
> person and the indestructible soul, and its rights and liberties; and because the
> biological determinism is incompatible with the idea of reason as a spiritual
> substance independent of the qualities of the body which houses it.

At the same time, however, such symbols are not simply self-evident.
Even the American Declaration of Independence begins with the affirmation "*We* hold these truths to be self-evident." Accordingly, "whatever
criticism can be launched rightly against the race symbolism under moral
and religious aspects, as an interpretation of reality the idea that men
are different, and that their differences may be due to differences in
their biological structure, is not more unrealistic than the idea that all
men are equal." Moreover, in a revolutionary upheaval the authority of
established symbols is, practically by definition, highly impaired so that
whatever symbols have currency are likely to prevail.

In the context of the totalitarian revolutions of the twentieth century, pride of place must go to what Voegelin here identified as "the
superstition of science," or scientism, to use the terminology of the last
chapter. Likewise the "positivist destruction of science" may be intelligibly linked to totalitarian domination with the observation that the
eclipse of an awareness, even among scholars, that social symbols create
theological and metaphysical problems, not quantitative and phenomenal ones, constitutes the background for the introduction of new social
symbols, expressing specific spiritual experiences, under the guise of
"science." This is why Bolsheviks called themselves "scientific socialists"
and revered Marx as the founder of scientific socialism and also why
Nazis considered their "race theories" to be scientific.

One of Arendt's insights regarding totalitarian domination is that the
regime, if that is the correct word, is less a structure than a movement,
which means that it "can have only a direction, and that any form of
legal or governmental structure can only be a handicap to a movement
which is being propelled with increasing speed in a certain direction."[62]
Voegelin offered his own account of the phenomenon:

> when science "progresses" farther and new symbols evolve on the basis of
> new materials, the older ones cannot defend themselves by the authority
> of a religious belief of intrinsic value, but they are exposed to attack and

---

62. Arendt, *Origins*, 388.

dissolution on the level of their superstition. The history of symbols during the last century offers to a detached view the spectacle of a somewhat hectic sequence of scientific fads.

Voegelin's observation regarding the sequence of scientific fads needs to be distinguished from the progress of genuine science. He did, after all, criticize Arendt for not being up-to-date in her choice of analytic instruments, and urged her to take a look at Toynbee. On the other hand, Strauss's answer to the problem of scientism or of "scientific fads" was to consider it as an aspect of historicism, the self-refuting nature of which can be demonstrated easily enough. In more positive terms, Straussian political science is based on the philosophical anthropology of the classical thinkers. For Voegelin, however, historicity was a fundamental dimension of human existence. This is why he was able to dismiss Aristotle's classification of regimes as no longer relevant to the analysis of contemporary political problems, whereas Strauss considered such a position premature, to say the least.

In this chapter we have seen in outline how Voegelin's political science sought to incorporate the historically contingent with the nonhistorical or essential. The following chapters will discuss the argument in detail, and we shall return to the question of historicity in Chapter 10.

5

Philosophical
Anthropology

———

On several occasions in the previous chapters, we drew attention to the fact that one of the central criteria by which Voegelin judged the merit of a text was the adequacy of the philosophical anthropology developed in it or presupposed by its author. Occasionally, Voegelin used the term *idea of man* to indicate the relationship of human being "to the realms of nature (organic, plant, and animal life) as well as to the source of all things, man's metaphysical origin as well as his physical, psychic, and spiritual origins in the world, the forces and powers that move man and that he moves, the fundamental trends and laws of his biological, psychic, cultural and social evolution, along with their essential capabilities and realities."[1]

In his review of Cairns's *Theory of Legal Science*, for example, Voegelin referred to the same range of topics as was just indicated in the quotation from Scheler. The context was one of establishing criteria of relevance. "The question of relevance and of the principle of selection is the crucial question with regard to the structure of social science," Voegelin said. But on this topic, we recall, Cairns's book was silent. "And it is silent for the good reason that Mr. Cairns has no overt philosophy of man and of his place in the society and the world at large that could tell him what is relevant in the world of man and society; the whole branch of knowledge that goes today under the name of philosophical anthropology is non-existent for the author." This was a grave omission, as Voegelin pointed out, because "unless we have an idea of man, we have no frame of reference for the designation of human phenomena as relevant or irrelevant. Man is engaged in the creation of social order physically, biologically, psychologically, intellectually, and spiritually."[2] Moreover, some of these engagements offer the opportunity for the formulation of more or less

1. Max Scheler, *Philosophical Perspectives*, trans. O. A. Haac, 65.
2. Voegelin, "The Theory of Legal Science," *CW*, 27:101.

general rules, but only on the basis of a frame of reference that establishes criteria of relevance.

Similar arguments were made in the course of Voegelin's analysis of other texts, methods, and approaches. Hovering always in the background was the historical context that Voegelin described as the era of postivistic destructiveness of science, which included philosophical anthropology understood, in turn, as part of a general ontology. A philosophical anthropology, therefore, would serve the minimal purpose of establishing the relationship between physical, biological, intellectual, and other activities insofar as such activities and their relationship influence the establishment of social order. This was why Voegelin was inclined to rank the work of a scholar such as Strauss much higher than that of Brecht or Arendt. Notwithstanding his reservations regarding Strauss's unqualified commitment to classical political philosophy, one at least found in Plato and Aristotle a coherent and extensive "theory of man." It was clear as well that Strauss made good use of classical anthropology in his analysis of the comparatively defective anthropologies he associated with "modern" political thinking.[3]

The importance of philosophical anthropology in the development of Voegelinian political science is that it integrated what conventionally would be called philosophy of history and philosophy of consciousness. In this chapter we are concerned chiefly with Voegelin's philosophy of consciousness—or rather, with his philosophy of consciousness as it existed in the mid-1940s. The implication of the last phrase is that Voegelin's philosophy of consciousness changed over the years; and it did. The necessity of such changes, furthermore, was an integral part of Voegelin's philosophy of history. This was indicated in a summary way in the famous opening sentence of *The New Science of Politics:* "The existence of man in political society is historical existence; and a theory of politics, if it penetrates to principles, must at the same time be a theory of history." As we shall see below, it was indicated more extensively in the foreword to *Anamnesis.*

Voegelin provided an account of the development of his philosophy of consciousness between the mid-1940s and the mid-1960s in a letter to his friend Robert Heilman, dated June 19, 1966.[4] The letter discussed some of the difficulties Voegelin was experiencing in the administration of the Political Science Institute in Munich, but most of it was devoted to a summary of the structure of his recently published book, *Anamnesis,*

---

3. "Modern" is in quotation marks because, as was indicated in the last chapter, it meant something different for Strauss than for Voegelin.

4. HI 17/9. Subsequent quotation in the text is from this source.

and to an account of his motives for writing it. Voegelin wrote the book, he said, for three reasons. First, no one in Germany read the books he had written in English, and as professor of political science in a chair previously held by Max Weber, and as director of the Political Science Institute, "I had to publish a book in German sometime as a sort of public obligation." Second, he had to work through a number of problems before he could complete *Order and History*, and these essays formed a coherent set of what might be called "working papers," or specialized studies, as he called them. "Third, however, and most important, I wanted to experiment with a new literary form in philosophy."

In the course of explaining what he meant by a new literary form, Voegelin made some very important remarks regarding the way he understood the development of his own work. He began with the observation that Heraclitus was "the first thinker to identify philosophy as an exploration of the psyche" or of consciousness. That kind of exegesis remained the centerpiece of philosophy, though it had been "overlaid" by a secondary meaning, namely "communicating the results of exegesis as well as its speculative consequences." The history of philosophy, he said, has moved between exegesis of consciousness and dogmatic summary of results. The latter task can be formulated as a system, a deduction from given premises, or a discursive exposition of problems to be found in the philosophical literature, but the former cannot: "original exegesis of consciousness," Voegelin said,

> can proceed only by the form of direct observation and meditative tracing of the structure of the psyche. Moreover, this structure is not a given to be described by any means of propositions, but [is] a process of the psyche itself that has to find its language symbols as it proceeds. And finally, the self-interpretation of consciousness cannot be done once for all, but is a process in the life-time of a human being. From these peculiarities stem the literary problems.

Heraclitus, for example, dealt with the literary problem by means of aphorism, whereas Christian meditation used the form of the *via negativa*, as did Descartes.

More than the choice of a literary form is involved, however, because the content of the meditation is bound to be shaped by the contingencies of the reigning orthodoxy. Every particular, concrete exegesis of consciousness "is undertaken historically in opposition to the prevalent dogmatism of the time." Because the exegesis is an attempt to recover or recollect "the human condition revealing itself in consciousness," there will be an inevitable moment of resistance to the dogmatic "debris of opaque symbols." On the one hand, this means the resistance will be colored by the historically accidental contents of the dogma that the exegesis of consciousness seeks to dissolve; on the other, it means that one cannot simply appropriate an earlier exegesis; on the contrary, it is necessary to begin with the existing and historically current "obstacles to human self-understanding." Chief among these obstacles was positivism, but it was not the only one.

So far as the new literary form of *Anamnesis* is concerned, Voegelin used neither the Heraclitian aphorism nor the *via negativa;* it was neither pre-Socratic, nor classic, nor Christian, though it had "certain affinities to the mysticism of Plotinus, and Dionysius Areopagitica, not to forget the Cloud of Unknowing."

> In my special case, I proceeded in the following manner: Parts I and III of the book contain two meditative exercises of about 75 pp. each. The first one I went through and wrote down in September–November 1943; the last one, in the second half of 1965. The first one, in Baton Rouge, was the breakthrough by which I recovered consciousness from the current theories of consciousness, specifically from Phaenomenology. The second one, begins as a rethinking of the Aristotelian exegesis of consciousness (in *Met.* I and II), and then expands into new areas of consciousness that had not come within the ken of classic philosophy but must be explored now, in order to clear consciousness of the above-mentioned dogmatism. Between the two meditations, I have placed, under the title "Experience and History," eight studies which demonstrate how the historical phenomena of order give rise to the type of analysis which culminates in the meditative exploration of consciousness. Hence, the whole book is held together by a double movement of empiricism: (1) the movement that runs from the historical phenomena of order to the structure of consciousness in which they originate, and (2) the movement that runs from the analysis of consciousness to the phenomena of order inasmuch as the structure of consciousness is the instrument of interpretation for the historical phenomena.

Voegelin's formulation of what he was undertaking to do in *Anamnesis* is a late formulation. Indeed, the "double movement" of which he spoke in the concluding sentence could easily be construed as a summary of his own understanding of Schelling's philosophy of consciousness and philosophy of history. Most of the present analysis of Voegelin's understanding of the foundations of political science focuses on the historical phenomena of order. In a 1966 letter to Dante Germino, Voegelin described the studies reproduced as part II of *Anamnesis* as a selection "from a mountain of studies about ten times what has been published, the selection being made under the aspect of bringing out the high-points of anamnetic reconstruction of a theory of consciousness, which happens to be the centerpiece of political science."[5] In the following chapters we will explore several sectors of the "mountain of studies," but first we will consider Voegelin's account of the centerpiece, the "instrument of interpretation for the historical phenomena" as it existed in 1943.[6]

We indicated above that the minimal purpose of philosophical anthropology is to establish the relationship among the physical, biological, psychological, intellectual, and spiritual "engagements" of human beings as they establish and maintain social and political order. This minimal purpose accords with the surface meaning of the term, namely the philosophical account of the full amplitude of human being, of "man" generically understood. It refers, therefore, to what Voegelin called a "branch of knowledge" that has existed at least from a time prior to the installation of the inscription over the temple to Apollo at Delphi that read *gnothi seauton*, know thyself, and that Voegelin identified as the exploration of the psyche. It refers as well to the ancillary reports on the results of the exploration. The accent, as Voegelin indicated, was heavily on this second meaning when the term was introduced in the late sixteenth century, by Otto Casmann. According to Casmann it referred to the *doctrina geminae naturae humanae*, the account of the dual nature of human being.[7] Human being was dual in the sense that it was both physical or material and spiritual or psychological, and philosophical anthropology was an account or, in Voegelin's language, a report of that nature. Kant subsequently gave the term further currency, and it has remained an element in philosophical discussions, especially in Germany, ever since.

Our present concern, however, is with the development of philosophical anthropology in the twentieth century. We begin with a consideration of philosophical anthropology as report, not meditation. Unlike earlier philosophical reports of human being, contemporary philosophical anthropology has not had the field to itself. Indeed, one may say that

5. HI 14/14. In fact, he said as much in the foreword to *Anamnesis: Zur Theorie der Geschichte und Politik*, 7–8.

6. That is, we will ignore Voegelin's analysis of consciousness as it was achieved in the mid-1960s, after his major studies of the historical phenomena had been completed. See, however, Kenneth Keulman, *The Balance of Consciousness*; Eugene Webb, *Philosophers of Consciousness*, chap. 3; Glenn Hughes, *Mystery and Myth in the Philosophy of Eric Voegelin*, chap. 1; Michael P. Morrissey, *Consciousness and Transcendence: The Theology of Eric Voegelin*; John J. Ranieri, *Eric Voegelin and the Good Society*, chaps. 1–2.

7. Casmann, *Psychologica anthropologica* (Hannover, 1594); *Secunda Pars anthropologicae* (Hannover, 1596).

it sprang into being in part as a response to the specialized human sciences or social sciences: linguistics, psychology, sociology, cultural anthropology, economics, and political science. Even though it was re- vived at the same time as the social sciences were developed, the re- lationship of philosophical anthropology to them has not always been clearly understood or defined. Each social science, having accumulated enormous amounts of information and having developed logically co- herent models within which that information could be understood, saw itself as autonomous not merely with respect to other social sciences but with respect to philosophical anthropology as well. This opinion was so self-evident to Cairns, for example, that, as was mentioned earlier, he was apparently unaware of the significance of Voegelin's critical remarks.[8]

It is for this reason that contemporary accounts of philosophical an- thropology emphasize the importance of a "coordinating discipline" necessary to repair the "loss of center" at the heart of the several so- cial sciences.[9] The great desideratum, according to this argument, is for a "unified concept of man" that would integrate the findings of the specialized social sciences into a coherent whole. The problem, in fact, is rather more complex. Considering only the well-known historical facts, behind the proliferation of the social sciences lies the separation of natural science from theology and philosophy, which was still a source of concern for Kant. Even more fundamental was the late medieval separation of theology from philosophy, understood now to include the subject matter studied by natural science. Accompanying this dogmatic distinction between reason and revelation and the triumph of science un- derstood as the analysis of natural phenomena was a countermovement, at least in political science, that rejected a phenomenalist interpretation of politics in terms of calculative reason, rational action, contract, and consent. Such an interpretative context was seen to be little more than a historical contingency reflecting the collective self-understanding of the industrial bourgeoisie. Vico, for example, argued that ages of reason were late developments in a civilizational cycle, not early ones, which raised the question: what are the elements in the nature of man that are responsible for political order or human culture prior to the achieve- ment of rational self-awareness? The countermovement to phenomenal- ist rationality and scientism consisted in an exploration and analysis of the natural conditions of human being, understood either in terms of

8. See Cairns, "Comment," *Louisiana Law Review* 4 (1942): 571–72.
9. H. O. Pappé, "Philosophical Anthropology," in *Encyclopedia of Philosophy* (New York: Macmillan, 1972).

external nature or in terms of internal nature, which is to say, in terms of the unconscious and its expression by nonrational and mythic ritual, by symbols, stories, cultic actions, and so on. More broadly, therefore, one might characterize philosophical anthropology as being the consequence of a desire to understand the whole of human being, including that which is conventionally separated out from positivist social science as irrational "religion" and "metaphysics."

According to Michael Landmann, three additional factors contributed to the reformulation of philosophical anthropology during the 1920s and 1930s. First was a dissatisfaction with the central place of epistemology in philosophy, which had already found a prewar expression in the *Lebensphilosophie* of Dilthey. Second was the phenomenological concern for the perceptual experience and reflective account of the "things themselves," as distinct from epistemologically defined objects of science. These first two additional considerations require of philosophical anthropology that a theory of consciousness also be formulated. Third was a general sense of crisis, which also had a prewar history, and a corresponding desire to find principles by which that crisis might be understood.[10] The development of philosophical anthropology, therefore, illustrated a more general observation made by Voegelin in the introduction to *The New Science of Politics:* "In an hour of crisis, when the order of a society flounders and disintegrates, the fundamental problems of political existence in history are more apt to come into view than in periods of comparative stability."[11] Philosophical anthropology, then, in its aspiration to be a foundation for the social sciences, may be understood as a means of comprehending, and thereby coming to terms with, the general sense of crisis.[12] Of the four men who may be said to have initiated and carried through the revival of philosophical anthropology, Helmuth Plessner, Adolf Portmann, Arnold Gehlen, and Max Scheler, it was the last named whose work, as David J. Levy said, formed "a point of departure" for Voegelin's own efforts.[13]

Scheler was not the only source of philosophical anthropology upon whom Voegelin drew, and Voegelin was hardly the only political scientist

10. Landmann, *Philosophical Anthropology,* trans. D. J. Parent (Philadelphia: Westminster, 1974), 55–59.

11. *NSP,* 1–2.

12. In 1936 Voegelin gave a course at the University of Vienna with the title "Philosophical Anthropology as Foundational Science (*Grundwissenschaft*)," HI 55/8.

13. Levy, *Political Order: Philosophical Anthropology, Modernity, and the Challenge of Ideology,* vii. See also Jürgen Gebhardt, "Eric Voegelin und die neuere Entwicklung der Geisteswissenschaften."

upon whom Scheler had an impact. Voegelin himself has indicated in his *Autobiographical Reflections* several of the people who "influenced" him. Our interest here, however, is in providing an analysis of the structure of Voegelin's political science, not in tracing the genesis of his arguments (which is, in any event, a rather pointless exercise).[14]

Scheler argued, as did many of his contemporaries, from the basis of Casmann's postulate of a "dual nature" to human being, but he modified it considerably in light of subsequent philosophical arguments and scientific discoveries. When God was understood literally and dogmatically to have made the world and its creatures differentiated as to kind, it made sense to discuss human nature as having constant, explicit, and permanent attributes. Historical changes were, by this understanding, contingent actualizations of the essential and unchanging attributes of human being. Under the pressure of phenomenalist theories of evolution, the commonsense evidence of social and technological change, and the development of "process" as a central theological and philosophical category, the understanding of human nature as a fixed, essential, finite attribute had been challenged.[15] In its place a new complex of questions has arisen, centered, as the title of Scheler's book indicated, on "the place of human beings in the cosmos."[16]

Like rocks and trees and dogs, human beings are physical beings; like trees and dogs, human living beings are alive beings; like dogs, human beings are animal beings. Commonsense distinctions of the modes of dependence upon, and orientation within, the cosmos indicated to Scheler a hierarchy of beings; the *differentia specifica* of human being was identified by him as "spirit." Spiritual being is, unlike animal being, not simply subject to the environment or to a genetically transmitted inheritance of instincts and behavioral repertoires. "Instead, it is 'free

14. See Voegelin, *Autobiographical Reflections*, chaps. 3–6, and Stephen Frederick Schneck, *Person and Polis: Max Scheler's Personalism as Political Theory*, 6. In a 1973 letter to Russell Nieli, Voegelin mentioned Cohen, Rickert, Husserl, Stefan George, French neo-Thomism, Jaspers, Heidegger, Hegel, Alfred Weber, and Toynbee as "influences" (HI 27/12).

15. Hannah Arendt's objection to Voegelin's summary description of a nature as what makes a thing a thing probably had this development of philosophy in mind; for Voegelin, however, philosophy as the communication of the results of the philosopher's exegesis of consciousness was a secondary matter. Human nature, in the sense of a consciousness seeking the exegesis of itself, obviously could not change, though the historically contingent formulations that gave expression to that exegesis just as obviously could.

16. The German title of *Man's Place in Nature* was *Die Stellung des Menschen im Kosmos*. Voegelin acquired a copy of this book the year it was published, 1928. Reference is to the English translation by Hans Meyerhoff.

from the environment' or, as we shall say, 'open to the world.' "[17] The human ability, as Scheler said, to say "no" to the immediate environment sustains the capacity to objectify it, to place a distance between man and nature so as to represent it and name it through signs, and finally to act into nature and redirect the causal connections of the cosmos to serve human purpose. As Helmut Plessner once put it, man does not just live his life, he leads it. This does not mean that human beings are boundlessly protean or that the cosmos is plastic (though human beings sometimes act as if this were so). On the contrary, the cosmos is in being prior to acts of human consciousness that explore its meaning: as Spinoza said, reality resists consciousness. The real mountain is an obstacle to be climbed; in peril halfway up, it is of no avail to imagine oneself at the summit or safely home in bed.

In Voegelin's copy of Scheler's book is a note that summarizes the argument made so far.[18] The first part is reproduced below:

Transcendental being

Human [being]	pragmatic understanding
	speech
	reason — creation of ideas
	spirit: anxiety, love, guilt, commitment, repentance,
	joy, rebellion, defiance
Animal [being]	motility
	instinct
	pragmatic intelligence
	communication
	playfulness (Huizinga)
Vegetative [being]	life, metabolism, reproduction regeneration, birth and
	death, waking and sleeping
	instinct: heliotropism
Inorganic [being]	atomic form, etc.

The list represents a hierarchy of being from physical or natural being to the being that is transcendent to human being.

The great insight of Scheler and of the other philosophical anthropologists was to have recovered a systematic awareness of this hierarchy

17. Scheler, *Man's Place*, 37. The distinction between environment, *Umwelt*, and world, *Welt* (or sometimes, *Lebenswelt*, life-world or lived world), is central to phenomenology. It was initially introduced as a technical term by Jacob von Uexkuell, upon whose work several philosophical anthropologists as well as phenomenologists have drawn.

18. The copy is in Voegelin's library at the University of Erlangen.

of being. The second part of Voegelin's note indicates his own reflective understanding of the significance of this hierarchy:

Principles of the Order of Being

1. ground or foundation
2. formation
3. participation
4. consubstantiality
5. independence (autonomy)
6. partial causality

These "principles" are even more tersely stated than the hierarchy set out in the first part. The meaning, however, seems to be tolerably clear. The order expressed in the hierarchy of being is summarized by means of the six interdependent principles.

Consider the following example: it is as physical beings that humans fall off mountains and crash to the valley floor like rocks; as animal beings, humans climb to the summit like mountain goats or mountain lions; as spiritual beings they conquer the summit or hear the voice of God when they get there, or are defeated or hear only the wind. Partial causality means that, to keep with this example, it is not enough to have courage and determination; one must also have (or better, be) a body that is physically capable of making the climb. Likewise and reciprocally, it is not enough simply to be physically capable of climbing a mountain, one must have the necessary commitment as well. Or again, one must be sufficiently autonomous with respect to the mountain to be able to consider climbing it, which in turn enables an alpinist to conquer it, unlike a mountain goat, who is simply capable of climbing it; but also human and mountain being are sufficiently consubstantial that the mountain is both physically there in reality and spiritually there as a challenge that in turn may defeat the climber.

In general one may say that philosophical anthropology integrates several modes of human experience rather than splits them apart into familiar dichotomies of culture and nature, mind and matter, heredity and environment, and so on. Such dichotomies express the "dual nature" of human being. They are not, therefore, independent entities suitable for analytic treatment. The symbol *dual nature*, in contrast, may be said to have a genuine ontological status and, as was noted in Chapter 4, can be the subject matter of a realistic theory.

It would be a philosophical error, therefore, to attempt to reduce the ontological reality, expressed in the symbol *dual nature*, to one or another of its constituent elements. Such one-sided accounts are, however, a comparatively late development in human history. For centuries prior to the triumph of modern phenomenalist natural science, the cosmos was understood in terms of life and its purposes. And, as Hans Jonas once remarked, it is far more evident that the world is filled with life than that it is made of inanimate "matter."[19]

A second insight from philosophical anthropology, then, is to caution against any kind of reductionism. A third part to Voegelin's note indicates the errors to be avoided:

Negative: no radical reduction is possible
no complete causality from above or below

One conclusion, therefore, is that reductionist theories that argue that x is really y must be fundamentally false insofar as they ignore both the individual and particular content of phenomena and the order of being. In terms of philosophical anthropology, it is as great a mistake to say that earth, wind, and matter are filled with life as it is to say that the meaning of life is that it is but a consequence of chance and necessity and the mutually interchangeable attributes of matter and energy.

This does not mean that all social scientists are of the opinion that the phenomena they study are really explicable in terms of physics. On the contrary, sociobiologists resist the claims of biologists just as sociologists resist the claims of sociobiologists; for that matter, biologists resist the reductionism of biochemists, and so on. Moreover, they all have effective enough arguments at their disposal to do so. However, defense of specialized sciences by scientific specialists is to be distinguished from justification in principle. The latter, as Levy observed, requires "an ontology that recognizes the relative autonomy of the various strata of being and justifies this recognition by rational argument."[20] Such an ontology is precisely what the philosophical anthropologists aimed at providing. The imagery and details of the several arguments differ, but all begin with a phenomenology that describes the ways in which reality is experienced and known by humans.[21] In the language employed

19. Jonas, *The Phenomenon of Life: Toward a Philosophical Biology*, 7–8.
20. Levy, *Political Order*, 17.
21. The formulation in the introduction to *OH*, vol. 1, of the quaternarian structure of being, a structure that excluded any ontological progress or regress but that, on the contrary, drew attention to a historical and more or less articulate apprehension, was clearly based on the philosophical anthropological work of Scheler and his contemporaries.

earlier, philosophical anthropology is required by its own internal logic to elaborate a philosophy of consciousness.

Scheler discussed the subject matter indicated by the term *philosophy of consciousness* under the category of "spirit." Human spirit opens human being to the world, enables man to make of it an object, and so on. Animals lack this potential, he said, and so are incapable of "concentrating" their intelligence in such a way as to achieve self-consciousness, "by which is meant the consciousness that the spiritual center has of itself." The human structures of self-consciousness and the capacity to objectify can account for a number of specifically human characteristics such as a sense of homogeneous space and of transcendence of the world as given. Most important, however, is that the center from which these spiritual acts are performed is not itself part of the world that is objectified as body, psyche, world, and so forth. Introspection, for example, can objectify acts of the psyche as taking place "in" time, but the intentionality that makes such acts appear to reflective consciousness, namely the spiritual act, cannot be so objectified. Instead, Scheler said, we "collect" ourselves as "persons." For the same reasons, other human beings cannot be objectified and at the same time remain persons. As persons they can be discerned only by love, by a commitment to another as irreplaceable.[22]

A final implication of Scheler's philosophy of consciousness must be noted. The structure of human nature was symbolized by the dichotomy of life and spirit. The specific character of the spirit was its capacity to objectify the world and its own psychophysical nature; but once human consciousness has done this, it "must also encounter the completely formal idea of an infinite absolute Being beyond this world." Once having separated themselves from nature and having transfigured it into an imaginative object, human beings are compelled to ask: where is my place in the cosmos? According to Scheler such questioning "belongs to his essence and constitutes the very act of becoming a man." Having discovered himself as spiritual, man can no longer pretend to be simply part of the world precisely because spiritual experience is accompanied by the insight and awareness that one's person transcends the forms of worldly being, namely space and time. Accordingly, there can be no answer to the question just raised that takes the form: man's place in the cosmos is this or that. Instead, the discovery that such answers are unavailable prompts further questions that express the experience of a consciousness of spiritual insight. The process is expressed in the classic questions of Leibniz: Why is there something and not nothing? Why is something as it is, and not different? These questions express

22. Scheler, *Man's Place*, 40, 47–48.

for both Scheler and Leibniz a (formal) consciousness of God, "where God is to be conceived as a being in itself (*causa sui*) to whom we attribute the predicate 'holy,' capable of manifesting itself in a thousand different ways."[23] The conclusion of Scheler's argument was that the process by which human beings seek to understand themselves leads to a consciousness of theophany. To use the language of Voegelin, in seeking to understand themselves, human beings become aware of the world-transcendent being, which they symbolize as "holy." Or, as he said in his note in Scheler's book on "Principles of the Order of Being," humans participate through spiritual formation in the ground or foundation of being.

Although neither Voegelin nor Scheler discussed the question in this context, it may be useful to recall Voegelin's distinction between philosophy as an exploration of consciousness and as a literary report on the results of the exploration. Terms such as *holy* or *foundation of being* fully make sense only within a meditative process in consciousness—within the act of exploration, as Voegelin put it. They should not, therefore, be misconstrued as being limited to abstract speculation or to the logical elaboration of a set of implications that may be derived from a more or less arbitrary hypothesis.

Scheler concluded his argument in *Man's Place* by distinguishing two attitudes possible in the face of the discovery that the cosmos was contingent and that one's own spiritual personality transcended it. One "could pause in wonder (*thaumazein*) and then set his spirit in motion to grasp the Absolute and to become a part of it," which Scheler symbolized by the term *metaphysics.* Alternatively one could "yield to the irresistible urge for safety or protection, not only for himself, but primarily for the group as a whole," which he identified with "religion."[24] Scheler's language in making this distinction was needlessly aggressive, though in principle the literary formulation of his meditative exploration of the psyche, namely that a coherent account of human being was required to include an account of the relationship of human being to the cosmic-transcendent ground of being, was accepted by Voegelin.

In addition to a philosophy of consciousness we indicated earlier that philosophical anthropology was led, by its own internal logic, to consider and develop a philosophy of history. This is a large and complex topic by itself and is discussed at length in the following chapters. Here we will indicate only the connection between philosophy of consciousness and philosophy of history. It may be brought to light by recollecting Scheler's

23. Ibid., 88, 89. See also Voegelin, *CW,* 12:43–44.
24. Scheler, *Man's Place,* 91.

fundamental questions, "what is man? what is his place in the cosmos?" Two things we know already: first, that a denotatively specific answer is not to be expected, and second, that the self-conscious expression of the necessity of a philosophy of consciousness that begins in "wonder" must be, historically speaking, a comparatively recent development. There is ample evidence of the overwhelming presence of historical societies without philosophy. Scheler said nothing of the significance of nonphilosophical human existence beyond the dismissive categorization that it sought safety and protection in "religion."

Scheler's response to his own two questions may be summarized as follows: man is the free but limited being; his place in the cosmos is between: between life and death, between beasts and gods, between freedom and necessity, between heredity and environment and any number of other dichotomous poles that express the tension of human life "between."[25] Within this Schelerian philosophical anthropology, politics appears as the human response to limited freedom. If freedom were more limited, by instinct for example or by genetic instructions, humans would be akin to Aristotle's gregarious herds or perhaps to dolphins or orcas. That freedom is limited, nevertheless, means that not everything is possible. Within the ontological constant of limited freedom, human beings can create a political order that more or less adequately responds to that attribute. Political order, one may say, is the historical actualization of limited freedom. It is an achievement, and so a contingency beset with threats of disorder and the danger of dissolution.

Reflection on the character of the variegated manifestations of human "nature" in history—that is, reflection on the character of political order—leads one to consider the patterns of transformation of political order. Analysis of these patterns of change is not simply a historiographic exercise or an account of one thing after another because of the significance of political order as the historical manifestation of human being. No account of political order, therefore, can be developed without at the same time introducing the full range of questions raised by philosophy of consciousness, whether Scheler's or some other's. It is for this reason that a philosophical anthropology requires a philosophy of history. One may say, therefore, that the term *philosophy of history* refers to the body of knowledge that, to use the formulation of Voegelin quoted in the previous chapter, accounts for the changing manifestations of human

25. In his later writings Voegelin often referred to Plato's use of the term *metaxy*. It is usually used in Greek as an adverb of place or of time and as a preposition. Voegelin adopted its occasional usage as a noun, *to metaxy*, and transformed it into a technical term: the In-Between. See Keulman, *Balance of Consciousness*, 162–63.

"nature" in history, where that "nature" is accounted for in philosophical anthropology.

The historicity of human being, evident in the arguments of Scheler and Voegelin both, means that the doctrinal attribution of specific and essential features to an equally specific, essential, and so unchanging human nature is untenable. Because human being includes consciousness as a process of exegesis of itself, the possibility of "essentialism" is effectively foreclosed. On the other hand, philosophy of history must also aim to prevent philosophy of consciousness from dissolving into historicism and simple relativism. This is a problem Voegelin encountered in a particularly complex way in his analysis of Schelling, as we shall see in Chapter 10 below. Scheler also avoided historicism. In the closing pages of *Man's Place*, he reflected on the process of reality as a mediation between human consciousness and the "formal" conception of God, or *deitas*. Beyond the formal *deitas*, Scheler said, was the nonobjective, nonobjectifiable, nonhistorical, nonconceptual Ground of Being. Regarding the Ground of Being, immanentist propositional language is inappropriate precisely because the term symbolized the experience of a cosmic-transcendent reality for which any immanent account would have to be analogical. For one reason or another we may find Scheler's account unsatisfying: mention was made earlier, for instance, of the aggressiveness of his account of "religion." Nevertheless, the direction of the argument, namely a meditation on the relationship of human being to the Ground of Being, indicates a coherent way of understanding human existence as more than the existence of a natural or simply historical being, but of a being that nevertheless does not lack natural and historical attributes.

Scheler sought to understand the place of human beings in the cosmos and the meaning of political order. The result of his reflections, his "report," was not historicist confusion but a reflection of the "primordial incompleteness"[26] of human being, which is necessarily reflected in the provisional nature of any report. In other words, the process of striving to understand, of raising and (provisionally) answering Scheler's questions (or equivalent questions), remains constant.[27] The raising and answering of those questions occurs historically, which is to say that every discovery or disclosure of reality is necessarily historical, whatever else it may be. The coherent recognition and account of this constancy is indicated by the term *philosophy of history*. As we will see in the following chapters, Voegelin appropriated several of Scheler's arguments and refined them for his own purposes within the context of political science.

---

26. Landmann, *Philosophical Anthropology*, 226.
27. Scheler, *Man's Place*, 51.

In the 1966 foreword to *Anamnesis*, Voegelin remarked that it was clear to him in the 1920s that "the *misère* of political science, namely its being mired in neo-Kantian theories of knowledge, value-relating methods, historicism, descriptive institutionalism, and ideological speculations on history, could be remedied only by a new philosophy of consciousness."[28] His first efforts at clarification of the problem, he said, were chiefly critical, but they were followed over the decades by "variegated work on the historical phenomena of order and the reduction of the phenomena of order to the logos of consciousness." Indeed, the final volume of *Order and History*, which Voegelin was revising at the time of his death in 1985, may be considered the last phase of a meditation that began more than half a century earlier. A decisive point in this process, we saw in the letter to Heilman quoted earlier, occurred in the fall of 1943. In a series of epistolary essays, stimulated by a discussion with Alfred Schütz on the topic of Husserl's phenomenology, Voegelin achieved a clear formulation of a "theory" of consciousness. The materials are collected as part I, "Recollection," in *Anamnesis*.[29]

There are four sections to part I: a memorial notice of Alfred Schütz, a letter to Schütz on Husserl, the essay "On the Theory of Consciousness," and a collection of twenty "Anamnetic Experiments." The three sections that followed the Schütz memorial, Voegelin said, "are a meditative unit."[30] Perhaps the simplest introduction to this complex series of texts is Voegelin's 1977 essay "Remembrance of Things Past," written for the English edition of *Anamnesis*.

"In 1943," Voegelin began, "I had arrived at a dead-end in my attempts to find a theory of man, society, and history that would permit an adequate interpretation of the phenomena in my chosen field of studies."[31] On the basis of his prewar studies as well as the analysis undertaken during the war, it was "clear beyond a doubt that the center of a philosophy

28. Voegelin, *Anamnesis*, 7; all passages quoted from the German edition are my translation.
29. See also *Autobiographical Reflections*, chap. 18.
30. *Anamnesis*, 17. A translation of the letter can be found in *Faith and Political Philosophy*, 19–34. Translations of the other two pieces are available in the English version of *Anamnesis*, trans. and ed. Gerhart Niemeyer. The term *anamnetic experiments* is taken from the English version. The original title was simply "Anamnesis." The unity of the three parts is even more strongly indicated in the manuscript inasmuch as "On the Theory of Consciousness" is called "Preamble to the Anamnesis" (*Vorbemerkung zur Anamnesis*, HI 62/1). The first English translation omits the letter to Schütz. The reason for this change is not evident from Voegelin's correspondence either with Notre Dame University Press or with the translator, Gerhart Niemeyer (HI 38/26, 27/13).
31. Voegelin, "Remembrance of Things Past," in *Anamnesis*, trans. Niemeyer, 3.

of politics had to be a theory of consciousness" because restrictions and deformations of consciousness were at the heart of the political mass movements Voegelin had observed at first hand and analyzed in his prewar books.

However, there were no "intellectual instruments" available to make sense of political movements and events. Of course, there were a vast array of "theories" of consciousness, which Voegelin characterized as "school philosophies" and about which he was well enough schooled. However, they were precisely what constituted the *"misère* of political science" because they were incapable of answering such questions as:

> why do important thinkers like Comte or Marx refuse to apperceive what they apperceive quite well? why do they expressly prohibit anybody to ask questions concerning the sectors of reality they have excluded from their personal horizon? why do they want to imprison themselves in their restricted horizon and to dogmatize their prison reality as the universal truth? and why do they want to lock up all mankind in the prison of their making?

The answer, Voegelin eventually discovered, was that the school philosophies were as defective in their own restrictions of consciousness as the mass political movements were in theirs. "But if that was true," Voegelin added, "I had observed the restriction, and recognized it as such, with the criteria of the observation coming from a consciousness with a larger horizon, which in this case happened to be my own." There was no question of invoking the intellectual apparatus of any school for an explanation along the lines of an abstract subject of cognition coming to terms with objective materials; the discovery, very simply, was that a concrete consciousness of a real human being named Eric Voegelin had confronted certain concrete deformations and understood them for what they were.

Voegelin's conclusion was straightforward: "an analysis of consciousness . . . has no instrument other than the concrete consciousness of the analyst." Accordingly, the quality of the instrument depended upon the breadth of what Voegelin called the horizon of the consciousness of the analyst, which in turn depended upon his desire to know, as Aristotle said, or, in Voegelin's more precise vocabulary, "on the analyst's willingness to reach out into all dimensions of the reality in which his conscious existence is an event." This understanding of consciousness lacks all a priori structures; it is a process or an action that expands, orders, articulates, and corrects itself; it is an effort to be open and responsive to reality; "it is an event in the reality of which as a part it partakes." Voegelin summarized his insight as the discovery, or rather, the rediscovery, of consciousness "in the concrete, in the personal, social, historical existence of man, as the specifically human mode of participation in reality." The consciousness characterized as restricted, whether applied to school philosophy, to political ideologies, or to mass political movements, was evidence, therefore, of a restrictive deformation of human existence.

These deformations can become the subject matter for an analysis by the human being whose consciousness is less restricted or, positively described, whose consciousness is open and responsive to reality. Such a person, whom we will identify in a shorthand way as a philosopher, has the task not merely of analyzing the deformations of school philosophy and of ideological politics but, as Voegelin put it in the 1966 letter to Heilman, of exploring his own consciousness and elaborating an exegesis of it that makes sense of the facts that have come to constitute the contemporary deformations. In 1943, Voegelin's answer emerged from his study of Husserl's phenomenology; it was precipitated, as he said, by a conversation with Schütz and occasioned by reading Husserl's *Crisis of the European Sciences,* first published, in part, in 1936.[32] On September 17, 1943, Voegelin wrote Schütz a long letter containing a critical analysis of Husserl's *Crisis.*

Voegelin was very impressed by Husserl's work. Compared with the work of contemporary philosophers and with other work of Husserl, the *Crisis* was truly great. Voegelin concluded his description of what was praiseworthy in Husserl's work by characterizing it "as the most significant epistemological performance of our time." Nevertheless, Voegelin was disappointed. However important epistemology may be "it does not exhaust the philosophical field." It is neither self-sufficient nor is it fundamental; at best it is "a prolegomenon to philosophy." In a letter to Leo Strauss, Voegelin was more blunt: "What I find missing in the present article [the *Crisis*], as well as in the other published work of Husserl, is a foundation of phenomenology in the larger context of a metaphysical system. The 'egological sphere' is for him an ultimate sphere beyond which he permits no questions. Well—I like to ask a few questions beyond."[33] In other words, Husserl was not open or receptive to reality insofar as he refused to consider experiences that led to what Scheler conventionally called "metaphysical questions." Moreover, Voegelin was persuaded that there was sufficient evidence to

32. An international philosophical yearbook, *Philosophia,* edited in Belgrade, published the first two parts. Reference is to *The Crisis of the European Sciences and Transcendental Phenomenology,* trans. David Carr. The complete work was first published in 1954. A copy of *Philosophia* is part of Voegelin's library at the University of Erlangen.
33. Voegelin to Strauss, September 26, 1943, in *Faith and Political Philosophy,* 19.

indicate that no metaphysics would be forthcoming from the mountain of Husserl's unpublished manuscripts.

The evidence was found in Husserl's conception of history, which Voegelin discussed in four related arguments. First, the only history of interest to Husserl was Greek antiquity and the period following the Renaissance.[34] "The Hellenistic period, Christianity, the Middle Ages—an insignificant time-period of merely two thousand years—are a superfluous interlude." The Indians and Chinese "are a slightly ridiculous curiosity on the periphery of the globe" whom Husserl dismissed as "merely anthropological types."[35] Husserl distinguished, therefore, between the full or complete representatives of humanity, namely Western society insofar as it has been formed by philosophy (in Husserl's sense) and the incomplete, anthropological types elsewhere. In Greek antiquity, according to Husserl, the "entelechy of humanity" achieved its breakthrough; with Descartes a new foundation was established. During the intervening two millennia, Voegelin dryly observed, "the entelechy obviously amused itself elsewhere." Perhaps, indeed, the spirituality of medieval Western man had reverted to the merely anthropological type? Finally, after Kant had corrected certain imperfections of Descartes, "we come to the final foundation in Husserlian transcendentalism." In short, Husserl proposed a typical three-phase structure to history: first the pre-Hellenic gloom before the entelechy stirred into life; second the period between the Greeks and Husserl, which suffered regressions as well as recoveries; and finally the Husserlian final foundation.

Second, Voegelin said, this "impoverished vision of the spiritual history of mankind" was an essential presupposition to Husserl's speculation, not an inadvertence. The whole purpose of Husserl's historical construction was to establish his own philosophical reflections as "final-foundational" and thereby to enable Husserl to understand past philosophers "better than they understood themselves." From this privileged position, Husserl could not be contradicted by mere historical evidence or philosophical arguments. "For the first time, in the evidence of the critical total view, the meaningful harmony of the course of history flashes up behind the 'historical facts.' " In plain language, Husserl claimed that, following his own final foundation, the meaning of history

34. Helmut R. Wagner made many of the same observations regarding Husserl in his article "Husserl and Historicism," esp. 707 ff. In January 1975, in the course of a sustained correspondence, Voegelin remarked that he had read the article, which Wagner had sent him, "both with great interest and, if I may say it, with some amusement, because apparently you ran into the same problems with 'orthodox' phenomenologists as I did in my time" (HI 39/21).

35. Husserl, *Crisis*, 16.

had been fully revealed; accordingly, everyone who was properly to be called a philosopher henceforth must be a Husserlian. More precisely, the community of mankind had been constricted by Husserl's speculation to the representative community of Husserlian philosophers, or "orthodox" phenomenologists, as Voegelin called them in his letter to Wagner. One could easily be reminded of similar claims by Hegel, Comte, and Marx and in September 1943 of similar evocations of an armed and active Aryan elite, which understood itself as representing "true humanity," at the head of an intramundane human collectivity.

The relationship between the systematic task of Husserl's transcendental philosophy of final foundation and the rest of humanity, including the merely anthropological types, was expressed in the formula that Husserlian philosophers were "functionaries of mankind."[36] Voegelin's third critical remark sought to clarify the significance of the term *functionaries of mankind.* He began by noting his distaste for functionaries of any sort, especially when they endow themselves with such grandiose titles. More seriously, for Husserl's formula to make sense, "mankind" would have had to be an intramundane collectivity of which individuals were instances or particles without any direct relation to a Ground of Being that might endow them with substantive, personal, and spiritual singularity. In Christian language, the humanity of the individual, or human dignity, which is dogmatically expressed in the statement that humans are made by God in the image of God, had been replaced by Husserl with a collective entelechy of philosophical reason. Voegelin called this position "Averroistic" because the most important literary source of the argument was apparently Averroës's commentary on Aristotle. Voegelin identified Averroës as the source of an intramundane understanding of human existence and of political life generally.[37] Several Averroistic variations are possible insofar as the collective soul can be identified with a variety of intramundane phenomena, the most familiar and dangerous of which have been associated with mass ideological political movements.

As was indicated above, for Husserl humanity preeminently meant European humanity, and especially the fully developed form of European humanity, namely the philosophers of antiquity and of the modern era. This Averroistic or "collectivist-historical" metaphysics had the political consequence of rendering relatively superfluous the "merely anthropological types" who are evidently not part of the collective

36. Ibid., 17, 71.
37. See, for example, the comments on "Siger de Brabant," *Philosophy and Phenomenological Research* 4 (1944): 507–26, and *HPI,* II:178–204.

philosophical entelechy. In contemporary language, Husserl was an apocalyptic progressive. And as a progressive he had to deal with the great problem of all unfolding entelechies: what to do with the earlier generations whose lives are but steps on the way to a final goal? Kant found in this question, which turned all prior humanity into the means by which the last generation attained its fulfillment, a source of "distaste."[38] But for Husserl, said Voegelin, the notion that Greek and modern philosophy was "only the historical manure from which the flower of the Husserlian final foundation blooms, does not seem 'distasteful' to him in the least." Again in contrast to Kant, who maintained a supposition of unending progress and thereby as well the proposition that every historical generation shares with every other the fate of imperfection, there was no unending progress because Husserl's final foundation was not to be infinitely postponed. Indeed, it had already been undertaken in Husserl's phenomenology.

In other and plainer words, Kant's consciousness of his own humanity, which was registered as an inner protest, a "distaste," was eclipsed in Husserl's messianic transposition of history into a new apocalypse of the human spirit vouchsafed in virtue of the final foundation. Moreover, the self-understanding of Husserlian phenomenologists as functionaries of mankind was clear evidence that Husserl was also the founder of a sect of collectivist intellectuals whose purpose was to preside over the final phase of history. Last, since the chief consequence of the final foundation was to ensure that the terminological apparatus of the historical entelechy rendered Husserl's interpretation of all prior philosophy privileged, no merely historical arguments or evidence could be introduced to contradict Husserl's version, which, *ex definitione*, could not be false.

Voegelin called such historiography "demonic" because "the historian absolutizes his own spiritual position with its historical limitedness, and 'really' does not write history, but misuses the material of history as historical support for his own position." A nondemonic history of human spirituality would aim to penetrate every historical spiritual position to the point where it opens upon "the experiences of transcendence of the thinker in question." The philosophical purpose, he said,

> of genuine historical reflection is to penetrate to the spiritual-historical form of the other to its experience of transcendence, and in such penetration to train and clarify one's own formation of transcendent experience. Spiritual-historical understanding is a catharsis, a *purificatio* in the mystical sense,

38. See Kant's "Idea of a Universal History with a Cosmopolitan Purpose," in *Kant's Political Writings*, trans. H. B. Nisbet, ed. H. Reiss (Cambridge: Cambridge University Press, 1970), 41–53.

with the personal goal of *illuminatio* and *unio mystica;* in fact if it deals systematically with great chains of material, it can lead to the working out of sequences of order in the historical revelation of spirit; and finally it can in this way produce in fact a philosophy of history. The guides to this understanding, however, which cannot allow any moment to be abandoned, are the "self-testimonies" of the thinker—those very self-testimonies that Husserl not only believes to have no rights, but that he systematically avoided as disturbing his teleology.

Voegelin's fourth critical point concerned a fundamental element in Husserl's speculation, his relationship to Descartes. It was Husserl's opinion, as has been noticed, that modern philosophy was imperfectly founded by Descartes, corrected by Kant, and then finally established by himself. Husserl's final foundation, therefore, was understood to have brought out the full truth of Descartes's original foundation. According to Husserl, Descartes's *Meditations* was an imperfect form of phenomenological reduction, the purpose of which is an *epoche* of the contents of the world so as to reconstitute the world as objective from the transcendental "egological" sphere. Husserl's critique, Voegelin said, was partially correct in that he drew attention to the fact that Descartes's *epoche* was not radical: the psychological "I" was made the starting point for the reconstitution of the world, and such a Cartesian "I" was part of the world. Husserl correctly saw that a transcendental ego, not a psychological one, was required. However, Husserl also argued, on the basis of his entelechy, that the purpose of the Cartesian reduction was simply epistemological and thus only a step on the way to Husserl's own transcendental philosophy. This, Voegelin said, was false.

According to Voegelin, Descartes's philosophical meditation had a far richer content than the *epoche* of the world undertaken in order to establish the epistemological sphere of the transcendental ego. The proper context for understanding the *Meditations,* Voegelin said, was the tradition of Augustinian meditation, the purpose of which is to turn the soul toward God.[39] Such a meditation begins with the attitude of the *contemptus mundi,* the willful elimination from one's consciousness of material and animate reality. The willed not-knowing of the world enables the soul to direct its attention to God. Fundamentally, the meditation is part of the biography of an individual, and the actual duration of the experience of transcendence is customarily brief. Derived from that experience, however, is the literary form of the meditation, the "report," which in turn can serve as a means to reenact the originary experience.

39. Compare the remarks of Étienne Gilson on "Cartesian Spiritualism" in *The Unity of Philosophical Experience* (London: Sheed and Ward, 1938), chap. 6.

Descartes was firmly part of that tradition of Christian meditation. However, the use to which Descartes put the meditative technique was not to maintain an attitude of "contempt" toward the world, the better to attain the point of transcendence, but to restore the reality of the world from the "Archimedean point" of transcendence. In Voegelin's words, Descartes's innovation was that "the sentiment of *contemptus mundi* gives way to the sentiment of interest in the world." Husserl, Voegelin said, was oblivious to the experiential content of transcendence and so misinterpreted Descartes's "proof" of God as a dogmatic proposition that he felt at liberty to reject. But in fact the scholastic "proofs" of God do not have the purpose of assuring the thinker who employs them of God's existence. It is, simply, a stylistic form or convention that contains not a logical demonstration but a purely descriptive report of the experience of transcendence and of the correlative experience of human finitude. "God cannot be in doubt," Voegelin pointed out, "for in the experience of doubt and of imperfection, God is implied. In the limit-experience of being finite there is given, along with this side of the limit, the beyond."[40]

Husserl's achievement may now be specified more exactly. He appropriated his own version of Descartes's transcendental ego, namely an ego that had been turned back toward the world, and he correctly criticized Descartes's conflation of the psychological "I," the soul as world-content, with this transcendental ego, a conflation that was obviously necessary if Descartes's sentiment expressed his "interest" in the world rather than the *contemptus mundi*. But, in fact, Husserl did not consider that the ego might be directed not toward the world but toward the point of transcendence for the very good reason that he never undertook the originary meditation, the "exploration of the psyche," of which Descartes's text is the exegetical report. Instead, he appropriated the literary results for his own epistemological purposes. Why Husserl did not reenact the originary experiences was unknown. The consequences, however, were clear: "he has taken the way out in the immanence of a historical problematic, and with the greatest care blocked himself off from the philosophical problem of transcendence—the decisive problem of philosophy." Voegelin ended his letter to Schütz by affirming once again his great respect for Husserl's achievement. He had done all that could be done "without rising in an originary way to the level of the fundamental problem of philosophizing," namely to respond to the *realissimum*, the world-transcendent Ground of Being.[41]

40. See also Voegelin's later remarks in *CW*, 12:300–301, 380–83.

41. Voegelin made many of these same arguments in much briefer compass in a review of Marvin Farber, *The Foundation of Phenomenology* (1943). Farber, incidentally,

The importance of Voegelin's letter lay as much in its being an illustration of his analytical procedure as in its direct assessment of Husserl's philosophy. So far as the immediate issue was concerned, it seems that Schütz was not entirely persuaded by Voegelin's analysis.[42] Even so, certain fundamental problems were clarified, particularly the difference between Husserl's phenomenology and classical philosophy. As Voegelin wrote later, "phenomenological philosophizing such as Husserl's is oriented in principle on the model of the experience of objects in the external world; classical philosophizing about political order is likewise oriented in principle on the model of noetic experience of transcendent divine being."[43] Husserl's understanding of consciousness on the model of sense perception was, therefore, restrictive. Accordingly, a comprehensive "philosophical epistemology" must take into account not merely abstract statements about the structure of consciousness but the act by which those statements are acknowledged by somebody as being true. "Their truth," he said, "rested on the concrete experiences of reality by concrete human beings who were able to articulate their experience of reality and of their own role as participants in it, and thus engender the language of consciousness. The truth of consciousness was both abstract and concrete."[44] Likewise, by excluding large sectors of humanity from participation in the historical development of meaning, namely the unfolding of the "entelechy of humanity" that culminated in Husserlian phenomenology, his philosophy of history was similarly restricted.

Voegelin's analysis and critical clarification of the issues, helpful as they were, remained insufficient. He still had to tackle the problem of formulating an alternative. This did not mean postulating an alternative hypothesis or "theory" to that of Husserl but undertaking an original exegesis of consciousness in opposition to Husserl, but with a restorative, and not merely critical, purpose. As Voegelin said in his foreword to *Anamnesis*, the most important result of his studies on the historical phenomena of order

---

was pleased with what was, in fact, a critical appraisal of Husserl's enterprise. Indeed, he went so far as to remark: "The extent of our agreement concerning the merit of phenomenology leads me to regard you as an active colleague in this field of scholarship and I hope you will think of yourself as such" (HI 61/17).

42. See Helmut R. Wagner, "Agreement in Discord: Alfred Schütz and Eric Voegelin," in *The Philosophy of Order: Essays on History, Consciousness, and Politics for Eric Voegelin on his Eightieth Birthday, January 3, 1981* (Stuttgart: Klett-Kotta, 1981), 74–90, and Wagner, *Alfred Schütz: An Intellectual Biography*, chap. 12.

43. Voegelin, "In Memoriam Alfred Schütz," in *Anamnesis*, 19.

44. Voegelin, "Remembrance of Things Past," in *Anamnesis*, trans. Niemeyer, 11.

was the insight that a "theory" of consciousness in the sense of generically valid propositions concerning a pregiven structure was impossible. For consciousness is not a given that can be described from the outside but an experience of participation in the ground of being, the logos of which has to be brought to clarity through the meditative exegesis of itself. The illusion of a "theory" [of consciousness] had to give way to the reality of the meditative process; and this process had to go through its phases of increasing experience and insight.[45]

Reflection on Husserl's apocalyptic construction of history indicated the direction in which Voegelin's efforts must go. If Husserl's philosophy of history served to exclude the "merely anthropological types" from consideration as human beings, if his vision of phenomenologists as "functionaries of mankind" had the purpose of attempting to ensure that all philosophers must become phenomenologists or risk decertification, if the purpose of this entire enterprise was to preside over the end of history as a functionary of mankind, then any alternative would have to begin by introducing, or rather by reintroducing, the historical dimension that Husserl sought to exclude. Concretely, therefore, the "phases of increasing experience and insight" consisted of the historical analyses that formed the "mountain of studies" about which Voegelin wrote in his letter to Germino, and a selection of which were included as part II of *Anamnesis.*

The "historical dimension" to which Voegelin adverted was not a piece of information about "the past." It was, he said, "the permanent presence of the process of reality in which man participates with his conscious existence." The Husserlian structure of a subject of cognition intending an object of thought is only one mode of consciousness. More fundamental is the consciousness that human beings have of being parts of a comprehensive reality; they express this awareness "by the symbols of birth and death, of a cosmic whole structured by realms of being, of a world of external objects and of the presence of divine reality in the cosmos, of mortality and immortality, of creation into the cosmic order and of salvation from its disorder, of descent into the depth of the *psyche* and the meditative ascent toward its beyond."[46] Voegelin then provided a highly concentrated summary: "man's conscious existence is an event within reality, and man's consciousness is quite conscious of being constituted by the reality of which it is conscious."

45. Voegelin, *Anamnesis,* 7.
46. Voegelin, "Remembrance of Things Past," in *Anamnesis,* trans. Niemeyer, 10, 11.

Voegelin's formula served to recapitulate his argument regarding the truth of reality experienced. If one acknowledged the formula as being true, the truth expressed in it must first of all have been recognized by a real person as being really true, and that person must have been able to express his or her experience of reality and of his or her own place as a participant in reality by using the language of consciousness. This is what Voegelin had indicated in his letter to Heilman as the "direct observation and meditative tracing of the structure of the psyche"; it was indicated earlier as well in his letter to Schütz when he spoke of the philosophers as guides to reality; indeed, as early as *On the Form of the American Mind* (1928), Voegelin spoke of "self-expressive" phenomena as constituting the subject matter of political science.[47] Yet it is also true that these self-testimonies and self-expressions do not always agree with one another. In the context of Voegelin's analysis of Husserl, "something had to be done. I had to get out of that 'apodictic horizon' as fast as possible."[48] In short, Voegelin found himself confronted with the question of why he was personally attracted by "larger horizons" and repelled by restrictive deformations.

The answer was not to be found simply in terms of a straightforward conflict between larger and smaller horizons or between hermeneutical circles of larger or smaller circumference; nor could it be found in terms of more and less adequate "theories" of consciousness. Nor was it simply a pragmatic problem of escaping harm at the hands of ideological activists with particularly narrow horizons and deformed consciousnesses. Voegelin's concern was philosophical, not pragmatic, and he realized that he had to rely not on "theory" but on his own resources. The answer had to be sought "concretely in the constitution of the responding and verifying consciousness. And that concrete consciousness was my own." An exploration of one's own consciousness is necessarily a recollection in the present of one's own past experience; moreover, the exploration would be concerned less with the recent events of one's life than with the early ones because one's "manner of response to learning and events was precisely the question to be clarified." As Voegelin said in the foreword to *Anamnesis*, "remembered, however, will be what has been forgotten; and we remember the forgotten—sometimes with considerable travail—because it should not remain forgotten."[49]

The purpose of the "anamnetic exploration" of consciousness, therefore, was to recapture whatever childhood experiences allowed themselves to be captured. Whatever experiences turned up did so "because

47. *CW*, 1:7–8.
48. Voegelin, "Remembrance of Things Past," in *Anamnesis*, trans. Niemeyer, 10.
49. Voegelin, *Anamnesis*, 11.

they were living forces in the present constitution of [one's] conscious-ness."[50] Moreover, Voegelin knew enough about the "self-testimonies" of classic, patristic, and Scholastic philosophy to be aware "that the philosophers who had founded philosophy on an analysis of conscious-ness were analyzing a few phenomena of consciousness besides the perception of objects in the external world."[51] One may add that even though Voegelin's remarks were an account of the procedure by which he clarified his own philosophical consciousness, they can, in principle, be extended to anyone. The result of his anamnetic analysis constituted the second text sent to Schütz.

The second and third parts of the "meditative unit" consist of the introductory essay "On the Theory of Consciousness" and the twenty "Anamnetic Experiments" along with some brief prefatory remarks to them. The "experiments" were written first, then edited into their present form with the prefatory note added.[52] Shortly thereafter Voegelin wrote "On the Theory of Consciousness." In *Anamnesis*, the introductory essay preceded the "experiments," which is the order of analysis here. The reason for this order is that the only context for the anamneses is the essay on the theory of consciousness. The anamneses themselves are, in the words of David Tresan, "raw."[53]

Occasionally Voegelin's style reflects the informal origin of these epistolary essays. "On the Theory of Consciousness," in particular, is repetitive and more loosely constructed than one of Voegelin's polished pieces. One has the feeling that Voegelin is working out his account in part through the effort of writing it down. There are, nevertheless, four distinct parts to the essay. The first discusses accounts of the structure of consciousness; the second deals with myth, and the third with "process theology"; and finally come the summary and conclusion.[54]

50. Voegelin, "Remembrance of Things Past," in *Anamnesis*, trans. Niemeyer, 12–13.

51. *Autobiographical Reflections*, 71.

52. The manuscript of these "anamnetic experiments" gives the dates October 10–13, 1943; the published version dates them October 25 to November 7, 1943 (HI 72/14; *Anamnesis*, 76).

53. Tresan is a psychiatrist practicing at the C. G. Jung Institute of Northern California. His comments on Voegelin's anamneses have helped me in my interpretation of them, though of course he bears no responsibility, professionally or personally, for my remarks.

54. The divisions are not all marked in the text but have been extracted from the logic of the development of the argument. See *Anamnesis*, "Zur Theorie des Bewusstseins," 37–60. Section 1: 37–44 (English, 14–21); section 2: 44–50 (English, 21–26); section 3: 50–54 (English, 26–30); section 4: 54–60 (English, 30–35). Subsequent quotations in the text are from this essay.

Voegelin's motive for writing was deeper than his desire to be clear about one of Husserl's articles. It came, he said, from a long-standing discontent "at the results of those philosophical investigations that have as their object the analysis of inner time-consciousness." Inner time-consciousness, or simply time-consciousness, became a topic for philosophical analysis during the nineteenth century and subsequently came to occupy the place held by meditation prior to the dissolution of Christian categories as acceptable expressions for thought. The analysis of the time-consciousness of an imaginary and truncated world-immanent human being was the secularized residue of Christian ascertainment of existence in meditation, the spiritual apex of which was formulated as Augustine's *intentio animi* toward God.

The grave defect of the later philosophical studies of time-consciousness or of stream-of-consciousness was that the elaborate conceptual constructions did not describe anything experienced. There is no stream of consciousness given to experience apart from a highly focused perception, namely the auditory perception of a tone, that can be described, without obvious distortion, by the metaphor of a stream or flow.[55] "The phenomenon of 'flow,'" Voegelin said, "can be made present only under very specific and favorable conditions, namely when the object of perception is so sensually simple that in turning to the object one can still economize enough attention to be conscious of one's consciousness of it." Because it is simplified, artificial, and abstracted from normal experience, however, auditory perception serves poorly as a model for the understanding of time as a whole. Nevertheless, it does reveal clearly the "fleetingness" of sense experience, which also means that one must rely on sense experience in order to make us aware of the "fleetingness" of consciousness. That is, if one were not already interested in the phenomenon of flow, then the question of fleetingness would not arise; if one were instead interested in consciousness as the spaceless, timeless world of meaning, sense, and the order of the soul, then one would not, in the first instance, devote such attention to the vanishing point of fleetingness. Voegelin concluded that a concern with "fleetingness" had the limited result of aiding one's understanding "of the roots of consciousness in the sphere of the body."

All philosophical anthropologists are agreed that the sphere of the body is the foundation for consciousness. Attention to bodily realities is therefore philosophically legitimate because, between birth and death, the body determines what parts of the world enter consciousness

55. The imagery of "flow" and "stream" was first examined by Voegelin in *On the Form of the American Mind, CW,* 1:chap. 1.

through it, not merely as a sensorium but as a determinant of the internal tensions and attentions of the world of consciousness. It would be an obvious error, however, to conclude from this that the body is the sole determinant of the structure of consciousness. Voegelin concluded from his initial reflections that the question of the constitution of consciousness as a "flow" or "stream" was badly formulated: the stream of consciousness was a limit phenomenon. "Consciousness as a whole does not flow." Accordingly, there was no point in searching for the constitution of a stream of consciousness or for its agent. The place to begin describing the structure of consciousness, Voegelin said, was in the phenomenon of "attention and the focusing of attention" or, as Scheler had called it, "concentration."

The most obvious characteristic or attribute of the power of concentration is that it is highly variable. When focused, one's horizon of attention narrows; the actual quantum of energy varies among individuals, and "consistent practice of concentration results in an increased capacity for concentration." Most important, this center of energy is engaged in a process that cannot be observed externally. "Rather it has the character of an inner 'illumination.'" The general meaning of luminosity, in this context, is that consciousness is experienceable from within. Past and future, therefore, were not to be understood as empty stretches into which data are entered. "Past and future are the present, luminous dimensions of the processes of the power of concentration." In his review of Cairns's book, Voegelin made the same point more directly in connection with the technological attitude that seeks to make the future as it wills.

> The implications of this new attitude, which has been in the making since the middle of the nineteenth century, can be made clearer by reflection on a sentence from a speech of Mussolini to his Blackshirts: "The past is behind us, the future is before us, we stand in the present in-between." Some may consider this sentence an oratorical flourish, but they would be mistaken. Not at all times is the past behind us and the future before us; that happens only when we are in the throes of a violent crisis. Normally the past and the future are present; we do not stand between them, but are moving in the continuous stream of history. The past reaches into our present as the civilizational heritage that has formed us and that we have to absorb into our lives as the precondition for the formation of the future, not in some distant time ahead of us, but in the present of our daily life and work.[56]

Considered the other way around, "in the luminous dimensions of past and future one becomes aware not of empty spaces but of the structures of finite processes between birth and death."

56. CW, 27:109.

Conceptual analyses of processes that transcend consciousness, including birth and death, lead to a number of "fundamental problems" or *aporias*. The reason for this outcome lies in the fact that there is inevitably a conflict between the finiteness of any conceptual model and the "infinite" or "transfinite" processes that transcend consciousness. Indeed, to introduce the negative metaphor of "infinity" is already "equivalent to saying that we have no experience of it as a 'totality.'" If, nevertheless, one does treat "infinity" as a kind of experiential possibility, the result is a derivative transformation or reduction (to use mathematical language) that is expressed as paradox, as in Zeno or in set theory, as Kantian antinomy, and so on.[57] The reason for the development of such conceptual paradoxes is that the process of consciousness is the only process humans know "from within." It is, therefore, the only experiential source for our conceptual understanding of processes that transcend consciousness. Leaving aside such things as birth and death, one learns, for example, that no causal series can begin "in time" because humans have no experience of such a beginning. "More precisely, the only time of which we have experience is the inner experience of the luminous dimension of consciousness, of the process that sinks away at both ends into inexperienceable darkness." The result of trying to characterize the structures of processes that transcend consciousness on the basis of finite experiences leads inevitably to "conflicts of expression" of which the Kantian antinomies are, historically, a familiar but late example. Yet we do have the experience of knowingly "not-knowing" those processes that transcend consciousness, and we are able to undertake to transform them so as to make them understandable in terms of the finite processes of consciousness. Voegelin's formulation necessarily reminds one of Socratic ignorance.

Because they are not experienced from within, processes that transcend consciousness cannot intelligibly be expressed in conceptual language without paradox—which in conceptual discourse amounts to contradiction and unintelligibility. More adequate for the expression of the experience of "knowingly not-knowing," as we have called it, are myths. "A mythical symbol," Voegelin said, "is a finite symbol that aims to render 'transparent' a transfinite process." By "transparent" Voegelin wished to indicate a nonliteralist intelligibility. For example, a creation myth, he said, renders the beginning of the transfinite process of the world "transparent" in the same way as an anthropomorphic image of God makes the experience of transcendence finitely expressible or

57. For details of this conceptual puzzle, see, for example, José Bernardete, *Infinity* (Oxford: Clarendon, 1964), chap. 1, or Leslie Armour, *Being and Idea* (Hildsheim: Georg Olms, 1992), chap. 8.

a Platonic speculation on pre- and postexistence of the soul provide a finite formula for the beyond before birth and after death.

Historically, Voegelin observed, there is a tendency to substitute for sensual and polytheistic myths single deities without sensual attributes. In particular Voegelin drew attention to Plato's use of myth. When, for one reason or another, sensual myths are no longer persuasive, philosophers typically reduce the mythic elements to one or another finite process or to elements in a complex speculation with a paradoxic or antinomic linguistic character. Plato, however, "consciously composed myths where another philosopher would use the instruments of speculation." One may prudently assume Plato did so, Voegelin said, in the knowledge that there was an equivalence between speculative and mythic symbols with respect to their ability to convey meaning. Because it is more widely accessible, myth may indeed be a "more precise instrument for conveying the excitement of the soul's experience of transcendence." Moreover, because Plato used two different myths, in the *Republic* and in the *Laws,* to convey a truth concerning the structure of the soul, Voegelin was led to consider the question of the "adequacy" of a myth in rendering the experience of transfinite processes "properly." The myths in question concerned the "metals" in the souls of the several classes in the *Republic* (414b–15d), which Plato called "a sort of Phoenician tale," and the myth of God as the player of human puppets in the *Laws* (644d–45b). The latter myth was held by Voegelin to be more adequate because it was not subordinate to any pragmatic purpose, such as keeping the community of the *Republic* intact, but was free to express the relationship between the soul and world-transcendent being without the distraction of an ulterior purpose.

The problem was complicated because both the *Republic* and the *Laws* were concerned with others and with the relationship between "I," the "other," and world-transcendent being. In principle, the other is a process transcending consciousness just as fully as the processes of nature, but with an important difference "insofar as we recognize in the 'other' a process that is in principle akin to our own process of consciousness." The problem lay not in the matter of transcendence, since natural processes were also transcendent to consciousness. Nor was it, as Husserl thought, a matter of constituting an alter ego because, as with the transcendence to consciousness of natural processes, others are not constituted at all. The experience by consciousness of an other is a given. In general, therefore, "the capacity of transcendence is as fundamental a characteristic of consciousness as luminosity; it is a given." The only problem concerns the way of symbolizing one's fellow creature.

On this topic, the history of myth can give a clear answer: the acknowledgment of human equality occurs along the same lines that express the transcendence of the body or of the spirit. Humans are equal either insofar as they are children of a common mother or insofar as they have been formed after the spiritual image of a common father. In either instance, and whatever the speculative idealization to which the variant myths may be subjected, the purpose remains to render in finite language the transcendence of consciousness by the other. Historically this process is enacted by the formation of finite communities that understand themselves as mythic representatives of human beings as such. The resulting conflicts between communities as well as within a single community regarding the appropriate image of human being is, clearly, a significant problem for political science.

An aspect of this problem that is of particular importance to the Western world is the modern rationalist dissolution of the myth. When the sensual myths of the Christian tradition were dissolved and spiritualized expressions of world-transcendent being, namely intellectual mysticism and philosophical speculation, remained accessible only to a few, "the inevitable result is the phenomenon of 'lostness' in a world that no longer has a locus of order in myth." The experiences of world-transcendent being do not disappear, but they do not generate symbols by which transfinite processes can properly be expressed in a comprehensible way, or "transparently," in myth. Instead, such experiences remain confined to spiritual phenomena such as fear and anxiety. Great political movements and wars, Voegelin said, are evidence of this lostness in two respects. First, the orgiastic character of these events is an entirely comprehensible response of a will paralyzed by anxiety. But, second, the need for orgiastic discharge arises only when there is no will to order, which in turn can be secured only where the meaning of order is sustained in a community myth, which is precisely what modern rationalism has dissolved. Voegelin also encountered the question of the relationship of myth and rational discourse, and of the depths that are expressed but not constituted in myth, in his analyses of Vico and Schelling. These questions are discussed below in Chapters 9 and 10.

Besides the general problem of "conflicts in expression" by which transfinite experiences are symbolized, and the more particular problem of myth, Voegelin discussed a third fundamental topic, "process theology." In fact, Voegelin's language throughout the essay has been the language of process theology. The section we are about to consider, therefore, constitutes a systematic reflection on what Voegelin had, in fact, been doing to that point.[58]

58. The section is found on pp. 50–54 of the original essay and pp. 26–30 of the English translation of *Anamnesis*.

By process theology, Voegelin meant the elaboration "of a system of symbols that seeks to express the relation between consciousness, the consciousness-transcending inner-worldly classes of being, and the world-transcendent Ground of Being using a language based on inner-worldly processes." Moreover, he added that it was his belief that a process theology and a metaphysics developed from it, "which interprets the transcendence-system of the world as the immanent process of a divine substance, is the only meaningful systematic philosophy." Voegelin's reference was to Schelling, whom he described as "the systematic starting point of this problem," but his words could equally be applied to Scheler.

We also noticed an equivalent systematic starting point in the questions of Leibniz, repeated in propositions such as: every being implies the mystery of its existence over the un-ground or abyss of its possible nonexistence. These questions and propositions can be dismissed by elaborating a speculative philosophy on the basis of certain restrictive assumptions, as was indicated earlier in the example of Husserl, but such destructive speculations can be resisted as well.

Voegelin described two experiential complexes on the basis of which resistance can be undertaken. The first is found in the experience of one's own structure of existence and of its relationship to the world-immanent order of being. The systematic description of that structure has been indicated by the term *philosophical anthropology.* "Human consciousness is not a process that occurs in the world side by side with other processes with contact maintained only by cognition; rather, it is founded on animal, organic, and inorganic being, and only on this basis is it consciousness of a human being." Because the existence of humans has the structure just described, it can transcend itself into the world and find there an order that it also experiences as its own foundation. The "fundamental experience" of consciousness is that human being is a microcosm. As to what that foundation "really" is, one can say only that it is a depth beyond specific, finite experience. Much as Scheler argued, the differentiation of "levels" of being—inorganic, organic, animal, and conscious—implies something common to them all that makes it possible for them all to appear in human existence, even though that common element cannot be specified precisely.

The second experiential complex is meditation. As was indicated earlier in connection with Voegelin's exegesis of Descartes, the spiritual aim of meditation is to enable the intention of consciousness to be directed toward world-transcendent being. As with the common cosmic substance that sustains the continuity of human existence in the world, world-transcendent being cannot be specified in phenomenally precise language. Both the depth of the soul and the beyond of the cosmos are experienced as unknown.

These two experiential complexes are intelligible if the differentiation of modes or levels of being is interpreted as a process that unfolds the identical substance that is eventually illuminated in human conscious-ness. "The meditative complex of experiences in which the reality of the Ground of Being is revealed then leads to the necessity of seeing the world-immanent process of being as conditioned by a process in the Ground of Being." The meaning of the question "why is there something and not nothing?" can now be specified at least in part. It refers to the unavoidable problem of process with respect to the experience of world-transcendent being.

The remaining pages of Voegelin's essay were devoted to a summary and conclusion. In place of the theory of a stream of consciousness, Voegelin spoke of a process of consciousness illuminated from within. To one who subscribed to the stream-of-consciousness theory, the ob-jection might be raised that the change in terminology did not bring additional insight. Voegelin agreed, but added that this was because nothing much had been said of this process of consciousness beyond the fact that it was a center of energy and was "luminous" when one turned one's attention toward it. Voegelin had argued that consciousness is experienced only from within; that experience, however, is neither bodily nor material, even though it exists only on the basis of somatic and material processes. In other words, "luminosity" attaches only to the experience of consciousness and not to natural being nor to that being that is the basis or "ground" of all experienceable particulars. In contrast to the "illumination" of consciousness, one may describe the being of the external world as metaphorically "opaque." Being external to consciousness and to oneself, it is not experienced from within. "Our human finite-being," Voegelin said, "always remains within being. At one point, in consciousness, this being has the attribute of luminosity, but luminosity is affixed only to this attribute." In other words, conscious-ness illuminates neither the fundamental being of nature nor world-transcendent being. In conventional philosophic language, this means that neither "metaphysical idealism" nor "metaphysical materialism" is tenable. Both attempt to reduce the whole of being, including world-transcendent being, to the categories of one or another "part" of being.

The foregoing considerations led Voegelin to formulate the following general principles for a philosophy of consciousness. First: "there is no absolute starting point for a philosophy of consciousness." All philoso-phizing about consciousness is itself an event in consciousness and so is conditioned by the considerations brought to light by philosophical anthropology. And so, for example, since there is no "pure" consciousness but only the consciousness of somebody, all philosophizing is an event in the philosopher's biography, in the history of his or her community with its particular symbolic language, in the history of humanity, and last, in the history of the cosmos. Human beings cannot, therefore, reflect upon consciousness as an object; reflection is, on the contrary, a particular orientation within consciousness.

Voegelin's final reflections returned to the question of Husserl's "radical" philosophy of consciousness. It was radical, Voegelin said, because it aimed at the impossible, namely to establish in consciousness and from consciousness a new foundation of the world. When characterized in that way, the question naturally arose as to why anyone would undertake such a grandiose exercise. The answer was to be found in the growing inadequacy of the received symbolic language used to describe human existence—the structures of inorganic matter, organic life, animal life, and so on. The "prevalent dogmatism of the time" and the "debris of opaque symbols," as Voegelin put it in his 1966 letter to Heilman, meant that so far as Husserl was concerned the available philosophical anthropology was simply inadequate. Accordingly, he undertook to forge his own; historically speaking, "a civilization and its symbols had fallen into crisis." Under the circumstances, the attempt to begin anew was indispensable for the development of symbols adequate to a description and analysis of the new reality of historical crisis. Protests in the name of tradition were simply evidence of "spiritual sterility." But at the same time, the legitimacy of a reaction against a spiritual crisis "says nothing about the value of the new beginning as a positive spiritual substance. There are good and bad reactions and sometimes the reaction is worse than the tradition against which it critically reacts." An understanding of a philosopher's motivation, therefore, was to be critically distinguished from an understanding of a philosopher's spiritual achievement.

Voegelin concluded by illustrating what such an appraisal of results would entail by comparing the response of Plato to the crisis of fifth-century Athens with that initiated by Descartes in the seventeenth century and developed more fully by Husserl. Such a comparison was legitimate insofar as the symbols created on the occasion of the reaction could be understood in the context of the new spiritual orientation or structure of consciousness to which they refer. The historically enduring value of Plato's reaction, for example, consisted not merely in his rejection of the myth of the polis but in his ability to articulate new and fundamental spiritual experiences by means of the philosophers' myth and create thereby a new spiritual world. When Plato's reaction was compared with that of Descartes and his successors, there was not much to choose between them so far as the radical negation of tradition was concerned. "But we must say as well that [with respect to the modern response] not much of a new spiritual creation nor of the development of a new symbolism can be observed." Following Descartes, not only was the traditional symbolism dissolved, so too were the underlying experiences excluded from the compass of philosophy. In Voegelin's view, Descartes and his successors abandoned the decisive problem of philosophy, "the creation of an order of symbols by which the place of human beings in the world is to be understood."[59] Husserl's transcendental ego in particular had the consequence for philosophy, understood in this large sense, of undermining its own possibility by speculatively destroying the coherence of the world, without which philosophy is impossible. Voegelin closed his essay with the following words: "The fundamental subjectivity of the egological sphere, which is Husserl's philosophical ultimatum and so nondiscussable, is the symptom of a spiritual nihilism that is perfectly acceptable as a reaction, but no more than that."

In the introduction to this analysis of Voegelin's essay, we noted that Voegelin identified his own motive as being one of dissatisfaction with the results of the philosophical analyses of time-consciousness. Like Husserl, then, he began his reflections as a reaction to disorder. But philosophy has as well a creative task, as Voegelin has observed, and the execution of that task depends in part on the "breadth of spirit" of the philosopher as well as on his skill at symbolizing his spiritual insights. Voegelin noticed this initially, as he said, in his rejection of restrictive deformations made evident in the arguments of other philosophers. But this negative or critical attitude had to be balanced by an account of the concrete consciousness that responded to reality, namely his own. In the "anamnetic experiments" to which we now turn, one can discover the constitution of Voegelin's consciousness as it is expressed in his own experiences of reality up to the date of composition.

The prefatory remarks to the twenty "anamnetic experiments" summarized the argument made in "On the Theory of Consciousness."[60] First, consciousness is not constituted as a stream or flow within the ego; second, while the intentionality of consciousness transcends itself into the world as perception, this is but one form of transcendence and must not be made thematic for a general theory of consciousness; third,

59. Voegelin's language regarding *die Stellung des Menschen in der Welt* echoed the title of Scheler's book.
60. References are to *Anamnesis*, pp. 61–76 in the German edition. The text is reproduced in Niemeyer's translation, pp. 36–51.

the experiences of the transcendence of consciousness, into the body, the external world, the community, history, and the Ground of Being, are given and, therefore, antecede any systematic reflections; fourth, systematic reflection commences from these given experiences; and fifth, such reflection is an event in the biography of a particular consciousness, additional to the given experiences of transcendence; it may lead to clarification of the problems of consciousness and its structure and, in meditation, may lead to insights with respect to the structure of reality.

Under no circumstances, therefore, is systematic reflection a radical beginning of philosophizing, nor can it lead to such a beginning. In his 1943 letter to Schütz dealing with Husserl's *Crisis*, Voegelin made matters very clear regarding what philosophers of history must not do, which was to make their own systematic and conscious reflections into the final criterion by which meaning is established. To do so, he said, was a "demonic" misappropriation of historical evidence. The proper procedure, for a philosopher of history or anybody else, is to explore one's own instrument for participating in the world of meaning, the cosmion, and to attend to this awareness when exploring the reality of the cosmos as a whole. In concrete terms, this means penetrating "every historical spiritual position" to the point

> where it is deeply rooted in the experiences of transcendence of the thinker in question. Only when the history of spirit is carried on with this methodolog-ical aim can it attain its philosophical aim, which is to understand the spirit in its historicity or, formulated in another way, to understand the historical forms of the spirit as variations on the theme of experience of transcendence. These variations succeed one another in an empirical and factual way, not ar-bitrarily; they do not constitute an anarchic series; they permit the recognition of sequences of order, even though the order is somewhat more complicated than the progress metaphysicians would wish it to be.

On this basis, Voegelin proceeded to his anamnesis, which attempted to make of his consciousness no more than the site of the "empirical and factual" variations. His *epoche* aimed at allowing whatever experiential teleology existed in his recollections to appear with a minimum of interference on his part and a minimum of interpretation.

Just as systematic reflection can never be the beginning of philosophiz-ing, neither can the radicalism of philosophizing be measured by the sys-tematic nature of the results. As Voegelin argued, the radical beginning of philosophizing is to be found, quite literally, in the biography of the philosophizing consciousness, in the experiences that lead consciousness toward systematic reflection and do so because they excite consciousness to the wonder of existence; accordingly, the radicalism of philosophical reflection will depend on the nature of the experiences and the excitements they engender along with the "attunement" of consciousness to its problems. The first task, leading to an eventual systematic exposition of the results, would be to recollect experiences that have engendered excitements leading to reflection. "Obviously, an anamnesis of this kind is a complicated process; it is only partly transparent and its results are far from unquestionable." In this context, an unquestionable interpretation would arise only on the basis of an arbitrary teleology. To use a formula Voegelin employed in his later writings, such unquestionability would amount to certain untruth rather than uncertain truth.

Bearing in mind these cautionary remarks, Voegelin did, nevertheless, add some interpretive notes to indicate which of the memories were "always present." Being always present, in the sense that their presence could not be dated, Voegelin said was an indication that such memories were important and that their meaning was clear. A second group was important as well, but the meaning was less clear, though it was clarified on the occasion of writing the memories down. A third group was less important, but reappeared in memory on the occasion of writing. A fourth group also appeared at this time, but the meaning was unclear to Voegelin, even after writing them down. Of a fifth group, Voegelin said nothing. His preliminary observation regarding this classification was that anamnesis can, in principle, either regress from present problems and their excitements in order to find the initial occasion for the outbreak of excitement or advance from the initial excitements and memories to current problems. The memories seem to be listed in the order of their biographical occurrence and were drawn from the first ten years of Voegelin's life. The content was selected as relevant in terms of excitements concerned with the transcendence of consciousness into space, time, matter, history, and also into imaginative or wish- or dream-time and wish- or dream-space. Several themes may coexist in a single recollection, though one can usually be seen to be dominant. In the presentation that follows, the recollections have been roughly classified according to theme. Interpretative observations follow the summary presentations.

Seven stories fell into the first two of Voegelin's classes and may be considered as the most important. Three were concerned primarily with space and four with time. Voegelin's earliest recollection, "The Months" (no. 1), was the response of his mother to a question by a saleslady in a bakery inquiring about his age. "Vierzehn Monate," fourteen months, his mother replied. Voegelin said he remembered feeling pride at being so splendid a thing as a *Monate*. "The word had weight; the sonority of the O with the subsequent nasal consonant may account for the fascination of something mysterious." A second, equally important memory of personal time, "Years" (no. 2), concerned the discovery of calendar years and the order of months, centered on the very agreeable time from Christmas, to New Year's, to his birthday, January 3. There was, one may say, both mystery and rhythmic order in time.

Two memories chiefly concerned history. The first was contained in young Eric's favorite schoolbook, called the *Book of Realities, Das Realienbuch* (no. 15). What particularly impressed him was that the history of the Prussian state was presented as moving backward from the present into the past, but as it did so the size of the kings who seemed to make up the state grew larger. Looming far in the background was the gigantic shadow of a prince, named "the Bear" because of his excellent qualities. Voegelin attributed his own ability to understand mythical images to this experience of reversed Prussian history. "I have always taken it for granted that the present was to be measured, as with Thucydides, in human terms; that with increasing distance men grew to the size of Solon and Lycurgus, that behind them there cavorted the heroes and that the horizon was securely and dependably closed with the gods."

The order of history, however, like the order of personal time, was mysterious as well as structured. In a second memory about history, "The Song of the Flag" (no. 17), Voegelin recalled a song that inspired children to dedicate their lives to the flag. The children were excited by the association of the song with the wreck of the gunboat *Iltis*, which sank with her flag flying and her doomed crew singing "The Song of the Flag." The flag still waves, Voegelin said, but "flags never had my whole sympathy." The flag that cracked in the wind grew quiet in the water. "Its color then faded and turned to a glimmer of silver. It really was no longer a flag but just a silvery waving. And then the waving, too, disappeared and there remained only a sound of calling stillness; sometimes softly, as from a distance, sometimes strong and close, so strong and close that it can hardly be distinguished from the call of the waves in which we go down." Perhaps even the great king, the "Bear," would go down like the flag.

One additional recollection regarding time, which had been long forgotten and appeared only on the occasion of writing down the anamnesis, concerned the Monk of Heisterbach (no. 4). This medieval worthy once had lived in a monastery, which in turn had become a romanesque ruin and then the goal of Sunday afternoon walks. The monk, Caesarius of Heisterbach, was the subject of many legends, chief among them being the story of a meditative walk that, to him, took place one afternoon but, to his fellow monks, took a hundred years. "I do not remember having felt an urge to pursue the meaning of that legend further in my mind. The event seemed to me wholly natural. But I do recall the temptation of the thought to let time stand still and then to return from lostness-in-thought into the world."

A final recollection focused on the topic of time concerned "Boats of the Cologne-Düsseldorf Line" (no. 10). These were first of all part of a festive world, luxury transport between great riverside hotels used by strange foreigners; their decks were aglow with lanterns, and people danced the night away. "It was a magic world sliding past, strange and mysterious forebodings of something intoxicating but unknown reached me." On Sundays, the Voegelin family used the boats for excursions, and the young man would watch the scenery steadily change and observe the gliding by of the land. "Sometimes I closed my eyes in order to interrupt the gliding and to see how after a minute the view had changed. But then I regretted it having done that; something precious seemed to have been lost in the not-observed gliding-by of this minute."

One additional "historical" memory, "The Kaiser" (no. 16), appeared under the same biographical circumstances, but Voegelin was unclear about its meaning. The kaiser was a familiar but remote icon: his picture was at home and at school, where Voegelin sang a song about him (to the tune of Papageno's song in *Die Zauberflöte*), but there existed little emotional depth to Voegelin's sentiments regarding his monarch. This attitude, Voegelin said, has remained with him; he kept a "psychically indifferent attitude to representatives of power." One day the kaiser came to the Rhineland; Voegelin was not allowed to join his mother and sister on a trip to Bonn to see him because he was being punished for having broken a window. However, the kaiser changed plans, bypassed Bonn, and came through Oberkassel where young Eric lived; as it happened, his automobile drove right in front of Voegelin's house. "In the evening I celebrated a triumph." Over the next few days Voegelin deduced from the conversation of the adults that he had not seen the kaiser after all, but only an equerry. "But I never let on."

The three important recollections regarding space were also tinged with ambiguity, paradox, and mystery. The first, called "The Loaf of Bread" (no. 14), concerned the problem of a baguette cut thickly on a slant to make pieces whose surfaces were of varying areas. "I always preferred to have my butter on the larger surface." But what happens when you cut a slice so thin that both sides look the same? And when does one side become greater? Voegelin's parents dismissed his questions as nonsense, and Voegelin thought that a wrong had been done to him. He concluded: "today I believe to have intellectually mastery of Zeno's paradoxes and their solution; but physically they are to me still a marvel, as they were then."

The second recollection, "St. Peter's Mountain" (*Der Petersberg;* no. 8), concerned a tiny house on top of a mountain visible from the Voegelins' home. He was shocked to learn that it was not tiny but a regular hotel, where people lived, and that if he went up there his own home would look like a toy. He had discovered "that space is a weird matter" and that the world he knew "looked differently if one stood at a different place in it." Space, said Voegelin, "was never something neutral, a quantitative extension; it always remained for me a problem of the soul." Moreover, this disturbance of the center of his world had implications for the relation of spatial position to psychic, spiritual, social, and political perspectives.

As an example of the latter, Voegelin distinguished the "Netherlanders" (no. 11), which referred to boats of the Netherland Line, carrying names from the Siegfried saga, from the "Dutchmen" (no. 12), who hawked herring and blue cheese and sold waffles at the fair each year. "That the blue cheese-vendors might come from Xanten was wholly unthinkable."[61] Similarly, the last recollection, of his emigration from Cologne to Vienna (no. 20), began with the excitement of his teacher, whom he revered, telling him that he was about to embark on an adventure; he discovered for himself what the move meant when he started school several weeks later in Vienna. A change in perspective occurred in "The Freighters" (no. 9) as well, and taught him "caution" in delicate questions of interpretation. These boats emitted thick black clouds of smoke, which Voegelin watched "partly with pleasure, partly with uneasiness—for when clouds appeared, then rain would follow, and I would have to stay in the house." One day he presented a weather report to his family: "tomorrow it would rain because today the freighters had produced many clouds." His parents laughed at him; he felt foolish and ashamed of his ignorance but learned the difference between two kinds of clouds. "I still love to see interesting relationships," Voegelin said, "but just when I see them in the most satisfactory and most beautiful way, the smoke of the freighters rises and clouds my pleasure."

Voegelin had one important recollection regarding what he called dream-space. This concerned another mountain, the Ölberg (no. 5), from the top of which one could see three other mountains, the big, middle, and small Breiberge, beyond which lay *Schlaraffenland*, a place of great indolence filled with enormous amounts of food, mostly desserts; the details were well known to him from fairy tales. There was only one

---

61. *Xanten* was the name of "the most glorious" of the Netherland boats, "a blue-gold mysterium" named for the castle of Siegmund to which Siegfried and Kriemhild returned before Siegfried was betrayed. See *Nibelungenlied*, chap. 11.

way to get there, and that was by eating one's way through the *Brei-berge*, the porridge-mountains. Getting to *Schlaraffenland* seemed worth some effort, but how much? It was difficult enough to climb the Ölberg; once one reached the summit of the Ölberg, the Breiberge were still far away; and even if you reached the Breiberge, there was still the problem of eating your way through the mountain of porridge. To make matters worse, Voegelin was sure that the Breiberge were made of *Griessbrei* (a kind of semolina mush similar to cream of wheat), and young Eric, like all sensible children, hated *Griessbrei*. He was only slightly relieved to learn from his father that he only had to eat through the small Breiberg. "I had a dark feeling that it might have to be the Big one. Most of all, I was afraid that I might get stuck in the middle of the mountain of porridge and suffocate. *Schlaraffenland* remained a beautiful dream; but the nightmare of the Breiberg has remained indissolubly linked with it. This area of timeless happiness appeared as a pleasure that was not worth the price."

Two other recollections also evoked a wish-space. The first of these, "The Old Seamstress" (no. 6), carried a meaning similar to "The Ölberg." The Voegelin family's seamstress, Mrs. Balters, read Voegelin stories from *The Leatherstocking Tales* by James Fenimore Cooper, but more important they conversed on grave theological topics. Mrs. Balters had excellent information regarding Paradise. As with *Schlaraffenland,* Voegelin was concerned about learning how to get there. He knew it was not in heaven above, because what was above was empty. Mrs. Balters informed him that, of course, it was not in heaven, but on earth, and you need not even die in order to get there. "That was most reassuring, because I could not imagine what dying was." Unfortunately, however, Paradise was a long way off to the east, "in Schina." Only a few people had ever successfully arrived there, and Mrs. Balters was not of their number. "The matter seemed hopeless to me; I gave up on Paradise." He did not, however, give up on "Schina."

The final memory of dream-space is called "The Cannons of Kronburg" (no. 19). Nothing of the larger story from which it was taken remained besides the fact that, when ships pass by Kronburg, the cannons say "boom." Kronburg itself is in the uttermost north. Ships pass by and no one asks where they come from or where they are going; there are no sounds as they pass. "No human beings; only the cannons; and they say 'boom!' with solemn sadness, at the end of the world."

The single story of dream-time has a mood quite different from "The Cannons of Kronburg." It was called "The Emperor's Nightingale" (no. 18), and Voegelin said that it was one of the most exciting fairy tales of his childhood. The emperor lay dying and Death sat on his chest, slowly removing the insignia of office. The Nightingale arrived and sung so gloriously that Death returned the emperor's sword and crown and allowed him to live. "The Nightingale still sings his heart-rending, breath-choking song against death. The significance a musical composition has for me is determined by the degree to which it brings back again this sweet anguish between death and life."

Two memories appeared on the occasion of Voegelin's writing down his recollections; neither, therefore, was in the category of being "always present." The first was called "Fools' Parade" (no. 3). Voegelin was about three and the time was Mardi Gras. It was the custom to march around in costume, form groups, carouse for a time, and drop away from the group. He was fascinated by the "dropping away." A parade came by, tightly bunched but for the last few rows of people; there it dissolved, as people moved off into side streets. The parade seemed intact, but Voegelin was disturbed by the phenomenon of crumbling. What would become of the parade if it dissolved into nothing? "I recall an oppressive feeling of a threat involved with this dropping away, an anxiety that the magic charm [that kept the parade together] could fade away."

The second, "The Comet" (no. 13), took place four or five years later on the occasion of the appearance of Halley's Comet. There was great excitement and the event was widely discussed, especially the possibility that the earth might pass through the comet's tail and, conceivably, bring the end of the world. Voegelin had his doubts about that, since the comet was so far away, but he still wondered what the end of the world would be like. He was told that houses would collapse and a lot of people would die, which was fearful indeed. He was relieved when the comet left. "Of this fear of the world's end, there remained a shudder of horror in the face of matter. 'The starry heaven above me' fills my heart with admiration only as long as I see it as a firmament with glittering points; when I think of what these points are, I am seized by a horror of the solitude in which globs of matter float around without meaning."

A final remembrance, "The Cloud Castle" (no. 7), Voegelin said, was filled with strong excitement, though he was still unclear about its meaning. The Cloud Castle, *Wolkenburg*, was always surrounded by clouds, as is proper; it was situated atop the Wolkenstein, the Cloud Peak, one of the Seven Mountains (The Ölberg, from the summit of which the Porridge Mountains were visible, beyond which lay *Schlaraffenland*, was also part of this group). The Knight of the Wolkenburg "dwells" there; there existed a saga about him, of which Voegelin knew nothing. The important thing was: he "dwelt" up there. This was highly unusual, because the great allure of the Wolkenstein was its inaccessibility. Besides the ever-present clouds at the top, there were quarries on the mountain and no one was allowed to climb it. From below nothing could be seen of the castle—if it existed at all. Voegelin at least did not doubt its existence. The uncertainty of the details, he said, may have accounted for the firm place it held in his soul. "The place was dark and moist, surrounded by rags of clouds; and the knight, a vague, sad, lost figure, traveling much on mysterious business, always returning in order to 'dwell' there for a while."

So far as I am aware, there has been very little discussion of Voegelin's anamneses. Apart from their rawness, as Tresan observed, there is the problem of their representativeness. Are the twenty recollections a selection? Were these charming or enigmatic stories of young Eric all that he could remember? If he selected these ones, because they seemed to him more significant in 1943, would he have selected different ones in 1973? Does the numerical order mean anything? What does one make of the surely extraordinary claim that Voegelin retained memory of an event that occurred when he was an infant of fourteen months? Was this recollection constructed from later events, or from third-party stories told to him at a later date?

The problem, it seems to me, is this: if Voegelin supplied his readers with sufficient context to make sense of the raw stories, he would be open to the criticism that he made of Husserl (though on a smaller historical scale), namely of telling the story he wants to tell about his own consciousness in 1943. On the other hand, assuming that the raw stories are provided in good faith, which seems reasonable enough, readers are left to their own devices, which means that the reader, rather than Voegelin, must deal with the problem of arbitrariness. It seems to me that the difficulty might be cleared up by a good psychologist in conversation with Voegelin, but that option has been permanently closed. A second-best approach might be to proceed upon the assumption, which we have already made, to a degree, that the experiences recollected in the anamneses are earlier manifestations of tendencies that appeared later in his scientific work.

The following remarks, in any event, are advanced very tentatively and without a great deal of confidence. We may begin with Voegelin's later observations that the twenty anamnetic sketches "added up to something like an intellectual autobiography up to the age of ten."[62] The question is: what, for example, does one make of the fact that, at fourteen months, Voegelin was highly pleased at being called "*Monate*"? Did it simply resonate with Leibniz's *Monade* when Voegelin announced

---

62. Voegelin, *Autobiographical Reflections*, 71.

this recollection to his astonished parents at age twenty? Because young Eric grew up on the banks of the Rhine, one might see in his later concern with process a reflection of his early experiences of the flow of the river, just as the many mountains in these memories might be taken as physical embodiments of Voegelin's desire to see things from above, like the Gods. The order of months and of parades, the danger of dissolution and "dropping away," and the solidity of his mother and his family all suggest a firm grounding in the ordinary realities upon which children necessarily rely.

Instead of reading back into Voegelin's childhood attitudes evident from his mature life, one might consider the stories more or less on their own and examine the relationship between the images that induce anxieties and the responses that overcome them. The "Song of the Flag" indicated that, in the end, human endeavors at building a political world, as cosmion, led to dissolution, just as the monastery of the monk of Heisterbach became a ruin and then the contemporary terminus for secular picnic pilgrimages on Sunday afternoons. Even though the history of the flag was exciting, it never retained Voegelin's whole sympathy; the monk, however, seemed capable of meditatively transcending the world of space and time entirely, which puts into perspective the dissolution of the flag in the waves.

The theme of history and of changes in interpretative perspective with respect to it was expressed in Voegelin's story of watching the riverside glide by then shutting his eyes: history glides by in one direction only. Moreover, it is filled with uncertainty (the kaiser changed his mind) and must be confirmed by authorities (the kaiser turned out to be an equerry); even then, authorities can be denied (young Eric never admitted he had not seen the kaiser) or their remarks devalued as being unjust (as when his questions about the two sides of a slice of bread were dismissed). He learned as well about changes in perspective regarding the boats, far-off hotels, the people and freighters from Holland, the "adventure" of moving to Vienna that turned out to be no adventure, the realization that clouds of smoke from the boats did not cause rain.

One could go on to consider other anxieties regarding the boats or history, the kaiser, getting to earthy paradise, the dissolution of the fool's parade, or the possibility of matter without spirit. They all contain similar accounts of puzzles and enigmas and difficulties that may be cleared up by insight. It is evident as well that Voegelin had developed an early distrust of magic. At the same time, however, these materials do more than record his more or less well formed understanding of his relation to authority, the state, the natural and imaginative world, and so on. Certainly there is more to these charming anecdotes than the record of idiosyncratic phobias and pleasures. To follow Voegelin's own indication, they were expressions of occasions when he experienced particularly meaningful realities.

Considered from this perspective, it is clear that a sense of wonder was a strong force in Voegelin's young soul. Of course, he took pride at being the sonorous *Monate,* felt foolish when he learned that smoke clouds do not cause rain, and felt he had been unjustly treated when his question about the two sides of a conic section of bread was considered to be nonsense. But the more pervasive experiences seem to center around the enticing curiousness of reality. The connections between smoke clouds and rain clouds *were* an "interesting relationship"; in later life, Voegelin still marveled at the physical representation of Zeno's paradoxes.

The order and disorder of a raucous parade were also expressed in his discoveries of the mystery of time and history. Events were singular and highly unpredictable: the kaiser could change his mind and drive down the other side of the river and turn out to be an equerry after all; the glorious flag sinks into the sea and becomes part of it. But at the same time events were ordered: the months of the year were regular, behind the present kings were the gigantic inhabitants of a mythic past to give them stability. In the same way, space was mysterious: perspective was always a "problem of the soul" whether it involved a mountaintop hotel or the downriver inhabitants of Xanten turning into cheese vendors.

Voegelin maintained a similar balance of consciousness regarding "religious" magic and the imagery of world-transcendence. The memory of the Porridge Mountains and the promise of *Schlaraffenland* led Voegelin to express the feeling that seemingly endless leisure and indolence were not worth striving for because of the nightmare that required his passage of the Breiberg, which might very well collapse on him. The "Chinese" Paradise promised by Mrs. Balters might have been too far away to make the effort of trying to get there plausible. Besides, it might be distant enough to turn out to be similar to Kronburg, silent except for the cannons.

The most fascinating recollections of transcendence, however, were those that expressed the real experience of moving beyond the world rather than the impossible or imaginary experience of actually getting beyond the world. Voegelin himself could contemplate at age five the possibility of leaving the world to be lost in thought like the Monk of Heisterbach; however, when he tried it, by shutting his eyes to interrupt the gliding by of the shoreline seen from the Sunday seat of a festive Cologne-Düsseldorf steamer, he regretted having lost the experience of perceiving the world slipping by. Even the process of world-transcendence had its price. Those boats themselves were magical, and

Voegelin was fearful of the transcendence of festive intoxication. Such a transcendence of the world, to use his later language, would be an experiential derailment, its transcendence an ersatz transcendence. Hence the boy's regret at shutting his eyes. In contrast, the ability of music to draw the soul beyond the world—and, indeed, to overcome death by its beauty—was expressed in the memory of "The Emperor's Nightingale." Similarly, the memories of the comet and of the Cloud Castle indicate the poles of consciousness in the process of transcending. In the first, the Kantian formula of the starry heavens above (with no mention of the other wonder, the moral law within) retained its power so long as one did not recall that the points of light were matter and void. The Cloud Castle, likewise, expressed the mystery of an invisible beyond. That it was not balanced in reflection by thoughts regarding the inaccessibility of the castle or the significance of the knight's mysterious comings and goings may account for its enigmatic meaning for Voegelin. On the other hand, its inaccessibility meant that it was unencumbered by the practical question of actually getting there, unlike "Chinese" paradise and *Schlaraffenland*, and so, perhaps, it was more firmly placed in his soul.

Voegelin's memories of wonder at the order and disorder of reality express the experience behind Leibniz's metaphysical questions. They confirm as well the classical philosophical experience that philosophy begins in wonder. In addition, the spiritual balance of order and disorder, of mysteriousness and pragmatism, of anxiety and overcoming it, of world-transcendence and world-immanence expresses experiences that Voegelin later described as the tension of existence "in-between." These anamnetic experiences indicated that Voegelin's consciousness was open to a wide range of reality. His was, to recall again Bergson's term, an open soul. But Voegelin's consciousness was concerned with verification of reality as well as being responsive to it. His was also, therefore, a balanced soul.

In the preceding chapters we have seen that Voegelin often criticized others for their inadequate or incomplete philosophical anthropologies or even for their obliviousness to the need for an "idea of man" in order to develop adequate criteria of relevance. In this chapter we have indicated that, at the center of any philosophical anthropology, was a philosophy of consciousness. We may conclude with a brief examination of Voegelin's account of one book that did present adequately a philosophical anthropology, Jan Huizinga's *Homo Ludens*.[63] In "his last great treatise," Huizinga proposed to consider play as "an irreducible element in the

63. Voegelin, review in *Journal of Politics* 10 (1948): 179–87.

nature of man" that becomes manifest in law and politics, science and philosophy, poetry and art or, more broadly, in the history of culture. For Huizinga, history was "the field in which the nature of man unfolds, both in its glory and its baseness." It was studied, therefore, neither out of mere curiosity nor simply to understand the pragmatic course of events, but to apprehend the sense of human existence itself. "Man as a whole exists historically," Voegelin said, "and therefore history must become a history of human culture, embracing all human manifestations." But when a field of study was so broadly understood, the possibility of being overwhelmed by detail was an obvious danger. As with Voegelin's remarks regarding Cairns, and as he had discussed at length in correspondence with Schütz, criteria of relevance, "a system of categories which permit [the historian] to order and select the materials," are required.

Huizinga presented such a set of criteria and more. "It is human nature itself which manifests itself in history; hence a philosophy of human nature is required for the interpretation of its historical manifestations. The *Homo Ludens* is the systematic presentation of Huizinga's philosophical anthropology." Huizinga's argument, in sum, was that human culture has been the historical achievement of *homo ludens*, not *homo sapiens*.

Voegelin characterized Huizinga as less an innovator than one who had resumed a theme from classical philosophy that had for centuries been ignored and forgotten. In particular, Plato's educational theory in the *Laws* developed the close connection between *paideia*, education, and *paidia*, play. All young creatures play, but human beings can order their play through rhythm and melody, which begins the choric education of children. It ends as the "serious play" of the polis in partnership with God (*Laws* 659d, 803c). Play confirms that animals are more than mechanical and that humans are more than reasonable—for play transcends reason. Play has a quality beyond what is given and everyday, which is another way of indicating that it is irreducible. Voegelin surveyed the questions Huizinga discussed and declared: "there is even more to his theory of play than his treatment of the problem would reveal. And this 'more' is of specific importance for a theory of politics."

Play was defined by Huizinga as a *superabundans*, an excess or overflow of spirit beyond necessity or the preservation of existence. In relation to this necessity of existence, play is not pragmatic action but the enacting of a role in an imaginative world. Voegelin pointed out, however, that the concept of *superabundans* should not be confined to play. Rather, it is an element of transcendence that can be found in inorganic and vegetative beings as well as in the specifically animal form of play. With these other forms of being, existence is heightened by qualities that have no pragmatic relationship to causal sequences: the patterns of snowflakes or clouds, the distinctive shapes of oak or holly leaves. "The aesthetic and moral values which attach to the order in the universe," Voegelin said, "as well as to colors and shapes in the organic realms are a *superabundans* beyond natural laws and physiological necessities." Voegelin proposed, therefore, distinguishing the generic pervasiveness of transcendence from the specific elements characteristic of play as one of the phenomena of transcendence in animals.

The separation of generic and specific is required for a coherent interpretation of political culture insofar as archaic cultures, including the Hellenic, understood their political order in terms of a cosmic analog. The significance of cosmological symbols "is inexplicable unless we allow for a continuity of meaning between the inorganic and human levels of being." This means that the cosmos is more than relations of space, time, and mass that are described by the equations of physics. The cosmos "also contains the *superabundans* of meaningful order, form, and rhythm which enters into the symbolization of human life in community." Bearing this "correction" of Huizinga's theory in mind, Voegelin indicated two important implications for political science.

First, play is an intermediate category between the necessity of existence and the actual intellectual and spiritual content of culture. Considered from above, play is not itself a meaning so much as a vehicle for worlds of meaning. Seen from below it is not a determinant of meaning, as in the Marxist sense of sub- and superstructure, but an independent element linking the spirit with animal nature by reason of its transcendence of necessity. This peculiar intermediate position accounts for the attitude of players who are both serious about playing and aware that they are "merely" playing. In the larger context of history, for example, it accounts for the existence of more than one cosmological, or more than one ecumenical, empire, at the same time, which "logically" ought to be impossible, but yet is accepted with equanimity by all the players. "Societies seem to play their game, abiding by their rules, without regard to what is happening on the level of pragmatic history." Likewise during the period of Western national states, one after another Western society discovered itself to be divinely chosen and would rather fight than give up the grandiose role that it gave itself.

A second insight concerned the new light shed by Huizinga on early civilization. On the one hand, he showed that Hellenic civilization, which is often understood to be directly antecedent to modern Western civilization, contains a large array of archaic elements that usually are ignored by modern historians. On the other hand, "we find a surprising closeness of structure between Hellenic and Sinic civilizations." Whatever the continuity between Hellas and the modern West, it is put into a new context when compared to the "broad band of meaning that links Hellas and China." The insights regarding equivalence of meaning of Chinese and Hellenic symbols are discussed at greater length in the following chapters. Huizinga's importance for philosophical anthropology, however, also lay in his elaboration of play as a category of mediation, of existence as "between."

Horace's aphorism "naturam expellas furca, tamen usque recurret" surely applies to the genesis of philosophical anthropology. Under pressure from the specialized social sciences as well as intellectual currents such as positivism and historicism, the concept of human nature was virtually expelled from the serious discussion of human being. Yet it returned, under the title *philosophical anthropology,* responding not only to intellectual inadequacies but also to a more general crisis of culture and of politics.

Voegelin's philosophical anthropology can perhaps best be understood as an extension of Scheler's, particularly Scheler's image of man as an ontologically unified process consisting, nevertheless, of ontologically distinguishable subprocesses: physical, biological, and spiritual.[64] Several interconnected implications were drawn from Scheler's argument: first, human being is "rooted" in animal, physical, and cosmic being; second, there can be no legitimate reduction of one "level" of being to another; third, any adequate philosophical anthropology must include a well-articulated philosophy of consciousness; fourth, such a philosophy of consciousness must be able to account for its own awareness of the world-transcendent Ground of Being; and fifth, the historically variegated accounts of consciousness of reality must be integrated by a philosophy of history.

Voegelin's philosophy of consciousness, in the form it had attained during the 1940s, was both a coherent account of the instrument of analysis he used in writing his *History of Political Ideas* and a sustained criticism

64. One might make the same argument with regard to Bergson. As did Scheler (*Man's Place,* 47–48), Bergson saw in love the highest commitment (*The Two Sources of Morality and Religion,* trans. R. Ashley Andra and Cloudesley Brereton [Garden City: Doubleday Anchor, 1935], 233); like Scheler, Bergson indicated to Voegelin "that human societies have moral cultures without benefit of theory" (HI 63/11). Moreover, Bergson was a central figure for Schütz, and his philosophy was the subject of several letters between the two. Other parallels are brought out in Ellis Sandoz, "Myth and Society in the Philosophy of Bergson," and Dante Germino, *Political Philosophy and the Open Society,* esp. chap. 9. Voegelin explained some of his differences to Germino in a letter of December 5, 1974, HI 14/14. See also Voegelin, *Autobiographical Reflections,* 36, 114, and Helmut R. Wagner with Ilja Srubar, *A Bergonian Bridge to Phenomenological Psychology.*

of Husserl. Considered in this latter aspect, Husserl's phenomenology, along with other attempts to reduce philosophy to epistemology, was an intellectual symptom of a general crisis in Western civilization no less important than the apocalyptic orgies of war and totalitarian political movements. Both Husserl and the political ideologues advanced their own restricted or deformed consciousness as the model of human consciousness as such, just as their respective philosophies of history were advanced as providing a comprehensive account of the meaning of history. In response, Voegelin elaborated his own theory of consciousness as well as described from within the early experiences of reality that continued to be present and so helped constitute its structure. In the course of his argument Voegelin noted the importance of mythical symbols for rendering transfinite experiences intelligible to finite consciousness, the systematic exposition of which he called *process theology*. The analysis of the process of his own consciousness indicated that it was, indeed, open to the full amplitude of reality, its mysteriousness, its order and disorder, and the several modes of transcendence.

For Voegelin, therefore, philosophical anthropology designated a comprehensive frame of reference within which information can be appraised as relevant to an account of political reality. Especially important in this respect was the insight that the problem of transcendence was the decisive problem for philosophy. Moreover, he indicated as well that a "genuine historical reflection" consists in following the process of development of this decisive problem as it was understood and experienced in the past and made evident in previous philosophical and nonphilosophical "self-testimonies." In this way, Voegelin said, one may undertake to work out a philosophy of history. In his *History of Political Ideas,* and indeed before that project got under way, Voegelin discovered in Jean Bodin a way of "reading" history that proved central to his own work.

6

The "Reader" of History

At the center of Voegelin's political science was his philosophical anthropology; at the center of his philosophical anthropology was his philosophy of consciousness; at the center of his philosophy of consciousness was the concrete consciousness of the individual, Eric Voegelin, political scientist. Voegelin put the matter more tersely in the opening words to *Anamnesis*: "The problems of human order in society and history originate in the order of consciousness. The philosophy of consciousness is, therefore, the centerpiece of a philosophy of politics."[1] The "problems of human order in society and history" are the subject matter of political science; by saying they *originate* in the order of consciousness Voegelin meant that "consciousness is the center from which radiates the concrete order of human existence into society and history." Accordingly, political science entails "the constant interchange between investigations of concrete phenomena of order and analyses of consciousness that make the human order in society and history intelligible." The organization of *Anamnesis* reflected these propositions and principles.

The book was divided into three sections. The first and last contain meditative exercises: we have already discussed the 1943 analysis of consciousness. Part III, "The Order of Consciousness," consisted of a single article—"What Is Political Reality?"—that Voegelin first presented as an address to the German Political Science Association in 1965. Voegelin characterized the last section as consisting of a "comprehensive and temporarily satisfactory new formulation of a philosophy of consciousness." The two meditative exegeses of consciousness, undertaken some twenty-two years apart, were related to a series of "special studies" collected under the heading *Experience and History*. These studies ranged from the justification of a new concept in political science, which Voegelin called historiogenesis, to speculative meditations on eternal being in

1. Voegelin, *Anamnesis*, 7.

212

time, as well as more or less conventional interpretations of political texts and political history that had been written over the previous quarter century. They were intended to "demonstrate how the historical phenomena of order give rise to the type of analysis that culminates in the meditative exploration of consciousness."[2] The 1943 meditation had as one of its purposes the recollection of the tensions, the dynamic, and the structure of consciousness under contemporary conditions, which included the "reports" of previous exegeses undertaken by Aristotle, Augustine, Descartes, Husserl, and others, that had attained the formal and dogmatic shape of several philosophical "schools." The recovery of the original experiences, presented in the anamneses, enabled Voegelin to pierce the shell of the "reports" and analyze the "historical phenomena of order" as they appeared in the texts and events discussed in the "special studies."

Voegelin's 1966 letter to Heilman indicated the connection between the study of the actual phenomena of order and the consciousness of the individual who undertakes the interpretation of the historical phenomena. In the more conventional language we have been using in this analysis of Eric Voegelin and the foundations of modern political science, philosophy of consciousness implies philosophy of history. But what is philosophy of history?

The phrase *philosophy of history* was used first as a technical term by Voltaire, in the middle of the eighteenth century. As a rule of thumb in the study of the "history of ideas," terminological innovations, such as *history of ideas* itself, have usually been introduced in response to historical and experiential novelties. This was true of Voltaire's invention.[3]

During the two or three centuries prior to the publication of Voltaire's *Essai sur les moeurs et l'esprit des nations* (1756) a complex configuration of historical events was understood by those who reflected upon them to convey that an epoch had ended. First of all, the Reformation had fractured the church in the West as an institutional representation of humanity. Frederick the Great expressed a new political consciousness when, in 1740, he offered Voltaire his views on the significance of the death of Charles VI. "The Emperor is dead," wrote Frederick, "now is the moment for a complete change in the old political system."[4] His remarks

2. Voegelin to Robert Heilman, June 19, 1966, HI 17/9.
3. This analysis of Voltaire is taken from *From Enlightenment to Revolution,* ed. John H. Hallowell, chap. 1. It corresponds to "Apostasy," in *HPI,* VI:31–70.
4. Frederick to Voltaire, October 26, 1740, in *Les Oeuvres complètes de Voltaire,* vol. 91 (Geneva: Institut et Musée Voltaire, 1970), 342.

reflected the fact that from as early as the Treaty of Utrecht (1713), a plurality of sovereign states in a quasi-constitutional balance with one another existed as ultimate political units with little or no relation to the empire. The new power configuration was accompanied by a new sense of community centered on the national body politic. For Frederick the new national power configuration and its balance seemed to have overwhelmed the symbolic significance of the empire, including its Roman heritage and the connection to Western universality. Western ecumenic expansion, which was akin to the new power configuration inasmuch as it was also a pragmatic development, had led to the discovery and settlement of the "new world" by Europeans. In 1658 a Jesuit, Martinio Martini, published his *Sinicae Historiae,* the first comprehensive Western history of China. Thus, a century or so later, awareness of the civilization of China had come within the ken of all educated Europeans, and trade with Asia was begun more or less on a basis of equality. More important, the immense size and civilizational grandeur of Asiatic societies put the *orbis terrarum* of classical antiquity in a new perspective and reintroduced the problem of "intercivilizational" contacts. For the first time in modern Europe, there was a widespread awareness that Christian civilization could be measured by standards other than its own. As a result, the necessity to elaborate an "idea of man" that could serve as a basis for understanding law, politics, and ethics, but that was not limited by what was increasingly seen to be the apparent parochialism of Christianity, was widely felt.

That something new was in the air, then, was obvious not just to scholars but to all who had the leisure to consider the question. One such, the marquise du Châtelet-Lorraine, expressed the new self-understanding in two queries, written in the margin of Bossuet's *Discours sur l'histoire universelle* (1681), which was the last "theology of history" written along the lines of Augustine's *City of God.*[5] In the first of her notes she questioned the significance of the Jews for "history," and in the second she wondered about the preeminence of Rome, as compared to the much greater significance that ought be accorded the Russian Empire. The marquise did not initiate a historiographic revolution so much as by her naïveté indicate that one had already occurred.

According to Bossuet, as to Augustine, history was guided by providence so that humans ought neither unduly to fear terrestrial misery nor unduly to admire terrestrial grandeur. Whatever the fortunes of a Christian people, whether for apparent good or ill, they were in the hands of God. One may say, therefore, that Bossuet's *Discours* was written on

5. See Karl Löwith, *Meaning in History,* chap. 5.

the basis of a Christian anthropology. The Christian account of human being thus provided the criteria of relevance for his selection of historical evidence presented in the *Discours.*

Bossuet's book was divided into three parts. The first began with the creation of the world and surveyed events from Adam to Charlemagne. He made no distinction in part I between what we might call profane and sacred events but rather conflated the two in a complex mixture of ages and epochs. The seventh and last age was initiated with the birth of Christ; the establishment of the Western Christian Empire by Charlemagne and its continuation by the French monarchy made this part an edifying manual for the instruction of Bossuet's royal and noble pupils. The second part corresponded to Saint Augustine's sacred history in the strict sense and consisted in a presentation of the unfolding of religious history, especially as concerned the Jews, the appearance of Christ, and the history of the church. The third part discussed the history of empires, understood as a story of educational tribulation for God's chosen people. The chief beneficiaries of imperial history, therefore, had been the Jews, though Bossuet also saw God's plan at work in the coincidence of the Roman imperial unification of the Mediterranean basin with the evangelical spreading of the Gospel and the establishment of the church. As late as 1681, then, the Christian "idea of man" was able to provide criteria for ordering history into a meaningful story.

By questioning the significance of the Jews and of Rome, the marquise du Châtelet was also challenging the Christian anthropology that provided the context within which the historical position of the Jews and of Rome was meaningfully situated. For the marquise, as for her witty correspondent, Voltaire, Christianity was an event "in" history, which in turn had to be meaningful on the basis of some other and larger context. In conventional terms, the marquise and Voltaire were looking for a story, an idea, an entelechy within which the concrete events of pragmatic and spiritual history unfolded in a meaningful sequence. Christianity had heretofore provided such a context inasmuch as it transfigured the pragmatic events of historical action and passion into the scenes of a spiritual drama of humanity. But Christianity was precisely what was being called into question. Whereas for Bossuet sacred and profane were intermingled but distinguishable, for the marquise and for Voltaire the distinction between the two was false. By this account, "really" there was but a singular secular history, an inner-worldly chain of events, an immanent stream of genesis that nevertheless contained or expressed a universal, meaningful order of human history. Anything else, Voltaire once remarked, was "a pack of tricks we play on the dead." In consequence, sheer quantitative greatness became the defining factor of significance. For the marquise, as for Frederick, Rome had no universalist symbolical meaning and so was retired to the status of a limited historical phenomenon.

Voltaire was impressed with the remarks of his quondam hostess and patron and undertook to respond to them in his *Essai*. His term *philosophy of history* was therefore polemical, developed in direct opposition to Bossuet's *theology of history*. Voltaire's criticism rested on two points: first, Bossuet's allegedly universal history was in fact not universal at all. He considered only four antique empires, after all, and said nothing of the Russians, as the marquise had observed. Nor, of course, were the Chinese or Indians included in this putative universe, even though Martini's *Sinicae Historiae* had been published over two decades before his *Discours*, and so presumably was available to him.[6] What was worse, said Voltaire, when Bossuet did consider the empires of antiquity, he made it appear as if they were concerned chiefly to instruct the Jews, which provided Voltaire with the occasion for a joke.[7] In contrast, Voltaire declared he "would speak of the Jews as of Scythians or Greeks." In point of fact, Bossuet was perfectly well aware that the significance of the Jews lay in the spiritual drama of religious life not in the secular changes of empire. Voltaire was obliged, therefore, to answer the question: if Bossuet's history was in fact parochial, not universal, in what did universal history consist?

Before considering Voltaire's response, we may note his second objection to Bossuet, namely that there was no evidence of providential guidance to the course of history. This apparently fatal objection depended for its force on a coherent analysis of the significance of providence. Unfortunately, Voltaire had only the haziest understanding of what Bossuet meant by the term. Very approximately, and in the context of his theology of history, divine providence for Bossuet symbolized the experience of anticipation of the Parousia. Faith and trust in God's ultimate deliverance and final salvation were clearly central elements in the Christian "idea of man." Both the Creation of the world by God and its eschatological transfiguration expressed the substance of Christian universality, but neither the Beginning nor the End was a historical event, properly speaking.

Voltaire's response to his second criticism of Bossuet, namely that his allegedly universal history had forgotten about the universe and

6. See the discussion of Bossuet in Edwin J. Van Kley, "Europe's 'Discovery' of China and the Writing of World History," *American Historical Review* 76 (1971): 358–85.
7. Voltaire, *Oeuvres complètes*, vol. 7 (Paris: Furne, 1846), 684 (*Dictionnaire philosophique*, article "Histoire," section 2).

substituted fable, was to claim that his *Essai* was merely a supplement and correction to Bossuet's *Discours*. In fact, however, it was an attempt to replace it root and branch. Voltaire allowed that Bossuet had provided a splendid account of antiquity, even though he overemphasized the importance of Israel. His first task, then, was to supply the missing data relative to China, India, Persia, and Islam and to continue Bossuet's European narrative from Charlemagne to Louis XIII.

Voltaire's criticism was not without value. Clearly China and India would have to be related to Western Christian history, but how? We may sharpen the theoretical issue by considering the following: Bossuet's universalism depended on the validity of his account of the Beginning and the End. Those two world-transcendent "events" were not part of the historical narrative but rather endowed it with its meaningful and providential form. By Bossuet's account, unity of meaning was ensured by the universality of the Christian spiritual drama: as with Augustine, sacred history governed the meaning of profane history. Yet this spiritual drama, its universalist form notwithstanding, ignored India and China. But then, by what right did it claim to be universal? How could the empirical or profane history of non-Christian societies and civilizations be integrated into the putatively universal Christian drama of humanity? That was the real question raised by Voltaire.

His response to it was to undertake an up-to-date quasi-encyclopedic survey of historical phenomena. Such an enterprise was questionable for two reasons. First, it would have to be revised as additional knowledge came to light. His polite jest, that history was a pack of tricks we play on the dead, was meant seriously after all. A second and more fundamental objection is that even if Voltaire (or any other historian) were able to provide a complete account of every historical event, the encyclopedic result would not necessarily contain any unity of meaning. Of course, the encyclopedic information contained in handbooks is useful, but criteria of meaning must be established on other grounds, as we have seen, namely those of philosophical anthropology, whether Christian or not. In fact, Voltaire did undertake to construct a unity of historical meaning on non- and indeed on anti-Christian grounds.

The purpose of his *Essai* was not, he said, to recount the detail of facts but to tell *l'histoire de l'esprit humaine*. The plot of this story of the human spirit was clear: it consisted in tracing "the steps by which we have advanced from the barbarian rusticity of [feudal] times to the *politesse* of our own." Voltaire was confident that his *Essai* would bring these steps to light because, as he said with deceptive candor, he had selected the facts with considerable care. Contemplating this array of facts, he believed all reasonable men would conclude that the story was, indeed, of the "extinction, rebirth, and progress of the human spirit."[8]

Voltaire's remark was a transparent *petitio principii.* The structure of his account, however, copied that of Bossuet. Parallel to the universal biblical story of the creation and descent of mankind was the aforementioned encyclopedic, textbook completeness; parallel to the providential presence of the Holy Spirit was the intramundane *esprit humain;* parallel to the apocalyptic transfiguration of the end of days was the ecumenic spread of *politesse;* the historical extinction, rebirth, and progress of the human spirit were the secular equivalent to the Christian drama of the fall of humanity in the story of Adam, the redemption of humanity in the story of Christ, and the transfiguration of humanity in the evocation of the Last Judgment.

Voltaire had, in short, constructed a complex series of categories that were both analogous to Christianity and derived from it. The purpose of doing so was to formulate a secular equivalent to the interpretative categories of Christian sacred history. In this way, he believed he could create a context within which the expanded array of historical materials that fell under his notice could be meaningfully presented. At the same time, he would avoid the "fables" of Christian doctrine, which he had rejected on other grounds.

Voltaire's philosophy of history, Voegelin said, was no mean achievement. It served as a model for the great speculations of Comte and Marx during the nineteenth century, and for their twentieth-century successors. Ignoring for a moment the question of intramundane spirituality, there remains the aforementioned methodological defect common to all historical speculations of the Voltairean type. All stories, whether putatively universal or not, express a unity of meaning. Indeed one may say that the essential or defining element of a story is that it contain and express a unity of meaning. Now, the attempt to create a universal story on the basis of an encyclopedic survey of historical evidence will necessarily be futile unless at the same time one can establish on principle the knowledge that the empirical survey is exhaustive. In other words, no unity of meaning can be established on the basis of a pretended encyclopedic survey unless history is ended and the whole of its course known. From the perspective of Voltaire's secular and intramundane position, this is impossible because, in principle, and ignoring other problems of method, only the past can be known. Moreover, the meaning of the past must be conditioned by the present perspective of the author. It is for this reason that the imposing stability of Christian anthropology

8. Voltaire, *Remarques,* in *Oeuvres complètes,* vol. 21 (1846), 264, 266 ff.

and Christian theology of history contrasts so strikingly with the instability of intramundane equivalents to sacred history and intramundane
anthropologies developed in the aftermath of the Enlightenment.

The dynamic of instability is clearly expressed in Voltaire's evocation
of the *esprit humaine*. In light of Christian anthropology, the human spirit,
left to its own devices, is apt to err or rebel. In light of Christian theology
of history, the intramundane historical consciousness is necessarily pre-
disposed toward novelty and the endless production of expressions of
a contemporary sense of epoch based on ever-changing intramundane
sentiments. But times change and so do sentiments. This is why Voltaire's
evocation of *politesse* as the goal toward which the labors of history were
directed looks so bizarre, even though a powdered and bewigged French
philosophe may provide a more agreeable image of perfected humanity
than a Comtian captain of industry, a Marxist "socialist man," or even
a Husserlian functionary of humanity. In fact, the theoretical fallacy lies
in the principle of any such evocation and not in its contingent content.
Moreover, the fallacy is not particularly difficult to understand, which
raises the obvious question: why did Voltaire commit it?

Voegelin provided a brief answer in *The New Science of Politics*.[9] By
transforming the Christian fulfillment by grace of the Holy Spirit in death
into the fulfillment of the polite intellectual by grace of the human spirit
in life, Voltaire had created an imaginary "eidos" or essence or meaning
to history. But, remarked Voegelin,

> Things are not things, nor do they have essences, by arbitrary declaration.
> The course of history as a whole is no object of experience; history has no
> eidos, because the course of history extends into the unknown future. The
> meaning of history, thus, is an illusion; and this illusionary eidos is created
> by treating a symbol of faith as if it were a proposition concerning an object
> of immanent experience.

Simply pointing out the fallacious intellectual act does not explain it but,
on the contrary, underlines the problem. One cannot assume that Voltaire
was too dull to understand the questionable nature of the enterprise,
nor that he understood it and went ahead anyway for some dark and
malevolent reason. "Obviously," Voegelin said, "such acts cannot be
explained simply by stupidity and dishonesty. A drive must rather be
assumed in the souls of these men, which blinded them to the fallacy."
One can analyze the nature of the "drive" by an examination of the
consciousness of one so driven. This may be accomplished by raising
the question: what is achieved when individuals undertake the fallacious

---

9. Quotations are taken from pp. 120–22.

construction? "On this point," Voegelin said, "there is no doubt. They achieve a certainty about the meaning of history, and about their own place in it, which otherwise they would not have had." Consciousness of certainty, then, eclipses whatever intellectual misgivings one such as Voltaire may have had regarding the incoherence of an argument that appears only to reflective consciousness anyway.

That there is a genuine existential problem involved and not merely an intellectual one is indicated as well by Bossuet's own polemical writings. His *Histoire des variations des Églises protestantes* (1688) was a defense of the accumulated wisdom of the church in the face of Protestant individualism. His argument was prudential, not intellectual or rational. Christianity, understood as a historical phenomenon and the source of community substance and cohesion in the West, required the institutional authority of the church to keep it intact. Without such authority the tradition that sustained the sacredness of religious scripture would dissolve. It was, therefore, less the contents of Protestant doctrines that troubled Bossuet than the fact that they were the occasion for schism, and schism, he held, would eventually lead to the historicization of Christianity and thereby to its eclipse.[10] Bossuet was of the opinion that the contemporary dynamics of Protestantism were comparable to the succession of heresies during the early Christian era. He quoted Tertullian's comment that what is permitted Valentinus or Marcion must be accorded the Valentinians and Marcionites, which is to say if sectarian founders claim a right to innovate they cannot also claim a right to prohibit subsequent innovation. The initial break with the church and with its orthodoxy inevitably leads to a general instability of both institutions and doctrines.

Voegelin was not concerned with problems of ecclesiastical unity and so, unlike Bishop Bossuet, was not compelled to argue in favor of the collective wisdom of the church, though he was very much aware of the importance and the significance of institutional stability for the maintenance of the Western or even the French cosmion. For Voegelin, changes in the social and political order, such as the fracturing of the Western church into Protestant, Anglican, and Roman Catholic churches, had a direct and evident impact on the order of consciousness of individuals such as Voltaire who sought to understand these political and social events. The anxieties expressed in Bossuet's polemical writing were, in turn, amply confirmed by the time of Voltaire. These observations indicate the connection between consciousness and politics and the necessity of linking the investigation of actual historical changes to the

---

10. *Histoire*, preface, in *Oeuvres complètes de Bossuet*, vol. 4 (London: Guérin, 1862), iii, iv. The *Histoire* itself is on 410 ff.

sentiments of the analyst, even when, as with Voltaire, the sentiments are inconsistent and confused. At the same time, Voltaire's objections to Bossuet and to Christian theology of history could not be met simply by pointing to the unhappy consequences of disbelief in the order of consciousness of enlightened intellectuals.

Voegelin provided his own summary reflections on the continuity of this historical process under the title "The Dynamics of Secularization," which is, of course, a vast and complex topic. The presentation of the outline of the problems involved at this point does no more than hint at its complexity. Other aspects of the question are treated in the following chapters. In sum, it was Voegelin's view that what we now refer to as the secularization of history, of which Voltaire's polemical "philosophy of history" was an important symptom, may more accurately be characterized as the dissociation of the constituent elements of medieval Western universalism, namely spirit, reason, and imperium. Regarding the last of these, the remark of Frederick the Great quoted earlier indicated that the imperium had fragmented into particular national realms. The dissolution of the spiritual-temporal unity of Christendom, articulated into empire and papacy and justified by the Gelasian doctrine of the two swords, by Augustine's theology of the two cities, and eventually by the words of Christ (Matt. 22:21) into the organizational opposition of church (or churches) and state (or states) left open not only the question of the spiritual representation of Western humanity but also the question of what would replace the empire as the basis for order among Western political units.

The second factor to dissociate from the medieval configuration was reason. Beginning in the thirteenth and fourteenth centuries, Averroism and nominalism began the development that ended with the autonomous secular reason and natural law of the seventeenth century. The social order that lent support to this intellectual movement consisted in the array of lawyers, scientists, and philosophers outside ecclesiastical orders, as well as the royal corps of administrators.

The third factor, the disintegration of the medieval spiritual power into one pole of the church-state pair, was perhaps the most complex. According to Voegelin's account, the spiritual ascendancy of the church was only in part a consequence of its spiritual heritage. It was also an effective civilizing organization by virtue of the institutional and administrative competencies that it had acquired through compromise with the surrounding classical and then barbarian civilizations. But by the late middle ages, Europe had begun to develop into a new civilizational order and the novel European communities (in the cities, for example) were entirely capable of continuing Western civilization without the economic and political leadership of the church. For one reason or another, the church did not liquidate its economic strength nor abandon its political position. Moreover, as guardian of the civilizational heritage of classical antiquity, the church was bound eventually to conflict with the civilizational achievements of the growing secular European civilization. In order to preserve its own spiritual mission under these new circumstances, the church would have had to reach a new compromise, similar in principle to that concluded with Roman civilization in antiquity. Specifically, it would have had to abandon those elements of its ancient tradition that were incompatible with the new civilization. Again, however, the evidence indicates that the church was unable to adjust.

Voegelin distinguished three general phases in the process by which the medieval unity of imperium, reason, and spirit dissociated into modern fragments. The first or "political" phase extended from 1300 to 1500. The refusal of the church to reduce its economic and political profile led first to fourteenth-century Anglicanism, then to fifteenth-century Gallicanism, and finally to the wholesale confiscations during the Protestant Reformation of the sixteenth century. The second phase, extending from about 1500 to 1700, was focused on the status of reason. The inevitable friction between the new astronomy and physics and the Babylonian cosmology preserved in the Old Testament led to the celebrated conflicts between Bruno and Galileo and the Inquisition. The third phase extended from around 1700 to the present and consists in the great spiritual clash between the modern, critical, and secular treatment of sacred texts and sacred history and the ecclesiastical interpretation of the meaning of faith. The spiritual phase of dissociation was exemplified in the conflict between Voltairean philosophy of history and Augustinian theology of history.

The development of political and of intellectual autonomy, Voegelin's first two phases, had a profound and devastating effect on the institutional position of the church and thereby induced deep structural fractures into the cultural integrity of Western civilization. The expropriation of church properties and the growth of sovereign political units acknowledging no legal superior did not by itself impair the spiritual mission and purpose of the church. The problem lay elsewhere. With the transformation of the medieval tension between spiritual and temporal authority into the modern political conflict between church and state came the privatization of spiritual institutions and the monopoly of the public sphere by the new sovereign political units. As early as the first Diet of Speier (1526) it was decreed that, in matters of faith, princes might act in such a manner that they could answer to God and emperor. By the

Peace of Augsburg (1555) the "monstrously cynical formula '*Cujus Regio, Ejus Religio,*'" as Toynbee put it, enshrined the destruction of any public representation of spiritual authority as a condition for public peace.[11]

The destruction of public authority in spiritual matters did not mean that Western society carried on as before, with the sole difference being that the traditional spiritual exercises were henceforth undertaken behind closed doors. On the contrary, the destruction of the church left a spiritual vacuum that was quickly filled by the new sources of spiritual order: the divine right of kings, nationalism, humanitarianism, liberalism, socialism, racism, pacifism, feminism, and so forth. The plethora of spiritual movements with which modern society has come to be afflicted would, indeed, have confirmed Bossuet's worst fears with respect to schism.

In Chapter 3 we considered some of the more ominous consequences of the triumph of autonomous reason in the guise of phenomenalist science. Here dogmatic resistance by the church and forcible suppression of speculation by the Inquisition led to the dogmatic counterdogma that science could provide a substitute for the spiritual integration of human life. As in the political sphere, the consequence was simply to introduce new spiritual forces, this time into the structure of the personality rather than into society more generally. Contemporary evidence, such as Voegelin's encounter with the behaviorists, illustrates the point clearly enough.

The gravest danger, however, has come from the third phase, the open conflict between Christian symbols and the rationalist and historical critique of them as myths and fables. This dedivinization of the world, as Max Weber called it, both destroyed the usefulness of mythical language to convey experiences of world-transcendent realities and obscured the fact that so-called scientific criticisms are often genuinely obscurantist myths presented by means of conceptual rather than sensual language.

Voegelin's judgment regarding Voltaire as a representative of this third wave of modernity was as mixed as his judgment regarding the response of the church. Regarding Voltaire, Voegelin was under no illusions concerning the "long list of his more reprehensible qualities."

> He was deficient in spiritual substance and he was vulgarly irreverent. His surprising range of solid knowledge was coupled with an equally surprising ignorance concerning the more intricate questions of philosophy and religion; as a result his judgment was frequently superficial, though delivered with authority. He has set the style for brilliantly precise misinformation, as well

11. Toynbee, *A Study of History*, 4:221.

as for the second-rater's smart detraction of the better man. He was ever ready to sacrifice intellectual solidity to a clever witticism. He introduced to the European scene the unhappy persuasion that a good writer can talk about everything, that every unsound utterance has to be considered an opinion, and that irresponsibility of thought is synonymous with freedom of thought. In short: he has done more than anybody else to make the darkness of enlightened reason descend on the Western world.

His positive qualities as a man of tolerance and common sense and his hatred of bigotry, obscurantism, and persecution were genuine. But this strength "lies in the twilight zone of procedural virtues." Voltaire's was a consciousness that "has lost the old faith sufficiently to see its shortcomings as an outsider and to attack them without compunction," but he had not gained "enough substance of the new faith to create its law." Such an intermediate stage of consciousness "is a realm not of the spirit, but between the spirits, where man can live for a moment in the illusion that he can, by discarding the old spirit, free himself of the evil which inevitably arises from the life of the spirit in the world, and that the new one will create a world without evil." Finally, Voegelin observed, whatever the dubiousness of Voltaire's anthropology as a systematic achievement,

> there can be no doubt that his compassion with the suffering creature was sincere. The religious wars of the sixteenth and seventeenth centuries, the innumerable individual persecutions perpetrated by the Catholic as well as the Protestant churches of all persuasions, were a stark reality. . . . The compassion with the suffering creature which is trampled underfoot by historical forces beyond its understanding and control is the great positive quality in Voltaire. And if his compassion had been less passionate and more spiritual, one might almost recognize a Franciscan in him. In the thirteenth century the mute creation had to be discovered and to be drawn into the orbit of spiritual sympathy; in the eighteenth century, man in society and history had to be recognized as part of the God-willed creation and to be accepted in compassion. It may be considered unfortunate that the institutions of the spirit had sunk so low at the time that a Voltaire had to devote himself to the task and to act with authority as the defender of man in historical society, but one cannot deny that he acted with grandeur the role of a *defensor humanitatis* against the professionals of the faith.

As is evident from his closing words, Voegelin's judgment regarding the church was mixed. On the one hand, he said that the defensive refusal by the church to employ the language of phenomenalist scientism in order to reduce the mystery of the world-transcendent drama of the soul to the psychodynamics of internal and world-immanent experience could only be admired. Less admirable was the church's refusal to undertake an active philosophical response. "A problem undeniably exists," wrote Voegelin,

> and it cannot be solved, like the problems of the first and second phases, by a belated acceptance of the new situation. It is not for us to offer a solution; but certainly a part of it would have to be a new Christian philosophy of history and of mythical symbols that would make intelligible, firstly: the new dimension of meaning that has accrued to the historical existence of Christianity through the fact that the Church has survived two civilizations; and that would make intelligible, secondly: the myth, as an objective language for the expression of a transcendental irruption, more adequate and exact as an instrument of expression than any rational system of symbols, [and] not to be misunderstood in a literalism that results from opacity nor reduced to an experiential level of psychology. Obviously it is a task that would require a new Thomas rather than a neo-Thomist.[12]

In order to deal with this problem, an act of "ecclesiastical statesmanship" comparable to that achieved by Saint Paul or Saint Thomas was required.

Voegelin was in no way an ecclesiastical statesman. The most that could be said of him along those lines is that, should an ecclesiastical statesman appear, he or she would profit from Voegelin's analysis of the source of the contemporary social, political, and spiritual disorders. The problem, which reappears in later chapters of this study, may be summarized and simplified as follows: modern, Western civilization does not understand itself as a postscript to antiquity. In their famous quarrel, the moderns as well as the ancients made valid and legitimate claims. The categories of meaning concerning the extinction, rebirth, and progress of the human spirit may be intellectually untenable, but they were applied to a wider range of historical materials than were the Christian categories from which they were derived. If the church did not discern the hand of God in the affairs of human beings, if, on the contrary, large blocks of human history were simply ignored or treated superficially, then humans would likely search for or perhaps invent new divinities that showed more interest in their affairs. No *deus absconditus* is ever likely to be an effective reality save but in the consciousness of a tiny minority. In its past, the early church was able to absorb and penetrate the civilizational culture of antiquity; after an equally difficult struggle, Saint Thomas was able to formulate an acceptable account of imperial Christianity. In contrast, Voegelin said, the modern church has not risen to the occasion but has, on the contrary, abandoned its *magisterium* and

---

12. Voegelin, *From Enlightenment to Revolution*, 32–33, 22.

withdrawn to lament the pride of modern human beings who refuse to submit to its authority.

Some may, indeed, lament that the authority of the church has declined or even disintegrated into a plurality of churches, but it is certain that it cannot be restored through expressions of regret. When Saint Paul, for example, declared in his epistle to the Romans that God has revealed himself to the Gentiles through his creation (Rom. 1:19–20), to the Israelites through the Written Law, and to all by the Law of Christ, graven on the hearts of men (Rom. 2:12 ff), he was able meaningfully to integrate the civilizational substance of the pagan, the Jewish, and the Christian communities. No such integration has been achieved by his modern Christian successors.

No political scientist would ever claim for himself that he was a new Thomas. We will see, however, in the chapters that follow, that in the course of reestablishing or of restoring the foundations of political science Voegelin was compelled to make sense of the failure of the church to respond to the genuine problems brought to light by Voltaire. When the traditional formulations of Christian sacred history omitted large sections of humanity from a putatively universal spiritual drama, something clearly was wrong. At the same time, Bossuet's fears were not simply those of episcopal traditionalism. A new Thomas would, therefore, develop a philosophy of history that was neither as empirically limited as the theology of history represented here by Bossuet nor as spiritually arid as the secular philosophy of history represented here by Voltaire. Such an enterprise, as was just indicated, would have three interrelated components. First, it would balance the universal spiritual insights of Bossuet with Voltaire's concern for an ecumenical survey of evidence. It would, moreover, be concerned for the historical vicissitudes of the church as an institution that has attempted to shelter the spiritual substance of Christianity from the corrosive influence of two civilizational courses. And, third, it would be sensitive to the intelligibility of mythical symbols as vehicles for the transmission of experiences of world-transcendent realities.

An adequate account of the implications of these three components, even for the rather focused questions of Voegelinian political science, cannot be made all at once. Among other things, the significance and empirical validity of terms such as *civilization* would have to be critically clarified and justified. To begin an analysis of this problem we will examine the political science of Jean Bodin (ca. 1529–1596). Bodin's analysis of the "problems of human order in society and history" of his own times was a model for Voegelin's. So too was Bodin's analysis of the order of consciousness.

In his *Autobiographical Reflections* Voegelin made the following recollection:

> I was again in Paris in 1934 for several weeks. At this time I was interested in the French sixteenth century and especially in the work of Jean Bodin. I collected materials for a comprehensive study of Bodin's work and in fact wrote it later to form part of the *History of Political Ideas,* but it has never been published. At that time, I worked through the catalogue of the Bibliothèque Nationale on French publications on the history and politics of the sixteenth century. So far as I remember, I had every single item in the catalogue in hand at least once. . . . But considerable piles of materials and the connection with the work of Bodin have never been published.[13]

In the political science of Bodin, Voegelin found a thinker who, a century before Bossuet and nearly two centuries before Voltaire, confronted and resolved a very similar complex of problems.

Bodin's lifetime fell into what Voegelin called the first phase in the process of dissociation of the medieval configuration of imperium, reason, and spirit. As we shall see, Bodin was fully alive to the spiritual experiences of world-transcendent reality and had a comprehensive understanding of reason. Regarding the third element of this complex, for Bodin religious schism was less a danger, as Bossuet put it, than a fact.[14] For Bodin, the breakdown of church and empire had already entailed the

13. Voegelin, *Autobiographical Reflections,* 36–37. See also RF 1:1/705/5/49, which contains a memorandum from Tracy B. Kittredge of the Rockefeller Foundation discussing, inter alia, Voegelin's work in Paris on sixteenth-century French politics. Voegelin, in fact, wrote two essays on Bodin. The first, nineteen pages in manuscript, was, on the basis of internal evidence, probably written in the early 1940s; the second, eighty-two pages in manuscript, was written during the summer of 1948, according to a report Voegelin submitted to the Social Science Council, December 7, 1948, HI 36/30. The two versions, no doubt, were intended for different versions of Voegelin's *History of Political Ideas;* both are given in the chapter "Bodin" in *HPI,* V:180–251, and quotations are from there unless otherwise indicated. In January 1936 Voegelin gave a speech in Vienna, "Das neue Bild von Person und Werk Jean Bodins, 1530–1596" (HI 56/6). Much of file 56/6 consists of Voegelin's notes on Bodin. There is, finally, in "Man in History and Nature," the chapter that precedes the chapter on Bodin in *HPI,* V, another short section on Bodin (158–63).

14. Between Bodin and Bossuet came first the Edict of Nantes (1598) and then its revocation (1685), which signaled the subordination of intellectual life and culture to the demands of royal rule and religious conformity. The *grand siècle,* it seems clear, sought to avoid the return of civil war at the cost of obscuring the achievements of Bodin and his contemporaries, not least of all with respect to reason. This conclusion, first made in the nineteenth century by Gabriel Monod, "Du progrès des études historiques en France depuis le XVIe siècle," was resumed nearly a century later by George Huppert, *The Idea of Perfect History: Historical Erudition and Historical Philosophy in Renaissance France,* 87 and chap. 10.

breakdown of the worldly premises upon which Augustinian historical speculation had rested. The church had symbolized the final era of sacred history, as the empire (however tenuously connected to the *imperium Romanum*) symbolized the final form of profane history. When church and empire could no longer symbolize historical finality, the question of the meaning of history had to be reopened. By the eighteenth century even kings and fashionable intellectuals were aware of the problem; in the sixteenth, Bodin, along with Vignier, La Popelinière, and Pasquier, had sensed that, although the course of history had separated from its Christian meaning, it nevertheless had an intelligible structure.[15] Central to the search for what in modern terms would be called a philosophy of history was the national self-consciousness of the French jurists of the sixteenth century. As George Huppert observed, "the educated French-man could not conceal the fact that the thousand-year-long history of the French was more important to him than the history of the Greeks and Romans; and, if the truth were known, to his mind even the history of the Jews paled in significance beside that of the French." The history of other European nations and cities had first to be considered, then the Arabs and Turks "who had played as large a role in the history of Mediterranean Europe as had the Romans and Greeks," and beyond them the Tartars, Huns, Russians, Africans, Americans, and Far Eastern nations as well.[16] To account for all this evidence a new perspective was needed.

Bodin's first major work, the *Methodos ad Facilem Historiarum Cognitionem* (1566),[17] was devoted to forging a new perspective in order to make the structure of *historia integra* again intelligible. His first task,

15. See George Huppert, "The Renaissance Background to Historicism"; Donald R. Kelley, "*Historia Integra:* François Baudouin and His Conception of History" and "The Development and Context of Bodin's Method," in Horst Denzer, ed., *Jean Bodin*, 123–50.

16. Huppert, *Idea of Perfect History*, 90–91.

17. Reprinted in *Oeuvres philosophiques de J. Bodin*, ed. Pierre Mesnard, 106–269; English translation by B. Reynolds, *Method for the Easy Comprehension of History*. Quotations, with occasional minor modifications, are from Reynolds's translation. Voegelin's chapters on Bodin considered many more aspects of his work then can be dealt with here. By Voegelin's reading, Bodin's philosophical principles "seem to have been settled in his midthirties, that is, about the time he wrote his *Methodus*. From this time on, the literary production of Bodin assumes the form of a recasting of his system. Hence it could be said rightly that the *Methodus* contains, on principle, the whole later thought of Bodin." Each of Bodin's works, Voegelin said, "has an enormous bulge, while the other parts of his system dwindle out of proportion, and sometimes are reduced to a few summarizing sentences" (*HPI*, V:185). In this chapter we focus on the *Methodus* and introduce the other works of Bodin only insofar as

which Bossuet later reversed, was to distinguish human history from natural and divine history. The former is the field of action for the human will; nature is studied in terms of necessity and cause; and divine history is concerned with the miraculous irruptions of world-transcendent divine power into the orderly sequences of nature. The three kinds of study lead to three distinct kinds of results. The truths of human history are probable; those of natural history are logically necessary; those of divine history are holy. The associated virtues are prudence, knowledge, and faith. Together they constitute wisdom, "man's supreme and final good." The structure of history as a whole seems to result from the interplay of these three kinds of history.

Bodin then focused on human history, which "mostly flows from the will of mankind." And the will of mankind introduced instability: "new laws, new customs, new institutions, new manners confront us." These novelties invariably lead to new errors unless action is led by nature or by divine prudence. At this point Bodin abandoned the term *will* and substituted *the mind of man.* Even though it is part of the eternal divine mind, "the mind of man" is nevertheless marred by "earthly stain," being "deeply immersed in unclean matter" and "so influenced by contact with it, and even distracted within itself by conflicting emotions." Accordingly, human beings can neither avoid error nor obtain justice without divine assistance.

Voegelin here detected "the Gnostic origin of Bodin's anthropology." By this interpretation, the divine substance descended into unclean earthly matter to become man. The resulting mixture required further intervention from above if confusion and illusion were subsequently to be avoided. But human history on its own, Voegelin said, "seems due to the fall of an eon into matter," which is a common enough Gnostic theme.[18] The concluding paragraph of chapter 1 of the *Methodus* contained additional evidence of Gnostic influences. There Bodin provided an alternative division of history for those who did not wish to include mathematics with the natural sciences:

> then he will make four divisions of history: human, of course, uncertain and confused; natural, which is definite, but sometimes uncertain on account of contact with matter or an evil deity, and therefore inconsistent; mathematical, more certain, because it is free from the mixture of matter, for in this way the ancients made the division between the two; finally, divine, most certain and by its very nature changeless. And this is all about the delimitation of history.

---

they illustrate aspects of Bodin's political science that Voegelin appropriated and incorporated in his own.

18. See Hans Jonas, *The Gnostic Religion,* 2d ed., 51–54, "Worlds and Aeons."

By this reasoning, number, which is free of matter, provided an additional level in the structure of history, more certain than natural history but less certain than divine. In any event, as John L. Brown observed, "Bodin's addition of 'mathematical history' (that is, based on numerology) is original with him and not to be found in any preceding examples of the *genre ars historica*."[19]

Whatever the significance of these Gnostic themes, the three levels of divine, natural, and human history are analogically present in the factors that determine the human mind, namely divine prudence, right reason, and sensuous matter. The interplay of these several factors provides human history with its structure, which introduces a final Gnostic touch. "Since," Bodin said,

> for acquiring prudence nothing is more important or more essential than history, because episodes in human life sometimes recur as in a circle, repeating themselves, we judge that attention must be given to this subject, especially by those who do not lead a secluded life, but are in touch with assemblies and societies of human beings.
>
> So of the three types of history let us for the moment abandon the divine to the theologians, the natural to the philosophers, while we concentrate lone and intently upon human actions and the rules governing them.

One may emphasize the Gnostic aspect of this passage in the following way: the cycles of order and disorder, which constitute the structure of history, occur independently of any human understanding that they take place. For those who do not lead a secluded life, understanding the structure of history is an important guide to action. Perhaps, indeed, the knowledge of the cycle will enable the statesman to break the cycle. In any event, it seems evident that Bodin's study of history, like Machiavelli's two generations earlier, had an activist inspiration.

The structure of history can be apprehended only if the field of observable phenomena is large enough. But how large is that? Bodin first considered the problem of the correct unit of analysis by distinguishing between individual and universal history. The former referred to the history of individual human beings or of individual peoples; the latter dealt with the deeds of several human beings or peoples, or at least of the most famous. It turned out, however, in chapter 2 of the *Methodus*, that universal history (called *historia communis* in chapter 1) "embraces the affairs of all, or of the most famous peoples, or of those whose deeds in war and peace have been handed down to us from an early age of their

19. Brown, *The "Methodus Facilem Historiarum Cognitionem" of Jean Bodin: A Critical Study*, 62.

national growth." The principle was clear: if the evidence was there, all things were included, which meant the origins of the world, the floods, the earliest beginnings of states and religions, and their ends, if they had ended. If the evidence was not all there, at least the most important materials were available. A vast accumulation of detail was not crucial: equally important to a proper identification of the subject matter was a correct method of interpretation. Here Bodin distinguished between a "writer" of history, a historiographer in the ordinary sense, and what he called a "reader" of history. The reader of history was concerned, Bodin said, with analysis of what the writer of history, who proceeded by the method of synthesis, had done. The subject matter of the reader was not the *res gestae* of specific historical individuals, whether these be particular or collective, but mankind, or in Bodin's terms, the republic of the world, the *respublica mundana*. In contemporary terms, Bodin was a philosopher of history rather than a historiographer.

After offering some bibliographic advice, Bodin made the following methodological observations: "the things that we have said about the arrangement of history are understood very easily on account of the analogy to cosmography." Cosmography included geography because much of the information available concerning the ancients and the Americans had been compiled by geographers. But more to the point, the reader of history, concerned with the structure of the whole, was aided because of the analogy between the structure of history and the structure of the cosmos. Indeed, he said, the science of cosmography and that of "reading" history are so close as often to seem identical. Cosmography begins with the study of celestial bodies and moves on to uranography, anemography, hydrography, and geography. The last named is further subdivided into circles, zones, continents; the continents are then studied by chorography, the science of regions, and then by topography and geometry. "Not otherwise," said Bodin, "shall we define and delimit universal history."[20] The fact that we end up dealing with the placement of copses, hedgerows, and willow plantations should not obscure Bodin's methodological point: universal history can be understood by analogy with cosmographic spatial deployments. From hedgerows to the heavens, we can proceed, by analogical reasoning, to analyze the meaningful structure of universal history.

Voegelin named the subject matter of universal history the "cosmic individual." According to him, Bodin developed his *Methodus* in order to understand this cosmic individual. His "method," therefore, was designed to bring to light the structure of universal history as it appeared

20. *Method,* trans. Reynolds, 26.

by way of the syntheses or accumulations of facts by erudite scholars. The strictness of the correspondence between cosmography and philosophy of history meant that universal history cannot be understood without considering the cosmographic conditions of the peoples who constitute the "individuals" about whom historiographers write. One of the most significant cosmographic conditions is the finite surface of the earth. In principle it can be studied by proceeding from uranography to geometry.

Löwith's distinction between meaning in history and the meaning of history may be helpful in understanding the problem that Bodin was dealing with and its significance for Voegelin's work. If historical, pragmatic events were manifestly meaningful, there would be no need to move from the writing of historical syntheses to the analytic reading of them. "History," Löwith said, "is meaningful only by indicating some transcendent purpose beyond the actual facts."[21] For Bodin that transcendent context was described by cosmography. History, therefore, could be understood by analogy with the spatial structure of the world. The most important aspect of cosmography, at least in its terrestrial subfield, was the fact that the world was finite and so could be exhaustively surveyed. The uranological sciences did add an element of the unknown, though some guidance, Bodin said, could be found in astrology.

The implication of the finitude of the globe so far as the reading of universal history is concerned is therefore enormous. In Voegelin's words:

> By means of his cosmographical analysis, Bodin slips finiteness of structure into his philosophy of history. The great problem of a philosophy of history—how to arrive at the meaning of a process of which we only know the closed past but not the open future—is solved by endowing the process of history with a spatial structure. The future is disregarded and the known past becomes the model of history, in its structure analogous to the cosmos.

The analogical relationship between the two sciences meant that, in concrete detail, Bodin's philosophy of history was concerned chiefly with the twin problems of space and time.

Human history, we know, is enacted within the space of the earth, which in turn is ordered by regions, each of which is inhabited by peoples differing in physiology and in character. These differences are reflected in variations in custom, religion, political institutions, and so on. In general, diversification of political, social, and cultural forms is

---

21. *Meaning in History*, 5. Thus, as we saw earlier, Voltaire's "transcendent purpose beyond the actual facts" was the development of the human spirit in the direction of *politesse*.

unintelligible unless one takes the influence of habitat into account. Now, the elements of Bodin's theory of the influence of climate on civilizations and on political institutions were not new.[22] Indeed, Bodin listed a large number of sources in chapter 10 of his book. What is new is the systematic arrangement of the data and Bodin's awareness that he was in command of a much larger body of information than his predecessors.[23]

Climatic factors influence human nature in such a way that the three principal human types, the wise, the prudent, and the strong, defined in terms of the predominance of a specific virtue are differentially distributed across the globe. The virtues, in turn, correspond to three parts of the soul (mind, reason, senses), to specific abilities (sacrifice and contemplation, the art of ruling, and military and manual service), to the chief supports of the state (principles, ordinances, and actions), and to the three estates (priests, rulers, and commons). The details concerning the interaction of stars, weather, blood, and bile are less important than the observation that the whole procedure is vaguely Platonic, with the difference that it is the purpose of the middle type, characterized by prudence, to rule. Those who "lead a secluded life," as Bodin put it in the quotation given earlier, are the highest insofar as they devote their lives to contemplation without action. As with Plato, the lowest are characterized by action without contemplation. The truly political man would mix the two, an evocation that was doubtless autobiographical. Moreover, it was fully compatible with the intention noted earlier of removing all eschatological speculation from human history. The philosopher is destined to lead a secluded life in "perpetual contemplation of the most beautiful things, as all Academicians would have it." But, Bodin added, that way of life "has nothing in common with military and civil affairs."

Bodin took over from Plato the hierarchy of human types and indicated his rivalry with him by displacing the philosopher-king as ruler, noting in passing that the disaster at Syracuse was evidence of Plato's mistake. Moreover, the plurality of human types existed, for Bodin, not simply within a single polis but as peoples distributed across the earth in different climatic circumstances. "What Plato did in his *Republic*," wrote Bodin, "we shall do for the republic of the world [*respublica mundana*], but a trifle differently."[24] In Bodin's view, a theory of politics, however

22. See M. J. Tooley, "Bodin and the Medieval Theory of Climate," *Speculum* 28 (1953): 64–84.

23. This element of self-conscious superiority as compared to the ancients led Brown to place Bodin strongly in the camp of the moderns. See Brown, *The Methodus*, 88, and Bodin's own remarks, *Method*, trans. Reynolds, 299–302.

24. Bodin, *Method*, trans. Reynolds, 117.

excellently it may be based on philosophical anthropology (and, we have seen, Bodin proposed to correct the Platonic hierarchy of types here as well), is limited, not to say defective, if it can be applied only to one polity. Bodin's expansion of the suitably modified Platonic theory was, in his view, a decisive improvement.

The "republic of the world" was Bodin's symbol for humanity diversified into historical peoples living in different regions. The details may appear quaint today,[25] but the intention is not: Bodin sought to understand the civilizational diversity of humanity as an intelligible whole living on a climatically diversified and finite planet. The "republic of the world" and its differentiation into characterological types was a formula that "gives meaning to the world of states," once the sheltering institutions of church and empire were under attack and the meaning of Western humanity as constituting the mythical body of Christ was no longer persuasive. In Voegelin's later essay he explained the significance of Bodin's insight at greater length:

> Mankind is not uniform because men are differentiated according to character types; no human being represents humanity as a whole; the potentiality of the human mind can only unfold historically through the various types; they supplement each other, and only their aggregate is the fullness of man. With the opening of the historical field beyond the Christian *corpus mysticum*, Bodin has made the systematic attempt of evoking a new mystical body of mankind, an idea of man that can be realized fully only through the differentiation into civilizational and political types in the course of history. This grandiose evocation, and the understanding of its theoretical necessity, makes Bodin the great founder of a modern political science.

Regional diversification, which enabled Bodin to include non-Christian peoples as individuals within universal history, did not, however, override the differences in rank among the several peoples.

To begin with, Europe had achieved greater historical importance than any other region of the earth. Within Europe, France combined the best features of north and south and was uniquely placed to create sound laws and become the political teacher of humanity. At the center of France lay Paris; at the center of Paris, its law school; at the center of the law school, the jurisconsult Bodin, writing his *Methodus*. It is easy to misunderstand France's specific contribution to the world republic as a claim to rule it; the ease of misunderstanding, moreover, alerts us to Bodin's pathos and his emotional commitments, to the possibility of French parochialism and of intellectual imperialism. On the other hand, Bodin's hierarchy

25. See ibid., 124–25.

is also a reflection of the hierarchy that appears to his reflective consciousness. In this respect it is almost a textbook example of Voegelin's observation in *Anamnesis* that "consciousness is the center from which radiates the concrete order of human existence into society and history."

Bodin's reflections on the temporal order of history may lead to similar misgivings. The title of the chapter dealing with this question indicates Bodin's argument: "Refutation of those who Postulate Four Monarchies and the Golden Age." The prophecy of the Book of Daniel, which had been interpreted by a host of famous and erudite men to refer to a specific succession of empires, was mistaken. Not that Daniel's authority was questionable, but his obscure and ambiguous words had been twisted. Even if his images of wild beasts did refer to monarchies, *monarchy* was a term with a meaning that was not to be used lightly or arbitrarily. Specifically, the Danielic prophets interpreted the four beasts as referring to the Assyrian, Persian, Macedonian, and Roman empires, with the Roman, which fell under the control of the Germans, being the last. But, said Bodin, the people who maintained this notion were Germans, which led him to conclude they did so for reasons of national glory, "for it is altogether strange to the interpretation of Daniel." The evidence was not new in Bodin's time, and it was overwhelming. As did Voltaire, Bodin pointed out the obvious: the Turks controlled most of the former Roman empire; the contemporary Spanish and Portuguese empires were larger than the German; the Germans could never have resisted Charles V without French aid. Bodin would not even mention the prince of Ethiopia, whose domain was greater than all Europe, nor the emperor of the Tartars, who ruled countless unconquered barbarians, except to say: "if you compare Germany with these you compare a fly to an elephant."[26] The rest of the argument continued in the same fashion: even if the Danielic prophecy were applicable to contemporary questions, which it was not, the German empire would not fulfill its conditions.[27] With so many gaps and errors, where is the universality? The Myth of the Golden Age, the chief alternative to the Danielic options, was similarly disposed of: what looked golden was, in fact, ignorant and barbaric when compared to Bodin's present.

26. Ibid., 292, 293.
27. Bodin's remarks on Daniel provoked a storm of controversy; for details see Brown, *The Methodus*, 70–74. In *Six livres de la République*, Bodin gave his reply. It is not contained in the French edition of 1583 available to me (Paris: Samaritaine, 1583), reprinted by Scientia, 1961. Bodin's response is, however, available in the more convenient translation by Richard Knolles, 1583; this text is widely available in the edition by Kenneth Douglas McRae, *Jean Bodin: The Six Bookes of a Commonweale*, 465–66.

Once all eschatological speculation has been expunged from profane history, once Christian sacred history as a source of meaning has been discarded, one must look "beyond the actual facts," as Löwith said, for a source of meaning. For Bodin, that source, with respect to time, was based on the Talmudic periodization of certain Rabbis named Elia and Catina. According to them (according to Bodin) the "elemental world" would last 6,000 years because God took six days to create it and "one day is with the Lord as a thousand years, and a thousand years is as one day" (2 Pet. 3:8). In principle this was not much different from Saint Augustine's speculation in *The City of God* (book XX:7). Bodin, however, divided the duration of the world into three ages of 2,000 years each, corresponding to the temporary predominance of one of the types of men: "for two thousand years men excelled in religion and wisdom and studied zealously the motion of the celestial stars and the universal power of nature. Likewise, in the next two thousand years they were occupied in establishing states, in enacting laws, and in leading forth colonies." In this period the men of the middle region predominated over the southerners. In the third era, beginning with the death of Christ, "various arts and handicrafts, formerly unknown, have come to light." This era of about a thousand years was accompanied by "the great disturbances of wars throughout the world, when of course pagan faith in Jupiter died and empires, so to speak, were overthrown and fell to the Scythians, the sons of Mars."[28] The sequence of the religious, political, and war-making technological ages bears some resemblance to the law of the three phases developed by Auguste Comte, two and a half centuries later.

The implications of Bodin's speculation would appear to be that the meaning of history was completely unfolded after all human potentialities had been actualized. The last human types to triumph apparently would be the technologically adept sons of Mars. Yet Bodin's argument was not so simple as that, because he suggested that this "conjecture" about the 6,000 years was oracular; many people "think Elias was a prophet," in which case, if such beliefs were true, matters became much more complex. "In the perpetual agitation of 6,000 there will come a change of the elemental world and . . . in the seventh millennium there will be quiet until, when 49,000 years have passed, a fiftieth millennium will bring the fall of the celestial spheres and the quiet of the Great Jubilee. But to investigate more subtly these matters, which cannot be grasped by human wit, or inferred from reason, or approved by the divine prophecy,

28. Bodin, *Method*, trans. Reynolds, 122–23.

seems not less stupid than impious."[29] It is not clear from the last sentence whether speculation of the Great Jubilee and so on was considered by Bodin to be stupid and impious, as Paul Lawrence Rose has argued,[30] or whether any additional and more subtle investigations would be stupid and impious.

For reasons to be discussed shortly, Bodin did not think that the meaning of history absorbed the meaning of life. Yet it is clear that he has tampered with Augustinian sacred history in a manner that deserves critical attention. For Augustine, the meaning of history is to be found in the world-transcendent drama that concerns the soul, not the rise and fall of empires in profane history. The placing of the *imperium Romanum* as the final form of profane history is of minor importance to Christian pilgrims toward the Heavenly City and can hardly be considered essential. It is, rather, a symbol for the time of waiting for the Second Coming, the advent of which is historically indeterminate. For Bodin, however, the meaning of history has become immanent to its 6,000-year course. Just as Bodin's evocation of the spatial structure of history carried with it the danger of turning into a parochial glorification of France and an egoistical glorification of the author of the *Methodus*, so did the temporal structure of history carry with it the danger that empirical history may pretend to the attributes of sacred history in the Augustinian sense. Indeed, that was precisely the temptation to which Voltaire succumbed or the danger to which he fell victim.

Bodin did not make Voltaire's mistake. Before indicating how he avoided it, we must emphasize the complexity of the question by drawing together some of the themes developed so far. Several times during

29. Ibid., 333. The "Rabbi Elias" was not an individual. The term *Elian* referred variously to the biblical prophet Elijah or to Elias, who was so closely associated with the Carmelites that they were sometimes called "Elians." Bodin had been a Carmelite monk during the 1540s but left, possibly after a trial for heresy, in 1548, to study law at Toulouse; for details see Pierre Mesnard, "Jean Bodin à Toulouse" and "Un rival heureux: De Cujas et de Bodin, Étienne Forcadel." On the Carmelite episode see H. Naef, "La jeunesse de Bodin ou les conversions oubliées," and E. Droz, "Le Carme Jean Bodin, hérétique." More broadly, "Elian" referred to an adherent of virtually any of the sixteenth-century prophetic movements and "spiritual libertines." Elian prophecies were, obviously, related to Joachite notions of the three ages. For details see W. J. Bouwsma, *Concordia Mundi: The Career and Thought of Guillaume Postel*, 163–66, 281–83; F. Secret, "De quelques courantes prophétiques et religieuses sous le règne de Henri III"; G. Demerson, "Un mythe des libertins spirituels: Le prophète Elie"; Marion L. Kuntz, *Guillaume Postel: Prophet of the Restitution of All Things, His Life and Thought*, 113 n. 363.

30. *Bodin and the Great God of Nature: The Moral and Religious Universe of a Judaiser*, 82 n. 45.

the course of this study of Voegelin's political science the problem of criteria of relevance has been considered. In conventional language, the development of criteria of relevance entails the elaboration of a philosophical anthropology and a philosophy of history. Historical examination of the term *philosophy of history* indicated that it originated as part of an intellectual movement devoted to the writing of secular history. Critical analysis of the internal logic and of the anthropological assumptions of secular history showed that the enterprise was more a question to be analyzed by political science than a part of it. Even so, the great insight of this type of historiography, namely its concern for the independence of meaning of non-Western and non-Christian peoples, was undeniable. Notwithstanding certain Gnostic elements, in Bodin, Voegelin found a thinker who had a Voltairean awareness of the meaningful plurality of peoples but who did not pretend that history had an eidos. At the same time, Bodin avoided the chief defect of Bossuet's theology of history, namely that it seemed to ignore uncongenial non-Christian evidence. For Bodin, the process of history has a structure analogous to that of the cosmos and independent of any Christian apocalyptic meaning. Accordingly, historical analysis (or philosophy of history) can indicate and express that structure both spatially (through France as the new omphalos) and temporally (through a tripartite division of history into 2,000-year epochs).

Voegelin's detection of Gnostic influences and the ease with which one can misunderstand Bodin's evocation of the spatial and temporal structure of history have been reflected in contemporary scholarship. For Roger Chauviré, Bodin's work was filled with "preposterous inventions." John Plamenatz declared him to be credulous; others have said he was a "blend of rationalism and superstition," or simply a kind of schizoid: "a profound political philosopher and a superstitious bigot."[31] More circumspect scholars have suggested that because he was only half-modern he asked the wrong questions.[32] Or, if he did ask the right questions, his expression was defective, which turned him into a

---

31. Chauviré, *Jean Bodin: Auteur de la République,* 486; Plamenatz, *Man and Society,* 1:93; Thomas I. Cook, *History of Political Philosophy from Plato to Burke,* 387; Beatrice Reynolds, "Introduction" to her translation of Bodin's *Method,* xxi; Harold Elmer Manz, "Jean Bodin and the Sorcerers," *Romanic Review* 15 (1924): 154.

32. Thus Donald R. Kelley regretted that Bodin was not "strictly historical" and so could not be included in his *Foundations of Modern Historical Scholarship: Language, Law, and History in the French Renaissance,* 12–13. Likewise, Edward Fueter excluded him from his earlier treatise, *Geschichte der neueren Historiographie,* 343, 435. See also George H. Sabine, *A History of Political Theory,* 3d ed., 400.

"predecessor" of somebody whose formulations better please modern scholarship.[33]

For Voegelin, such judgments and the approach that justified them were of no use in political science. "The interpretation of a thinker," he said, "must be based on the actual content of his work; it must not attach itself to particular doctrines (for instance, [in the case of Bodin] the theory of sovereignty)[34] but penetrate to the motivating center of his thought that endows the particular doctrines with their meaning; and it must place the thinker and work in their civilizational environment." By implication, then, one must abandon simpleminded dichotomies, such as the distinction between ancient and modern or medieval and modern, and consider modernity as a process of dissolution of the medieval spiritual-temporal order that occurs at earlier times and with greater speed in some places than in others. Bodin, for Voegelin, was thoroughly modern, though he belonged to the Mediterranean phase of postmedieval history; and this Mediterranean cultural or civilizational complex itself broke down a generation after Bodin with the rise of the Atlantic cultural area and its exuberant political expansion accompanied by a spiritual retrogression for which Voltaire was a symptom. "From the position of our transalpine modernity," Voegelin remarked, "it requires a special effort adequately to reconstruct the systematic thought of Bodin, which holds together a wealth of materials and problems, far surpassing in range our contemporary attempts at systematic thought."

The "motivating center" of Bodin's thought, and the source not only of the aforementioned Gnostic pathos but also of a spiritual sensitivity that was missing from Voltaire, was his mysticism. Bodin's philosophical anthropology was grounded in a mystical vision. According to Voegelin's understanding, Bodin argued that the one true God was revealed equally to the Hebrew prophets, to the sages of "pagan" antiquity, to Jesus, and to the saints. "A community of initiates," Voegelin said,

> grows through the ages, and what fascinates Bodin is the fate that the divine messengers suffer at the hands of the superstitious mass when they fulfill

33. See, for instance, Étienne-Maurice Fournol, *Bodin, prédécesseur de Montesquieu;* W. Dunning, "Jean Bodin on Sovereignty"; F. J. C. Hearnshaw, "Bodin and the Genesis of the Doctrine of Sovereignty," 94.

34. The otherwise impeccable scholarship of Julian Franklin, for instance, is probably the most notable for having discussed sovereignty in this way. See his *Jean Bodin and the Sixteenth Century Revolution in the Methodology of Law and History, Jean Bodin and the Rise of Absolutist Theory,* and "Sovereignty and the Mixed Constitution: Bodin and His Critics."

their ineluctable duty. Not only are they calumniated and persecuted in their own time; even if their message takes effect it will degenerate into superstition when the historical, human form of the revelation is taken for its essence, and when fanatical literalism obscures the function of the message, that is, the purification of the mind and the direction of the soul toward God.

The evocation of a socially inevitable drama of the prophetic message, its diffusion from a solitary center to the religion of the people, and the return from the historical religion to the solitude of the prophetic soul concerned Bodin all his life.

The obvious answer, the withdrawal of the contemplative mystic from civil society, has an equally obvious appeal. However, the price would be the degeneration of public life "into a spiritually stagnant welfare administration with a department of rites." This was not Bodin's intention because such a solution ignored the social nature of human life. Accordingly, because human existence is social, the good for both man and society is always mixed. In life, the human mind cannot become pure; it can only be purified. "The mind cannot enjoy pure contemplation before it shall have been entirely wrested from the body."[35] Short of death, therefore, as Plato indicated in his image of the cave (*Republic* 514a), the philosopher-mystic has the duty of sharing his or her insights with fellow citizens.

The parallel with Plato, indicated clearly enough in the title of Bodin's most famous book, *Six livres de la République*, extended to the central feature of his political science, that the well-ordered soul is the source of order in the polity. "The Platonic Eros, which carries the soul toward the vision of the Agathon, has its parallel in Bodin's purging of the mind and its conversion toward God." For Voegelin, this recovery of something close to Platonic experience raised an ancillary question: to what extent was the order of the Bodinian soul formed by the mystical tradition and to what extent was it original? To answer this question Voegelin turned to a famous passage in *De la démonomanie des sorciers* (1580), where Bodin told the story of the appearance of a demon to a "friend." Voegelin accepted the view, not universally shared by Bodin scholars, that the story was autobiographical and assembled the evidence from neo-Platonic and Pseudo-Dionysian sources to indicate the antecedents to Bodin's mystical-philosophical anthropology and his classification of human types. It was, he said, "a peculiar Platonic-Jewish-Christian mixture. . . . The aggregate . . . does not fit into the anthropology of any of the conflicting Christian churches of the age; and in anticipation we

35. Bodin, *Method*, trans. Reynolds, 34.

may say that a politics based on this anthropology will not fit into the conventional categories of constitutionalism or democratic ideas."[36]

Mysticism was also the "motivating center" of Bodin's *Colloquium Heptaplomeres*.[37] The subject matter of the *Heptaplomeres* is the relationship between the one true religion and the many historical religions. Dramatically, seven men converse at the home of a wealthy Venetian merchant. They are all highly cultivated, tactful, and polite; they have vast comparative knowledge of religious doctrines and practices, and the food supplied by their host is excellent. In the course of the dialogue, only five of the seven speakers represent historical religions. Had only they been present, one might anticipate the result to be a dogmatic deadlock. Bodin added two other interlocutors, Toralba and Senamus. The former claims a special authority for his religion because it was the oldest and most natural; Senamus represents a kind of humanist spiritualism: for him all religions are representative of the one true spiritual religion so that he is equally at home as a Jew among Jews or a Greek among Greeks. The conclusion to be drawn at the level of the story presented in the *Heptaplomeres* is that religious tolerance is a very practical attitude for well-fed scholars attending a splendid international conference in one of the world's great cities.

Such a conclusion, notwithstanding its potential appeal to contemporary intellectuals, ignores the serious purpose of the drama in order to concentrate on its literary form. According to Voegelin's interpretation, the setting and the dialogue constitute a symbolic play. The intention animating the play "is no less than the claim of his mystical religiousness to be the true religion, which ought to determine the spiritual order of the polity." Bodin's famous doctrine of tolerance, then, was in no way

36. The story is found in Bodin, *De la démonomanie des sorciers,* bk. I, chap. 2. A discussion of the medieval and Renaissance background to Bodin's imagery is found in F. von Bezold, "Jean Bodin als Okkultist und seine *Démonomanie.*" Christopher Baxter restated the von Bezold thesis, that the story was autobiographical, in his "Jean Bodin's Daemon and His Conversion to Judaism," in Denzer, ed., *Jean Bodin,* 1–22. Rose has provided details regarding other Jewish sources in *Bodin and the Great God of Nature,* 164–74. On the other hand, Maryanne Cline Horowitz, "Judaism in Jean Bodin," 113, suggested Bodin may indeed have described the experience of a friend and proposed Guillaume Postel as a candidate.

37. Bodin, *Colloquium of the Seven about the Secrets of the Sublime,* trans. Marion Leathers Daniels Kuntz, esp. xlvii–lxvi. See also Bodin, *Colloque entre sept scavans qui sont de differens sentimens,* trans. and ed. François Berriot, xlv–xlvi. For an account of other factors that influenced the composition of the *Colloquium* see C. R. Baxter, "Problems of the Religious Wars," 177; Haim Hillel Ben-Sasson, "Jewish-Christian Disputation in the Setting of Humanism and Reformation in the German Empire"; and Horowitz, "Judaism and Jean Bodin."

based on relativism or indifference to spiritual truth. On the contrary, the establishment of the core of true religion was a public concern, not simply because the historical religions were engaged in civil war but because humanity is a spiritual whole and part of a harmonious cosmos. The twin sources of Bodin's tolerance, as evident in the drama of the *Heptaplomeres* as well as in the soul of its author, were contemplative mysticism and extensive knowledge of comparative religion. "Contemplative mysticism," Voegelin wrote in his first essay on Bodin, "with its culminating experience in the *fruitio Dei*, is essentially ahistoric and adogmatic, which means in practice that the confessional and institutional differences that underlie the turmoil of the sixteenth century become indifferent." Comparative knowledge, in the context of the *Heptaplomeres*, may have the same effect. Voegelin called this attitude "contemplative realism."

The Bodinian prophet was in turn charged with special responsibility for the spiritual health of the community because God graciously provided him with superior spiritual gifts. One may conclude, therefore, that Bodin's tolerance was directed toward the expression of experiences of world-transcendent reality in dogma and cult and not toward spiritual perversion or indifference. "The work of Bodin," Voegelin said, "holds a unique place in modern political history insofar as it makes the conscious attempt at founding the idea of political order on mystical culture." The immediate purpose of Bodin's mysticism and the tolerance of dogmatic disagreement that flowed from it was to moderate the religious wars of France.[38] In the event, of course, he was unsuccessful, an outcome to which he was evidently resigned.[39]

The spiritual penetration of the order of the cosmos seemed to be a suitable means to create political order because, for Bodin, the cosmos was the model that political order was supposed to emulate. To put the matter the other way around, the order of nature, when contemplated by a properly formed Bodinian consciousness, resembled a well-ordered state. In his prefatory dedication to the *Theatrum Naturae*, Bodin looked back on his achievement in the *République*. There he had collected the laws of the world, but he had found no agreement in them concerning the certainties of order: what was called justice in one place and was there

38. Thus the famous lines that closed his *Universae Naturae Theatrum*, "Here ends the *Theatrum Naturae*, written by Jean Bodin while all France was ablaze in civil war" (633).

39. For details, see Paul Lawrence Rose, "The *Politique* and the Prophet: Bodin and the Catholic League, 1589–1594" and "Bodin and the Bourbon Succession to the French Throne, 1584–1594"; Owen Ulph, "Jean Bodin and the Estates-General of 1576"; Ernst Hinrichs, "Das Furstenbild Bodins und die Krise der französichen Renaissance monarchie," in Denzer, ed., *Jean Bodin*, 281–302.

praised was elsewhere a culpable offence. The law, then, was uncertain, "but nothing is uncertain in nature" because it was cosmos, order, and with form, and not simply confused, chaotic, formless matter. This was the true order, he said, and worthy of our contemplation because it would purge us of all impiousness and turn us toward the adoration of the one true God.[40] Following the purge of consciousness, one saw as well that the cosmos was an intelligible order of spirits, each with a proper rank and corresponding responsibilities. "Just as a wise prince will organize his republic so that his magistrates and officials are always prepared for all things, so too has the provident creator of the cosmos placed his angels everywhere, each in his station, that is, in the heavens, in the airs, in the waters, in the subterranean realms, in the villages and cities, to perform their duties; and he has assigned good and bad angels to the animals, plants, minerals, elements, and to every individual in order to reward and to punish."[41] The two aspects of Bodin's political science were complementary. First, the spiritual contemplation of cosmic order provided a standard by which to measure the political disorders of the day; and second, the spiritual animation of the cosmos was the substantive basis of a properly ordered political society.

The nature to which Bodin looked for spiritual guidance was, as it was for Copernicus as well, the Hellenic closed cosmos. Bodin's work was the last occasion "that Hellenic nature determines in a representative manner the ideas of man and politics." Accordingly, "Bodin's work marks the end of the humanistic phase of politics."[42] Bodin's humanism was evident clearly in his rejection of, or indifference to, Copernicus's mathematical investigation of this same cosmos.

It was self-evident neither to Bodin nor to Voegelin that the mathematical simplicity achieved by the hypothesis of heliocentrism was "more true" than mathematical complexity. As was pointed out in Chapter 3, the desire for mathematical simplicity was motivated by intellectual activism, not by the contemplation of the order of nature. What *is* self-evident is that the heliocentric model in no way alters the experience of meaningful cosmic rhythms: the sun still rises in the east, spring follows winter, the equinoxes precess. If one was concerned with contemplating the order of nature, as was Bodin, and if one sought clarity concerning the participation by humans in that order by developing analogical accounts, then the project of mathematical simplicity would have no appeal.

40. Bodin, *Universae Naturae Theatrum*, 1.
41. Ibid., 528; see also 632–63.
42. Voegelin, "Man in Nature and History," in *HPI*, V:137–38.

In the *Apologie de René Herpin pour la République de J. Bodin*, Bodin raised the obvious and pertinent question: "how does it serve to correct the tables of the celestial movements [of the ancients] whether the earth be mobile or immobile? Whether there be epicycles or no? By placing the sun in the center? For that the pilot leaves port for to course upon the high seas, and if he thinks that the port moves off and that his ship moves not, as the poet says, *urbesque domusque recedant,* there will ever be the same distance from the ship to the port as from the port to the ship."[43] Bodin had Copernicus in mind, as was shown not only by the context but by his using the same passage from Virgil as had the astronomer. Copernicus argued in favor of spaceship earth; Bodin considered the argument nonsense.[44] Bodin's point, however, was methodological: one could assume a heliocentric cosmos in order to simplify calculations, but if one was not initially interested in calculations, nothing would be gained thereby.

Moreover, Bodin had his own excellent reasons for preferring to assume that the earth was the center of the cosmos: God had said that no man shall see his face but only his back. That is, God would be understood only by the contemplation of his works, and for that reason placed man not off in a dark corner of the cosmos but in its very center, "the better to behold in contemplation the universe of things and through the works, as through spectacles, shall he behold the Sun, that is, God Himself."[45] The analogy would be persuasive only for those who had eyes to see, that is, for a consciousness that had been properly purged and was capable of apprehending the cosmic chain of command proceeding downward from God to his archangels and angels, from them to men and from men to women and beasts. In Voegelin's view, it was the hierarchic conception of the animated cosmos that provided the decisive reason to reject the comparatively homogeneous theory of Copernicus.

Bodin had a considerable impact on the formation of Voegelin's political science. Possibly its most important effect was found in what Voegelin called Bodin's "contemplative realism." One may say that such an attitude, sentiment, or experience is specific and proper to the consciousness of the political scientist. "The tolerance of contemplative realism," Voegelin said, "permits giving due weight to social reality as well as to religious experience. The Reformers despised the 'secular' authority. For

43. *Apologie* 30v; the 1581 edition was bound with the edition of the *République* and reprinted in facsimile by Scientia in 1961.
44. Copernicus, *De Revolutionibus* I.8; Virgil, *Aeneid* III.72.
45. Bodin, *Universae Naturae Theatrum,* 633.

Bodin the natural sphere is as much human as the solitude of the *fruitio Dei;* the spheres differ in essence and in rank, but nature must not be despised." More specifically, Voegelin said, Bodin was "a cosmological thinker. That means he accepted the structure of the cosmos, including the realm of politics; he is aware that this structure is an object of description, not of explanation. . . . Man with his natural and spiritual structure in historical evolution is an ultimate structural feature of the cosmos beyond explanation."[46] In this context, Bodin's great achievement was to have adapted "the Mediterranean speculation on cosmic hierarchy," particularly as it had been developed by Maimonides, "to the theory of the nation state," and especially to its legal construction.[47]

In coming to terms with the range of secondary accounts of Bodin, Voegelin indicated another dimension of his importance. First, one must attend to the "actual content" of a thinker's work as a whole and not to particular doctrines of interest to later scholars. This meant, second, that the objective of analysis of texts or doctrines was to penetrate to the motivating or experiential center that generated the document. For Bodin, that meant understanding what was meant by a spiritually animated cosmos, a *cosmos empsychos.* Most emphatically did Bodin exemplify Voegelin's principle that human society "is as a whole a little world, a cosmion, illuminated with meaning from within by the human beings who continuously create and bear it as the mode and condition of their self-realization." For Bodin politics was cosmological because the cosmos was experienced and understood in his consciousness as a spiritual-political hierarchy.[48]

Third, we recall that Voegelin's discussion of Bodin began with the observation that modern political history begins with the dissolution of Western medieval universalism. The disintegration of the *sacrum imperium,* Voegelin's "first phase" of modernity, was completed by Bodin's day. The end of the *imperium* did not, however, mean the end of Western spirituality or of the culture of reason. On the contrary, the disintegration of the medieval complex under the double impact of the new evidence regarding non-Christian peoples and the destructiveness of Christian dogmatic religious wars was an opportunity to reconsider, on the basis of reason, the major problems of political order, which were centered on the problem of human spirituality. Two implications followed. On the one

46. In *NSP,* 5, Voegelin provided a very Bodinian account of the prescientific participation of human existence in reality to "the dispassionate gaze on the order of being in the theoretical attitude."
47. Voegelin, *CW,* 27:27–31. See also Voegelin, *Die politischen Religionen,* 30–31.
48. *NSP,* 27.

hand, empirical evidence from non-European histories and societies was central to political science and, as Voegelin said in his *Autobiographical Reflections,* his study of Bodin introduced him to the importance of Asiatic events for the Europeans.[49] On the other hand, in order to make sense of these data one must become a Bodinian "reader of history," which is to say, a Voegelinian philosopher of history.

In an earlier section of this chapter we quoted Voegelin's observation that a "new Thomas" would have to develop a Christian philosophy of history that took into account both the question of spiritual universalism and wide-ranging historical evidence. If such a philosophy of history was sensitive to myth as a symbolism that was capable of conveying experiences of world-transcendent reality in the same sense that, say, biblical revelation did so, it would also be capable of understanding the role of the church in Western Christendom. Bodin was, in this respect, a model political scientist. Moreover, so far as Voegelin's own political science was concerned, the content of the *Methodus* reaffirmed the desire, present from childhood, to seek out "larger horizons." In the actual scholarly activities that Voegelin undertook to understand Bodin's political science, the trail of evidence led him to consider Bodin's sixteenth-century context, which happened to include the victory of Temür over Bayezid in 1402. In the following chapter we discuss Voegelin's later arguments regarding the range of evidence that a genuine and empirical political science must consider.

49. A brief account of one aspect of Bodin's concern with Asia is Clarence Dana Rovillard, *The Turk in French History, Thought, and Literature, 1520–1660,* 19–20, 476–81.

7

The Range of Evidence

In his correspondence with Schütz regarding Husserl's *Crisis of European Sciences*, discussed in Chapter 5, Voegelin objected to Husserl's characterization of the Chinese and Hindus as "merely anthropological types" and to his dismissive attitude toward Chinese and Hindu speculation. Such views were not merely in questionable taste; more important, they were, Voegelin said, unscientific. As we have seen in Chapter 3, Voegelin's understanding of science was influenced strongly by Max Weber. Weber's distinction between science and ideology remained a permanent element in Voegelin's political science, despite the latter's reservations regarding Weber's methodology. Equally important was the range of Weber's comparative knowledge. "So far as I am concerned," Voegelin wrote in his *Autobiographical Reflections*,

> Weber established once and for all that one cannot be a successful scholar in the field of social and political science unless one knows what one is talking about. And that means acquiring the comparative civilizational knowledge not only of modern civilization but also of medieval and ancient civilization, and not only of Western civilization but also of Near Eastern and Far Eastern civilizations. That also means keeping that knowledge up to date through contact with the specialist sciences in the various fields. Anybody who does not do that has no claim to call himself an empiricist and certainly is defective in his competence as a scholar in this field.[1]

In addition to Weber, Voegelin mentioned that Auguste Comte and Oswald Spengler also had mastered an impressive amount of solid comparative knowledge. As with Voltaire, however, the contexts within which their knowledge appeared were theoretically questionable. Voegelin also mentioned Eduard Meyer, the great historian of antiquity, Arnold Toynbee, for whom Meyer was also an authority, and Alfred Weber, Max

1. *Autobiographical Reflections,* 13.

247

Weber's brother, as having insisted on the importance of mastering non-Western sources. We will discuss Voegelin's reading of Toynbee, in particular, in the following chapter.

Voegelin learned a great deal from Weber, Meyer, Toynbee, and the others. It is also true that, on the basis of his study of Bodin alone, he spoke with authority when he insisted on the importance of acquiring wide-ranging comparative knowledge. Voegelin himself had studied in France, Britain, and the United States during the 1920s. The importance of these experiences gained away from the taken-for-granted intellectual debates and problems of German scholarship was evident to Voegelin. Speaking of his trip to America, he wrote:

> The great event was the fact of being thrown into a world for which the great neo-Kantian methodological debates, which I considered the most important things intellectually, were of no importance. . . . In brief, there was a world in which this other world in which I had grown up was intellectually, morally, and spiritually irrelevant. That there should be such a plurality of worlds had a devastating effect on me. The experience broke for good (at least I hope it did) my Central European or generally European provincialism without letting me fall into an American provincialism.[2]

This *expérience vécue* confirmed as an immediate experience of reality what he had learned through the study of Weber's comparative civilizational analysis.

The first major problem that Voegelin examined in the area of what is conventionally called intercivilizational encounters concerned the influence of Asiatic political and military events on the history and political thought of Europe. As we saw, Voegelin began his investigations in connection with his studies of Bodin in the early 1930s. The first fruit of this interest, as we noticed briefly in the previous chapter, was an article published in 1937 on the image of Tamerlane.[3]

---

2. Ibid., 32–33.

3. In the late 1930s, when he was applying for teaching positions in the United States, Voegelin had emphasized that one of his areas of interest was early Asiatic political ideas. See, for example, Voegelin to Harold Lasswell, April 12, 1938; Voegelin to Robert B. Hall, Institute for Far Eastern Studies, University of Michigan, November 17, 1938 (HI 38/20, 19/6). In April 1938 Voegelin wrote to Friedrich von Hayek that he expected to have a *book* on the Mongols ready by the fall of that year (HI 17/3). Of his forced residence in Zurich, Voegelin wrote to W. Y. Elliott that he discovered in the Zurich city library texts by seventeenth-century German historians who, as a matter of course, wrote of "Genghizkhanism" as akin to Judaism, Paganism, and Mohammedanism. "The wars of Tamerlane," he said, "are considered to be a chapter in the ecclesiastical history of the Mediterranean. That fits nicely

Among the great conquerors to have emerged from the steppes of inner Asia, Tamerlane is remembered chiefly because his life inspired the imagination of literary artists.[4] In contrast, Chenggis Qan is known both to historians and to history, even though Timür, or Temür to give him his proper name, caused more deaths and devastation and brought more territory under his sway.[5] Temür modeled his career on that of Chenggis. We will discuss some of the more impressive early Mongol achievements below. For the present it is perhaps sufficient to note that, in several respects, the period of Mongol rule, especially in Persia, was destructive.

In 1335, the last of Chenggis's successors in Iran, Abu Daid, died. By the middle of the fourteenth century, the Chaghatai Qanate of Central Asia was divided into a "traditional" Mongol realm, Mughulistan, in the east, and Transoxania in the west. The latter, to use the useful distinction of Joseph Fletcher, "cohabited"; the former remained nomadized. "To cohabit," he wrote, "was to become a Turk and a Muslim. To nomadize meant staying in or returning to the steppe and remaining a Mongol and a believer in the universal sky-god Tenggeri."[6] In Mughulistan the Chaghatai qans, descended from Chenggis's second son, Chaghatai, ruled, but in Transoxania rule was divided between Chaghatai qans with nominal authority and several amirs with varying degrees of power.

Temür was said to have been born in 1335, in Transoxania. He belonged to the cohabiting Barlas tribe, ethnic Mongols who had converted

---

with my problems of political religions, and I am quite delighted now about the delay in Zürich" (Voegelin to Elliott, August 20, 1938, HI 11/2). The original article, "Das Timurbild des Humanisten: Eine Studie zur politische Mythenbildung," was published in 1937. The text used here is the nearly identical reprint in *Anamnesis*, 153–78.

4. Apart from Marlowe, whose *Tamburlaine* is discussed below, the life of Tamerlane was the subject of a play in French by Jacques Pradon (1691), of operas by Scarlatti (1706) and Handel (1724), and of a poem by Edgar Allan Poe (1827).

5. Tamerlane is more correctly identified by his Turkic name. The Western version, Tamerlane, is derived from the Persian, Timur-i lang, Temür the lame. In the words of Clavijo, who was certainly in a position to know, "Timour Beg is the proper name of that lord, and not Tamerlane, as we call him; for Timour Beg is as much to say, in his language, the same as the *Lord of iron*; because *Beg* means *Lord*, and *Timour* is *iron*. Tamerlane, on the contrary is an insulting name; and means *lame*, because he became lame on the left side, and was wounded in the two small fingers of the right hand, from blows which were given him when he was stealing some sheep one night" (*Narrative of the Embassy of Ruy Gonzalez de Clavijo to the Court of Timour at Samarcand*, A.D. *1403–6*, trans. Clement R. Markham, 77–78).

6. Fletcher, "The Mongols: Ecological and Social Perspectives," 50. We shall have occasion to discuss Mongol theology as well as other aspects of Fletcher's insightful article below.

to Islam and spoke Turkish. Temür followed a path to power similar to that taken earlier by Chenggis: from chieftaincy of his own tribe, he developed a strong personal following and forged alliances with other tribal leaders. By 1370 he ruled Transoxania and was seeking further fields to conquer, not least of all because of a need to keep his very effective military organization busy.[7] As a result, Temür's armies were almost constantly in the field, sometimes overrunning, conquering, and devastating the same territory several times. Even to a specialist historian, "a chronological narrative of Temür's campaigns would be extremely confusing, and it will not be attempted here."[8] One campaign was greatly significant for Europe though of relatively small importance to Temür, the invasion and conquest of Anatolia.

By the mid-fourteenth century, the Ottoman sultans had replaced the empire of Nicaea in northwestern Anatolia. In 1368 they conquered Bulgaria. After his father was killed on the battlefield at Kosovo in 1389, where the Serbs had been defeated, Sultan Bayezid completed the annexation of Bulgaria and Serbia. During the early 1390s he completed the conquest of Asia Minor, and in 1396 at Nicopolis he destroyed the flower of Hungarian and Bergundian chivalry, who had combined in a crusade to recover the lost territory of Christendom on the lower Danube. Bayezid then turned his attention to the great Byzantine city of Constantinople and began a siege.

Temür, meanwhile, was contemplating an extensive expansion into Eastern Europe and proposed a division with Bayezid along the Dnieper River. Bayezid refused and directed his attention to Constantinople, leaving Temür to deal with his adversaries alone.[9] He crushed the Qipchaq army, disrupted the long-distance trade between Europe and East Asia, which severely hurt the economy of the Golden Horde farther north, and then undertook a two-year campaign of plunder in India. By the spring of 1399 he was preparing to deal with his adversaries in the west. During the fall of 1400 he was in Syria, and in March 1401 his troops pillaged Damascus. "For Temür," wrote Roemer,

> the Syrian campaign reaped a rich reward in terms of goods and valuables confiscated and slaves captured. For the country itself it meant economic

7. An excellent contemporary account of Temür's political achievement and of his technique of rule is Beatrice Forbes Manz, *The Rise and Rule of Tamerlane*. See also her earlier "The Ulus Chaghatay before and after Temür's Rise to Power: The Transformation from Tribal Confederation to Army of Conquest."

8. David O. Morgan, *Medieval Persia, 1040–1797*, 88. See also René Grousset, *The Empire of the Steppes: A History of Central Asia*, trans. Naomi Walford, chap. 11; H. R. Roemer, "Timür in Iran."

9. For details see Ahmed Zeki Velidi Togan, "Timurs Osteuropapolitik."

ruin, the devastation of its cities, the decimation of its population and the destruction of countless businesses and trades. This state of collapse, which was to last for many years, suited Temür's plans perfectly. Together with the unstable political situation inside Egypt, it offered, for the time being at least, the best possible guarantee against dangerous activities on the part of the Mamlüks, let alone any revival of the idea of an alliance between them and the Ottomans.[10]

Apparently Temür no longer felt threatened by the Mamlüks in Egypt, but before turning his attention to the Ottomans he had to secure his rear. During the summer of 1401 he took Baghdad by storm, demolished its fortifications and public buildings, and put the entire population, minus the Muslim theologians and dervishes, to the sword.

The confrontation with Bayezid proceeded slowly but relentlessly. As René Grousset observed, "both leaders . . . watched and spied upon one another, hesitant to engage in battle and so hazard what they had gained, one from the conquest of Asia, the other from that of the Balkans."[11] Each had clients who were enemies of the other, so pretexts were easy to come by. Following an exchange of insults, the two met late in July 1402 at Chubuq, near Ankara. Temür again won decisively, captured Bayezid, and retained him in his retinue in a barred litter (not an iron cage). The conquest of western Anatolia was quickly undertaken, and Bayezid's son, Süleyman, declared his submission. Temür abruptly withdrew, now secure in the knowledge that Anatolia had been economically and politically neutralized.[12] So far as the European powers were concerned, the intervention of Temür unexpectedly and inexplicably granted to the city another half century of existence in Christian hands.

Before considering the impact of these events on Europe, a brief notice of Temür's religious views may be in order. According to Roemer, "Temür remained strongly attached to Mongol traditions" notwithstanding the frequency with which he stressed his Muslim faithfulness.[13] Perhaps faithful to his status as a "cohabiter," Temür followed both Mongol customary law and Islamic religious law, according to circumstance. Likewise on occasion he emphasized his kinship to Chenggis but also to

10. "Timür in Iran," 76.
11. *Empire of the Steppes*, 449.
12. For details, see G. Roloff, "Die Schlacht bei Angora (1402)," and M. M. Alexandrescu-Dersca, *La campagne de Timur en Anatolie (1402)*. A shorter account may be found in Speros Vryonis Jr., *The Decline of Medieval Hellenism in Asia Minor and the Process of Islamicization from the Eleventh through the Fifteenth Century*, 140–42.
13. Roemer, "Timür in Iran," 88. He received a Mongol burial. See V. V. Bartold, "The Burial of Timür." The invasion of India, for example, was justified in terms of religious devotion.

the Prophet, Muhammad, which placed him "in the unique position of being connected with the two most powerful dynastic lines in thirteenth and fourteenth century Iran and Central Asia."[14]

In seeking to understand the ferocity with which he conducted his campaigns, Jean Aubin emphasized that Temür, like Chenggis, worshiped the sun god, Tenggeri, and obtained his victories by the grace of Heaven. "Temür," he wrote, "considered himself to be the executor of divine decrees." He also received revelations from God by way of angels. The results were, perhaps, predictable: "imbued with his own authority of divine right, subject neither to obligation nor sanction, never deflected by defeat, the Great Emir considered terror as *the* means of government."[15] Grousset compared Temür to Chenggis on several occasions and concluded that Temür was worse not simply because he did more damage but also because he was culturally more civilized. "The early Mongols," Grousset observed, "were simple savages, whereas Tamerlane was a cultured Turk and a great lover of Persian poetry who yet destroyed the flower of Iranian civilization, a devout Muslim who sacked all the capitals of the Muslim world."[16] Moreover, Grousset attributed Temür's greater thoroughness to this same Islamic civility.

> The Mongols were mere barbarians who killed simply because for centuries this had been the instructive behavior of nomad herdsmen toward sedentary farmers. To this ferocity Tamerlane added a taste for religious murder. He killed from piety. He represents a synthesis, probably unprecedented in history, of Mongol barbarity and Muslim fanaticism, and symbolizes that advanced form of primitive slaughter which is murder committed for the sake of an abstract ideology, as a duty and a sacred mission.[17]

A final consideration with respect to the consequences of Temür's syncretism of Mongol and Islamic religious experiences was brought to light by the fourteenth-century Arab traveler Ibn Battūta. The Sultan

14. Thomas W. Lentz and Glenn D. Lowry, *Timur and the Princely Vision: Persian Art and Culture in the Fifteenth Century*, 28. In addition, the inscription on his tomb declared his mother to be Alanqoa, who was associated with the Virgin Mary and was, like the mother of Jesus, supernaturally impregnated.

15. Aubin, "Comment Tamerlan prenait les villes," 87–88, 122.

16. *Empire of the Steppes*, 431. At the same time, Temür created his own capital, Samarqand, a very unnomadic thing to do, adorned it with the treasure of his conquests, and surrounded it with villages named after the ancient Islamic cities he so thoroughly sacked. See Roemer, "Timür in Iran," 86.

17. *Empire of the Steppes*, 434. It is perhaps worth pointing out that Grousset wrote his masterful study prior to the day when commandants of extermination camps could also be sensitive interpreters of Bach. See Rudolf Hoess, *Commandant of Auschwitz*.

of Transoxania, he wrote, is "a man of great destruction, possessed of numerous troops and regiments of cavalry, a vast kingdom and immense power, and just in his government. His territories lie between four of the great kings of the earth, namely the king of China, the king of India, the king of al-'Iraq, and the king of Üzbak, all of whom send him gifts and hold him in high respect and honor."[18] Temür thus grew up in the symbolic middle of the world, surrounded by great kingdoms or empires. One by one he visited them and subdued their rulers, except for China. In 1368 the Ming dynasty had expelled the Mongols. In 1404 Temür convened a *quriltai* near Samarqand, reviewed his troops, conducted a splendid festival, and prepared to visit the greatest territory the Mongols had ruled.[19] He died en route in February 1405, and the expedition to China was abandoned. By any standard, the military achievements of Temür were enormous. He was undoubtedly one of the greatest generals in the history of the world and also one of the most brutal. "All in all," wrote David O. Morgan, "he remains one of the most complex, puzzling and unattractive figures in the history of Persia and Central Asia."[20] It is not, therefore, surprising that when accounts of his activities reached Western Europe they made a deep and lasting though, as befits a myth of this kind, diffuse impression.

In a prefatory note to the original article on the image of Temür, Voegelin stated that he became aware of the great significance that the Mongol empire had for European political thinking as a result of his study of Renaissance political theory.[21] Specifically, as he recalled some thirty-five years later, the figure of Temür was invoked as a rival to Alexander and Caesar and an exemplar of political greatness. "Practically every author of importance," he said, "dealt with these events, which were completely outside the normal experience of politics in the

18. H. A. R. Gibb, trans., *The Travels of Ibn Battūta*, A.D. *1325–1354*, 3:556.

19. For a report on the festivities and preparation, see Clavijo, *Narrative of the Embassy to the Court of Timür.* See also the Timurid account translated by Roemer in *Staatsschreiben der Timuridzeit: Das Saraf-namä des Abdallah Marwarid,* vol. 3 (Akademie der Wissenschaften und der Literatur, Veröffentlichungen der orientalischen Kommission, 1952), 21–23.

20. *Medieval Persia*, 93.

21. In 1940 Voegelin wrote to Mrs. William H. Moore that his concern with the Mongols "was aroused about ten years ago when I worked in the Bibliothèque Nationale on French political theory of the 16th century" (HI 8/50). He continued his work at the National-Bibliothek and the Universitätsbibliothek in Vienna (HI 61/4). These remarks written closer to the period of his studies confirm the recollection presented later in *Autobiographical Reflections.* Consider also Toynbee's remarks, *History*, 4:491.

West and introduced an inexplicable rise to power, which affected the very existence of Western civilization, as a factor into world history."[22] Even though the Mongols first appeared in European literature in the thirteenth century, Voegelin began his analysis with texts dating from two hundred years later because, he said, it was then that Europeans first began to construct a story based on the evidence but not limited to it. Voegelin planned a series of four articles, of which the first, which followed the prefatory note, would deal with the image of Temür as reflected in fifteenth- and sixteenth-century Mediterranean humanist literature. A second article would continue the analysis through the next two centuries. Here the emphasis would be on the work of French philologists and their efforts to translate Arabic and Persian sources. A third would treat the acquisition of ancient Far Eastern and Mongolian sources starting in the Romantic period and continuing up to the twentieth century. Voegelin anticipated that this third study would enable him to undertake a reinterpretation of the diplomatic correspondence between the Mongol qans and the European powers and to provide a glimpse of Mongol constitutional theory. A fourth and final study would draw together the most recent work on the Mongols and offer a new interpretation of the creation of the Mongol empire in terms of the problems associated with national political organizations.[23]

The beginning of humanist interest in Temür, Voegelin said, was found in the work of Poggio Bracciolini (1380–1459), who was twenty-two when Temür defeated Bayezid in 1402.[24] For the last years of his life Poggio

22. *Autobiographical Reflections,* 36.
23. Voegelin, "Vorbemurkung" to "Das Timurbild der Humanisten," 545–46.
24. Voegelin relied on sixteenth- and eighteenth-century editions. The edition consulted here was Poggius Bracciolini, *Opera Omnia,* ed. Ricardo Fubini. Recently, approaching the topic from the side of Arabic questions, Walter J. Fischel (*Ibn Khaldun in Egypt: His Public Functions and Historical Research, 1382–1406: A Study in Islamic Historiography,* 106–8) has brought to light the prehumanist sources of the *vita tamerlani.* They include Jean, Archbishop of Sultaniya, who had been sent on a diplomatic mission by Temür in 1402 to the court of Charles II of France; Gonzales de Clavijo, of whom mention has already been made; Johann Schiltberger, a Bavarian mercenary who had served with Bayezid until taken prisoner in 1402, after which he served Temür; Byzantine chroniclers; and several Italian merchants in the Levant, including Emmanuel Piloti, Paole Zane, and Bertrando di Mignanelli. The last mentioned, according to Fischel (108 n. 44), wrote a *Vita Tamerlani* in 1416. See also Johann Schiltberger, *The Bondage and Travels of Johann Schiltberger in Europe, Asia, and Africa, 1396–1427,* 22–23, 128, and J. Delaville le Roulx, "Rapports de Tamerlan avec les Chrétiens." In his 1940 letter to Mrs. Moore mentioned earlier, Voegelin wrote of the importance of Oriental historiography: "The most interesting part of my work concerns the problem of historiography. The standard monographs on the question

was chancellor and official historiographer of Florence. The context within which Temür's name was first raised was, therefore, complex. To begin with, there was Poggio's position as historiographer and man of letters. In a letter, written about midcentury, he compared the relative worth of the military and the literary life. He did not want to make a choice, but he did allow that fame could no longer be guaranteed by military glory alone. After all, he said, consider how soon Temür had been forgotten, though his activities far outstripped all the conquests of antiquity.[25] Accordingly, he argued, it is better not to depend on others for the preservation of one's name.[26] Such an argument is significant for several reasons. First of all, it is evidence that the Christian concern for the destiny of one's soul had been replaced by a concern for the earthly immortality of lasting fame. Second, the guarantors of fame were historiographers such as Poggio himself. Third, however, was the sentiment that the deeds of his own time, namely those of Temür, surpassed those of antiquity.

A second strand of meaning linked fame and fortune. Granted that the historiographer was, in the nature of things, superior to the man of action owing to his capacity to bestow immortality, in addition, the realm of action was intrinsically miserable insofar as the victor purchased his success at the cost of another's defeat. Moreover, no victory was final: the hero of today may be defeated tomorrow. All action, Poggio said, was

---

have the writing of history begin with Machiavelli and explain it with the renewed interest in antiquity. On the basis of my materials I can say by now that this thesis is only partially correct. While the renewed contact with Greek and Roman historians is doubtless an important influence, the contemporary Eastern historiography is at least equally important. While the Western writing of history has still the chronicle style, or is mythical, the historians of the Mongol empire in Persia, and of the Tamerlane period, write pragmatic highly critical history, and produce even treatises on the methods of history which compare with the best of our time. The same is true for the Byzantine historians of the 14th and 15th centuries. I think I am able to show that the Eastern historians were well known to the first Western historiographers, and that the Eastern methods were taken over and contributed decisively to the Western writing of history. Though I have collected the materials concerning these problems I am unable, for the reasons stated above, to prepare them for publication right now."

25. According to Fletcher, the reason for the relative ignorance of the Latin West with respect to Temür was a consequence both of his inability to pass on intact his conquests and of the dynamic nature of his empire, which required constant military activity to continue in existence, not administrative regularity ("The Mongols," 36 ff.). Manz, *Rise and Rule of Tamerlane*, is in agreement with this observation. Poggio's remarks are in *Opera Omnia*, ed. Ricardo Fubini, 1:344–46.

26. See also Machiavelli, *The Prince*, chaps. 6–7. The concern with fame in the context of military and literary achievements was a common topic. See Jacob Burkhardt, *The Civilization of the Renaissance in Italy*, trans. S. G. C. Middlemore, 128–34.

governed by fortune, "which exalts one as the *secunda* [the favored one] and curses another as the *adversa.*"[27] This, he said, was the significance of Temür's defeat of Bayezid. By the same token, Poggio's attitude toward the significance of power carried with it the implication that, in fact, the great power that Temür embodied could have extinguished the civilization of Europe. Temür could have become a successful Xerxes,[28] an image that evoked Herodotus's story of the age-old struggle between Europe and Asia. As Voegelin observed in *History of Political Ideas,* with Poggio's account "the West emerges from the enclosure of its imperial finality into the openness of a world scene on which mightier empires threaten the existence of Europe; Asia becomes again a determinant in the meaning of history and politics."[29] At the same time as Temür adopted the role of Xerxes in this drama, the role of Athens was unfilled, which added an additional significance to, and fascination with, the Asiatic conqueror.

These reflections led Poggio to a third strand of meaning. Even though the name of Temür could be forgotten (but not by Poggio), the power he embodied and the threat that another Temür might pose to Europe indicated that the apparent isolation of European history was an illusion. Like Voltaire and the marquise du Châtelet two centuries later, Poggio was concerned about the disturbing reality of "parallel" Asiatic histories that ran their course outside the categories of Christian universalism and its linear construction of history. Poggio was a humanist and thoroughly familiar with the heroic deeds of antiquity. Not surprisingly, therefore, he used the classical imagery to describe the contemporary hero, emphasizing the claim that, by comparison to the so-called heroes of antiquity, Temür was a giant among mere mortals. Here Voegelin detected not simply evidence that Poggio was fed up with the glories of antiquity, a typical theme of the quarrel of the ancients and the moderns, but also evidence of the first stirrings of a new political myth.

Poggio cast the story of Temür's life into the form of a series of significant dates and illustrative anecdotes. Poggio thus told the story of Temür's lowly parentage, early conquests at home and of his near neighbors, the expansion into Transoxania and Asia Minor, the victory at Ankara and the fate of Bayezid, his technique of camp construction, the discipline of his soldiers, the victories over Syria and Egypt, the storming of Damascus, the art of siege, the story of the three tents,[30] the comparison

---

27. *Anamnesis,* 156.

28. Poggio, "De Varietate Fortunae," in *Opera Omnia,* 2:539–40. The sentiment was still evident in Le Roulx's "Rapports de Tamelan avec les Chrétiens," 395–96.

29. "Man in History and Nature," in *HPI,* V:142.

30. When assaulting a city, according to this story, Temür would set out on successive days a white, a red, and a black tent. If the city capitulated before the

with Hannibal, the victorious return to Samarqand, the complaint that he has no great historian to celebrate his deeds, and the decline of the empire after his death.[31] Poggio's catalog of events provided the raw material for the deliberate construction of an image of ruthless power and limitless conquest. Temür grew to symbolize the great conqueror, the destroyer of cities and peoples who used human beings as raw material to build a city of splendor that would be an everlasting monument to himself. The purpose of politics by this account was to enable the Temürs of the world to express their outsized personalities. There was no mention of the Christian meaning of history or even of a concern for national survival. It was apparently enough that Temür had the capacity to create pyramids from the skulls of his victims to assure him of greatness, if not remembrance.

Eventually, the anecdotes crystallized into a quasi-formulaic mythic evocation. The first such enhanced "Life of Tamerlane" was written by Eneas Silvio Piccolomini (1405–1464), elected Pius II in 1458. Here the author reworked the historical materials to emphasize Temür's lowly origin, meteoric rise, and grand victories. A series of anecdotes illustrated his courage, efficiency, and cruelty; central among them was a story where Temür said of himself that he was superhuman, the scourge of God and punisher of sins, *ira Dei et ultor peccatorum.* The result of this process of selection and enhancement was to present an image of nihilistic grandeur, of expansive power without further meaning undertaken with no concern for the misery inflicted upon the defeated. The humanists' image of Temür combined personal charisma, organizational creativity, and annihilating power with the idea that such a combination was also the execution of divine will. Voegelin then provided summary analyses of the more significant *vitae* written during the sixteenth century and remarked that Temür bore the same relationship to the Renaissance and its historical culture that Alexander and his expeditions did to the culture of the Hellenistic period or that Caesar and his conquests did to the culture of world empires.[32]

Several conclusions may be drawn from Voegelin's article. The first, and most obvious, is that Poggio and his humanist successors were aware of the independent course of Asiatic history. This was often formulated

---

white tent, Temür would treat the inhabitants with mercy; if it waited until the day of the red tent, only the officers, magistrates, and political leaders would be executed; on the third day, the black tent signified that all would be killed. The story is told in many sources including Bodin's *Colloquium,* 84, and Marlowe's *Tamburlaine the Great.* This last source has received a good deal of attention from literary scholars. See W. L. Godshalk, *The Marlovian World Picture,* 103–4 and references cited in n. 3.

31. *Anamnesis,* 162–63.

32. Ibid., 174, 175.

in terms of significant parallels between contemporary events and those of antiquity. For example, the comparison of Temür and Hannibal, a typical element of the genre, carried with it the imagery of a grave threat to Rome, this time the Rome of the popes, not of the Republic. The Ottoman conquest of Constantinople in 1453 reinforced the secular humanistic construction of history and correspondingly undermined the Christian meaning. Second, the parallel meanings did not correspond to the single time line of Western, Christian historiography. The sacred history of Augustine was effectively ignored, and newly made over classical images were introduced. Events and personal characteristics were selected and enhanced in order to construct a new mythic image of a destroyer-and-creator, a terror of the world beyond the horizon of Christian categories and, as it were, beyond good and evil. The mystery of power and of political empire building was to be understood not in terms of Christian historiography and its single time line, but in terms of fame and fortune. Politics, to use a formula of Machiavelli, consisted in the acquiring of a state (or an empire or, indeed, the ecumene) on the basis of one's own effort and ability, Machiavelli's *virtù*.

The impact of Asiatic events on European political speculation and historiography is of interest not only to specialists in the Renaissance.[33] In 1951 Voegelin published a long section of the chapter on Machiavelli from *History of Political Ideas*.[34] Here he reviewed the circumstances of Machiavelli's biography, the significance to him of the French invasion of Italy in 1494, and the intellectual context within which his writings should be understood. Three elements combined to constitute that context: the first was a tradition of secular statecraft that began with the restoration of the pope's authority in the papal states a century and a half earlier. The second was the systematic reflection on the problem of restoring order under conditions of political disorder and rebellion by means of absolute temporal rule. And third was the development of humanist historiography.

A section entitled "The Asiatic Background" followed; here Voegelin reviewed the relevant events in Asiatic political history and provided a summary of his article on the image of Temür. So far as Machiavelli was

33. Even so, these same specialists seem largely unaware of, or remain uninfluenced by, Voegelin's analysis. Temür is unmentioned, for instance, by Hans Baron in his standard work, *The Crisis of the Early Italian Renaissance: Civic Humanism and Republican Liberty in an Age of Classicism and Tyranny*, rev. ed. Likewise, the more focused study by Donald J. Wilcox, *The Development of Florentine Humanist Historiography in the Fifteenth Century*, contains no mention of Temür, notwithstanding the extended discussion of the "theoretical" aspects of Poggio's historical writing.

34. Voegelin, "Machiavelli's Prince: Background and Formation."

concerned, the French invasion illustrated the meaning of the myth of Tamerlane. Stronger political and military force can crush a weaker political order "however high its rank may be in the realm of civilizational values."[35] This kind of event is not a natural disaster but a political one, at least for the defeated civilizational or cultural entity. But victory and defeat did not end the story. The stronger power was then faced with the necessity of restoring order on the basis of its own internal "civilizational values." In Voegelin's words, "the *virtù* of the conquering prince becomes the source of order; and since the Christian, transcendental order of existence had become a dead letter for the Italian thinkers of the fifteenth century, the *virtù ordinata* of the prince, as the principle of the only order that is experienced as real, acquires human-divine, heroic proportions."[36] One may conclude, therefore, that the founding virtue of a prince is more likely to be effective under conditions characterized by the experiential atrophy of divine transcendent order.

In the particular case of Machiavelli, the mythic evocation of a savior-prince to rid Italy of the French barbarians is at the center of his work "in the same sense in which the evocation of the philosopher-king is the center of Plato's work." According to Voegelin, the myth of the hero is presupposed by the theory of both the *Prince* and the *Discourses*. "The myth itself is fully and consciously unfolded only in the *Vita di Castruccio Castracani* (1520)." Voegelin then listed the main phases in the *Vita*, observing that they followed the pattern of the heroic myth of Temür. From his unknown birth to his triumphant victories, Castruccio looked like a Luccan Temür and, in Machiavelli's view, a potential savior of Italy. In fact, Machiavelli ignored some well-known facts of Castruccio's life, invented others, endowed him with the attributes of men such as Caesar Borgia and with the opinions of Machiavelli himself. Voegelin paid special attention to the summary of Castruccio's character:

35. Often, of course, Temür did nothing to restore order, which is the source of his bad reputation. Alexandrescu-Dersca, *La campagne de Timur en Anatolie,* for example, laid great stress on the sheer destructiveness of his achievements. Manz, *Rise and Rule of Tamerlane,* pointed to a possible explanation: "other great steppe conquerors had also arisen on the borderlands between steppe and sown, but most consolidated their hold first over the steppe. Temür on the other hand overran the steppe but never aspired to rule it" (2).

36. Voegelin, "Machiavelli's Prince," 165. The actual text quoted varies somewhat from the published article; in the Voegelin-Archiv at the University of Munich, a copy of the article with Voegelin's corrections is preserved. It is flagged with a note from Voegelin's typewriter: "The emendations in this reprint are not afterthoughts of the author. They restore the text of the MS. E.V." We have, accordingly, followed the original version from "The Order of Power: Machiavelli," in *HPI,* IV:31–87.

He was dear to his friends and terrible to his enemies; just to his subjects and faithless with foreigners; he never tried to conquer by force when he could conquer by fraud, for he used to say that by victory, not the method of gaining it, you acquire fame. Nobody was ever bolder in approaching dangers, and nobody more skillful in escaping them. He used to say that men should try everything and fear nothing, and that God is a lover of strong men, for as anyone may see, he always punishes the weak by means of the strong.[37]

Voegelin ended his article with the following observation: "The closing remark of this characterization is of special interest because it introduces the element of the *ira Dei* that we know from the *Vita Tamerlani;* the victorious prince becomes the *ultor peccatorum* [punisher of sins]. Neither in the *Principe* nor in the *Discorsi* has Machiavelli become so explicit in according to power and *virtù* the meaning of a providential order of politics."

Machiavelli has often been criticized for teaching immorality or evil. Voegelin's perspective on this problem was similar to the position he developed with respect to Bodin, discussed earlier. Because human existence is social, one is responsible for the consequences of one's actions on the lives of others. The spiritual insight of Plato, that it is better to suffer than to commit evil (*Gorgias* 474b), does not exhaust the political questions that statesmen or princes must consider. "A statesman," Voegelin remarked, "who does not answer an attack on his country with the order to shoot back will not be praised for the spiritual refinement of his morality in turning the other cheek, but he will justly be cursed for his criminal irresponsibility. Spiritual morality is a problem in human existence, precisely because there is a good deal more to human existence than spirit."[38] The "good deal more" refers, precisely, to the social, psychological, vital, somatic, physical, and other aspects of human being discussed earlier in terms of philosophical anthropology. These attributes may be ordered in terms of "value" (to use Scheler's language), but the ordering does not abolish the lower merely through acknowledging the higher as being higher.

The surface meaning of Machiavelli's "immorality" may therefore be specified as follows: he has recognized that the pursuit of spiritual truths may conflict with other matters, such as preserving one's own

---

37. The most accessible version is probably Machiavelli, "Life of Castruccio of Lucca . . . ," in *The Prince and Other Works,* trans. and ed. Allan H. Gilbert (New York: Hendricks, 1964), 205. Voegelin's translation in "Machiavelli's Prince," 168, has been altered slightly.

38. Voegelin, "Conclusion" to "The Order of Power: Machiavelli," *HPI,* IV:82–87. Subsequent quotations are from this source.

existence or community. "Every political order," Voegelin observed, "is in some part an accident of existence. The mystery of existential cruelty and guilt is at the bottom of the best order. . . . By social convention this mystery of guilt is not admitted to public consciousness." Consequently, when a political philosopher reminds his readers of this mystery, they will consider him immoral. Machiavelli was neither the first nor the last political philosopher to suffer moralizing, conventionalist opprobrium.

Even if one understands the reasons for Machiavelli's unsavory reputation, there remains the uneasiness that derives from his cold-bloodedness and apparent unconcern for the spiritual implications of his advice to new princes. Voegelin accounted for this uneasiness by arguing that Machiavelli was indeed concerned with spirituality, but it was an intramundane spirituality that, he said, derived from Polybius. "For Machiavelli, the expediency and immorality of action do not affect the destiny of the soul; his is holy, and has found its destiny, when it manifests its *virtù* in the world." That is, Machiavelli recovered a "pagan myth of nature" as a horizon within which he developed his political philosophy.

To understand the significance of Machiavelli's achievement for our present concern with the problem of historical evidence, we must recall the "background" factors about which Voegelin wrote in his published article. The disintegration of the medieval *sacrum imperium,* the creation of humanist historiography, the Asiatic events, and the traumatic invasion of the French in 1494 had made it clear, for those who had eyes to see, that "a world scene of politics had opened, with a structure of its own." When the Augustinian meaning of history was no longer meaningful, "the 'natural' structure of history, in the ancient sense, becomes visible again. The Myth of Nature, in fact," Voegelin said, "is not a piece of obsolete nonsense; it only is defective insofar as the problems of the spirit are not sufficiently differentiated." The alleged strangeness of Machiavelli's so-called immorality, then, is a consequence of the retreat in the differentiation of spiritual experience from that previously achieved through medieval Christianity or Hellenic philosophy. But in comparison to the Augustinian philosophy of history, such criticisms do not apply. In addition to the comparative narrowness of the historical horizon of the Christian philosophy of history, which was discussed in Chapter 6, the Augustinian account also "neglects the problem of the natural course of a political civilization." In this context, Machiavelli's "reintroduction of the problem of the cycle marks the beginning of a modern interpretation of history and politics that leads through Vico to the more recent elaboration of the problem by Eduard Meyer, Spengler, and Toynbee."[39] We will discuss the question of cycles and the "natural course of a political civilization" in the following two chapters.

In this section, we have discussed Voegelin's arguments regarding the image of Temür in Renaissance humanism generally as a significant background element in Machiavelli's evocation of a new prince. It would be fair to say that Voegelin's observations have not had much of an impact on the way that political scientists have studied Machiavelli's political philosophy generally, or on the more focused interpretation of the "Life of Castruccio Castracani."[40] Voegelin's argument and evidence have, however, been confirmed from what at first blush may seem an unlikely quarter.

39. A century after Poggio, the French humanist Louis LeRoy, writing during the period of the religious wars that also motivated Bodin's reflections, refined a fear of Asiatic power with an acute awareness of French internal disorder into speculative construction of successive civilizational epochs the course of which is beyond the *virtù* of any particular founder. Each epoch is initiated by the advent of a great conqueror, but his destructive action is followed by discoveries, inventions, and the advancement of knowledge. The initiator of the modern epoch, according to LeRoy, was none other than Temür. As with Machiavelli, in place of the Christian drama of fall and redemption, LeRoy substituted an intramundane world-historical cycle based upon the rhythms of nature, upon a myth of human destiny and, on a grander scale, of eternal return. "Not the drama of the soul [but the rhythm of nature] furnishes for LeRoy the categories of historical articulation. This is the first clear, though somewhat restrained, manifestation of the sentiments that later express themselves fully in the person and work of Nietzsche," Voegelin wrote in *HPI*, V:149. In a footnote, he drew attention to the differences between his interpretation and that of J. B. Bury, whose *The Idea of Progress*, 44–49, provided a well-known but in Voegelin's view erroneous interpretation. Werner L. Gundersheimer's *The Life and Works of Louis Le Roy*, notes the importance of Temür (112–13) but is unaware of his earlier importance for LeRoy's Italian predecessors.
40. For Guido A. Guarino, Machiavelli's "Life" was simply "a highly imaginative and fictionalized account of the Duke's life" ("Two Views of a Renaissance Tyrant," 285); Peter E. Bondanella showed that Machiavelli's Castruccio was "a mythological figure, an archetypal prince," and part of a "literary myth," but he provided no analysis of the sources of the myth ("Castruccio Castracani: Machiavelli's Archetypal Prince"); other studies stress the historical inaccuracies of Machiavelli's portrait but do not account for why Machiavelli might have introduced them; see Louis Green, "Machiavelli's *Vita di Castruccio Castracani* and Its Luccese Model"; Theodore A. Sumberg, "Machiavelli's Castruccio Castracani"; Jeffrey T. Schnapp, "Machiavellian Foundlings: Castruccio Castracani and the Aphorism." J. H. Whitfield, "Machiavelli and Castruccio," in his *Discourses on Machiavelli*, 111–39, says nothing of the *Vita Tamerlani* as a model for the "Life of Castruccio." For a full, scholarly, and contemporary account devoid of any mythic considerations, see Louis Green, *Castruccio Castracani: A Study on the Origins and Character of a Fourteenth Century Italian Despotism.*

For more than a century, scholars in the field of English literature have investigated the sources used by Christopher Marlowe for his play *Tamburlaine the Great*. Three matters appear to have been settled: first, that what J. S. Cunningham called "a prototype Tamerlane narrative," and Voegelin called a mythic image of Tamerlane, was current in Western Europe within a century of Temür's defeat of Bayezid; second, that the story developed in part I of Marlowe's play was taken from two main sources, Petrus Perondinus's *Vita Magni Tamerlanis* (1553) and George Whetstone's *English Myrror* (1586); third, that additional and minor sources were used for part II of the play.[41] Whetstone's account, in turn, was based on earlier studies by Pedro Mexia, Battista Fregoso, Eneas Silvio Piccolomini (Pope Pius II), B. Sacchi, M. Palmieri, and A. Cambini.[42] All these authors were discussed in Voegelin's survey of the humanists. Some critics have expressed astonishment that Marlowe had read so widely in a highly specialized area and at the same time carried his learning so lightly. The initial conclusion was that this discovery of Marlowe's sources was simply additional evidence of his dramatic and poetic skill.[43] Hugh Dick has argued that, without detracting from Marlowe's literary skill, many of these sources had been digested for him by Richard Knolles and that it was likely he took advantage of the opportunity to consult Knolles's enormous *Generall Historie of the Turkes*, which was not published until 1603, a decade after Marlowe's murder.[44] One may conclude from this evidence, then, that by the time Marlowe wrote his

41. Cunningham, "Introduction" to his edition of Christopher Marlowe, *Tamburlaine the Great*, 10; see also Hallett Smith, "Tamburlaine and the Renaissance"; John Bakeless, *The Tragicall History of Christopher Marlowe*, 1:chap. 7; Una M. Ellis-Fermor, *Christopher Marlowe*, 17–61; H. C. Hart, "Tamburlaine and Primaudaye"; Leslie Spence, "The Influence of Marlowe's Sources on *Tamburlaine I*" and "Tamburlaine and Marlowe," for useful, though somewhat dated studies. Johnstone Parr, *Tamburlaine's Malady and Other Essays on Astrology in Elizabethan Drama*, provides additional information on the more recondite influences on Marlowe's life and work. See also Samuel C. Chew, *The Crescent and the Rose: Islam and England during the Renaissance*, chap. 11.

42. Thomas C. Izard, "The Principal Sources for Marlowe's *Tamburlaine*"; see also Roy W. Battenhouse, *Marlowe's Tamburlaine: A Study in Renaissance Moral Philosophy*, 129–49.

43. Ethel Seaton, "Fresh Sources for Marlowe," 401.

44. Dick, "*Tamburlaine* Sources Once More." Knolles was the translator of Bodin's *Six Bookes of the Republic*. See K. D. McRae, "The Life and Background of Richard Knolles," in his edition of Bodin's *The Six Bookes of a Commonweale*, A52–62. Temür appears in Bodin's *Republic* as the slayer of the tyrant "Baiazet" (see McRae's trans., 221, 600); Dick has suggested that Bodin may have been influenced by Temür's legendary tolerance of conflicting faiths ("*Tamburlaine* Sources Once More," 155–56 n. 4). See also Chew, *The Crescent and the Rose*, 111–13.

play during the late 1580s the name of Temür was indeed surrounded by a complex of meanings concerning destiny, history, human will, and action of heroic proportions.[45]

Literary analysis of the content and action of *Tamburlaine* provides indirect evidence to support Voegelin's interpretation of the impact of the image of Temür on Machiavelli. In the early 1950s, for example, Irving Ribner published a series of articles on *Tamburlaine* and related topics. His own intensive analysis of the play and of its mythic hero confirmed Voegelin's argument. "Marlowe's play," he wrote, "treats *Tamburlaine* completely within the tradition developed by the humanist historians. . . . Marlowe's *Tamburlaine* is essentially that of Poggio Bracciolini and his followers, and he is also the type of man whom Machiavelli envisaged as the savior of Italy. A significant relation between Marlowe's *Tamburlaine* and Machiavelli's *Prince* is that they both draw in large part upon a common ideological source."[46] According to Ribner, then, Temür was, for Marlowe, a Machiavellian savior-prince.[47] More generally one may conclude that even the study of so undoubted a European topic as the work of Machiavelli requires an understanding of the impact of Asiatic history if his political thinking is properly to be interpreted. Such a conclusion, it seems fair to say, is not widely shared by contemporary historians of Renaissance political thought or by political philosophers. The persuasive nature of Voegelin's argument therefore contains a reflection on contemporary scholarship.

The second article Voegelin published dealing with the impact of Asiatic events on Europe concerned the Mongols. His critical preparation of the letters of the Mongol qans to the European powers was well underway by 1937.[48] By 1938 the plan announced in the prefatory note

45. Eugene Waith, *The Herculean Hero in Marlowe, Chapman, Shakespeare, and Dryden* and *Ideas of Greatness: Heroic Drama in England.*

46. Ribner, "Marlowe and Machiavelli," 354–55. Ribner and Voegelin exchanged several letters during this time, and Ribner sent Voegelin inscribed offprints of his articles. Ribner cited Voegelin's articles on Temür and on Machiavelli as a matter of course (HI 30/9).

47. Ribner, "The Idea of History in Marlowe's *Tamburlaine*"; "*Tamburlaine* and *The Wars of Cyrus*"; *The English History Play in the Age of Shakespeare,* rev. ed., 60–61; *Jacobean Tragedy: The Quest for Moral Order,* 4; "Marlowe's 'Tragicke Glasse,'" 93–96. See also Claude J. Summers, *Christopher Marlowe and the Politics of Power* and "Tamburlaine's Opponents and Machiavelli's *Prince*," and Michael Quinn, "The Freedom of Tamburlaine."

48. In May 1936, Voegelin lectured on the Mongols at the University of Graz under the title "Die Führer Asiens gegen Europa," *Grazer Urania,* 17, 19 (May 1, 1939), HI 55/9.

to his article on the image of Temür had expanded. At this time Voegelin contemplated publishing one book on the influence of the Mongol empires on European thought from the twelfth century to the twentieth and another variously characterized as being devoted to Mongol constitutional thought or to "the political concept of the Mongol Empire."[49] In the event, he published a thirty-five-page article in *Byzantion*.[50] The article was divided into five sections: (1) introduction; (2) a *présentation de texte;* (3) analysis of the preambles; (4) analysis of the contents; (5) conclusion.

The significance of the documents, Voegelin said, was twofold: "They contain the principal ideas underlying Mongol constitutional law, as well as the framework of Mongol political theory." The historical context may be summarized briefly. Around the middle of the eleventh century, the Saljūq Türkmen, recently converted to orthodox Sunni Islam, began a westward migration from Transoxania, on the eastern borders of the Islamic world, the Dar al-Islam, toward Syria and Asia Minor. Led by two brothers, Toghrïl Beg and Chaghri Beg, the Saljūqs moved first into Khurasan, in northeast Iran. In 1055 Toghrïl captured Baghdad, "liberated" the caliph from Shiite influences, and consolidated Saljūq control. Twenty years later, on a punitive expedition against Ghuzz tribesmen on the borders of Anatolia, the Saljūq army met and defeated at Manzikert a Byzantine force, taking the emperor captive and destroying imperial control in eastern and central Anatolia. The twenty years following the ascent of Malik-Shah to the sultanate in 1072 constituted the zenith of the Saljūq empire. The Saljūqs brought a degree of administrative stability to the region, notwithstanding the activities of their unruly nomadic kinsmen, the Ghuzz, to the west. As Morgan observed, "the Saljūqs were not, by the standards of the region, destructive conquerors."[51]

On the far western front, the Latin powers responded with the first crusade in 1096, which restored the coast of Asia Minor and western Anatolia to Byzantine rule. Internally the unity of the empire did not survive the death of Malik-Shah; succession struggles weakened the authority of the sultan and ended the unified empire. In 1097 Sanjar became governor of Khurasan, and he remained in control for sixty years, but the western provinces were much less stable, owing in part to

49. HI 19/7, 27/30.
50. Voegelin, "The Mongol Orders of Submission to European Powers, 1245–1255." Apparently the text was first submitted to *Speculum,* HI 19/6, 10/19. The transcript (fifty-eight pages) is available in HI, along with the German version subsequently published in *Anamnesis,* 179–222. Reference is to the published English text, unless otherwise noted.
51. Morgan, *Medieval Persia,* 33. For the earlier period see Vryonis, *Decline of Medieval Hellenism in Asia Minor,* 69–103.

the newly established crusader states in Syria and Palestine, but more to the internal dynastic squabbles of the contending candidates for the sultanate. It is important to recall that, whereas from the perspective of a European reading of history the crusades were a great assault to retake the Holy Land from Islam, from the perspective of Sanjar, the danger lay to the east.

In 1125, the Jürchen of Manchuria displaced the Khitan rulers of Mongolia and North China. One Khitan prince, Yeh-lü Ta-shih, moved west at the head of what has come to be known as the Qara-Khitai or "Black Cathay." In 1141 the Qara-Khitai defeated Sanjar near Samarqand (incidentally giving birth to the legend of Prester John, the Christian priest-king who was thought to be coming to the aid of the crusaders)[52] and gained control of Transoxania. Early in the thirteenth century, the Qara-Khitai were themselves partially displaced, this time by the Khwarazm, an Islamic people from the Oxus valley near the south shore of the Aral Sea. The Khwarazm-shah, however, was unable to consolidate his rule before having to confront the Mongols in 1218.[53]

Accounts of the initial contacts between the Khwarazm-shah Muhammad and Chenggis Qan are confusing and contradictory.[54] They may have begun as early as 1215; by 1218, however, Chenggis had dispatched a small force to deal with an old enemy from Mongolia, Küchlüg, who had seized the Qara-Khitai throne a few years earlier. Küchlüg converted to Buddhism from Nestorian Christianity and promptly began to persecute his Muslim subjects. The Mongol general, Jebei, entered the Qara-Khitai lands and declared the persecution over, and the Muslims rose against Küchlüg. Morgan observed: "The great Central Asian realm was, therefore, added to the Mongol Empire, it would seem, by the desire of its inhabitants: an event unique in Mongol history."[55] The destruction of Küchlüg, however, meant that the Mongol realm now bordered that of the Khwarazm-shah.

Chenggis opened diplomatic relations by indicating that the Mongols wished to trade with the lands to the west. He then declared that he

52. For details of this complex personage, see Charles E. Nowell, "The Historical Prester John."
53. See C. E. Bosworth, "Political and Dynastic History of the Iranian World (A.D. 1000–1217)."
54. Even so, Owen Lattimore, "The Geography of Chingis Khan," stressed the importance of Chinggis's decision to head west before turning his attention toward China, on his southern border, unlike his barbarian predecessors who, by invading China at the outset of their imperial expansion, ended their activities by finding themselves absorbed by China.
55. *Medieval Persia*, 56.

considered Muhammud "on a level with the dearest of my sons," which the sultan found deeply offensive.[56] Sometime that same year, 1218, a Mongol caravan was seized at the border town of Utrar and the merchants executed on the grounds that they were spies. An ambassador sent to ensure the Khwarazm made amends was likewise killed, which act created, in Mongol eyes, a state of war. Once Chenggis had secured his own eastern flank, the invasion westward began. In 1219 the Mongols invaded Transoxania; the Khwarazm-shah fled, and the Mongols pressed on into Khurasan. Chenggis's youngest son, Tolui, was in charge of the Khurasan campaign, and he executed his task "with a thoroughness from which that region has never recovered."[57] In 1223 Chenggis returned to Mongolia, and he died a few years later.

His imperial organization, however, continued to expand, chiefly into China. In fact, Chenggis's last campaign was against the Hsi-Hsia of northwest China. The northern Chin empire was defeated after his death, in 1234; the conquest of the southern Sung empire was not completed until 1279 by his grandson Qubilai. In the west, the land just north of Persia remained under Mongol control, to which was added Anatolia, following the battle of Köse Dagh in 1243. A few years later Chenggis's grandson and Tolui's son, Hülagü, subdued the rest of Iran and established the Il-Khan dynasty.[58]

The military operations of greatest concern to the Europeans, however, took place farther north. Nominally under the direction of Batu, grandson of Chenggis, the troops were in fact led by his great general, Sübedei, who was then around sixty years of age. Operations began in 1234 against the Qipchaq living on the southern Russian steppe but were quickly followed by an expedition against the Russian principalities. Moscow, then a relatively small town, was sacked in February 1238; Kiev was destroyed in December 1240, and the principality of Galicia was ravaged. During the winter of 1240–1241 the Mongols crossed the Vistula and advanced on Cracow, defeating a Polish army en route. In April 1241 a larger European army, consisting of Poles, German crusaders, and Teutonic knights was wiped out at Liegnitz. Meanwhile, Batu and Sübedei had invaded Hungary. King Béla IV advanced to meet the enemy, and on April 11 Sübedei won a splendid victory, followed by the usual executions, rapes, pillage, and pursuit of King Béla. In July,

56. Quoted in J. A. Boyle, "Dynastic and Political History of the Il-Khans," in Boyle, ed., *The Cambridge History of Iran,* 5:304.
57. Ibid., 312.
58. Il-Khan means "subject khan" and indicated that the Mongol rulers of Persia were subordinate to the Great Qan in the east.

elements of the army had reached Klosterneuberg, a few miles from Vienna, and in December 1241 Batu himself crossed the frozen Danube.

The western expansion of the Mongols reached its height in the winter of 1241–1242 with the devastation of Hungary. Among other things it ended, for the time being, the possibility of an alliance between the Mongols and the Latin West against the Muslims. Much to the relief and puzzlement of the Europeans, in the spring of 1242 the Mongols precipitously withdrew to the east. News, in fact, had just reached the Mongol armies of the death of the Great Qan, Ögödei. According to Mongol constitutional procedures, the presence of princes and military commanders was required at the *quriltai*, the convocation to elect a new qan. Shortly thereafter the newly elected Pope Innocent IV, apparently more sensitive to the threat the Mongols posed to European Christendom than the defeated Hungarian king, Béla IV, had been, dispatched three sets of envoys to treat with the Mongols.[59] The most successful journey was undertaken by a Franciscan, John of Pian di Carpine, who traveled to the Mongol capital, Qara Qorum, by way of Siberia. A second mission, headed by a Dominican, Ascelin, took a southern route and eventually encountered the Mongol commander, Baiju, in May 1247. His message was eventually conveyed to Qara Qorum, and instructions were relayed to Baiju, who in turn wrote the pope.[60] A third, under another Dominican, Andrew of Longjumeau, also reached a Mongol army near Tabriz, just west of the Caspian Sea. A fourth delegation, under the Franciscan John of Portugal, was commissioned, but it is unclear whether the mission was undertaken.[61] Andrew encountered a Nestorian priest, Simeon (or Rabban Ata), who advised him to counsel the Christian emperor to submit to the Mongols. The message was duly delivered in the spring of 1247. As a leading historian of these events has remarked, "to all evidence the papal missions had achieved no other purpose than that of bringing back reliable, first-hand information of what Innocent IV must have considered a most dangerous foe."[62]

59. Denis Sinor, "Les relations entre les Mongols et l'Europe jusqu'à la mort d'Arghoun et de Béla IV," 42–49, 61. See also Jean Richard, "Les causes des victoires Mongoles d'après les historiens occidentaux du XIIIe siècle."

60. Gregory G. Guzman, "Simon of Saint-Quentin and the Dominican Mission of the Mongol Baiju."

61. Bertold Altaner, *Die Dominikanermission des 13. Jahrhunderts*, 124; Jean Richard, "Mongols and Franks," 46–47.

62. Denis Sinor, "The Mongols and Western Europe," 521–22. An accessible account of the Mongol invasions and the subsequent activity is Igor de Rachewiltz, *Papal Envoys to the Great Khans*. See also Jean Richard, "Les Mongols et l'Occident: Deux siècles de contacts." The most important documents can be found in Christopher

Louis IX of France proceeded to open his own communications with the Mongols in December 1245 when he met with two of their envoys on Cyprus and proposed an alliance against the Saracens.[63] The Mongol emissaries returned east, along with three Dominicans, but the political situation had changed drastically with the death of the Great Qan Güyük. By the time the Dominicans returned west again in 1251 they brought not a treaty of alliance but a routine demand for submission. Last, the famous mission of the Franciscan William of Rubrick in 1253–1255, though undertaken largely for intelligence rather than for diplomatic purposes,[64] resulted in his conveying to Louis yet another demand for submission. So far as the Mongols were concerned, the "Franks" were simply more grist for their mill. As with Temür, that is, the affairs of the Latin Christian West seemed to be relatively unimportant.[65]

Voegelin provided a brief summary of these diplomatic events and added a philological description of the genesis of the documents and of the relatively abundant reports and discussions of the missions. His own contribution consisted of an analysis of the contents of the documents, which, he said, had "attracted scant attention, and their importance for our knowledge of Mongol political and legal concepts has scarcely been stressed. Nobody has ever made an attempt to inquire into the juridical nature of the documents, or to analyze the constitutional theory they set forth."[66] The original documents, as distinct from the mission reports that imperfectly preserved Latin versions of Persian texts, were discovered

---

Dawson, ed., *The Mongol Missions: Narratives and Letters of the Franciscan Missionaries in Mongolia and China in the Thirteenth and Fourteenth Centuries,* trans. a Nun of Stanbrook Abbey. Another useful collection of documents in English translation is Bertold Spuler, *History of the Mongols: Based on Eastern and Western Accounts of the Thirteenth and Fourteenth Centuries,* trans. H. and S. Drummond, esp. 68–69 for another translation of the Order of God. Still another translation, by M. J. Hanak, was made available to me by Paul Caringella. Grousset's still useful general history, *Empire of the Steppes,* was published about the same time as Voegelin completed his own study. It has been supplemented by many specialized studies as well as by the first volume of *The Cambridge History of Early Inner Asia,* ed. Denis Sinor. Unfortunately for our present interests, the first volume deals with the pre-Mongol period of Inner Asian history. Also useful are J. J. Saunders, *The History of the Mongol Conquests,* and David O. Morgan, *The Mongols.*

63. Jean Richard, "La politique orientale de Saint Louis: La Croisade de 1248," in his *Les relations entre l'Orient et l'Occident au Moyen Age,* 200–203.

64. According to Richard, "Les causes des victoires," 107–8, the earlier mission of John of Pian di Carpine was also as much an intelligence as a diplomatic mission.

65. Luc Kwanten, *Imperial Nomads: A History of Central Asia, 500–1500,* 174.

66. Voegelin, "The Mongol Orders," 382.

in the spring of 1921 in the Secret Archives of the Vatican by Father Cyril Korolevskyj. In 1923 Paul Pelliot published the first of a series of texts and commentaries on the Mongols and the papacy.[67] Voegelin relied on Pelliot's texts for his own commentary.

Before considering Voegelin's commentary directly, we will examine briefly the current scholarship. Virtually all the scholarly commentary prior to Pelliot's publication was concerned with geographical information, philological questions, or the place of the missions in the pragmatic history of the West, of the Mongols, or of the religious orders entrusted with the missions. With a few notable exceptions, which compared the Mongol constitutional order to that of China, most of the political commentary consisted in severe but superficial censures of Mongol "arrogance" toward the Latin West and toward Christendom in general as well as expressions of horror at the spectacular bloodthirstiness of the Mongols, their treachery in combat, and their generally unchivalrous character.[68]

Even so accomplished a contemporary scholar as Morgan admitted he was puzzled. Writing of Tolui's subjugation of Khurasan in 1223, he said:

> One can only speculate about why the Mongols chose to behave in so atrocious a fashion. No doubt they felt that they were punishing the misdeeds of the Khwarazm-shah, though the punishment can hardly be said to have fitted the crime. Probably more important, they were removing permanently any possibility there might have been of a center of power existing in Persia that could have rivalled Chenggis Qan himself. Lastly it may well be that, in the Mongol's steppe-oriented minds, the destruction of cities and agriculture was still a matter of little or no real consequence.[69]

67. Antoine Mostaert and Francis Woodman Cleaves, "Trois documents Mongols des Archives Secrètes Vaticanes," 420 n. 1; Pelliot, "Les Mongols et la Papauté."
68. The chief exception, Abel-Rémusat, a nineteenth-century French Orientalist, advanced the view that cultural diffusion from China by way of the Mongols was chiefly responsible for the technical advances in the West that brought to an end the European middle ages. Bertold Spuler has speculated on the existence of an independent influence on Mongol thought coming from Nestorian Christianity. The argument, revived in the West by Dante, for example, held that a single ecumenical church implied a single political empire as its correlate. Spuler, *The Muslim World: A Historical Survey*, part II, *The Mongol Period*, trans. F. R. C. Bagley, 5. For other considerations, see P. B. Golden, "Imperial Ideology and the Sources of Political Unity amongst the Pre-Cinggisid Nomads of Western Eurasia"; Igor de Rachewiltz, "Some Remarks on the Ideological Foundations of Chingis Khan's Empire" and "Yeh-lü Ch'u-ts'ai (1189–1243): Buddhist Idealist and Confucian Statesman"; and V. Minorsky, "The Middle East in Western Politics in the 13th, 14th, and 15th Centuries." See also Richard, "Les causes des victoires," 109 ff., and H. F. Schurmann, "Mongolian Tributary Practices of the Thirteenth Century."
69. *Medieval Persia*, 57–58.

Let us consider these observations. It is no doubt true that the destruction of the Persian empire, starting with the slaughter in Khurasan, removed any potential rival, but there were ways of practicing Realpolitik other than by systematic extinction. Second, modern historians no less than contemporary observers of the events might be of the opinion that the "punishment" did not fit the "crime." But surely the problem is to understand how, in Mongol eyes, the punishment perfectly fitted the crime and why the desire to preserve one's independence or to conduct normal hostilities or normal politics was, in Mongol eyes, a crime in the first place. Third, the explanation offered, that steppe-dwelling Mongols had no use for cities and agriculture, while true, does not explain why they went to the trouble of destroying cities, wrecking irrigation works, and destroying an agricultural order. Besides, these same steppe dwellers behaved rather differently in China: Yeh-hü Ch'u-ts'ai explained to Chenggis's successor, Ögödei, the importance of taxes with the famous words: "the empire was created on horseback, but it will not be governed on horseback."[70] Moreover, other steppe dwellers, notably the Türkmen, behaved rather differently in Iran.

These considerations may have led J. J. Saunders to emphasize the religious differences between Mongol and Muslim as being decisive in determining the difference between the Arab invaders of the seventh century and the Mongols.

> The Caliphs were not Bedouin sheiks, but townsmen from the commercial aristocracy of Mecca: the Khans were nomad tribal chiefs writ large, who revelled in the freedom of the boundless steppes and thought of towns as prisons. Indeed, the massacre and destruction of the Mongols perpetrated in city after city (in Nishapur in 1221, we are told, not only men, women and children but the very cats and dogs in the streets were slaughtered), exercises in genocide to which no parallel is to be found in the Arab conquests, may possibly be ascribed, not so much to a cold and callous military design to terrorize their foes into submission, as to a blind unreasoning fear and hatred of urban civilization.[71]

Saunders did not explain the origin of the Mongol's blind unreasoning fear and hatred of urban civilization, which suggests that the real question is not to understand how unreasonable the Mongols were, but rather to see how what appeared to Saunders, to Morgan, and to countless other observers as unreasonable and bloodthirsty was, to the Mongols, something else.

70. Quoted in de Rachewiltz, "Yeh-lü Ch'u-ts'ai," 195. See also Saunders, *History of the Mongol Conquests*, 67.
71. Saunders, *Muslims and Mongols: Essays on Medieval Asia*, ed. W. G. Rice, 48.

A preliminary answer may be found in Joseph Fletcher's account of what he called the ecological and social considerations that conditioned Mongol activities.[72] When Fletcher's work is combined with Voegelin's textual analysis, a fairly clear picture results.

The chief difference between Mongols and Turks, according to Fletcher, is the speed with which the Mongols came upon Muslim culture, and the numbers in which they came. The Türkmen came in small groups, as refugees from the East Asian steppes, by way of the great deserts of inner Asia. The experience of life in the desert taught the Türkmen nomads how to accommodate their way of life to that of sedentary city dwellers. The objectives of the nomads were to control the sedentary world and to extort wealth from it. Violence would, on occasion, prove useful in this regard, but the long-term objective was *not* to destroy the sources of wealth upon which they preyed.

Steppe, as distinct from desert, nomads had a much different perspective. "Steppe nomads," said Fletcher,

> lived apart from settled peoples, and friendly contacts between them were less the rule. Nomad and farmer or townsman were not usually acquaintances. Geography did not force steppe pastoralists and settled folk together in seasonal reunions. It separated them. At the eastern end of the Steppe zone, where the lines between nomad and sedentary were most sharply drawn, Mongolia and China confronted one another through much of history as worlds apart. The ordinary steppe nomad had little or no motive to develop an understanding of agrarian agriculture or of urban society, and he did not view his fortunes as tied to their prosperity.[73]

That is, the conventional distinction between the desert and the sown must be modified to account for the equally important difference between the steppe and the desert. Bearing this distinction in mind, it is significant that the Mongols moved directly from steppe experience into the sedentary agricultural world of Iran, without having passed through the experience of what Fletcher called "cohabitation."

> Unlike the Turks, they entered the desert habitat suddenly, en masse, in centrally-planned campaigns, phases of a concerted and temporally compact effort. There was no time to acculturate themselves to the desert habitat; so they carried with them, directly into the Middle East [and Europe], attitudes nurtured in the East Asian steppe: disdain for peasants, who like the animals that the Mongols herded, lived directly off what grew from the soil.[74]

72. Fletcher, "The Mongols," 11–50. Toynbee's remarks on Mongol nomadism are also pertinent here; see *History*, 3:12–13, 23–25, 396, 452.
73. "The Mongols," 41. See also David O. Morgan, "The Mongol Armies in Persia."
74. "The Mongols," 42.

In short, the havoc wrought by the Mongols in their encounter with sedentary agrarian societies "proceeded logically from the legacy of steppe wisdom about how nomads could best obtain what they wanted from the agrarian world." To the contemporary observers of the desert pattern of nomadic-sedentary extortion, the destructive violence of the Mongols seemed, indeed, as irrational as it does to many historians today.

In the context of understanding the tremendous destruction accomplished by the Mongols, Voegelin's contribution was twofold. First, he indicated the legal constitutional form taken by the Mongol's "steppe wisdom." Second, he indicated how Mongol constitutionalism was integrated with what Fletcher called, uncritically and anachronistically, the Mongols' "ideology of universal dominion."[75]

In the manuscript for the second section of his article, which presented the textual evidence, Voegelin provided his own translations; the published version reproduced the French translation of Pelliot and the Latin translations from the mission documents. Because nothing came of the diplomatic exchange and no negotiations properly speaking were undertaken, Voegelin remarked, little attention had been paid to the contents of the documents. Using Pelliot's philological arguments,[76] Voegelin began with an analysis of the formular preambles to the letters. He argued that some of the documents were not, in fact, "letters," which is to say, ordinary diplomatic correspondence between the Mongol imperial court

---

75. Ibid. Fletcher added a footnote to Voegelin's article at this point.

76. Voegelin knew no Central Asian language. The philological problems still remain formidable. As Denis Sinor remarked, "what makes the task of the historian even more complicated is the necessity for him to penetrate into the mysteries of Chinese and Persian philology in order to solve his problems. . . . If he is not an expert in each of these fields (along with Islamic, Greek, Slavic and Slavonic)—and who can claim to be one?—he has to rely on second-hand information, which is, in most cases, utterly inadequate to provide him with the solid basis on which he can build. . . . As reliable translations are very rare, each little mosaic stone brought into the picture must be hammered into place with hard work" (*Orientalism and History*, 108). See also the remarks of Thomas T. Allsen, *Mongol Imperialism: The Policies of the Grand Qan Möngke in China, Russia, and the Islamic Lands, 1251–1259*, preface. Likewise Morgan, *The Mongols*, 5, relied on Mongolian, Chinese, Persian, Arabic, Turkish, Japanese, Russian, Armenian, Georgian, and Latin sources. Saunders in his *History of Mongol Conquests*, 1, observed, "in bulk, the original sources are not unmanageable, but they are extant in so many languages that only a linguistic prodigy could claim a mastery of them all." And Morgan, in "The Mongol Empire: A Review Article," commented, "Pelliot was such a prodigy, and there is said still to be one or two, though not, so far as I know, on this side of the Atlantic. Most of those who elect to study the Mongol Empire must choose their end of Asia, west or east, and learn the languages accordingly. . . . And as any orientalist will tell you, there is no short cut!" (125).

and the Western powers, but *edicts*[77] from the Mongols to the Westerners. Other documents were indeed letters, but they were from subordinate Mongol military commanders such as Baiju to the Western leaders. The collection as a whole, however, constituted a set of "legal instruments revealing essential features of Mongol public law and political ideas." More specifically:

> The so-called "Letters" are in part orders of submission issued by the Khans to the European powers, observing carefully what in Mongol opinion was due process of law, and in part formal instruments of information and commentary on fundamental rules of the constitutional law of the Empire, attached to the orders of submission in order that the addressees might not plead ignorance of Mongol law when they did not obey the orders received. The juridical structure of the instruments is surprisingly clear. The legal rules are organized and classified with a high degree of rationality into general substantive law, general rules concerning sanctions for the case of contravention, individual orders, legal instructions, and laws of procedure.[78]

Voegelin indicated that the formulas followed a typical pattern or structure: (1) reference to God; (2) a reference to the emperor; (3) the name of the writer; (4) the name of the addressee; (5) a formula of order or instruction; (6) a formula requiring compliance to (5) by the addressee. He then proceeded to discuss the sequence of legal rules and their formular expression. The general substantive law was expressed in the following formula: "God on high [is] over everything, the very immortal God, and over the earth, Chenggis Qan the only lord and master."[79] The intention of this "Order of God," as it has been designated, was twofold. First, the order revealed dogmatically the existence of a parallel between the monarchical regime of Heaven and the earthly monarchy of the Mongols. The second intentional element was pragmatic as well as dogmatic: insofar as the earthly part of the cosmos has not yet actually conformed to

77. This was Voegelin's translation of the Mongol legal concept *yarlik* or *yarlïgh*, to use more contemporary transliteration. For recent discussion, see John Andrew Boyle, "The Il-Khans of Persia and the Princes of Europe," 37–38; Mostaert and Cleaves, "Trois documents Mongols," 469–70; George Vernadsky, "The Scope and Contents of Chenggis Qan's *Yasa*."

78. Voegelin, "The Mongol Orders," 402–3. Voegelin was correct to have stressed the novelty of his approach to these documents. In 1934, Wladyslaw Kotwicz, "Formules initiales des documents mongols aux XIIIe et XIVe siècles," discussed many of the same formulas that Pelliot had first noticed but did not mention their legal significance. His 1934 paper was developed from a report delivered in 1923. See also Kotwicz, "Les Mongols, promoteurs de l'idée de paix universelle au début du XIIIe siècle."

79. Voegelin relied on the Latin translation, "The Mongol Orders," 403; the version given above is the Hanak translation.

the revealed Order of God, Chenggis Qan (or his successor in law)[80] has been charged with acting in such a way that the world of human beings, the political realm per se, might be brought into conformity with divine rule in Heaven. Considered pragmatically, the Order of God constitutes a claim by Chenggis Qan to rule the world—a claim that was resisted by the Latin Western (and Muslim) powers, who were of the view that they might just as well govern themselves, and that has been denounced by so many Western commentators as "arrogant." The Latin and Muslim perspective on Mongol religious devotions was highly unsympathetic. In order to understand why, in Mongol opinion, the desire of the Franks and Muslims to govern themselves was considered criminal, a brief consideration of Mongol theology is required.

It is customary to refer to Mongol religion as "shamanistic," which is adequate enough provided that one bears in mind a few ancillary doctrines.[81] The shaman was a mediator between the mundane world and its spirits and the higher, more divine order of the Eternal Heaven (*Möngke Tengri*), identified with the visible blue vault of the sky, and accessible by way of sacred high places such as mountaintops. Tengri was a single, universal, and, most important, a victory-granting sky-god. Tengri's last attribute in particular shaped Mongol political and legal procedures. Whatever the historical genesis of this Mongol belief,[82] the purpose of Mongol rule was understood to be the establishment of Tengri's order. Because Tengri was a universal cosmic God, so too must Tengri's earthly order be, if not universal, then ecumenic. In any particular case of an ambitious ruler who sought to conquer the world, legitimization would likely come first through the mediation of the shaman, though confirmation through military victory was the most visible demonstration of Tengri's favor. As Saunders said of Chenggis Qan, he "was something more than a brilliant soldier and outstanding chieftain to his people: he was the spokesman of Heaven, the executor of the Divine Will, perhaps even a mortal god, for his cult flourished in Mongolia down to our own day."[83] In any event, the conviction that

80. Mongol law was, in fact, quite specific regarding both patrilinial and lateral succession. See Fletcher, "The Mongols," 17–18, 23–28, and A. K. S. Lambton, "Concepts of Authority in Persia: Eleventh to Nineteenth Centuries, A.D.," 99–100.

81. For details, see J. A. Boyle, "Turkish and Mongol Shamanism in the Middle Ages" and "A Form of Horse-sacrifice amongst the 13th- and 14th-Century Mongols"; Morgan, *The Mongols*, 40–44.

82. Fletcher is of the opinion that it was ultimately derived from the early proto-historic Aryans. See "The Mongols," 30–32, esp. n. 13.

83. In Saunders, *Muslims and Mongols*, 44. See also Mori Masao, "The T'u-chüeh Concept of Sovereign"; Jean-Paul Roux, "Tängri: Essai sur le Ciel-Dieu des peuples

Tengri was fighting for the Mongols, who in turn were charged with the mission of unifying mankind and bringing peace to the world, provided them with a spiritual purpose that was also a legal instrument. Even after the Mamlüks defeated the Mongols at Ain Jalut in 1260 and they sought to forge another alliance with the Franks, it was clear that the Mongol request was in fact a command. "Behind the request for military help" apparently found in a letter from Hülagü to Louis IX, "one discerns the threat that if this help is not forthcoming, the French king will one day also experience the fate meted out to the disobedient."[84]

The contradiction or tension between the essential, substantive, and revealed Order of God and the actual state of affairs that in pragmatic fact consisted of an expanding Central Asian power organization entering into relations with remote foreign powers to the west was responsible for the need to issue the legal instruments, the "edicts," in the first place. To explain this dynamic, Voegelin introduced two novel technical terms: "When the power of the [Mongol] Empire spreads *de facto,* the *de jure* potential membership of foreign powers is transformed into *de jure* actual membership in the Empire."[85] All powers on earth are, by the Mongol law, de jure potential and subordinate members of the empire. When the actual power of the Mongol qan first comes into contact with the power of another ruler, there is neither peace nor war. Rather, the foreigner is given an opportunity to acknowledge his place as a de jure actual subordinate part of the empire. By doing so, the foreign power thereby also becomes a de facto member of the empire. By refusing, such a power becomes a de jure rebel; any subsequent conflict between the empire and the foreign power is less a war between sovereign states than a police action undertaken by the empire in order to enforce the Order of God.[86]

---

altaïques"; N. Pallisen, "Die alte Religion der Mongolen und der Kultus Tschingis-Chans"; Osman Turan, "The Ideal of World Dominion among the Medieval Turks"; Lambton, "Concepts of Authority in Persia," 99–100; Saunders, *History of the Mongol Conquests,* 95; Allsen, *Mongol Imperialism,* 42.

84. Paul Meyvaert, "An Unknown Letter of Hülagü, Il-Khan of Persia, to King Louis IX of France," 249. See also Saunders, *Muslims and Mongols,* chap. 3, and Lillian Herlands Hornstein, "The Historical Background of *The King of Tars.*"

85. Voegelin, "The Mongol Orders," 404.

86. It should be pointed out that the Mongols, as other politically organized peoples, did not always follow the law of their own constitution. Latin chronicles have emphasized instances of Mongol "treachery" often enough to make it a staple constituent of the European image of the "Tartars." At the same time, it is likely that many of these writers were imperfectly acquainted with the details of Mongol constitutionalism. For one account, see the summary by Gregory G. Guzman, "Simon of Saint-Quentin as Historian of the Mongols and Seljuk Turks."

The procedure for integrating de jure potential member powers into the empire was strictly governed by the same law to which the qan himself was subject. It was the duty of the qan, given to him by God, to institute a world empire. The edicts, thus, were legally regulated procedures by which the Mongols informed the rest of the world that the time had come for the foreigners to pass from potential to actual membership. The various options of obedience and disobedience were spelled out along with appropriate threats of sanction in the case of noncompliance. Since the order came from God, the entire process was sacred. The Order of God was announced to foreigners as the Word of God; the expansion of the Mongol military power was not therefore understood to be a secular political enterprise at all but might more accurately be called an armed missionary activity. "The Empire-in-the-Making thus is in all its phases a divine revelation, starting with the Order of God."[87] Chenggis Qan was the entitled Son of God, and his successors were understood to be executors of a divine mandate. Their edicts, accordingly, could be understood as having been issued equally from God as from the Mongol court. The peculiar status of the Mongol edicts as well as of the Order of God also helps explain the great brutality of the Mongol style of armed missionary activity. As Fletcher observed, a conquering warrior, guided by the Order of God, "would hold no bias against violence and slaughter, nor would it [the Order of God] insist upon any institutional limits to the absoluteness of his autocracy" for the simple reason that the apparent and unlimited autocracy of the qan was, in fact, an analog to the real, unlimited, and divine autocracy of Tengri.[88]

The first and most obvious conclusion Voegelin drew was that the Mongol documents were in no way "primitive" or even "arrogant." On the contrary. They were "well considered legal acts showing a remarkable juridical technique."[89] The legal notion of an *imperium mundi in statu nascendi,* he said, was strange and quite foreign to Western international relations, "but it is not obscure." Its contents were juridically rational; that is, they proceeded from a basic principle through a set of general rules, individual orders, and procedures for promulgation and enforcement. Moreover the logical structure was capable of explication "by such technical terms as potential and actual Empire and *de jure* potential and *de jure* actual membership of the Empire."[90]

87. Voegelin, "The Mongol Orders," 409.
88. Fletcher, "The Mongols," 31.
89. Voegelin, "The Mongol Orders," 411. As Denis Sinor observed, "the Mongols were playing a different game of which neither Islam nor Europe were capable of discovering the rules" ("Les relations entre les Mongols et l'Europe," 61).
90. Voegelin, "The Mongol Orders," 411–12.

His second conclusion drew upon the first. Analysis of the formular structure of the preambles to these documents enabled Voegelin to distinguish two kinds of correspondence, provisionally identified as "edicts" and "letters." The letters, more closely considered, turned out not to be "diplomatic notes," in the sense of Western international relations, nor were they private mail. Rather, in the context of the *imperium mundi in statu nascendi*, they were executive orders addressed to specific representative individuals (such as the pope or the king of the Franks) indicating the formally correct legal procedures to be followed in obedience to the Order of God. Voegelin ended by conjecturing that the Order of God and the formular instructions were probably sections of the *Yasa* of Chenggis Qan.[91]

Specialists in Mongol and Central Asian history have, generally speaking, acknowledged the pioneering work Voegelin undertook.[92] According to Jean Richard, for example, Voegelin's analysis of the correspondence was "a very precise study" designed to describe "the political doctrine of which they were the expression, that of an *imperium mundi in statu nascendi*." Likewise, Igor de Rachewiltz remarked that Voegelin's "perceptive analysis" was "a considerable advance over its predecessors." Specifically, Voegelin was the first to explain "why the Mongols until the time of Qubilai, i.e., two generations after Chingis Khan, could not conceive of international relations on the basis of parity with foreign countries and why the tone of their letters to foreign leaders was that of an arrogant feudal lord to an insubordinate vassal."[93] Considered simply as a contribution to a rather obscure area of political science, Voegelin's study was, therefore, well received. One may

91. This view was confirmed by several specialists. See Allsen, *Mongol Imperialism,* 114; Vernadsky, "The Scope and Contents of Chingis Khan's *Yasa*," 344–45, 359–60; Igor de Rachewiltz, "Some Remarks on the Ideological Foundation of Chingis Khan's Empire," 25; Saunders, *History of the Mongol Conquests,* 95.

92. Allsen, *Mongol Imperialism,* 42 n. 78; Morgan, *The Mongols,* 181 n. 16. Morgan's account is, in fact, less subtle than Voegelin's, notwithstanding his familiarity with Voegelin's work. For example, Morgan stated that, for the Mongols, "any ruler who had not submitted to them, whether or not he had ever heard of the Mongols, had the status of a rebel against the divinely ordained government of the world" (*The Mongols,* 181). According to Voegelin's analysis, ignorant peoples were only potential rebels inasmuch as, in their ignorance, they were merely potential de jure members of the empire. Once they had heard of the empire and had been instructed on the proper legal procedures to acknowledge their actual de jure membership, then and only then did the possibility of rebellion arise.

93. Richard, "Ultimatums Mongols et lettres apocrypes: L'Occident et les motifs de Guerre des Tartares," 214; de Rachewiltz, "Some Remarks on the Ideological Foundations of Chingis Khan's Empire," 24–25.

note, as well, that Voegelin's training as a lawyer provided him with a mode of analysis denied to most of the specialists in Mongolian studies.

The immediate pragmatic significance of the contacts between the Mongols and Western Christendom was to dispel somewhat their mutual ignorance. Old legends of Prester John and Alexander the Great and fantastic travelers' tales were discounted, if not wholly dissolved. "The image of the Tartars was increasingly clarified and, if fond hopes for a conversion fell victim to this process, the faithfulness of the information enabled the West for the first time in centuries to become aware of a culture and even of a scale of values fundamentally different than their own."[94] It is evident that the Mongols were a clear and present danger to the eastern marches of Europe. Whether they could project their horse-bound power into Western Europe is less clear, insofar as there undoubtedly existed a limit to the effectiveness of light nomad cavalry, even before the introduction of gunpowder, namely the ability of the land under occupation to supply sufficient forage to provision the very large remuda, with remounts and other stock, that such armies necessarily employed. Thus, as Denis Sinor proposed, "military victory could not resolve the conflict between the pastoral and the sedentary civilization. The nomads were able to invade but were unable to maintain their hold permanently over the conquered territories without relinquishing their trump card, their strong cavalry." And of course, the sedentary civilizations beyond the borders of inner Asia could not support large numbers of cavalry either.[95]

Fletcher supplemented Sinor's economic and logistical argument with additional considerations that, he argued, restored the "old wisdom, found, for example, in Grousset, [that] attributed the Mongols' halt to

94. Denis Sinor, "Le Mongol vu par l'Occident," in *1274: Année Charnière,* 66; see also Guzman, "Simon of Saint-Quentin and the Dominican Mission," 232.

95. Denis Sinor, "Introduction: The Concept of Inner Asia," in Sinor, ed., *The Cambridge History of Early Inner Asia,* 10. What may be called the Sinor thesis was sustained in the final battle fought (and lost) by the Mongols in the Middle East, against the Mamlūks at Ayn Jalut. As John Mason Smith Jr. observed, "had the Mongols possessed better horses, they would not have needed so many of them, and might have solved both their logistical and tactical problems. But they could not keep better horses without abandoning nomadism" ("Ayn Jalut: Mamlūk Success or Mongol Failure?" 345). See also David O. Morgan, "The Mongols in Syria, 1260–1300," in Peter W. Edbury, ed., *Crusade and Settlement: Papers Read at the First Conference of the Society for the Study of the Crusades and the Latin East and Presented to R. C. Smail,* 231–35; R. P. Linder, "Nomadism, Horses, and Huns"; Peter Jackson, "The Crisis in the Holy Land in 1260."

the politics of succession."[96] According to Fletcher, Sinor's argument was incomplete (however suggestive) because lack of fodder did not prevent the Mongols from undertaking cavalry campaigns in Vietnamese rice paddies or introducing new weapons, such as the elephant, in Burma. "The old wisdom," he said,

> is best. The Mongols stopped where they were in India and Europe in 1242 because of Ögödei's death at the end of 1241. They stopped where they were in the Middle East in 1260 because of Möngke's death in August of 1259. The decease of a steppe emperor, as all of the Mongols knew, was no small matter. The classic pattern of the steppe empire . . . was one so closely tied to the ruler's person that when he died, it stood in real danger of collapse. If it were to be preserved, the preservation would have to be based on political maneuvering, struggle, and probably civil war. All of these followed the deaths of Ögödei and Möngke. The Mongols had little choice but to break off their campaigns.[97]

Notwithstanding these factual military and economic considerations, the significance for Voegelin's political science of the thirteenth-century Mongol invasions as well as of the historically later episode with Temür lay elsewhere.[98] A first approximation may be found in the old opposition between the desert (and the steppe) and the sown. In the biblical book of Genesis, for instance, the story of Cain and Abel expressed, inter alia, the victory of an agricultural over a pastoral economy; but the story of the deception of Isaac by Jacob, and Esau's anger at having to live by the sword, suggests that sedentary success does not dispel anxiety. As Sinor observed,

> Need may then be felt for a barrier to be erected between the winner and the loser. They may be built of stone, as the Great Wall of China or Hadrian's Wall, but such constructions may crumble or may be taken by assault. It is better to build a dam in the hearts of men, which can resist the ravages of time and neutralize the assaults even of common sense. Prejudice is virtually impregnable.[99]

96. "The Mongols," 45. The reference is to Grousset's *Empire of the Steppes*, 267–68: "meanwhile in Mongolia, on December 11, 1241, the grand Khan Ogödäi had died. The question of the succession which then arose caused the Mongols to evacuate Hungary. . . . There is no doubt that this saved the west from the gravest danger it had faced since Attila."
97. "The Mongols," 47.
98. There were, of course, significant differences, both internal and external, between the Mongols and the Timurid empires. Chief among them, as Beatrice Forbes Manz has pointed out, is that Temür overran but did not attempt to rule the steppe (*Rise and Rule of Tamerlane*, 2). One reason, as was suggested earlier, may have been that Temür had "cohabited" with Islamic civilization.
99. Sinor, "Introduction," in Sinor, ed., *The Cambridge History of Early Inner Asia*, 17; see also Sinor, "The Greed of the Northern Barbarian."

The Mongols, in short, became for Western Christendom the incarnation of the barbarian. Again to quote Sinor:

> It could hardly be otherwise, since the Barbarian and the Civilized are opposed and complementary, neither can be defined without an understanding of the other and the gap between the two has proved unbridgeable: "What peace can there be between hyena and dog? And what peace between the rich and the poor?" Inner Asia is the antithesis to "our" civilized world. Its history is that of the Barbarian.[100]

There remains, however, a fundamental ambivalence about "the barbarian."[101]

Voegelin dealt with both elements of this ambivalence. The constitutional law of the Mongols, as "outsiders" to the familiar Western tradition, reappeared in *The New Science of Politics*[102] as an example of a political order that understood itself as the representative of a transcendent truth. As with the empire of the Ancient Near East as well as of China, the Mongols "understood themselves as representatives of a transcendent order, the order of the cosmos." In such imperial organizations, "one uniformly finds the order of the empire interpreted as a representative of cosmic order in the medium of human society." Inevitably, there will arise opposition to such enterprises. Accordingly, insofar as the existence of the empire is not automatic, it must be established, preserved, defended, and, in the Mongol case, expanded by human effort: "those who are on the side of order represent truth, while their enemies represent disorder and falsehood." The first instance introduced by Voegelin on this occasion was the Behistun inscription, which celebrated the victories of Truth through the agency of Darius I.[103] The representatives of the Lie, the pragmatic enemies of Darius and of the God he served, Ahuramazda, had nothing to say. Having been silenced by military defeat, they were in no position to erect their own monuments. The exchange with the Mongols, in this context, preserved both sides of a conversation where each party claimed to represent humanity, or at least a significant and representative part of it, and therewith the truth of human existence as well.

---

100. Sinor, "Introduction," in Sinor, ed., *The Cambridge History of Early Inner Asia,* 18. The quotation is from Ecclesiasticus 13, 18.

101. See the splendid essay by Walter J. Ong, "The Barbarian Within: Outsiders inside Society Today," in his *The Barbarian Within and Other Fugitive Essays and Studies,* esp. 264–85.

102. *NSP,* 52–59. Subsequent quotations are from these pages.

103. Quoted in *NSP,* 55–56. The text and translation is in L. W. King and R. C. Thompson, *The Sculptures and Inscriptions of Darius the Great on the Rock of Behistun in Persia.*

Voegelin introduced as evidence the edict of Güyük to Innocent IV.[104] Apparently the pope had requested that the qan receive baptism and cease his massacres of the Christians of Eastern Europe. The qan replied that these requests made no sense to him. He had followed the legal procedures of the Mongol constitution punctiliously; he had informed the Europeans of the Order of God, and they chose to disobey it.

> God, therefore, resolved on destroying them and on delivering them into our hands. For otherwise, because if God would not do [it], what could man do to man? But you men of the west believe yourselves alone to be Christians while you despise all other men. But in what manner can you know on whom will God deign confer his graces? We, however, worshipping God, laid waste by virtue of God's power, the entire earth from East to West. And if this were not by virtue of God's power, what could men do? If you, however, pursue peace and are willing to surrender onto us your forces, you, pope, with the Christian potentates, in no way delay coming to me for the sake of making peace; and at that time we shall know whether you want to be at peace with us. If in truth you will not believe God and our letter and will not listen to our counsel, and will not come to us, then we shall know for sure that you wish to be at war with us. What the future holds beyond that, we do not know, only God knows it. Chinggis Qan, first emperor. The second, Ögödei Qan. The third, Güyük Qan.

Voegelin commented: "this meeting of truth with truth has a familiar ring." In fact, he said, the Behistun Inscription and the Order of God "are not oddities of the remote past but instances of a structure in politics that may occur at any time, and especially in our own. The self-understanding of a society as the representative of cosmic order originates in the period of the cosmological empires in the technical sense, but it is not confined to this period." The symbolization of cosmic representation survived into the twentieth century, for example, in Manchu China. More important for an understanding of twentieth-century politics, and indeed what gives the Order of God its familiar ring, was the ideological representation of truth in, for example, the communist movement.[105] "Consciousness of this representation," Voegelin wrote:

> leads to the same political and legal constructions as in the other instances of imperial representation of truth. Its order is in harmony with the truth

104. A Latin translation was provided in Voegelin's "The Mongol Orders," 388; an English translation from the Latin is in the Dawson collection, *The Mongol Missions*, 85–86, and another English translation, direct from the Persian, is appended to Rachewiltz, *Papal Envoys*, 213–14. The version given is the Hanak translation, slightly modified.

105. G. L. Seidler, "The Political Doctrine of the Mongols," in his *The Emergence of the Eastern World*, 165–67, spoke in a similar context of "political messianism."

of history; its aim is the establishment of the realm of freedom and peace; the opponents run counter to the truth of history and will be defeated in the end; nobody can be at war with the Soviet Union legitimately but must be a representative of untruth in history, or, in contemporary language, an aggressor; and the victims are not conquered but liberated from their oppressors and therewith from the untruth of their existence.

Analysis of the Mongol documents and of their structural similarity to, in this instance, Marxist dialectics cleared up the matter of Mongol "arrogance" and military brutality, but by doing so it opened a new problem, namely whether the military conflict between the Mongols and their sedentary neighbors on the periphery of inner Asia was the sole test of truth. Simply by raising this question one indicated, at least provisionally, the answer. To use the terminology Voegelin later developed, the compact consciousness of reality characteristic of cosmological empires is differentiated, by raising the question, into a truth beyond the pragmatic configuration of power. That is, in order to question the validity of the claim of, for instance, the Mongols, the questioner must, at least implicitly, establish himself or herself "as the representative of the truth in whose name we are questioning." The source of that truth, on the basis of which the questioner questions, may be but dimly apprehended—but it must be there.[106]

The analysis of the Mongol documents was Voegelin's most extensive work on Oriental materials before the publication of the first volume of *Order and History*. Of course, the pragmatic interdependence of Asiatic and European events had been noticed before, at least by scholars. In a famous footnote, for example, Edward Gibbon commented on the report by Matthew Paris that fear of the Mongols prevented the Swedes and Dutch from sending their ships to England in pursuit of herring; the absence of an export market had predictable consequences. "It is whimsical enough," wrote Gibbon, "that the orders of a Mongol khan, who reigned on the borders of China, should have lowered the price of herrings in the English market."[107] Likewise, more recently, H. J. Mackinder speculated that the Angles and Saxons may have been pushed overseas to found England as the remote consequence of the migrations of remote nomadic peoples in inner Asia.[108] Near the beginning of his analysis of "medieval

106. *NSP*, 60. In *NSP*, 61 ff., Voegelin went on to discuss Plato's version of this insight or differentiation in the *Republic*, 368c–d, as the "anthropological principle."
107. Gibbon, *The Decline and Fall of the Roman Empire*, 6:286 n. 1. Gibbon's source was Matthew Paris's thirteenth-century *Historia*. See J. A. Giles's edition, *Matthew Paris's English History, from the Year 1235 to 1273*, 1:131–32.
108. Mackinder, "The Geographical Pivot of History."

political ideas" in his own *History of Political Ideas*, Voegelin discussed the importance of the Asiatic migrations for the more immediately important *Völkerwanderung* of the Germanic tribes. "The two migration processes, the Germanic and the Asiatic, and their interaction since the fourth century A.D. determined the general framework for the history of medieval institutions and ideas."[109] The commonsensical conclusion seems obvious enough: the pragmatic interdependence of European and Asiatic events was simply a fact. Moreover, the interdependence was more than that where ignorant armies clash by night. The study of the image of Temür indicated that the military events could be invested with mythic significance and then appropriated by Western political philosophers for what might be termed domestic consumption. Once part of the stock of Western political ideas or of the climate of opinion, the military and political events of remote peoples and places could be invested with their own symbolic significance.

But what did this pragmatic and symbolic interdependence mean for Voegelin's political science and philosophy of history? Was there, for instance, such a thing as "world history"? And if so, who or what was its subject? Or, if not, were there perhaps parallel Asiatic and European histories? But then how was any intelligible communication possible? Answers to these and other related questions have been indicated indirectly in the course of this and the preceding chapter. In this chapter we followed the sequence outlined in Voegelin's prefatory note to his article on the image of Temür. Historically, however, the sequence was reversed: the conquests of Chenggis Qan were, in some measure, a model for Temür; the link between Temür's conquests and Machiavelli's new prince was in part textual and in part interpretative. The case that Poggio's initiative with the *vita Tamerlani* became part of the stock of knowledge upon which Machiavelli (and Marlowe) drew seems clear enough. In addition, however, Temür behaved in many ways as a Machiavellian new prince. For example, Temür shifted the center of power over the tribes from the ruling families to men who owed their position to him.[110] By so doing, he separated tribal politics from the politics of the new confederation. He maintained elements of the traditional Mongol order by ensuring his sons and grandsons were appointed governors. Defeated enemies were conscripted into his own forces, and defeated rulers and

109. *HPI*, II:31. See also the remarks of L. Halphen in *The Cambridge Ancient History*, vol. XII, *The Imperial Crisis and Recovery*, A.D. 193–324 (Cambridge: Cambridge University Press, 1939), 108.

110. This insight was developed at length by Beatrice Forbes Manz, *Rise and Rule of Tamerlane*. See also her "The Ulus Chaghatay," esp. 94–100, for a brief analysis of Temür's exercise of Machiavellian *virtù* in his introduction of new modes and orders.

their companions accompanied him on his campaigns.[111] Temür also deliberately used ritual and ceremony "to make himself appear larger than life, cloaking an aura of power, a Machiavellian commonplace."[112] The integration of Asiatic political events into Voegelin's political science certainly provided evidence of his actual pursuit of "wider horizons." In addition, however, the range of evidence that Voegelin considered to be relevant to political science had implications for his developing philosophy of history.

One may see this in the following way: in Chapter 6, we began by considering the origin and development of secular history. The modern secular philosophers of history were sensitive to the necessity of wide comparative knowledge, and they insisted that profane history meant something other and more than awaiting divine intervention to bring about the end of the world. At the same time, they neglected significant areas of reality experienced and symbolized as world-transcendent. In the language used in Chapter 5, they had restricted horizons and defective philosophical anthropologies. The exception was Bodin. His philosophical anthropology was based on the mystical experience of divine transcendence, which he symbolized as "true religion." Bodin also argued that wide-ranging comparative information, the "writing of history," was required for a philosophical "reading of history." In this way the true religion could be apprehended by way of the several historical religions. Bodin's greatest significance for Voegelin's political science, however, was to indicate that, if reading of history was neglected, then true religion would be lost. In contemporary language, if philosophy of history was neglected then philosophical anthropology would be defective. Why? Because the evidence indicated as clearly as possible that human being is historical. Philosophical anthropology required philosophy of history in order to be adequate to the subject matter it considered.

In the following chapter we consider again the question of profane history, this time in the context of historical configurations and "cycles."

111. Fletcher argued ("The Mongols," 28–32) that this attribute of the imperial organizations created by steppe nomads was inherent in their predatory relationship to settled, agrarian societies. In addition, however, such activities would appear to Machiavelli to be the successful "acquiring" by a new prince.

112. Lentz and Lowry, *Timur and the Princely Vision*, 32.

8

Intelligible Units
of Analysis

I n December 1930, Voegelin delivered a four-lecture series in Geneva on the topic "National Types of Mind and the Limits to Interstate Relations."[1] This relatively early effort at formulating a coherent account of national differences is a useful starting point for discussion of the subject matter indicated by the title of this chapter, not least of all because Voegelin was constrained to express himself in relatively straightforward and commonsense English rather than in German, and so did not have immediately at hand the familiar expressions of a German scientific vocabulary. During the course of his lectures, Voegelin raised an important methodological question: what is the most appropriate way of gathering and dividing historical evidence in order for it to be as intelligible as possible? Such an enterprise entails reflection on such heretofore unproblematic topics as, for example, "the Mongols" or "the Franks" or "the Timurids." That is, raising the question of intelligible units of analysis entails a reconsideration of some of the topics first introduced in Chapter 6. At the same time, this chapter continues the discussion of the previous chapter, on the range of evidence germane to political science, by posing the obvious question: how does one make sense of comparative materials? *Comparative,* in this context, refers to evidence suitable to distinguish, say, France and Germany in 1935 but also the France of 1935 from the France of 1735. In addition, as will become clear toward the end of this chapter, the question of intelligible units includes the dimension of spirituality both in the sense of a "national

---

1. A typescript is available in HI 52/10, where it is identified by the opening words of the first lecture, "To discuss the problems of national types of mind. . . ." The title given here is taken from a list of publications Voegelin appended to his letter of June 19, 1931, to John V. Van Sickle in the Paris office of the Rockefeller Foundation. It is held in the Rockefeller Foundation Archives, RF/705/5/46. The language Voegelin employed on this occasion was similar to the language he used in his first book, *On the Form of the American Mind* (1928), *CW,* vol. 1.

spirit" and in the sense of a spiritual dimension of human existence that transcends not only the particular national community but also society as such.

Voegelin began his first lecture with the straightforward observation that "we recognize as self-evident the differences between a Frenchman and a German, a Frenchman and an Englishman, and even, in spite of the frequently asserted Anglo-Saxon racial unity, the difference between an Englishman and an American." In addition to these commonsense distinctions, there are distinctions that follow from a scientific treatment of the topic. In this case the science involved was initially identified as sociology. In turn, he said, sociology as a contemporary discipline with an independent subject matter is to be distinguished from the treatment of social questions within the context of a general philosophy.

For example, in the *Republic* Plato presented his well-known analysis of the parts of the soul and the hierarchic relationship of those parts. Of greater interest for Voegelin's current problem, however, was the "application of the analysis to the problem of national types." For Plato the spiritual dimension was central. He was "of the opinion that the peoples known to him could be classified according to the tripartite structure of the soul." Accordingly, the Phoenicians were said to be dominated by the acquisitive or appetitive part, the Scythians by the spirited or courageous part, and the Greeks by the noetic part (*Republic* 435e ff.). The methodological lesson Voegelin drew from the Platonic typology was fundamental: in order to have a variation in intensity of one or another part of the soul in each of the specific national characters, "the types have to be units of substantive similarity." In other words, for the several "mental types" to be interpreted in an intelligible way is possible "only when [the mental type] is substantially homogeneous with the interpreting mind." If the several existing "national minds," conceptualized as mental types, were entirely unrelated to the mental type of the interpreter, they would also be entirely unintelligible. As did Bodin, Plato considered his own national type of mind—in Plato's case, the Greek—to be superior to the others. Thus, as reason in a well-ordered individual soul governs the lower parts, namely spiritedness and appetite, so are Greeks to be distinguished from barbarians. This tendency to elevate one's own national type was not entirely accidental and, as we shall indicate shortly, presents recurring methodological problems for political science.

The contemporary inquiry into "cultural types" began with the expansion of the historical horizon, as was evident enough from the earlier discussion of the historical speculations of Bossuet and Voltaire.

By the nineteenth century, the amount of historical materials available compelled a reorganization of them. Comte, for example, chose as his principle of organization the growth of scientific reason and arranged the evidence under three types of mind and culture that together formed a chronological order. A closer examination of the succession of the religious, metaphysical, and positivistic ages, Voegelin said, indicated that the range of evidence was, in fact, meager: "his relatively clear horizon does not stretch farther than perhaps the Renaissance, and all previous history disappears in one undifferentiated mass of theology."

Hegel, in contrast, had a much larger horizon. Using the development of freedom as his principle to construct mental types, Hegel ordered his evidence from Oriental antiquity, where one was free, through Hellenic antiquity, where a few were free, to the modern European state, where all are free. With the introduction of ethnographic material, the horizon expanded once more to include primitive societies; with the amendments to Hegel's speculation offered by Marx and Engels, the third age of freedom for all was still to be achieved.

All these type studies, Voegelin said, considered simply as means of ordering evidence into an intelligible unit, "use the same fundamental scheme of construction: the single types are well characterized and held together by an evolutionary principle, which gives a chronological order to the types, and, at the same time, makes them intelligible by marking their place in the evolution." The difficulty with all such schemata is that they reduce the autonomy, independence, or self-sufficiency of the several types of mind to a place in the evolutionary series. The unit of intelligibility is not, in fact, the single type but the series.

There is, therefore, a conflict of principle with the Platonic postulate of intelligibility, namely "substantial homogeneity [of the types] with the interpreter's mind." In contrast, when historical evidence of types is conceived as the embodiment of a principle of evolution, the Platonic understanding of intelligible types and interpreters' minds becomes impossible. Moreover there can be no autonomous and contemporaneous units: either all the types have reached the same evolutionary point or existing differences must be recast as lags in evolution. Either way the significance of Voegelin's initial commonsense observation regarding the differences between the French and the English would be destroyed. The French must now be understood as being ahead of the English or behind them in a common evolutionary series.

Reflecting upon these kinds of evolutionary schemata, Voegelin observed: "These speculative philosophers certainly wanted to understand something, only the something was not the other one, but their own selves." In particular they sought to understand their own place in the evolutionary series they evoked.[2] The common modern procedure consisted in evoking a law of the mind that can explain history. Evidence was then selected in conformity to this law and introduced as proof that historical experience indeed shows the same mental development as the speculator's idea within its own mental realm.

Voegelin made, in effect, two comments at this point. The first was that the selection of historical evidence and its transformation into an entity, an "idea" or "stage" intelligible only within the mental realm of the speculator, inevitably has the consequence not of providing insight or intelligibility of understanding but of justifying actual historical action taken within the speculator's historical environment. Both Comte and Hegel, for instance, glorified both their own times as the positivist age and the age of the modern state, "with a little extra glorification of France and Prussia respectively on the side." This result was, in principle, equivalent to the Platonic discovery that the Greeks were rational above all others whereas the barbarians were characterized by predominance of other and lower aspects of the soul. Considered as a mode of political action, therefore, and not as a means of understanding historical evidence, the purpose of such speculations as those of Comte or Hegel is to justify the existence of the individual speculator, his age, and perhaps even his nation, not merely in terms of naked self-assertion in the world but rather in terms of the right of a real or virtual body politic to existence within the realm of the spirit, which is to say, within a context of meaning greater than that of the everyday and commonsense world. In terms of the everyday world, nevertheless, and distinct from the realm of the spirit, the act of asserting a right to exist will clearly have political implications. Voegelin considered this matter in his third lecture, on the limits to interstate relations.

A second comment followed from Voegelin's insight that the "something" that such speculative thinkers sought to understand was their own selves. "The grandeur of these conceptions," Voegelin said, "does not lie at all in the material interpreted, but exclusively in the law of the mind which is used as a means of interpretation. When it is not a law of the mind of a great philosopher, the whole interpretation business becomes a farce." He provided an interesting example of an interpretation of American history by way of illustration. This anonymous author told a story of pre-Revolutionary darkness followed by a period of greatness that was in turn followed by a period of corruption. Colorful examples were provided to illustrate the truth of the author's insight. "And,

---

2. Readers of *OH*, vol. 4, will recognize an early version of Voegelin's concept of "Historiogenesis."

indeed, you could not say that he was wrong in his interpretations—the only argument against it is its utter stupidity, when we take into consideration the materials he selected and particularly those he neglected." To use the language of Leo Strauss, Voegelin was quite clear that historicism, whether the product of a narrow and inflexible or of a capacious and elastic mind, was a dead end.

Inasmuch as the subject matter of Voegelin's lecture was international relations, it is not surprising that he went on to contrast the more or less peaceful relations characteristic of an ongoing state system constituted under the guidance of the intellectual imperialism of a Comte or a Hegel with the Marxian evocation that contemplates the abolition or dissolution of the entire state organization as such.

Voegelin concluded by observing that the dead end of historical speculations of the Hegelian or Comtian type has been proved by the simple accumulation of evidence. No matter how grand the mental apparatus of a philosopher, it is still historically (as well as biologically) finite. Additional evidence inevitably will accumulate after the death of the individual whose "law of the mind" ordered the historical material into a meaningful whole. Once again new techniques to organize the historical evidence would have to be found. In a rather awkward sentence, Voegelin observed: "we do not attempt anymore to organize the history of mankind as a whole in one unit of speculation, and apply the new technique to work out a multitude of coordinated structural units which are not concatenated by an evolutionary principle." Instead, a new science, which in Germany was named the sociology or morphology of culture, was developed.

Voegelin chose as the most obvious example Oswald Spengler. Spengler assumed the existence of a number of units of culture, identified them, and described their several styles.

> Spengler believed that cultures were strictly isolated; that every one developed her own unique style in a plant-like manner, with periods of youth, maturity, senescence and decay; out of the nothing a type of culture would spring up and into the nothing it would go. The single types were not related one to the other, there was no principle linking them perhaps into a chain, or evolving higher forms of humanity as they followed one or the other in course of time. Spengler went even so far in his tendency to work out the strict isolation as to say: a type of culture never could be understood by anybody not belonging to it.

The reason Spengler went "too far," of course, is that if it were true that cultural units were isolated, then they would be unintelligible even to Spengler the morphologist of culture. That is, Spengler did not pay sufficient attention to the Platonic insight regarding the substantive homogeneity of the subject matter under investigation with the mind of the investigator. Consequently, his fundamental dogma concerning the unintelligibility of another culture destroyed the basis of the science he wished to establish.

In contrast, Voegelin sought to combine the insights of a Spenglerian morphology, the results of which were by no means negligible, with the Platonic postulate of substantial homogeneity. "The science of types of mind," he said, "acknowledges the substantial homogeneity of all the cultural units to be investigated, as well as the fundamental differences between them according to the principle of mind that is embodied in every one, and gives them their morphé, their unique style from the innermost and essential phenomenon to the last and almost negligible detail." The close of his first lecture established what might be termed the epistemological profile of the science of types of mind. In his second lecture he summarized the procedure of describing the national types.

What is involved here is a genuine methodological issue, not one of providing a catalog of examples of how the French and Americans differ with respect to clothing, food, gardens, and the choice of paint for ferryboats. These everyday appearances are clearly manifestations of something; the question is: what? As in *On the Form of the American Mind,* Voegelin said that one must look to "the central sphere," the realm "where the mind expresses itself in speculations on the meaning of life, the place of man in society and the universe, etc." Here the discursive form is already congruent with the analytical discourse of science so that the distance between the subject matter and the subject doing the interpretation is minimal. Second, this sphere "contains the explicit self-expression of a nation's mind either in reflected or unreflected form," the understanding of which is, after all, the whole point of the inquiry.

More explicitly stated, the subject matter studied by a science of types of mind is "the nation's attitude towards the essential questions of life." These include such things as: what is considered of greatest value or importance? what is the proper attitude toward death? or God? or other persons? or other national units? Bearing in mind the two epistemological requirements—first that the substantial similarity of two minds, including that of the scientist, means that both have the same fundamental structure, and second, that this structure is formed in every part by a morphological principle that maintains the autonomy of each—it would seem that the science of types of mind must deal with a unique problem: "Mind as an object is not given objectively like a piece of external nature because there is no system of coordinates beyond it. . . . Mind is the only object which is not given as a datum to a knower of other substance than its own; it is identical in substance with the knowing subject." This is, in the end, the source of the methodological difficulties expressed earlier in Plato's dichotomy of Greek and barbarian or in the glorification of his own age and nation by Comte or Hegel.

The problem, therefore, is that the scientist "in spite of being rooted, educated, and with all his active powers inescapably caught in his own national mind" must aim "to transcend it intellectually in order to have to his own [national mind] the same distance as to the foreign ones." What Voegelin sought was not a supercelestial or pseudo-objective perspective on "all" national minds, since that had already been in principle excluded; rather the scientist "can only by mutual comparison make visible the differences as morphological differences of an identical structure." Voegelin indicated immediately that this was a long and complex task and the results to date were fragmentary. He illustrated the technical difficulties involved with reference to his own work on the American mind.

In his third lecture Voegelin used the term *political science,* in place of *sociology* or the awkward circumlocution *science of types of mind.* Political science does not, he said once again, examine its subject matter externally, as does physics. Rather, it is part of the thing it studies. He then offered a preliminary definition. "Political science," he said, "is, therefore, rational discourse directed objectively towards the phenomena of politics in an attempt to classify them, but always under the more or less conscious control of the national beliefs" of the political scientist. If this contextual and participatory perspective is not kept in mind, the inevitable result will be to introduce more problems than are already present. Specifically, once the participatory aspect of political science is forgotten or eclipsed, the discourse of the political scientist turns into no more than an expression of the interpreter's national mind and thereby a justification in the actual world of the right of the political scientist's nation to exist, to prosper, and perhaps to triumph over all others. We are back, once again, with the problem of the barbarians or of the glorification of his own age by a Comte or a Hegel.

The injunction to be aware of the limitations to one's own perspective, which followed from the necessity of having one, was more than a statement regarding intellectual honesty. The additional dimension can be indicated with reference to the appropriate units of analysis. Voegelin's contemporaries, as Voegelin himself, lived in a general political regime the chief elements of which were nation-states. The discourse conditioned by participation in such a regime also had its limitations, whatever the personal intellectual honesty of the political scientist employing it. The methodological issue was not, therefore, one of individual integrity regarding the pursuit of truth rather than the pursuit of individual or national greatness and power.

For instance, the modern nation-state, as a typical body politic, emerged from the medieval empire as the latter dissolved. Now, all empires constitute "a type of political existence with a type of theory of its own." Specifically, empires do not usually develop a theory of sovereignty: "the typical empire-theory is that of imperial peace." In contrast "the characteristic feature of our political existence is, or I should say almost always has been, the theory of sovereignty." One may connect the two sides of the problem, namely that of types of mind and that of forms of political existence, with the observation that "a political existence is conceived as a unit in terms of its type of mind as to be found in its belief." There are, of course, a variety of political existences: empires, poleis, tribes, nation-states, and so on; and these must be understood and studied on their own terms, in accord with the Platonic postulate.

The methodological problems Voegelin discussed in this lecture of 1930 preoccupied him in his later work as well. In the context of his philosophy of consciousness, for instance, one can see in this early formulation the concepts of compactness and differentiation that Voegelin developed twenty years later. In the course of considering the range of evidence needed to establish a theoretically adequate philosophy of history, the problem was encountered in another form. The subject at hand is concerned with what in political science is conventionally referred to as international relations or comparative politics. The methodological question of interest to Voegelin here is the following: granted that the study of national minds is appropriate in the context of a specific type of general regime such as the nation-state, how is this limited complex (of national mind and national state) related to broader questions explored by philosophy of history? The direction in which an answer would be sought was toward the aforementioned wider horizons—of consciousness and of historically relevant information. What Voegelin encountered, however, was several different forms of parochialism.

Voegelin clarified some of the issues involved in an expansion of a science of national types of mind to a philosophy of history in response to a letter from Karl Loewenstein. Loewenstein had asked Voegelin, among others, to take part in a roundtable panel at the 1942 meeting of the American Political Science Association, which would be devoted to the problem of comparative government. In late August, Voegelin replied.[3]

3. HI 23/23.

After offering his apologies for the lateness of his reply, Voegelin declared he was somewhat puzzled by Loewenstein's request. "The so-called Field of Comparative Government," he said, is not a science but a "college-institution." It is a category useful to impart information concerning foreign governments to students who otherwise would remain ignorant. Such texts as exist in the field are more or less useful, but they do not, properly speaking, do any comparing. In place of the traditional but spurious course on comparative government, Voegelin said he offered a two-term course, with the first term devoted to the "Crisis of Democracy" and the second to "Totalitarian Government."

If one nevertheless were to raise the question as to the substance of the field of comparative government, one would conclude that it "is not a science at all but a pragmatic unit of knowledge to which several sciences contribute," including population statistics, economics, law, political history, history of institutions and ideas, economic and social theory, psychology, theory of the political myth, the science of religions, theology, metaphysics, and so on.

A focus on political institutions is useful enough, he said, during periods of stability, as for instance between 1870 and 1914.

> Since the First World War and the Russian Revolution it becomes increasingly futile; now that the Revolution has extended to Italy and Japan, to Germany and France, has engulfed continental Europe, and is overdue in England and the Empire construction, the approach is meaningless. Not that we do not need the description of institutions, but it has to be incidental to the analysis of World-Revolution. Comparative Government should be today a critique of our civilization, centering around the political phenomena.

A genuine science of comparative government would, therefore, entail an initial mastery of the appropriate languages and subordinate or constitutive sciences.

> The problems of the Revolution have not arisen yesterday. We possess the great critiques of our civilization by Nietzsche and Max Weber, and for me at least they are the indispensable starting-point for every work in the field; the science of mass psychology, of political mythology, of political and economic history, of the several national laws, etc. are all well developed. Nobody who is not an exceptional personality can hope to master the fantastic complex empirically and theoretically in its entirety; but everybody can do his work on special phases in accordance with his interests and predilections. We do not have to search for problems with a lamp; from the point of view of the scholar the present ghastly crisis offers experience and problems as hardly another period in the whole history of mankind; wherever you look you will see problems of first-rate scientific importance—if you can see. The only limit for the scholar which I am able to see is physical exhaustion.

Voegelin's letter to Loewenstein is significant in several respects. In his 1930 lecture he mentioned the difficulty in simply acquiring mastery of the empirical materials so as to be able, for instance, to compare the American and French minds. In his own study of the American mind, he did, in fact, use evidence from many of the sciences he named in his letter. At the same time, it was clear that the categories *crisis of democracy* and *totalitarian government* were more faithful to the actual political conditions than a comparison of national minds, no matter how far-ranging.[4] The reason for the change of focus, he said, was the revolutionary changes in political affairs following World War I. By contemporary standards, discussing "national minds" in the context of comparative politics was as obsolete and parochial as focusing on political institutions.

There was plenty of evidence that parochialism and attachment to obsolete ways were not confined to American political science departments. A few years later Voegelin discussed this same problem area, though this time the focus was on the limited horizon imposed by the English mind with respect to existing political realities.[5] Early in 1950, T. M. Knox, the editor of the *Philosophical Quarterly*, wrote Voegelin asking him to review a number of books and articles by well-known Oxford or Oxford-connected philosophers.[6] Voegelin agreed, but said he would be unable to do so until he had finished two current projects, his *History of Political Ideas,* then projected to fill four volumes, and his Walgreen Lectures, which would be published as *The New Science of Politics.* In August 1952, the article was finally dispatched. Before considering in detail the books he was asked to review, Voegelin provided "a sketch of the task of political philosophy in our time, a task that is vigorously tackled elsewhere. By comparing the sketch with the performance of the Oxford Philosophers the reader can draw his own conclusions."[7]

4. Voegelin used the popular term *crisis of democracy* in his 1930 lectures as well and developed its theoretical meaning by way of a brief criticism of Harold Laski and Carl Schmitt.

5. Voegelin, "The Oxford Political Philosophers" (1953). Subsequent quotations, unless otherwise indicated, are from this review.

6. HI 29/3. The texts Knox had in mind were: R. G. Collingwood, *The New Leviathan* (1942); A. D. Lindsay, *The Modern Democratic State* (1943); E. F. Carritt, *Ethical Political Thinking* (1947); T. D. Weldon, *States and Morals* (1946); J. D. Mabbott, *The State and the Citizen;* G. R. G. Mure, "The Organic State," *Philosophy* 24 (1949); and the series of primary texts published as *Blackwell's Political Texts.* The published article also considered Lindsay's *The Essentials of Democracy* (1929) and Collingwood's *The Idea of History* (1946).

7. HI 29/3.

Voegelin began his article by referring to political events, not texts. The twentieth-century wars and revolutions were, he said, the culmination of a five-hundred-year process that has convulsed the whole of Western civilization. Such an upheaval has changed not only Western political institutions but also, as the contrast between Voltaire and Bossuet showed so graphically, the sentiments that justified them emotionally and the discourses that interpreted their meaning. Under contemporary conditions, when knowledge of the course of Western history had become clearer, political philosophy had the task of "sifting the debris," of "testing in light of contemporary experience the validity of problems and symbols still taken for granted a generation ago," and of "repairing the edifice of critical theory that has become badly dilapidated in the course of the so-called modern centuries."

The political institution that was formed during this time and that may be said to characterize the period was, of course, the national state. The conventional assumption regarding the nation-state is that all sovereign power units ought to be nations and that all nations ought to be organized for sovereign dominion over a specific territory and population, that is, as states. Furthermore, it has also conventionally been assumed that nation-states ought to be democratic. The use of the auxiliary verb *ought* in the foregoing formulations of the problem indicates that these conventional beliefs are also more or less unrealistic. In fact not all candidates for nationhood are capable of forming states and not all existing power units are nations. Nor, of course, are these power units, whether nation-states or not, necessarily democratic. Accordingly, "a philosophy of politics that insists on being a theory of the state is rapidly moving into the shadow of obsolescence, as the theory of the polis did when the age of empire had come." Second, since the insistence on democracy as the proper form of political organization is clearly inappropriate even for Western society, "a second problem of political philosophy [is] to separate the essential from the historically contingent and to break with the habit of treating the institutions of a particular national state as if they truly manifested the nature of man."

Furthermore, the genesis of the nation-state was accompanied, as was clearly evident in Voegelin's discussion of Bossuet and Voltaire, by a spiritual as well as a political-institutional change. The transformation of the medieval temporal power into the modern secular state set the spiritual life of Western humanity adrift on the open sea of unbounded potentiality. The resulting development of immanentist creed movements or "ideologies," ranging from the relatively benign forms of nationalism and liberalism to the more murderous forms of Bolshevism and National Socialism, has been part of the same historical process from its inception.

The third task of political philosophy, then, was to recognize the spiritual dimension to political life. This meant acknowledging, for example, that the provision of civil rights and democratic equality derives less from the institutions of the secular state than from Stoic cosmology and Christian faith. As a practical matter, therefore, the secular state "does not make sense to men who do not live in this cultural tradition." Theoretically, political philosophy is compelled by existing political phenomena to undertake a third task, "a critical examination of the compact symbolism that has grown in the period of the secular state," and then, to replace that symbolism "by a considerably more differentiated body of concepts." The "compact symbolism" Voegelin referred to here was conditioned by the restricted horizon of the national (or, indeed, historical) mind of those who employed it. In this instance the reference was to the English mind; more generally the comment applied equally to the conventional terminology of political science. Establishing and gaining acceptance for a "more differentiated body of concepts" was, of course, the great desideratum.

It may have been unavoidable that the limited self-understanding characteristic of the national and secular state has served as the linguistic basis for the concepts of political science. However, it is in the nature of all such self-understandings to be unaware of themselves as problematic, incomplete, or contingent formulations, so that when this characteristic was transmitted into the discourse of political science as well, the consequence was that political scientists spoke easily for example of church and state in Byzantium or even in Hellas. That is, the limitations of the self-understanding of the national and secular state were transferred to the putatively conceptual discourse of political science. Reproducing the limitations of social and political self-understanding within the medium of conceptually explicit political science was a recipe for error.

In order to indicate what a more adequate or "conceptually differentiated" political science might entail, Voegelin then described a twofold historical process as constituting the context within which the tasks of political science were to be undertaken. On the one hand there was the institutional growth of the national state; on the other, the spiritual growth of several immanentist creed movements. That both of these were widely accepted as given in the nature of things and not understood as contingent historical configurations was evidence of a third problem: "the destruction of classic and medieval philosophical culture; in particular philosophical anthropology was destroyed so thoroughly that we have not recovered from the blow to this day." The development of more adequate and "differentiated" theoretical concepts to replace the more compact or less differentiated symbolism characteristic of the era of the secular state depended, precisely, on a recovery of the principles of an adequate philosophical anthropology.

"Differentiation" of concepts, one may say, consists in the development of rationally connected language terms within the context of political science that is itself conditioned by the "wider horizons" toward which Voegelin indicated he was drawn. In the absence of comprehensive philosophical anthropology, a particular and contingent configuration of political institutions, such as the democratic and secular nation-state, could easily be mistaken for a "manifestation of the nature of man." Once one accepts such an uncritical opinion as true, there is very little reason to consider evidence beyond the horizon of the nation-state in question as being relevant to politics as an expression of human nature in any larger sense. Under these conditions, it is hard to imagine what that "larger sense" might be. In this way, parochialism regarding the range of evidence appropriate to political science reinforced neglect of philosophical anthropology. The same may be said, of course, with respect to neglected historical evidence, such as was discussed in the previous chapter regarding Temür or the Mongols.

Voegelin summarized his views on the current tasks of political science as being both negative and positive. The negative or critical task was to submit to analysis the compact symbols by means of which the thinkers of the national state period expressed their convictions about political order. The task of political science was positive insofar as criticism must receive its direction from the goal of developing an account of political reality that did not mistake itself for the justification of a particular configuration of institutions. As with his criticism of Comte and Hegel in his 1930 lecture, it was impermissible simply to use the language of political science or philosophy of history to glorify or justify the existence or expansion of one's own political regime, state, or empire. The double task of criticism and reorientation had, Voegelin said, assumed a variety of forms and been undertaken by individuals in a wide range of sciences and under quite distinct institutional conditions. The last factor is of particular significance for political science.

Where national political institutions have not been seen as authoritative and perhaps not even as legitimate, where class structures are either fluid or rigidly polarized rather than solid but flexible, where immanentist creed movements have corroded social order to the point where the movement rather than the nation has endowed political life with meaning and purpose, "there a science of principle will develop, and especially of philosophical anthropology, to the neglect of the analysis of institutions." Voegelin's example to illustrate this development was Germany. In contrast, British institutions embodied centuries of moderate and effective political experience; there class conflict had been prudently managed and immanentist creeds had not seriously corrupted the Western civilizational tradition. And there as well political principles and philosophical anthropology were scarcely distinguishable from the state of England or from the model of an English gentleman. Voegelin's observation may be generalized easily enough: where political practices are in great disarray, the question of principles soon becomes acute; where political institutions provide safety, simplicity, and familiar shelter from the vicissitudes of daily life and foreign dangers, they are easily enough understood as the incarnation of justice and right order.

Having established the context of analysis, Voegelin proceeded to examine the texts of the Oxford political philosophers. With the possible exception of G. R. C. Mure, all were "willing to accept the mystery of incarnation: that the principles of right political order have become historical flesh more perfectly in England than anywhere else at any time." This attitude, Voegelin said, had nothing to do either with complacency or with jingoism, though it did reflect the "Renaissance pathos of the national state," which considered that particular political form to be "the supreme organizational form of human societies after the breakdown of Church and Empire." Measured in that light, the Anglo-Saxon democracies did appear at the innermost circle of civilized humanity. What remained unexamined, but for Voegelin highly questionable, was the "idea of man" professed by the humanists during the Renaissance, which "idea" found expression in the national state.

Perhaps the humanist "idea of man" was superior to that of the classical political philosophers who developed their anthropology on the basis of the *bios theoretikos;* perhaps it was superior as well to the Christian conception of politics as being oriented in the direction of the sanctification of life. But in order to find out, a close examination of the argument in its favor is required. No such argument was explicitly provided in any of the texts under review. They did, however, make certain assumptions about human being and the manifestation of human nature in political institutions. To make these assumptions explicit and to subject them to analysis Voegelin focused on a central element in the humanist account of politics and of human being, namely the principle of liberty of conscience.

Voegelin criticized several authors for their use of vague and anachronistic terminology. A sharper analytic problem underlay those remarks, however. By freedom of conscience was meant the political right to act according to one's conscience and without governmental interference. Conscience itself was understood as the act of judgment regarding conduct taken in light of rational moral knowledge. Conscience was not, however, infallible; it might err for reasons ranging from stupidity and ignorance to thoughtless moral obtuseness and spiritual perversion. It was this last factor in particular, or rather the silence on the part of the Oxford political philosophers with respect to it, that attracted Voegelin's attention.

The issue may be sharpened by the following consideration: supposing one's conscience were badly in error, would it be morally right to follow it? The silence with respect to this problem was "remarkable," Voegelin said, especially as "it is one of the glories of English political philosophy to have faced the question of conscience and its suppression unflinchingly in the person of Hobbes." In his analysis of Puritanism, Hobbes showed that the good conscience of the Puritans was in fact a manifestation of the *libido dominandi* and not, as the Puritans claimed, of the *amor Dei*. "This diagnosis," Voegelin said, "tears the problem of moral conscience wide open; beyond conscience lies the spiritual personality of the man who has it." Hobbes's analysis of the problem was followed by his solution, namely the suppression of the destructive exuberance of the spiritually disoriented consciences of the Puritans by the rigid enforcement of a civil theology by Leviathan. In the intellectual, if not actual, success of Hobbes's solution lay an explanation of the silences and reticences of the Oxford political philosophers. By Voegelin's analysis, the distinguished Oxonians were expressions of, rather than reflections upon, the English mind. Indeed, they were, within their own horizons, considerably less astute than Hobbes, who in this respect may be considered to have defined the main elements of the English mind so far as politics is concerned. The Oxonians, that is, operated well within the horizon that Hobbes had created.

In consequence, the Oxford political philosophers, as had British statesmen and politicians, simply adopted Hobbes's civil theology as constituting in principle the appropriate language for political discussion per se. As a result, "contemporary political debate is only to a minor extent theoretical discussion, while to a larger extent it is a cautiously moving elaboration of civil theology and its adaptation, if possible, to the disquieting events of the age." When, regrettably, the events of the age did not conform to the civil theology of England, the result was felt in the systematically poor analyses by leading English civil theologians of genuine texts of political philosophy. In terms of the methodological issues raised in his 1930 lectures, Voegelin was not criticizing the Oxford political philosophers for operating within the context of the English mind, for such a perspective was unavoidable. Rather he was pointing out that they were unaware of the need to attempt to transcend it. To the extent that the authors of the great texts in political philosophy had aimed at transcending the parochialism of their own national mind (or of contingent historical circumstances), then analyses of their work that were oblivious of the authors' intentions were bound to be poor. In terms of the language used earlier, the application of relatively compact analytic and interpretative language to relatively differentiated texts was bound to produce inferior understanding and superficial interpretation. The most apparent explanation for such defects lay in the aforementioned ignorance of philosophical anthropology. This ignorance, in turn, was conditioned, not to say nourished, by the practical success and stability of British political institutions that, in turn, were celebrated by the Oxonians as *the* standard of political achievement, which was, of course, precisely the difficulty Voegelin found with Comte and Hegel.

Voegelin provided several examples of the problems that followed when a scholar, for one reason or another, deprived himself, or was deprived of, conceptually differentiated analytical instruments. Probably the most important and easily understood consequence is that such an individual, having forfeited the authority needed to oppose the surrounding civil theology, "cannot gain the necessary critical distance from his object and must surrender to the stream of history." For the political scientist concerned with the question of conscience, this act of self-deprivation poses a problem:

> Does ignorance cause us to hold certain beliefs with a good conscience, or does our will to hold certain beliefs cause us to remain ignorant with regard to disturbing facts? And if the latter should be the case, does the end of holding a certain belief justify the means of ignorance? Is there not a truth, higher than a civilizational creed, binding a philosopher's conscience? Is he really entitled to hold a belief concerning the meaning of history, though he perfectly well knows (or ought to know) that the meaning of history, its essence or eidos, is unknown because history extends into the future and hence is not a "thing" whose eidos can be known? And is, therefore, political Gnosis which confers on us knowledge of the unknowable a philosophical attitude at all? And if it is not, does not our indulgence in Gnostic speculation destroy the truth of philosophy? And if we are doing that, are we not actively engaged, with the best of consciences, in the destruction of the civilization that we praise, like any Communist or National Socialist?

No more than his criticism of Hannah Arendt did Voegelin's words carry the implication that the gentlemen at Oxford were in the same camp as the Nazis and Communists. On the contrary, their opposition to the more virulent and murderous acts of self-deprivation was, in fact, emphasized. The trauma of the World Wars, Voegelin said, was the real cause of the distressing state of political philosophy at Oxford. "The threat to national existence causes the withdrawal into the citadel of national political values, their defiant reassertion, and the condemnation of anything alien to them." As a theoretical position, however, the differentiation of England from the rest of humanity amounts to an "appalling impoverishment" of intellectual and spiritual resources.

The example of G. R. G. Mure provided a small ray of hope that all was not lost. "Here at last is a real philosopher, rushing to the defence when a particularly ignorant attack on classic philosophy arouses his wrath." Mure simply restated the principles underlying Aristotle's theory of the polis, having been provoked by Karl Popper's *The Open Society and Its Enemies*. What Voegelin found especially significant was "that a restatement of philosophical fundamentals in matters of politics comes as a surprise, almost a feat of heroism in a hostile environment."[8] Voegelin did not directly elaborate the theme of the relationship of philosophy or of political science to the specific conditions of the English mind. He concluded instead with a statement of principle regarding "the decisive issue in a philosophy of politics." Using Aristotle's language (as did Mure), Voegelin recalled that the polis was a human community providing "the opportunity for full actualization of human nature. The fully actualized man is the *spoudaios*, the mature man, who has developed his dianoetic excellences and whose life is oriented by his noetic self." No theory of conscience that ignored the fact that a conscience is only as good as the person whose conscience it is, or that was developed without a sustaining philosophical anthropology, could be anything but "a parlor game in which one can indulge as long as the surrounding society contains enough Christian substances to make at least the worst sort of good consciences socially ineffective." Even so, the parlor games played by the English mind only added to the confusions of the day. "This is no time," said Voegelin,

> to pat the viciously ignorant on the back for being "sincere," or abiding by their "conscience." This is a time for the philosopher to be aware of his authority, and to assert it, even if that brings him into conflict with an environment infested by dubious ideologies and political theologies—so that the word of Marcus Aurelius will apply to him: "The philosopher—the priest and servant of the gods."

In a letter to Elizabeth deWaal, a longtime friend, Voegelin explained the seeming harshness of his views of the Oxford gentlemen. DeWaal had earlier objected to Voegelin's tone in his discussion of the Homeric

---

8. Voegelin's opinion of Popper's work was not high. See, for example, his letter to Strauss of April 18, 1950, in *Faith and Political Philosophy*, 67–69, or the discussion below of his 1954 review of works by John Wild and R. B. Levinson.

heroes. Voegelin adduced some philological evidence to the effect that Homer distinguished between the nobility's social status and their moral stature. He also mentioned Plato in this connection, for whom "the great poetry of Homer throws the golden veil of his magnificent verse around persons and actions which are contemptible, and thereby may induce acceptance of the standards of morality of the persons thus glorified." His own attitude toward the Oxford political philosophers, he said, was akin to that of Plato toward the Homeric heroes.

> I enclose an article on the "Oxford Political Philosophers." You will per- haps find it also contemptuous in tone. But you will find in it also some explanations why sometimes a tone should be contemptuous, and not be genteel under pretext of innocuous "disagreement with other authors." I just recall a phrase from the author of the *Screwtape Letters:* It is advisable to keep an open mind with regard to technical inventions, kitchen-appliances, and the like; to keep an open mind with regard to the Ten Commandments is "moral imbecility." There seems to be point where unequivocal expression of contempt is in order; a point at which the pretext of amiable conversation about intellectual matters with "colleagues" would be collaboration in crime.[9]

Voegelin's "contemptuous" tone was, therefore, deliberately achieved in order to convey his judgment regarding the political consequences of the spiritual complacency and blankness of the Oxonians. They were concerned neither with a comprehensive range of phenomenal evidence nor with developing an intelligible and rationally defensible philosophi- cal anthropology. Parochialism and spiritual ignorance proved mutually sustaining.

In the following chapter we will consider more systematically Voe- gelin's account of the emergence of national communities as schismatic politico-religious bodies. The general direction is evident enough from Voegelin's argument in "The Oxford Political Philosophers." That is, parochial responses to particular national difficulties are misunderstood as general answers to universal problems. Likewise the ideas that are advanced are thought to be political theories of widespread validity. During the nineteenth century, the issue arose and was debated with unusual acumen and spiritedness in the dispute between Gladstone, on the one side, and Manning and Newman on the other.[10] The occasion was

9. HI 39/17.
10. Voegelin's account is in "The English Quest for the Concrete," in *HPI*, VI:161– 63. Subsequent quotations are from this source. See also V. Alan McClelland, "Glad- stone and Manning: A Question of Authority," in Peter J. Jagger, ed., *Gladstone, Politics, and Religion*, 148–70, or E. R. Norman, *Anti-Catholicism in Victorian England*, for more recent analyses of the problem.

the Papal Syllabus of 1864 and the Vatican Council of 1871. Gladstone criticized the Catholic leaders because they refused "contentedly and thankfully" to accept the benefits of civil order, including the supremacy of the state. On the contrary, Gladstone said, the Catholic hierarchy prides itself on refusing to submit to the civil order. For Voegelin, there was little more at issue than the heritage of the parochial state coming into conflict with "spiritual substance of universal validity and claim."[11]

Newman's answer, Voegelin said, was clear and to the point. Duty is not to be measured by utility, expedience, nor the convenience of the state, but conscience, where the latter is understood as the "voice of God. . . . Conscience is the aboriginal Vicar of Christ." For Gladstone and, indeed, for the Oxford political philosophers, the conflict was simply political: the churches had become irritants, as had any claim to universal spiritual significance.

The Oxford political philosophers were not alone in their parochialism. Over the next few years Voegelin reviewed several scholarly works that, in one way or another, expressed a common defect, a parochialism that construed the intelligible units of analysis too narrowly. John Bowles's *Western Political Thought* for example, did succeed in avoiding one of the perennial defects of texts on the "history of political thought" because "it takes the problem of continuity in history seriously" and begins not with the Greeks but with the neolithicum and moves on to the ancient Near Eastern civilizations before considering the Greeks.[12] However, like the Oxford political philosophers, "the author is severely handicapped by his almost chauvinistic Anglomania." The purpose of political philosophy, in consequence, was to enhance the reader's understanding of "the good life," which happily had been achieved in England. In Bowles's philosophy of history, Voegelin said, "the life of intellect and spirit has no autonomous value" and is to be avoided insofar as it diverts

11. Voegelin wondered whether Gladstone would be as complacent regarding the submissiveness of the churches when the state involved was not England but one under the hand of Nazis or Bolsheviks. He added a personal note, and relayed a conversation he had in 1934 with the master of an Oxford College, "one of the finest contemporary English minds. The conversation turned on National Socialism and the plight of the churches in Germany. My interlocutor took a detached view of the question and opined that the German churches were in a position similar to that of the English and would have to submit to the order of the state like the English. To the consideration that submission to the English civil order was perhaps less of a problem for a Christian church than submission to a National Socialist order, he seemed impermeable. For him, the problem of spiritual substance seemed completely superseded by the dogmatism of the English institutional arrangements."

12. Voegelin, "A Simplification of History," *Review of Politics* 9 (1949): 262–63.

one's attention from acquisition and toward "a transcendental destiny of the soul." Voegelin ended his appraisal with a splendid summary.

> The whole history of mankind has only two really important revolutions: the neolithic revolution that brought grain-crops and the domestication of animals, and the industrial revolution. The rise and fall of civilizations is an affair about which people of "good sense" do not bother; the pessimism with regard to the fate of our civilization is a Continental aberration which Englishmen should avoid. In fact, our civilization is as vital as we can desire it to be; we are rid of the religious obsession that plagued the Middle Ages and we have the advancement of science that gives us all the power that we want for increasing the good life. In a sense, we are back to the harmony with nature in which lived our primitive ancestors: when magic failed they turned to religion; now "the attempt to master nature begins again. . . . Science may be said in some sense to be magic that works." In conclusion, let us not overlook that Hellenic civilization most probably declined because "the actinic rays of the Levantine sun were in the long run harmful"; by contrast we may assume that good, old England has a better chance of survival, surrounded as she seems to be by a dense fog.

As with the anonymous example of American political history mentioned in his 1930 lecture, "the only argument against it is its utter stupidity."

Another example, certainly less stupid but still methodologically questionable, was Ewart Lewis's edition of a source book for medieval political ideas. It was, Voegelin said, in many respects an excellent compendium. However, with respect to its principles of selection, which were derived from the earlier multivolume collection of the Carlyles, certain unavoidable but familiar difficulties arose.[13] Like Lewis's predecessors and the Oxford political philosophers, politics was conceived in the light of English constitutionalism, "institutional devices, derivation of authority, and distribution of jurisdiction among organs of government." Unfortunately, not all political orders conformed to the English pattern, and in some respects that lack of conformity extended to medieval politics. For example, Voegelin wrote, Lewis's summary of Jordan of Osnabrück

> concludes with the sentence "For political theory in the more technical sense, the treatise has little significance, but it is a striking illustration of what was perhaps the most deeply-rooted and persistent of medieval ways of thinking about the empire." The observation is excellent—but it raises the issue whether the "technical sense" of political theory should not be revised in

13. Voegelin, "Medieval Political Sources" (1954). "The Carlyles" referred to R. W. and A. J. Carlyle, *A History of Medieval Political Theory in the West*.

such a manner that it will cover "the most deeply-rooted and persistent ways of thinking" about politics which characterize a period. If the author preferred the "more technical sense" as her historiographic principle nevertheless, some critical justification of the preference would have been indicated.

Lewis, however, provided no such justification. Voegelin then indicated that his own principle of selection of medieval texts would "treat medieval political culture in the light of principles that emerge from the sources themselves," so as to take into account the succession of orders, from the Clunaic through the Cistercian to the Mendicant, the growth of heretical sectarian movements, the "new philosophy of history of Joachim of Flora," Dante, and Scotus Erigena. Voegelin's judgment regarding Lewis's achievement was, therefore, suitably restrained: "The work can be accepted as excellent by those who want to measure the political thought of mankind by English constitutional techniques, and those who prefer critical standards of historiography will still find it useful as far as it goes." The conclusion to be drawn from these reflections of Voegelin on the work of other political philosophers or historians of political thought was that a combination of the "Renaissance pathos of the national state" and the "Renaissance idea of man" limited the perspective of the authors and thereby restricted the range of experiences deemed relevant to a comprehensive science of politics. The result was to generate an intellectual miasma that might surround not just those excellent admirers of British constitutionalism.

Corresponding in many instances to a commitment to the political myth of British constitutionalism was the personal aspect of the English mind, of which we earlier spoke, namely "gentlemanliness." Voegelin poked fun at Bowles for his embrace of good sense and his rejection of continental aberrations; his praise of Mure alone among the Oxford political philosophers was that he was a "real philosopher," as distinct from a gentleman philosopher, much as a real farmer is distinct from a gentleman farmer. The problem with gentlemen philosophers or gentlemen political scientists (if one may use such terminology) is that they presume that others are also gentlemen (or ladies).

In his review of Albert R. Chandler's *Rosenberg's Nazi Myth*, the peculiar limitations of philosophical gentility were clearly illustrated. Alfred Rosenberg's *Myth of the Twentieth Century* was, Voegelin said, the most important literary document of National Socialism, excepting only *Mein Kampf.* Taking the text as "a body of doctrine, fallacious in principles and inaccurate in detail," and subjecting it to logical analysis and exposition can result only "in informing the reader about the painfully obvious." The genuine problems raised by Rosenberg's *Myth*—"the rise of intra-mundane religiousness, of its causes, of its social appeal, of the apparent helplessness of the Christian churches in the face of this threat"—were all overlooked. "Does Chandler really believe," Voegelin asked, "that problems of this magnitude can be met by the well-bred question: 'After comparing Nazi "religion" and Christianity, who can doubt which degrades humanity and which exalts it?' "[14] There are questions that must be raised in the pursuit of understanding even if they would not be raised by well-bred but spiritually insensitive gentlemen.

Voegelin was not simply making a sociological point regarding the limited imaginative horizons of gentlemen, or of persons of good breeding. In his letter to deWaal, Voegelin spoke of *criminal collaboration* as the proper term to describe what others might call gentlemanly disagreement. The seriousness of the issues involved was brought out in Voegelin's review of John Wild and R. B. Levinson to which reference has already been made.[15] The context for understanding Platonic political science was clear: "The world wars in which we are engaged are wars of the spirit, as Nietzsche prophetically styled them. The warfare on the battlefield was preceded, and is accompanied, by the literary warfare of the ideologists against the classic and Christian substance of Western civilization." Several ideological interpretations of classical texts had appeared during the 1930s and 1940s and had been warmly received by "the so-called liberals." The scholars, on the other hand,

> expressed their anger with more or less politeness. As representative I quote a sentence from a lecture by Mure, before the Royal Institute of Philosophy, on occasion of Popper's treatise: "One would say, indeed, that he had flung scholarship to the winds in the pursuit of his thesis, could one be sure that he had had any to fling." My own attitude should be reported for what it is worth. I read Winspear's treatise at the time of its publication, because I considered it my duty to know what a Marxist ideologist would do to Plato; and I considered my duty done by reading that one sample. I have not seen Crossman's *Plato Today*, because I had read previously one of his other books. Chapman and Fite I have sampled but not read. My intention to follow the same course in the case of Popper was frustrated, because too many students wanted my more detailed criticism of the work.

Voegelin's point was that, under circumstances other than literary warfare against ideologists, a scholar would not be compelled to waste his or her time reading such documents.

When, therefore, Wild and Levinson felt they had to defend Plato and, as it were, the honor of philosophy against ideological abuse, their books

---

14. Voegelin, review in *American Journal of Sociology* (1946).
15. Voegelin, review of Wild, *Plato's Modern Enemies*, and Levinson, *In Defence of Plato* (1954).

appeared as symptoms of the corrosion of intellectual institutions. Wild and Levinson, he said, had done a public service. "We are in their debt for their performance of a tiresome but necessary task. And they have raised a warning signal for ideologists that the time when they could get away with everything is over." There is, however, an additional task to be undertaken:

> If, for instance, the charge that Plato is an enemy of the open society (in Popper's sense of the word) is examined and effectively refuted, as is done by both Wild and Levinson, and if nothing more is said about the matter, then the critic has made the fateful admission that the "open society" is an issue at all and that it would be a bad thing if Plato were found guilty of being its enemy. The detailed examination, therefore, should be followed (or preceded) by an explanation of why the question as such is nonsensical. Plato was not a democrat or a fascist, not a totalitarian or humanitarian, not a friend or an enemy of the open society, for the good reason that he was a philosopher and not a political ideologist.

In the case of Popper's "open society," for instance, there is more than a misuse or perversion of Bergson's symbol, though both Wild and Levinson overlooked Popper's misinterpretation. Indeed, Voegelin said, Bergson's "open society" "could have been put to good use in the detailed refutation of charges against Plato. And, more important, it would have shown, in a model case, the root of the evil, that is, the hatred of the ideologist for the authority of the spirit." One conclusion at least may be drawn with respect to Voegelin's understanding of the limitations of the gentleman philosopher: when he quoted Marcus Aurelius in the conclusion to his analysis of the Oxford political philosophers, that the philosopher was the priest and servant of the gods, he was offering a serious description.

In this section, we began by considering some of the methodological questions that Voegelin formulated on the occasion of his 1930 lecture on national types of mind. In answer to the question "how does one understand scientifically the politics of those separated from the analyst by time or culture or national mind?" Voegelin briefly developed his answer: a combination of sympathetic and participatory understanding and rational analysis of structures of meaning. This was hardly his last word on the topic. The examples that followed, from the APSA panel on comparative politics to the analysis of the Oxford political philosophers, Bowles, and Lewis, were negative instances of conventionally respectable but parochially limited approaches.

In his 1930 lecture Voegelin raised the Platonic question regarding the consubstantiality of interpreter and subject matter as well as the

Spenglerian one of morphology. The first question has been considered in this study in terms of the necessity of acknowledging and accounting for the spiritual element in the "idea of man" or philosophical anthropology embraced by the political scientist—or at least expressed by way of his or her work. In his early work Voegelin discussed this topic using the term *mind* rather than *spirit*, but in both usages he sought to indicate a dimension of meaning transcending the everyday.

In the previous chapter we saw that, whatever one makes of morphology, the evidence to be categorized by *morphe* must, in principle, be drawn from as wide a range of sources as possible. In summary, one must, therefore, be open to the full range of evidence, on the one hand, but also have a solid understanding of philosophical anthropology in order to avoid the twin dangers of capitulation in the face of events or retreat to the senior common room and the pseudo-safety of one's gentlemanly companions. In short, Voegelin was restating the necessity of a political scientist being a "reader of history" in Bodin's sense.

Arnold J. Toynbee was probably the most famous twentieth-century "reader of history."[16] Voegelin acquired the first three volumes of *A Study of History* in 1939 and volumes 4, 5, and 6 in 1943.[17] His first public remarks on Toynbee's work appeared as a paper on "cycle theory" presented to the Southern Political Science Association (SPSA) in 1946. Before considering Voegelin's analysis, let us first indicate the direction of Toynbee's argument.

Toynbee opened his *Study* with a reflection on the impact that industrial society has had upon the writing of history, and on the connection between industrial society and what Voegelin called national mind. Toynbee's equivalent terms were "the national standpoint" or the "Principle of Nationality." The appeal of the national standpoint is that it seems to provide an intelligible field about which a history could be written. In contrast, the writing of a universal history on the basis of

16. Toynbee's opus magnum, *A Study of History*, was published in five stages between 1934 and 1961. The first three volumes appeared in 1934; the next three in 1939. After the interruption caused by the war, volumes 7–10 were published in 1954. A historical atlas and gazetteer appeared as volume 11 in 1959, and Toynbee's *Reconsiderations* was published as volume 12 in 1961. The completed work ran to 7,170 pages. In 1980 a bibliography of and about Toynbee was published by Oxford University Press; it contained more than 3,000 entries and ran to more than 300 pages. S. Fiona Morton, *A Bibliography of Arnold J. Toynbee.*

17. Voegelin's personal copies contained the bills from Claitor's Book Store, Baton Rouge, for the 1939 reprint of the second edition of vols. 1–3 of 1935 and from G. E. Stechert and Co., New York, for vols. 4–6, for the 1940 reprint of the 1939 edition.

"industrial principles" appears to be impossible, not least of all because the professional division of labor among historians made renunciation of the required synoptic vision virtually a requirement if one were to be considered a professional historian in the first place. On the other hand, writing the history of a new national state created by the Treaty of Versailles brings into focus the absurdity of taking contingent political configurations such as Czechoslovakia or Yugoslavia as intelligible universes about which history could be written. The same observation could be made of the so-called great powers such as France or Britain, which in turn raises the question as to whether there exists "an intelligible field of historical study independent of the local and temporary standpoints and activities of historians."[18]

Taking the familiar example of Great Britain, Toynbee argued that it was an integral part of a larger entity. Such political communities as Britain or France "are simply articulations of the true social entities and are not independent entities in themselves."[19] These "true social entities" are greater than the political articulations of nation-states or city-states such as Athens, but less than "the whole of Mankind," and so are not properly speaking universal. Neither are they coextensive with the habitable and navigable surface of the earth and so cannot be called ecumenic either. Toynbee called these true social entities "civilizations" and drew the provisional conclusion that they constituted the intelligible field of historical study for which he was searching.

Toynbee's argument and approach to historical evidence were a distinct innovation in English historiography. Two studies by contemporary historians indicate the context of his departure from conventional scholarship quite clearly. In 1936 H. A. L. Fisher made the following observation in *A History of Europe:*

> During the hundred years of the Tatar peace (1269–1368) technicians and missionaries from the west were welcome in China. Then the veil suddenly fell. The Mongol power was broken, the missionary stations were obliterated, and with central Asia once more plunged in chaos, China retreated into impenetrable darkness and the sternest isolation.[20]

A year later C. W. Previté-Orton made a similar remark:

> Two contemporary circumstances, however, closed once more the routes of the Far East to Europeans for many generations. One was the overthrow of

18. *History,* 1:10, 16.
19. Ibid., 1:45.
20. H. A. L. Fisher, *A History of Europe,* 412; see also Toynbee, *History,* 12:199 and references.

the Mongol dynasty in China by the native, anti-Christian Ming dynasty in 1368; the other, in 1369, was the accession to power in Turkestan of the fervent Musulman and ferocious conqueror, Tamerlane. The Christian missions were practically destroyed, and amid wars and massacres Christian merchants could no longer venture beyond the Volga. The Far East retreated once more into legend.[21]

Leaving aside the fact that *Europe* was a term adopted by fifteenth-century geographers from the usage of ancient Hellas in order to make sense of discoveries brought to light by the new art of oceanic navigation, we have already seen in the previous chapter that neither Temür nor the new Mongol rulers of China understood their existence as either isolated or legendary. One is reminded of a real or apocryphal BBC weather forecast: fog in the Channel; the continent is cut off.

Early in life Toynbee wrote in a letter, "I am going to research and become a vast historical Gelehrte." His use of the German for *scholar* was apt, for one of his most significant models was Eduard Meyer. "Meyer," wrote Toynbee's biographer, "did for the ancients what Toynbee in-tended to do for both ancients and moderns; that is, he wove the whole together into a single tapestry, having first mastered more detail than any ordinary mind could cope with." According to Toynbee, Meyer taught him that Greece and Rome were "a whole that was complete in itself with its own Dark Age, Middle Age, and Modern Age. This unitary view of Greek and Roman history, which Eduard Meyer had given me, led me to look for a unitary name to describe the society whose history this was."[22] The unitary name he settled upon was "Hellenic Civilization." He subsequently identified twenty other societies of the same species, each of which was itself an intelligible unit of study.

"Civilizations," according to Toynbee in 1939, furnished the intel-ligible units of history. Moreover, it was his view that civilizations were not merely morphologically comparable but were "philosophically equivalent."[23] This meant that it was impossible to arrange civilizations on a scale so that some would be, in some general sense, higher than others; on the contrary, each could be measured only in terms of the degree to which it achieved its own particular goal. The internal growth

21. C. W. Previté-Orton, *A History of Europe from 1198 to 1378*, 185. Previté-Orton's study was one of an eight-volume series, by different authors, that was intended to be a standard history of Europe. In Toynbee's terminology, it was European history written according to "industrial principles," that is, on the basis of the division of labor.

22. William H. McNeill, *Arnold J. Toynbee: A Life*, 31 (the letter, quoted on the same page, was to R. S. Darbyshire, May 21, 1911); Toynbee, *History*, 10:233.

23. *History*, 1:175.

and decay of civilization provided the content to the subject matter of the historian's investigation. Toynbee identified "the particular beats of a general rhythmical pulsation which runs through the Universe" with the Chinese symbolism of yin and yang. More specifically, the "integration of custom" was identified with the static yin and the "differentiation of civilization" with the dynamic yang.[24] This symbolism was then expanded into Toynbee's well-known concepts of challenge and response, withdrawal and return, apparentation and affiliation, and so on. At the same time, the dead end of sheer repetition was avoided by the introduction of yet another image, that of the wheel and the chariot: the repetitive and circular motion of the wheel achieved the nonrepetitive and linear motion of the chariot.[25] In this respect, at least, Toynbee had provided a decisive improvement over Spengler.[26]

In commonsense language, which Toynbee also used in his interpretation of an enormous amount of historical evidence, the rhythm of growth and decay resulted from the fact that every civilization emerged from a successful response by a society to an external or environmental challenge. New challenges were bound to arise. They might be internal to the civilization or not, but so long as they were met by the action of what Toynbee called a "creative minority," the civilization would flourish. It would decline, however, when the challenges grew too great even for a creative minority to handle or when they were met not by a creative but by a dominant minority, a ruling group too strong to be replaced by an internal creative minority but too inflexible to deal with the new situation. The rhythm was continuous in the sense that even disintegration was not final. Rather it was itself a symptom of what Toynbee called the Palingensia, or rebirth, of communities (such as churches) that might become the "chrysalis" of a new civilization. This new civilization, moreover, exists on a higher spiritual level than its predecessor in the sense that it more adequately realizes and represents to itself the image of human being. In this respect as well Toynbee had

24. Ibid., 1:205, 244, 201 n. 4. In response, Fisher, whom we have cited as a typical and parochial British historian, considered Toynbee to have overgeneralized on the basis of inadequate evidence and particularly disliked his use of the yin-yang symbolism. See Fisher's review of vol. 1–3 in *Nineteenth Century and After* (December 1934): 671–72, and Toynbee, *History*, 12:199.

25. *History*, 4:34–36, 6:324–25. In Voegelin's personal copy of *History*, these passages were marked with paper slips and pencil lines alongside Toynbee's text.

26. See Friedrich Engel-Janosi, "Toynbee and the Tradition of Universal History," 67–68. In his personal copy of *History*, 4:12–13, Voegelin inserted a slip with the words "Spengler refuted." See also Toynbee, *Civilization on Trial*, 9–10.

improved upon Spengler—for whom, as we saw at the beginning of this chapter, civilizations were mutually exclusive monads.[27]

Notwithstanding their disagreements, Spengler and Toynbee, not unreasonably, have been linked together. In the aforementioned SPSA paper of 1946 on "cycle theory" Voegelin provided a useful account of the ties between them.[28] The term *cycle theory* itself refers to a topic for which Spengler's *Decline of the West* is broadly representative, namely a complex of opinions and sentiments concerning the growth, flowering, and decline of civilizations, or "cultures" as Spengler called them. The typical course is also a necessary one, and "Western civilization" was not exempt, notwithstanding the fact that persons such as Spengler have brought the inevitable course of things to public consciousness, for it turns out that it is late in the day and "Western civilization," according to him, happens to be in a period of cultural decline just prior to complete collapse.[29]

Not everyone found Spengler's message congenial even without submitting his arguments to analysis. As one might expect on doctrinal grounds alone, opposition arose based on the biblical religions and Islam but also from believers in the secular and progressive or "Enlightenment" doctrines of unilinear change in the direction of self-salvation through the application of "reason," as well as from adherents to the Marxist variation, redemption through revolution. "Cycle theory" in the broad sense of the term also encountered opposition from conventional specialist historians, as we have seen already in connection with Toynbee, and from positivists and utilitarians of various kinds. The context of reception to cycle theory has therefore been complex.

On closer examination, however, *cycle theory* turns out to be something of a misnomer. Not even Spengler's argument was really about a cycle. There was, for example, no repetition. On the contrary, Spengler's

27. One must note, however, that the acknowledgment of a spiritual hierarchy did not fit easily with Toynbee's earlier dictum that all civilizations were "philosophically equivalent." We will see how Toynbee dealt with this problem below, along with Voegelin's analysis of it.

28. HI 62/15.

29. The German title of Spengler's book indicates this melancholic mood clearly: *Der Untergang des Abendlandes* literally means "The Going-down of the Evening-lands." It may be appropriate to observe that many studies of economic "cycles" are also infused with anxiety and dread. See the recent example of James Dale Davidson and William Rees-Mogg, *The Great Reckoning: How to Protect Yourself in the Coming Depression,* 11. For a more general account see Arthur Herman, *The Idea of Decline in Western History.*

account in fact looks more like the opposite to a cycle. In his view, when a civilization has run its course, that's it. After an indefinite and monotonous "fellahim" period, the civilization disappears, overcome by external and catastrophic forces. As we have already seen, Toynbee's account is even less a "cycle theory."

Granted the term *cycle theory* is vague and imprecise, and so properly speaking is also not a theory, the term does nevertheless express a genuine configuration of sentiments, opinions, and ideas that are correctly associated with Spengler and Toynbee. The origins of the cycle symbolism, Voegelin said (following Toynbee), were to be found in Babylonian cosmological speculation.[30] It was introduced into Hellenic philosophy by Aristotle (*Problemata* 916a 18) in a way that strikes modern readers as a *jeu d'esprit* rather than as an expression of anxiety,[31] and reappeared in Europe with the recovery of Aristotle and the introduction of Islamic philosophy in the late thirteenth century. Thereafter "cycle" symbolism recurred, in Voegelin's words, "as symptoms of a weakening Christian civilization and as attempts to regain non-Christian sectors of human experience."[32] Considered as a symbolization, therefore, "cycle theory" is the symbolic expression of a reality experienced by those who employ it. Voegelin characterized that reality, on this occasion, as "non-Christian." He then indicated the contents of this non-Christian sector of experience more directly by drawing a comparison between the twentieth-century "cycle theorists" and an ancient predecessor.

Unlike Aristotle, who could calmly discuss whether "human life is a circle," Spengler and even Toynbee were anxious over the fate of "Western civilization." Toynbee himself indicated at least indirectly why he, as Spengler, might be anxious.[33] He raised the question as to whether

30. Noted by Voegelin in his copy of *History*, 4:36–37.

31. According to Voegelin, Aristotle's attitude was evidence that his speculation took place "on the level of the myth of nature, as the substance of which man and society are a part" (HI 62/15).

32. In the previous chapter we saw with LeRoy and Machiavelli the attempt to revive a "myth of nature" to account for the meaning of the rhythm of rise and fall. Toynbee's invocation of the yin/yang symbolism served the same purpose.

33. That Toynbee was anxious *en détail* as well as *en gros* is clear from his correspondence. In a list of "well known slogans" he wrote to Sir David Davies (September 21, 1961) Toynbee made the following aperçus: "We have no right to liquidate the human race because we ourselves choose to commit suicide over national interests or ideologies. If one prefers being dead to being red, one can put one's own head in a gas oven without having to commit genocide as well as suicide. If the human race allows itself to survive, it has 2000 million years ahead of it, and the longest totalitarian regime so far, the Christian one, only lasted 1300 years (ca 382–1682)" (Toynbee Papers, Bodleian Library, Oxford, Box 80).

the catastrophic experience takes place at the time of civilizational disintegration or at the beginning, when a civilizational response, yang, is needed to master a catastrophe that has disturbed the tranquil yin state. The question was suggested to Toynbee by a consideration of the *Statesman* (271e–272a), where Plato tells a myth about the divine helmsman who lets go of the rudder of the world so that it begins to rotate, as it were, backward. "The sinister change in human fortunes," said Toynbee, "was not the change from the growth of a civilization to its breakdown but was the antecedent transition to the genesis of a civilization from the static condition of a primitive society in its Yin-state."[34]

Voegelin accepted Toynbee's use of the Platonic myth and applied it as an interpretative model to the course of Western civilization. In Voegelin's view, Western civilization originated in a "terrific catastrophe," namely the Great Migration, the *Völkerwanderung* of the Germanic tribes, which eventually became the "creative minority" of Western civilization. Pushed west before the nomads of Inner Asia, the tribes were forced into contact with the Romans. So brutal was the encounter that many of them perished without a trace. The "anxiety of extinction" at the hands of the Asiatics was, Voegelin argued, the core experience that motivated the Western creative minority. The pragmatic danger lasted until the last of the Asiatic waves, the Magyars, was fought to a standstill in the tenth century at Lechfeld, though the symbolism persisted far beyond the occasion of its initial formation.

According to Voegelin, the document that gave expression to the historical experience of the *Völkerwanderung* was the *Nibelungenlied*, the first crystallization of a myth of Western defeat, because of fratricidal disunity, by the Asiatics.[35] It was not the experiences of the Germanic "creative minority" that centrally concerned Spengler and Toynbee, however. Rather, the fate of the yin-like Roman (or Greco-Roman) civilization was the chief source of clues for the construction of the course that all civilizations must undergo.

In Voegelin's view, the use of Rome as a model civilization continued the great debate on the decline and fall of the Roman empire that began in the eighteenth century and continued until the generation before Spengler and Toynbee in the work of Eduard Meyer and Michael Rostovtzeff. Unlike the Germanic tribes of the *Völkerwanderung*, the

---

34. *History,* 4:585.

35. The Mongol invasions, as we saw earlier, left no comparable epic, though the "Asiatic background" to Machiavelli's savior prince was an experiential commonplace among the humanists.

anxiety of extinction was focused not on physical annihilation so much as on moral or spiritual disintegration. As Leo Strauss remarked with respect to Spengler, "the crisis of the West consists in the West's having become uncertain of its purpose."[36]

Several strands of interpretation must be distinguished here. Most important is the fact that, in order for the discussion of the Roman decline to serve as a suitable means of analysis and criticism of the Western world, Western history had to be understood as autonomous from Roman history. This was possible only after the national states had become established in opposition to the "Roman" institutions of church and empire. The sentiments accompanying the break, by which term one indicates the convulsions of the wars of religion and the consolidation of the national states, were bound to be deeply ambivalent, for if Rome could decline and fall so could its successor, however it might be identified.

A second interpretative insight has already been discussed in connection with Voltaire's dispute with Bossuet. If Western history or the history of post-Roman civilization was autonomous, that understanding could not easily be reconciled with the Augustinian notion of profane history as a waiting for the Second Coming. As we have seen, the meaning of "profane" Western history was a matter of great concern to large numbers of human beings who were not about to be told, politely or rudely, that the meaning of their collective life was to sit tight and wait. They could very clearly see that something decisive was happening before their eyes. We will consider this question again in the following chapter. For the present, it is enough to emphasize that the interpretative discovery of autonomous and intelligible units of history, which following Toynbee we call civilizations, only brings other questions into focus.

When, for example, Eduard Meyer applied the modern terminology of antiquity, middle ages, renaissance, and enlightenment to the course of Hellenic history in the first edition of his *Geschichte des Altertums*, he applied categories developed from the interpretation of universal history to a particular civilization. Likewise, when he discovered the cycle of Babylonian history, which had been practically unknown until then, he raised a real and pressing problem: if Babylonian and Hellenic histories were, so to speak, closed cycles, what happens to universal history? If Babylonian and Hellenic histories are intelligible units, what are they intelligible units *of*? Critics may find Toynbee's answer, particularly in the first six volumes, unsatisfactory, but as Voegelin pointed out to one

36. Strauss, *The City and Man*, 3. M. Rostovtzeff made practically the same point in his *Social and Economic History of the Roman Empire*, 2d ed., 1:541.

of them, James K. Feibleman, "the inability of an author to give an acceptable theoretical form to his problem does not imply that he has not hit upon a real problem."[37] In his 1946 paper Voegelin concluded by referring to Vico's philosophy of myth and to Schelling's analysis of spiritual history. We will discuss Vico and Schelling as sources of Voegelin's political science in the following chapters. The balance of this chapter is devoted to Voegelin's analysis of Toynbee's discovery of the problem of intelligible units of history.

The first major reappearance of the problem occurred when Voegelin reworked the early chapters of his *History of Political Ideas* into the first volume of *Order and History*. Volume 1, *Israel and Revelation*, appeared in 1956 but was written prior to the publication of volumes 7–10 of Toynbee's *Study*.[38] Chapter 3, section 1, of *Israel and Revelation* is entitled "The Structure of Civilization Courses." There one may find Voegelin's first major attempt to provide "an acceptable theoretical form" to the real problem that Toynbee had raised.

Voegelin began by considering the criticism raised by the Egyptologist Henri Frankfort of Toynbee's account of Egyptian history, particularly of the significance Toynbee attributed to the First Intermediate Period (2200–2050 B.C.) as the "time of troubles" of the Egyptian civilization course. According to Frankfort, Toynbee's application of the pattern he found in the course of Greco-Roman history to the history of the Ancient Near East, was illegitimate, "a generalization from insufficient materials," in Voegelin's summary.[39] The problem specifically was that the Greco-Roman "time of troubles" saw the birth of what Toynbee termed an internal proletariat that, in turn, became originator and bearer of new religious movements, especially Christianity. If one applied this interpretation of Greco-Roman history to Egyptian history of the First Intermediate Period, one must look to the Egyptian lower classes to find an internal proletariat and to a new religion, which Toynbee identified as the "Osirian church."

In Frankfort's view, there never was an internal proletariat and the cult of Osiris was not a "church," in the sense of an organized body of believers. Moreover it originated in the upper classes of Egyptian society. Accordingly, Toynbee's interpretation of Egyptian history based on the surmise of what the "normal" course would have been like was purely hypothetical. The Greco-Roman pattern of growth, disintegration, and

37. HI 12/11; see also his comment to Gurian, HI 15/27.
38. See *OH*, 1:15.
39. *OH*, 1:53.

dissolution did not apply: in Egypt, according to Frankfort, an initial civilizational form once created remained intact, notwithstanding its internal variation, over two millennia.

Voegelin observed that both Frankfort and Toynbee could support their interpretations with "a respectable array of authorities" and a good deal of empirical evidence. Such disagreements, he said, could not be resolved simply on the basis of evidence because they were caused "by the use of insufficiently analyzed concepts." Accordingly, it was necessary to distinguish aspects of reality that Toynbee or Frankfort did not distinguish. In particular, the creation, consolidation, and destruction of political institutions is to be distinguished from the dominant experience and symbolization of spiritual order. The constituent elements, in turn, can combine to result in what Frankfort called the "style" or the "form" of a civilization. On the basis of these distinctions Voegelin indicated that Toynbee was correct to diagnose a "time of troubles" in the sense of a breakdown in political institutions, but there was no new spiritual experience as a result, and Frankfort was therefore correct to insist upon the fact. Yet Toynbee was not entirely wrong to sense "an experiential climate, pregnant with new religious possibilities."[40]

Voegelin provided an analysis of a famous contemporary text, "The Song of the Harper," to indicate how the political disorder of the First Intermediate Period also posed a challenge to the spiritual order of the Egyptian civilizational "form," namely the Pharonic foundation of Egyptian society. Politically, that foundation had been shaken by the events of the "time of troubles"; spiritually, "The Song of the Harper" indicated a skepticism with respect to the lastingness of the Pharonic order and the ritual integration of the society into the changes of the cosmos, but it did not indicate a radical break or a new spiritual insight that the source of cosmic order was itself transcendent to the cosmos and, accordingly, the human consciousness that was aware of this reality was necessarily directly in touch with this cosmic transcendent source of order. In *Order and History* Voegelin called this experience a "leap in being."[41]

We must leave consideration of the term *leap in being* to another occasion. Our present concern is the conclusion Voegelin drew from his analysis of the dispute between Toynbee and Frankfort with respect to civilizational courses. First, he pointed out that the debate over civilizational courses would remain inconclusive so long as it consisted only in the classification of phenomena. Second, therefore, was the observation that a combination of theoretical analysis of political institutions *and*

40. *OH,* 1:57.
41. *OH,* 1:10.

of experiences of spiritual order is necessary if one is to gain insight into the "constants of history."[42] Third, the procedure of creating "historical constants" simply on the basis of type concepts of phenomenal regularities is theoretically untenable because, as we have seen with respect to Spengler, "civilizations are not self-contained units repeating a pattern of growth and decline." Using Frankfort's term, a civilization is the "form" in which a society takes part in an ongoing spiritual reality. "A civilizational form," Voegelin said, "has historical singularity, never to be absorbed by phenomenal regularities, because the form is an act in the drama of mankind that unknowably is enacted into the future." Finally, Voegelin concluded, the importance of understanding spiritual order or the "dramatic" enactment of human existence should not be misunderstood as implying that the search for, and description of, the phenomenally typical in the course of civilizations is a waste of time. On the contrary: one must begin with what appears in order to understand the constants of history for which the phenomena are evidence.[43]

In "The Song of the Harper" Voegelin detected a spiritual climate with the potential of creating new religious possibilities. In the example of the Israelites there was actually born a new historical form. Voegelin referred to the process by which a new form was made articulate as the "differentiation" of experience. In contrast, as was noted earlier, Toynbee spoke of the "differentiation of civilization" from the "integration of custom" or the passage to yang from yin.[44] For Voegelin, in order to be "differentiated," human experience of reality must have been fully present from the beginning, but in a form that Voegelin referred to as compact, not "integrated." In order for the full range of reality to be experienced, whether in differentiated or compact form, human nature

42. *OH*, 1:63. Gurian criticized Toynbee on just these grounds in a review of vols. 1–6 of *A Study of History* in *Review of Politics* 4 (1942): 508–14. Voegelin wrote Gurian: "Your critique is amply justified; one could say even a few more pungent things about the empiricism of volume I, revelling in the time calculations of Sir James Jeans" (HI 15/27).

43. *OH*, 1:63. For Voegelin, this was the pith and substance of his own "empirical" method. Notwithstanding Toynbee's greatness as a historian, Voegelin wrote to Stephen McKnight, he still employed an a priori rather than an empirical method. Voegelin's empiricism, for example, led him to the discovery of the "ecumenic age" on the basis of textual sources and the self-understanding of the human beings who lived through such an age, and not on the basis of a "theory" (HI 25/2). In a similar vein, M. A. Fitzsimmonds observed that Toynbee's "learning . . . illustrates his theories" and his theories were grounded in a "vision of history" that Toynbee experienced in the 1920s (Fitzsimmonds's review of vols. 7–10 of *A Study of History*, in *Review of Politics* 19 [1957]: 544–53). Toynbee agreed with the date (*History*, 7:ix–x).

44. *History*, 1:244.

must be constant. In "The Song of the Harper," Voegelin argued, one finds a symptom of the search for spiritual order seeking to move beyond the traditional and compact cosmological form toward a more differentiated spiritual form where the searching consciousness would have been able to experience the source of spiritual order beyond the cosmos. In this particular instance the author of the text did not succeed in creating the symbols to express the insights of a "differentiated" consciousness. He was, however, able to express his doubts about the spiritual order of the cosmos because he could see clearly enough that it had broken down. Indeed, that is what "the Harper" was complaining about.

We will return to this question of differentiation after considering the analysis of Toynbee's account of the Israelites. To anticipate the direction of the argument, Voegelin's criticism of Toynbee's account anticipated Toynbee's own misgivings that eventually caused him to change direction with the publication of volume 7 of the *History*, which Voegelin considered "one of the most fascinating documents of the life of the spirit in our time."[45]

The first section of chapter 4 of *Israel and Revelation*, entitled "Israel and the Civilizational Courses," resumed the discussion of "The Structure of Civilizational Courses" of chapter 3. Here the major theoretical questions centered on "the status of Israel as a peculiar people." The "peculiarity" in question had the historical consequence of making "a break in the pattern of civilizational courses," so that Israel constituted a new kind of historical agent, neither a civilization nor a people within a civilization. "Hence," said Voegelin, "we can speak of an Egyptian or a Mesopotamian but not of an Israelite civilization."[46] Yet Toynbee did argue that a Syriac civilization was constituted from such peoples as the Israelites, Phoenicians, Philistines, and so on. Even so, the difficulties remain: first, only the Israelites produced the spiritual literature collected as the Jewish Bible or as the Old Testament of the Christian Bible; second, the course of Israelite history began before the Syriac civilization crystallized into existence and moved in a surprising direction through the prophets and Christianity when the Syriac civilizational area was conquered successively by the Assyrians, Babylonians, Persians, Macedonians, and Romans.

Voegelin illustrated the problem in detail by constructing three chronological tables. The first presented the Old Testament events from the age of the Patriarchs, through the exodus to the conquest of Canaan, the

45. HI 37/29. Voegelin wrote this remark in a letter to Toynbee.
46. *OH*, 1:116.

establishment and split of the Kingdom, the Babylonian exile, the return to Jerusalem and the building of the second temple, and the returns of the prophets Nehemiah and Ezra. A second table listed the waves of migration through the Syriac civilizational area, from the early Semites of the third millennium B.C. to the Romans. A third indicated the dates of the main phases of the course of the Syriac civilization according to Toynbee's analysis.

Some events, such as the conquest of Canaan, appeared in all three tables, though the meaning in each is different. According to the Bible the conquest was the fulfillment of a divine promise; according to the second table it was one of several ethnic migrations into the area; according to table three, it was an invasion that helped destroy Egyptian and Hittite rule in order for the Syriac civilization to grow. More important, however, some events that loom large in the biblical narrative do not appear in the other two chronological tables. In particular, Moses is missing both from the chronology of migrations and from Toynbee's account of the course of Syriac civilization.

It is not perhaps surprising that the escape of a group of indentured laborers through the marshes at the north end of the Red Sea did not count as a major migration, but the omission of Moses and the account of the events in Exodus from Toynbee's narrative was "rather a shock," Voegelin allowed, because, according to Toynbee, " 'religions' are the 'products' of disintegrating societies" and one would naturally have thought that Moses had some connection with religion. According to Toynbee, however, the only religious products of the Syriac civilizational decay were the prophets and Judaism, which were "produced" some three to seven hundred years after Moses.

The first thing to be done, therefore, was to understand why Toynbee distinguished Moses from the Syriac religious figures. He made the distinction by postulating an " 'ascending' process of spiritual enlightenment."[47] On this line he placed the Prophets (and "above" them, Jesus) and Moses; "below" Moses and Abraham, and, eventually, with the

---

47. Toynbee, *History*, 5:119 n. 4. The word *ascending* is put in quotation marks by Toynbee, presumably to indicate that no genuine ascent or spiritual hierarchy is intended. That is, the quotation marks constituted the tribute paid by Toynbee to his doctrine of "philosophical equivalence." But he paid such tribute only by choosing to use the word *ascent*, with its hierarchic implications, in the first place. In short, Toynbee wished to have it both ways, which is to say, he had not thought through the philosophical anthropology of the position he was developing. In contrast, for Voegelin, a genuine "ascent" was conceptualized in terms of the differentiation of consciousness.

"primitive religion of Israel," one discovers "the *jinn* inhabiting and animating a volcano in North-Western Arabia."[48] The traditional biblical figures were related, therefore, but only on the basis of this postulated line. They were emphatically not related to a single civilization nor to a legitimate or internal line of meaning such as is expressed in the biblical narratives. On the contrary, each was a product of antecedent and unconnected civilizational conditions, namely the time of troubles. Accordingly, Moses emerged from (or was produced by) the time of troubles associated with the decline of the Egyptian New Kingdom; Abraham, from the Babylonian disintegration after Hammurabi. For his part, Jesus was produced by the disintegrating Hellenic civilization, and the Yaweh-*jinn* was produced by nature itself, which is no doubt fitting for a worship so primitive.

If one followed Toynbee in this interpretation, Voegelin observed, one finds the beginning of the history of Israel with the conquest of Canaan, a line of enlightenment running from a *jinn* to Jesus. Abraham turns into a Babylonian and Moses becomes an Egyptian. Looking upon this "odd assortment," he said, one wonders "what has become of the Israel whose history is preserved in the Old Testament?"[49] Furthermore, since Toynbee's constructions "certainly make good sense in terms of a study of civilizations," we once again conclude that one cannot speak of Israelite civilization. But that merely sharpens the question: what does one make of the history of Israel that is preserved in the Bible? On the one hand, it seems to be true enough that, considered as pragmatic history, the observation made earlier by Voltaire was undoubtedly correct: Moses leading the Israelites out of Egypt was a trivial event. But on the other, Jews (and Christians and Muslims for that matter) have the habit of outlasting the rise and fall of the political units that loom so importantly over the landscape of pragmatic history. One must somehow accommodate the spiritual realities expressed in the biblical narrative, because eliminating them makes nonsense of history as such. The events symbolized in the Exodus or the Covenant do, after all, mean something: even the most spiritually insensitive pragmatic historian is compelled to acknowledge that the recollection of those events and their meaning turned the Israelites into a new type of political society. Human beings who understood their individual and collective existence in terms of the symbolism of the Covenant or of Sheol, the desert and the Promised Land, were transformed by the experience. To ignore that fact is to do bad history in any sense of the term.

48. *History,* 6:39.
49. *OH,* 1:120.

Voegelin, therefore, began "empirically," with the traditional biblical language expressing the Israelite self-understanding. The meaning of the events recounted from the beginning of Genesis to the end of the second book of Kings can properly be characterized as "an account of Israel's relation with God." Events are experienced not in terms of pragmatic political power but as acts of obedience or of disobedience to God's will. The narrative itself is, to use a later term, sacred history, and single events are paradigmatic illustrations of God's way with human beings. Accordingly, once a story has become part of the Israelite oral tradition it can be elaborated and reworked in order to bring out more truly its essential meaning. "A pragmatic historian, to be sure, would regret such transformations as a falsification of sources, but the writer of sacred history will understand them as an increase of truth." The conclusion, which we have already encountered during the course of this study of Voegelin's political science, is obvious enough: history in its most comprehensive sense "is a complicated fabric of which two strands become visible in the two chronologies."[50]

Voegelin's initial and anachronistic description of Israelite "sacred history" was more precisely described as a form of existence analogous to the cosmological form of the Egyptians. That is, where the Egyptians understood the meaning of their political order in terms of ritual integration with the rhythms of the cosmos, the Israelites understood theirs in terms of obedience to God. The discovery of God as the source of order beyond the order of the cosmic rhythms, the "leap in being," to use Voegelin's preferred term, resulted in the new type of political society. In turn, Israel became the carrier of a new experiential truth in history. In order for this new spiritual insight regarding the cosmic-transcendent source of order to be passed on to the next generation, it was necessary to create the appropriate symbolic record, to recount the discovery itself and the subsequent confirmations of it during the course of Israelite history. The Old Testament, therefore, is best understood by political science as the symbolic record that created and maintained the Israelites in pragmatic historical existence.

Recall now the arguments of Spengler and Toynbee. According to Spengler, civilizations flower but once in the historical landscape; according to Toynbee, each civilization has a history, but the history of such histories is not somehow a more meaningful history. On the contrary, the pragmatic narrative seems to be a meaningless sequence of power relations, a "slaughter-bench" as Hegel called it. According to Spengler, the end point is a kind of ahistorical, boring, and vegetative

50. *OH*, 1:122, 123.

existence; according to Toynbee it is no less boring, namely "1,743 million repetitions of the relations between our Western Society and the other societies that are alive today!"[51] In the face of such an imaginative dead end, Voegelin said, it would be useful to shut down the imagination and apply one's intellect to the problem. The defect of both Spengler's and Toynbee's accounts appears in light of the previous remarks on history as a symbolic or inner form of existence. Spengler and Toynbee have ignored this dimension of reality, and thereby ignored an important— perhaps *the* important—meaning of Israelite history.

Voegelin's analysis has cleared up this particular defect in the Spengler-Toynbee enterprise, at least in principle, but by so doing he has also provided the prelude to another question that was encountered implicitly in connection with Toynbee's postulated line of spiritual enlightenment. Why, in the face of the clear biblical symbolism regarding the Exodus, the Covenant, obedience to God's commandments, and so on, was it necessary to ignore the Bible and search for explanations elsewhere? According to Voegelin the reason for the defect in their accounts must be sought in the historical situation in which the theory was formed. Both Spengler and Toynbee are burdened with the remnants of certain humanistic traditions. In its late liberal-bourgeois form, this "tradition" postulated that civilizations were mystical entities that produced cultural phenomena such as myths and religions, arts and sciences. Neither of the two thinkers accepted the principle that experiences of spiritual order as well as their symbolic expressions are not products of a civilization but its constitutive forms. They still lived in an intellectual climate where "religious founders" kept busy founding "religions." In fact such persons were concerned with the ordering of human souls and, if successful, with founding communities of human beings who lived under the order discovered as true. If, however, the Israelite discovery of history as a form of existence was disregarded, then the form in which a society exists under God would also be rejected. "The conception of history as a sequence of civilizational cycles suffers from the Eclipse of God, as a Jewish thinker [Martin Buber] has recently called this spiritual defect. Spengler and Toynbee return, indeed, to the Sheol of civilizations, from which Moses had led his people into the freedom of history."[52] Simply on methodological grounds then, the Israelite understanding of history is more comprehensive than the civilizational "cycle theory" in either

51. *History*, 1:463. Boredom is a major theme for a latecomer to these exercises in imagination, Francis Fukuyama. One is reminded of the resignation expressed by the characters in Sartre's play *Huit Clos:* "eh bien! continuons."
52. *OH*, 1:125–26.

Spengler's or Toynbee's formulation. Accordingly, it is to be preferred, and the defective notion of civilizational changes "producing" religious enlighteners must be rejected.

However justified this methodological decision may be, it does not abolish all the problems connected to the Israelite conception, nor does it provide a solution to the question of intelligible units of analysis. The problem lies in the ambiguity of the term *history* in this new context provided by Israelite experience. On the one hand, without the sense of a society moving through time "on a meaningful course toward a divinely promised state of perfection," there would be no "historical" societies but only cosmological civilizations existing in time. But, on the other hand, restricting "history" to the Israelite form seems to lead to the conclusion that, for example, Egypt had no history.[53] Any solution must include the methodological insight regarding the inner spiritual form of societies. A society such as the Egyptian, which understands its own spiritual order as participation in the divine and visible order of the cosmos, does not exist in historical form. But if this is so, how can an Egyptian society have any history at all?

To answer this question one must have recourse to Voegelin's general interpretative principle introduced earlier, the matter of compactness and differentiation. In "The Song of the Harp Player," Voegelin, Toynbee, and Frankfort agree, one finds, to be sure, the symbolization of a search for spiritual order beyond the divine cosmos, but it was a search that was not successful. The author of the text decides, more or less, to internalize his skepticism with respect to the truth of Pharonic political order and eat, drink, and be merry. Unfortunately he is also aware that he cannot be merry, and his hedonism is joyless and boring because life is senseless. For this reason Voegelin characterized the state of his consciousness as "pregnant with new religious possibilities" but no more. With the Israelite experience of history as a form of spiritual order, namely the understanding of social existence in terms of obedience to God, the new religious possibility was "differentiated" out of the "compact" cosmological symbolism. The actual experience of differentiation was identified earlier with the term *leap in being.*

Egyptian history, following this principle of interpretation, is still history, even though it occurs in cosmological form: "The Song of the Harper" was a genuine search for spiritual order that, in the event, failed in its objective, which was, conceptually speaking, to achieve the

---

53. *OH*, 1:126–27. In *OH* 4:chap. 1, Voegelin revised this understanding of the ambiguity of the term *history* with the discovery of the concept of "historiogenesis." For a brief analysis see Barry Cooper, *The Political Theory of Eric Voegelin*, chap. 4.

differentiation of consciousness following from the "leap in being." More generally, therefore, the "history" of Egypt, understood as a search for spiritual order, cannot be known as history until there is a successful differentiation such as is found in the Israelite experience. Thus, in principle, the presence of history can be discovered in retrospect only from a position in which the historical form of existence has been distinguished or differentiated.

This hermeneutical principle can be amplified in a commonsense way: when the spiritual order of the soul and society is concerned with the will of God, then the actions of individuals and society are understood and experienced in terms of fulfilling the divine will or not. This action, experience, and understanding create what Voegelin called a "historical present." From the historical present, the past takes on a meaning it did not have at the time of its actual occurrence. Israelite life in Egypt prior to the exodus was, let us say, the workaday travail of indentured laborers on large-scale public works. The experience of the exodus transfigured Egypt into the Sheol, the house of bondage and spiritual death. The exodus, then, incorporated a stream of past events into a meaningful present. Moreover, in principle, one might expect the historical present to expand to include all humanity insofar as the historical form expressed the experience of fulfilling the will of God. As Voegelin observed, "history tends to become world-history, as it did on this first occasion in the Old Testament, with its magnificent sweep of the historical narrative from the creation of the world to the fall of Jerusalem."[54] This expansive tendency, in turn, brings its own problems, of which Voegelin mentioned three.

First, the inclusion of the past in the historical present through retrospective interpretation is not an arbitrary construction but a genuine discovery. In Egypt, for example, imperial expansion was accompanied by the knowledge that the conquered people were human beings created by the same god who created the Egyptians even before the foreigners came within the Egyptian empire. Conceptually, the Egyptian texts indicated that human society is greater than the nuclear society of the expanding cosmological empire.

A second complex of questions emerged from the multiplicity of historical presents of which the Israelite was the first but not the last. Each present has its own past; each is related to the others as part of that past (as for example the Christian with the Israelite or the Islamic with the Christian) or as an unrelated but parallel present (as for example Hellenic philosophy with both the Israelite and the Christian). Voegelin

54. *OH*, 1:128.

worked out the details of this set of problems in his later work, using the language of equivalence of experience and symbolization.[55] Here we need mention only that these several presents could be related to one another only because the literary sources involved—the Old Testament, Plato's *Republic*, the *Gospels*, Augustine's *City of God*, and so on—actually report real events that Voegelin summarized conceptually as the manifold of historical presents.

The third problem to emerge from Voegelin's analysis bears directly upon the Spengler-Toynbee "cycle theory." A society that exists in historical form, we said, understands the meaning of its actions in terms of obedience to God's will. Its history tells the story of how it came to this position and, as a story, is part of the symbolism by which a society in historical form constitutes itself. The Israelites, for example, continued in existence in part because they remembered the stories of the Bible. Considered as a symbol, however, any such story is exposed to the possibility of a loss of meaning or substance. As we have seen several times in the course of this study, the past of mankind may be related to a present formed by the experiences and opinions of progressivist intellectuals rather than the experience of trying to remain obedient to God, or to live a life of reason.

In this context the Spengler-Toynbee "cycle theory" is a clear expression of a historical form that has lost touch with the substantive historical meaning first expressed through the biblical text. Here one encounters again the experiential question: If there is no meaningful present to which the past of mankind can be related, why write history at all? If all one finds is the boredom of vegetative states or the typical and recurrent situations and responses, why bother to undertake such an enormous historiographic exercise as *A Study of History*? Voegelin's answer is that both Spengler and Toynbee were concerned not about a meaningful present and what that meaning might be but rather about a meaningless one. That is, the concern with civilizational decline or with witnessing a meaningful present swallowed by civilizational cycles reflects the anxiety of losing the historical form entirely. Their efforts showed that contact with the historical form was not entirely lost after all. The task remained, however, to relate the ever more comprehensive past of humanity to the meaningful present. Such remained the task of Voegelinian political science.

In the fall of 1955, after the publication of volumes 7–10 of Toynbee's *Study*, Voegelin took part in a symposium devoted to an examination of

55. See in particular *CW*, 12:chaps. 3, 5.

"the intent of Toynbee's *History.*"[56] Voegelin's contribution to the volume may be considered a postscript to the analysis presented in *Israel and Revelation.* In presenting this postscript, we begin as we did above, with Toynbee's own argument.

Starting with volume 7 and the third wave of publications, Toynbee modified his basic methodology. Looking back on the whole ten-volume work, he stated:

> Civilizations proved, so it seemed to me, to be intelligible units of study so long as I was studying their geneses, growths, and breakdowns; but when I came to study their disintegrations I found that, at this stage, their histories—like those of the national subdivisions of the modern Western World—were no longer intelligible in isolation. A disintegrating civilization was apt to enter into intimate relations with one or more other representatives of its species; and these encounters between civilizations gave birth to societies of another species: higher religions.[57]

In the first six volumes, Toynbee tried to explain the emergence of the higher religions in terms of civilizations; starting with volume 7, the implication of the higher religions as "chrysalises" by which disintegrating civilizations metamorphosized into new ones indicated several things. First, it meant that the "churches" that performed the function of "chrysalis," and so served as a bridge between generations of civilizations, constituted a higher species of society than the civilization whose disintegration they survived. In its survival, the church preserved

56. Voegelin's contribution, "Toynbee's *History* as a Search for Truth," was published as part of the proceedings, *The Intent of Toynbee's History,* ed. Edward J. Gargan. Subsequent references are to this text. It was Gargan's opinion that Toynbee was "almost the only one in the West, with two possible exceptions, prepared to appreciate [Voegelin's] accomplishment," and he hoped that Toynbee's *Reconsiderations* (vol. 12 of *History*), would "contain some reference to Voegelin's work." At the time, Toynbee had neither met Voegelin nor read his work. Gargan to Toynbee, November 15, 1957, Milo (Toynbee's secretary) to Gargan, November 21, 1957, Toynbee Papers, Bodleian Library, Oxford, Box 81.

57. *History,* 12:26. By "higher religions," Toynbee meant the following: "Higher religions are attempts to put individual human souls into direct communion with absolute spiritual Reality, without the mediation of either non-human nature or the human society—whichever it may be—in which the soul in search of God is a participant in consequence of man being a social creature. And, for this reason, the discoverers—or recipients—of a higher religion are moved to extricate it from a religious traditional social matrix and to embody it in new institutions . . . that will no longer be integral parts of the structure of some civilization but will be independent societies of a new kind" (12:218). In a letter to Voegelin, Toynbee indicated that he had a "feeling" as early as the writing of vol. 1 that he was being "drawn into a field which had been beyond my horizon when I was planning the book" (HI 37/29).

something of the civilization that had just disintegrated around it. But what? This was not clear. What was clear is that civilizations served the higher religions notwithstanding the fact that civilizations also served as intelligible units of study so far as their genesis, growth, and breakdown were concerned, though not, as Toynbee said, so far as the stage of disintegration was concerned.[58] Moreover, the dynamics of the genesis of a higher religion, namely the encounter of two or more civilizations, meant that the intelligible field of study for the higher religions must be larger than that of the civilizations. Concerning the several churches generated by the higher religions, they were, Toynbee said (following Saint Augustine), projections of the single *civitas Dei.* Accordingly, the species of society of which this single commonwealth was the sole representative is of a spiritually higher order than the species of society represented by civilization. One may say, therefore, that the birth of a civilization is invariably a catastrophe for a church whereas the breakdown of a civilization is merely the opportunity for the birth of a church.[59]

Voegelin summarized Toynbee's observations:

> The work that has begun with the definition of civilizational societies as "the intelligible fields of historical study" ends with the declaration that they are unintelligible. The definition thus is as invalidated as a definition can be. Nevertheless, the execution of the program contained in the definition preserves its validity intact on its own level of operations. I need not elaborate to make it clear that, whatever the substantive merits of the new position may be, the conceptual work leaves much to be desired.[60]

The "substantive merits" of the new position consisted in the recognition by Toynbee that his initial definition of the intelligible units of history was wrong. In this respect the reformulations of volume 7 are a decisive improvement. Yet the shoddy "conceptual work" remained. In his 1947 letter to Feibleman, quoted above, Voegelin seemed to excuse Toynbee for his poor theoretical craftsmanship. In the 1955 essay, Voegelin's analysis exposed the source of Toynbee's inability to give a proper theoretical formulation to his problem. It lay not in his technical deficiencies as a philosopher so much as in "a further difficulty of a personal nature."[61]

Toynbee's *Study,* Voegelin said, was "an inquiry in the classical sense of a *zetema,* a search for truth both cognitive and existential."[62] The two

58. *History,* 8:88.
59. Ibid., 7:526.
60. "Toynbee's *History,*" 192.
61. Ibid., 184.
62. Ibid., 183.

aspects of the search were related insofar as the validity of cognitive definitions would depend upon the degree of existential insight the author had achieved. Accordingly, definitions developed at the outset may prove defective and undergo qualification and modification as the inquiry unfolds in accord with the logic of existential insight. This may be "inconvenient" for "a reader who identifies truth with information," but the inconvenience is inevitable. The problem, therefore, is not the aforementioned conceptual deficiencies.

The problem rather lies in the incompleteness of Toynbee's existential search. The existential logic ensures that the *zetema* reaches its goal in a view of reality, even if the cognitive apparatus may prove to be defective in one way or another. In contrast to the Platonic *zetema*,[63] Toynbee's search did not reach its goal, which is to say Toynbee stopped en route. Instead of attaining a vision of reality similar or equivalent to the Platonic *philia* of the *sophon* or the Augustianian *intentio animi* toward God, Toynbee engaged in a peculiar dialogue with Martin Wight. What is peculiar about this dialogue is that Wight spoke from a spiritually and intellectually superior position, and Toynbee knew it, at least to the extent that by reproducing Wight's argument he "reveals as penultimate the position which Toynbee chooses to make his last one."[64] By engaging

---

63. *OH*, 3:82–88.

64. Voegelin, "Toynbee's *History*," 185. Voegelin was intrigued by Martin Wight and in 1956 asked Peter Fleiss, who had met him, to provide him with information (HI 12/25). A few weeks later, in response to a request from Richard C. Cornuelle of the William Volker Fund for names of European scholars who might be invited to a summer conference supported by the fund, Voegelin strongly recommended Wight, even though he did not know him personally. "Toynbee let him read the section on the Universal Churches in his Vol. VII of the *Study of History*, and then incorporated, much to his credit, Wight's comments. Much to Toynbee's credit I say, because Wight in his little finger knows more about these things than the whole Toynbee. The result is somewhat ludicrous, insofar as the text brings the dilettantistic ruminations of Toynbee on the subject, while the notes and appendices bring the competent comments of Wight. That man really knows something about philosophy of history and politics, and seems to have a very good knowledge of contemporary literature" (HI 42/1). In "Toynbee's *History*," Voegelin said one might be "tempted" by the notion that Toynbee had invented Wight as "a figure designed to cast light a few steps ahead on the path, the *epanodos* [cf. Plato, *Rep.* 532b], which the author did not choose to ascend further" (185). In fact, Wight was one of Toynbee's collaborators at Chatham House (1936–1938 and 1946–1949), a longtime friend, his literary executor, and a Roman Catholic. See Christian B. Peper, ed., *An Historian's Conscience: The Correspondence of Arnold J. Toynbee and Columba Cary-Elwes, Monk of Ampleforth*, 247 n. 3, 342 n. 2; Toynbee, *History*, 7:737–48; Martin Wight, "Arnold Toynbee: An Appreciation"; Hedley Bull, "Martin Wight and the Study of International Relations," in Wight, *Systems of States*, ed. Hedley Bull, 1–20.

in a dialogue with Wight, Toynbee had undertaken "something like an act of atonement" for his own *mauvaise foi* because, said Voegelin, "we cannot, when engaged in a search for truth, stop where the view is pleasant and declare a way-station to be the summit without betraying the Guide who has brought us thus far." Specifically, Toynbee's pleasant stopping place was one where he might survey the "four universal living religions" and offer them some unsolicited advice on how they might constitute a "symphony" of Higher Religions and bring peace on earth. Wight quite properly characterized it as a kind of syncretism that looked like a capitulation "to a Hindu mode of thought."[65]

The cognitive value of civilizations as the intelligible units of analysis, as we saw, rested on the solid evidence furnished by scholars such as Eduard Meyer. Notwithstanding the limitations of the Greco-Roman model, the insights it furnished for other civilizations "have been surprisingly successful."[66] The limit to the cognitive validity of Toynbee's argument came, as he indicated indirectly, with the discovery of another intelligible unit of study, "independent entities with a claim to be studied on their own merits" that transcend the society from which these "entities" have emerged, namely the universal churches that appear during the process of civilizational disintegration. Toynbee considered the possibility that the churches were simply by-products of civilizational disintegration, but, unlike Spengler, he rejected the possibility of a spiritually meaningless organic rhythm of growth and decay. He did not, however, create the cognitive instruments to describe the spiritual insights advanced by the universal churches. Indeed, Toynbee was convinced that the symbolization of spiritual truth was simply impossible. As he said in a letter to Hedley Bull, "I remain the agnostic that I became when I was an undergraduate, yet, though, as you note, I do not share Martin [Wight]'s Christian religious faith, I do share his conviction that religion is the most important thing in human life, and consequently I am his fellow-heretic from the standpoint that is now prevalent in the non-Communist as well as in the Communist world."[67]

This position was, to say the least, unsatisfactory. On the one hand, Toynbee had come to a position where, following Augustine, the several universal churches were representative of the one *civitas Dei*, but on the

65. Voegelin, "Toynbee's *History*," 185; Toynbee, *History*, 7:428, 745. For his part, Toynbee considered Wight to be a "perfectionist" who gave him "the impression that he was nearer to orthodox Christianity (belief in the creeds) than I was. But he never gave me any positive information about his own religious beliefs" (Toynbee to Hedley Bull, February 7, 1974, Toynbee Papers, Box 86).

66. Voegelin, "Toynbee's *History*," 188.

67. *History*, 6:325; Toynbee to Bull, April 18, 1974, Toynbee Papers, Box 86.

other he had apparently no way of knowing what the spiritual truth so symbolized might be. The final objective, he said, "would be to attain to a fuller vision of God the Dweller in the Innermost. In the present *Study* we cannot aspire to do more than follow our pair of explorers—if Science and Religion can be imagined as setting out hand-in-hand—on the first stages of this new quest for the *Visio Beatifica*." By "science" Toynbee meant, more or less, reason and philosophy; by "religion" he meant something like spiritual intuition. In any event, Martin Wight challenged Toynbee's imprecise formulation on its own terms with the observation that, if he was to be concerned at all with spiritual truths, that is, with a "fuller vision of God the Dweller in the Innermost," then it would be necessary to achieve the proper "formulation," and "such a formulation is the proper work of Reason."[68] Toynbee replied that he could escape the implications of Wight's criticism by following the example of Plato!

Toynbee justified, at least in his own eyes, the choice of so inapt an example as Plato by the following remarks:

> I have set my face against the precipitation of a new theology through a fresh attempt to formulate in the language of Reason the truths of Poetry and Prophecy. I do not accept your postulate that a reconciliation between Reason and the Subconscious must be communicated by the Reason in some systematized formulation. Plato, for example, scrupulously refrained from attempting this. He yokes Reason and Intuition to his winged chariot side by side, without ever trying to disguise either one of them in any trappings that belong to the other. In my belief it is because he drives this pair of horses in double harness that he succeeds in flying so high. I appeal to Plato's example.[69]

Toynbee has "set his face" against theology; he does not "accept" Wight's "postulate," and he states his own "belief" regarding Plato's imagery. And that, so far as he is concerned, is that. Accordingly, "debate must cease," even though a few words remain to be said by way of characterizing Toynbee's attitude after Wight subjected his "position" to analysis. In Voegelin's words we are facing "a dilettantism with regard to questions of reason and revelation, philosophy and religion, metaphysics and theology, intuition and science, as well as communication, that could easily be overcome by anybody who wanted to overcome it."[70] For one reason or another Toynbee did not wish to deal with the problem.

Voegelin was making not a psychological point but a methodological one. Toynbee was spiritually sensitive enough to apprehend the word

68. *History*, 7:501; for Wight's comments see 7:501 n. 1.
69. Ibid., 7:501 n. 1.
70. "Toynbee's *History*," 197.

of God as it has become manifest though dogmatic symbols such as "Reason" and "Intuition" or through ecclesiastical institutions such as the aforementioned universal churches, but "he does not hear the word as spoken to him personally." That Toynbee was aware of the fact is clear from his concluding prayer.[71] It is a prayer not from a man named Arnold Toynbee to God, but from the united and syncretistic religions to the constellation of their historical symbols: Christ Tammuz, Christ Adonis, Christ Osiris, Mother Mary, Mary Isis, Mother Cybele, Noble Lucretius, Valiant Zarathustra, Strong Zeno, Pious Confucius, Blessed Socrates, and the rest.

In March 1958, Toynbee wrote to Voegelin asking for a copy of the paper he had presented at Loyola.[72] Voegelin sent it to him a few months later, and Toynbee replied in *Reconsiderations* by calmly acknowledging the validity of Voegelin's remarks: "Voegelin criticizes me . . . for having failed, so far, to construct the new intellectual framework that the new plan requires for its execution. This is a charge to which I plead guilty. In volumes VII–X of this book I did try to carry out the new plan within the original framework. This was a mistake in procedure." The blandness of Toynbee's reply may be taken as evidence of his intellectual humility and great tolerance for criticism. But, Voegelin said on another occasion, "intellectual humility is sometimes difficult to distinguish from intellectual evasiveness." In any event, Toynbee's reply did not respond to Voegelin's critical analysis. Martin Wight has observed that Toynbee's "greatest weakness was an inability to learn from criticism of his premises or method."[73] That seems evident enough from volume 12.

There was no doubt in Voegelin's mind that Toynbee was "a great historian."[74] Apart from its sheer magnitude and the brilliance of specific studies embedded in it, Toynbee's work was notable for three not inconsiderable achievements. First, "as a result, the history of mankind has gained a lateral dimension, the breadth of movement that is so regrettably lacking in the Europocentric, unilinear constructions." Second, he found a way beyond "the worst aberrations of the preceding generations," most notably "the annihilation of mankind and history through the restriction of historical study to the morphology of civilizations," as is evident in Spengler's work. Third, Toynbee succeeded in placing "the substance of history beyond the gnosis of progress."[75] And last, as

71. *History*, 10:143–44.
72. HI 37/29.
73. *History*, 12:651; *OH*, 2:23; Wight, "Arnold Toynbee," 12.
74. HI 25/2.
75. *OH*, 2:21.

emerged from Voegelin's analysis, there are other intelligible units of history suitable for the scientific investigation of the historian besides those societies called civilizations.[76] Toynbee's limitations, no less than his undoubted achievements, enabled Voegelin to reopen the question of sacred history and to show how the spiritual history of humanity was a central concern of political science. As was indicated earlier, the work of Vico was instrumental in Voegelin's recovery of an understanding of sacred history. It is to that question we turn in the following chapter.

76. See Voegelin's remarks in "Les perspectives d'avenir de la civilisation occidentale."

9

Vico and the New Science of Politics

———

In November 1943 the political theory panel of the Research Committee of the American Political Science Association met in Washington to discuss current research needs and achievements. Voegelin took part and presented a report that subsequently was published in the *American Political Science Review* under the title "Political Theory and the Pattern of General History."[1] As is customary when scholars examine the "state of the discipline," most of the contributors provided useful histories of recent scholarship. Voegelin's contribution provided evidence of the methodological context within which he considered his own work to be situated.

Examples of treatises in the field of "the general history of political ideas," he said, were the books by William Archibald Dunning, Charles Howard McIlwain, George H. Sabine, and Thomas I. Cook.[2] By "general history," Voegelin meant to distinguish this category of writing from specialized monographic treatments of individual thinkers and time periods, and from analyses of traditional political problems such as sovereignty, authority, constitutional government, and so on. The topics covered by a "general history," he said, were international in scope, but the literary form "is almost an American monopoly."[3]

---

1. It was reprinted in Ernest S. Griffith, ed., *Research in Political Science* (Chapel Hill: University of North Carolina Press, 1948), 190–201. Citations in the text are from the *APSR* version.

2. Dunning, *A History of Political Theories, Ancient and Medieval* (New York: Macmillan, 1902), *A History of Political Theories from Luther to Montesquieu* (New York: Macmillan, 1905), and *A History of Political Theories from Rousseau to Spencer* (New York: Macmillan, 1920); McIlwain, *The Growth of Political Thought in the West, from the Greeks to the End of the Middle Ages* (New York: Macmillan, 1932); Sabine, *A History of Political Theory* (New York: Holt Rinehart and Winston, 1937); Cook, *History of Political Philosophy.*

3. Voegelin did not explicitly discuss why this was so, though it is clear from his analyses of American jurisprudence in *The Form of the American Mind* that he would

Dunning's three-volume study was the first to survey the general history of political ideas. It was written, at least in part, in opposition to the work of the French historian Paul Janet. Janet's *Histoire de la science politique dans ses rapports avec la morale*[4] was, in Dunning's view, too restricted. It was restricted first of all because it considered the ethical doctrines of philosophers as constituting the core of political theory. But ethics, according to Dunning (and to Voegelin), was only a part, however important, of political theory. Janet was restricted in another sense as well. Because of a real difference in the coherence of a major text in political science compared with an unsystematic piece of opinion literature, to say nothing of works of the imagination, Janet concluded that the degree of scientific achievement constituted an appropriate measure of relevance for inclusion in a history of political thought. Only systematic argument or "doctrine" deserved to be included. Third, the emphasis on ethical content and on doctrinal form led Janet to create a restrictive ethical continuum, with the "ethical absolutism" of Plato and Aristotle at one end and the technical rationality of Machiavelli at the other. In the middle, and constituting a "true" system of political science by which the others could be measured, were the "ideas" contained in the Declaration of the Rights of Man and the Citizen. This splendid French document was held by Janet to embody the most perfect framework within which all human beings could develop their moral destiny as free and rational agents. Fortunately, Janet did not consistently apply the principle that the aim of human history was to embody the principles of the 1791 Declaration, and materials other than those that could meaningfully be placed on a line of progress leading to it were also included. There was, for instance, a "preliminary chapter" dealing with China and India "for no other good reason than that the Chinese and Hindus exist; an integration of the Far Eastern body of thought into a general pattern of history is not attempted."

Before considering the content of Dunning's history of political ideas, Voegelin made the point that the "general history of political ideas" was a "young science" if it could be dated from Dunning's differentiation of his enterprise from that of Janet. As with many such innovations, the new science was clear about what is to be included as subject matter, but the details and structure were still controversial. In 1944, when Voegelin wrote, there was even less agreement than there was in Dunning's day a generation before. There were two reasons for this: first, there had

---

have found a practical and prudential motivation. See, on this question, David M. Ricci, *The Tragedy of Political Science: Politics, Scholarship and Democracy,* 67–69.

4. Paris: Lacan, 1887, 3d ed., 2 vols.

been an enormous increase in the sheer historical evidence that a scholar was obliged to master; second, there had been a substantial revision in the understanding of the conventional structure of history. Accordingly, it was advisable to outline "the ways in which the development of historical science has affected the more special problems of a general history of political ideas."

Historians of political ideas, as other intellectual historians and other historians in general, conventionally considered history to be analogous to a straight line along which "mankind," the subject matter containing the ideas, moves "in continuity through the ancient, modern and medieval phases." The theological origin of the straight-line "idea" was, as we saw with Bossuet, empirically adequate so long as one remained within the medieval spiritual horizon and identified Christian universalism with the historical horizon of the Western world. In other words, the straight-line "idea" was persuasive only if in good conscience one might ignore parallel non-Western histories or remain ignorant of the history of the preclassical civilizations. However, by indicating the conditions under which the straight-line "idea" was useful, Voegelin also indicated the sources of the disturbance to its usefulness.

As indicated in Chapter 7, when considering the range of evidence with which political science is concerned, the postmedieval historiographers were acutely aware that the linear "idea" was questionable. It was, of course, possible to substitute for the Old Testament of Christian sacred history the history of classic antiquity; in this way the Renaissance was understood somewhat literally as the rebirth of classic antiquity on an improved level. More systematically considered, the new epoch corresponded to the era marked by the appearance of the New Testament, and the middle ages became correspondingly "dark." But, as we have seen in connection with the image of Temür, there was also resistance by historiographers such as Poggio to the notion that Alexander and Caesar were the greatest embodiments of military and political action and virtue. In addition, the impact of the navigational exploits of the Western Europeans shifted political activity away from the Mediterranean basin and toward the Atlantic seaboard, which effectively eclipsed the problems introduced by the Renaissance awareness of the parallel and impressive Asiatic events and ensured that a linear but now secular pattern retained its legitimacy.

According to Voegelin, it was not until the generation after Hegel that the problem of parallel non-Western historical activity again became central. The pragmatic importance of the non-European power of Russia in European affairs was clearly evident after the Congress of Vienna. The work of Orientalists brought new knowledge of parallel Near and Far

Eastern civilizations into the public realm once again, and as was indicated in the last chapter, the work of Spengler and Toynbee on the internal cycles of a plurality of civilizations severely qualified the conventional linear pattern. These by now familiar observations constituted a prelude to a new question. "In what manner," Voegelin asked, "do these changes in the pattern of political history affect the history of political ideas?" The answer, he continued, "will depend on our definition of the political ideas of which we intend to write a history, and of their relation to the political environment in which they grow."

Voegelin then provided a survey of possible answers. First, one must entertain the possibility that the history of political ideas is without form and structure of any kind. If so, a so-called history of political ideas is properly identified as a chronological encyclopedia of successive opinions. A minimum understanding of history, namely that it is "the unfolding of a pattern of meaning in time," would be violated by such a compendium. On the other hand, there is the view of Janet, that only highly integrated doctrines and "systems" deserve to be considered because only the great thinkers achieve results that can properly be called "scientific." The conclusion to be drawn from this approach is that "the pattern of political history would have little bearing on the pattern of a history of political ideas."[5] The first option would have made the entire enterprise of a general history futile and so may be dismissed out of hand. The example of Temür, and the impact of his political activities on Machiavelli's evocation of a savior-prince, has indicated as well that the second conclusion is erroneous. The real problem is to specify the relationship between the history of political ideas and political history in a philosophically defensible way.

In this context, Dunning's methodological advance over Janet was clear: he distinguished "political theory," by which he meant opinions, sentiments, and ideas, "whether integrated into a scientific system or not, which tends to explain the origin, nature and scope of the authority of rulership," from Janet's more narrow and systematic "political science." Dunning proceeded on the methodological assumption that a "theory" mattered not because it was systematic or scientific but because it was "in touch" with actual political history and existing political institutions. With two exceptions, "the history of theory thus is subordinated for its pattern to the structure of political history." The first and minor exception was that Dunning excluded those "ideas" that were unrelated to the

5. In contemporary political science, the first assumption is made by some members of the so-called Cambridge school, while the second assumption seems to guide the work of some "Straussians."

existence of a state, such as the "ideas" of tribal or clan organization, families, and so on. This exception was not particularly important, at least so far as the history of Western political ideas was concerned, because in fact most "political theory," in the broad sense initially employed by Dunning, was indeed related to the state, if that term is also broadly construed.

The second exception was more significant because Dunning believed that the structure of political history was "progressive." He did not mean by this term the conceit of Voltaire, who glorified his own *politesse*, or even Janet's esteem for the Declaration of the Rights of Man and the Citizen. Rather, he meant the differentiation of an autonomous political sphere "from ethical, theological, legal, and other contexts." In Dunning's version of the Renaissance pathos encountered with the Oxford political philosophers, this differentiation was achieved first among the Greeks and then again among the Renaissance moderns. On these grounds Far Eastern and Asiatic theory was eliminated from the field. This exclusion did little to damage the integrity of Western political theory because the connections between the two, Voegelin agreed, were "thin," notwithstanding evidence supporting the importance of the imagery of Temür. More serious, however, was the elimination of the pre-Hellenic Near East, which Dunning's near contemporary, Eduard Meyer, had included in his own history of antiquity. Such an exclusion was more serious because, Voegelin observed, "a good deal of Western political thought is deeply rooted in the Mesopotamian, Persian, and Israelite pre-history."

The most important problem with his approach, however, was that apart from the late medieval question of the separation of church and state, Dunning was compelled by his principles of interpretation to exclude a large amount of medieval material on the grounds that no "political history" took place. In Voegelin's view this position was untenable even when Dunning held it and certainly had to be revised in 1944. By so doing,

> we can deal adequately, not only with the later phases of civilizations which show the differentiation of spheres, considered progressive by Dunning, but also with the equally important early phase of a civilizational cycle, in which the temporal power, as in the Middle Ages, is considered one order in the embracing mystical body of Western Christian mankind. The elimination as irrelevant of a phase of history which is in direct and broad continuity with our own, because its structure of political ideas differs from ours, cannot be justified by any standard of scientific method.

Sabine corrected this defect by abandoning Dunning's commitment to "progress" and consistently applying his own principle "that political theory is a function of politics and that, therefore, the pattern of a history of theory has to follow the pattern of political history." Neither the restricted standard of Janet's science nor the restricted conception of Dunning's politics was admissible. The historian, according to Sabine, must "follow the structure of theory as it reveals itself in history" whether it takes the form of science or of "an undifferentiated complex of community order" that includes such things as ethics, law, and religion. By so doing, Sabine organized the historical materials into three major parts. The first was on the polis, the second on the universal community, and the last on the national state. "With the elaboration of this methodological position," Voegelin said, "the problem of principles has come to a rest." Commitment to a linear progressive "ancient-medieval-modern" model had finally been abandoned and the "structure of a history of political theory is unconditionally subordinated to the structure of political history."[6]

Finally, on the basis of Sabine's principle, Voegelin enumerated the chief problems with which "the historian of political theory" was currently concerned. According to Voegelin, three questions were involved: (1) the choice of a pattern, such as that of Toynbee, on the basis of which the materials may be organized; (2) the classification and integration of new materials on the basis of the pattern adopted; (3) the revision of the pattern on the basis of interpreting new materials that do not conform to the categories of the original organization.

Voegelin spent the remaining three and a half pages of his report discussing the problem of harmonizing the history of political theory with political history. The pattern of history presupposed in his discussion was conditioned by Toynbee and by the studies found in the *Cambridge Ancient History* and *Cambridge Medieval History*. His purpose was to emphasize the fact that there existed a wealth of specialized studies in the area of political theory as well as in the area of political history, so that even though a scholar was faced with mastering a great deal of newly uncovered historical evidence, the material was presented in an accessible form. Accordingly, "the historian of political theory . . . has the fascinating opportunity of trying his hand at bringing the two complexes of knowledge together." Voegelin then provided half a dozen examples of major problem areas at which the cooperative efforts of scholars were being directed.

To begin with, the history of political theory could no longer begin with the Greeks. It had become clear, and not just from the work of

6. Sabine's "historicism" has been criticized by Strauss on just these grounds. See Sabine, "What Is a Political Theory?" 2, and Strauss, *What Is Political Philosophy?* chap. 1 and 223–28.

Sabine, that Aristotle brought an end to the theory of the polis and that Alexander and the Stoa initiated something new. But the connection between the Hellenistic imperial expansion and the pre-Hellenic empires of the Ancient Near East was less clearly developed. What stood in the way of such an interpretation were a number of cherished beliefs connected to a linear conception of history. First, the notion that the Hellenistic period was some sort of amalgam of the Near Eastern and Hellenic historical streams would have to be given up. Second, the Mesopotamian, Persian, and Egyptian political ideas would have to be considered on a par with the Hellenic, not dismissed as "Oriental" or "preclassical." Third, the interpretation of governmental authority would no longer be the central question in political theory. Its importance for periods of relative stability might remain undiminished, but "in the initial phases of civilizational cycles, the problems of community-substance, of its creation, its delimitation, and its articulation," were at least of equal significance; likewise, during periods of crisis, dissolution, and regeneration of the "community-creating political myth," questions of community substance or meaning came to the fore. Accordingly, the integration of a history of political ideas to the process of political history would entail an account "of the ideas concerned with the mythical creation of communities, and of the far-reaching theological ramifications of those ideas." On the side of "ideas," therefore, the political scientist had to consider a great deal more than what Janet or even Dunning considered relevant to their respective disciplines.

The focus on the evocation of political communities would also influence the interpretation of established political communities. In this respect, it was now understood that Plato's political philosophy was not so much a theory of the *polis* as a theory of "the lethal crisis of the *polis*" and a call for spiritual renovation and renewal. Likewise, the material in the *Cambridge Ancient History* and in more recent monographic literature on the sacramental aspects of the regime made a reinterpretation of ancient political ideas not only possible but evidently necessary.

The appearance of Christianity in the context of Roman imperial politics and Roman imperial political thought introduced additional methodological problems. "The cautious evasion of religious problems and of the creation of the mystical Body of Christ is untenable" because those topics deal with the substance of the Christian community. Without a concern with the *pneuma* of Christ, one is left with the problem of the reception of Stoic ethical theory and the problem of accommodation with temporal authority, neither of which touch the essential elements of the Christian evocation nor render the struggle with paganism intelligible. "It will not do," said Voegelin, "to eliminate from the field of political theory the theory of the community within which the structural political problems arise by classifying it as religious. Precisely the so-called non-political ideas, as for instance the eschatological sentiments and ideas, are the great source of political fermentation and revolution throughout Western history to this day."

Finally, there is the problem of treating the medieval materials. On the one hand, there is considerable new knowledge of the migration period, much of which was in fact digested and presented in the pre-war volumes of Toynbee's *History*. It is possible, therefore, to consider Teutonic political ideas in a way that could not be conceived either by Dunning or by the Carlyles in their standard multivolume study. Furthermore, the organization of medieval political thought in light of the spiritual movements associated with the Franciscans and Joachim of Flora, which mark the beginning of a new evocation, has become possible in light of Alois Dempf's great study, *Sacrum Imperium*. Specifically one may now pay proper attention to the beginning of the evocation of new mystical bodies replacing the mystical Body of Christ that subsequently crystallized as the national state, and to the growth of "parallel" sectarian communities that became part of the general history of political ideas in the West after the Reformation. The integration of medieval "parallel" histories was an example of a more or less familiar topic; less familiar ones would include Byzantine, Islamic, and Jewish medieval "parallel" histories. Voegelin's general methodological point was clear: "The field of research is wide open; there is no lack of problems, only a lack of strength to deal with them all at once."

Voegelin's *History of Political Ideas* brought together the two "complexes of knowledge" identified in 1944 as the history of political ideas and political history. With respect to the history of political ideas, the debate across the centuries between Voltaire and Bossuet ended, as it were, with Enlightened opinion triumphant. Several important spiritual consequences followed. First, the "idea" of transcendental spiritual universalism was replaced by the "idea" of an intramundane universalism of reason. As we saw earlier, this new "idea" was justified in terms of commonsense morality motivated by the sentiment of compassion for humanity and directed by social utility. We also noted that it was based on the assumption, derived from the impressive achievements of Newton, that knowledge had to be based on the methods of physics if it were to count as science. In order for Voltaire to sustain such an opinion, he had to reject the experience, still present in Bossuet, of the cognition of faith. He did so, as we saw, by his attack on the linguistic expression of that experience in the form of Christian doctrine and, in particular, in the Christian theology of history that Bossuet had accepted along with its doctrinal form. Finally, we recall that Voltaire did not simply reject Bossuet's doctrine and substitute his own, but turned the experience of the cognition of faith into a psychological accident. This position Voegelin called "spiritual obscurantism."

Because it was based on a denial of the cognitive value of the experiences of faith, the development from spiritual obscurantism to dogmatic atheism was predictable in the sense that it followed an obvious *logique du coeur.* First, if faith was not an act of cognition, then it was necessarily an act of imagination. In contrast to Voltaire, who was forced to confront the doctrine of Bossuet, the intellectuals who followed Voltaire's lead assumed the validity of his spiritual obscurantism and took it as a starting point for further speculation. For such persons, the conclusion to be drawn was clear: the alleged spiritual experiences really had no valid content to them, which is to say they were not, properly speaking, experiences of anything. Thus did the assertive materialism of Holbach and Helvétius follow the tentativeness of Voltaire.[7] Likewise, the sentiment of Newtonian usefulness could be elaborated into a Benthamic moral calculus. The importance of this development of political ideas, however, was that it constituted the generalization or popularization of a new philosophical anthropology rather than a penetrating theoretical insight or discovery.

The process of generalization both eclipsed the spiritual universalism of Christianity (along with its doctrinal form) and substituted for it the more vivacious spirituality of the particular and parochial community. As was indicated in Chapter 6, by the eighteenth century the national bodies politic had attained considerable internal administrative coherence and self-understanding. Increasingly they began to substitute themselves for the mystical Body of Christ; that is, they understood themselves as spiritual forces in their own right. They did so by asserting the claim to be autonomous mystical bodies endowed with the authority and prerogatives of the by now weakened institutions of imperial Christianity. Heretofore the institutions of church and empire and the imagery of Christian universality that they embodied were strong enough or persuasive enough to maintain the appearance of a single Western historical process unfolding by way of a manifold of national variations.

One symptom of the disintegration of the Western body politic into a collection of schismatic politico-religious bodies was the growth of a new set of conventions by which Europeans expressed their disdain for one

---

7. See Voegelin, *From Enlightenment to Revolution,* ed. John H. Hallowell, chaps. 2–3, for details; reprinted in *HPI,* VIII:chap. 1.

another's national particularities.[8] To the English, for example, the German spirit was obscure whereas the French spirit typically substituted logic for common sense; to the French, the German spirit was without civilization and the English was opportunistic; to the Germans, the French were superficial and the English were uncultured. The significance of such amenities lay not in their accuracy regarding the several national characteristics but in their being symptoms of a newly respectable spiritual parochialism and a growing mutual unintelligibility.

The respectability of this parochial recrimination, in turn, was a reflection of the political history of Europe. By the eighteenth century, as we saw in Chapter 6, the several national communities were in a position to evoke "ideas" of themselves as replacements for the no longer meaningful Christian and Imperial "idea." Voegelin termed the process by which the new mystical bodies of the nations gained respectability "apostatic revolt." Voltaire's was the most articulate voice of apostasy; that he was heard is evident from the changes in the history of Western political ideas but also from the course of political history. Not only did the several parochial national bodies politic substitute themselves for the mystical Body of Christ, they also began to insulate themselves against one another, as the litany of uncomplimentary epithets indicated above clearly shows. In place of the parochial religious tensions and a cycle of wars of the sixteenth century, one finds parochial national tensions and wars that have not come to an end four centuries later.

Regarding the actual configuration of so-called national characteristics, the chief determinant, as we have noticed on several occasions, was the constellation of ideas and sentiments, which varied from nation to nation, *at the time* of the particular apostatic revolt. In the French example, the apostasy of Voltaire took the form of a revolt in the name of universal reason against Catholic universalism. In England, the anti-Catholic attitude had long been settled by the Anglican schism and the Puritan revolution. Because there was no institutional guardian of the Western spiritual tradition in existence, there could be no intellectual expression of it as one finds in Bossuet. Instead the English conflict was between Protestant, personal, and idiosyncratic interpretation of Scripture and secularized individualism. The conflict was muted because the established Church of England was without significant spiritual force in the first place. Accordingly, as we saw with the Oxford political philosophers, all sides were chiefly concerned with maintaining respectability, civility, and "gentlemanliness." In England there was neither the enthusiasm nor the spiritual zest needed to produce a "counter-religion"

8. This account follows Voegelin's argument in the chapter "The Schismatic Nations," in *HPI*, VI:71–81. See also Hazard, *The European Mind*, 385 ff.

of Reason or Positivism or Humanitarianism as there was in France. Between the solidity and resiliency of English social forms, including the Church of England, and the personal freedom of the individual within those forms, the life of the spirit, Voegelin said, "moves in an even twilight of preservation and euthanasia."

In contrast, the German apostasy was complicated by three interrelated tensions. First, the ongoing Catholic-Protestant conflict overlapped with regionally dominant principalities in such a way that neither could form the new body politic to the exclusion of the other. Second was the tension between the imperial tradition and the plurality of minor territorial principalities, on the one hand, and the trend toward national unification and closure analogous to the Atlantic nations of France and England, on the other. Third, social differences remained between the colonized territories of the east and the old settlement areas of the south and west that was ended only precariously by the nineteenth-century Prussian-led wars of national unification.

Differences in the political history of the European political societies made uniform apostatic developments unlikely in the extreme. In Germany, for example, the absence in the nineteenth century of both national political institutions and uniform religious commitments precluded a national revolution in the name of reason as had taken place earlier in France. Likewise, German Protestantism was not characterized by idiosyncratic scriptural interpretation and so never developed into the corresponding secular forms of individualism that, in turn, helped shape English parliamentary political institutions. Whereas in England Parliament became, in Toynbee's language, "idolized," in Germany it was never more than a technique of rule without deep attachments of sentiment.[9] There was, accordingly, in Germany no parallel to the French relationship between reason and revelation or to the English one between parliamentary government and secular individualism. Instead, Voegelin said, one finds a plurality of political institutions juxtaposed to a long sweep of metaphysical and mystical speculation moving from Kant and Herder through Fichte, Hegel, Schelling, and Marx. The speculative efforts of the German thinkers, unlike their counterparts in France and England, could not penetrate or inform the institutions of a national polity because none existed.[10]

The relationship of "juxtaposition" between the events of political history and the history of political ideas meant that one might simply

9. See Toynbee, *History,* 4:414–18.
10. See John H. Hallowell, *The Decline of Liberalism as an Ideology, with Particular Reference to German Politico-Legal Thought* (Berkeley: University of California Press, 1943), and Voegelin's review (1944).

accept or reject existing political institutions rather than have them give internal coherence to the national body politic. Hegel and Marx are conventionally identified as typifying the two alternatives. The gap between events and ideas was bridged by the wars of national unification, but Bismarck's *Realpolitik* was not, in Voegelin's view, equivalent to the English or French revolutions and consequently did not solidify and articulate the national substance as a body politic either. Voegelin believed that an opportunity for a national revolution was missed in 1918 because Marxism paralyzed the workers' parties and they alone might have supplied the necessary strength to carry such a revolution through. "The overdue revolution was finally realized, in 1933, borne by the middle-class of an industrialized society and resulting in a national as well as an international catastrophe."[11] That the Nazi revolution was a disaster must not obscure the fact that it was part of a pattern common to the division of the West into national states of which the English and French revolutions were simply prior instances.

The term *closure,* which Voegelin associated with the English, French, and German revolutions, contained both a spiritual and a legal or institutional dimension. The former, which is conventionally related to the history of political ideas, referred to the complex of problems relating to the new schismatic and apostatic meanings of the preschismatic past. The latter, which conventionally belongs to political history and resulted in the political form of the sovereign state, referred to the complex of problems concerning the political relations among the several new sovereign entities issuing in the disintegration of Western society in the great wars of the twentieth century.

On the basis of these distinctions between spiritual and legal closure, Voegelin summarized the differences between the French, English, and German examples. In the first two, the institutional establishment of a unified national state preceded the spiritual closure, whereas in Germany the sequence was reversed. Accordingly, in France and England the process of spiritual closure could take for granted the existence of the political state, whereas in Germany the simultaneous development of both phases introduced additional disturbances. For example, the wisdom of Bismarck's policy in forcing Germany in the direction of a national state remained a live issue long after the actual political unification had been attained. So far as the central European areas are concerned, it is far from clear, even in the last decade of the twentieth century, that an imperial-federal construction would not be a more appropriate political form.

11. *HPI,* VI:78.

Another example of the twofold consequences of closure has been considered already in Voegelin's analysis of the Oxford political philosophers. The development of political ideas in the direction of increased parochialism was quite clearly not confined to England, however. Problems in political order and disorder that are properly understood as being specific to a particular national community have been widely misunderstood as having universal significance. In France, for example, the conflict between enlightened "reason" and Catholic doctrine and the superiority of the former over the latter became generalized beyond the eighteenth-century context into a legitimating source for France's famous *mission civilatrice*, which amounted to the imposition of "reason" on other people whether they were convinced of its reasonableness or not.

To this account of the English, French, and German responses to the problem of disintegrating Western Christian society and the differentiation of distinctive national characteristics, Voegelin added an analysis of the Italian. The structure of Italian political ideas no less than Italian political institutions presents a strong contrast to transalpine developments. The territorial states of the north, even in Germany, had long superseded the city-state, whereas in Italy the culture of the city-state remained the dominant political form until late in the nineteenth century.

The difference in political culture between the north and Italy led to a number of intricate complexities. On the one hand, the political and economic revolutions of thirteenth- and fourteenth-century Italy anticipated developments on the scale of the transalpine national state, sometimes by centuries. The use of a balance of power as a means of limiting political disorder among the several Italian states, for instance, was well developed long before the technique was used among the northern territorial states. Italian political thinkers, therefore, had good reason to consider their fellows the most sophisticated practitioners of the political arts. On the other hand, the superior military power of the French and Spanish national states, especially after the appeal by Milan to Charles VII in 1494, meant an end to an independent Italian political culture.[12] Notwithstanding their great skill in the practice of politics on the Italian peninsula, it was also clear that the city-states were no match for the territorial states in more serious conflicts.

Accordingly, the conventional term for the period between the French invasion of 1494 and the Risorgimento of the nineteenth century is *decadence*. The term is justified, but only with respect to the weakness of Italy

12. See Voegelin, "Machiavelli's Prince," esp. 142–45.

as a military and political power as compared to other European nations. Certainly the existence of political thinkers of the stature of Machiavelli, Guicciardini, Campanella, and Vico means that the term is inadequate as a general description of the consequences of the French invasion. One must, for instance, take account of Machiavelli's characterization of the French as barbarians. Only if one makes the equally conventional but also unjustified assumption that the national state is necessarily the goal toward which all peoples aspire can one conclude that the Italian failure to achieve that goal was a genuine failure and a symptom of weakness.

Granted that the conflict of political cultures is not settled simply in terms of who commands the larger battalions—in this case, the foreigners—it is also true that, within Italy, the trend toward a national culture during the fourteenth century was effectively reversed and a period of what has been termed "municipalization" began. Regional differences accordingly were stressed rather than merely acknowledged, and, under the pressure of the Counter-Reformation, many sensitive and energetic individuals emigrated to more congenial places. The political and intellectual contexts must both be borne in mind when considering the work of Giambattista Vico.[13]

"The work of Vico," Voegelin wrote, "is recognized today as the magnificent beginning of a modern philosophy of history and politics."[14] His lasting achievement was to establish a "new foundation of a science of politics and ideas." Nevertheless, Vico's work "remained almost unknown in its own time and exerted little, immediate influence." The first

13. Unless otherwise indicated, quotations from Voegelin are taken from the chapter "Giambattista Vico—*La scienza nuova*," in *HPI*, VI:82–148. The original text of Vico is in the Scrittori d'Italia series, ed. Fausto Nicolini, Giovanni Gentile, and Benedetto Croce, *Opere di G. B. Vico*. The *Autobiography* and *The New Science* were translated by T. G. Bergin and M. H. Fisch. Citations to Vico's *New Science* will be given in parentheses in the text and refer to the standard paragraph numbers. Other translations will be cited in footnotes. The only discussion of Vico and Voegelin I have come across is concerned chiefly with Voegelin's remarks in *OH* and *Anamnesis* and is brief. See Riccardo Caporali, "Vico in Voegelin."

14. Voegelin, review of the Bergin-Fisch translation of *The New Science* (1949). Thirty years later, however, B. A. Hadock was still of the opinion that "Vico's position in the history of political thought has yet to be established. . . . This lacuna is perfectly intelligible. Vico did not write a 'classic' of political philosophy" ("Vico on Political Wisdom," 165). On the other hand, consider Isaiah Berlin, *Against the Current: Essays in the History of Ideas*, 4. Adrienne Fulco made a more defensible claim, that "what is lacking is an overview of Vico's political ideas and an evaluation of his role as a political theorist" ("Vico and Political Science," in Giorgio Tagliacozzo, ed., *Vico: Past and Present*, 175).

question to be considered, then, is the reason for Vico's importance if his influence has been so slight.

Part of the answer lies in the style of Vico's writing. Like Bodin, Vico is not an easy read.[15] One reason is the "municipalization" of literary Italian: there simply was no national standard for intellectual discourse. More important, however, was the complexity of the subject matter. The substance of his work was a philosophy of history, but it was presented by way of erudite philological studies, theories of language and aesthetics, and analyses of Roman law and political institutions. Because he was anxious to avoid the attention of the Inquisition, there are also present in his work a host of spurious authorities alongside silences regarding his real sources.[16] Moreover, the style of historiography to which Vico conformed was one that found merit in collecting materials rather than in presenting a systematic exposition of methods or interpretative results.[17] The task of distinguishing the principles of Vico's method from

15. "Vico's Italian," wrote Leon Pompa, "is undeniably very difficult indeed. His works were invariably written at great speed; he used sentences of great length, which are often tortuous, chaotic and incorrect in construction; he expressed himself frequently with grim irony, which can sometimes confuse the sense of what he says; his works are illuminated by brilliant aphorisms together with a deliberate play upon words, while interlaced to the point of incomprehensibility by obscure and condensed intellectual allusions; he used ordinary language in an idiosyncratic and technical way without offering the help of many definitions" ("Preface," in *Vico: Selected Writings*, xiii). Isaiah Berlin made a similar remark: "Vico's elaborate, convoluted, 'baroque' prose, archaic even in its own time, with its constant digressions, occult references, esoteric allusions, and lack of any apparent order or easily intelligible structure, faced the reader with a huge and impassable jungle, which discouraged even the intellectually enterprising" ("Corsi e ricorsi," 481). See also Hazard, *The European Mind*, 414.

16. See Max H. Fisch, "The Academy of the Investigators." The most complete examination of the presence and activities of the Inquisition in Vico's Naples is Gino Bedani, *Vico Revisited: Orthodoxy, Naturalism, and Science in the Scienza Nuova*, chap. 1. Bedani also drew attention to class-based opposition to Vico from ecclesiastical landowners who were not above seeking assistance from the Inquisition against upstarts in the *ceto civile*, the civil or administrative class (153–54, 278). The consequences for Vico's "art of writing" have been accordingly emphasized by Straussian readers. See Frederick Vaughan, *The Political Philosophy of Giambattista Vico*, and Theodore A. Sumberg, "Reading Vico Three Times," both of whom are highly skeptical of Vico's claim to be a faithful son of the church. On the other hand, as Thomas Berry observed, "an accusation of this kind is so insidious that any proofs offered to the contrary might be taken by some as a manifestation of the perfection with which he accomplished this deception, which, it is suggested, was partially conscious and partially subconscious on his part" (*The Historical Theory of Giambattista Vico*, 12).

17. Kelley, *Foundations of Modern Historical Scholarship*, 301–5.

the materials to which he applied it is accordingly both subtle and complex.

Perhaps the greatest obstacle to understanding Vico was the intimate and meditative character of *The New Science*, particularly when it is read in conjunction with his *Autobiography*. In this respect Vico found a worthy successor in Voegelin. Just as Voegelin argued that his own consciousness was the instrument by which he and political scientists generally undertook the task of analysis, so Vico's story of his own life turned into a verification of the principles of *The New Science*.[18] The book published by that name is not a single, systematic treatise. Rather it is a compendium of Vico's thought, begun in 1708, when the author was forty, and continued until his death in 1744 when the "third" *New Science* was published. In fact, there were so many revisions that the "third" edition is sometimes called the ninth version. So far as Vico's language is concerned, the later texts, based upon even more years of meditation, were written in an increasingly personal style, "which was turning into a private language as its author withdrew further into himself."[19] One may say, therefore, that for thirty-six years Vico developed through meditation a philosophy of the spirit in history for which the several publications were interim reports. The earlier versions were not, however, simply superseded by the later ones. Rather, the successive phases "also contain elements which have to be considered as simultaneous parts of a system." The combination of systematic simultaneity and successive clarification over a very long time provides the most serious obstacle to an adequate analysis.

Voegelin, as other Vico scholars, divided the development of his thought into three phases. First was the criticism of Descartes's scientism, marked by the publication of the *Metaphysics* in 1710.[20] The second phase may be dated from 1720–1721 and the publication of a treatise that Vico referred to as his *Diritto universale*.[21] This work continued Vico's critical reflections on the basis of the metaphysical insights he had developed in

18. This dimension of Vico's philosophy is exposed brilliantly by Donald Phillip Verene, *The New Art of Autobiography: An Essay on the Life of Giambattista Vico Written by Himself*, esp. 87, 160, 219. See also H. S. Harris, "Philosophy and Poetry: The War Renewed."

19. Peter Burke, *Vico* (Oxford: Oxford University Press, 1985), 30–31. When reference is made in the text to paragraphs of *The New Science*, it is to the "third" *NS*.

20. *De antiquissima italorum sapentia ex linguae latinae originibus eruenda: Liber primus: Metaphysicus*, in *Opere*, 1:127 ff. In English: *Selected Writings*, trans. Pompa, 47 ff., and L. M. Palmer, *On the Most Ancient Wisdom of the Italians*, trans. L. M. Palmer. To summarize Vico's criticism boldly, he argued that Descartes's was an "insane method" because it applied geometry to the "caprice, rashness, occasion and fortune" of human life and so produced rational lunatics (*Most Ancient Wisdom*, 99).

21. Three texts were involved: the *Synopsi del Diritto universale*, 1720; the *De uno universi juris principio et fine uno*, 1720; and the two-part *De Constantia Jurisprudentis*,

his polemic against Descartes. The subject matter of his analysis on this occasion was the theory of natural law expounded by Grotius, Selden, and Pufendorf, all northerners, all Protestants. He deployed an enormous philological knowledge to show that the origins of Roman political institutions were far different from what the natural law theorists imagined and that, as we shall see, the origin, development, and disintegration of Roman institutions followed the course of the human mind. The natural-law advocates, as Descartes, made the error of assuming that because a law is given in the context of one set of institutions, namely their own, it must be equally "objective" in any context whatsoever. Vico argued this was an error because it ignored the connection between "the historically conditioned character of institutions and the content of natural law."[22] Such erroneous assumptions led to such oddities as conceiving of the origin of society and civilization through a contract that presupposed the attributes of eighteenth-century bourgeois civility.

This "conceit of scholars," *boria dei dotti*, is more than just a minor flaw; it is an "impious conceit," because it is based on the premise that humans can attain wisdom, or even insights, unassisted by God. In fact, such persons become skeptics, not wise because their rationality is directed toward the prerational foundations of social life. "Thinking themselves wise, the philosophers became fools."[23]

Such an approach, Vico said, was futile because it cut human beings off from participation in divine truth, and dangerously corrupting because the young in particular would follow it and grow contemptuous of prudence and common sense. They would turn into smug skeptics, keen only to apply their "insane method" mechanically.[24]

The second part of the *De Constantia* used the term *new science* for the first time, in reference to philology. Philology was understood as the science that explores the origins of things by exploring the origins of their names, for the "things" of society, namely religious and legal institutions, are signified by names and flow from the mind of man. The third phase was marked by the publication of the first version of *The New Science*, in 1725. In this work, the course of Roman history, discussed in *De Constantia*, was typified as a course to which the histories of all peoples conform, an "ideal eternal history," Vico called it. The second and third editions of *The New Science* enlarged and modified the position of 1725.

1721. They have been republished in a three-volume modern edition, *Opere* 2:1–3 (1936).

22. Leon Pompa, *Vico: A Study of the "New Science,"* 2d ed., 39.

23. Mark Lilla, *G. B. Vico: The Making of an Anti-Modern*, 152.

24. Vico, letter to Francesco Estevan, January 12, 1729, *Opere*, 5:214. See also the exegesis of Michael Mooney, *Vico in the Tradition of Rhetoric*, 101–3.

In 1941, when Voegelin had substantially finished his chapter on Vico, the secondary literature was still quite modest.[25] The most important study was Croce's 1911 book, *The Philosophy of Giambattista Vico*. Voegelin expressed misgivings about Croce's interpretation, which he characterized as secularist and progressive, and argued that Vico's greatness lay in his Christian awareness of the problems of the spirit, not in his efforts at constructing a secular philosophy of history along the lines of Voltaire.[26] Vico was aware, Voegelin said, that "the great irruptions of transcendental reality do not fall into patterns that can be constructed regarding the historical courses of human civilizations." Accordingly, he avoided the error of attempting to find the meaning of history in the humanly intelligible structures of profane history.

Voegelin summarized his own understanding of Vico with the remark that his was a "well-constructed theory of politics and history" and so had at its core a philosophical anthropology. "Having established this central theory," Voegelin said,

> Vico interprets the course of history as an unfolding in time of the potentiality of the human mind. The various actualizations of the mind in society receive their meaning in history as the intelligible phases in the unfolding of a potentiality. The philosophical anthropology and the unfolding of the mind in a temporal process of the community are the inseparable parts of Vico's theory.

The details of presentation through the collection of materials, therefore, were bound to be superseded by advances in historical knowledge, the refinement of philological techniques, and so on. The "ideas" of Vico's philosophical anthropology and his philosophy of history as the intelligible unfolding of the human mind, no less than its meditative form, are

25. HI 11/7, Voegelin to Engel-Janosi, September 24, 1941. In the past five or six decades the secondary literature on Vico has grown enormously. As one observer said, "Vico has become not only a relic but an icon, not only a classic but a commodity" and, as happens to all commodities, Vico has been industrialized as well. See Donald R. Kelley, "Giovanni Battista Vico," in George Stade, ed., *European Writers: The Age of Reason and Enlightenment*, 312. Much of this secondary material (and I make no claim to have read more than a large sample) is either useful enough scholarly exegesis of a historical kind or the appropriation of Vico's text or themes. At its best, the second type of appropriation can result in *Finnegans Wake*, but mostly it results in papers by various *dotti* on "Vico and the Hermeneutics of Critical Sociology" and the like.

26. This division between Vico scholars who emphasize the Christian spirituality at the core of Vico's work and those who emphasize his heterodoxy and historicism has persisted to the present. In this dispute, Voegelin is on the side of Momigliano and Rossi, not Berlin and Pompa—who, in turn, disagree about other matters.

what attracted Voegelin's attention. His focus, however, remained Vico's position "in a general history of political ideas."

To begin with, the name *New Science* echoed both Bacon's *Novum Organum* (1620) and Galileo's *Dialogues on Two New Sciences* (1638). For Vico, however, the *Scienza nuova* was a "true science of substance in opposition to a science of physical phenomena, while, at the same time, it is a science of politics in emulation of the imposing science of nature." In his *Autobiography,* for example, Vico said of his book: "By this work, to the glory of the Catholic religion, the principles of all gentile wisdom human and divine have been discovered in this our age and in the bosom of the true Church, and Vico has thereby procured for our Italy the advantage of not envying Protestant Holland, England or Germany their three princes of this science."[27] Such a claim raised the obvious question: what had Vico accomplished that outweighed both the achievements of natural science and the northerners' new theories of natural law?

Voegelin's brief answer was: "the insight into, and reversal of, the Western apostatic movement." The content of *The New Science,* therefore, was both an analysis of "the hubris of disoriented man who is obsessed by his *amor sui*" and an antidote to it. Vico's position within an unbroken Catholic tradition combined with his Italian sentiment of resistance to the pretensions of northerners provided him with the necessary strength to undertake his massive and isolated act of resistance. Vico was not, for that reason, "anachronistic" or "antimodern." Voegelin's reasoning was akin to that deployed earlier when he indicated that Italy could not properly be called decadent for failing to have formed itself into a territorial state. In the same way, philosophers are not obliged to move through the penumbra of Voltairean spiritual obscurantism to the darkness of progressivism, utilitarianism, romanticism, materialism, and all the rest in order to discover something is amiss. Vico's "genius" was able to anticipate fruits of apostasy without having to begin the *voyage au bout de la nuit.* In the words of A. Robert Caponigri, Vico "diagnosed the crisis of the modern spirit even before it had arisen."[28]

Voegelin began his exegeses of the stages of Vico's forty-year meditation with a close analysis of the argument leading to Vico's most famous aphorism: *verum esse ipsum factum.*[29] The "Latins," according to

27. Vico, *Autobiography,* 173; *Opere,* 5:53.
28. Caponigri, "Vico and the Theory of History," 184.
29. The formula is found initially in book I.1 of Vico's *Metaphysics* and has been the topic of considerable scholarly attention, most of which, however, ignores the context to which Voegelin drew attention. See, for example, James C. Morrison,

Vico, used the terms *verum* (truth) and *factum* (deed, thing done, "fact") interchangeably. This is indicated by the synonymous use of the terms "understand," "read perfectly," and "know plainly." The significance of Vico's observation arises from his assumption that words symbolize ideas as ideas symbolize things. Accordingly, reading means the collection of the elements of things in order to create a perfect idea that, when possessed, amounts to the possession of the thing. Perfect understanding, therefore, amounts to the identity of fact and idea. From this conclusion Vico justified the distinction between divine and human knowledge. God is the first truth because he is the first maker; God can read things perfectly and so know them because he orders them, whereas human beings can only think (*cogitare*) about them. Humans participate in reason rather than possess it, as God does.

The doctrine of the Latins must, however, be modified, Vico said, if it is to be acceptable to Christians. The Latins could identify *verum* and *factum* because they assumed that the world was eternal and that God operated on it from the outside. Christians, however, hold that the world is created and that God may act in it through grace and providence. A Christian philosopher, therefore, would make a further distinction between the created truth, which is identical with the *factum*, and the uncreated truth, which is not made but begotten (*genitum*). The Bible, accordingly, called the truth of God *Verbum*, the Word. In this divine Word, the truth and the comprehension of the elements of all potential worlds are identical.

Voegelin's exegesis of this passage indicated the methodological steps undertaken by Vico consistently throughout his speculation. First, he began with reference to the actual use of specific terms by a specific people, in this case, the "Latins." By so doing he avoided the conceit of scholars that human beings are isolated individuals capable of attaining the truth through solitary reflection. Accordingly, one looks first to myth, poetry, and civil institutions as they exist historically and unreflectively. The philosopher, properly speaking, begins meditative reflection by first considering the unreflective symbols as they appear historically and then undertaking the speculative interpretation of their meaning (*NS*, 51, 400 ff.). Myths, for Vico, provide the initial self-interpretation or articulation of society, which then serves as the basis for subsequent action and interpretative revision.[30] In short, myth is the chief vehicle to ensure the continuity of societies.[31]

"Vico's Principle of *Verum* Is *Factum* and the Problem of Historicism," but also Lilla, *G. B. Vico*, 25–36.

30. Mooney, *Vico in the Tradition of Rhetoric*, 241–44.

31. Emil Kauder, "Ideal History: Remarks on the Foundation of the Wave Theory," 212.

Second, Vico's speculation proceeds on the basis of the epistemological principle that true understanding is possible only if the knower is also the doer or maker. Of course, this is possible only for God, whose creation can be understood by humans only externally, or phenomenally. Human understanding, however, admits of different degrees of certainty, depending on the closeness of the analogy to divine creation. In the *Metaphysics* mathematics seemed to be most certain because it proceeded from definitions made by the mathematician. In *The New Science* the realm of the mind in history became the field of certainty as well because human beings are the doers or makers as well as the knowers of history. We will consider the significance of this change below.

Third was the contextualization of the epistemological principle as pagan, and the distinction between created truth, which is made, and uncreated truth, which is begotten. This distinction, Voegelin said, has been overlooked by many interpreters of Vico, but it was central because it preserved the Christian tension between the world-transcendent being of God and the being of the world.[32] Accordingly, God created the world from his wisdom, revealed himself to the world through the Word and guides, and preserves the world through grace and providence, but is not absorbed by the world and even less by any part of the world such as history.

Voegelin drew attention to two important implications, one theoretical, the other practical. First, history cannot be a process of self-reflective fulfillment, and its meaning cannot be penetrated by the reflective consciousness of an individual thinker. The distinction between what is begotten and what is made, between *gentium* and *factum,* enabled Vico to maintain the distinction between profane history, which is apprehended by the science of the *verum creatum,* and a sacred history that rests on the authority of the revealed Logos, which is "beyond the *factum creatum* and cannot be penetrated by the human mind." In principle, therefore, the attempt to "Hegelianize" Vico is to follow a false scent. Voegelin would have agreed with George Huppert, therefore, that Vico "was a distant disciple of the sixteenth-century jurists and historians, a straggler in the history of ideas, echoing Bodin, not announcing Hegel."[33] Second, still

---

32. See, however, A. Robert Caponigri, *Time and Idea: The Theory of History in Giambattista Vico,* 107; Arnaldo Momigliano, *Essays in Ancient and Modern Historiography,* 273; Paolo Rossi, *The Dark Abyss of Time: The History of the Earth and the History of the Nations from Hooke to Vico,* trans. Lydia G. Cochrane, 175, 252–53; Lilla, *G. B. Vico,* 8–9, 95, 152.

33. Huppert, *Idea of Perfect History,* 166. See also Elio Gianturco, "Bodin and Vico"; Girolamo Cotroneo, "A Renaissance Source of the *Scienza Nuova:* Jean Bodin's *Methodus,*" in Giorgio Tagliacozzo, ed., *Giambattista Vico: An International Symposium,* 51–59; and Paul Avis, *Foundations of Modern Historical Thought, from Machiavelli to Vico*

less can one claim the authority of Vico in support of an activist effort at creating a truth through the pseudo making associated with political activity. The process of history, even for pagan philosophy, is unreflected. Political action, which is not a making, properly speaking, creates a historical *factum*, to be sure, but the *verum* it contains is beyond the actor's intentions and foresight and is apprehended only retrospectively. Reflective reason in action, Vico said explicitly, does not produce reason in history but a barbarism worse than that of the sensuous or "heroic" barbarians (*NS*, 1106).

In addition to his philological method and the context furnished by Christianity, Vico's Neoplatonism provided a second and philosophical premise on the basis of which the materials were shaped into the speculative arguments of *The New Science*.[34] Owing to the heterodoxy of such views and to the vigilance of the Holy Inquisition, Vico did not stress this source, and his argument was rather obscure. He advanced it in chapter 4 of the *Metaphysics*. As with the discussion of the *verum-factum* principle in chapter 1 of that book, Vico began with some philological observations on the identical meaning of *essentia* (essence) as used by the Scholastics with *vis* (force) and *potestas* (power) as used by the Latins. This observation led him to make additional conjectures and arguments of a Neoplatonic cast. The philosophers of Italian antiquity, he said, considered the essences of all things to be eternal and infinite *virtutes* (excellences, virtues). Because of the characteristics of these excellences, namely their eternity and infinity, the vulgar called them immortal gods and worshiped them accordingly. The wise, however, attributed these characteristics to a single, highest divinity (*pro uno summo Nimine ac-ciepiebant*) beyond appearance. Metaphysics, accordingly, was, Vico said, for the ancients the true science because it dealt with what Vico called the *conatus* (striving or endeavor) and the *virtus extensionis* (extended or expanded virtue) of the visible and apparent phenomena.[35] In contrast,

---

(London: Croom Helm, 1986). Leon Pompa, *Human Nature and Historical Knowledge: Hume, Hegel, and Vico*, 132–42.

34. Croce, "The Sources of Vico's Theory of Knowledge," reprinted as appendix III to his *The Philosophy of Giambattista Vico*, 279 ff. Vico's other modern editor, Nicolini, declared Neoplatonism to be "blood of his blood" (quoted in Caponigri, *Time and Idea*, 16), and other scholars have likewise emphasized the Neoplatonic elements in the *New Science*. See David Lachterman, "Vico, Doria, and Synthetic Geometry"; Linda Gardiner-Janic, "G. B. Vico and the Artes Historiae," in Tagliacozzo, ed., *Vico: Past and Present*, 89–98; and A. Tucker, "Plato and Vico: A Platonic Reinterpretation of Vico"; see also Thomas Berry, *Historical Theory of Giambattista Vico*, chaps. 4, 5, 9.

35. The notion of *conatus* was central to Hobbes and Spinoza as well as to Vico. In Vico's usage, it symbolized both the participation by humans in the divine order

physics dealt with observing the appearances of bodies and motions, that is, with phenomena.[36] Thus, Vico concluded, beyond the extension and movement of bodies apprehended by physics lay the unextended principle of extension and the unmoved principle of motion, both of which were apprehended by metaphysics. These principles, the virtues, are in God, who is the *factor* (maker) of nature, the infinite and eternal being in whom knowledge and the power of creation (*potestas*) are united.

According to Voegelin, the importance of Vico's Neoplatonism, at least for a general history of political ideas, was in part a historical contingency. A configuration of facts came to Vico's attention and precipitated a crisis, in the sense that the traditional intellectual instruments available to him were inadequate to account for the new situation. The facts constituting the new situation were: (1) the growth of mathematized science; (2) the evocation of a new image of man by means of the Cartesian *cogito* that crystallized in the Protestant doctrines of natural law; (3) the enlarged historical horizon.

In the area of political science, the more general intellectual crisis, as we argued earlier in Chapter 3, took the form of a direct application of the ideal of mathematical or quasi-mathematical science to the problems of human life in society.[37] So long as science was understood as the science of phenomena, of "physics" in Vico's terminology, the science of substance, including political science—or "metaphysics" in Vico's terminology—remained impossible. His Neoplatonism, then, was not embraced because Vico sought the excitement of heresy but because it was available to demolish the option of applying the scientific ideal of phenomenalist physics to problems of spiritual and political substance.

Likewise Vico's attack on the Cartesian *cogito* was conditioned by its importance in Vico's time. The *cogito* was not, in his view, a point of certainty where the substance of human being would be immediately given. On the contrary, it was a phenomenon, and the *cogitare* was not the creative evocation of symbols that express a hidden human substance but a reflective "thinking about" something. Just as Neoplatonism indicated the reality of a depth of nature beyond its appearance, so did Vico find in the world of poetry, myth, and political institutions a deeper stratum of human substance.

---

and the divine assistance needed by humans to rise from the status of *stulti*, fools, to *sapiens*. See Lilla, *G. B. Vico*, 11, 45, 59, 81, 207; Bedani, *Vico Revisited*, 267–74. *Conatus* is discussed in more detail below.

36. "Uti corpus et motus sunt proprium physicae subjectum, ita conatus et virtus extensionis sint materia propria metaphysices"; *Opere*, 1:151.

37. Berlin, *Against the Current*, 94; Bedani, *Vico Revisited*, 174.

The third factor, the enlargement of the historical horizon, has been discussed in previous chapters of this study. The option no longer lay between Augustinian truth and pagan falsehood. "The 'Hermetic' authors who admired age-old Egypt, writers who cited the wisdom of the Chaldeans, the Jesuits who praised China, had raised a series of problems, set new ideas in circulation, awakened curiosities, and opened discussions. These problems called for a response."[38] Vico responded not by postulating an imaginative secular history combining the characteristics of nature and grace so that the same intramundane process that appeared in the rise and fall of civilizations or empires was also a process of salvation. Rather, he transferred the Neoplatonic model of nature to the history of a people. China no less than France or Rome had a history that ran its course in accord with the "nature" of the particular human community involved. The several courses may run in parallel or in succession, but they are run by finite communities, not by "mankind" or by "humanity." Vico was not, therefore, compelled to find an imaginary meaning of history in the rise and fall of nations. On the contrary, the meaning of the whole of history was still symbolized by the term *sacred history*. Accordingly, for Vico, sacred history remained "the criterion and the focal point of the problems raised by profane history."[39] Vico was concerned, then, with a "typical" course of history that could be empirically observed, and the Neoplatonic "nature" of a people was Vico's term for the substantive unit of intelligibility. His term for the empirically observable and typical course was *storia ideale eternale*, "ideal eternal history." The term was not, however, intended to be a substitute for Christian sacred history so that the question of a universal meaning beyond the finite, simultaneous, and successive courses remained beyond the scope of his new science.

By Voegelin's interpretation of Vico's Neoplatonism, then, he belongs to a tradition that looked back to Bodin by way of Ficino and Bruno, and ahead to Schelling. Indeed, as we remarked in Chapter 3, during the nineteenth century Schelling characterized the period from Descartes to Hegel as a giant aberration and was concerned to resume problems of the spirit where they had been left by Bruno. Moreover, Vico's position in the history of Western political ideas has suffered from a fate similar to that of Bodin. Because of the triumph of Cartesian and Newtonian mathematized science, those who opposed it inevitably bear the odium

38. Rossi, *Dark Abyss of Time*, 151. See also John Milbank, *The Religious Dimension in the Thought of Giambattista Vico, 1668–1744*, chap. 1.
39. Rossi, *Dark Abyss of Time*, 175.

of reaction, pessimism, or simply eccentricity. Voegelin's methodological point, which was Vico's as well, was obvious enough and has been made previously in other contexts: it is inadmissible in a critical history of ideas to endow one epoch, such as the epoch of mathematized science and reason, or of Voltairean *politesse,* with such authority and significance that all other periods must be understood in terms of a movement toward, or defection from, the authoritative period. Vico's Neoplatonism inoculated him against the authoritative status of the phenomenal network of mathematical or quasi-mathematical relations. Behind phenomena lay the reality of nature; behind motion lay the unmoved principle of motion. At the same time, the Neoplatonism of Vico's model of nature was, as we noted earlier, incompatible with Christian orthodoxy, particularly as understood by the Inquisition. This meant that the transfer of the model, developed in the critical context of the *Metaphysics,* to the speculations of *The New Science* was a complex operation.

The complexity is apparent when one raises the question of the relationship of the historical courses of the several peoples to the created world within which they occur. Two principles that bear on this question, which is central to Vico's science of history, follow from his most basic Christian affirmation, that human being in history has been created in the image of God. First is the ontological principle, "that the process of the human mind in history is part of the process of divine creation"; second, epistemologically, "the operation of the human mind in history can be understood as an analogue of the operation of God in his creation." Thus arose Vico's famous formula, in *The New Science* (331), to which we will return, that man is creator of the civil world as God is creator of the natural world. This human creation may be known from the inside by the human mind, as nature is known through phenomena.

The civil world is therefore intelligible, but not in isolation from divine creation.[40] The relationship between human and divine creation was the subject of the *Diritto universale* and constituted the initial formulation of Vico's philosophical anthropology. In the "Proloquium," Vico explained that he came across a statement of Varro in chapter 31 of book 4 of Saint Augustine's *City of God,* where the latter observed that, had he the power to give the Romans a religion, he would choose a God *"ex formula naturae,"* namely "one, incorporeal and infinite, not innumerable finite idols." Upon reading the passage Vico suddenly understood that law was by nature a formula, that is, a true idea, through which the

40. This point of Voegelin is also emphasized in A. Robert Caponigri, *"Umanita* and *Civilita:* Civil Education in Vico."

truth of God is displayed.[41] In Voegelin's language, legal institutions may be "transparent for the truth of God," which is to say that divine truth may appear in the world by way of such institutions when they are understood as finite analogues to divine creation as well as part of it.

Vico opened the *Diritto universale* with what he said was a paraphrase from Augustine's *Confessions*, that God is infinite power, knowledge, and will.[42] Because humans are made in the image of God, they share these characteristics, rather than fully possess them. Vico explained the mode of human participation in the divine in terms of the distinction between body and mind: (1) human beings are both body and mind; (2) mind, being of the spirit, cannot be circumscribed by corporeal limitations; but (3) the body is, nonetheless, a corporeal limitation; therefore, (4) human being is "finite knowledge, will and power that strives towards infinity" (chap. 10).[43] In an important and highly Thomistic passage in chapter 11, Vico argued that, because infinite being is God, human being tends to return to God, or at least would have followed this tendency had humanity not suffered corruption, with the result that human will opposes human reason. The resulting domination of will over reason is called cupidity, which breeds error and perturbations of the soul, especially the *amor sui*, love of self. Cupidity, furthermore, seeks satisfaction in the pursuit of the things useful to the body (chaps. 10–21). His argument, to this point, was essentially that of Hobbes.

Vico, however, linked the process of human creation, including the disorientation of cupidity and the *amor sui*, to the permanent presence in history of divine providence. The "principium omnis humanitatis," the principle of all humanity, which was the title of chapter 33, is that human beings can never completely lose sight of God so that even when we deceive ourselves, we do so under some image of truth. Accordingly, the seeds of eternal truth were not quite extinct even in corrupted humanity, and, with divine grace, they could operate against the corruption of nature (chap. 34).[44] In individual humans, he went on, the force of truth

41. "Igitur jus naturale est formula, est idea veri, quae verum nobis exhibet Deum. Igitur verus Deus, ut verae religionis, ita veri juris, verae jurisprudentiae principum est"; *Opere*, 2–1:33.

42. Vico, *Il diritto universale*, in *Opere*, 2:ii, chap. 2, p. 43. Further citations to this source are given in parentheses in the text by chapter. Vico did not provide a specific citation. See, however, Augustine, *Confessions* XIII.xi.

43. Vico's language in chaps. 2 and 10 was nearly identical. In chap. 2 he wrote: "Deus . . . est Posse, Nosse, Velle infinitum," and in chap. 10 his words were: "Homo . . . hinc est nosse, velle, posse finitum, quod tendid ad infinitum." For a similar exegesis, see Caponigri, *Time and Idea*, 77–79.

44. The title of this chapter was "Vis veri," the force of truth.

is reason and, to the extent that it is present, is called virtue. When it directs the utilitarian interests of the many it is called justice (chap. 43). Utilitarian interests are measured by reason, which participates in eternal truth (chap. 44), and are not, therefore, the cause of justice but its occasion (chap. 46).[45] Grotius, however, did not see that utility was never the principle of human society; nor was it necessity, fear, or indigence, as Epicurus, Machiavelli, Hobbes, Spinoza, and Bayle believed. Rather, such conditions were also occasions on which human beings, who are by nature social, were induced to actualize their social nature and realize justice (chap. 46).

Voegelin's commentary on this aspect of Vico's theory emphasized his rejection of the psychology of disorientation as a basis for political science. Even if one lived in a society characterized by Hobbesian competition or the *amor sui*, that did not mean, either for Vico or for Voegelin, that one is compelled to adopt the prevailing anthropology and erect a spiritual disease into a human norm. The basis for this position for both men is as old as philosophy: human spirituality retains its autonomy even in the face of an empirical failure to live in truth. In Vico's traditional Christian language, human beings are made in the image of God even if they deny it in revolt; in Vico's equally traditional philosophical language, human beings are linked through reason to the infinite transcendent reality.

The corollary Vico drew from this more or less traditional position was, Voegelin said, "of the utmost importance for the method of history." Just as self-deception takes place under the image of truth, so too for the history of political ideas: "the structure of the spirit cannot be abolished through revolt against the spirit; the revolt itself must assume the structure of the spirit." This was why, for example, Voltaire could not produce an empirical science of universal history but only a pseudo-sacred history of the progressivist type. Vico's discovery of the principle of the persistence of an identical structure throughout all modifications, defections, and perversions of the spirit "is the basis for a *history* of ideas, understood as an intelligible line of meaning in time." Without this principle, the manifestations of the human mind would be disconnected events, *partes extra partes*. Voegelin applied this principle to his analysis of texts in political science all his life.

Vico also integrated spirit with material or utilitarian interests and necessities. He readily acknowledged interests to be the great motive power of history but did not make the mistake of concluding that the

---

45. The title of this chapter is "Utilitas Occasio, Honestas est Caussa Juris et Societatis humanae."

necessities were the determinants of spiritual order. On the contrary, they were, as we saw, the occasions for the appearance of human spirituality. Whether the cooperation between spiritual order and material interests is called the operation of providence was secondary to the acknowledgment of a recognizable spiritual order that rises above the interplay of material interests. This relationship "is a stark fact of history however we interpret it," Voegelin said.

In the *Diritto universale* Vico developed his own interpretation of this "stark fact" in his initial theory of the *recursus*, which was distinct from the *ricorso* of *The New Science*. The *recursus* was the course of history as it proceeded from God and returned to God, whereas the *recorso* was the course of the nations after the migrations that followed the premigration course of the nations of antiquity. The *recursus*, in other words, was the historical analogue to the anthropological structure set forth in chapter 11 of the *Diritto universale:* human being tends to return to God as it has proceeded from God. At the same time, however, the *recursus* showed the same sequence of phases as one finds in the *storia eternale ideale* of *The New Science*, beginning with the prehistoric solitary life of corrupted man (chap. 98), akin to the "feral state" of *The New Science*. From this hypothetical beginning emerged the social unit of the family (chaps. 100–103) that in turn differentiated into a clientele and a clan (*gens*) that protected them (chap. 104). This whole process of differentiation, Vico said, was guided by providential counsel. All history thereafter was conditioned by the structure of the *gens* and was therefore properly described as the course of "gentillician" history.

Political history proper began with the formation of the gentillician republic, consisting of the heads of the *gentes* united in the face of a threat from the clientele. The regime consisted of an elected king, which developed in turn into an aristocratic and then a democratic republic; the instability of the latter led to the seizure of power by a regal *princeps* and then a tyrannical one, which was followed by disintegration and the rise of Christianity.

This account, however, contained a fundamental difficulty.[46] Christianity for Vico was clearly part of the tendency, indicated in chapter 11 of the *Diritto universale*, of human being to return to God. Taken by itself this *recursus* may indicate Vico's orthodoxy. At the same time, however, it indicated that his philosophy of history is incomplete. One may, for example, raise the same kind of questions with respect to Vico's argument as were asked of Toynbee's fantasy of 1,743 million civilizations: What

46. Noticed as well by Frank E. Manuel, *The Eighteenth Century Confronts the Gods*, 167.

happens to gentillician history after the return to God in Christianity? Will the cycle go round again? Will there be a successor to Christianity that provides an even closer return to God? Will the sequence be repeated asymptotically? In short, what is the relation of the *recursus* to the *corso* of any particular people? Was there a subject to the *recursus*, such as "humanity," analogous to the subject of the *corso*, namely the nation? And if so, what was its relationship to the nations and their *corsi*?

Vico's answers to what may be called the question of the relationship between *recursus* and *corso* were incomplete and tentative. Voegelin's analysis of them brought several topics into focus and by so doing raised issues that he himself was unable to resolve until many years later. In the *History of Political Ideas,* Voegelin argued that Vico's philosophy of history became increasingly clear regarding the fundamental questions because he was able to clarify analytically the ambiguities of the successive formulations. Vico's intellectual *corso* was, in this respect, recapitulated by Voegelin. Contemporary Vico scholars have not, so far as I know, discussed this problem. Most, indeed, appear to be oblivious to its existence.[47] Instead commentators have usually considered a derivative question, the degree to which Vico's views agreed and conflicted with Roman Catholic orthodoxy regarding biblical chronology. In Paolo Rossi's words, for example: "as Vico was to see clearly, the problem of the great age of the Egyptians and the Chaldeans had become indissolubly tied, after the middle of the seventeenth century, to that of the immense age of China: China's antiquity also threatened the authority of the Bible and cast doubt on the universal Deluge."[48] Vico's way around the problem was to dismiss it as secondary compared to his postulate of an irrational and savage origin of human society, namely giants devoid of reason and possessed of a vigorous imagination (*NS*, 377 ff., 502 ff.). For Voegelin, the doctrinal question regarding chronological anomalies between the Bible and, for example, Egyptian or Assyrian civilization was secondary. This means as well that Voegelin's science of politics depended on the scientific (and Protestant) textual-critical analyses of the Bible in order to be developed at all. The difference in this respect is that the doctrinal conflict with biblical chronology had been transmogrified by Voegelin's day into a broader conflict between doctrine generally and the expression of human and political spirituality.[49]

47. Lilla, *G. B. Vico,* 221, may be an exception, though he does not seem to see its importance.
48. Rossi, *Dark Abyss of Time,* 140.
49. See Bedani, *Vico Revisited,* 109–10.

In the *Diritto universale* the problem of *corso* and *recursus* received its initial shape. At one point (chap. 219), Vico compared the course of mankind, the *genus humanum*, to the phases of individual life. "Thus youngsters (*pueri*) are distinguished by being governed by their desires, adolescents overflow with imagination, men (*viri*) judge with reason and the elderly (*senes*) with firm prudence." So too with the phases of humanity: because of its original vice, it began in a solitary and most needy position and had to grow in an easy fashion, by unchecked liberty; then, through imagination it was obliged to discover the necessary, the useful, and the pleasant things of life. This was the age of the poets and, in short, the time of inventions and civil life; it was followed by the age of reason and wisdom "when the philosophers taught the duties of human life." The succession of ages was the same as that of *The New Science*, and the characterization of them corresponded to the elements of will and knowledge in Vico's philosophical anthropology. In addition, there is a parallel with Saint Augustine's succession of ages from infancy to senescence.

The first two elements drew the connection between the *corso* of a people, from its mythic evocation to the dissolution of the myth by analytic reason, and the nature of human life; the third, Augustinian, element introduced humanity, the *genus humanum*, as the subject of the *corso*. The problem, therefore, is this: if the theory were concerned only with the history of a people from its mythic evocation to its disintegration, then the question of a universal meaning, a meaning for the whole of the *genus humanum*, would not arise and the cycle could continue, in the fashion of the early Toynbee, ad infinitum. But because the element of the universality of meaning was in fact introduced, the question of Augustinian sacred history could not be avoided.[50] The problem is: how to reconcile the finite *corso* of a people with the *genus humanum* as its subject?

In the "first" *New Science* the emphasis on the problem of the *corso* was on the finite course of a people and away from the topic of the *genus humanum*. The contents of the *corso* may be summarized as proceeding from myth to reason. The initial mythic evocation crystallized in religious and legal institutions, which were then subjected to reflective analysis. "When the reflective penetration is completed," Voegelin observed, "the *akme* of the course is reached; the *akme* is the perfect state of the nation when the arts and sciences, which have their origin in religion and law, all serve religion and law."[51] And the *akme* is passed when reflection turns against its origins and religion and law are lost to a people. When the

---

50. See Rossi, *Dark Abyss of Time*, 252–53.
51. See Vico, *Opere*, 3:11; *Selected Writings*, 83.

"civilizational personality" embodied in religion and law is dissolved in what we would call demythologization or even deconstruction, there is nothing worth defending and, at the same time, the possibility of governing oneself is lost. The result is a return to the heroic age where there is no equality between the weak and the strong.

In the "third" *New Science*, Vico discussed the *corso-recursus* problem again. This time he emphasized less the critique of the age than the anticipation of the current barbarism of reflection being followed by a barbarism of heroes. The parallelism between the ancient *corso* and the modern one was discussed in detail in book 5. In addition, however, "we shall show how the Best and Greatest God has caused the counsels of his providence, by which he has conducted all the human institutions of all nations to serve the ineffable decrees of his grace" (*NS*, 1046). The "counsels of his providence," we noted earlier, guide all gentillician history; the "ineffable decrees of his grace," in contrast, concern sacred history. But how does the one "serve" the other? Vico's answer was given in the next paragraph:

> When, working in superhuman ways, God had revealed and confirmed the truth of the Christian religion by opposing the virtue of the martyrs to the power of Rome, and the teaching of the Fathers, together with the miracles, to the vain wisdom of Greece, and when armed nations were about to arise on every hand destined to combat the true divinity of its Founder, he permitted a new order of humanity to be born among the nations in order that [the true religion] might be firmly established according to the natural course of human institutions themselves. (*NS*, 1047)

In other words, the second *corso*, the *ricorso*, had as its purpose the securing of the historical existence of Christianity, which thereby supplanted the pagan myth. The second course is still typical, but it is enacted, in Voegelin's words, at "a higher level of spiritual consciousness."

The *recursus* of the *Diritto universale* was, therefore, linked to the *recorso* of *The New Science* in the following way. The *recursus* ended with the senescence of mankind in the Roman empire, which was indeed the *saeculum senescens* of Augustine. The *ricorso* unfolded within the spiritual context established by the *recursus*. In terms of Augustine's theology of history, the *ricorso* constituted the natural structure of the *saeculum senescens;* in Vico's philosophy of history, the *ricorso* was the instrument by which providence sustained the *recursus*. Vico's theory of the *corsi*, therefore, was an attempt to harmonize systematically the universalist meaning of Augustinian sacred history with the finite meaning of the profane rise and fall of civilizations under the conditions provided by the wider historical horizons of the eighteenth century.

To see the significance of Vico's achievement, Voegelin drew attention to the fact that other options were available. First, one could have attempted to evoke a new Christ who would inaugurate a new period of spiritual meaning, as was done, for example, by Joachim of Flora.[52] But such efforts were bound to fail. Practically, saviors do not materialize at the bidding of speculative systems; theoretically, it is impossible to deal with the problem of a meaning to profane history by tampering with sacred meaning because the latter is the domain of God, not of the philosopher, prophet, or revolutionary activist. Second, there was the option of Spengler, namely to discard the whole question of sacred history and look for meaning in the intramundane rise and fall of nations. The abolition of mankind as the subject of history and its replacement by a plurality of civilizations or cultures is in this respect admirable if only for the relentlessness with which Spengler pushed his *logique du coeur*. The third option, that of Voltaire, as we indicated, was to transfer the sacred meaning of Christian history to the most recent phase of Western civilization.

Vico's solution, to build a gentillician *recorso* into the *saeculum senescens* of Augustine, was not without its own problems. It did have the advantage of ensuring that spiritual events were not deprived of their unique meaning. The fact remained, however, that the institutional success of Christianity meant that Augustinian sacred history had become part of the profane history of Western civilization. Vico acknowledged this by distinguishing the *corso* from the *ricorso* and by indicating that the latter developed at the level of spirituality gained by the *recursus*. Even so, by characterizing Christianity as the "myth" of the postmigration nations, Vico strongly emphasized the repetitive nature of the second *corso*. As Voegelin observed, "the *recorso* ought to have a *recursus;* and where would the *recursus* lead us if not to a new Christ?" Vico obviously would have had hesitations about evoking a new Christ.

Voegelin pointed to the source of Vico's hesitation in the theoretical conflict between a profane cycle and a sacred straight line.[53] It was the

52. See *NSP,* chap. 4, for details, and HI 50/1, "Notes on Philosophy of History."
53. Voegelin later introduced the concept of "historiogenesis" to describe the straight-line image of historical change as well as to indicate the anxieties that it expressed and was designed to assuage (*OH,* 4:chap. 1). Bedani pointed out that, in Vico's day, orthodox Christians, both Roman Catholic and Protestant, were concerned that Christianity was a historical development from Judaism, rather than the completion of it, so that scholars were particularly concerned with the integration of Israelite and pagan chronologies and myths. See Bedani, *Vico Revisited,* chap. 7, and Momigliano, "Vico's *Scienza Nuova:* Roman 'Besioni' and Roman 'Eroi,' " *History and Theory* 5 (1966): 3–23.

same difficulty encountered by Toynbee, and it stemmed from the same source: inadequate sample size. Vico, as Toynbee, based his "ideal eternal history" on the course of a single civilization, the Greco-Roman. Even so, Vico has been praised for the profundity of his insights given the scarcity of evidence upon which to base his generalizations. He knew next to nothing of primitive societies and had a vague and incomplete knowledge of medieval Europe. Basing his speculation only upon classical philology and Roman law, it was, said Erich Auerbach,

> almost a miracle that a man, at the beginning of the eighteenth century in Naples, with such material for his research, could create a vision of world history based on the discovery of the magic character of primitive civilization . . . there are few similar examples, in the history of human thought, of isolated creation, due to such an extent to the particular quality of the author's mind. He combined an almost mystical faith in the eternal order of human history with a tremendous power of productive imagination in the interpretation of myth, ancient poetry and law.[54]

Notwithstanding Vico's gifts, it was also true that they were deployed on the basis of an assumption or a conviction that Roman culture and history were complete, complex, and universal, a culture "that had patiently run the entire gamut of the human *corso,* from barbaric and crude beginnings to a state of high refinement."[55] That is, Rome's national gentillician history acquired in retrospect for Vico the universality required for his new science.

The plain fact is, however, that the development from heroic Homeric kingship to the empire and Christianity did not fit all civilizational courses. Such regularity as exists, Voegelin said, is confined to "the dynamics of pragmatic history" and does not extend either to "the history of the myth" that provides sacramental coherence and meaning to a civilization or to "the evolution of the spirit in the history of mankind," for which something like Voegelin's concepts of compactness and differentiation would be required to give an adequate account.[56] At

54. Auerbach, "Vico and Aesthetic Historism," 117–18.
55. Mooney, *Vico in the Tradition of Rhetoric*, 184.
56. Mark Lilla proposed an ingenious alternative interpretation: *The New Science* shows how Providence guides all nations through an ideal eternal history similar in principle to that of Rome. "All nations once were Rome," he said, "and therefore can return to their 'Roman' roots as an alternative to modern political life" (*G. B. Vico*, 9). According to Lilla, Vico was an "anti-modern," which may be acceptable enough, but at the same time Lilla meant that Vico rejected the insights of ancient Greek as well as of modern Cartesian philosophy, and this for Lilla was less than acceptable (*G. B. Vico*, 153, 203–9, 216, 226). In Voegelin's later terminology, Lilla's

the time of writing the chapter on Vico, however, Voegelin was more conscious of the problem than aware of the solution to it. For this reason, perhaps, his formulation of the issues was less precise than it became in his subsequent work.

At the time of *History of Political Ideas,* Voegelin simply noted that Vico had blended the course of pragmatic Roman history with that part of the "spiritual evolution of mankind" that had occurred during that time. In one respect, Vico's approach was methodologically sound: every civilization has its myth; its *akme* is attained when the myth is rationally comprehended; its decline begins with the rational criticism of the civilizational myth. The effects of the history of myth on the course of the pragmatic history of a civilization are to be distinguished, however, from the problems associated with the fact that a myth is evoked in the first place, that it has a specific spiritual meaning, and that it is intelligible to speak of a humanity that has a spiritual history that lasts through the pragmatic cycles. In commonsense terms, the fact that human beings today can find spiritual meaning in the philosophy of Plato or in the message of the Gospel without participating in the course of Greco-Roman history indicates that such problems transcend the pragmatic regularities of a civilizational course. In Voegelin's terminology, they belong to "the philosophy of the theogonic process."

Voegelin did not indicate directly what he meant by this term. In the discussion of Saint Augustine's sacred history that followed, a few hints were made. It is clear what is to be avoided: when constructing a theory of a *typical* civilizational course it is inadmissible to include as one of the constituent elements the mythical structure of a *specific* civilization, whether Greek, Hebrew, Roman, or whatever. Saint Augustine's sacred history, namely the history of Israel and Christianity, was, in Voegelin's words, a "well-circumscribed phase" of the spiritual history of mankind. There was, quite clearly, an inherent "evolution of religious conscious-ness" independent of the *corsi* of the Egyptian, Mesopotamian, Persian, Roman, and other civilizations.

The difficulties with both Augustine and Vico did not arise, in Voe-gelin's view, from the distinction between spiritual and pragmatic his-tory but rather from not insisting upon it more strongly. Vico failed to distinguish sufficiently the specific problems of the pagan myth from

---

historiogenetic myth divided evidence into ancient and modern, which division is itself questionable, and made Vico "anti-modern," not "ancient," and so merely a negative reflection of modernity. Lilla, in this respect followed Strauss, not Meyer or Toynbee or, indeed, Voegelin and Vico in his understanding that ancient and modern were not to be conceptualized as divisions *internal* to the course of a civilization.

the typical pragmatic *corso* just as Augustine failed to distinguish sacred history sufficiently from the course of pragmatic Israelite and Roman history. We discussed one aspect of the Augustinian problem in connection with Voltaire's legitimate criticism of Bossuet. Augustine's idea of a *saeculum senescens* combined the spiritual meaning of the age between the death and the Second Coming of Christ with the pragmatic "old age" of the Roman empire. When he wrote, there was plenty of evidence that the Roman empire was drawing toward its close, but there was nothing senescent about the spirit—in this case the spirit of Christ. Moreover, the Christian spirit was perfectly capable of establishing a social institution, a community, to embody and preserve its substance, namely the church that did, in pragmatic fact, survive the disintegration of the Greco-Roman world. As Toynbee indicated, it became the chrysalis of a new civilization, Western civilization.

Vico's construction likewise failed sufficiently to distinguish sacred and profane history. Like Augustine, he modeled the *recursus* of the ancient course of history on "the coincidence of the Roman pragmatic course with the phase of spiritual history that culminates in Christianity."[57] The result was to impart to the second *corso* the mood of a spiritual twilight that found expression in the several ambiguities already noted but was ultimately derived from Saint Augustine's experience of the pragmatic twilight of Rome at the hands of Alaric the Visigoth.

Voegelin's criticisms of Vico, and of Augustine for that matter, were balanced by a keen awareness of their achievements. Vico, in particular, had achieved a rare balance of accepting the insights of a theory but not pressing the logic of its argument so far that the consequences became dubious.

Notwithstanding Vico's contribution to the question of the universal history of humanity, the theory of the *corsi* is the most important immediate contribution to political science. The chief topic of *The New Science* is the *corso*, and Vico's greatest innovation is the evocation of a typical course, the *storia eterna ideale*, to which, he said, the histories of all nations conform. Even so, given the meditative context within which Vico developed his argument, the result was not a rationally closed system so much as a speculation whose formulations converge toward, rather than attain, a final form. In this interpretation of Vico, much as in the interpretation of Bodin, one finds Voegelin explicating his own

57. Voegelin revisited this question of the "coincidence" of Roman imperial and Christian spiritual history in vol. 4 of *Order and History*. By 1974, however, the terms of his analysis had changed, as had the insights drawn from them.

philosophy of history and consciousness by way of the texts written by his predecessors.

The most important of Vico's principles has already been introduced. Paragraph 331 of *The New Science* contained "the eternal light, which never fails us, of this truth beyond doubt: that this world of history is most certainly made by men, and hence we can find, we must find, its principles in the modifications of our own human mind." This Neoplatonic principle established the analogy between the world of nature and the world of history: as God "makes" nature, so humans "make" history; as God knows nature from the inside, so humans know history. The most obvious question raised by Vico's formulation is this: what happened to the distinction, within the world of civil society or within the historical world, between sacred and profane history? What is the relationship between God and sacred history, if divine making and knowing are confined to nature? To deal with this problem one first must acknowledge that the extreme and dualistic contrast between nature and history or the "world of civil society" is formulated in such a way that, in fact, it may well be misinterpreted to mean that the study of history is an intramundane science and Vico an "ordinary" historicist.[58]

We have already seen, however, that for Vico the distinction between sacred and profane history was fundamental. Accordingly, this initial formulation in paragraph 331 needs to be balanced by other statements to understand what Vico had in mind. One indication is given in the next sentences of paragraph 331: "Whoever reflects on this [Neoplatonic principle] cannot but marvel that the philosophers should have bent all their energies to the study of the world of nature, which, since God made it, He alone knows; and that they should have neglected the world of nations or civil world, which, since men had made it, men could come to know." Vico explained this oddity as "a consequence of that infirmity of the human mind by which, immersed and buried in the body, it naturally inclines to take notice of bodily things, and finds the effort to attend to itself too laborious." In other words, Vico, having undertaken the "effort" of attending to the concerns of the spirit, has reached a position where he can "marvel" at the attention paid by philosophers, who are concerned with the things of the body, to nature. Looking back, as it were, the contrast between natural and spiritual concerns seemed much greater than the contrasts within the spiritual, historical, or civil world.

To put it another way, Vico's emphasis is as much on the "effort" or the process of clarification as it is on the results attained by that effort. A metaphysics of nature and a spiritual metaphysics or a metaphysics

58. Compare Caponigri, *Time and Idea,* ix–x, 107; Berlin, *Vico and Herder* (London: Hogarth, 1976), 140–41.

of mind are not simply alternative positions, the one false and the other true. They are historical phases of the same process. This is evident first of all in the commonsense observation that it would have been impossible for Vico to "marvel" at the errors of the philosophers of nature and so to transcend them unless they (and he) had undertaken the study of nature in the first place.

One is reminded here of several observations of Voegelin: (1) that the instrument for the analysis of consciousness was the consciousness of the analyst; (2) that in consequence the quality of the instrument will depend upon the analyst's desire to know; (3) philosophy is both an exegesis of consciousness and a report on the results. One may conclude, then, that Vico's explanation of his own efforts at attending to spiritual things amounted to a statement that the quality of his own analytical instrument had improved and that the "reports" he issued indicate the several improvements.

Textual evidence for a change in Vico's own consciousness (to use Voegelin's terminology) is found in a comparison of the argument of the *Metaphysics* of 1710 with that of paragraph 331 of *The New Science* published more than thirty years later. In both works very similar wording was used to indicate antithetical conclusions. In the earlier work, mathematics was said to be more certain than ethics because the premises of the former were made by the mind in a mode that was as independent of matter as possible, whereas with ethics, and so with the whole of the civic and historical world, the movements of the mind were deeply buried in bodily matter.[59] During the course of his thirty-year meditation, however, Vico had sufficiently purified or clarified his own reflective self-understanding that greater certainty could later be accorded his new science than mathematics.

Voegelin substantiated this interpretation by reference to an intermediate text, the "first" *New Science* (1725). There the stark contrast between the natural and the historical was modified by more precise language. In book I, chapter 11, entitled "The need to seek the principles of the nature of nations by means of a metaphysics elevated to contemplate a certain common mind possessed by all peoples," Vico discussed the various uncertainties that surrounded the "first men, from whom the gentile nations later arose," their feral migrations, customs, and woes. "In view of these uncertainties," Vico said,

> when meditating upon the principles of this Science we must, with very great effort, clothe ourselves in a nature in many ways similar to that of those first men. Hence, we must reduce ourselves to a state of extreme ignorance of all

59. See Vico, "Metaphysics," in *Selected Writings*, 55–56; Lilla, *G. B. Vico*, 27.

human and divine learning, as if, for the purposes of this enquiry, there had been neither philosophers nor philologists to help us. And whoever wishes to profit from this Science must reduce himself to such a state, in order that, in the course of his meditations, he should be neither distracted nor influenced by preconceptions for long held in common. For all these doubts combined can cast no doubt whatsoever upon this one truth, which must be the first in such a science, since in this long, dense night of darkness, one light alone glows: that the world of the gentile nations has certainly been made by men. Hence, in this vast ocean of doubt, one small island appears, upon which we may stand firm: that the principles of this Science must be rediscovered within the nature of our human mind and in the power of our understanding, by elevating the metaphysics of the human mind—which has hitherto contemplated the mind of individual man, in order to lead it to God as eternal truth, which is the most universal theory in divine philosophy—to contemplate the common sense of mankind as a certain human mind of nations, in order to lead it to God as eternal providence, which should be the most universal practice in divine philosophy. In this way, without a single hypothesis (for metaphysics disowns hypotheses) this Science must, in fact, seek its principles among the modifications of our human mind in the descendants of Cain, before the Flood, and in those of Ham and Japhet, after it.[60]

In this passage, we find not the dualism of the natural and the historical but the more precise indication that "the world of the gentile nations," or gentillician history only, has been made by human beings. The principles of gentillician history are found in the nature of the human mind, as in *The New Science,* but, through a series of parallel constructions, Vico indicated that the human mind was itself open to the divine. More specifically, the "metaphysics of the human mind" has been heretofore a contemplation of the *mind of individuals* undertaken in order to lead them toward God as eternal *truth,* which is the most universal *theory* in divine philosophy; but now it has become the contemplation of the *senso commune del genere umano,* the *common sense of mankind,* undertaken in order to lead them toward God as eternal *providence,* which is the most universal *practice* in divine philosophy.

The metaphysics of the mind, Vico went on to say, is not a hypothetical enterprise but a process of contemplation that leads toward the insight that the structure of history is an operation of providence unfolding in and through the human mind. Voegelin summarized this passage in a way that described his own political science: "The contemplation of the civilizational course reveals the providential structure, and the con-templator himself [Vico or Voegelin] is part of the providential course."

60. Vico, "The First New Science," in *Selected Writings,* 99. The first two sentences of this quotation correspond to para. 330 of *The New Science;* the remainder corresponds to para. 331.

Accordingly, the human mind that grasps the principles of history or the order of history, to use Voegelin's later term, is not the constituent of an immanentist philosophy. Rather, it is the means by which providence appears in history; the mind of such a philosopher is able to contemplate the order of history because it contains a providential core that guides it toward historical understanding. In Voegelin's later language, one would say that the consciousness of the philosopher of history is a participating partner in the order of providence.

Turning, then, to the question of historical order rather than the mind that apprehended it, Voegelin considered Vico's remark that one of the principal aspects of *The New Science* is that it is "a rational civil theology of divine providence" (*NS*, 342). The meaning of this phrase is far from self-evident.[61] As a first indication of what is meant, Vico noted that the contents of such a civil theology consisted in the "demonstration, so to speak, of what providence has wrought in history." It will, therefore, be a history of the order that providence has imparted to "this great city of the human race. For though this world has been created in time and particular, the institutions established therein by providence are universal and eternal" (*NS*, 342). The *order* of providence, being universal and eternal, cannot be grasped on the basis of an empirical survey or on the basis of individual psychology but only as "a history of human ideas" (*NS*, 347) concerning the necessity and utility of human life. We have already seen that, for Vico, necessity and utility are the *occasions* on which the eternal idea of a just order becomes clarified; necessity and utility are, in Voegelin's words, "human instruments through which Providence operates in order to achieve the meaningful course of man in history." The ideas are not, therefore, the eternal order, nor is the embodiment of utility and necessity in social institutions. The "ideas" concerning necessity and utility, which are embodied in human institutions, constitute the material that occasions the apprehension by the philosopher of the eternal order.

In other words, providence is present from the start, in the (chiefly bodily) experiences of utility and necessity. Then it is immediate and usually at cross-purposes to human intentions (*NS*, 342); it becomes less inchoate when embodied in social institutions and grasped intellectually as "ideas." Finally, these ideas are themselves the occasion for the appearance of the providential order. In Voegelin's words, "Divine Providence creates a meaning in history beyond the humanly created ideas. This meaning, which is immanent in the course as a whole but

61. James C. Morrison, "How to Interpret Divine Providence in Vico's *New Science*."

transcends every single phase of it, is re-created by the historian in his contemplation." The meaning of history that results from this act of contemplation reproduces the providential element of the *corso*.

The decisive test for the New Science, therefore, is the following: "that, since these institutions have been established by divine providence, the course of the institutions of the nations had to be, must now be, and will have to be such as our Science demonstrates" (*NS*, 348). The New Science has the task of reproducing the providential strand of the human fabric, namely the *storia eterna ideale*, "the ideal eternal history traversed in time by the history of every nation in its rise, progress, [mature] state, decadence and end" (*NS*, 349). The historian who meditates this New Science "narrates to himself this ideal eternal history insofar as he makes it for himself by that proof that 'it had, has, and will have to be.'" The reference to the assertion in paragraph 348 that the institutional course must be as it was, was followed by a reference to the principle of paragraph 331, that "this world of nations has certainly been made by men" so that the changes it manifests must be found "within the modification of our own human mind." Combining the two observations or principles, Vico concluded that "history cannot be more certain than when he who makes the things also tells of them himself." Just as the science of geometry creates and contemplates a world of quantity out of its constituent elements of points, lines, surfaces, and figures, so too does *The New Science* create and contemplate the world of the nations, "but with a reality greater by just so much as the [constituent] institutions having to do with human affairs are more real" than the lines and figures of geometry. The demonstrations of the New Science that narrate this history "should therefore, O reader, give you a divine pleasure for it is only in God that knowing and making are the same thing" (*NS*, 349).

Vico's understanding of the problems of the meaning of history and of the existence of meaning in history were central to Voegelin's political science. Vico's methodological superiority to Voltaire, in this respect, consisted in his distinction between the meaning of history as a whole, which can be "known" only by revelation, and the meaning of the finite but trans-individual *corso* that can be known by his New Science. Unlike Voltaire, Vico assumed the existence of intellectual and spiritual meanings in history; these meanings can appear only as the consequence of intellectual and spiritual action. And action requires an agent. But who? It cannot be an individual because the meaning of the *corso* transcends the individual. Vico introduced Providence as the nonhuman agent. But then how can humans understand a meaning created by this nonhuman agent? Because Providence is also present in the individual mind, even if the individual is unaware of it.

So far as the individual was concerned, the operations of Providence were symbolized by the term *conatus*. As was noted above, the word was used extensively in seventeenth-century theological discourse, particularly by Hobbes and Spinoza. Vico's usage, however, was entirely his own inasmuch as it had none of the conventional determinist connotations. Initially, he said, human nature emerged from animal spirits through the power of *conatus* (*NS*, 340, 504) that directed and animated human motion away from corruption and toward the good. Indeed, it was similar to the Platonic image of God as the player of the human puppets developed in *The Laws* (644d). In particular, the gentle pull of the puppet's golden cord needs the cooperation and support of human beings if it is to be effective. Likewise the disposition toward the good needs human cooperation to be effective. *Conatus* symbolized for Vico the link between the divine and the human. As Mark Lilla said, "the divine power of *conatus* . . . draws man back to God and perfects him."[62] The reality so experienced meant, in more conventional Christian imagery, that humanity had not been abandoned by God, even after the Fall (*NS*, 1098).

The experience of *conatus* is particularly intense in the meditative contemplation of the philosopher and the practitioner of Vico's new science. Specifically, the philosopher becomes aware of the presence of providential meaning in the *corso*, and this reflective awareness appears as intelligibility or reasonableness. This was the meaning of Vico's enigmatic statement quoted earlier, that his New Science aimed to provide a rational civil theology of divine providence (*NS*, 342).

Voegelin accepted Vico's analytic formulation of the problem: there was, in fact, a transindividual meaning to be discerned in the *corso* that, in his later work, Voegelin identified as "configurations of history."[63] One may summarize Vico's argument in favor of *conatus* and, a fortiori, in favor of Providence as follows: given the existence of transindividual meaning in the structure of the *corso*, what are the necessary metaphysical and anthropological assumptions to explain the fact or occasion of such meaning? Vico's assumption, to repeat, was identified as a transindividual Providence that directs the generations of human beings along a line of meaning and that is also present in the soul of the philosopher in such a way that it becomes intelligible through human contemplation of the *corso*. "This solution," Voegelin said, "is classical insofar as—in the present state of science—we cannot improve its structure." This did not mean that the metaphysical symbols were fixed. On the contrary.

62. *G. B. Vico*, 59.
63. *CW*, 12:chap. 4.

"Providence" did not indicate a doctrinal formula. Indeed, during the nineteenth century a whole series of alternative symbols—psychological, biological, organic—was introduced to provide a collective subject to experience the transindividual meaning that unfolded in the history of a group. The choice of symbols, Voegelin added, did not alter the structure of the problem, which was to symbolize the merging of the individual with the substance of the cosmos—with the "it-reality," to use a term Voegelin employed in volume 5 of *Order and History*. In fact, Vico's symbol is methodologically preferable to the nineteenth-century alternatives because it expressed and preserved the nonempirical or nonexistent characteristic of the problem. It should occasion no surprise, therefore, that the "rational civil theology of divine providence" should be accompanied by "a divine pleasure." In Voegelin's words, "we can well understand the tone of mystical joy in his announcements to the reader and his divine pleasure in tracing, as the tool of Providence, the line of meaning drawn by the finger of God in history." Such divine pleasure was shared by Voegelin, the reader of Vico, as well as by Vico, the reader of history.

The most important concept that translates the principle of ideal eternal history into a recognizable intellectual operation, by Voegelin's interpretation, is centered on the term *senso commune*, common sense or common meaning. In setting out the axiomatic elements of the New Science, Vico defined *senso commune* as follows: "judgment without reflection, shared by an entire class, an entire people, an entire nation, or the entire human race" (*NS*, 142). This definition formed the basis, Vico said, for "a new art of criticism regarding the founders of nations" and so regarding gentillician history as well. Specifically, the *senso commune* was "the criterion taught to the nations by divine providence to define what is certain in the natural law of the gentes" (*NS*, 145). Common sense, in Lilla's view, was the "link between individual *conatus* and the ideal eternal history of nations." It is the social rather than individual expression of divine *conatus* and begins with the desire to share experiences with others. "Once man is socialized," he went on, "common sense operates a set of customs holding society together and propelling it along a divinely established path of development. Those customs are religion, marriage and property."[64] There is, therefore, a parallel in the effort of *conatus* working in the individual, as it draws him or her from *stultus* to *sapiens*, and in the societies, as through the operations of customs common sense draws them in an orderly fashion from barbarism to

64. *G. B. Vico*, 156.

civilization. In the language of contemporary political science, Vico's *senso commune* constituted the substance of a civilizational or gentillician myth.

The civilizational *corso* began with the foundational myth, the unreflective consensual judgment regarding the meaning of fundamental things. In other words, the *senso commune* embodied in the basic political and religious institutions of the nation *are* the stock of meaning that, during the historical *corso*, is increasingly penetrated by reason until the achievement of what Vico called the *akme*,[65] the perfect balance between reason and the unreflected initial stock of meanings. The development of the *corso*, therefore, consists in the refinement or, to use Voegelin's term, the differentiation of the existing civilizational substance. The later, rational period does not add to the stock of meaning; it merely gives the existing substance a new form. In this way, Voegelin wrote, the concept of the *senso commune* "established the great principle of civilizational interpretation that the history of a civilization is the history of the exhaustion of its initial myth and of such mythical elements as may have entered the course from other sources."

Voegelin drew several important conclusions from Vico and from the criticism Vico made in the "First New Science" of the stoics, Epicureans, Grotius, Plato, and Selden.[66] Vico's principle of civilizational interpretation, that the "vulgar wisdom" of the nation, its common sense or primordial myth, was both passionate and meaningful in its partnership with the divine, meant that none of the elements ought be considered in isolation. A philosophy of history based on a psychology of the passions alone would ignore the order of history; likewise one based on an eternal idea of justice alone would overlook the concrete and passionate motivations of political actors who nevertheless manage to realize a meaningful political order. Nor may one begin from the life of philosophical reflection because the actual forces of historical growth, namely utility and necessity, are far from the contemplative attitude of the philosopher. The philosopher of history likewise must not assume human beings are essentially good, because that assumption leads one to overlook the political tension between the evil of force and violence and the actualization of political order that nevertheless relies on force to exist. Finally, Voegelin concluded, Vico cautioned against mistaking the problems of spiritual or sacred history for the problems of pragmatic or gentillician history. That is, for both Vico and Voegelin, the course of a civilization resulted from the cooperation between, or

65. *"First" New Science*, I:2; in *Selected Writings*, 83.
66. *"First" New Science*, II:3–5, in ibid., 105–10.

the partnership of, the providential and the human, the architect and the artificer.

Vico's and Voegelin's position was designed as well to avoid a complex array of errors. For example, Vico stated that it was wrong for philosophers to have meditated solely upon a civilized human nature, that is, a human nature changed by religion and law because, in Voegelin's words, religions and legal institutions "are precisely the medium within which the function of philosophy grows as a rational penetration of the initial mythical substance." What the philosophers have not done is meditate on the human nature that produced religion and law that in turn produced philosophers. By this argument, philosophy had no autonomous authority but rather derived what authority it had from the civilizational substance on which it reflected. This derivative status of philosophy accounted as well for the greater emphasis Vico gave to Rome as compared to Greece. Roman superiority so far as political order was concerned derived from the superiority of common sense to philosophy, the former being more deeply rooted in human nature than the latter. Or, what amounts to the same thing, human being is more *stultus* than *sapiens*. When this general as well as historical situation of philosophy was forgotten or ignored, speculation moved either in the direction of naively erecting one's own civilizational myth into an absolute or in the direction of reflective idiosyncrasy.

The philosopher of history, therefore, is obliged to understand his own historicity, which means bringing the mythical meaning or substance of his own civilization within his rational grasp and orienting himself within the *senso commune*. The philosopher of history cannot transcend the myth by a feat of personal creativity because it is a transpersonal reality to begin with. But, added Voegelin, "he can transcend it speculatively by exploring the origin and the course of the myth and by accepting the myth consciously as the transpersonal substance by which his personal meditation lives." This observation applied to Vico's personal situation as an interpreter of Western civilization, and also to Voegelin's, and anyone else's.

Vico in particular lived reflectively within the civilizational myth both of the Roman *corso* and of the Christian *ricorso*. This is why he could neither continue the Augustinian orthodoxy nor turn into a philosopher of profane history. Both constituent elements must, for Vico, be acknowledged and understood. The problem, however, is that sacred history cannot be understood in the way that gentillician history can be, namely by meditation on the *storia eterna ideale*. Vico's own personality inclined toward the joy of experiencing the knowing and making of gentillician history; that same joy cannot occur with respect to sacred history because the generative word speaks itself. In commonsense language, Vico can transcend gentillician history through the ecstatic experience of the philosophizing intellect actively grasping its meaning. With respect to Christianity the element of agency is reversed. No philosopher can transcend Christianity by an act of speculation. Accordingly, there is no penetration of the mythic substance by the rational intellect. On the contrary, with sacred history the meaning penetrates the individual in the passion of faith. In Voegelin's discussion of the inclinations of Vico's personality and its relation to the New Science, one cannot but notice an autobiographical mood to his analysis, as we have pointed out several times in passing.

The political structure of the *corso*, being the most intellectually accessible element of Vico's political philosophy, is also the best known. It begins when those in whom the *senso commune* providentially is found awaken to the fact and establish a civilizational community. The *corso* itself consists in the foundation, development, transformation, and dissolution of the community. The phases of the *corso* may be briefly summarized.

The first phase, of creative action, was called by Vico the poetic age; it was further divided into a prehistoric feral state, a divine age, and a heroic age. Human beings emerge from a feral state, with the aid of divine providence, to the worship of pagan gods. The myth of the first age is created by those who, Vico said, are intelligent and become the heads of families. The others, who are servile and stupid, become agricultural *clientes*. They, in turn, grow rebellious, which motivates the heads of families to become an aristocratic estate and turns the *clientes* into plebeians. In this way the aristocratic state is created. The patrician myth still lives among the rulers, but the lower estate resists their rule and, in a complicated process, forces them to extend the sacramental union. In this way the second major phase, of reflection, which Vico called the human age, began.

Politically, the human age is characterized by the development of a free or popular republic. Spiritually, the power of the myth declines, and reasoned ethical arguments take its place. Virtuous acts result no longer from unreflective religious inspiration but from the rational analysis of the idea of virtue, and the secret and sacred law is replaced by a rational codified law before which all are equal. Political competition in a popular republic is between parties or factions, not estates; because it has no inherent limitation, it may grow fierce enough to endanger the regime. Under such conditions, three outcomes are possible: (1) a Caesarian monarch may compel submission; (2) the divided republic may be conquered by stronger and united neighbors; or (3) it may disintegrate into a new barbarism, the individualist barbarism of reflection. And then only Providence can "relieve the horror by awakening again the mythical powers in man, thus opening a new *corso*." The conclusion Voegelin drew was similar to the conclusion he drew from his study of Toynbee, namely that their achievement was not so much in elaborating the details of the *corso* as in showing that it was the intelligible unit of analysis.

It follows that, for Vico, none of the regimes that constitutes each of the several constituents of the *corso* is inherently preferable or more just. His political philosophy consists in a description of the sequences of ideal necessity, not in justifying ethical preferences. The phases of the *corso* are connected insofar as they are transformations of a single political substance that changes through the movement from evocation to foundation to dissolution. Vico's term for this substance was *mente eroica*, the heroic spirit or desire for justice. Without it, Vico's theory of the *corso* would be no more than a theory of culture accompanied by a sequence of forms of government connected only through the psychology of the degeneration of rulers. With it, the element of political identity is added to the *corso*. The *mente eroica* is found initially with the earliest evocation of the *senso commune* and continues as the love of one's own religious and legal institutions along with the conscious will to preserve them in existence. So long as it exists, the community preserves its political existence through the successive regimes from that of the heroic creators of the myth through to the spirit of popular republican laws and the Caesarian monarch who concentrates the whole *mente eroica* in his own being. When no person can be found capable of embodying the idea of justice, the substance that was created by the initial evocation is truly exhausted. A general disorder or Toynbeean interregnum follows until such time as another providential source of founding creativity appears.

Voegelin concluded his chapter on Vico with remarks intended to support the proposition that Vico was "one of the founders of modern political science." He had the advantage of living at a time when the "intellectual and spiritual disaster" known to us as the Age of Reason or the Age of Enlightenment was just beginning its *corso*. This was an advantage because the intellectual and spiritual profile was clear and unimpeded by pragmatic consequences. In opposition to the Age of Enlightenment Vico developed five counterpositions.

First, against natural science, Vico's New Science attempted to restore a science of substance, a science of the mind and spirit, in opposition to the opinion that the science of natural phenomena was the sole model for science. Second, in opposition to the Cartesian *cogito*, Vico's analysis of the historicity of existence began the recovery of philosophical anthropology. In opposition to the meditative isolation of the *cogito*, Vico argued that reason is not an independent creative principle but operates only within the context of mythic creativity, both in the sense of the *senso commune* of gentillician history and in the awareness of the "transcendental irruptions in sacred history." Third, against the opinion that human beings are fundamentally good, Vico argued that they need providential aid to establish order. Fourth, as a corollary, the "contract theory" is simply false, as is, fifth, the doctrine of progress. Or rather, the sentiments that sustain the doctrine, namely the desire for self-salvation, were effectively eclipsed by his theory of the inevitability of the *corso*. Vico was, in Voegelin's words, "the first of the great diagnosticians of the Western crisis," and he saw that the most significant symptom of that crisis was the sentiment that relied on the individual human being as the source of order. Vico saw that the isolation of the individual was but a prelude to Caesarian monarchy.

The arguments that sustained Vico's five counterpositions help distinguish his *new* science of the *corso* from the existing or "old" ones, notwithstanding the fact that the sentiments of the "old" science are still with us as progressivism, socialism, and so on. In other words, what is generally seen as being modern today was already analyzed as being "old" by Vico's new science. "Modern political science, in the sense of Vico's new science," concluded Voegelin, "is a comparatively insignificant island in a sea of 'old' ideas." The principle of the *corso* and the category of the *mente eroica* as the substance that remained identical throughout the sequence disposed of the principle of classifying the forms of government and debating their relative merits. This is, perhaps, a signal indication of where Voegelin and Strauss part company. At the same time, the insight that the *corso* was the proper unit of analysis was limited, as was Toynbee's insight, because it amounted to a generalization of the Roman model and of the Augustinian understanding of spiritual history, the twin constituents of Vico's *senso commune*. "Here," Voegelin wrote,

> is the wide-open field of the new political science. With the increase of knowledge in empirical history, and with the increasing penetration of the theoretical problems of spiritual, evocative, and pragmatic history, we have to expect a development of the new science far beyond the scope envisaged

by Vico, an enlargement of which the studies of Schelling and Bergson, of Spengler and Toynbee, are hardly more than a beginning.

By the mid-1940s Voegelin was in the midst of developing just such a new science of politics. The arguments and analyses of the chapter on Vico in *History of Political Ideas* were presupposed in Voegelin's report to the American Political Science Association in 1943.

10

Schelling

———

The analysis in the previous chapters has made clear the principle by which Voegelin organized the materials in *History of Political Ideas*. First, he attended to the formative and evocative changes of sentiments and attitudes that are most apparent in the political realm; second, as a result of these political initiatives and activities, he analyzed the impact of new spiritual forces on other realms of human activity, chiefly philosophy, literature, and the arts. That is, in the political evocation of a cosmion, human beings engage the whole of the personality so that all aspects of the civilizational order bear the imprint of that effort. This does not mean, however, that the whole of the cosmion is a static entity, with clear lines connecting the political institutions with other spiritual or intellectual phenomena, but it does mean that the division of historical periods is to be sought in the sphere of sentiments, attitudes, and experiences that, in turn, influence the integration and disintegration of political institutions.

At the beginning of the modern historical period, it was a relatively simple matter to identify the personal and social forces that sought to acquire legitimate status in the world understood as existing within the age of Christ. The entry of the new worldly forces into the Christian order was accompanied by more or less coherent accounts of the newcomers' place and of their relationship to the world-transcendent divine order. Not surprisingly, as Voegelin remarked in his account of this activity, the newcomers were inclined to ascribe honorable and important functions to themselves as organizing centers for their own community, for a collection of related communities, for the Western world, or for the whole of humanity. All these structural changes in the order of mundane forces did not, however, alter the overarching structure of the one Christian age.

With the disintegration of the modern historical period, matters become complex in the extreme. For a comparison, one may consider the disintegration of the polis and of polis culture, which was in some respects similar to the disintegration of the modern period but took place on a smaller scale. Even there, however, the process was one of simultaneous integration and dissolution. As early as the texts of

Heraclitus one can find evidence that "the most distinguished citizen could not find a status in the community in keeping with his spiritual rank," but the polis was not destroyed as a political institution for another century and a half, a period of time that is conventionally identified as the golden age of Hellas.[1] Similarly, as we have seen with the discussion of the origin and growth of philosophy of history, the personality of a man such as Voltaire could combine a remarkable openness toward the integration of non-Christian and non-European social and spiritual order into a meaningful history with an equally remarkable superficiality.

If, following Voegelin, we identify the beginning of the modern period with the experience of spiritual maturation, one might expect to encounter a different complex of problems in connection with the period of disintegration. Moreover, from the Hellenic case, we need not expect to see a general collapse: the institutional polis outlasted the spiritual death warrant delivered by Heraclitus. Even so, in the case of disintegration one would expect that the questions dominating the public scene would be those that express and so reveal disorientation and confusion, "while the successful attempts at spiritual and intellectual orientation are relegated to socially obscure corners."[2] Accordingly, if one is to consider experiences of orientation rather than disorientation one must isolate those ideas that are systematically central and so furnish "a stable point of orientation" by which the surrounding disorientation, confusion, and chaos may be understood.

In this respect, for Voegelin, Schelling (1775–1854) was a central figure, not merely in terms of nineteenth-century philosophy but also in terms of resuming the *philosophia perennis.* Voegelin placed his chapter on Schelling at the center of the section entitled "Last Orientation" and described him as "one of the greatest philosophers of all times," but one whose life spanned an age of spiritual and intellectual desolation. This biographical contingency made his work even more important for Voegelin.[3] In the 1943 essay "On the Theory of Consciousness," Voegelin said that Schelling was the starting point for a philosophy

1. Voegelin, "Introduction" to "The Structure of the *Saeculum,*" in *HPI,* II:105–12. See also *OH,* 2:220 ff.

2. "Introductory Remarks" to "Last Orientation," in *HPI,* VII:175–77.

3. Voegelin had completed the Schelling chapter by mid-July 1945. A few days later he wrote to Robert J. Harris, his chairman at LSU, and mentioned the fact, adding that it was "a most important part" of his analysis of the nineteenth-century materials (HI 16/15). Some weeks earlier he had finished the chapter on phenomenalism and drew attention to the fact that he had done so six weeks prior to the atomic bombing of Hiroshima, which, he said, was a significant occasion in the development of phenomenalist obsession.

of consciousness.[4] Finally, in his *Autobiographical Reflections*, Voegelin indicated that it was "while working on the chapter on Schelling, [that] it dawned on me that the conception of history of ideas was an ideological deformation of reality." Ideas were derived from symbols that had been removed from the experiential context that gave them meaning; moreover, the term was inappropriate as a designation of "an Egyptian coronation ritual, or the recitation of the *enuma Elish* on occasion of Sumerian New Year festivals."[5] By 1989 when these words were published, Voegelin had been considering Schelling's philosophy for nearly half a century. In 1945 Schelling's immediate importance for Voegelin's political science lay in the fact that Schelling took up again the problem of natural philosophy where it had been left by Bruno and recast it as a philosophy of the unconscious. Moreover, there is nothing in this chapter by Voegelin that indicates he had abandoned the format of a history of ideas, though the emphasis is clearly on the importance of experience. Accordingly, we will consider Voegelin's interpretation of Schelling in the context of the history of ideas, much as Voegelin himself, much later, would speak about "permanent values in the process of history," even though the language of "values" was tied to contingent acts of will and so had nothing permanent about it. Indeed, in the same essay where Voegelin spoke about "permanent values" he added that the language of values was "the *caput mortuum* of a bygone era of methodology." The use of theoretically questionable terminology may be excused, if not justified, on the grounds that no alternative language "has yet reached the stage of common acceptance," and one does, after all, wish to be understood.[6]

In the discussion of phenomenalism in Chapter 3 we drew attention, following Voegelin, to the philosophical dilettantism of those who indulged in the act of substituting a field of phenomenal relations for substantive reality. It remains a gross philosophical error to look upon a theory of biological phenomena, for example, as an account of human spirituality, no matter how many individuals believe it. The acceptance of a half-baked opinion on a mass scale does not make it any less half baked. More technically stated, the substance and structure of the various ontic realms must be properly distinguished and related using appropriate language terms in order to count as a rational or philosophically competent "report." Moreover, if the "report" is to be adequate to the reality about which the philosopher presumes to report, an awareness of

---

4. *Anamnesis*, 50–54.

5. Voegelin, *Autobiographical Reflections*, 63.

6. Voegelin, "Equivalencies of Experience and Symbolization in History," *CW*, 12:115.

the order of the spirit is essential. On the other hand, if the order of the spirit is not a living reality in the consciousness of a philosopher, then the "report," whatever its merits in other respects, will be fundamentally impaired. Indeed, if we take rationality in a "report" to mean a coherent account of the full amplitude of reality, from matter to spirit, then any "report" that fails to represent the structure of reality will properly be called irrational. Finally, Voegelin drew attention to the fact that spiritual insights were preserved in communities by institutions devoted to the task. Saint Thomas had the Dominican order; Bodin had the majesty of the law in a royal state. In contrast, one might consider a modern intellectual such as Voltaire. Not only was he not much of a philosopher technically speaking, even his genuine virtues could not form part of a tradition because there was no institutional environment within which his sentiments could be handed over. The result, increasingly, has been that the spiritual realist "finds himself in an intellectual and social environment that is no longer receptive to the rational, technically competent thought of a spiritually well-ordered personality."[7]

The consequences of isolation and ineffectiveness were known to Voegelin as a matter of biographical fact. When the public stage was filled with different varieties of irrationalism, there could be no continuity of analysis regarding genuine philosophical problems. Instead one finds a succession of uncritical opinions advanced with sincerity, certainty, and great fanfare. It is impossible for the spiritual realist to take part without becoming a partisan, which, in turn, would mean abandoning the standards of realism by which such a person lives. By standing sufficiently apart from the disorder to analyze it, the realist remains socially ineffective. On the one hand, this means escaping the fate of Bruno, but on the other it also means, as Voegelin said in the closing words of his article on scientism, "that we who are living today shall never experience freedom of the spirit in society."[8] This consideration raises an interesting question: in the grand scheme of things is it better to have received the social consideration that leads to an auto-da-fé or the uncomprehending praise of the ignorant coupled with their pragmatic misuse of one's arguments. As Leo Strauss said to Voegelin in an analogous context, God knows which is right.[9]

In Chapter 3, we described the dissolution, under the impact of the new astronomy and natural science, of the unstable and precarious

---

7. Voegelin, "Schelling," in *HPI*, VII:193–242. Subsequent quotations from Voegelin, unless otherwise indicated, are from this chapter.

8. "Origins of Scientism," 494.

9. Letter of June 4, 1951, in *Faith and Political Philosophy*, 91.

synthesis of Christian spirituality with alchemy and astrology. Bruno distinguished clearly between the new science of phenomena and a substantive philosophy of nature; in place of a discredited alchemy he posited the existence of an *anima mundi* or a *cosmos empsychos*, a spiritual substance that lives even in material being and culminates in the reflective spirit of human being. As Copernicus, Bruno was motivated by a desire to order the world in accord with the speculative form of the mind. Moreover, Bruno was able to create a speculative analogue to the cosmos because he experienced his own existence as participating in an animated nature from the depth of matter to the One.

In the context of Bruno's speculation, Descartes's achievement was to have argued successfully against the unity of spirit and nature. The success of Cartesianism, from this perspective, was a work of destruction. "The result was the foundation of a critical epistemology that culminated in Kant, but we have to agree with Schelling that the Cartesian position was a fatal fall from the level of speculation that had been reached by Bruno." Kant himself was in an intermediate position comparable, in Voegelin's view, to the state of flux that existed during the controversy between Kepler and Fludd. The reason was that Kant's thing-in-itself is both inaccessible under the phenomenal surface of causal relations and immediately present to practical reason, which indicated "that there exists a problem of substantial identity between nature and reason that can be ignored, as it was by the neo-Kantian critique of methods of science, but cannot be abolished." The end product of the classic age of modern philosophy was its bifurcation into materialism and idealism, the one having reduced human spirituality to a manifestation of matter, the other having transfigured nature into a projection of the subjective ego. The first option was that of the French materialists; the second, that of Fichte.

The significance of this development is clearly expressed in Schelling's mature appraisal of Fichte.

As for the appearance of this idealism among us, it is only the expressed secret of the whole tendency that has increasingly prevailed in other sciences, in arts, in public life. What has been the aim of all modern theology but a gradual idealizing of Christianity, which is to say an emptying of its substance? Just as in life and in public opinion, where character, ability, and strength have been increasingly devalued, and so-called humanity, for which those other things must, after all, serve as a basis, now counts for everything, so also with God. Only a concept of God from which everything of might and power had been removed could suit this time: a God whose highest power or expression of life consists in thinking or knowing, everything else being only an empty schematizing of himself; a world that is nothing but an image, indeed, an image of an image, a naught of naught, a shadow of a shadow;

men who are also only images, only dreams of shadows; a people who, in the good natured effort to attain so-called enlightenment, really arrived at the dissolution of all into darkness, and lost also that barbarous principle (let the right word be used here in any case) that, when conquered but not annihilated, is the foundation of all greatness and beauty—such phenomena are indeed necessarily contemporaneous, even as we have witnessed them together.[10]

More than a criticism of Fichte was implied by Schelling's words. It was, in effect, a criticism of the age and even an anticipation of much of the critical effort of nineteenth-century thinkers. Voegelin cited it with approval.

The idealization of Christianity had emptied it: here one finds the starting point for Kierkegaard's criticism of bourgeois religiousness and his efforts at restoring a sense of Christian spirituality; it is also the starting point for Marx's attack on the opium of the people and an early formulation of Nietzsche's pronouncement on the death of God. For Schelling the death of God meant that God had ceased to live in human hearts and had been reduced to a thinking and knowing god. As a result all God's "might and power" had been lost and divine creation had become an "empty schematizing." Then followed Schelling's formulations— image of an image, shadow of a shadow, and so on—that recall Bruno's "accidences of the accidences." With the human beings who are "dreams of shadows," Voegelin said, "we recognize the phenomenalists in their world of phenomenal obsessions and actions." Finally there are the humanitarians filled with compassion and sentimentality, but devoid of strength and virtue, who have conquered barbarism only by mouthing high-sounding words. They are Vico's barbarians of reflection whose hollowness is an invitation to the sensuous barbarians to commence the attack, and a premonition of Nietzsche's contempt for the last man.

Voegelin's admiration for Schelling's achievement was not confined to a warm agreement with his criticism of the Enlightenment or of Cartesian rationalism. It is evident from the care Voegelin took in explicating the details of Schelling's metaphysics that he found in it what he had been looking for, particularly as concerned that aspect of philosophical anthropology dealing with the transition from the somatic or preconscious or, indeed, unconscious to consciousness.

Voegelin began his analysis with a presentation of several of Schelling's "aphorisms on reason":

10. F. W. J. Schelling, *The Age of the World*, trans. F. de W. Bolman Jr., 234. The translation is slightly altered.

(1) Not we, not you or I, know about God. For reason, insofar as it affirms God, can affirm *nothing* else, and in this act it annihilates itself as a particularity, as something that is *outside God*.

(2) The "I think," "I am," is since Descartes the fundamental error of all knowledge; thinking is not my thinking, and being is not my being, for all is only of God, or of the All.

(3) Reason is not a faculty, or tool, and it cannot be used: indeed there is no reason that we have, there is only a reason that has us.

(4) Reason does not *have* the idea of God, it *is* this idea, and nothing else.

(5) There is no ascent of knowledge to God, but only an immediate recognition; not an immediate recognition by man, but of the divine by the divine.

These aphorisms indicate that, for Schelling, there is in reality no substantive distinction between subject or ego and object and nonego. The terms are simply abstractions. In reality or substantively, there is only the One, God, the cosmos, which can never be an object of knowledge because in reality consciousness cannot get "outside" in order to posit God as object for an ego.

Voegelin accepted the rationality of Schelling's formulation; that is, it was an adequate linguistic expression of his exegesis of consciousness. In a letter to Robert Heilman in May 1952, Voegelin furnished his friend a commonsense explanation of the problem. He was responding to a suggestion from Heilman, who had read the typescript of *Order and History* seeking to remove any stylistic infelicities, regarding a proposed improvement. Voegelin was explaining why he was not prepared to accept one of Heilman's suggestions, although

> it stirred up extremely interesting problems in a philosophy of language. Let me give you an example: "This horror induced Plato . . . to make the true order of society dependent on the rule of men whose proper attunement to divine being manifests itself in their true theology."
>
> You suggest to change the end of the sentence to: " . . . in their possessing (or mastering) the true theology." I did not follow your suggestion, though I am fully aware that it would bring a substantial improvement in style, for the following reason: In the history of philosophy, from Plato to Schelling, there rages the great debate on the question: who possesses whom? Does man possess a theology or does a theology possess man? The issue was most strikingly brought into focus when Descartes' *Cogito ergo sum* provoked Baader's counter-formula *Cogitor ergo sum.* The immanentist "I think" as the source of self-assertive being is countered by the transcendentalist "I am thought" (by God) as the source of dependent being. If I insert the verb *possess* into the passage in question I prejudge a theoretical issue that is a major topic in the work—and besides I would prejudge it in the wrong direction. The only permissible solution would be cumbersome dialectical formula ("possess, while being possessed by" or something of the sort) that

would divert attention from the main purpose of the sentence. So I left it, though with regrets.[11]

The question of "who possesses whom," evident in the aphorisms on reason with which Voegelin began his discussion of Schelling, is both subtle and complex. Moreover, it was central to Voegelin's understanding of Schelling. Voegelin remained close to Schelling's text in his exegesis, and Schelling, like Vico and Bodin, was not an easy writer to understand.

In order to consider this "extremely interesting problem" in more detail, we will examine the 1961 Aquinas Lecture of Emil Fackenheim, which explored the metaphysical and anthropological issues raised by both Schelling and Voegelin.[12] Fackenheim's philosophical language was different from Voegelin's, though cognate with it. Moreover, just as Voegelin's political science began with the concrete political situation, so for Fackenheim "history is a predicament for a man who must live it." Human beings seek a perspective *on* history, which means they must be capable of somehow rising *above* history in order to achieve sufficient distance for the imagery of a perspective to be meaningful. The great problem accordingly is to distinguish what is merely fashionable or conventional from what is sufficiently exempt from contingency that one can speak of its "timelessness," rather like Voegelin spoke of "permanent values." This problem is particularly acute, Fackenheim said, not just because of the extent of pragmatic changes, or the famous "acceleration of history" about which Toynbee spoke. Matters have been made worse because of the "spiritual effects" that have actually accompanied the development of historical self-consciousness in the West.

In its most vulgar manifestation, historical self-consciousness is no more than historical relativism. Because we are aware that what seemed unquestionably true in the past looks highly questionable today or that what is accepted in one civilizational context is rejected in another, one might think that history discloses nothing but a variety of *Weltanschauungen* with no criteria for determining which is preferable. This is the starting point from which Glaukon and Adiemantus began their conversation with Socrates. In contrast to the spiritual drama of the *Republic*, the modern conversation has not ascended toward the vision of the *agathon* but has remained bound to the contingencies of history. Fackenheim

11. HI 17/9.
12. Fackenheim, *Metaphysics and Historicity* (Milwaukee: Marquette University Press, 1961). Subsequent quotations in the text are from the reprint of this lecture in Fackenheim, *The God Within: Kant, Schelling, and Historicity*, ed. J. Burbridge, chap. 8.

then provided an account of this process while leaving in abeyance for the moment the question of whether the actual development of historical self-consciousness was also its necessary development.

In this account, Fackenheim adopted the voice or style of Hegel's movement, *Bewegung,* of consciousness.[13] From the insights afforded by historical relativism, broadly understood, historical self-consciousness drew the conclusion that great purposes and great achievements have been based on great confidence and on great faith. As in the Bible, faith is the substance of things hoped for and proof of things not seen (Heb. 11:1). So, for example, one has faith in God because God is the truth; by the same argument, one has faith in progress because progress is the truth.[14] Looked at from the perspective of what may be called naive or unreflective historical self-consciousness, the problem is that such faith, such confidence, is missing.

The absence of faith leads naive historical self-consciousness into a position of "skeptical paralysis," an attitude of doom and gloom, demoralization, nay-saying, and a generalized lack of energy. Fackenheim did not indicate what moved consciousness on to the next position—boredom perhaps—which he called "pragmatic make-believe." In order to escape the paralysis of historical skepticism, but without recovering the experience of faith in God, consciousness, through an act of will, makes a determination to believe in something. It does so not because what it believes in is truth, but because whatever it believes in is a useful means of moving away from, or beyond, a position that has grown intolerable. Unfortunately such a believer is never unaware that he or she nevertheless does not believe, which leads to a new attitude, called by Fackenheim "ideological fanaticism."

Like the commitment of faith, ideological commitment is without qualification. But like pragmatic make-believe, ideological commitment is also conscious of being historically contingent. At this point the structural similarity between faith in God and faith in progress is clarified by a consideration of the more fundamental and more significant difference between the two kinds of faith. Ideological faith has no basis, no ground, outside history, and history, as contingent, is no ground at all. The form of historical self-consciousness that Fackenheim identified as pragmatic

13. Fackenheim was, in fact, an astute analyst of Hegel. See his *The Religious Dimension in Hegel's Thought* or *Encounters between Judaism and Modern Philosophy: A Preface to Future Jewish Thought,* chap. 3, "Moses and the Hegelians."

14. This is not to say that there is, *in reality,* no difference between faith in God and faith in progress, which would be absurd, but only that, in both instances the *structure* of the experience, indicated by the biblical formula, is the same.

make-believe knows this, even while denying it. Indeed, in order to deny it, it must know what it denies. That is why it is both self-conscious and "make-believe."

Yet, this consciousness is unable or unwilling to return to skeptical paralysis, let alone to faith in God. As with Hegel, the development of consciousness moves in one direction. What lay ahead was an intensification of the element of make-believe. Again, ideological consciousness is aware of what it is doing to itself as it grows increasingly fanatical. In Fackenheim's words, "unlike faith [in God], ideology must by its very nature become fanatical." When ideological commitments are challenged, there is no retreat to a truth untouched by historical contingency. One must push ahead "in" history and *make* it after one's own image of truth. "That is," said Fackenheim, "in order to resolve its internal conflict between absolute assertion and historical scepticism, it must engage in a total war from which it hopes to emerge as the only ideology left on earth." Under such conditions, ideological fanaticism might return to pragmatic make-believe. It would still be divorced from, or alienated from, the truth of reality, and it would know it, but if anyone pointed this out, which would be a hostile act, a quick recovery of ideological fanaticism would extinguish the opposition.

Fackenheim was very much aware of the political implications of his remarks, but his primary concern was to raise the nonhistorical questions of whether historical self-consciousness must lead to ideological fanaticism.[15] In order to answer this question, Fackenheim turned to "that most ancient of all philosophical enterprises, metaphysics," because metaphysics has steadfastly claimed that, however grave the predicament of history, human beings can rise above it, as did Glaukon and Adiemantus, toward "a grasp of timeless [and so not historically contingent] truth." Yet, since the time of Schelling, he said, the view has been advanced that, far from transcending history, metaphysical truth is tied to it. One of the consequences of this position is that it calls into question the notion of a permanent human nature: "What if the distinction between permanent nature and historical change is a false distinction: if man's very being is historical?"[16] Fackenheim called the account of this position the "doctrine of historicity."

15. Fackenheim here referred to Hermann Rauschning, *The Revolution of Nihilism* (New York: Longman's, 1939), and Hannah Arendt's *Origins of Totalitarianism*.

16. Fackenheim was precise in his use of philosophical terminology and so avoided the kinds of criticism, discussed in Chapter 4, that Voegelin directed at Arendt. See, however, the discussion between Fackenheim and Strauss: Strauss, *What Is Political Philosophy?* 57; Fackenheim, *The God Within*, 151.

Bearing in mind whatever qualifications Voegelin might advance, at least in his later work, regarding the status of "doctrine," Fackenheim is surely correct to say that the doctrine of historicity cannot simply be refuted *ex definitione*, that is, by a doctrine of substance or of nature that begins from much different premises and rests on much different assumptions and experiences.

Fackenheim drew a simple and commonsensical distinction between the doctrine of historicity and the study of history. The latter enterprise may show that human beings are subject to historical change and even, as with Toynbee's *Study of History*, that these changes are patterned, typical, or configured, but there is no implication that human being, qua being, is transfigured by this change. To take a more "philosophical" example: the traditional atheistic denial of the being of God does not touch the question of historicity, whereas Nietzsche's assertion, that God is dead, does. Fackenheim's first task, therefore, was to ensure that the doctrine of historicity is comprehended in the terms it required for proper understanding.

He divided this task into two parts: first, to describe the metaphysical assumption that allowed the doctrine to arise and, second, to indicate the metaphysical categories that maintained it. Only then, he said, could one raise the question of "whether the doctrine of historicity necessitates the surrender of the age-old idea of timeless metaphysical truth."

The first presupposition is that human action, which constitutes history, is free, whereas natural processes are not: they are caused and they happen. In short, there is a qualitative or ontological difference between history and nature. The assumption that action is free requires a second one as well, because it could be argued that the capacity for freedom presupposes that history is unable to alter this capacity, which would mean that freedom could be construed simply as part of the "nature" of man. This second assumption, which earlier was raised as a question, implies that there are no permanent natures distinct from the processes in which they are involved. In short, the second assumption is that human *being* is indistinguishable from human *acting*. By acting, therefore, human being constitutes itself. Fackenheim then described the implications in detail:

> To assert this is not to deny that man is largely the product of natural processes. Nor is it even to deny that he is the product of divine creation, or subject to divine influence after creation. But it is to assert that, apart from history, man's very being, *qua* being and *qua* human, is deficient. Man is what he becomes and has become; and the processes of becoming which make him distinctively human are historical. But what makes history distinctively historical is human action.

On the basis of the assumption that human being is historical, the study of human being, or philosophical anthropology, cannot be divorced from the study of human history.

Having identified the assumptions necessary for the doctrine of historicity to arise, Fackenheim then proceeded with his second and more difficult task, to provide an intelligible account of a process of self-constitution or, as he preferred to say, of self-making. To begin with, he said, such a process looks akin to the story of Baron von Münchhausen, who, after falling into a swamp, pulled himself out by his hair. But, Fackenheim went on, "a metaphysical doctrine may well seem unintelligible, and yet in fact be unintelligible only in terms of a metaphysics which is its rival." It would be necessary, then, to distinguish between the assumptions governing the "major" metaphysical tradition, for which the notion of self-making is unintelligible, and the "minor" tradition for which it makes sense.

Fackenheim began by considering the accounts of God that the two traditions furnished. The major tradition understands God as pure being, as creator of the world ex nihilo; the minor understands God as pure freedom who, in the act of creating ex nihilo, is differentiated into actuality. Philosophers who constituted the minor tradition included Boehme and, most important, Schelling. Indeed, Schelling was the source of the term Fackenheim used to describe the minor tradition. The major tradition, he said, was ontological and the minor was, strictly speaking, meontological.[17]

The meontological concept of God generates its own nonstatic, developmental, or "dialectical" logic, the terms of which are altered as the several moments of the process are (self-) constituted. More to the point, the major or ontological understanding of a self-constituting process can only be historical, whereas a meontological understanding of one process in particular, namely God, is more than historical without being eternal. Fackenheim called this in-between position "quasi-historical" and justified it by the following argument: the moment of nothingness prior to creation must be distinguished from actuality in order for there to be any process at all, but the two moments must also be an identity if the process is to be divine rather than merely historical or sequential.

17. F. W. J. Schelling, *Sämmtliche Werke*, pt. II, vol. 1, 288 ff., 306 ff.; hereafter abbreviated as *SW*. In *The Ages of the World*, 108, Schelling drew attention to the "grammatical" and "quite simple distinction between not being at all [*nicht Sein*] (*me einai*) and being which is not [*nicht seiend Sein*] (*me On einai*), which is to be learned from Plutarch if nowhere else."

But while *at least* quasi-historical, this process can also be *no more than* quasi-historical. This is because it must wholly transcend temporality. For while, because it is self-making, it appropriates the past into presentness, because [being divine] it is absolute, it appropriates the past absolutely and without remainder. And while, because it is a self-making, it anticipates the future as possibility, because [being divine] it is absolute, its anticipating of possibility is indistinguishable from its production of actuality. Indeed, it is senseless to speak here of either anticipating or possibility. Absolute or divine self-making, then, is only quasi-historical because it is eternal, or wholly present, a process symbolizable only as circular: for it is an absolute returning upon itself. And yet this eternity *is* quasi-historical. Something really goes on. Its end is, and yet is not, identical with its beginning.

In contrast to the ontological concept, the meontological concept of eternity preserves the moment of direction within it as what Schelling called a "self-renewing movement."[18]

This divine self-making does not, however, generate history. That is why Fackenheim called it quasi-historical. On the other hand historicity must be distinguished from mere temporality on the grounds that the former included the concept of self-making but the latter did not. Past and future are appropriated as recollection or reenactment and as anticipation. In the context of self-making, the past is other than the present effects of earlier events, and the future is other than possibility because both past and future enter into the constitution of human being. The historical present is likewise an active integration of future possibilities with past actualities and not merely the vanishing point of passage. For human being understood as self-making, such acts fulfill the condition that they constitute what an individual *is*, not what an individual *does*.

Historical acts nevertheless take place in the world amid natural events, and even though historical being is distinct from both temporality and eternity, it may lapse into a condition that approaches mere passage of time and attain heights that are near to transhistorical eternity. But so long as temporality is neither negated nor fully enveloping, historicity remains in-between and human. The concept that enabled Fackenheim to distinguish human historicity from the quasi-historical eternity of divine self-making and from mere temporality was the concept of situation. The situation necessary to situate a self-making must be other than the process of human self-making in order to ensure finiteness, but not wholly other, so as to be able to influence the inner structure or constitution of self-making. By so doing, the situation thereby loses some of its otherness. The relationship between historical or human

18. Schelling, *Ages of the World*, 116.

self-making and the situation is, therefore, dialectical. Again, human historicity is in-between. One may see this in a negative way as well because, if one ignores one or another element of the dialectic, then typically one falls into either the error of idealism, which regards all limits as self-limitations, or into the error of naturalism (or materialism), which regards the otherness of the situation as (eventually) constituting the self.[19]

The most obvious way in which human beings are limited is by the natural situation, which sets obvious and unbreakable limits to human self-making. In commonsense terms, one might say that human beings are, at least in the beginning, "dependent" on nature. They cannot simply be dependent, however, or they would never be capable of appropriating the past and future.

There is, therefore, more than one type of situation. Indeed, how the dialectical relation manifests itself depends on the type of situation in which the self-making is situated. Human action is not circumscribed only by natural events. Even floods and earthquakes, however, have human significance because they provide opportunities for initiative and not just occasions for a determined reaction. This is even more obvious with historical events—wars and elections, for example. The philosophical problem, therefore, concerns not the *existence* of historical situations in addition to natural ones, but the question of whether they are able to affect the very being of a human. If humans are understood simply in terms of a permanent nature, then historical situations affect only accidental manifestations; but if human being is understood in terms of self-constitution or self-making, the concept of historical situation is ontological as well as historical.

Fackenheim discussed the issue in terms of the individual's biological development and in terms of the collective actions of human beings, which is what we usually mean by history. So far as the individual is concerned, past actions, from the lowest form of subconscious influence, such as overcoming childlike innocence by facing up to sorrow, to the highest form of conscious recollection, such as being capable of doing higher math after having done lower math, in some measure affect the present human being. If human being is a self-making, then personality

19. Dualism between a self and a self-awareness is likewise unsustainable because initially the "self" would be passive with respect to self-awareness; but if it were also a self-making, then self-awareness would be wholly active and so able to overcome its limitations simply by becoming aware of them, and in this way eventually it would be able to overcome finitude. This is why Schelling called dualism "merely a system in which reason mutilates itself and realizes its despair" (*SW*, pt. I, vol. 7, 354).

is the history that begins with birth and ends with death, and "identity" is a process that integrates past acts of self-constitution into present ones.

Second, however, the actions of individuals are affected by the acting of others, including past acts. The possibility of citizenship in a polis, for instance, is not open to contemporary human beings. If human beings have a permanent nature, then the historical specificities of the twentieth century are irrelevant to that nature and to its essential possibilities. All one need do, under these circumstances, is recollect the occasion when the essential possibilities were first discovered and formulated, which may be symbolized as devotion to the study of Aristotle's *Ethics* and *Politics*. However, if human being is self-making, then circumscribing what contemporary human beings can experience and do will also circumscribe what humans can be and are.

As with the concept of the natural situation, the historical situation must also remain other than the situated, but not in the same way as nature because, with respect to the historical situation, both the situating and the situated are human action. The difference between the natural and the historical situation is that, even though both limit human being, the attitude of human being toward natural limits can only be acceptance, whereas the limits of a historical situation can also be appropriated as augmentation. For example, a lost childhood is forever lost, but one can appropriate Plato's work, cause it to lose its otherness, and by so doing augment, which is to say improve, oneself. The togetherness of both limitation and augmentation alone constitutes a situation as historical. Corresponding, as Hannah Arendt might have said, to the fact of birth is the possibility of novelty and initiative, of a new beginning, which constitutes the essential structure of a historical situation, whereas novelty in a natural situation is merely accidental. As a consequence, any initiative enlarges the scope of subsequent acting. And if human being is self-making, this implies that the scope of human being differs from one situation to the next and so, to the extent that human being is situated, that very humanity changes from age to age. This provisional conclusion is an echo of Vico.

Fackenheim then returned to his original question: if human being is a historically situated self-making, all activities, including metaphysics, must be historically situated. The case against a timeless metaphysical truth must therefore be overwhelming because metaphysics is only a form of self-making, and a transhistorical form of self-making appears to be impossible, if the self-making is historically situated. Such a conclusion means that metaphysics consists in aiming at what *seems* to be a timeless truth. This means that all metaphysical arguments really are just *Weltanschauungen*, though they are not recognized as such by the metaphysician; they are recognized as *Weltanschauungen*, however, by the historian. So the historian displaces the metaphysician, knowing that his own history of *Weltanschauungen* is also historically situated and thus subject to revision, but also that his position with respect to the history of *Weltanschauungen* is final in that no metaphysics beyond the history of *Weltanschauungen* is possible. This position, which refuses to distinguish between historical and metaphysical questions, is properly called historicism.[20]

Historicism, however, is untenable, and if historicity entails historicism, then the metaphysics of historicity is likewise untenable.[21] If the doctrine of historicity is not to collapse into historicism, it must make room for transhistorical possibilities of self-making. Once granted in principle, the claim of a transhistorical possibility cannot be confined only to philosophy. It must be extended, for example, to art.

More to the point, so far as the argument of Fackenheim was concerned, was his observation that it is easier to refute historicism than to understand it in a way that avoids the obvious inconsistency. According to Fackenheim, Hegel provided such a response. By his interpretation of Hegel, human being is a self-making made up of both finite and situated (and therefore human) aspects and infinite and nonsituated (and therefore philosophical) aspects. Both aspects, Hegel said, "seek each other and flee each other . . . I am the struggle between them."[22] Hegel's formulation referred to the experience that Voegelin has called the tension of existence. In the end, both Fackenheim and Voegelin would agree, Hegel let go of the "struggle" between the finite and the infinite and absorbed the former into the latter.[23] If historicity is to be maintained, however, human being must be understood as a tension or as "aspects" or "moments" that both seek each other and flee each other. The finite and infinite aspects must seek each other because human identity requires, if not an integration of the two, at least a search for integration; and the two aspects must flee each other because if ever they were integrated the

20. Fackenheim here cited Strauss, *What Is Political Philosophy?* 57.

21. Fackenheim here cited Strauss's arguments against historicism, which may be summarized by the observation: "History may stand in need of being rewritten in every age. The philosophy which recognizes this truth cannot itself stand in need of being so rewritten." That is, historicism cannot be true because, if it were, its truth would be universal and hence would invalidate its own principles. It is, therefore, not so much self-refuting as self-canceling.

22. Hegel, *Lectures on the Philosophy of Religion*, trans. E. B. Speirs and J. B. Sanderson, 1:65.

23. Fackenheim and Voegelin would not have agreed on *why* Hegel abandoned the struggle, however. I have discussed this rather complex point in *End of History*, 328 ff.

result would be either an all-too-human and self-canceling historicism or a superhuman Hegelian elevation of philosophy to wisdom. If human existence is understood as a self-making, then the unresolvable struggle or tension is what human being *is*.

This understanding, which conventionally is identified with existentialism, introduces a new question. If human existence is such a struggle or tension, then philosophy, which seeks to understand the struggle, must be a unique form of it. Such an understanding of philosophy, Fackenheim said, implies a revolutionary metaphysical cognition: the self-as-struggle that knows itself as struggle cannot detach itself from the struggle. There is no standpoint available for a dispassionate subject to gaze upon a world of equally dispassionate objects. Rather, philosophy too must define itself as an attempt to transcend the tension by understanding it.

> These attempts must be radically individual, made by each person for himself. But the knowledge attained through them is radically universal. For this is not a person's mere knowledge of his personal situation. It is his knowledge that he is both in principle situated and yet able to recognize his situatedness. This knowledge is universal; and the person who has acquired it has risen to philosophical self-understanding.

Philosophical consciousness, as Voegelin said, is always somebody's consciousness, and that person, as philosopher, becomes a representative human being. The correlate of such representativeness, Fackenheim observed, is that a new "situation" arises, beyond that of nature and history, which he called the human situation. It is not an "objective fact" because that would distort its individual aspect, nor is it merely personal, because, when it is acknowledged, it is understood to be universally human.

The human situation is not a source of additional limitations but the ontological ground of both the natural and the historical situations that in turn are understood as specific manifestations of the human situation but are irreducible to it. If the concept of the human situation is accepted, it leads to an important revision of the concept of self-making. So long as only natural and historical situations are granted, the autonomy of the self-making qua self-making is not challenged, and human being qua human and qua being can be understood, at least collectively, as a wholly autonomous human product. However, once the concept of human situation is accepted, this is no longer possible. Like the naturally situating, the other is not human; but like the historically situating, it contributes to the internal constitution of human being. The revision made necessary by the discovery of the human situation is this: human being must be understood as something more than a mere product and yet as something less than a self-making; it must be, rather than radical self-constitution, an accepting or choosing of something already constituted and yet also not fully constituted because the acceptance or choosing by human being is part of its essence.

Fackenheim's description of the dialectic between the self that is chosen and the self that does the choosing is very subtle. One is reminded of Saint Thomas's account of grace or of Voegelin's account of Christian faith.[24] It amounts, Fackenheim said, to the choice between the self and the authentic self. That is, the doctrine of self-making becomes, with the discovery of the human situation, a doctrine of self-choosing. In turn, this change in perspective entails the aforementioned change in metaphysical knowledge. If human being is simply self-making, then it is possible that metaphysical truths are affected by this self-making as well, and metaphysics as such collapses into historicism. But once human being is understood as humanly situated self-choosing, this possibility is precluded, because what situates a human being is not a human product but the condition for all human producing. Metaphysics, from this perspective, therefore, is the recognition or acknowledgment of the other as other par excellence, as an Other, Paul Ricoeur said, who draws near.[25]

This recognition means that the Other is not totally unknown, but yet not known, for if known it would cease to situate. Yet the recognition of mystery means it is not totally mysterious, just as ignorance that knows the grounds of its ignorance is not wholly ignorant. Traditionally, one would speak here of Socratic ignorance, an awareness of one's ignorance. Likewise the Other that, or rather who, is pointed to in ignorance is not wholly unknown but rather is given (several) names. "But the names," Fackenheim said, "express Mystery. They do not disclose it." After a hundred pages of close argument, the doctrine of self-making has come to a position where it must acknowledge that a reality other than man has a share in the constitution of human being, and it is neither less than human nor merely human, which has been implied by doctrines of human nature all along.

Fackenheim's analysis of the formal structure of a metaphysics of historicity clarified a major problem: because existence is individual, history is significant. If, therefore, reason is able to reach conclusions

24. Thomas, *Summa contra gentiles* III.151–53; Voegelin, *NSP,* 122, and the reference to Thomas, *Summa theologiae* II-II, qu. 4, art. 1. See also Søren Kierkegaard, *Either/Or,* trans. W. Lowrie, 2:218–19.

25. Ricoeur, *Freud and Philosophy: An Essay on Interpretation,* trans. Denis Savage, 524 ff.

that apply to the whole of existence, it can do so only by means of what, with some hesitation, Voegelin called a philosophy of existence, a reformulation of the problem discussed in Chapter 5 under the title of philosophical anthropology.[26] The specific achievement of Schelling that Voegelin appropriated for his own political science is suggested by a comparison of Kant and Schelling with respect to the question of revelation. Kant, as is well known, argued that reason is confined to experience. In place of what escaped experience, namely revelation, Kant substituted "philosophy of religion." Instead of asking whether God exists, philosophy of religion asks what religious experience is. The Kantian philosopher, wrote Fackenheim, "now seeks to understand in systematic unity all experience without exception. Among the data of experience is religious experience, which includes the experience of revelation. The [Kantian] philosopher must interpret, not the experience in terms of the revelation, but the revelation in terms of the experience."[27] But just this "autonomy of reason," as it is usually called, was for Schelling questionable, as it was for Voegelin as well.

Instead of "knowledge of God," which Kantian philosophy had dismissed, Schelling found "the life of the divine substance, animating the world and man as part of the world." The universal process animates the differentiation of specific relations among God, nature, and reason. As with Bruno, Schelling's speculation centered on the revelation of God in the universe. Unlike Bruno, however, Schelling had available a more adequate terminology so that he could distinguish the fundamental substance from the partial phases—God, nature, and reason—into which the whole process was articulated. "The fundamental substance is, therefore, neither matter nor spirit, neither a transcendent God nor an immanent nature, but the identity of the process in which the One becomes the articulated universe." Instead of breaking the process up into discrete units or phrases, Voegelin said, one must follow Schelling's description of the tensions of the soul: freedom and necessity, darkness and light, lower and higher, and so on.

The details of Schelling's *Potenzenlehre*, "perhaps the profoundest piece of philosophical thought ever elaborated," are secondary, for Voegelin's purposes, when compared to the significance of his philosophical

26. The importance of a philosophy of existence for Fackenheim was indicated, toward the end of *Metaphysics and Historicity,* by the number of references to Kierkegaard and Heidegger. See also Voegelin's comments on the title of his article, "The Philosophy of Existence: Plato's *Georgias*," in *Faith and Political Philosophy*, 62 ff., and Hannah Arendt, "What Is Existenz Philosophy," in *Essays in Understanding, 1930–1954*, ed., J. Kohn, 163–87.

27. Fackenheim, "Schelling's Philosophy of Religion," in *The God Within*, 94.

anthropology.[28] "Everything," Schelling said, "absolutely everything—even what is by nature external—must previously have become inward for us before we can represent it externally or objectively. If the ancient era whose image he wishes to sketch for us, does not dawn again within the historian, then he will never truly, never plastically, never vitally, represent it."[29] The past, nature, and so on, is experienced imaginatively (or inwardly) before it is understood. This is possible because of the substantive unity of the individual life and the cosmos, an ontological assumption that enables the anamnesis of the entire process to take place.

Of course, the past of human life and of the cosmos as a whole is in shadow, but it is not completely dark. "A light in this darkness," said Schelling,

> is that just as man, according to the old and nearly threadbare saying, is the world on a small scale, so the process of human life, from the utmost depths to its highest consummation, must agree with the processes of universal life. It is certain that whoever could write the history of his own life from its very ground would have thereby grasped the history of the universe in a brief synopsis.[30]

The human soul is, therefore, coextensive with the universe, including its creation, and the philosopher is simply the one who performs the recollection by way of mythology, revelation, the empirical sciences of nature and history, as well as by philosophical speculation itself.

Voegelin did not exaggerate the importance of Schelling in his *Autobiographical Reflections*, notwithstanding the fact that, in his later published observations, Voegelin's appraisal was much more critical.[31] Indeed, his exegesis of Schelling's philosophy of history sounds very much like passages from his own *Order and History*. Myth and philosophy, said Voegelin, "are the vessels of divine self-affirmation in the world through man" and are as much a part of cosmic history as is the history of human action. History, therefore, means both the course of events and the understanding of them as the meaningful unfolding of the cosmos. The internalization of the external process is possible, as we have already noted, because the soul that does the internalizing participates

28. Like Voegelin, Fackenheim had a high opinion of Schelling's work, calling his *Philosophy of Revelation* "one of the profoundest works in modern religious thought, equal in importance to the work of Kant, Schleiermacher and Hegel" (*The God Within*, 93).

29. Schelling, *Ages of the World*, 87.

30. Ibid., 93–94.

31. See the account of these later observations in Gerald L. Day, "Eric Voegelin and the Schelling Renaissance."

in the unfolding of the cosmos by endowing it with meaning, which it then discovers within itself. This "thesis," as Voegelin called it, may be summarized as follows: "the process of the universe can be made intelligible through an anamnesis by which the meaning of the external process is extracted from the unconscious in man."

The anamnesis, however, cannot be completed and transfigured into something like Hegelian science or "actual knowledge" because it is still a "striving for consciousness through anamnesis," which Schelling called "dialectic."[32] For Schelling, there can be no "end of history" because "the unconscious is pregnant with the time that has not yet become past." In Schelling's words,

> it seems all the more necessary to me first to recollect the nature of all that happens, how everything begins in darkness, since no one sees the goal, and the individual occurrence is never intelligible by itself, but only the entire event when it has completely transpired. We must also recall that all history, not only in reality but also in narration, can only be relived; it cannot be communicated by a universal concept all at once, as it were. Whoever wishes a knowledge of history must make the long journey, dwell upon each moment, submit himself to the gradualness of the development. The darkness of the spirit [the past] cannot be overcome suddenly, nor with a single blow.[33]

The truth that emerges from this speculation is never finalized as a complete vision or as a system. Rather it is a moment of a reflective process that must constantly be verified with reference to the anamnetic dialogue whose beginning and end are unknown.

At this point Voegelin introduced a new term, "protodialectical experience," in order to "designate the experience of the emergence of a content from the unconscious, still in the state of flux and vagueness before its solidification into language symbols." The experience, Voegelin said, is accompanied by various emotional "tones" such as anxiety, joy, release, melancholy, and so on, an awareness of which would be useful not only for the interpretation of Schelling's speculation but "generally for a philosophy of existence," including Voegelin's own.

For Schelling, however, the transition from unconsciousness to consciousness and reflection is a model for "the interpretation of the universal process" and is accompanied by vivid images of ecstasy, suffering, procreation, anxiety, and so on, all of which express the experience of the creative process. It is a process characterized, as Voegelin explained in the letter to Heilman from which we quoted earlier in this chapter, by

32. Schelling, *Ages of the World*, 86. See also Cooper, *The End of History*, 336 ff.
33. Schelling, *Ages of the World*, 94.

both passion and action; the individual in whom it occurs is both agent and patient, a link between the conscious and the unconscious.

Schelling's language was highly charged with striking imagery. Let us begin with the moment of passion and the suffering of pain, "something universal and necessary in all life, the inevitable point of transition to freedom." One must recollect such pain, both physical and moral, both human and divine, because "suffering is generally the way to glory, not only with regard to man, but also in respect to the creator. God leads human nature through no other course than that through which his own nature must pass. Participation in everything blind, dark, and suffering of God's nature is necessary in order to raise him to highest consciousness. Each being must learn to know its own depths; this is impossible without suffering." The moment of suffering, however, is followed by the moment of agency, of potency and action. It begins slowly, "as a gentle attracting, like that which precedes awakening from deep sleep." The powers are then "aroused to sluggish, blind activity. Powerful and shapeless births arise" and existence "struggles as in heavy dreams" that arise from the past. The conflict grows and these nocturnal births "pass like wild fantasies" through the soul, which experiences "all the horrors" of its own being. The conflicting tendencies in the soul are now experienced as angst.

> Meanwhile the orgasm of powers increases more and more, and lets the integrating power fear total dissociation, complete dissolution. But as soon as this power yields to life, it discerns itself as already past, the higher form of its nature and the quiet purity of the spirit arise before it as in a flash. Now, in contrast to the blind contracting will, this purity is an essential unity in which freedom, understanding, and discrimination dwell.

Finally, Schelling said, there is a balance between agent and patient, conscious and unconscious.

> The basic power of all initial and original creating *must* be an unconscious and necessary one, since no personality really flows into it. So, in human works, the higher the power of reality perceived, the more impersonally did they arise. If poetic or other works appear to be inspired, then a blind power must also appear in them. For only such a blind power can be inspired. All conscious creating presupposes another, which is unconscious, and the former is only a development, an explication of the latter.[34]

In dialectical language, the language of Schelling's philosophical "report" rather than in protodialectical imagery, one would say that the unconscious is not posited by consciousness as a solid ground but is

---

34. Ibid., 225–27.

something that human beings find opening beneath them, as a depth or darkness upon which they are nevertheless dependent. Whatever the human yearning for spiritual perfection, the nature, the raw being beneath human existence, can never be fully spiritualized or "conquered." This aspect of existence, for reflective consciousness, is colored by melancholia. Happiness, therefore, is a moment that rises above the ground of sadness and is experienced as grace, an inner return to spiritual perfection to be sure, but a fleeting one.

On the basis of such a philosophical anthropology, Schelling developed his account of political existence within the order of being. The fleetingness of the inner return to the divine, Schelling said, was expressed in the ancient myth of a Golden Age that is always behind us.[35] We ought not, therefore, waste our time in a futile search for it through endless advancement into the future. Schelling's reference to Kant's dream of perpetual peace indicated a road not to be taken. Of course human beings were not alone in the world, but the path to spiritual perfection was by way of the inner return. It did not lead to community action. Because human beings cannot (except fleetingly) exist in unity with God (and then only as individual souls that have undertaken the inner return), the myth of the fall of humanity is an adequate expression of its lost unity. In place of the lost unity, of the Golden Age or of the Garden of Eden, "behind" us, one finds a second-order natural unity, a remnant of the lost unity with the divine, the state.

The state, in Schelling's understanding, is considerably removed from what it might have been for Fichte or Hegel and is closer to that of Augustine: an intelligible order that is both a reflection of sin and the fall of humanity and a response to sin and the fall. The political order is the actualization of the intelligible order of the whole in the existing and historical world. The state, for Schelling, is not a constant political institution in history or a "regime." Rather it is a form of political existence that is part of the theogonic process of history by which a meontological Divinity externalizes itself into the cosmos and history, which moment is followed by a return to itself. The state, in this strict or theoretical sense, provides a shelter within which art, science, and religion may freely develop. "The church is not external to such a state but within it. The church can be 'external' only in a state with merely profane purposes and institutions; but such a state is no longer a state."[36] Such an institution is, to use Voegelin's term, a "power-state."

35. Schelling, "System der gesamten Philosophie und der Natur-philosophie inbesondere," in *SW*, 6:563. Most of this edition is available in the 1974–1976 reprint of *SW*.
36. Schelling, "System der gesamten Philosophie," *SW*, 6:576.

Political order, the state in the strict sense or, as Voegelin on occasion said, the idea of the state, indicated a reality that, in Schelling's words, "is older than all actually existing human beings and does not derive from actuality."[37] Schelling's political science, and Voegelin's for that matter, is concerned with political order as part of the whole of human existence in society at any particular historical period.

In contrast, the power-state is concerned only with the external and can achieve no more than external order. Voegelin then made explicit Schelling's criticism of Kant. In *Perpetual Peace*, written in 1795, at the height of the terror of the French Revolution, Kant tried to reconcile the "external" state, Voegelin's power-state, with the highest freedom of the individual. He introduced several ingenious arguments but was forced, in the end, to conclude that perpetual peace is *unausführbar*, unable to be put into practice, which provides Hegel with the opportunity for a rare joke: perpetual peace really means perpetual war. Likewise Schelling said that the power-state can neither sustain the highest and inner freedom nor maintain genuine unity. Instead, it can become only an "organic whole," as Fichte apparently sought in his evocation of the "closed commercial state." But an organic whole must follow the course of all organic beings: "to flourish, mature, grow old, and die," a course inevitably punctuated by war and conflict, and by additional evils that accompany the merely external struggle to exist.

In order to clarify Schelling's argument, Voegelin introduced a distinction between the state, or the idea of the state, and the power-state. It may be advisable to make a similar distinction with respect to the church. We have already quoted Schelling's remark that the state, understood as the order of political existence, includes the church. Because it is based on divine revelation, the church aims at producing "like-mindedness" or an inner unity among human beings. For purposes of clarity, let us call this church the "true church" or the "spiritual church." In contrast there exists, alongside the power-state, the institutional or hierarchical church. The distinction to be drawn is similar to that made several times by Saint Augustine in *The City of God* between the true *civitas Dei* and the ecclesiastical institution intermingled in the world with the *civitas terrena*.

By Schelling's account, the institutional hierarchic church was unable to resist the advancement of the external power of the state because it was itself, at its height during feudal times, also an external power. The political history of Christian Europe, therefore, can be understood

37. Schelling, "Philosophische Einleitung in die Philosophie der Mythologie oder Darstellung der rein-rationalen Philosophie," *SW*, 11:528.

as the story of a "movement from a feudalized, hierarchical church to a secularized, nonspiritual power-state." With the destruction of the single external hierarchy during the Reformation, the power-state, without any internal or spiritual purpose at all, displaced the medieval institutions that at least retained the dignity of a compromise with the "true church." The result has been a growth in tyranny directly in proportion to the degree to which a concern with internal unity was dispensed with.

So far as analysis of the modern power-state is concerned, Schelling established the principle that political science is not exhausted by an account of institutions and their history—the development from absolute to constitutional monarchy, the rule of law, the balance of executive, judicial, and legislative power, and so on. On the contrary, Voegelin said by way of summary, "the secular state must be understood in its very secularity, that is, in its relation to the spiritual substance of the community." The primary political problem for the political science of Schelling and of Voegelin is not the internal organization of the regime but the relation of the power-state to the community substance. In that relation are to be found nearly all contemporary political issues: stability and instability, rise and decay of regimes, their evolution and crises.[38] "If," wrote Voegelin, "the secularized state is not placed in the context of the spiritual history of the modern world, the political phenomena of an age of crisis must remain utterly incomprehensible, and their discussion must be reduced either to a dreary description of external events, or to ravings about the bad people who do not like good, liberal, enlightened democracy." If we may summarize the central problem of Voegelin's and of Schelling's political science it would be cast in terms of the relation of the "idea" of the state or of the true state, which includes a true or spiritual church, to actually existing political institutions. Voegelin illustrated the problem by examining Schelling's analysis in *The Philosophy of Revelation* of the tension in the ancient polis between official polytheism and the mystery religions.

The Olympian gods were the polis gods, ruling over the present age and over the poleis of the Athenians, the Spartans, the Corinthians, and so on. The Olympian religion was in conflict with what Voegelin called the logos-religion of the so-called pre-Socratic philosophers; the break was openly acknowledged by Socrates' contempt for the prejudices of

---

38. The catalog looks like an updated version of Book V of Aristotle's *Politics*. Just as Aristotle found the problem of equality and inequality at the root of *stasis* and *metaboule politike,* so did Schelling, though characteristically he cast his observations in historical language: all historical human beings differ from one another, and so are unequal, notwithstanding their generic equality as historically existing persons.

the "first accusers," *protoi kategoroi*, in *The Apology* (18b ff.), and the end of the polis religion was institutionalized in the apolitism of the Cynic, Stoic, and Epicurean schools. The Olympian gods were also challenged by the chthonic and other divinities of the mystery religions. Behind this well-known historical development, Schelling sought, in Voegelin's words, to understand "the evolution of the consciousness of crisis and the latent willingness to surrender the gods, and the polis with them, in the Dionysian element of the mysteries."

Schelling discovered three aspects of Dionysos. The Zagreus was the ancient god of nature and the underworld; the Bacchos was the contemporary celebrant at the public orgiastic festivals; the Iacchos or Iakchos was the Dionysos of the Demeter mysteries and ruler of the age beyond the life of the polis and of the Olympians. Just as, in the "orthodox" account, Zeus was victorious over Chronos, so will Dionysos-Iakchos succeed Zeus. The "content" of the Dionysos mystery, transfigured into dialectical language, is "the knowledge of the theogonic process and the presentiment of the end of the polytheistic world." The process itself has the sequence of (1) the underworld ruler of the darkness and depth, Dionysos-Zagreus, metamorphosing into (2) the Dionysos-Bacchos of the living, and (3) finally transfiguring through death and resurrection into the spiritual god, Dionysos-Iakchos. By this interpretation, the specific Greek consciousness of crisis was aware that the theogonic process could not be fulfilled in the political and cult life of the polis but must attain spiritual fulfillment beyond the polis.

This is a bold, perhaps an overbold, interpretation of Greek religion. No classicists of a philological bent are likely to find it acceptable, though some of Schelling's interpretations find resonance among classicists of an anthropological persuasion.[39] For Voegelin, however, it is not the cultic existence of a trinitarian Dionysos that is of greatest importance but that Schelling's reflections on Dionysos enabled him to develop a speculative philosophy of the unconscious that, in turn, Voegelin appropriated and modified. Shelling argued, in effect, that the god enacted through his myths a primordial process that was experienced directly in the consciousnesses of his followers. Let us, then, consider some of the "anthropological" arguments of contemporary classicists.[40]

---

39. The distinction is made by Walter F. Otto, *Dionysus: Myth and Cult*, trans. R. B. Palmer, 7. Obviously one cannot say that *no* philological classicist has *ever* made use of Schelling's approach, but a search of the major contemporary texts, editions, and commentaries does not turn up his name.

40. A useful general survey of classical scholarship regarding the topic is Park McGinty, *Interpretation and Dionysus: Method in the Study of a God*.

According to Walter Otto, for example, Dionysos-Zagreus is the great hunter who becomes hunted; he is the *anthroporraistes*, the "render of men" or, more exactly, the "crusher of human beings" who is himself crushed or rent. "The meaning of the myth," said Otto, "is this: The god himself suffers the horrors which he commits. That which the myth tells in words, the *cultus* repeats in regular sacrificial actions."[41] Dionysos has long been known for his ambiguities and oddities, the antitheses of ecstasy and horror, vitality and destruction. This god, said Otto, "the most delightful of all the gods, is at the same time the most frightful. No single Greek god even approaches Dionysos in the horror of his epithets, which bear witness to a savagery that is absolutely without mercy." In fact, Dionysos is not a true Olympian at all. As the son of a mortal he is akin to a creature such as Herakles who must, as it were, earn his place on Mount Olympus through great deeds. But at the same time, he was born again, from the body of Zeus. "This is the reason," said Otto, "why he is, in a great and complete sense, a god—the god of duality, as the myth of his birth expresses so beautifully and so truly. As a true god he symbolizes an entire world whose spirit reappears in ever new forms and unites in an eternal unity the sublime with the simple, the human with the animal, the vegetative and the elemental."[42]

The duality of Dionysos, furthermore, belongs as much to death as to life. Indeed, Heraclitus declared Dionysos and Hades, the god of the underworld, to be the same (frg. 15). Likewise, according to Carl Kerényi, "the myth of Dionysos expressed the reality of *zoë*, its indestructibility, and its peculiar dialectical bond with death."[43] In terms of Voegelin's philosophy of consciousness, the duality of Dionysos-Zagreus expressed a heightened or ecstatic "protodialectical experience" between life and death.

Turning now to Dionysos-Bacchos one finds most obviously the god of intoxication. He is, however, more than that: he is the god who is mad, the god of mania. For his sake, his attending maenads are mad. Madness, too, is a protodialectical experience, but what does it mean? Otto argues that, like the myth of Dionysos-Zagreus and the rites of the rending

41. Otto, *Dionysus*, 107. A *zagreus*, in Greek, is a hunter who captures living animals rather than one who kills them; he is a catcher of game. The purpose of live capture was to enable the captive animals to be ritually torn apart or "rent" and devoured raw.

42. Ibid., 113, 202.

43. Kerényi, *Dionysos: Archetypal Image of Indestructible Life,* trans. R. Manheim, 238. In Greek, *zoë* indicates life without further characterization or limit, whereas *bios* meant a "characterized life." See Kerényi, xxxi–xxxvii; the "indestructible life" of the title of his book is *zoë*, which naturally included death. Kerényi does not, however, distinguish Dionysos-Zagreus as sharply as Schelling.

maenads, mania too expresses an ecstatic experience of *zoë* between life (*bios*) and death. "He who begets something which is alive must dive down into the primeval depths in which the forces of life dwell. And when he rises to the surface, there is a gleam of madness in his eyes because in those depths death lives cheek by jowl with life."[44]

Simply in commonsense terms, whenever there are signs of life, death is also near. In everyday experiences one can say, without paradox, that one is most alive when near to death. In ritual, the experience of ecstasy and intoxication may be expressed as a meeting or an embrace of death and life. The experience, to use the distinction introduced earlier, is not that of a *bios* that has grown old and is tottering toward its end, but the border between love and death, the *eros* and *thanatos* about which Freud had so much to say. The Dionysian mania "arises from the depths of life, which have become fathomless because of death," and Dionysos, said Otto, lives in those depths. Hence his madness. "This unfathomable world of Dionysos," he continued, "is called mad with good reason. It is the world of which Schelling was thinking when he spoke of the 'self-destroying madness' which 'still remains the heart of all things.' "[45] Kerényi describes the mania in more clinical, but not in dissenting or contradictory, language as "a kind of visionary attempt to explain a state in which man's vital powers are enhanced to the utmost, in which consciousness and the unconscious merge as in a breakthrough."[46]

Of the three persons of the Dionysian trinity, Dionysos-Iakchos seems to be the least known to modern classicists. Indeed, what is known seems to be remote from Schelling's argument. Dionysos-Iakchos can be found at Knossos as *i-wa'ko* and had Egyptian analogues as well. These latter were helpful in moderating the scorching power of the star, Sirius, the rising of which signaled the advent of the hot season, the rising of the Nile, and the increase of fevers and epidemics. The Egyptian priests took fire from the altar of Iachim and used it against the destructive fire of Sirius. "Through Dionysos," said Kerényi, "this fire was transformed into the 'pure light of high summer' " and the "light of Zeus."[47] Schelling, however, saw in Dionysos-Iakchos something more, and in Aeschylus's play *Prometheus Bound* found textual support for it.

---

44. Otto, *Dionysus*, 136–37.
45. Ibid., 139–41; cf. Schelling, *Ages of the World*, 148, 227–29.
46. Kerényi, *Dionysos*, 134.
47. Ibid., 77–78. In the *Frogs* (lines 340–42) Aristophanes confirms that Iakchos "kindles the flaming torches, brandishing one in each hand / the light-bringing star of the nocturnal mysteries."

As with the trinitarian Dionysos, Schelling's interpretation of the "eschatological consciousness" of the Athenians has not found a great deal of favor among today's classical scholars. According to Schelling, eschatological consciousness increased among the Athenians between the period of the reforms of Cleisthenes in 508/7 and the Battle of Marathon in 490. The story of a controversy over *Prometheus Bound* was seen by Schelling as highly significant. The audience, apparently, was enraged because it believed he had profaned the Dionysian mystery. There was controversy as well over just what mystery had been profaned and over Aeschylus's defense, that he could not have been guilty because he had not been initiated.

Schelling presented the familiar Hesiodic story that is retold by Aeschylus. Probably, had the entire trilogy, which modern classicists call the *Promethia*, survived, the meaning of the whole would have been surrounded by less conjecture. Even so, the story line recounted by Schelling may well indicate what was involved politically. As we did earlier, we will first present Schelling's version and then suggest what aspects of it are confirmed by contemporary "anthropological" classical scholars. Last we will indicate what Voegelin drew from Schelling's account.

The bare bones of the story are familiar enough: Prometheus, whose name means "forethinker," was a Titan, a pre-Olympian divinity, who nevertheless had supported Zeus in his victorious struggle against the other Titans. But Prometheus had also given aid and comfort to the humans by bringing them the gift of fire from heaven, and for this act Zeus punished him by binding him to a rock in the Caucasus and sending an eagle to rip out his liver each day, which, being as immortal as the rest of him, grew back each night. Prometheus endured because he knew a secret hidden from Zeus. Zeus was in love with Thetis, a Nereid, but she was fated to bear a son greater than his father. If Zeus married her, he would suffer what he inflicted on his father, Chronos. Prometheus then struck a deal with Zeus: in exchange for his liberation he would reveal the secret. Aeschylus's version, we shall argue, was probably more complex than this Hesiodic summary.

Schelling believed that the secret was the mystery. Just prior to the famous scene near the end of the Aeschylus play, where Hermes visits Prometheus, the latter expresses to the chorus his contempt for Zeus: "Let him do and govern as he wills for the short time he has. / He will not rule the gods for long" (939–41). A few lines later, after exchanging insults with Hermes, Prometheus declared: "Have I not seen two tyrants already hurled from their thrones? / And very soon I shall see a third one, today's, fall to earth / more shamefully than his precursors, and sooner"

(956–59). By Schelling's reading, if the reign of Zeus was limited, so too was the cult of the Olympians and, therefore, the existence of the polis as well. He drew from this line of reasoning the conclusion that only one element of the mystery was publicly acceptable: Dionysos was the Bacchos of the present polis. The expectation of, and yearning for, the death of the god and his resurrection as Dionysos-Iakchos, however, was not acceptable.

The eschatological consciousness was confined to the mystery religions. Publicly it appeared only indirectly through the development of philosophy and the symbolization of God and the soul as transcending the polis and Olympian pantheism. The direction of philosophy was, therefore, to move the soul beyond the political realm entirely, to use political symbols to express experiences of realities beyond the limits of polis life. This new attitude was expressed not only in the famous "irony" of Socrates; when read as an ongoing spiritual drama, it also pervades the entire Platonic corpus.

At least some of Schelling's bold interpretation can be discovered in contemporary scholarship. Generally speaking the issue has been debated in terms of the "Zeus problem" within the dramas of Aeschylus. In its most specific instance, this "problem" concerns the harmonization of Zeus the tyrant with the Zeus reconciled with Prometheus in the second and third plays of the *Prometheia*. On occasion, the problem is expanded to include the treatment of Zeus in other Aeschylean dramas. For want of a better term, one may characterize many commentaries as being partisan, in the sense that they take the side of Prometheus or of Zeus.[48] The problem, particularly for the admirers of Zeus, concerns his evident injustice; it must somehow be changed or reduced, and this is usually accomplished by imaginative reconstructions of the two lost plays of the trilogy, the titles of which, *The Unbinding of Prometheus* and *Prometheus the Fire-bearer*, seem to indicate reconciliation. The argument in favor of Zeus's repenting is usually cast in terms of a change that reflects the evolution of the Greek or Athenian image of Zeus. This may make sense if one is concerned about the difference between the Zeus of Hesiod and the reconciled Zeus of Aeschylus, but it is more difficult to argue this position with respect to a change between the first and last plays of a single trilogy.

D. J. Conacher proposed a straightforward "political" interpretation. In the first episode (lines 193–396) Prometheus tells how he chose the side of Zeus, against his fellow Titans, in the struggle with Chronos.

---

48. A useful recent survey of the question is D. J. Conacher, *Aeschylus' Prometheus Bound: A Literary Commentary*, chap. 6.

Gaia, his mother, foretold that Zeus would win by guile, not brute strength. The Titans were offered "guile" in the form of Prometheus, but he was rejected; Zeus accepted him and his counsel, and won (212–21). By implication, had the Titans chosen Prometheus, they would have been the victors.[49] The element of political contingency is continued, by this reading, with Prometheus's fall (224–25), which was the simple result of "a tyrant's occupational mistrust of friends."[50] At the end of the play, Prometheus was sent to join his fellow Titans in Tartarus, but the other Titans were to be liberated. By this interpretation, then, the story is simply one of changing fortunes, changing alliances, power, and its connection to intelligence. If Zeus and Prometheus are to be reconciled, the element of political contingency must be given its due. At the same time, if Gaia's prophecies about force and guile—or, conceptually, about power and intelligence—remain valid, then Zeus must have survived on the basis of something more than brute strength—represented by Kratos and Bia (strength and violence) in the prologue and by the concluding cataclysm. Indeed, this has already been suggested inasmuch as Zeus had sufficient intelligence or foresight to see the advantage of the intelligence or foresight of Prometheus. A generation ago, Gilbert Murray suggested that Zeus had access to *zynesis*, understanding, and so was capable of learning.[51] If Zeus, who embodies force and power, is yet intelligent enough to change his mind, perhaps Prometheus, who embodies intelligence, can be forced to change his.

This problem was also discussed, indirectly to be sure, by Carl Kerényi. He began by reflecting on the differences between the biblical creation of *the* world by God and the creation, or more accurately the founding, of *a* world by a poet. A world in this second sense owes its foundation not only to the human poet but also to the stuff "from which the world is built and by virtue of which it is not a mere figment of thought but a subsisting 'order.' " This order, *kosmos* in Greek, was established by the protodialectical unions and marriages, births and battles, that constitute the mythical history of the beginnings that, taken in their entirety, are a theogeny. The order of *Prometheus Bound* is the world of Zeus; what is unparalleled in the play is that this world "is called into question on the strength of Prometheus' suffering and . . . of his knowledge."[52] His knowledge, indeed, is part of what raises his suffering above the

---

49. This version of Gaia's prophecies in *Prometheus* is Aeschylus's alone; it is absent from Hesiod (*Theogony*, lines 626–28).

50. Conacher, *Aeschylus' Prometheus Bound*, 39.

51. Murray, *Aeschylus: The Creator of Tragedy*, 101.

52. Kerényi, *Prometheus: Archetypal Image of Human Existence*, trans. R. Manheim, 33, 88.

bodily suffering of animals and connects it to his sense of injustice. In this respect Prometheus has adopted the experiential standpoint of human, not divine, being; more broadly, the trilogy called into question the world of Zeus.

Prometheus's prophecies to Io (907 ff.), whom Zeus has condemned to wander the earth in the form of a heifer, that she will bear a son who will overthrow Zeus, are to Kerényi, nothing short of astonishing:

> What amazing prophecies are these! Words unique in pagan Greek literature, expressing something very close to the expectation of a savior. . . . At the end of Zeus' work of world building it is also anticipated that he will marry, and with this marriage what he has founded will come to an end. An amazing possibility dawns: the possibility of a salvation from the intolerable oppression of the environing world, a transcending of the order of Zeus by something stronger which will grow from within it, for the order of Zeus encompasses all things that grow.

Kerényi's excitement at voicing this interpretation is clear; as he makes no mention of Schelling, we may infer he has rediscovered what Schelling had previously learned. Prometheus, he concluded, had taken an "imaginative step beyond the world, beyond the cosmos, and shows the essentially limited character of the realm of Zeus."[53] In order for Zeus's realm to be both "essentially limited" and yet also constitute the order of the world, the limitation must appear only within the context of a world-transcending eschatological vision.

Kerényi discussed this final problem (again indirectly) in his commentary on the textual aspects of the "Zeus problem." Hermes told Prometheus, near the end of *Prometheus Bound* (1020–29), what his defiance of Zeus would mean: Zeus's eagle feasting daily on his blackened liver, providing endless agony "until a god will freely suffer for you, / will take on him your pain, and in your stead / descend to where the sun is turned to darkness, / the black depths of death." In *Prometheus Bound,* we anticipate sheer suffering accompanied by the aforementioned sense, on Prometheus's part, of injustice. In *The Unbinding of Prometheus* the torment of a constantly renovated wound is accompanied by witnesses, his now liberated fellow Titans. He explains to them what happens to him and his helplessness: "I cannot keep that fell bird from my breast, / Reft of myself I wait the torturing hour / Looking for end of ill in hoping death."[54] The sufferings of

53. Ibid., 104, 105.
54. The few lines from *The Unbinding of Prometheus* are preserved in Cicero's *Tusculan Disputations* II.10.

Prometheus, now observed by the Titans, Kerényi said, "have taken on a new intensity." The Titans have, themselves, suffered at the hand of Zeus, and now they are onlookers at even greater pain. At this point, for the first time, "Prometheus clamors for death to put an end to his pain."[55] The *amor mortis* that Cicero quoted was new, and the source of the "intensity."

So long as Prometheus understood himself in terms of the immortal gods, he was not fully immersed in human existence and so could abide the injustice of Zeus in *Prometheus Bound*. But now, condemned to bear the bitter fate, the dolor, of human life, namely bodily pain, his immortality is rendered meaningless. Injustice *accompanied* by pain is fully human and can be concluded only by death. Hence Prometheus discovers the *amor mortis* at the same time as he abandons his last hope, that Zeus will be overthrown. Notwithstanding his cunning, intelligence, and foresight, Prometheus has been *forced* by imposed suffering to change. He has not been persuaded; no appeal either to his intelligence or to his foresight was made. This position, akin to that of Zeus, who embodies force but is not devoid of intelligence, Kerényi said, is "in between" (a characteristic Voegelinian term), in this instance "between full divinity and human vulnerability and suffering."[56] The only resolution seems to be that prophesied by Hermes at the end of *Prometheus Bound*, that another god die and suffer for Prometheus.

Kerényi provided reasons to think of Herakles and Chiron as teaming up to effect the release and deliverance of Prometheus. For two reasons one should speak of this release as a redemption and not merely as an unbinding. First, because Chiron voluntarily purchased the freedom of Prometheus at the cost of his own. But second, and more important, because "the possibility of a substitution proves that this is an existential suffering, not identified with any one person but inherent in existence." That is, because there is no gap in the ranks of the gods who undergo suffering, the significance of the change is more than theogonic; this addition Kerényi called "existential." Considered in terms of a theogonic myth, the fact that Chiron is not Prometheus and so is not in revolt against the order of Zeus is also significant. In this respect, Chiron is close to the suffering servant of Deutero-Isaiah. Herakles, by mistake, had caused incurable suffering in the beloved and respected physician; like Zeus, Chiron was a son of Kronos, and like Prometheus he was in pain and unable to die. Even less than Prometheus did he "deserve" to suffer endlessly; and this "innocence," if we may use a somewhat alien

---

55. Kerényi, *Prometheus,* 116.
56. Ibid., 118.

notion, was, in the vision or insight of Aeschylus, what made him a more satisfactory sacrifice.

This excursus into contemporary speculative classical scholarship (as distinct from nonspeculative, but indispensable, classical philology) has indicated that, however unusual Schelling's remarks may have been, they were not without foundation and plausibility. For Voegelin, in any case, the separation of official, orthodox, polis religion from the eschatological mystery-religions and from the polis-transcendent direction of philosophy was characteristic of "true" Greek politics in Schelling's sense. It informed his analysis of the Greek texts that later were included in volumes 2 and 3 of *Order and History*. Earlier in this chapter we quoted from Voegelin's 1945 correspondence with Robert Harris at LSU indicating the importance of Schelling for "the nineteenth century materials." Eighteen months later he wrote to W. Y. Elliott at Harvard that he had rewritten the Plato section in the *History* after having completed his studies of Vico and Schelling. In April 1947, he wrote to Friedrich von Hayek that the whole project of the *History of Political Ideas* had been delayed "because I had to insert long sections on the late work of Plato (*Timaeus* and *Critias*) which I had not understood properly before I had worked through Vico and Schelling. But now this last obstacle is overcome." Indeed, later that year he published his first article on Plato, a study of a portion of the *Timaeus*.[57]

Voegelin began with the observation, still true, that even though the *Timaeus* and *Critias* are explicitly identified as continuations of the much-studied *Republic*, they have largely been ignored by interpreters of Plato's political science. The reason for this neglect, he said, is that the content of the dialogues "is cast into the form of mythical poems; and the techniques for the interpretation of myths have only quite recently been developed to a point where the analysis of the late Platonic myths can be approached with some hope of success." Voegelin was concerned in particular with the "Egyptian myth" that opens the *Timaeus* (*Tim.* 17–27b).

The *Timaeus*, we said, was a continuation of the *Republic*, which immediately suggests that the argument of the *Republic* was incomplete and so in need of continuation. According to Voegelin, the "idea of the polis" was not fully developed in the dramatically earlier dialogue. In the *Republic*, he said, Plato developed the "idea of the polis" in two distinct forms, as the paradigm set up in heaven and as the *politeia* of

---

57. HI 16/15, 11/2, 17/3. Voegelin's "Plato's Egyptian Myth" formed the basis for the treatment of the *Timaeus* and *Critias* in *OH*, vol. 3, though Voegelin's attention to Schelling was more critical in the later work. Quotations in the following paragraphs are from this article.

a well-ordered soul (*Rep.* 591–92). The third form, the idea as the order of an *actual* polis, was surrounded by ambiguities, ironies, contradictions, paradoxes, and jokes. To use a modern image, Voegelin said, the description of a well-ordered and actual polis might be understood as the projection of an actual well-ordered soul. "The uneasiness about the status of the idea is the sentiment which leads from the *Republic* to the *Timaeus*." This "uneasiness" is evident when one asks: "what is the meaning of a well-ordered polis when its evocation is not the first step to its embodiment in reality?" The conventional answers, that it is a utopia or an ideal or the opinion of an alienated intellectual, were all rejected by Voegelin in favor of the view that the *Timaeus* transferred the well-ordered polis of the *Republic* from the status of myth to the status of an order in political reality. In this respect, he said, the results in the *Timaeus* were akin to the Augustinian notion of sacred history or to secular equivalents such as Marx's historical dialectics that effected an imaginary transfiguration of history.

Because the Christian Augustinian symbolism of a transcendent destiny of the soul in its pilgrimage toward the City of God was unavailable (as was the Marxist derivative), Plato was constrained to articulate his speculative transposition within the myth of nature and the rhythms of the cosmos. That is, if the idea is not *now* embodied in a polis and yet is (somehow) the "measure" of what is now embodied, it must have once existed (or will exist again), and we must be able to account for its present disembodiment. By Voegelin's interpretation, then, Plato in the *Timaeus* provides a "myth of the polis, as the 'measure' of society which in its crystallization and decay follows the cosmic rhythm of order and disorder." The literary device that Plato used to convey this evocation of a measure that is embodied and disembodied, and so exists beyond the time of the evocative soul of the philosopher, is found in the dramatic context of the *Republic* and its connection to the dramatic sequel, the *Timaeus*.

By the dramatic context of the *Republic* and the *Timaeus*, the following considerations are meant. First, the *Republic* was not an original dialogue but a report by Socrates of a discussion that took place a day earlier, presented, as the opening pages of the *Timaeus* indicate, to Critias, Timaeus, Hermocrates, and a fourth unnamed person. In the *Timaeus* the unnamed person is absent, apparently owing to illness. Socrates reviewed some of the topics of the *Republic,* ignored others, and gained the assent of Timaeus that he had gone over the main points (*Tim.* 19a). Socrates then described his own sentiments: the account in the *Republic* was like the portrait of a beautiful creature at rest; one desires to see it in motion as well. So far as the polis of speech of the *Republic* is concerned, this meant considering its struggles and wars with its neighbors. "In brief," said Voegelin, "what we should like to have is an epic celebrating the historical struggles of the polis." Socrates, however, cannot undertake such a task, but neither could the poets or sophists, for reasons made plain in the *Republic* and elsewhere. Thus he turns to his companions.

Hermocrates replies that, in fact, on the way home the night before, Critias remarked that Socrates's report in the *Republic* recalled to his mind a logos brought forward from long ago about the early city. Critias heard the logos from his grandfather, also named Critias, and his grandfather from Solon, who was a friend of Dropides, the father of Critias the elder, and so the great-grandfather of the present Critias. Solon in turn had heard the logos from the priests at Sais, in the Nile delta. Sais had been founded by a god that they thought was identical to Athena, making them, the Saites, related to the Athenians. Solon and the priests exchanged logoi, and he found that they had knowledge of things far earlier than the most remote memories of the Greeks. The Greeks, said one of the priests, were like children, "young in soul" (22b). The reason, he explained, is that at long intervals the earth undergoes catastrophes, usually by fire or water. These are retained in memory in the form of the myth (*mythos*), the truth of which is that the catastrophes have been caused by deviation (*parallaxis*) in the heavenly bodies (22d). When this happens, the priests of Sais explained, only a few survive, and with them, the memory of the terrible events. Owing to its favorable geography and climate, Egypt escaped these periodic catastrophes, which enabled the Egyptians to recall them. In contrast, Athenians such as Solon recall nothing prior to the last deluge (23b). Hence the youthfulness of their souls. More specifically, the priest of Sais went on, the Athenians did not know that the previous Athens, which was founded 1,000 years before Sais, the records of which go back 8,000 years, was peopled by the most beautiful, well-governed, and victorious people. The laws and institutions of Sais, in fact, were copied from the Athens of 9,000 years earlier. The greatest achievement of the early Athens, Solon heard, was the defeat of Atlantis, a mighty island empire west of the Pillars of Herakles that was subsequently destroyed by an earthquake, along with the Athenians who, by their victory, saved the entire Mediterranean world from slavery (25d).

The sequence, from Socrates's evocation of the philosopher's polis of speech in the *Republic* to the contemporary Critias, to the older Critias, the logoi of Solon and the Saitic priests, "broadens the collective memory." Moreover, the polis itself becomes increasingly real as it proceeds from the medium of speech in the *Republic* to the imitation of Sais, to the original Athens of the preceding aeon. The ascent in time to the original

Athens is balanced by the descent of the idea into the Socratic present, and the sequence of logoi that concludes with the logos of the priests explaining a *mythos* of the Athenians is carefully interwoven with the sequence of youth and age.

The chronologically as well as civilizationally young Solon received the logos from the chronologically and civilizationally old men of Sais. Solon, now an old man, hands it on to a boy, the elder Critias, son of his friend Dropides. The younger Critias, at a festival when boys are admitted to the phratries, hears the story from the ninety-year-old elder Critias, after the boy's friend Amynander praises the poems of Solon. In the dialogue *Timaeus*, then, the logos of Solon is embedded in the report by the present Critias of a conversation between the older Critias and the young Amynander. On the present occasion, the evening reported in the *Timaeus*, the dialogue of the older Critias is blended by the younger Critias into the present conversation, which in turn continues the conversation of the *Republic*, a report by Socrates at which the younger Critias, who is now himself an old man, was present.

The present Critias did not, however, continue the sequence and hand the story over to the younger generation, which, in the *Republic*, was represented by Glaukon and Adeimantus. Instead, Critias himself had to recover the story of his youthful memories by anamnesis, after hearing the report by Socrates in the *Republic*. He began the anamnesis on the walk home, continued it during the night, and just after dawn related the logos to Timaeus and Hermocrates (20c–d, 26b–c). "The old man Critias," Voegelin observed, "thus is informed through the memory of the young Critias. Youth is the repository of the idea, and age can get access to it through anamnesis." In the *Statesman*, Voegelin said, "the symbolism expressing the insight was explicitly treated: the world was released by the gods as young and perfect but grew worse the farther it was removed in time from its divine origin, and the youth of the origin has to be recovered through the anamnesis of age." This is what Critias did, which implies that the era of the *Timaeus* is near the end of the 9,000-year cycle at the beginning of which the victory of Athens over Atlantis took place.

The time of the *Timaeus* is during the old age of the world, which is a time for old men to recapture through anamnesis the youth of the idea. The dramatic setting of the *Timaeus*, like the setting of the report delivered by Socrates the previous night, the *Republic*, is an evening of old men. The Socrates of the *Timaeus* and the reporter of the *Republic*, unlike the Socrates who converses with the young men in the *Republic*, is concerned with the mature confirmation, not the youthful conversion, of his interlocutors. The confirmation of the *Timaeus*, said Voegelin, "adds the historic dimension to the polis" of the idea advanced in the *Republic* as the "projection" of the Socratic soul. Critias's summary, his recounting of the logos of Solon, can now be expounded in detail. "And," said Critias, "the polis and its citizens, which you [Socrates] described yesterday [in the *Republic*] in the order of myth (*en mytho*) we shall now transpose into the order of reality. We will imagine that the polis is the ancient polis of Athens, and declare that the citizens you [Socrates] imagined [in the *Republic*] are in truth our progenitors, as the priest said" (26d). That is, the citizens of the *Republic* are the same citizens who live in the Athens of the previous aeon. Socrates agrees with the logos of Critias and adds that it is all-important that his logos be not a *mythos* but a true logos (*alethinos logos*). If nothing else, Voegelin's close reading of the text indicates the great subtlety of Plato's poetic art.

In order to indicate the meaning of this poetic achievement, Voegelin said, we must undertake an analysis not only of the speeches and actions of the dramatis personae but also of the experiences of the author who created them. This means that there is, for Voegelin, no historical signif- icance to the interlocutors, the Egyptian logos of Solon, the war between Athens and Atlantis, and so on. Adopting this ahistorical perspective on the *Timaeus* and on its connection to the *Republic*, "we are prepared to interpret the dialogue as a drama within the soul of Plato." From this interpretative position, the Socrates who, in the *Timaeus*, is dissatisfied with the polis of speech of the *Republic* expresses the experiences of Plato, or is the "projection" of the Platonic soul. Likewise the Critias who undertakes the anamnetic search for the true or full idea of the polis also expresses the experiences of the Platonic soul. Schelling's interpretation of the Aeschylean soul was, in short, a model of Voegelin's interpretation of the Platonic. "It is Plato," wrote Voegelin, "who finds Atlantis through anamnesis; and the youth in which he finds it is neither that of Critias [the dramatic character or the historical person], nor his own [youth] in a biographical sense, but the collective unconscious which is also living in him." The *collective* aspect of this unconscious is symbolized by the logos of its transmission; the transmission from *remote antiquity* indicates a threefold dimension of depth: first, the "collective soul" of the Athenian people, in the transmission from Solon to the younger Critias; second, beyond Athens, the "generic collective soul of mankind" in the transmis- sion from old Athens to Sais, from which the logos of Solon originated; and third, beyond the generic soul of mankind, "the primordial life of the cosmos" from which human being sprang, in the transmission from the gods. The mythic forces of the Socratic soul in the *Republic*, namely Eros, Thanatos, and Dike, and the paradigm set up in heaven are, in the *Timaeus*, "authenticated by the assent of the unconscious."

In other words, the philosopher, listening to the logos told by Critias in the *Timaeus*, understands its truth upon hearing it. The mythic forces that "orient the individual soul towards the Agathon" in the *Republic* are now supplemented by the mythic forces of the collective soul that "reach, in its depth, into the life of the cosmos." In the *Timaeus*, the life of the individual soul, which animates the speculation of the *Republic*, is supplemented by other forces. Socrates, in the *Timaeus*, represents the life of the individual soul, and he is present as having motivated the present dramatic gathering, but he effectively is silent. The task that Socrates began in the *Republic*, and that brings the interlocutors together for the *Timaeus*, is carried forward by others. The significance of the dramatic presence of characters other than Socrates is Plato's way of acknowledging, or assenting to, his debt to natural cosmic, human, and Athenian rhythms. In this respect Bodin, with his *Republic*, the *Theatrum Naturae*, and the *Colloquium Heptaplomeres*, followed Plato's *zetema* from the individual soul through his society to humanity and the divine cosmos.

In the dialogues named after them, Timaeus and Critias were the main speakers. Timaeus, the astronomer, described the creation of the cosmos down to the appearance of human being, which reflected "Plato's acknowledgment of his debt to the Pythagoreans who awakened in him the sense for the fundamental measure and rhythm of nature." The task was carried further, then, by Critias, who told of the heroic prehistory of Athens and of its war with Atlantis, which was "Plato's acknowledgment of his debt to Athens, and its aristocracy to which he belongs." Critias retold a logos he heard from the older Critias, his grandfather and a representative of the generation of Marathon. Voegelin concluded his reflection on this aspect of Plato's symbolism with the observation that the idea of the polis had grown "because in the life of the soul the solitude of contemplation," symbolized by the Socrates of the *Republic*, "is now in harmony with the transpersonal rhythms of the people, of the human race and of the cosmos." Accordingly, the contemplative philosopher was no longer simply in revolt against the actuality of Athenian history, symbolized in the murder of Socrates by the Athenians; rather, the philosopher had recovered "strength and support in the youth of the unconscious," which, again as with Bodin, provided a more comprehensive context than the sheer conflict between the philosopher and the city.

The concluding section of this article contained Voegelin's reflections on the role of Plato, who was now understood as the poetic creator of the myth. The Solon of the *Timaeus*, which was provisionally identified with Plato, did not, Voegelin said, represent the whole Platonic personality but only one aspect or "stratum" that, in the *Republic,* was symbolized by Socrates. In the *Timaeus,* Socrates, or what one might call the political element of the Platonic soul, declared, as we pointed out above, that he was not equal to the task of singing the praise of the polis (*Tim.* 19d) and neither were the poets. In the *Timaeus,* Socrates hands the task of singing the praise of the polis over to Timaeus and Critias, who, Voegelin argued, represent "the strata of the unconscious (the 'Egypt,' the 'youth') from which Plato has, through anamnesis, extracted the saga of Atlantis." The *Timaeus,* in other words, moved beyond the active politics presented, with considerable qualification, in the *Republic.* This was indicated dramatically by having the Socrates-Plato of the *Republic* lapse into silence in the *Timaeus* and disappear altogether in the *Laws.* In the *Timaeus,* however, Timaeus-Plato "will sing the poem of the idea."

The poetry of the idea is the aforementioned *alethinos logos* that transformed the Socratic *polis en logois* of the *Republic* into a myth in the *Timaeus.* The source of the truth of the logos in the *Timaeus* is "the symbolic 'youth' or 'Egypt' of the unconscious. In comparison with this truth, which is drawn most reliably from the depth of the soul itself, all other realities pale into the secondary truth of appearance or fable." In short, the poetry of the idea in the *Timaeus* did to the *Republic* what the myth of the Socratic soul in the *Republic* did to the mimetic truth of the Homeric epic, namely turn what once was a truth into an untruth, a "myth."

Voegelin concluded his article with a "Note" drawing attention to the parallels between Plato and Schelling. Systematically, both philosophers explored the relations between the idea and the unconscious. In addition Voegelin made a remark that reminds one of Vico and Toynbee. The reader, he said, "should observe in particular the parallel in the historical positions of the two philosophers: in both cases the philosophy of the unconscious becomes of systematic importance in the course of a reaction against the preceding Age of Enlightenment." The criticism of mimetic poetry in the *Republic,* or rather of its enlightened misuse, is evidence of "the advancement from the myth of the people to the new level of spiritual conscious." This "advancement," which Voegelin later called differentiation of consciousness, had two distinct aspects. First, it was "an event in the spiritual history of mankind" that was followed by other "events" such as the establishment of Christianity. But, second, it was a typical rather than a unique event: "the break of the mystic with the traditional forms of expression is an event which recurs in every civilization in its late phase of disintegration when the traditional forms are losing their value as adequate instruments of expression because the substance which they can express adequately is dissolving, while the substance of the mystical personality cannot be expressed in them adequately at all." With the arrival of Vico's "barbarism of reflection," mimetic art will necessarily fall into crisis because the social reality of which it is the mimesis is disintegrating or otherwise undergoing a crisis.

These general observations, which were developed on the basis, as Voegelin said in his letter to Elliott, of his studies of Vico and Schelling, provided the context for Voegelin's interpretation of Plato. They apply as well, however, to Voegelin's analysis of Schelling's argument regarding the conflict between official, orthodox polis religion and the eschatological mystery religions that Schelling discovered in his analysis of Aeschylus. More specifically, the division between orthodoxy and mystery religion indicated, to Schelling and to Voegelin, a significant difference between Hellenic and medieval Christian politics. For Christianity, eschatological consciousness was at the symbolic center of religious practice—the death and resurrection of Christ—so the Hellenic solution to the problem of the disruption that accompanied eschatological spiritual movements was ruled out. Instead, Christian spirituality was accompanied by what Voegelin called "subeschatologies," heterodox perhaps, but tolerable, and so capable of institutional integration into the hierarchy and discipline of the church. On occasion, however, they could be dealt with by the church only by persecution and suppression. With the institutional breakdown of the church the conflicts between the several "subeschatologies" became public and political, most recently, according to Voegelin, in the secular form of ideological wars and revolutions.

In Hellas, eschatological consciousness was never a source of political revolution. There was no Hellenic Joachim who sought to transform the civilization inwardly through the eschatological invocation of a Third Realm. The Third Dionysos, the Dionysos-Iakchos, was confined to the mysteries. But the god was there, and Schelling found him. Or, more scientifically stated, Schelling was able to recollect by his own anamnesis the experience of the presence of Dionysos-Iakchos, to reconstitute it in his own soul and to report on the event, which, Voegelin said, "leads us back to the historical existence of Schelling himself." On the basis of Schelling's own argument, history is the amalgamation of the materials, the evidence obtained by available historical and philological means, with the meaning that welled up from the depth of Schelling's unconscious. In Chapter 5, we saw this same argument applied by Voegelin to his own consciousness rather than to that of another. Just as Voegelin had become aware of his own experiential search for "wider horizons," so too was Schelling able to discover the spiritual movement toward Dionysos-Iakchos through actual experience. Specifically, Voegelin said, he saw in the evocation of Dionysos-Iakchos a "spiritual foreshadowing" of Christianity. Schelling was able to undertake this imaginative enterprise, Voegelin said, "because he stood himself in the parallel situation of the Christian crisis." The Roman Catholic or Petrine church had been followed by the post-Reformation Pauline churches; what was to come was a third, Johannine Christianity.

Notwithstanding some Joachitic touches, Schelling did not await an incarnation of the new spirit in a new leader.[58] He expressed his sentiments instead in a desire for a more profound understanding of the experiential problem that sustained a desire for a new leader, for the renovation of the Pauline into the Johannine church, or for new mythic creations. The source of a desire for a mythic resolution of the spiritual crisis was to be found in the destruction of the creativeness of the mythic imagination, a destruction, Voegelin said, "that is inevitable when the 'world' is a *saeculum senescens*." The implication of the Augustinian term was that during the old age of the world there is no world-immanent meaning, which is to say that Voegelin understood his own historical position to be akin to that of the dramatis personae of the *Republic* and the *Timaeus*. At the same time, however, we have noted that Voegelin pointed out several times in the course of writing *History of Political Ideas* that such an understanding was not accepted by ever-growing numbers of Europeans, beginning in the thirteenth century. However true it may be that the soul "has to find the fulfillment of life beyond life," it remains true that some purposes are to be found in "a living nature" and that those experiences also demand expression. Such demands, Schelling concluded, are met by myths that represent and express the purposes of intramundane existence.

Within any particular community mobilized in pursuit of one or another intramundane aim, one finds myths of founders and protectors, of heroes and saviors, of civilizing missions, manifest destinies, and the natural evolution of a people. Moreover, such myths often coexist with the community-transcending symbolism of the mystical body of Christ. "We are," Voegelin observed, "living in a mixed religious system of Christian monotheistic spirituality and a polytheism of particular

---

58. In *OH*, 3:193, Voegelin criticized Schelling not for his Joachitic allegiances but for a "gnostic inclination to intellectualize the unconscious and to reduce its movement to the formula of a dialectical process." Voegelin did not indicate which of Schelling's texts he had in mind; in any case, Voegelin advanced this criticism of Schelling on solid Schellingian grounds, namely the insight that "protodialectical experiences" are impenetrable by consciousness, an insight Voegelin said was more adequately safeguarded by Plato, whose "myth always preserves its character as the transparent flower of the unconscious."

communities and movements." So long as humanity as a whole is not envisaged as having an intramundane purpose and thereby requiring a suitable intramundane monotheism, such syncretism may impose strains, but they are not intolerable: the fate of "the nations" has been separable since Augustine's day from the spiritual destiny of humanity.

Schelling, however, was not a nationalist or narrow community sectarian. For him the spiritual crisis concerned humanity and civilization as a whole. It could be met only with a mythic evocation of nature as the source of a common intramundane destiny. Voegelin called this effort by Schelling "a curious inversion of the Dionysian evolution." In Schelling's argument, Dionysos-Iakchos is the image of the future divinity beyond the polytheism of the polis. It is a movement *away* from the natural imagery of Dionysos-Zagreus and the intermediate form of Dionysos-Bacchos. In the Christian era, speculation of the Joachitic type must evoke a god (or a leader) who is more worldly than the Holy Spirit. Likewise, within the experiential horizon of the Dionysian age, Schelling reversed the differentiation of consciousness from the Third Dionysos back to Dionysos-Bacchos. "This inversion," said Voegelin, "is precisely what Schelling envisages as the solution of the civilizational crisis." The general outline of his solution was presented in Schelling's philosophy of art.

The age, Schelling said, lacks art comparable to that of the Greeks. The absence was felt especially in the lack of genuine tragedy. The problem, he said, is not that there is no talent, but that the material for the artist to work is missing. It is too raw, too elemental. In order for an artist to operate properly, the material must already be "organic" or "symbolic." But why is there no symbolic material available? Because, Schelling said, there are no natural symbols, no myths that live in the hearts and souls of human beings, as once the gods lived in the polis. Myths relate images to nature, where symbols are generated and to which they refer. "The things of nature mean and are at the same time," he said. "The glorious thing about the ancient gods of mythology is that they were not just individuals, not just historical beings as are the figures of modern poetry. They were not transient appearances but eternal essences of nature who intervene and act in history and at the same time have their ground in eternal nature, who are generic by being individuals."[59] The first step toward the restoration of a genuine mythology, and so of a genuine art, must be the recovery of a symbolic view of nature.

Because such a mythic consciousness cannot be gained in a society of diffuse individuals or divided nations, the precondition for the new

59. Schelling, *SW*, 6:571 ff.

mythology is the reunification of humanity. Under present conditions, only a partial mythology is possible, "not a universal and generically symbolic one." But the example of a polis indicated that, where a political community exists in spiritual unity with "a truly public life," then a "true and universally valid poetry can emerge."[60] In order to combine the spiritual unity of a polis with the universality of the Christian logos, Voegelin said, "Schelling dreams of a public state under the condominium of Dionysos-Bacchus and the spirit of Christ." Under the influence of Dionysos-Bacchos alone, we recall, Promethean consciousness lived in expectation of the end of the era and experienced the transcendence of melancholia only fleetingly; under the new dispensation existence in community will be permanently transfigured as a state of grace.

Voegelin had serious reservations concerning Schelling's enterprise of unifying humanity; he even had criticisms of Schelling's analysis of the civilizational crisis that Schelling undoubtedly experienced. His importance for Voegelin's political science, however, is undeniable and lay in the multidimensional balance of his diagnostic consciousness and in his technical ability to translate this balance into a dialectically coherent whole. There were at least seven dimensions or aspects to the balance of Schelling's consciousness. First, although he was himself a Protestant, he saw both the historical necessity of the Roman Catholic Church as well as its continuing importance. His Christianity, however, did not lead him back to any denominational church but beyond it into the more gnostic Johannine myth. His understanding of the Christian return to identity with God, however, led neither to a gnostic enthusiasm nor to a complacent union with the divine but to an increased sensitivity to the Promethean "moment" of grace. Fourth, his spiritualism did not lead him out of nature to an ethereal beyond but rather inspired him to evoke the vision of a God who anxiously suffers, as humans suffer, in the ascent from raw nature to the vision of purity. Fifth, Schelling's love for the Greeks did not turn into romanticism or idealization of the classical life because he was also aware of the crisis of polytheism. Likewise his consciousness of the crisis of Christianity did not move him to withdraw into an "otherworldly" asceticism but was balanced by his longing for a new myth of nature. His speculation on the third realm under the condominium of the spirits of Christ and Dionysos-Bacchos did not lead to any Joachitic eschatological fantasies but was moderated by the insight that the spiritual substance of any community grows through germination and development in the souls of individuals.

60. Schelling, *SW*, 6:572.

For Voegelin, this balancing of the many tensions of existence typified Schelling's philosophy. Finally, this entire complex of existential tension was balanced by the experience of salvation, by the reality of a cosmic-transcendent spirit. "The reader," wrote Voegelin,

> will remember Schelling's description of the universal process as a movement of God from nature, which he posited as his ground, to the articulation in the universe with its climax in man, and to the *anima mundi,* the third potency, which is the general form of the universe. This process of the universe has a direction insofar as it moves from nature to spirit, and the direction is determined by the longing for liberation and salvation from the suffering of existence in the quiet of being without desire.

The reader may remember as well Fackenheim's description of the dialectical moments of the meontological divinity and the anthropology derived from it. Finally, readers of Voegelin's *New Science of Politics* may recall Voegelin's account of the generation of science.

> Science starts from the pre-scientific existence of man, from his participation in the world with his body, soul, intellect, and spirit, from his primary grip on all the realms of being that is assured to him because his own nature is their epitome. And from this primary cognitive participation, turgid with passion, rises the arduous way, the *methodos,* toward the dispassionate gaze on the order of being in the theoretical attitude.[61]

The connection between the experience of the cosmic-transcendent spirit and the method of political science confirms the rationality of both Voegelin's approach to the study of politics and Schelling's metaphysics of historicity. It is possible, furthermore, to say something about the experience of the desire for salvation or deliverance, the experience Fackenheim described as self-choosing. On the one hand, redemption must come to the soul "by something else, which is outside it, completely independent of it, and elevated above it." But what kind of reality is this "other"? First, like Aristotle's famous unmoved mover, this other is not generated in continuity with any potency in nature; it must likewise be free of passion and desire, neither real nor unreal, "but only the eternal Freedom to be," and beyond being. "That the highest is above all being, is said with one accord in all higher and better doctrines. The feeling dwells with us all, that necessity follows all existence as its fate. . . . A profound feeling tells us that the true, the eternal freedom, dwells only above being." Schelling immediately added that, for most people,

61. *NSP,* 5.

who have never experienced that freedom of the soul, to be a subject, a personality, seems the highest.

> Therefore they ask: What, then, could be considered as above all being, or what is it which neither is nor is not? And they answer smugly: Nothing.
>
> Indeed, it is a nothing, but as the pure godhead is a nothing . . . because nothing can belong to it in a way distinguished from its nature, and, again, it is above all nothing because it is itself everything.
>
> Indeed, it is a nothing, but just as pure freedom is a nothing, like the will which wills nothing, which does not hunger for anything, to which all things are indifferent, and which is therefore moved by none. Such a will is nothing and everything. It is nothing inasmuch as it neither desires to become active itself nor longs for any actuality. It is everything because all power certainly comes from it as from eternal freedom alone, because it has all things under it, rules everything, and is ruled by nothing.[62]

This Nothing, Voegelin said, "is the supratrinitarian godhead of the mystics." By postulating the dissolution of existence in this Nothing as the goal for which existence strives, Schelling continued a tradition that stretched back to Augustine. "Every creature," Schelling wrote, "and especially man, really only strives to return to the position of willing nothing," even if human beings "give themselves up to all desires, for even the latter longs only for the condition where he has nothing more to will, although such a situation flees before him, and the more eagerly it is followed, the farther it draws away from him."[63]

Voegelin remarked on the similarity of this passage to Pascal's analysis of *divertissements* in his *Pensées*. There Pascal showed that escape into the life of passion was motivated by *ressentiment* against the ennui, the *tristesse*, and the anxiety, *la crainte*, at the heart of existence. But the consolation of the miseries of existence that is granted by the *divertissements* is itself the greatest misery because "it is precisely this consolation that hinders us from thinking about ourselves and advances us on the road to perdition."[64]

Pascal and Schelling issued the same warning, but the true goal, Voegelin said, may be distinguished by a change of "tone" in Schelling. It leads not to the Christian *summum bonum* of beatitude but to "a desire for depersonalization into a nirvana." The potential of seeking a nirvana, which had always been present in Western mysticism, had been effectively foreclosed by the strength of Christian orthodoxy. In this respect,

62. Schelling, *Ages of the World,* 121–22.
63. Ibid., 123.
64. Voegelin, "Nietzsche and Pascal," ed. Peter J. Opitz, 155. This essay is republished in *HPI*, VII:251–303. See *Les Pensées de Pascal*, no. 232.

Schelling represented a transition away from the "great mystical tradition" of Eckhardt, Nicholas of Cusa, and Boehme. The experiential source of Schelling's turn away from the Christian mystical tradition was "the experience of the Will in its world-immanent independence, in defiance of a God who trails existence fatally with a necessity that can never be conquered within life."[65] A generation later, Schopenhauer obscured the Western mystical desire for depersonalization by incorporating Oriental sources directly into his speculation.

Voegelin concluded his discussion of Schelling by drawing a parallel between his position and that of Plato in a way similar to what he wrote in the "Note" appended to "Plato's Egyptian Myth."

> In both instances, the religious crisis has reached the stage of enlightenment, and in both instances the enlightenment is followed by a great philosopher who restores the order of thought by means of a new vision of the soul. The atrophy of polytheism, the Age of the Sophists, and the Platonic myth of the soul have their parallel in the atrophy of Christianity, the Age of Enlightenment, and Schelling's philosophy of existence.

The parallels, however, did not lead Voegelin to construct a fanciful notion of the two being "philosophical contemporaries" in the sequence of a Toynbee-like cycle.

Indeed, not only can the differences between Schelling and Plato not be ignored, they are themselves highly significant. For Plato, the life and death of Socrates was the experience that awakened his consciousness of the soul and of its ordering structure as the authoritative source of speculation. Schelling, however, lived within a "tradition" that was established by the Hellenic discovery. Moreover, Schelling also lived within the "aion of Christ" and the meaning that history and the world have received through the soul of Christ. "Schelling's philosophy of existence has to be characterized, therefore, as a new level of critical consciousness within Christian history." The difference between the experiential and symbolic range of the two philosophers was expressed as well in the fact that Plato relied on myth to express "the meaning of existence beyond the limits that are drawn by the political type of the polis," whereas Schelling's soul "has penetrated universe and history; he does not need the myth" but is capable of translating his experience of the relations of the soul and the cosmos directly into the language of dialectical speculation. In other words, Plato was able to construct a "myth of the myth," as Voegelin characterized the achievement in

---

65. Voegelin here paraphrased the quotation given above, that "necessity follows all existence as its fate." Schelling, *Ages of the World*, 121.

Order and History, whereas Schelling constructed a reflective and de-liberate *Philosophie der Mythologie.*[66] As has already been indicated, it was Voegelin's view that the Platonic myth preserved and expressed the ambiguities of the unconscious more adequately than Schelling's transfiguration, or tendency to transfigure, protodialectical experiences into conscious, dialectical formulas.

Whatever the relative rank of their achievements, both Plato and Schelling were compelled to break with previous symbolism in order to achieve new critical insights. In the example of Schelling, the break was indicated by the expression of his experience of a Third Christianity, which referred not to an external, phenomenal Joachitic third realm but to an internal development of Christianity "through Catholicism and Protestantism to a spiritual Christianity beyond ecclesiastical dis-cipline." The several external or institutional churches were not to be replaced by a new and final church; they were, on the contrary, to be un-derstood "as symbols, comparable on their level to Hellenic mythology, to be overcome by the free Christianity of the individual souls." Schelling saw himself neither as a Joachitic prophet nor as the founder of a sect but was, in Voegelin's terms, a "spiritual realist" who expressed in his speculative philosophy the "existential fact that he, as an individual, is beyond the churches because the meaning of the churches has become actualized in history to the point where it has become part of the past in his soul."[67] The symbols of a Third Christianity, therefore, did not refer to a pragmatic missionary project but to "the projection into dialectical symbols of a direction to be found in his existence."

Voegelin went out of his way to insist on the reality of the experience in the soul of the man, F. W. J. Schelling, of "direction" and, indeed, of orientation, by noting Schelling's criticism of the view, which has not faded away, that religious experience is a useful support for morality. Such an opinion, Schelling said, turns God into a "patent-medicine that everybody can use in order to fortify their morality, that otherwise takes so much effort to maintain." Like Marx, Schelling saw that religion might be used as an "opium for the people," but unlike Marx he did not commit "the gross blinder of mistaking a phenomenal misuse for the substance of faith." Instead, Schelling pointed to the source of the blunder, the opinion that there is such a thing as a morality of human existence for

66. Voegelin, *OH,* 3:183, 194 ff.
67. Voegelin's remark about Schelling was strongly autobiographical as well. On occasion he playfully expressed this sentiment with remarks about being a "pre-Reformation" or "pre-Nicene" Christian, which were often treated as solemn doctrinal pronunciamentos.

which religious experience might be enlisted as support. The very term *morality,* he said, is a product of the Enlightenment. "In reality there is only virtue, *virtus,* a divine quality in the soul," but no morality that an individual might give to itself. "In this sense I shall gladly admit to anyone who wishes to maintain it that morality is excluded from my system."[68]

For Voegelin, Schelling's importance in the history of political science is that he was the first to have achieved a critical consciousness of the source of speculation in the sphere of "protodialectical experiences." He transformed speculation from the operation of the intellect within a tradition into a dialectical art that legitimized its activities not with respect to external texts but with respect to the consciousness of reality experienced by the philosopher. One may see, therefore, why Schelling was considered by Voegelin to be so significant: he enabled Voegelin to achieve clarity regarding the philosophy of consciousness that informed his own political science.

Schelling's importance did not end there, however. As did Voegelin himself, Schelling achieved this new awareness by reflecting on the progress of science. "The new critical science of the phenomena of nature made impossible the uncritical method of dealing with the substance of nature." Schelling began by assuming the validity of Bruno's "spiritualized nature," but he recast the formulation so that the term *nature* meant the unconscious basis for the conscious life of the spirit. "The philosophy of the unconscious," Voegelin said, "is the historical answer to the search [from Descartes to Kant] for access to the substances of nature." Between consciousness and the unconscious, as Voegelin indicated earlier, one finds the aforementioned protodialectical experiences and their several emotional "tones"—anxiety, joy, wonder, and so on—that serve as a source of meaning to be "projected into the universe and into history" with a wide variety of results.

The conclusion Voegelin drew was fundamental for his own political science and for the strategy of interpretation of texts and of other evidence that he employed. History, Voegelin said, was established by Schelling as "the science of the soul." First, Schelling's insight opened up the possibility of the critical understanding of myth. But, second, myth became a key to the exploration of the unconscious.

Projection of meaning and stimulation by materials interpenetrate, so that the materials receive their meaning from the existence of the interpreter, while they in their turn touch the unconscious and bring to the level of

68. Schelling, *SW,* 6:557.

consciousness meanings that otherwise would have remained submerged. History receives meaning from the soul, while the soul discovers the historical meanings as strata in its existence.

Finally, Voegelin compared Schelling's achievement to that of Saint Thomas. The latter undertook to "harmonize the tensions of the European high civilization" before they were resolved into the new orders of intramundane and particularist communities. Schelling, in turn, undertook "to bind into a balanced whole the tensions of the European late civilization" before they were resolved into the "crisis of our time."

Voegelin, too, has a place in this illustrious company. It fell to him to analyze "the crisis of our time," which he characterized as the violent dissociation of the elements that Schelling was able to hold together in balance by the strength of his soul. As a result of that dissociation, Voegelin said,

> we see the *disjecta membra* of his experiences scattered through the following generations: the experiences of the will and the nirvana in Schopenhauer; the craving for the inner return in Kierkegaard; the psychology of the unconscious in Freud; the experiences of Dionysos and of immanent grace in Nietzsche; the social critique of the age and the longing for the Third Realm in the mass movements of Communism and National Socialism; the ominous orgiastic experiences with their anxiety in Nietzsche, in Freud, and in the orgasms of destruction and self-destruction of the General Wars. This scattering of the elements is the signature of the crisis, as their balance was the signature of Schelling's greatness.

Like his great predecessors, Thomas, Augustine, and Plato, Schelling marked the end of an age, a pause in "the sequence of civilizational epochs," and his philosophy established "a new level of consciousness and critique." More specifically for Voegelin's political science, Schelling's achievement "becomes of increasing importance in a time of crisis as the point of orientation for those who wish to gain a solid foothold in the surrounding mess of decadent traditions, conflicting eschatologies, phenomenal speculation and obsessions, ideologies and creeds, blind hatreds, and orgiastic destructions." As Schelling built his science of the soul and of history on Bruno's spiritualized nature, so Voegelin built his political science on the foundation Schelling had left.

Concluding Remarks

A*namnesis* is, in several respects, a pivotal book in the evolution, the development, or the perfection of Voegelin's political science. In simple bibliographic terms, it fell almost exactly in the middle between the third and fourth volumes of *Order and History*. Volume 4, in turn, announced a major break in the program Voegelin had outlined in the first volume of the series and had carried out for some 1,300 pages. Moreover, much of the material in volumes 2 and 3 had been adapted with very minor changes from the typescript of *History of Political Ideas*. Finally, even though the work reported in volume 1 was chronologically the last of the first three volumes of *Order and History* to have been written, the general style of analysis was substantially a continuation of the approach used in *History*.

The pivotal position of *Anamnesis* was indicated in its opening sentence, though its importance can easily be overlooked. There Voegelin wrote: "The problems of human order in society and history arise from the order of consciousness. Philosophy of consciousness is, therefore, the essential element in a philosophy of politics." For contrast one might consider the somewhat different emphasis indicated with the first words of *The New Science of Politics*: "The existence of man in political society is historical existence; and a theory of politics, if it penetrates to principles, must at the same time be a theory of history." If its "theoretical implications are unfolded consistently," political science "will in fact become a philosophy of history." In other words, the focus of *History of Political Ideas* and the initial impetus of *Order and History* was to develop a philosophy of history that was to be an integral element of modern political science, or of the new science of politics outlined in Voegelin's Walgreen Lectures. With *Anamnesis*, however, the emphasis shifted to philosophy of consciousness.

We characterized *Anamnesis* as pivotal, which is meant to indicate that Voegelin's work after its publication had an intelligibly distinct orientation. This can be seen from Voegelin's June 1966 letter to Robert Heilman, from which we have already quoted. There he drew attention to the continuity of philosophy of history and philosophy of consciousness, but also to a change in accent or in emphasis that was expressed in the organization of the book. To recapitulate: part I was the textual report of the "anamnetic experiments" of 1943, which, we argued, were an integral part of his philosophical anthropology. On the basis of this philosophical anthropology, Voegelin undertook to order the vast range of materials that constituted *History of Political Ideas*. In *Anamnesis*, a representative sample was contained in Part II, "Experience and History." Here we have considered a number of important analytical divisions of Voegelin's philosophy of history as they emerged from the problems he encountered in writing *History*. That is, we have considered at some length the problems covered in the first two sections of *Anamnesis*.

We began by considering the biographical facts of Voegelin's escape from the Third Reich and his settlement in the United States. As a mere biographical event, the writing of *History of Political Ideas* was Voegelin's war effort, that is, his way of understanding and coming to terms with the war as a pragmatic symptom of a profound spiritual disorder. From this center of biographical motivation one can likewise understand Voegelin's criticism of the crude positivism of ordinary American political science, as well as his disagreements with Arendt and Strauss, as efforts at critical clarification that served to bring into focus what he took to be the real problems and issues. At the same time, Voegelin's desire for what he called wider horizons, from the range of Asiatic evidence to the problem of intelligible units of analysis, left a body of solid analytical work.

The transition from the problems associated with the history of political ideas or, more broadly, with the phenomena of order, which we have said were covered in a selective and representative way in Part II of *Anamnesis*, to the problems considered in Part III, "The Order of Consciousness," has been prepared by the extensive analytic reflections that preceded it. In considering *History of Political Ideas* we drew attention in particular to the work of Bodin, Vico, and Schelling as philosophers who combined "experience and history," the title of Part II of *Anamnesis*, in a way that Voegelin found particularly helpful for the development of his own work.

The foundations of modern political science, as they appear through the work of Eric Voegelin, are constituted by two distinct but related complexes of materials. First, one must attend to the work of the great thinkers whose names provide the titles to the chapters of the standard textbooks in political science. Second, however, as Voegelin argued at great length and as we indicated in Chapters 7 and 8 of this study, the political scientist must pay equal attention to the configurations of empirical political history because, for the great political scientists of the past, political history provided the immediate context, the experienced reality upon which they began their reflections. Just as Voegelin indicated that his political science began from the immediate experiences of everyday political reality, so too did the work of Plato or Bodin.

The meditative explorations of volume 4 of *Order and History*, of the later essays, and of volume 5 of *Order and History* were all undertaken on the basis of philosophical *and* historical materials to which Voegelin first gave form in *History of Political Ideas* and in the other work he undertook during the time between 1938 and the mid-1950s. We must reserve for another occasion the systematic discussion of the intellectual mansion Voegelin erected on these impressive foundations.

Bibliography

A complete bibliography of Voegelin's works and of works about Voegelin is available in Geoffrey Price, "Eric Voegelin: A Classified Bibliography." Periodic updates are provided in "Voegelin Research News" available at <Voegelin_Research_News@Man.ac.uk> or at <http//vax2.concordia.ca/vorenews>. Linda Bernard has provided a register of the Voegelin Papers at the Hoover Institution, Stanford.

The following bibliography chiefly covers material cited in this study and other works examined but not directly cited. See also the list of works cited by Abbreviation, p. xv.

1. Works by Eric Voegelin

A. Books

Anamnesis: Zur Theorie der Geschichte und Politik. Munich: Piper, 1966.
Anamnesis. Translated by Gerhart Niemeyer. 1978. Rpt. Columbia: University of Missouri Press, 1990.
Autobiographical Reflections. Edited with an introduction by Ellis Sandoz. 1989. Available: Columbia: University of Missouri Press, 1999.
Der autoritäre Staat: Ein Versuch über das österreichische Staatsproblem. Vienna: Springer, 1936.
Faith and Political Philosophy: The Correspondence between Leo Strauss and Eric Voegelin, 1934–1964. Edited and translated by Peter Emberley and Barry Cooper. University Park: Pennsylvania State University Press, 1993.
From Enlightenment to Revolution. Edited by J. H. Hallowell. Durham: Duke University Press, 1975.
The New Science of Politics: An Introduction. Chicago: University of Chicago Press, 1952.
Political Religions. Translated by T. J. Di Napoli and P. Easterly. Lewiston: Mellen, 1985.
Die politischen Religionen. Stockholm: Bermann-Fischer Verlag, 1939.
Rasse und Staat. Tübingen: J. C. B. Mohr, 1933.
Die Rassenidee in der Geistesgeschichte von Ray bis Carus. Berlin: Junkler und Dunnhaupt, 1933.

B. Articles

"Extended Strategy: A New Technique in Dynamic Relations." *Journal of Politics* 2 (1940): 189–200.

"The Growth of the Race Idea." *Review of Politics* 2 (1940): 283–317.

"Kelsen's Pure Theory of Law." *Political Science Quarterly* 42 (1927): 268–76.

"Liberalism and Its History." Translated by Mary and Keith Algozin. *Review of Politics* 36 (1974): 504–20.

"Machiavelli's Prince: Background and Formation." *Review of Politics* 13 (1951): 142–68.

"The Mongol Orders of Submission to European Powers, 1245–1255." *Byzantion* 15 (1940–1941): 378–413.

"Nietzsche and Pascal." Edited by Peter Opitz. *Nietzsche-Studien* 25 (1966): 126–71.

"Nietzsche, the Crisis, and the War." *Journal of Politics* 6 (1944): 177–212.

"The Origins of Scientism." *Social Research* 15 (1948): 462–94.

"Les perspectives d'avenir de la civilisation occidentale." In *L'histoire et ses interprétations: Entretiens autour de Arnold Toynbee,* edited by R. Aron. The Hague: Mouton, 1961.

"The Philosophy of Existence: Plato's *Gorgias.*" *Review of Politics* 11 (1949): 477–98.

"Plato's Egyptian Myth." *Journal of Politics* 9 (1947): 307–24.

"Political Theory and the Pattern of General History." *American Political Science Review* 38 (1944): 746–54.

"Siger de Brabant." *Philosophy and Phenomenological Research* 4 (1944): 507–26.

"Das Sollen im System Kants." In *Gessellschaft, Staat, und Recht: Unter-suchungen zur Reinen Rechtslehre: Festschrift für Hans Kelsen zum 50. Geburtstag,* edited by Alfred Verdross. Vienna: Springer, 1931.

"Some Problems of German Hegemony." *Journal of Politics* 3 (1940): 154–68.

"Das Timurbild der Humanisten: Eine Studie zur politische Mythenbil-dung." *Zeitschrift für öffentliches Recht* 17 (1937): 545–82.

"Toynbee's *History* as a Search for Truth." In *The Intent of Toynbee's History,* edited by Edward T. Gargan, 183–98. Chicago: Loyola University Press, 1961.

C. Book Reviews

1938. Review of J. Boissonet, *La misère par la surabondance: Karl Marx, père de la crise mondiale* (Paris: Sirey, 1938). *American Economic Review* 29:572.

1939. Review of Gaetano Mosca, *The Ruling Class* (New York: McGraw Hill, 1939). *Journal of Politics* 1:434–36.

1941. "Right and Might." Review of James B. Scott, *Law, the State, and the International Community* (New York: Columbia University Press, 1939). *Review of Politics* 3:122–23.

———. "Two Recent Contributions to the Science of Law." Review of N. S. Timasheff, *Introduction to the Sociology of Law* (Cambridge: Harvard Sociological Studies, vol. 3, 1940), and E. Bodenheimer, *Jurisprudence: The Philosophy and Method of the Law* (New York: McGraw-Hill Book Co., 1940). *Review of Politics* 3:399–404.

1942. "The Theory of Legal Science: A Review." Review of H. Cairns, *The Theory of Legal Science* (Chapel Hill: University of North Carolina Press, 1941). *Louisiana Law Review* 4:554–71.

———. Review of Maxine Y. Sweezy, *The Structure of the Nazi Economy* (Cambridge: Harvard University Press, 1941), and E. Frankel, *The Dual State: A Contribution to the Theory of Dictatorship* (New York, Oxford, Toronto: Oxford University Press, 1941). *Journal of Politics* 4:554–71.

1943. Review of Marvin Farber, *The Foundation of Phenomenology: Edmund Husserl and the Quest for a Rigorous Science of Phenomenology* (Cambridge: Harvard University Press, 1943). *Social Research* 11:384–87.

———. Review of Alec de Montmorency, *The Enigma of Admiral Darlan* (New York: E. P. Dutton, 1943). *American Political Science Review* 37:751–52.

1944. Review of John H. Hallowell, *The Decline of Liberalism as an Ideology, with Particular Reference to German Politico-Legal Thought* (Berkeley, Los Angeles: University of California Press, 1943). *Journal of Politics* 6:107–9.

1945. Review of Count Carlo Sforza, *Contemporary Italy: Its Intellectual and Moral Origins* (New York: E. P. Dutton, 1944). *Journal of Politics* 7:94–97.

1946. Review of Albert R. Chandler, *Rosenberg's Nazi Myth* (Ithaca: Cornell University Press, 1945). *American Journal of Sociology* 52:161.

———. Review of Gerhart Eisler, Albert Norden, and Albert Schreiner, *The Lessons of Germany: A Guide to Her History* (New York: International Publishers, 1945). *American Political Science Review* 40:385–86.

———. "Zu Sanders *Allgemeine Staatslehre*." Review of F. Sanders, *Allgemeine Staatslehre: Eine Grundlegung* (Brno, Prague, Leipzig, Vienna: Rudolf M. Rohrer, 1936). *Österreichische Zeitschrift für öffentliches Recht*, N.F. 1:106–35.

———. Review of Fred L. Schuman, *Soviet Politics, at Home and Abroad* (New York: Knopf, 1946). *Journal of Politics* 8:212–20.

1947. Review of Ernst Cassirer, *The Myth of the State* (New Haven: Yale University Press, 1946). *Journal of Politics* 9:445–47.

———. Review of D. Fellman, ed., *Post-War Governments of Europe* (Gainesville: Journal of Politics, University of Florida, 1946). *American Political Science Review* 41:595–96.

———. Review of F. S. C. Northrop, *The Meeting of East and West: An Inquiry Concerning World Understanding* (New York: Macmillan, 1945). *Social Research* 14:244–49.

———. Review of Rudolph Schlesinger, *Soviet Legal Theory: Its Background and Development* (New York: Oxford University Press, 1945). *Journal of Politics* 9:129–31.

1948. Review of Johan Huizinga, *Homo Ludens: Versuch zu einer Bestimmung des Spielelements in der Kultur* (Basel: Burg, 1944). *Journal of Politics* 10:179–87.

1949. Review of John Bowle, *Western Political Thought: An Historical Introduction from the Origins to Rousseau* (London: Jonathan Cape, 1947). *Review of Politics* 11:262–63.

———. Review of Leo Strauss, *On Tyranny: An Interpretation of Xenophon's Hiero* (New York: Political Science Classics, 1948). *Review of Politics* 11:241–44.

———. Review of Giambattista Vico, *The New Science*, translated by Thomas G. Bergin and Max H. Fisch (Ithaca: Cornell University Press, 1948). *Catholic Historical Review* 35:75–76.

1953. "The Origins of Totalitarianism." Review of Hannah Arendt, *The Origins of Totalitarianism* (New York: Harcourt, Brace, 1951). *Review of Politics* 15:68–85.

———. "The Oxford Political Philosophers." Review of A. D. Lindsay, *The Essentials of Democracy* (Philadelphia: Swarthmore College, 1929) and *The Modern Democratic State* (Oxford: Oxford University Press, 1943); R. G. Collingwood, *The New Leviathan, or Man, Society, Civilization, and Barbarism* (Oxford: Oxford University Press, 1942) and *The Idea of History* (Oxford: Oxford University Press, 1946); J. D. Mabbott, *The State and the Citizen: An Introduction to Political Philosophy* (London: Hutchinson, 1948); T. D. Weldon, *States and Morals: A Study of Political Conflicts* (London: John Murray, 1946); E. F. Carritt, *Ethical and Political Thinking* (Oxford: Oxford University Press, 1947); G. R. G. Mure, "The Organic State," *Philosophy* 24 (1949): 205–18; R. B. MacCallum, "Introduction," in J. S. Mill, *On Liberty, and Considerations on Representative Government*, Blackwell's Political Texts (Oxford: B. H. Blackwell, 1946); J. W. Gough, "Introduction," in John Locke, *The Second Treatise of Civil Government, and A Letter Concerning Toleration*, Blackwell's Political Texts (Oxford: B. H. Blackwell, 1946); Max Beloff,

"Introduction," in Alexander Hamilton, James Madison, and John Jay, *The Federalist, or The New Constitution,* Blackwell's Political Texts (Oxford: B. H. Blackwell, 1948); Wilfrid Harrison, "Introduction," in Jeremy Bentham, *A Fragment on Government and an Introduction to the Principles of Morals and Legislation,* Blackwell's Political Texts (Oxford: B. H. Blackwell, 1948); Michael Oakeshott, "Introduction," in Thomas Hobbes, *Leviathan,* Blackwell's Political Texts (Oxford: B. H. Blackwell, 1946); and A. P. D'Entrèves, "Introduction," in Aquinas, *Selected Political Writings,* Blackwell's Political Texts (Oxford: B. H. Blackwell, 1948). *Philosophical Quarterly* 3:97–114.

———. Review of F. Wagner, *Geschichtswissenschaft* (Freiburg, Munich: Karl Albert, 1951). *American Political Science Review* 47:261–62.

1954. "Medieval Political Sources." Review of Ewart Lewis, *Mediaeval Political Ideas* (New York: Alfred Knopf, 1954). *Yale Review,* n.s. 44:616–18.

———. Review of John Wild, *Plato's Modern Enemies and the Theory of Natural Law* (Chicago: Chicago University Press, 1953), and R. B. Levinson, *In Defence of Plato* (Cambridge: Harvard University Press, 1953). *American Political Science Review* 48:859–62.

1955. Review of R. Polin, *Politique et philosophie chez Thomas Hobbes* (Paris: Presses Universitaires de France, 1953). *American Political Science Review* 49:597–98.

2. Other Sources Cited

Alexandresar-Dersca, M. M. *La campagne de Timur en Anatolie (1402).* 1942. Rpt. London: Variorum, 1979.

Allsen, Thomas T. *Mongol Imperialism: The Policies of the Grand Qan Möngke in China, Russia, and the Islamic Lands, 1251–1259.* Berkeley: University of California Press, 1987.

Altaner, Bertold. *Die Dominikanermission des 13. Jahrhunderts.* Habelschwerdt: Breslauer Studien zur historischen Theologie, 1923.

Andrewes, A. *Greek Society.* Harmondsworth: Penguin, 1967.

———. *The Greek Tyrants.* New York: Harper, 1963.

Arendt, Hannah. *Between Past and Future: Eight Exercises in Political Thought.* New York: Viking, 1968.

———. *Essays in Understanding, 1930–1954.* Edited by J. Kohn. New York: Harcourt, Brace, 1993.

———. *The Human Condition.* Chicago: University of Chicago Press, 1958.

———. "Ideology and Terror: A Novel Form of Government." *Review of Politics* 15 (1953): 303–27.

———. "The Image of Hell." *Commentary* 2 (1946): 292–93.

————. *The Origins of Totalitarianism*. New York: Harcourt, Brace, 1951. New ed. New York: Harcourt, Brace, 1966.

————. "What Is Existenz Philosophy?" *Partisan Review* 13 (1946): 34–56.

Aubin, Jean. "Comment Tamerlan prenait les villes." *Studia Islamica* 19 (1963): 82–94.

Auerbach, Eric. "Vico and Aesthetic Historicism." *Journal of Aesthetics and Art Criticism* 8 (1949–1950): 112–28.

Bakeless, John. *The Tragicall History of Christopher Marlowe*. 2 vols. Cambridge: Harvard University Press, 1942.

Baron, Hans. *The Crisis of the Early Italian Renaissance: Civic Humanism and Republican Liberty in an Age of Classicism and Tyranny*. Rev. ed. Princeton: Princeton University Press, 1966.

Bartold, V. V. "The Burial of Timür." *Iran* 12 (1974): 81–83.

Bataillon, M., ed. *Aspects du libertinisme au XVIe siècle*. Paris: Vrin, 1974.

Battenhouse, Roy W. *Marlowe's Tamburlaine: A Study in Renaissance Moral Philosophy*. Nashville: Vanderbilt University Press, 1964.

Baxter, C. R. "Problems of the Religious Wars." In *French Literature and Its Background*, vol. 1, *The Sixteenth Century*, edited by John Cruickshank. London: Oxford University Press, 1968.

Bedani, Gino. *Vico Revisited: Orthodoxy, Naturalism, and Science in the Scienza Nuova*. Oxford: Berg, 1989.

Ben-Sasson, Haim Hillel. "Jewish-Christian Disputation in the Setting of Humanism and Reformation in the German Empire." *Harvard Theological Review* 59 (1966): 366–90.

Berkeley, George. *Works*. 6 vols. Edited by T. E. Jessop. London: Thomas Nelson, 1949.

Berlin, Isaiah. *Against the Current: Essays in the History of Ideas*. Oxford: Clarendon, 1991.

————. "Corsi e Ricorsi." *Journal of Modern History* 50 (1978): 472–92.

Berry, Thomas. *The Historical Theory of Giambattista Vico*. Washington, D.C.: Catholic University of America Press, 1949.

Bezold, F. von. "Jean Bodin als Okkultist und seine *Démonomanie*." *Historische Zeitschrift* 105 (1910): 46–52.

Bodin, Jean. *Apologie de René Herpin*. Paris: Samaritaine, 1581.

————. *Colloque entre sept scavans qui sont de differens sentimens*. Translated and edited by François Berriot. Geneva: Droz, 1984.

————. *Colloquium of the Seven about the Secrets of the Sublime*. Translated by Marion Leathers Daniels Kuntz. Princeton: Princeton University Press, 1975.

————. *De la démonomanie des sorciers*. Paris: du Puys, 1581.

————. *Method for the Easy Comprehension of History*. Translated by B. Reynolds. New York: Columbia University Press, 1945.

————. *Oeuvres philosophiques de J. Bodin.* Edited by Pierre Mesnard. Paris: Vrin, 1951.

————. *The Six Bookes of a Commonweale.* Translated by Richard Knolles. 1583. Rpt. Edited by Kenneth Douglas McRae. Cambridge: Harvard University Press, 1962.

————. *Six livres de la République.* Paris: Samaritaine, 1583.

————. *Universae Naturae Theatrum.* Lyons: Roussin, 1596.

Bondanella, Peter E. "Castruccio Castracani: Machiavelli's Archetypal Prince." *Italica* 49 (1972): 302–14.

Bosworth, C. E. "Political and Dynastic History of the Iranian World, A.D. 1000–1217." In *The Cambridge History of Iran,* vol. 5, *The Saljüg and Mongol Periods,* edited by J. A. Boyle, 185–202. Cambridge: Cambridge University Press, 1968.

Bouwsma, W. J. *Concordia Mundi: The Career and Thought of Guillaume Postel.* Cambridge: Harvard University Press, 1957.

Boyle, John Andrew. "A Form of Horse-sacrifice amongst the 13th- and 14th-Century Mongols." *Central Asiatic Journal* 10 (1965): 145–50.

————. "The Il-Khans of Persia and the Princes of Europe." *Central Asiatic Journal* 20 (1976): 28–39.

————. "Turkish and Mongol Shamanism in the Middle Ages." *Folklore* 83 (1972): 177–93.

————, ed. *The Cambridge History of Iran,* vol. 5, *The Saljüg and Mongol Periods.* Cambridge: Cambridge University Press, 1968.

Bracciolini, Poggius. *Opera Omnia.* Edited by Ricardo Fubini. 4 vols. Torino: Bottega d'Erasmo, 1964.

Brecht, Arnold. *The Political Education of Arnold Brecht: An Autobiography, 1884–1970.* Princeton: Princeton University Press, 1970.

————. *Political Theory: The Foundations of Twentieth-Century Political Thought.* Princeton: Princeton University Press, 1959.

Brown, G. *The "Methodus Facilem Historiarum Cognitionem" of Jean Bodin: A Critical Study.* Washington, D.C.: Catholic University Press, 1939.

Bube, Peter. *Vico.* Oxford: Oxford University Press, 1985.

Burkhardt, Jacob. *The Civilization of the Renaissance in Italy.* Translated by S. G. C. Middlemore. New York: Mentor, 1961.

Bury, J. B. *The Idea of Progress.* New York: Macmillan, 1935.

Cantril, Hadley. *The Invasion from Mars: A Study in the Psychology of Panic.* Princeton: Princeton University Press, 1940.

Caponigri, A. Robert. *Time and Idea: The Theory of History in Giambattista Vico.* Notre Dame: University of Notre Dame Press, 1953.

————. "*Umanita* and *Civilita:* Civil Education in Vico." *Review of Politics* 31 (1969): 477–94.

————. "Vico and the Theory of History." *Giornale di metafisica* 9 (1954): 172–94.

Caporali, Riccardo. "Vico in Voegelin." *Bollettino del Centro di Studi Vichiani* 20 (1990): 195–99.

Carlyle, R. W., and A. J. Carlyle. *A History of Medieval Political Theory in the West*. 6 vols. London: Macmillan, 1903–1936.

Chauviré, Roger. *Jean Bodin: Auteur de la République*. 1914. Rpt. Geneva: Slatkine, 1969.

Chew, Samuel C. *The Crescent and the Rose: Islam and England during the Renaissance*. 1937. New York: Octagon, 1965.

Clark, Henry, ed. *The Ethics of Experience and Behavior Control*. Los Angeles: University of Southern California Center for the Humanities, 1976.

Clavijo, Ruy Gonzales de. *Narrative of the Embassy of Ruy Gonzales de Clavijo to the Court of Timour at Samarcand, A.D. 1403–6*. Translated by Clement R. Markham. Hakluyt Society, First Series, no. 26, 1859. Rpt. New York: Bert Franklin, n.d.

Cole, R. Taylor. *The Recollections of R. Taylor Cole*. Durham: Duke University Press, 1983.

Conacher, D. J. *Aeschylus' Prometheus Bound: A Literary Commentary*. Toronto: University of Toronto Press, 1980.

Cook, Thomas I. *History of Political Philosophy from Plato to Burke*. New York: Prentice Hall, 1936.

Cooper, Barry. *Action into Nature: An Essay on the Meaning of Technology*. Notre Dame: University of Notre Dame Press, 1991.

————. *The End of History: An Essay on Modern Hegelianism*. Toronto: University of Toronto Press, 1984.

————. *The Political Theory of Eric Voegelin*. Toronto: Mellen, 1986.

————. *The Restoration of Political Science and the Crisis of Modernity*. Toronto: Mellen, 1989.

Croce, Benedetto. *The Philosophy of Giambattista Vico*. Translated by R. G. Collingwood. 1913. Rpt. New York: Russell and Russell, 1964.

Davidson, James Dale, and William Rees-Mogg. *The Great Reckoning: How to Protect Yourself in the Coming Depression*. New York: Simon and Schuster, 1993.

Dawson, Christopher, ed. *The Mongol Missions: Narratives and Letters of the Franciscan Missionaries in Mongolia and China in the Thirteenth and Fourteenth Centuries*. Translated by a Nun of Stanbrook Abbey. London: Sheed and Ward, 1955.

Day, Gerald L. "Eric Voegelin and the Schelling Renaissance." Paper presented at the Annual Meeting, American Political Science Association, Washington, D.C., August 29, 1997.

Demerson, G. "Un mythe des libertins spirituels: Le prophète Elie." In *Aspects du libertinisme au XVIe siècle,* edited by M. Bataillon, 105–20. Paris: Vrin, 1974.

Dempf, Alois. *Sacrum Imperium: Geschichtes- und Staatsphilosophie des Mittelalters und der Politischen Renaissance.* 1929. Munich: Oldenbourg, 1962.

Denzer, Horst, ed. *Jean Bodin.* Munich: Beck, 1973.

Dick, Hugh G. "*Tamburlaine* Sources Once More." *Studies in Philology* 46 (1949): 154–66.

Droz, E. "Le Carme Jean Bodin, hérétique." *Bibliothèque d'humanisme et de renaissance* 10 (1948): 77–94.

Dunning, W. "Jean Bodin on Sovereignty." *Political Science Quarterly* 2 (1896): 82–104.

Edbury, Peter W., ed. *Crusade and Settlement: Papers Read at the First Conference of the Society for the Study of the Crusades and the Latin East and Presented to R. C. Smail.* Cardiff: University College of Cardiff Press, 1985.

Ellis-Fermor, Una M. *Christopher Marlowe.* London: Methuen, 1927.

Engel-Janosi, Friedrich. "Toynbee and the Tradition of Universal History." In *The Intent of Toynbee's History,* edited by Edward J. Gargan. Chicago: Loyola University Press, 1961.

Fackenheim, Emil. *Encounters between Judaism and Modern Philosophy: A Preface to Future Jewish Thought.* New York: Basic Books, 1973.

———. *The God Within: Kant, Schelling, and Historicity.* Edited by J. Burbridge. Toronto: University of Toronto Press, 1996.

———. *The Religious Dimension in Hegel's Thought.* Bloomington: Indiana University Press, 1967.

Fisch, M. "The Academy of Investigators." In *Science, Medicine, and History: Essays on the Evolution of Scientific Thought and Medical Practice Written in Honour of Charles Singer,* edited by E. Ashworth Underwood, 521–63. London: Oxford University Press, 1953.

Fischel, Walter J. *Ibn Khaldun in Egypt: His Public Functions and Historical Research, 1382–1406: A Study in Islamic Historiography.* Berkeley: University of California Press, 1967.

Fisher, H. A. L. *A History of Europe.* London: Arnold, 1936.

Fletcher, Joseph. "The Mongols: Ecological and Social Perspectives." *Harvard Journal of Asiatic Studies* 46 (1986): 34–61.

Fournol, Étienne-Maurice. *Bodin, prédécesseur de Montesquieu.* 1896. Rpt. Geneva: Slatkine, 1970.

Franklin, Julian. *Jean Bodin and the Rise of Absolutist Theory.* Cambridge: Cambridge University Press, 1973.

————. *Jean Bodin and the Sixteenth Century Revolution in the Methodology of Law and History*. New York: Columbia University Press, 1963.

————. "Sovereignty and the Mixed Constitution: Bodin and His Critics." In *The Cambridge History of Political Thought, 1450–1700*, edited by J. H. Burns. Cambridge: Cambridge University Press, 1991.

Friedrich, Carl, ed. *Totalitarianism: Proceedings of a Conference Held at the American Academy of Arts and Sciences, March, 1953*. Cambridge: Harvard University Press, 1954.

Fueter, Edward. *Geschichte der neueren Historiographie*. Munich and Berlin: Druck, 1911.

Fussell, Paul. *The Great War and Modern Memory*. Oxford: Oxford University Press, 1977.

Gadamer, Hans-Georg. *Truth and Method*. London: Sheed and Ward, 1975.

Garin, Eugenio. *Astrology in the Renaissance: The Zodiac of Life*. Translated by C. Jackson and J. Allen. London: Routledge and Kegan Paul, 1983.

Gebhardt, Jürgen. "Eric Voegelin und die neuere Entwicklung der Geisteswissenschaften." *Zeitschrift für Politik* 36 (1989): 251–63.

————. "The Vocation of a Scholar." In *International and Interdisciplinary Perspectives on Eric Voegelin*, edited by Stephen A. McKnight and Geoffrey L. Price, 10–39. Columbia: University of Missouri Press, 1997.

Germino, Dante. *Political Philosophy and the Open Society*. Baton Rouge: Louisiana State University Press, 1982.

Gianturco, Elio. "Bodin and Vico." *Revue des littératures comparées* 22 (1948): 272–90.

Gibb, H. A. R., trans. *The Travels of Ibn Battūta*, A.D. *1325–1354*. 3 vols. Cambridge: Published for the Hakluyt Society by the University Press, 1971.

Gibbon, Edward. *The Decline and Fall of the Roman Empire*. 6 vols. New York: Dutton, 1920.

Giles, G. A., ed. *Matthew Paris's English History, from the Year 1235 to 1273*. 3 vols. London: Bohn, 1852–1854.

Godshalk, W. L. *The Marlovian World Picture*. The Hague: Mouton, 1974.

Golden, P. B. "Imperial Ideology and the Sources of Political Unity amongst the Pre-Chinggisid Nomads of Western Eurasia." *Archivum Eurasiae Medii Aevi* 2 (1982): 37–76.

Gould, Stephen Jay. *Ontogeny and Phylogeny*. Cambridge: Harvard University Press, 1977.

Green, Louis. *Castruccio Castracani: A Study on the Origins and Character of a Fourteenth-Century Italian Despotism*. Oxford: Clarendon, 1986.

————. "Machiavelli's *Vita di Castruccio Castracani* and Its Luccese Model." *Italian Studies* 42 (1987): 37–55.

Grousset, René. *The Empire of the Steppes: A History of Central Asia.* Translated by Naomi Walford. 1939. Rpt. New Brunswick: Rutgers University Press, 1970.

Guarino, Guido A. "Two Views of a Renaissance Tyrant." *Symposium* 10 (1956): 272–93.

Gundersheimer, Werner L. *The Life and Works of Louis Le Roy.* Geneva: Droz, 1966.

Guzman, Gregory G. "Simon of Saint-Quentin and the Dominican Mission to the Mongol Baiju." *Speculum* 46 (1971): 232–49.

———. "Simon of Saint-Quentin as Historian of the Mongols and Seljuk Turks." *Medievalia et Humanistica: Studies in Medieval and Renaissance Culture* n.s. 3 (1972): 155–78.

Hadock, B. A. "Vico on Political Wisdom." *European Studies Review* 8 (1978): 150–68.

Hammond, N. G. L. *A History of Greece to 322* B.C. 2d ed. Oxford: Clarendon, 1967.

Harris, H. S. "Philosophy and Poetry: The War Renewed." *Clio* 23 (1994): 395–407.

Hart, H. C. "Tamberlaine and Primaudaye." *Notes and Queries*, 10th series, 5 (January–June 1906): 484–87, 504–6.

Hayek, Fredrich A. *The Road to Serfdom.* Chicago: University of Chicago Press, 1944.

Hazard, Paul. *The European Mind, 1680–1715.* Translated by J. L. May. 1935. Rpt. London: Hollis and Carter, 1953.

Hearnshaw, F. J. C. "Bodin and the Genesis of the Doctrine of Sovereignty." In *Tudor Studies Presented . . . to Albert Frederick Polland*, edited by R. E. Seton-Watson. 1924. Rpt. New York: Russell and Russell, 1970.

Hegel, G. W. F. *Lectures on the Philosophy of Religion.* 3 vols. Translated by E. B. Speirs and J. B. Sanderson. London: Kegan, Paul, Trench Truebener and Co., 1865.

Heilke, Thomas. "Science, Philosophy, and Resistance: On Eric Voegelin's Practice of Opposition." *Review of Politics* 56 (1994): 727–52.

———. *Voegelin on the Idea of Race: An Analysis of Modern European Racism.* Baton Rouge: Louisiana State University Press, 1990.

Heilman, Robert B. "Eric Voegelin: Reminiscences." *Southern Review* 32 (1996): 147–65.

———. "The State of Letters: Baton Rouge and L.S.U. Forty Years After." *Sewanee Review* 88 (1980): 126–43.

Herman, Arthur. *The Idea of Decline in Western History.* New York: Free Press, 1997.

Hoess, Rudolf. *Commandant of Auschwitz.* London: Pan, 1974.

Hornstein, Lillian Herlands. "The Historical Background of *The King of Tars*." *Speculum* 16 (1941): 411–14.

Horowitz, Maryanne Cline. "Judaism in Jean Bodin." *Sixteenth-Century Journal* 13 (1982): 109–27.

Hughes, Glenn. *Mystery and Myth in the Philosophy of Eric Voegelin.* Columbia: University of Missouri Press, 1993.

Huppert, George. *The Idea of Perfect History: Historical Erudition and Historical Philosophy in Renaissance France.* Urbana: University of Illinois Press, 1970.

———. "The Renaissance Background to Historicism." *History and Theory* 5 (1966): 46–60.

Husserl, Edmund. *The Crisis of the European Sciences and Transcendental Phenomenology.* Translated by David Carr. Evanston: Northwestern University Press, 1970.

Hutchinson, Keith. "Toward a Political Iconology of the Copernican Revolution." In *Astrology, Science, and Society: Historical Essays,* edited by Patrick Curry, 95–141. Wolfeboro: Boydell Press, 1987.

Izard, Thomas C. "The Principal Sources for Marlowe's *Tamburlaine*." *Modern Language Notes* 58 (1943): 411–17.

Jackson, Peter. "The Crisis in the Holy Land in 1260." *English Historical Review* 95 (1980): 481–513.

Jagger, Peter J., ed. *Gladstone, Politics, and Religion.* London: Macmillan, 1985.

Jonas, Hans. *The Gnostic Religion.* 2d. ed. Boston: Beacon, 1963.

———. *The Imperative of Responsibility: In Search of an Ethics for the Technological Age.* Chicago: University of Chicago Press, 1984.

———. *The Phenomenon of Life: Toward a Philosophical Biology.* 1966. Rpt. Chicago: University of Chicago Press, 1982.

———. *Philosophical Essays: From Ancient Creed to Technological Man.* New York: Prentice Hall, 1974.

Kauder, Emil. "Ideal History: Remarks on the Foundation of the Wave Theory." *Anglican Theological Review* 28 (1946): 210–28.

Kelley, Donald R. *Foundations of Modern Historical Scholarship: Language, Law, and History in the French Renaissance.* New York: Columbia University Press, 1970.

———. "*Historia Integra:* François Baudoin and His Conception of History." *Journal of the History of Ideas* 25 (1964): 35–57.

Kerényi, Carl. *Dionysos: Archetypal Image of Indestructible Life.* Translated by R. Manheim. Princeton: Princeton University Press, 1976.

———. *Prometheus: Archetypal Image of Human Existence.* Translated by R. Manheim. New York: Pantheon, 1963.

Keulman, Kenneth. *The Balance of Consciousness.* University Park: Pennsylvania State University Press, 1990.

Kierkegaard, Søren. *Either/Or.* 2 vols. Translated by W. Lowrie. New York: Doubleday, 1959.

King, L. W., and R. C. Thompson. *The Sculptures and Inscriptions of Darius the Great on the Rock of Behistun in Persia.* London: British Museum, 1907.

Kotwicz, Wladyslaw. "Formules initiales des documents mongols aux XIIIe et XIVe siècles." *Rocznik Orjentaistyczny* 10 (1934): 131–57.

———. "Les Mongols, promoteurs de l'idée de paix universelle au début du XIIIe siècle." *Rocznik Orjentaistyczny* 16 (1958): 428–34.

Koyré, Alexandre. *From the Closed World to the Infinite Universe.* Baltimore: Johns Hopkins University Press, 1957.

Kuntz, Marion L. *Guillaume Postel: Prophet of the Restitution of All Things: His Life and Thought.* The Hague: Martinus Nijhoff, 1981.

Kwanten, Luc. *Imperial Nomads: A History of Central Asia, 500–1500.* Philadelphia: University of Pennsylvania Press, 1979.

Lachterman, David. "Vico, Doria, and Synthetic Geometry." *Bollettino del Centro Studi Vichiani* 10 (1980): 22–35.

Lambton, A. K. S. "Concepts of Authority in Persia: Eleventh to Nineteenth Centuries, A.D." *Iran* 26 (1988): 90–110.

Lattimore, Owen. "The Geography of Chingis Khan." *Geographical Journal* 129 (1963): 1–7.

Lentz, Thomas W., and Glenn D. Lowry. *Timur and the Princely Vision: Persian Art and Culture in the Fifteenth Century.* Washington, D.C.: Smithsonian Institution Press, 1989.

Le Roulx, J. Delaville. "Rapports de Tamerlan avec les Chrétiens." *La France en Orient au XIVe siècle, I, Bibliothèque des Écoles Françaises d'Athens et de Rome* XIV (1886): 391–95.

Levy, David. *Political Order: Philosophical Anthropology, Modernity, and the Challenge of Ideology.* Baton Rouge: Louisiana State University Press, 1987.

Lilla, Mark. *G. B. Vico: The Making of an Anti-Modern.* Cambridge: Harvard University Press, 1993.

Linder, R. P. "Nomadism, Horses, and Huns." *Past and Present* 92 (1981): 3–19.

Löwith, Karl. *Meaning in History.* Chicago: University of Chicago Press, 1949.

Mackinder, H. J. "The Geographical Pivot of History." *Geographical Journal* 23 (1904): 421–44.

Manuel, Frank E. *The Eighteenth Century Confronts the Gods.* Cambridge: Cambridge University Press, 1959.

Manz, Beatrice Forbes. *The Rise and Rule of Tamerlane.* Cambridge: Cambridge University Press, 1989.

———. "The Ulus Chaghatay before and after Temür's Rise to Power: The Transformation from Tribal Confederation to Army of Conquest." *Central Asiatic Journal* 27 (1983): 78–100.

Manz, Harold Elmer. "Jean Bodin and the Sorcerers." *Romanic Review* 15 (1924): 115–32.

Marlowe, Christopher. *Tamburlaine the Great.* Edited by J. S. Cunningham. Baltimore: Johns Hopkins University Press, 1981.

Masao, Mori. "The T'u-chüeh Concept of Sovereign." *Acta Asiatica* 41 (1981): 47–75.

McGinty, Park. *Interpretation and Dionysus: Method in the Study of a God.* The Hague: Mouton, 1978.

McKnight, Stephen A. "Eric Voegelin, the Renaissance *Prisca Theologica* Tradition, and Changing Perspectives on the Gnostic Features of Modernity." In *International and Interdisciplinary Perspectives on Eric Voegelin,* edited by Stephen A. McKnight and Geoffrey L. Price, 135–58. Columbia: University of Missouri Press, 1997.

———. *Sacralizing the Secular: The Renaissance Origins of Modernity.* Baton Rouge: Louisiana State University Press, 1989.

McNeill, William H. *Arnold J. Toynbee: A Life.* New York: Oxford University Press, 1989.

Mesnard, Pierre. "Jean Bodin à Toulouse." *Bibliothèque d'humanisme et de renaissance, traveaux et documents* 12 (1950): 31–59.

———. "Un rival heureux: De Cujas et de Bodin, Étienne Forcadel." *Zeitschrift der Savigny-Stiftung für Rechtgeschichte* 67 (1950): 440–58.

Meyvaert, Paul. "An Unknown Letter of Hülagü, Il-Khan of Persia, to King Louis IX of France." *Viator* 11 (1980): 236–54.

Milbank, John. *The Religious Dimension in the Thought of Giambattista Vico, 1668–1744.* Lewiston: Mellen, 1991.

Minorsky, V. "The Middle East in Western Politics in the 13th, 14th, and 15th Centuries." *Journal of the Royal Central Asian Society* 27 (1940): 427–38.

Momigliano, Arnaldo. *Essays in Ancient and Modern Historiography.* Oxford: Blackwell, 1977.

Monod, Gabriel. "Du progrès des études historiques en France depuis le XVIe siècle." *Revue historique* 1 (1876): 5–38.

Mooney, Michael. *Vico in the Tradition of Rhetoric.* Princeton: Princeton University Press, 1985.

Morgan, David O. *Medieval Persia, 1040–1797.* London: Longman, 1988.

———. "The Mongol Armies in Persia." *Der Islam* 56 (1979): 81–96.

———. "The Mongol Empire: A Review Article." *Bulletin of the School of Oriental and African Studies* 44 (1981): 120–36.

———. *The Mongols.* Oxford: Oxford University Press, 1986.

Morrison, James C. "How to Interpret Divine Providence in Vico's *New Science.*" *Philosophy and Rhetoric* 12 (1979): 256–61.

———. "Vico's Principle of *Verum* Is *Factum* and the Problem of Historicism." *Journal of the History of Ideas* 39 (1978): 578–95.

Morrissey, Michael P. *Consciousness and Transcendence: The Theology of Eric Voegelin.* Notre Dame: University of Notre Dame Press, 1994.

Morton, S. Fiona. *A Bibliography of Arnold J. Toynbee.* Oxford: Oxford University Press, 1980.

Mostaert, Antoine, and Francis Woodman Cleaves. "Trois documents Mongols des Archives Secrètes Vaticaines." *Harvard Journal of Asiatic Studies* 15 (1952): 419–507.

Murray, Gilbert. *Aeschylus: The Creator of Tragedy.* Oxford: Clarendon, 1940.

Naef, H. "La jeunesse de Bodin ou les conversions oubliées." *Bibliothèque d'humanisme et de renaissance* 8 (1946): 137–55.

Norman, E. R. *Anti-Catholicism in Victorian England.* London: George Allen and Unwin, 1968.

Nowell, Charles E. "The Historical Prester John." *Speculum* 28 (1953): 435–45.

Oakeshott, Michael. *Rationalism in Politics and Other Essays.* Edited by Timothy Fuller. Indianapolis: Liberty Press, 1991.

Ong, Walter J. *The Barbarian Within and Other Fugitive Essays and Studies.* New York: Macmillan, 1962.

Opitz, Peter J. "Max Weber und Eric Voegelin." In *Politisches Denken: Jahrbuch, 1992,* edited by Volker Gerhardt et al., 29–52. Stuttgart: Metzler, 1992.

Otto, Walter F. *Dionysus: Myth and Cult.* Translated by R. B. Palmer. Bloomington: Indiana University Press, 1965.

Pallisen, N. "Die alte Religion der Mongolen und der Kultus Tschingis-Chans." *Numen* 3 (1956): 178–229.

Parel, Anthony J. *The Machiavellian Cosmos.* New Haven: Yale University Press, 1992.

Parr, Johnstone. *Tamburlaine's Malady and Other Essays on Astrology in Elizabethan Drama.* University: University of Alabama Press, 1953.

Pascal, René. *Les Pensées de Pascal.* Edited by Francis Kaplan. Paris: Cerf, 1982.

Pelliot, Paul. "Les Mongols et la Paputé." *Revue d'Orient Chrétien* 23 (1923): 1–28; 24 (1924): 225–35; 28 (1931): 3–84.

Peper, Christian B., ed. *An Historian's Conscience: The Correspondence of Arnold J. Toynbee and Columba Cary-Elwes, Monk of Ampleforth.* Boston: Beacon, 1986.

Plamenatz, John. *Man and Society.* 2 vols. London: Longmans, 1973.

Pompa, Leon. *Human Nature and Historical Knowledge: Hume, Hegel, and Vico.* Cambridge: Cambridge University Press, 1990.

———. *Vico: A Study of the "New Science."* 2d ed. Cambridge: Cambridge University Press, 1990.

Previté-Orton, C. W. *A History of Europe from 1198 to 1378.* London: Methuen, 1937.

Price, Geoffrey. "Eric Voegelin: A Classified Bibliography." *Bulletin of the John Rylands University Library of Manchester* 76 (1994): 1–180.

Quinn, Michael. "The Freedom of Tamburlaine." *Modern Language Quarterly* 21 (1960): 315–20.

Rachewiltz, Igor de. *Papal Envoys to the Great Khans.* Stanford: Stanford University Press, 1971.

———. "Some Remarks on the Ideological Foundations of Chingis Khan's Empire." *Papers on Far Eastern History* 7 (1973): 21–31.

———. "Yeh-lü Ch'u-ts'ai (1188–1243): Buddhist Idealist and Confucian Statesman." In *Confucian Portraits,* edited by A. F. Wright and D. Twitchett, 194–95. Stanford: Stanford University Press, 1962.

Ranieri, John J. *Eric Voegelin and the Good Society.* Columbia: University of Missouri Press, 1995.

Ribner, Irving. *The English History Play in the Age of Shakespeare.* Rev. ed. New York: Barnes and Noble, 1965.

———. "The Idea of History in Marlowe's Tamberlaine." *English Literary History* 20 (1953): 251–66.

———. *Jacobean Tragedy: The Quest for Moral Order.* London: Methuen, 1962.

———. "Marlowe and Machiavelli." *Comparative Literature* 6 (1954): 354–66.

———. "Marlowe's 'Tragicke Glasse.'" In *Essays on Shakespeare and Elizabethan Drama in Honor of Hardin Craig,* edited by R. Hosley. Columbia: University of Missouri Press, 1962.

———. "*Tamburlaine* and *The Wars of Cyrus.*" *Journal of English and German Philology* 53 (1954): 569–73.

Ricci, M. *The Tragedy of Political Science: Politics, Scholarship, and Democracy.* New Haven: Yale University Press, 1984.

Richard, Jean. "Les causes des victoires Mongols d'après les historiens occidenteaux du XIIIe siècle." *Central Asiatic Journal* 23 (1979): 104–17.

———. "Mongols and Franks." *Journal of Asian History* 3 (1969): 46–58.

453

Bibliography

———. "Les Mongols et l'Occident: Deux siècles de contacts." In C.N.R.S., *1274: Année charnière, mutations et continuités,* 85–96. Paris: C.N.R.S., 1977.

———. *Les relations entre l'Orient et l'Occident au Moyen Age.* London: Variorum, 1977.

———. "Utimatums Mongols et lettres apocrypes: L'Occident et les motifs de Guerre des Tartares." *Central Asiatic Journal* 17 (1973): 203–21.

Ricoeur, Paul. *Freud and Philosophy: An Essay on Interpretation.* Translated by Denis Savage. New Haven: Yale University Press, 1970.

Riegel, Léon. *Guerre et littérature: Le bouleversement des consciences dans la littérature romanesque inspirée par la Grande Guerre (Littérature françoise, anglo-saxonne et allemande), 1910–30.* Paris: Klincksieck, 1978.

Ringer, Fritz. *The Decline of the German Mandarins: The German Academic Community, 1890–1933.* Cambridge: Harvard University Press, 1969.

Roemer, H. R. "Timür in Iran." In *The Cambridge History of Iran,* vol. 6, *The Timurid and Safavid Periods,* edited by Peter Jackson. Cambridge: Cambridge University Press, 1986.

Roloff, G. "Die Schlacht bei Angora (1402)." *Historische Zeitschrift* 161 (1940): 244–66.

Rose, Paul Lawrence. "Bodin and the Bourbon Succession to the French Throne, 1584–1594." *Sixteenth-Century Journal* 9 (1978): 75–98.

———. *Bodin and the Great God of Nature: The Moral and Religious Universe of a Judaiser.* Geneva: Droz, 1980.

———. "The *Politique* and the Prophet: Bodin and the Catholic League, 1589–1594." *Historical Journal* 21 (1978): 783–808.

Rossi, Paolo. *The Dark Abyss of Time: The History of the Earth and the History of the Nations from Hooke to Vico.* Translated by Lydia G. Cochrane. Chicago: University of Chicago Press, 1984.

Rostovtzeff, M. *The Social and Economic History of the Roman Empire.* 2d ed. 2 vols. Oxford: Clarendon, 1957.

Roux, Jean-Paul. "Tängri: Essai sur le Ciel-Dieu des peuples altaïques." *Revue de l'histoire des religions* 149 (1956): 49–82, 197–230; 150 (1957): 27–54, 173–212.

Rovillard, Clarence Dana. *The Turk in French History, Thought, and Literature, 1520–1660.* Paris: Vrin, 1940.

Sabine, George H. *A History of Political Theory.* 3d ed. New York: Holt, Rinehart and Winston, 1961.

———. "What Is a Political Theory?" *Journal of Politics* 1 (1934): 1–18.

Sandoz, Ellis. "Myth and Society in the Philosophy of Bergson." *Social Research* 30 (1963): 171–202.

———. "Voegelin Read Anew: Political Philosophy in the Age of Ideology." *Modern Age* 17 (1973): 257–63.

Saunders, J. J. *The History of the Mongol Conquests.* London: Routledge and Kegan Paul, 1971.

———. *Muslims and Mongols: Essays on Medieval Asia.* Edited by W. G. Rice. Christchurch: University of Canterbury Press, 1977.

Scheler, Max. *Man's Place in Nature.* Translated by Hans Meyerhoff. Boston: Beacon, 1961.

———. *Philosophical Perspectives.* Translated by O. A. Haac. Boston: Beacon, 1958.

Schelling, F. W. J. *The Ages of the World.* Translated by F. de W. Bolman Jr. 1942. Rpt. New York: AMS Press, 1967.

———. *Sämmtliche Werke,* 14 vols. Stuttgart and Augsburg: Cotta, 1856–1861. Rpt. Darmstadt: Wissenschaftliche Buchgesellschaft, 1974–1976.

Schiltberger, Johann. *The Bondage and Travels of Johann Schiltberger in Europe, Asia, and Africa, 1396–1427.* London: Hakluyt Society, 1879.

Schnapp, Jeffrey T. "Machiavellian Foundlings: Castruccio Castracani and the Aphorism." *Renaissance Quarterly* 45 (1992): 653–76.

Schneck, Stephen Fredrick. *Person and Polis: Max Scheler's Personalism as Political Theory.* Albany: State University of New York Press, 1987.

Schurmann, H. F. "Mongolian Tributary Practices of the Thirteenth Century." *Harvard Journal of Asiatic Studies* 19 (1956): 304–89.

Schutz, Alfred. *Collected Papers.* 3 vols. Edited by M. Natanson. The Hague: Martinus Nijhoff, 1962.

Seaton, Edith. "Fresh Sources for Marlowe." *Review of English Studies* 5 (1929): 401–26.

Sebba, Gregor. *The Collected Essays of Gregor Sebba: Truth, History, and the Imagination.* Edited by H. Sebba, A. A. Bueno, H. Boers. Baton Rouge: Louisiana University Press, 1991.

Sebba, Gregor, and Peter Opitz, eds. *The Philosophy of Order: Essays on History, Consciousness, and Politics for Eric Voegelin on His Eightieth Birthday, January 3, 1981.* Stuttgart: Klett-Cotta, 1981.

Secret, F. "De quelques courantes prophétiques et religieuses sous le règne de Henri III." *Revue de l'histoire des religions* 172 (1967): 1–32.

Seidler, G. L. *The Emergence of the Eastern World.* Oxford: Pergamon, 1968.

Sinor, Denis. "The Greed of the Northern Barbarian." In *Aspects of Altaic Civilization,* ed. Larry V. Clark and Paul A. Draghi. Indiana University Uralic and Altaic Series, 134 (1978): 171–82.

———. "The Mongols and Western Europe." In *A History of the Crusades,* edited by Kenneth M. Setton. Vol. III, *The Fourteenth and Fifteenth Centuries,* edited by Harry W. Hazard. Madison: University of Wisconsin Press, 1975.

———. *Orientalism and History.* 2d ed. Bloomington: Indiana University Press, 1970.

———. "Les relations entre les Mongols et l'Europe jusqu'à la mort d'Arghoun et de Béla IV." *Journal of World History* 3 (1956–1957): 42–61.

———, ed. *The Cambridge History of Early Inner Asia.* Cambridge: Cambridge University Press, 1990.

Smith, Hallett. "Tamburlaine and the Renaissance." In *Elizabethan Studies and Other Essays in Honor of George F. Reynolds*, 126–31. University of Colorado Studies, Series B, vol. 2. Boulder, 1945.

Smith, Mason, Jr. "Ayn Jalut: Mamlük Success or Mongol Failure?" *Harvard Journal of Asiatic Studies* 44 (1984): 320–62.

Snell, Bruno. *The Discovery of the Mind: The Greek Origins of European Thought.* Translated by T. G. Rosenmeyer. 1939. Rpt. Cambridge: Harvard University Press, 1953.

Snow, Dale E. *Schelling and the End of Idealism.* Albany: State University of New York Press, 1996.

Spence, Leslie. "The Influence of Marlowe's Sources on *Tamburlaine I.*" *Modern Philology* 24 (1926): 181–99.

———. "Tamberlaine and Marlowe." *PMLA* 42 (1927): 604–22.

Spuler, Bertold. *History of the Mongols: Based on Eastern and Western Accounts of the Thirteenth and Fourteenth Centuries.* Translated by H. and S. Drummond. Berkeley and Los Angeles: University of California Press, 1972.

———. *The Muslim World: A Historical Survey.* Part II. *The Mongol Period.* Translated by F. R. C. Bagley. 1953. Rpt. Leiden: Brill, 1969.

Stade, George, ed. *European Writers: The Age of Reason and Enlightenment.* New York: Charles Scribner's Sons, 1984.

Strauss, Leo. *The City and Man.* Chicago: Rand McNally, 1964.

———. *On Tyranny: Revised and Expanded Edition, Including the Strauss-Kojève Correspondence.* Edited by Victor Gourevitch and Michael S. Roth. New York: Macmillan, 1991.

———. "Political Philosophy and History." *Journal of the History of Ideas* 10 (1949): 30–50.

———. *What Is Political Philosophy? and Other Studies.* Glencoe: Free Press, 1959.

Sumberg, Theodore A. "Machiavelli's Castruccio Castracani." *Interpretation* 16 (1988): 285–93.

———. "Reading Vico Three Times." *Interpretation* 17 (1990): 347–54.

Summers, Claude J. *Christopher Marlowe and the Politics of Power.* Salzburg: Instüt für Englische Sprache und Literatur, 1979.

———. "Tamburlaine's Opponents and Machiavelli's *Prince.*" *English Literary History* 51 (1974): 256–58.

Tagliacozzo, Giorgio, ed. *Giambattista Vico: An International Symposium.* Baltimore: Johns Hopkins University Press, 1989.

———. *Vico: Past and Present.* Atlantic Highlands: Humanities Press, 1981.

Thorndike, Lynn. "The True Place of Astrology in the History of Science." *Isis* 46 (1955): 273–78.

Togan, Ahmed Zeki Velidi. "Timurs Osteuropapolitik." *Zeitschrift der deutschen morgenländischen Gesellschaft* 108 (1958): 279–98.

Toynbee, Arnold. *Civilization on Trial.* Oxford: Oxford University Press, 1948.

———. *A Study of History.* 12 vols. Oxford: Oxford University Press, 1934–1961.

Tucker, A. "Plato and Vico: A Platonic Reinterpretation of Vico." *Idealistic Studies* 23 (1993): 139–50.

Turan, Osman. "The Ideal of World Dominion among the Medieval Turks." *Studia Islamica* 4 (1955): 77–90.

Ulph, Owen. "Jean Bodin and the Estates-General of 1576." *Journal of Modern History* 19 (1947): 289–96.

Vaughan, Frederick. *The Political Philosophy of Giambattista Vico.* The Hague: Martinus Nijhoff, 1972.

Verene, Donald Phillip. *The New Art of Autobiography: An Essay on the Life of Giambattista Vico Written by Himself.* Oxford: Clarendon, 1991.

Vernadsky, George. "The Scope and Contents of Chenggis Qan's *Yasa.*" *Harvard Journal of Asiatic Studies* 3 (1938): 337–60.

Vico, Giambattista. *Autobiography.* Translated by Thomas G. Bergin and Max H. Fisch. Ithaca: Cornell University Press, 1944.

———. *New Science.* Translated by T. G. Bergin and M. H. Fisch. Ithaca: Cornell University Press, 1984.

———. *On the Most Ancient Wisdom of the Italians.* Translated by L. M. Palmer. Ithaca: Cornell University Press, 1988.

———. *Opere di G. B. Vico.* 6 vols. Edited by Fausto Nicolini, Giovanni Gentile, and Benedetto Croce. Bari: Laterza, 1911–1941.

———. *Vico: Selected Writings.* Translated and edited by Leon Pompa. Cambridge: Cambridge University Press, 1982.

Vryonis, Speros, Jr. *The Decline of Medieval Hellenism in Asia Minor and the Process of Islamicization from the Eleventh through the Fifteenth Century.* Berkeley: University of California Press, 1971.

Wagner, Helmut R. *Alfred Schütz: An Intellectual Biography.* Chicago: University of Chicago Press, 1983.

———. "Husserl and Historicism." *Social Research* 39 (1972): 696–719.

Wagner, Helmut R., with Ilja Srubar. *A Bergsonian Bridge to Phenomenological Psychology.* Washington, D.C.: University Press of America, 1984.

Waith, Eugene. *The Herculean Hero in Marlowe, Chapman, Shakespeare, and Dryden.* New York: Columbia University Press, 1962.

———. *Ideas of Greatness: Heroic Drama in England.* London: Routledge and Kegan Paul, 1971.

Webb, Eugene. *Philosophers of Consciousness.* Seattle: University of Washington Press, 1988.

Whitfield, J. H. *Discourses on Machiavelli.* Cambridge: Heffer, 1969.

Wight, Martin. "Arnold Toynbee: An Appreciation." *International Affairs* 52 (1976): 10–12.

———. *Systems of States.* Edited by Hedley Bull. Leicester: Leicester University Press, 1977.

Wilcox, Donald J. *The Development of Florentine Humanist Historiography in the Fifteenth-Century.* Cambridge: Harvard University Press, 1969.

3. Manuscript Collections

Cambridge. Harvard University Archives. Carl Friedrich papers; W. Y. Elliott papers.

Chicago. University of Chicago Archives. Leo Strauss papers.

Erlangen. University of Erlangen-Nürnberg. Voegelin-Bibliotek.

Munich. Geschwister-Scholl-Institut für Politische Wissenschaft. Eric-Voegelin-Archiv.

North Tarrytown, N.Y. Rockefeller Foundation. Rockefeller Archive Center, correspondence.

Notre Dame. University of Notre Dame Archives. Review of Politics, correspondence.

Oxford. Bodleian Library. A. J. Toynbee papers.

Stanford. The Hoover Institution. Voegelin papers.

Index

459